Exam 70-526: *Microsoft .NET Framework 2.0 Windows-Based Client Development*

Note: Exam objectives are subject to change at any time without prior notice and at Microsoft's sole discretion. Please visit the Microsoft Learning Certification Web site (*www.microsoft.com/learning/mcp/*) for the most current listing of exam objectives.

Microsoft

MCTS Self-Paced Training Kit (Exam 70-526):

Microsoft® .NET Framework 2.0 Windows®-Based Client Development

*Matthew A. Stoecker
and Steven J. Stein,
with Tony Northrup*

PUBLISHED BY
Microsoft Press
A Division of Microsoft Corporation
One Microsoft Way
Redmond, Washington 98052-6399

Library of Congress Control Number 2006932075

ISBN-13: 978-0-7356-2333-0
ISBN-10: 0-7356-2333-3

Printed and bound in the United States of America.

1 2 3 4 5 6 7 8 9   QWT   0 9 8 7 6

Distributed in Canada by H.B. Fenn and Company Ltd.

A CIP catalogue record for this book is available from the British Library.

Microsoft Press books are available through booksellers and distributors worldwide. For further information about international editions, contact your local Microsoft Corporation office or contact Microsoft Press International directly at fax (425) 936-7329. Visit our Web site at www.microsoft.com/mspress. Send comments to tkinput@microsoft.com.

Acquisitions Editor: Ken Jones
Project Editor: Denise Bankaitis
Technical Editor: Tony Northrup

Body Part No. X12-48734

About the Authors

Matthew A. Stoecker

Matthew Stoecker started programming in BASIC on a TRS-80 at the age of nine. In 2001, he joined Microsoft Corp. as a writer and programmer writing about Microsoft Visual Basic .NET. He has authored numerous technical articles about Visual Basic .NET and Microsoft Visual C# and has written or contributed to multiple books about these languages. He holds a Ph.D. in microbiology that he hopes he will never have to use again and lives in Bellevue, Washington.

Steven J. Stein, MCP

Steve began working with and programming computers as a hobby in the early 1980s. He spent many years in the automotive electronics industry, but as the personal computer revolution took hold and the need for automating routine business tasks became a necessity, he returned to programming and writing macros. Steve has been producing documentation and code samples at Microsoft since early 2000 and has been a programmer writer on the Visual Studio team for the last 5 years. He currently resides in Mill Creek, Washington, with his extreme coding partner Jackson (okay, he's just a cat but he's learning to use the command-line compiler!). Among other things, Steve is an avid skier, hiker, and motorcycle rider. He can often be found at the remotest part of some ski area or riding his motorcycle on a local, twisty back road.

Contents at a Glance

Table of Contents

What do you think of this book? **We want to hear from you!**	Microsoft is interested in hearing your feedback about this publication so we can continually improve our books and learning resources for you. To participate in a brief online survey, please visit: *www.microsoft.com/learning/booksurvey/*

5   Configuring Connections and Connecting to Data 197

Introduction

This training kit is designed for developers who plan to take Microsoft Certified Technical Specialist (MCTS) exam 70-526, as well as for developers who need to know how to develop Microsoft Windows–based applications using the Microsoft .NET Framework 2.0. We assume that before you begin using this kit you have a working knowledge of Windows and Microsoft Visual Basic or C#.

By using this training kit, you'll learn how to do the following:

- Create a user interface (UI) for a Windows Forms application by using standard controls.
- Integrate data in a Windows Forms application.
- Implement printing and reporting functionality in a Windows Forms application.
- Enhance usability.
- Implement asynchronous programming techniques to improve the user experience.
- Develop Windows Forms controls.
- Configure and deploy applications.

Hardware Requirements

The following hardware is required to complete the practice exercises:

- Computer with a 600 MHz or faster processor
- 192 MB of RAM or more
- 2 GB of available hard disk space
- DVD-ROM drive
- 1,024 x 768 or higher resolution display with 256 colors
- Keyboard and Microsoft mouse or compatible pointing device

Software Requirements

The following software is required to complete the practice exercises:

- One of the following operating systems:
  - ❑ Windows 2000 with Service Pack 4
  - ❑ Windows XP with Service Pack 2
  - ❑ Windows XP Professional x64 Edition (WOW)
  - ❑ Windows Server 2003 with Service Pack 1
  - ❑ Windows Server 2003, x64 Editions (WOW)
  - ❑ Windows Server 2003 R2
  - ❑ Windows Server 2003 R2, x64 Editions (WOW)
  - ❑ Microsoft Windows Vista
- Microsoft Visual Studio 2005 (A 90-day evaluation edition of Visual Studio 2005 Professional Edition is included on DVD with this book.)

Using the CD and DVD

A companion CD and an evaluation software DVD are included with this training kit. The companion CD contains the following:

- **Practice tests**   You can reinforce your understanding of how to create .NET Framework 2.0 applications by using electronic practice tests you customize to meet your needs from the pool of Lesson Review questions in this book. Or you can practice for the 70-526 certification exam by using tests created from a pool of 300 realistic exam questions, which is enough to give you many different practice exams to ensure that you're prepared.

- **Code**   Most chapters in this book include sample files associated with the lab exercises at the end of every lesson. For some exercises, you will be instructed to open a project prior to starting the exercise. For other exercises, you will create a project on your own and be able to reference a completed project on the CD in the event you experience a problem following the exercise.

- **An eBook**   An electronic version (eBook) of this book is included for times when you don't want to carry the printed book with you. The eBook is in Portable Document Format (PDF), and you can view it by using Adobe Acrobat or Adobe Reader.

The evaluation software DVD contains a 90-day evaluation edition of Visual Studio 2005 Professional Edition, in case you want to use it with this book.

How to Install the Practice Tests

To install the practice test software from the companion CD to your hard disk, do the following:

1. Insert the companion CD into your CD drive, and accept the license agreement. A CD menu appears.

NOTE If the CD menu doesn't appear

If the CD menu or the license agreement doesn't appear, AutoRun might be disabled on your computer. Refer to the Readme.txt file on the CD-ROM for alternate installation instructions.

---

2. Click the Practice Tests item, and follow the instructions on the screen.

How to Use the Practice Tests

To start the practice test software, follow these steps:

1. Click Start/All Programs/Microsoft Press Training Kit Exam Prep. A window appears that shows all the Microsoft Press training kit exam prep suites installed on your computer.

2. Double-click the lesson review or practice test you want to use.

NOTE Lesson reviews vs. practice tests

Select the (70-526) Microsoft .NET Framework 2.0–Windows-Based Client Development Foundation *lesson review* to use the questions from the "Lesson Review" sections of this book. Select the (70-526) Microsoft .NET Framework 2.0–Windows-Based Client Development *practice test* to use a pool of 300 questions similar to those in the 70-526 certification exam.

Lesson Review Options

When you start a lesson review, the Custom Mode dialog box appears so that you can configure your test. You can click OK to accept the defaults, or you can customize the number of questions you want, how the practice test software works, which exam objectives you want the questions to relate to, and whether you want your lesson review to be timed. If you're retaking a test, you can select whether you want to see all the questions again or only those questions you missed or didn't answer.

After you click OK, your lesson review starts.

- To take the test, answer the questions and use the Next, Previous, and Go To buttons to move from question to question.

- After you answer an individual question, if you want to see which answers are correct—along with an explanation of each correct answer—click Explanation.

- If you'd rather wait until the end of the test to see how you did, answer all the questions and then click Score Test. You'll see a summary of the exam objectives you chose and the percentage of questions you got right overall and per objective. You can print a copy of your test, review your answers, or retake the test.

Practice Test Options

When you start a practice test, you choose whether to take the test in Certification Mode, Study Mode, or Custom Mode.

- **Certification Mode**   Closely resembles the experience of taking a certification exam. The test has a set number of questions, it's timed, and you can't pause and restart the timer.

- **Study Mode**   Creates an untimed test in which you can review the correct answers and the explanations after you answer each question.

- **Custom Mode**   Gives you full control over the test options so that you can customize them as you like.

In all modes, the user interface you see when taking the test is basically the same but with different options enabled or disabled, depending on the mode. The main options are discussed in the previous section, "Lesson Review Options."

When you review your answer to an individual practice test question, a "References" section is provided that lists where in the training kit you can find the information that relates to that question and provides links to other sources of information. After you click Test Results to score your entire practice test, you can click the Learning Plan tab to see a list of references for every objective.

How to Uninstall the Practice Tests

To uninstall the practice test software for a training kit, use the Add Or Remove Programs option in Windows Control Panel.

Microsoft Certified Professional Program

The Microsoft certifications provide the best method to prove your command of current Microsoft products and technologies. The exams and corresponding certifications are developed to validate your mastery of critical competencies as you design and develop, or implement and support, solutions with Microsoft products and technologies. Computer professionals who become Microsoft-certified are recognized as experts and are sought after industry-wide. Certification brings a variety of benefits to the individual and to employers and organizations.

MORE INFO   All the Microsoft certifications

For a full list of Microsoft certifications, go to *www.microsoft.com/learning/mcp/default.asp*.

Technical Support

Every effort has been made to ensure the accuracy of this book and the contents of the companion CD. If you have comments, questions, or ideas regarding this book or the companion CD, please send them to Microsoft Press by using either of the following methods:

E-mail: tkinput@microsoft.com

Postal Mail:

Microsoft Press
Attn: MCTS Self-Paced Training Kit (Exam 70-526): Microsoft .NET Framework 2.0–
Windows-Based Client Development *Editor*
One Microsoft Way
Redmond, WA 98052–6399

For additional support information regarding this book and the CD-ROM (including answers to commonly asked questions about installation and use), visit the Microsoft Press Technical Support Web site at *www.microsoft.com/learning/support/books/*. To connect directly to the Microsoft Knowledge Base and enter a query, visit *http://support .microsoft.com/search/*. For support information regarding Microsoft software, please connect to *http://support.microsoft.com*.

Evaluation Edition Software Support

The 90-day evaluation edition provided with this training kit is not the full retail product and is provided only for the purposes of training and evaluation. Microsoft and Microsoft Technical Support do not support this evaluation edition.

Information about any issues relating to the use of this evaluation edition with this training kit is posted to the Support section of the Microsoft Press Web site (*www.microsoft.com/learning/support/books/*). For information about ordering the full version of any Microsoft software, please call Microsoft Sales at (800) 426-9400 or visit *www.microsoft.com.*

Chapter 1

Windows Forms and the User Interface

This chapter introduces you to Windows Forms. Windows Forms are the basis for most Microsoft Windows applications and can be configured to provide a variety of user interface (UI) options. The developer can create forms of various sizes and shapes and customize them to the user's needs. Forms are hosts for *controls*, which provide the main functionality of the user interface. Special controls called *container controls* can be used to control the layout of the user interface.

Exam objectives in this chapter:

- Add and configure a Windows Form.
    - Add a Windows Form to a project at design time.
    - Configure a Windows Form to control accessibility, appearance, behavior, configuration, data, design, focus, layout, style, and other functionality.
- Manage control layout on a Windows Form.
    - Group and arrange controls by using the *Panel* control, *GroupBox* control, *TabControl* control, *FlowLayoutPanel* control, and *TableLayoutPanel* control.
    - Use the *SplitContainer* control to create dynamic container areas.
- Add and configure a *Windows Forms* control.
    - Use the integrated development environment (IDE) to add a control to a Windows Form or other container control of a project at design time.
    - Add controls to a Windows Form at run time.

Lessons in this chapter:

Before You Begin

To complete the lessons in this chapter, you must be familiar with Microsoft Visual Basic or Microsoft Visual C# and be comfortable with the following tasks:

- Opening Microsoft Visual Studio and creating a Windows Forms project
- Dragging controls from the Toolbox to the designer
- Setting properties in the Properties window

Real World

Matt Stoecker

When I develop a Windows Forms application, I pay special attention to the design of the user interface. A well-thought-out user interface that flows logically can help provide a consistent user experience from application to application and make it easy for users to learn new applications. Familiarity and common themes translate into increased productivity.

Lesson 1: Adding and Configuring Windows Forms

This lesson describes how to create and configure Windows Forms. You will learn how to create forms and refer to them in code, alter the visual properties of the form, and control the behavior of the form at run time.

After this lesson, you will be able to:

- Add a Windows Form to a project at design time.
- Add a new Windows Form at run time.
- Resize a window at design time or run time.
- Identify and set the properties that determine a form's appearance and behavior at run time.
- Refer to the default instance of a form in code.
- Create a non-rectangular form.

Estimated lesson time: 45 minutes

Overview of Windows Forms

Windows Forms are the basic building block of the user interface. They provide a container that hosts controls and menus and allow you to present an application in a familiar and consistent fashion. Forms can receive user input in the form of keystrokes or mouse interactions and can display data to the user through hosted controls. Although it is possible to create applications that do not contain forms, such as console applications or services, most applications that require sustained user interaction will include at least one Windows Form, and complex applications frequently require several forms to allow the program to execute in a consistent and logical fashion.

When you create a new Windows Forms project, a form named Form1 is added to your project by default. You can edit your form by adding controls and other visual elements in the designer, which is a graphic representation of a designable, visual element (such as a *Form*) that appears in the Visual Studio Integrated Development Environment (IDE). The Visual Studio IDE is shown in Figure 1-1.

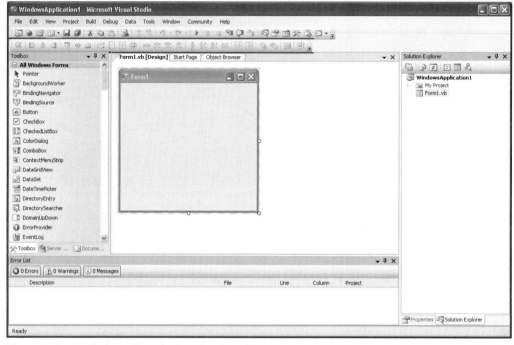

Figure 1-1   A Windows Form in the Visual Studio IDE

Adding Forms to Your Project

Most projects will require more than one form. You can add and configure additional forms at design time, or you can create instances of pre-designed forms in code at run time.

▶ **To add a new form to your project at design time**

1. From the Project menu, select Add Windows Form. The Add New Item dialog box opens.

2. Select Windows Form and type a name for the new form in the Name box. Click Add to add the form to the development environment.

   You can add and configure as many forms as your application needs at design time. You can also create new instances of forms in your code. This method is most often employed when you want to display a form that has already been designed. In Visual Basic, you can access default instances of a form by referring to that form by name. For example, if you have a form named Form1 in your application, you can refer to it directly by its name, Form1.

▶ **To access the default instance of a form at run time (Visual Basic only)**

1. Refer to the form by its name. You can call methods or access properties from this default instance. For example:

```
' VB
Form1.Text = "This is my form"
Form1.Show()
```

2. If referring to a form from within that form's code, you cannot use the default instance. You must use the special keyword *Me* (Visual Basic) or *this* (C#) to access the form's properties and methods.

▶ **To access a form's methods and properties from inside its code**

1. Use the keyword *Me* (Visual Basic) or *this*(C#). For example:

```
' VB
Me.Text = "J and J's Wine Shop - Main Page"
```

```
// C#
this.Text = "J and J's Wine Shop - Main Page";
```

2. You can also create new instances of forms at run time by declaring a variable that represents a type of form and creating an instance of that form.

▶ **To add a form to your application at run time**

1. Declare and instantiate a variable that represents your form. This example assumes that you have already designed a form named Form1 in your project:

```
' VB
Dim myForm As Form1
myForm = New Form1()
' Displays the new form
myForm.Show()
```

```
// C#
Form1 myForm;
myForm = new Form1();
// Displays the new form
myForm.Show();
```

Properties of Windows Forms

The visual appearance of your user interface is an important part of your application. A user interface that is poorly designed is difficult to learn and will, therefore, increase training time and expense. You can modify the appearance of your user interface by using Windows Forms properties.

Windows Forms contain a variety of properties that allow you to customize the look and feel of the form. You can view and change these properties in the Properties window of the designer, as shown in Figure 1-2.

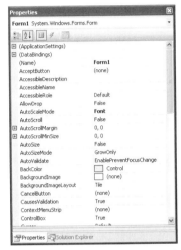

Figure 1-2   The Properties window

Table 1-1 summarizes some of the Windows Forms properties that are important in the look and feel of the application. Note that this is not an exhaustive list of all Windows Forms properties but, rather, a selected subset.

Table 1-1   Some Properties of the *Form* Class

Property	Description
(Name)	Sets the name of the *Form* class shown in the designer. This property can be set only at design time.
Backcolor	Indicates the background color of the form.
BackgroundImage	Indicates the background image of the form.
BackgroundImageLayout	Determines how the image indicated by the *Background-Image* property will be laid out on the form. If no background image is selected, this property has no effect.
ControlBox	Determines whether the form has a Control/System menu box.

Table 1-1 Some Properties of the *Form* Class

Property	Description
Cursor	Indicates the cursor that appears when the cursor is moved over the form.
Enabled	Determines whether the form is able to receive user input. If *Enabled* is set to *False*, all controls contained by the form are likewise disabled.
Font	Sets the default font for the form. All controls contained by the form will also adopt this font unless their *Font* property is set separately.
ForeColor	Indicates the forecolor of the form, which is the color used to display text. All controls contained by the form will also adopt this forecolor unless their forecolor property is set separately.
FormBorderStyle	Indicates the appearance and behavior of the form border and title bar.
HelpButton	Indicates whether the form has a Help button.
Icon	Indicates the icon that is used to represent this form.
Location	When the *StartPosition* property is set to *Manual*, this property indicates the starting location of the form relative to the upper left-hand corner of the screen.
MaximizeBox	Indicates whether the form has a MaximizeBox.
MaximumSize	Determines the maximum size for the form. If this property is set to a size of *(0,0)* the form has no upper size limit.
MinimizeBox	Indicates whether the form has a MinimizeBox.
MinimumSize	Determines the minimum size to which the user can resize the form.

Table 1-1   Some Properties of the *Form* Class

Property	Description
Opacity	Represents the opacity, or conversely the transparency of the form from 0% to 100%. A form with 100% opacity is completely opaque, and a form with 0% opacity is completely transparent.
Size	Gets and sets the initial size of the form.
StartPosition	Indicates the position of the form when the form is first displayed.
Text	Determines the text caption of the form.
TopMost	Indicates whether the form always appears above all other forms that do not have this property set to *True*.
Visible	Determines whether the form is visible when running.
WindowState	Determines whether the form is minimized, maximized, or set to the size indicated by the *Size* property when first shown.

Modifying the Look and Feel of the Form

You can use the Property Grid to set properties of the form at design time. Properties set in this manner will retain their values until the application starts, at which time they can be set in code.

Most properties of a form can also be set at run time. The generalized scheme for setting a simple property is to use the assignment operator (=) to assign a value to a property. The following example demonstrates how to set the *Text* property of a form.

```
' VB
Form1.Text = "This is Form 1"
```

```
// C#
Form1.Text = "This is Form 1";
```

Some properties, such as the *Font* or *Size* properties, are more complex. Their value is represented by an instance of a class or structure. For these properties, you can either set the property to an existing instance of the class, or create a new instance that specifies any subvalues of the property and assign it to the property as shown in the following pseudocode example:

```
' VB
PropertyY = New Class(value,value)
```

```
// C#
PropertyY = new Class(value,value);
```

The (*Name*) property, which represents the name of the *Form* class, is an exception. This property is used within the namespace to uniquely identify the class that the *Form* is an instance of and, in the case of Visual Basic, is used to access the default instance of the form.

Setting the Title of the Form

The name of the form is the name that is used to refer to the *Form* class or the default instance of a form (Visual Basic only) in code, but it is also useful for the form to have a title that is visible to users. This title might be the same as the name of the form but is more often a description of the form itself, such as Data Entry. The title can also be used to convey information to the user, such as "Processing Entries – My Application" or "Customer Entry – My Application". The title appears in the title bar and on the taskbar.

You can change the title of a form by changing the *Text* property. To change the title of a form at design time, set the *Text* property of the form in the Property Grid. To change the title of a form at run time, set the *Text* property of the form in code, as shown in the following code:

```
' VB
Form1.Text = "Please enter your address"
```

```
// C#
Form1.Text = "Please enter your address";
```

Setting the Border Style of the Form

The border style of a form determines how the border of the form looks and, to a certain extent, how a form behaves at run time. Depending on the setting, the *FormBorderStyle* property can control how the border appears, whether a form is resizable by the user at run time, and whether various control boxes appear (although these are also determined by other form properties). The *FormBorderStyle* property has seven possible values, which are explained in Table 1-2.

Table 1-2   Values for the *FormBorderStyle* Property

Value	Description
None	The form has no border and has no minimize, maximize, help, or control boxes.
FixedSingle	The form has a single border and cannot be resized by the user. It can have a minimize, maximize, help, or control box as determined by other properties.
Fixed3D	The form's border has a three-dimensional appearance and cannot be resized by the user. It can have a minimize, maximize, help, or control box as determined by other properties.
FixedDialog	The form has a single border and cannot be resized by the user. Additionally, it has no control box. It can have a minimize, maximize, or help box as determined by other properties.
Sizable	This is the default setting for a form. It is resizable by the user and can contain a minimize, maximize, or help box as determined by other properties.
FixedToolWindow	The form has a single border and cannot be resized by the user. The window contains no boxes except the close box.
SizableToolWindow	The form has a single border and is resizable by the user. The window contains no boxes except the close box.

The *FormBorderStyle* property can be set at either design time or run time. To change the border style of a form at design time, set the *FormBorderStyle* property in the Property Grid. To change the border style of a form at run time, set the *FormBorderStyle* property in code as shown in the following example:

```
' VB
aForm.FormBorderStyle = FormBorderStyle.Fixed3D
```

```
// C#
aForm.FormBorderStyle = FormBorderStyle.Fixed3D;
```

Setting the Startup State of the Form

The *WindowState* property determines what state the form is in when it first opens. The *WindowState* property has three possible values: *Normal*, *Minimized*, and *Maximized*. The default setting is *Normal*. When the *WindowState* property is set to *Normal*, the form will start at the size determined by the *Size* property. When the *WindowState* property is set to *Minimized*, the form will start up minimized in the taskbar. When the *WindowState* property is set to *Maximized*, the form will start up maximized. Although this property can be set at run time, doing so will have no effect on the state of the form. Thus, it is useful to set this property in the Property Grid only at design time.

Resizing the Form

When the *WindowState* property is set to *Normal*, it will start at the size determined by the *Size* property. The *Size* property is actually an instance of the Size structure which has two members, *Width* and *Height*. You can resize the form by setting the *Size* property in the Property Grid, or you can set the *Width* and *Height* separately by expanding the *Size* property and setting the values for the individual fields.

You can also resize the form by grabbing and dragging the lower right-hand corner, the lower edge, or the right-hand edge of the form in the designer. As the form is visibly resized in the designer, the *Size* property is automatically set to the new size.

The form can be resized at run time by setting the *Size* property in code. The *Width* and *Height* fields of the *Size* property are also exposed as properties of the form itself. You can set either the individual *Width* and *Height* properties or the *Size* property to a new instance of the *Size* structure as shown in the following example:

```
' VB
' Set the Width and Height separately
aForm.Width = 300
aForm.Height = 200
' Set the Size property to a new instance of the Size structure
aForm.Size = New Size(300,200)

// C#
// Set the Width and Height separately
aForm.Width = 300;
aForm.Height = 200;
// Set the Size property to a new instance of the Size structure
aForm.Size = new Size(300,200);
```

Note that if the form's *StartPosition* property is set to *WindowsDefaultBounds*, the size will be set to the window's default rather than to the size indicated by the *Size* property.

Specifying the Startup Location of the Form

The startup location of the form is determined by a combination of two properties. The first property is the *StartPosition* property, which determines where in the screen the form will be when first started. The *StartPosition* property can be set to any of the values contained within the *FormStartPosition* enumeration. The *FormStartPosition* enumeration values are listed in Table 1-3.

Table 1-3   *StartPosition* Property Settings

Value	Description
Manual	The starting location of the form is set by the form's *Location* property. (See the following options.)
CenterScreen	The form starts up in the center of the screen.
WindowsDefaultLocation	The form is positioned at the Windows default location and set to the size determined by the *Size* property.
WindowsDefaultBounds	The form is positioned at the Windows default location and the size is determined by the Windows default size.
CenterParent	The form's starting position is set to the center of the parent form.

If the *StartPosition* property is set to manual, the form's starting position is set to the location specified by the form's *Location* property, which is dictated by the location of the form's upper left-hand corner. For example, to start the form in the upper left-hand corner of the screen, set the *StartLocation* property to *Manual* and the *Location* property to (*0,0*). To start the form 400 pixels to the right and 200 pixels below the upper-left hand corner of the screen, set the *Location* property to (*400,200*).

Keeping a Form on Top of the User Interface

At times, you might want to designate a form to stay on top of other forms in the user interface. For example, you might design a form that presented important information about the program's execution that you always want the user to be able to see. You can set a form to always be on top of the user interface by setting the *TopMost* property to *True*. When the *TopMost* property is *True*, the form will always appear in front of any forms that have the *TopMost* property set to *False*, which is the default setting. Note that if you have more than one form with the *TopMost* property set to *True*, they can cover up each other.

Opacity and Transparency in Forms

You can use the *Opacity* property to create striking visual effects in your form. The *Opacity* property sets the transparency of the form. When set in the Property Grid, the opacity value can range from 0% to 100%, indicating the degree of opacity. An opacity of 100% indicates a form that is completely opaque (solid and visible), and a value of 0% indicates a form that is completely transparent. Values between 0% and 100% result in a partially transparent form.

You can also set the *Opacity* property in code. When the *Opacity* property is set in code, it is set to a value between 0 and 1, with 0 representing complete transparency and 1 representing complete opacity. The following example demonstrates how to set a form's opacity to 50%:

```
' VB
aForm.Opacity = 0.5
```

```
// C#
aForm.Opacity = 0.5;
```

The *Opacity* property can be useful when it is necessary to keep one form in the foreground but monitor action in a background form or create interesting visual effects. In most cases, a control inherits the opacity of the form that hosts it.

Setting the Startup Form

If your Windows Forms application contains multiple forms, you must designate one as the startup form. The startup form is the first form to be loaded on execution of your application. The method for setting the startup form depends on whether you are programming in Visual Basic or C#.

In Visual Basic, you can designate a form as the startup form by setting the Startup Form project property, which is done in the project Properties window, as shown in Figure 1-3:

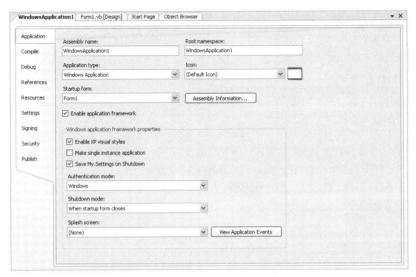

Figure 1-3   The Visual Basic project Properties window

▶ **To set the Startup form in Visual Basic**

1. In Solution Explorer, click the name of your project. The project name is high-lighted.

2. In the Project menu, choose applicationName Properties, where applicationName represents the name of your project.

3. On the Application tab, under Startup form, choose the appropriate form from the drop-down menu.

   Setting the startup form in C# is slightly more complicated. The startup object is specified in the *Main* method. By default, this method is located in a class called *Program.cs*, which is automatically created by Visual Studio. The *Program.cs* class contains, by default, a *Main* method, as follows:

```
static void Main()
{
    Application.EnableVisualStyles();
    Application.SetCompatibleTextRenderingDefault(false);
    Application.Run(new Form1());
}
```

   The startup object is indicated by the line

```
Application.Run(new Form1());
```

   You can set the startup form for the project by changing this line in the Program.cs class to the form that you want to start the application. For example, if you wanted a form called myForm to be the startup form, you would change this line to read as follows:

```
Application.Run(new myForm());
```

▶ **To set the Startup form in C#**

1. In Solution Explorer, double-click Program.cs to view the code. The code window opens.

2. Locate the *Main* method, and then locate the line that reads:

```
Application.Run(new Form());
```

where Form represents the name of the form that is currently the startup form.

3. Change Form to the name of the form you want to set as the startup form.

Making the Startup Form Invisible

At times you might want the startup form to be invisible at run time. For example, you might want a form to execute a time-consuming process when starting and not appear until that process is complete. The *Visible* property determines whether a form is visible at run time. You can set the *Visible* property either in the Property Grid or in code. If you set *Visible* to *False* in the property window, the form will be invisible at startup.

To make a form invisible during execution, set the *Visible* property to *False* in code, as shown in the following example:

```
' VB
aForm.Visible = False

// C#
aForm.Visible = false;
```

Quick Check

1. How can you specify the Startup Location of a Form?
2. How do you set the Startup Form?

Quick Check Answers

1. Use the Form.StartPosition to indicate the starting position of a Form.
2. In Visual Basic, you can set the Startup form by setting the value in the Application tab of the project properties. In C# you must locate the Application.Run method and change the startup form there.

Creating Non-Rectangular Windows Forms

For advanced visual effects, you might want to create forms that are non-rectangular. For example, you might want to create an oval form or a form in the shape of your company's logo. Although creating a non-rectangular form is easy, there are several considerations for the final look and feel of the form.

You can create a non-rectangular form by setting the *Region* property of the form in the *Form_Load* event handler. Because the change in shape of the form actually occurs at run time, you are unable to view the form in its actual shape at design time. Thus, you might have to start the application and view the form several times as you fine-tune the appearance and placement of controls.

The *Region* property is an instance of *System.Drawing.Region*. This class represents an area of the screen that is the interior of a graphics shape defined by rectangles and graphics paths. The easiest way to create a non-rectagular region is to create a new instance of the *GraphicsPath* class, and then create the new *Region* from it. The following code demonstrates a simple example.

```
' VB
Dim myPath As New System.Drawing.Drawing2D.GraphicsPath
' This line of code adds an ellipse to the graphics path that inscribes the
' rectangle defined by the form's width and height
myPath.AddEllipse(0, 0, Me.Width, Me.Height)
' Creates a new Region from the GraphicsPath
Dim myRegion As New Region(myPath)
' Sets the form's Region property to the new region
Me.Region = myRegion
```

```
// C#
System.Drawing.Drawing2D.GraphicsPath myPath = new System.Drawing.Drawing2D.GraphicsPath();
// This line of code adds an ellipse to the graphics path that inscribes
// the rectangle defined by the form's width and height
myPath.AddEllipse(0, 0, this.Width, this.Height);
// Creates a new Region from the GraphicsPath
Region myRegion = new Region(myPath);
// Sets the form's Region property to the new region
this.Region = myRegion;
```

The *System.Drawing* and *System.Drawing.Drawing2D* classes will be discussed in further detail in Chapter 14, "Creating Windows Forms Controls."

Because non-rectangular forms will have limited borders (if any), it is generally a good idea to set the *FormBorderStyle* property of the form to *None*. This prevents any parts of the form that intersect the original rectangle edges of the form from having a different and unwanted appearance. However, with the *FormBorderStyle* property set to

None, there will be no way for the user to resize, move, or close the form, and you must build these features into your design. A simple non-rectangular form is shown in Figure 1-4.

Figure 1-4   An elliptical form with a Close Form button

▶ **To create a non-rectangular form**

1. In the Property Grid, set the *FormBorderStyle* to *None*.

2. Double-click the form in the designer to open the default *Form_Load* event handler.

3. In the *Form_Load* event handler, create a new instance of the *Region* class as shown in the previous example.

4. If desired, add close, move, or resize functionality to the form because the user might not be able to access the form's borders or title bar.

5. Set the form as the startup form and press F5 to view the form. Fine-tune the appearance and placement of controls as necessary.

Lab: Customizing a Windows Form

In this lab, you will practice customizing a Windows Form by applying techniques that you learned in the preceding lesson. In Exercise 1, you will create a Windows Form and customize the appearance by setting properties and writing code. In Exercise 2, you will create a form with a non-rectangular shape. This lab guides you through the steps involved. If you prefer to do an unguided lab, please see the "Case Scenarios" section at the end of this chapter.

▶ **Exercise 1: Customize a Rectangular Windows Form**

1. Open Visual Studio 2005 and create a new Windows Forms project. The project opens with a default form named Form1 in the Designer.

2. In the Designer, select the form. The properties for the form are displayed in the Property Grid.

3. In the Property Grid, set the following properties to the values specified in the following table:

Property	Value
Text	Trey Research
FormBorderStyle	Fixed3D
StartPosition	Manual
Location	100,200
Opacity	75%

4. From the Toolbox, drag three buttons onto the Form and position them conveniently.

5. Select each button in turn and, in the Properties window, set the *Text* property of the buttons to *Border Style*, *Resize*, and *Opacity*. When finished, your form should look similar to Figure 1-5.

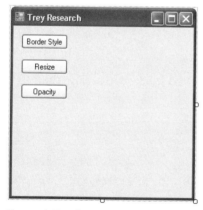

Figure 1-5   The practice form

6. In the designer, double-click the button labeled Border Style to open the code window to the event handler for *Button1.Click*. Add the following line of code to this method:

```vb
' VB
Me.FormBorderStyle = FormBorderStyle.Sizable
```

```csharp
// C#
this.FormBorderStyle = FormBorderStyle.Sizable;
```

7. Return to the Designer, and then double-click the Resize button and add the following line:

```vb
' VB
Me.Size = New Size(300, 500)
```

```csharp
// C#
this.Size = new Size(300, 500);
```

8. Return to the Designer, and then double-click the Opacity button and add the following line:

```vb
' VB
Me.Opacity = 1
```

```csharp
// C#
this.Opacity = 1;
```

9. Press F5 to run the application. Click each button and observe the effect on the appearance of the form.

▶ **Exercise 2: Create a Non-Rectangular Windows Form**

1. In this exercise, you will create a triangular Windows Form.

2. Open Visual Studio 2005 and create a new Windows Forms project. The project opens with a default form named Form1 in the designer.

3. In the Property Grid, set the *FormBorderStyle* property to *None* and the *Back-Color* property to *Red*. This will make the form easier to see when you test the application.

4. Drag a Button from the Property Grid to the upper left-hand corner of the form. Set the *Text* property of the button to *Close Form*.

5. Double-click the Close Form button and add the following code to the *Button1_Click* event handler:

```vb
' VB
Me.Close()
```

```csharp
// C#
this.Close();
```

6. In the Designer, double-click the form to open the *Form1_Load* event handler. Add the following code to this method. This code sets the form's region to the shape of a triangle by defining a polygon with three corners.

```vb
' VB
Dim myPath As New System.Drawing.Drawing2D.GraphicsPath()
myPath.AddPolygon(New Point() { New Point(0, 0), New Point(0, Me.Height), _
  New Point(Me.Width, 0) })
Dim myRegion As New Region(myPath)
Me.Region = myRegion
```

```csharp
// C#
System.Drawing.Drawing2D.GraphicsPath myPath = new
  System.Drawing.Drawing2D.GraphicsPath();
myPath.AddPolygon(new Point[] { new Point(0, 0), new Point(0, this.Height),
  new Point(this.Width, 0) });
Region myRegion = new Region(myPath);
this.Region = myRegion;
```

Press F5 to run the application. A triangular-shaped form is displayed.

Lesson Summary

Forms are the basic building blocks of a Windows application and serve as the foundation for the user interface. The form can act as a host for controls and can contain methods, properties, and events. Forms can be added at design time, or new instances of forms can be added in code at run time.

- You can alter the look, feel, and behavior of a form by changing the form's properties. Properties such as *Text*, *FormBorderStyle*, *WindowState*, *Size*, *StartPosition*, *TopMost*, *Visible*, and *Opacity* allow you to create a variety of visual styles and effects.

- You can designate the startup form in the project properties window for Visual Basic or by changing the startup form in the *Main* method. This method is usually found in the *Program.cs* class, which is auto-generated.

- You can create non-rectangular forms by creating a new instance of the *Region* class and then setting the form's *Region* property to that new instance.

Lesson Review

The following questions are intended to reinforce key information presented in this lesson. The questions are also available on the companion CD if you prefer to review them in electronic form.

NOTE Answers

Answers to these questions and explanations of why each answer choice is correct or incorrect are located in the "Answers" section at the end of the book.

---

1. Which of the following code snippets demonstrates how to add a new instance of a Windows Form named Form1 at run time?

   A. ' VB
   ```
   Dim myForm As Form1
   myForm = Form1.CreateForm()
   ```

   ```
   // C#
   Form1 myForm;
   myForm = Form1.CreateForm();
   ```

   B. ' VB
   ```
   Dim myForm As Form1
   myForm.Show()
   ```

   ```
   // C#
   Form1 myForm;
   myForm.Show();
   ```

   C. ' VB
   ```
   myForm = Form1
   myForm.Show()
   ```

   ```
   // C#
   myForm = Form1;
   myForm.Show();
   ```

   D. ' VB
   ```
   Dim myForm As Form1
   myForm = New Form1()
   ```

   ```
   // C#
   Form1 myForm;
   myForm = new Form1();
   ```

2. Which of the following code snippets correctly demonstrates how to set a form to a non-rectangular shape?

   A. ' VB
   ```
   Dim aPath As New System.Drawing.Drawing2D.GraphicsPath
   aPath.AddEllipse(0, 0, Me.Width, Me.Height)
   Me.Region = New Region();
   ```

   ```
   // C#
   System.Drawing.Drawing2D.GraphicsPath aPath = new
   System.Drawing.Drawing2D.GraphicsPath();
   aPath.AddEllipse(0, 0, Me.Width, Me.Height);
   this.Region = new Region();
   ```

B.
```vb
' VB
Dim aPath As New System.Drawing.Drawing2D.GraphicsPath
aPath.AddEllipse(0, 0, Me.Width, Me.Height)
```

```csharp
// C#
System.Drawing.Drawing2D.GraphicsPath aPath = new
System.Drawing.Drawing2D.GraphicsPath();
aPath.AddEllipse (0, 0, Me.Width, Me.Height);
```

C.
```vb
' VB
Dim aPath As New System.Drawing.Drawing2D.GraphicsPath
aPath.AddEllipse(0, 0, Me.Width, Me.Height)
Me.Region = New Region(aPath)
```

```csharp
// C#
System.Drawing.Drawing2D.GraphicsPath aPath = new
System.Drawing.Drawing2D.GraphicsPath();
aPath.AddEllipse(0, 0, Me.Width, Me.Height);
this.Region = new Region(aPath);
```

D.
```vb
' VB
Dim aPath As New System.Drawing.Drawing2D.GraphicsPath
aPath.AddEllipse(0, 0, Me.Width, Me.Height)
Me.Region = aPath
```

```csharp
// C#
System.Drawing.Drawing2D.GraphicsPath aPath = new
System.Drawing.Drawing2D.GraphicsPath();
aPath.AddEllipse(0, 0, Me.Width, Me.Height)
this.Region = aPath;
```

3. Which of the following code samples correctly sets the title, border style, size, and opacity of a form?

A.
```vb
' VB
Me.Text = "My Form"
Me.FormBorderStyle = FormBorderStyle.Fixed3D
Me.Size = New Size(300, 300)
Me.Opacity = 0.5
```

```csharp
// C#
this.Text = "My Form";
this.FormBorderStyle = FormBorderStyle.Fixed3D;
this.Size = new Size(300, 300);
this.Opacity = 0.5;
```

B.
```vb
' VB
Me.Text = "My Form"
Me.BorderStyle = "Fixed3D'
Me.Size = New Size(300, 300)
Me.Opacity = 0.5
```

```csharp
// C#
this.Text = "My Form";
```

```
this.BorderStyle = "Fixed3D";
this.Size = new Size(300, 300);
this.Opacity = 0.5;
```

C.
```
' VB
Me.Text = "My Form"
Me.FormBorderStyle = FormBorderStyle.Fixed3D
Me.Size = (300,300)
Me.Opacity = "100%"
```

```
// C#
this.Text = "My Form";
this.FormBorderStyle = FormBorderStyle.Fixed3D;
this.Size = (300,300);
this.Opacity = "100%";
```

D.
```
' VB
Me.Title = "My Form"
Me.FormBorderStyle = FormBorderStyle.Fixed3D
Me.Size = New Size(300,300)
Me.Opacity = "100%"
```

```
// C#
this.Title = "My Form";
this.FormBorderStyle = FormBorderStyle.Fixed3D;
this.Size = new Size(300,300);
this.Opacity = "100%";
```

Lesson 2: Managing Control Layout with Container Controls

This lesson describes how to add and configure container controls. You will learn how to add controls to a form or to a container control and to configure various kinds of container controls to create dynamic and varied layouts for controls in your form.

After this lesson, you will be able to:

- Add a control to a form or container control at design time.
- Add a control to a form or container at run time.
- Group and arrange controls with the *Panel* control.
- Group and arrange controls with the *GroupBox* control.
- Group and arrange controls with the *TabControl* control.
- Group and arrange controls with the *FlowLayoutPanel* control.
- Group and arrange controls with the *TableLayoutPanel* control.
- Create dynamic container areas with the *SplitContainer* control.

Estimated lesson time: 45 minutes

Overview of Container Controls

Container controls are specialized controls that serve as a customizable container for other controls. Examples of container controls include the *Panel*, *FlowLayoutPanel*, and *SplitContainer* controls. Container controls give the form logical and physical subdivisions that can group other controls into consistent user interface subunits. For example, you might contain a set of related *RadioButton* controls in a *GroupBox* control. The use of container controls helps create a sense of style or information flow in your user interface and allows you to manipulate contained controls in a consistent fashion.

When a container control holds other controls, changes to the properties of the container control can affect the contained controls. For example, if the *Enabled* property of a panel is set to *False*, all of the controls contained within the panel are disabled. Likewise, changes to properties related to the user interface, such as *BackColor*, *Visible*, or *Font*, are also applied to the contained controls. Note that you can still manually change any property inside a contained control, but if the container is disabled, all controls inside that container will be inaccessible regardless of their individual property settings.

The Controls Collection

Each form and container control has a property called *Controls*, which represents the collection of controls contained by that form or control. When a control is added to a form or container control at design time, the Designer automatically adds it to the controls collection of that form or container control and sets the location property as appropriate. You can also dynamically add a new control at run time by manually creating a new control and adding the control to the controls collection.

To Add a Control to a Form or Container Control in the Designer

There are four ways to add a control to a form or container control in the Designer:

■ Drag the control from the Toolbox to the surface of the form or container control.

■ Select a control in the Toolbox, and then draw it on the form with the mouse.

■ Select a control in the Toolbox and double-click the form.

■ Double-click the control in the Toolbox.

To Add a Control to a Form or Container Control at Run Time

To add a control to a form or container control at run time, manually instantiate a new control and add it to the Controls collection of the form, as shown in the following example. You must set any properties of the control, such as the *Location* or *Text* properties, before adding it to the controls collection. The following sample code assumes that you have added a *Panel* container named Panel1.

```vb
' VB
Dim aButton As New Button()
' Sets the relative location in the containing control or form
aButton.Location = New Point(20,20)
aButton.Text = "Test Button"
' Adds the button to a panel called Panel1
Panel1.Controls.Add(aButton)
' Adds the button to a form called Form1
Me.Controls.Add(aButton)
```

```csharp
// C#
Button aButton = new Button();
// Sets the relative location in the containing control or form
aButton.Location = new Point(20,20);
aButton.Text = "Test Button";
// Adds the button to a panel called Panel1
Panel1.Controls.Add(aButton);
// Adds the button to a form called Form1
this.Controls.Add(aButton);
```

The *Anchor* Property

The *Anchor* and *Dock* properties of a control dictate how it behaves inside its form or parent control. The *Anchor* property allows you to define a constant distance between one or more edges of a control and one or more edges of a form or other container. Thus, if a user resizes a form at run time, the control edges will always maintain a specific distance from the edges. The default setting for the *Anchor* property is *Top, Left*, meaning that the top and left edges of the control always maintain a constant distance from the top and left edges of the form. If the *Anchor* property were set to *Bottom, Right*, for example, the control would "float" when the form was resized to maintain the constant distance between the bottom and right-hand edges of the form. If opposite properties are set for the *Anchor* property, such as *Top* and *Bottom*, the control will stretch to maintain the constant distance of the control edges to the form edges.

You can set the *Anchor* property to any combination of *Top, Bottom, Left, Right*, or none of these. In the Properties window, you are presented with a visual interface that aids in choosing the value for the *Anchor* property. This interface is shown in Figure 1-6.

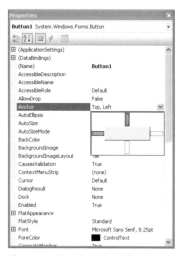

Figure 1-6   Choosing the *Anchor* property

The *Dock* Property

The *Dock* property enables you to attach your control to the edge of a parent control. The parent control can be a form or a container control such as a *Panel* control or a *TabControl* control.

Like the *Anchor* property, the *Dock* property provides a special visual interface that allows you to graphically choose the property value. This interface is shown in Figure 1-7.

Figure 1-7   Choosing the *Dock* property

To set the *Dock* property, click the section of the interface that corresponds to where you want your control to dock. For example, to dock your control to the right-hand side of the form, click the bar on the right of the interface. To release docking, choose None. Clicking the center of the *Dock* property interface sets the *Dock* property to a value of *Fill*, which means the the control will dock to all four sides of the form and fill the control in which it resides.

The *GroupBox* Control

The *GroupBox* control is a container control that appears as a subdivision of the form surrounded by a border. It does not provide scrollbars, like the *Panel* control, nor does it provide any kind of specialized layout capabilities. A *GroupBox* can have a caption, which is set by the *Text* property, or it can appear without a caption when the *Text* property is set to an empty string.

The most common use for *GroupBox* controls is for grouping *RadioButton* controls. *RadioButton* controls placed within a single *GroupBox* are mutually exclusive but are not exclusive of other *RadioButtons* in the form or other *GroupBox* controls. *RadioButtons* will be discussed in greater detail in Chapter 3, "Advanced Windows

Forms Controls." Table 1-4 describes *Text*, the most important unique property of the *GroupBox* control.

Table 1-4   The Text Property of the *GroupBox* Control

Property	Description
Text	Represents the caption of the GroupBox enclosure. If no caption is desired, this property should be set to an empty string.

The *Panel* Control

The *Panel* control creates a subsection of a form that can host other controls. The *Panel* can be indistinguishable from the rest of the surrounding form, or it can be surrounded by a border as determined by the *BorderStyle* property. A *Panel* can have a *BorderStyle* property of *None*, which indicates no border; *FixedSingle*, which indicates a single edge around the *Panel;* or *Fixed3D*, which represents a border with a three-dimensional appearance.

The *Panel* control is a scrollable control, which means that it supports horizontal and vertical scroll bars. Controls can be hosted in the *Panel* outside of its visible bounds. When the *AutoScroll* property is set to *True*, scroll bars will automatically be available if any controls are placed outside of the visible bounds of the control. If the *AutoScroll* property is set to *False*, controls outside the visible bounds of the panel are inaccessible. Important properties of the *Panel* control are shown in Table 1-5.

Table 1-5   Important Properties of the *Panel* Control

Property	Description
AutoScroll	Determines if the *Panel* will display scroll bars when controls are hosted outside the visible bounds of the *Panel*. Scroll bars are displayed when this property is set to *True* and are not displayed when it is set to *False*.
BorderStyle	Represents the visual appearance of the *Panel* border. This property can be set to *None*, which indicates no border; *FixedSingle*, which creates a single-line border; or *Fixed3D*, which creates a border with a three-dimensional appearance.

The *FlowLayoutPanel* Control

The *FlowLayoutPanel* is a subclass of the *Panel* control. Like the *Panel* control, it is most commonly used to create a distinct subsection of the form that hosts related controls. Unlike the *Panel* control, however, the *FlowLayoutPanel* dynamically repositions the controls it hosts when it is resized at either design time or run time. This provides a great aid to user interface design because control positions are automatically adjusted as the size and dimensions of the *FlowLayoutPanel* are adjusted, and it provides dynamic realignment of the user interface (much like an HTML page) if the *FlowLayoutPanel* is resized at run time.

Like the *Panel* control, the *FlowLayoutPanel* control is a scrollable control. Scroll bars are enabled when *AutoScroll* is set to *True* and are disabled when *AutoScroll* is set to *False*.

The default flow direction of the *FlowLayoutPanel* is from left to right, meaning that controls placed in the *FlowLayoutPanel* will locate in the upper left-hand corner and then flow to the right until they reach the edge of the panel. This behavior is controlled by the *FlowDirection* property. The *FlowDirection* property can be set to four possible values: *LeftToRight*, which is the default; *RightToLeft*, which provides flow from right to left; *TopDown*, in which the controls flow from the top of the control to the bottom; and *BottomUp*, in which controls flow from the bottom to the top of the *FlowLayoutPanel*.

Once the end of a row (in the case of *LeftToRight* and *RightToLeft FlowDirections*) or column (in the case of *TopDown* and *BottomUp FlowDirections*) is reached, the flow will wrap or not wrap to the next row or column as determined by the value of the *WrapContents* property. If *WrapContents* is set to *True* (which is the default), controls will automatically wrap to the next column or row. If set to *False*, controls will not automatically form new rows or columns.

You can manually create breaks in the flow of the controls that are analogous to line breaks in text. When the *WrapContents* property of a *FlowLayoutPanel* control is set to *False*, you must manually set flow breaks to manage the flow, but you can also set flow breaks when *WrapContents* is set to *True* if you desire individual breaks. You can set a flow break on a control by calling the *SetFlowBreak* method of the *FlowLayoutPanel*.

▶ **To set a flow break on a control hosted in a *FlowLayoutPanel***

1. Set the flow break by using the *SetFlowBreak* method as shown in the following example (which assumes a *FlowLayoutPanel* control named Flp and a Button named aButton have already been created):

```
' VB
Flp.SetFlowBreak(aButton, True)
```

```
// C#
Flp.SetFlowBreak(aButton, true);
```

2. Regardless of whether there is room in the *FlowLayoutPanel* to continue the flow of controls, a control that has had a flow break set by this method will start a new row (or column, depending on the value of the *FlowDirection* property) in the *FlowLayoutPanel*.

3. You can query a particular control to determine if it has had a flow break set for it by calling the *GetFlowBreak* method as shown in the following example:

```
' VB
If Flp.GetFlowBreak(aButton) Then
' Continue processing
End If
```

```
// C#
if (Flp.GetFlowBreak(aButton))
{ // Continue processing
}
```

Table 1-6 lists important properties and methods of the *FlowLayoutPanel* control.

Table 1-6   Important Members of the *FlowLayoutPanel* Control

Property/Method	Description
AutoScroll	Property. Determines if the *FlowLayoutPanel* will display scroll bars when controls are hosted outside the visible bounds of the *Panel*. Scroll bars are displayed when set to *True* and are not displayed when set to *False*.
BorderStyle	Property. Represents the visual appearance of the *Panel* border. It can be set to *None*, which indicates no border; *FixedSingle*, which creates a single-line border; or *Fixed3D* which creates a border with a three-dimensional appearance.

Table 1-6   Important Members of the *FlowLayoutPanel* Control

Property/Method	Description
FlowDirection	Property. Determines the direction of flow in the *FlowLayoutPanel*. Can be set to *LeftToRight*, *Right-ToLeft*, *TopBottom*, or *BottomUp*.
WrapContents	Property. Determines whether controls will automatically wrap to the next column or row when the *FlowLayoutPanel* is resized.
GetFlowBreak	Method. This method returns a Boolean value that indicates whether a particular control has had a flow break set.
SetFlowBreak	Method. This method sets a flow break on a control contained in the *FlowLayoutPanel*.

The *TableLayoutPanel* Control

Like the *FlowLayoutPanel* control, the *TableLayoutPanel* control is a specialized panel that aids in the design and layout of the user interface. The *TableLayoutPanel* is essentially a table that provides cells for the individual hosting of controls. Like other panels, it is a scrollable container that provides scroll bars when the *AutoScroll* property is set to *True*.

At design time, the *TableLayoutPanel* appears on the form as a table of individual cells. You can drag controls from the Toolbox into each of the cells. Generally, only one control can be hosted in a single cell although, for complicated user interface designs, you can nest other container controls inside *TableLayoutPanel* cells, each of which can host multiple controls.

At run time, the appearance of the cells is determined by the *CellBorderStyle* property. This property can be set to *None*, which displays no cell lines, or to *Single*, *Inset*, *Inset-Double*, *Outset*, *OutsetDouble*, or *OutsetPartial*, each of which provides a distinctive look and feel to the table cells.

The columns and rows of the *TableLayoutPanel* control are managed by the *ColumnStyle* and *RowStyle* collections. At design time, you can set the styles of the rows and columns by choosing the *ColumnStyles* or *RowStyles* collection in the Property Grid and launching the Columns And Rows Styles editor, shown in Figure 1-8.

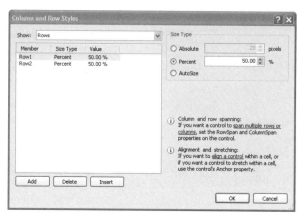

Figure 1-8 The Columns and Rows Styles editor

You can alter column and row size styles with this editor. Column and row styles can be set to *Absolute*, which indicates a fixed size in pixels, or they can be set to *Relative*, which indicates a percentage of the size of all columns or rows whose style is set to *Relative*. Columns and rows can also be set to *AutoSize*. When set to this value, the columns and rows will automatically adjust to the correct size.

Column and row styles can also be set manually in code by accessing the *ColumnStyles* and *RowStyles* collections in code. You can access the style for a particular column or row by the index of that column or row. Styles can be set as shown in the following example:

```vb
' VB
TableLayoutPanel1.ColumnStyles(0).SizeType = SizeType.Absolute
TableLayoutPanel1.ColumnStyles(0).Width = 20
TableLayoutPanel1.RowStyles(0).SizeType = SizeType.Percent
TableLayoutPanel1.RowStyles(0).Height = 50
```

```csharp
// C#
TableLayoutPanel1.ColumnStyles[0].SizeType = SizeType.Absolute;
TableLayoutPanel1.ColumnStyles[0].Width = 20;
TableLayoutPanel1.RowStyles[0].SizeType = SizeType.Percent;
TableLayoutPanel1.RowStyles[0].Height = 50;
```

If you set a row or column style to a size type of anything other than *SizeType.Absolute*, you can also set the *Width* (for columns) or *Height* (for rows). These values are set in either pixels or percentages as is appropriate for the *SizeType* of the *ColumnStyle*.

When adding new controls to a *TableLayoutPanel* at run time, you can use either of two overloads of the *TableLayoutPanel.Controls.Add* method. The first is the standard *Add* method, as follows:

```
' VB
TableLayoutPanel1.Controls.Add(aButton)
```

```
// C#
TableLayoutPanel1.Controls.Add(aButton);
```

This method simply adds the control to the controls collection of the *TableLayoutPanel*, and the control is inserted into the next open cell in the table. If there are no more open cells, the behavior of the *TableLayoutPanel* is determined by the value of the *GrowStyle* property. If the *GrowStyle* property is set to *AddRows*, additional rows will be added to accommodate new controls. If the *GrowStyle* property is set to *AddColumns*, new columns will be added when needed. If the *GrowStyle* property is set to *FixedSize*, no new cells may be added. If you attempt to add a control to a *TableLayoutPanel* with a *GrowStyle* value of *FixedSize*, an exception will be thrown.

You can also add a control to a specific cell by using the *Controls.Add* method, as follows:

```
' VB
TableLayoutPanel1.Controls.Add(aButton,3,3)
```

```
// C#
TableLayoutPanel1.Controls.Add(aButton,3,3);
```

Columns in a *TableLayoutPanel* are numbers starting at 1, while rows start at 0. Thus, the example shown above adds aButton to the cell in column 3 at row 3, which is actually the 3rd column and the 4th row the user sees. Note, however, that if a cell is already occupied by a control, your control might not be added to that cell. Controls added to cells at design time generally have precedence over controls added at run time. In these cases, the control is simply added to the next available cell. If you add the control to a cell that contains another control that has been added at run time, the cell already in that position will usually be moved down to the next available cell in favor of the control just added. As always, careful testing is important.

▶ **To add a control to a *TableLayoutPanel* control at run time**

 1. Declare and instantiate a new control in code.

2. Use the *TableLayoutPanel.Controls.Add* method to add the control. An example follows:

```
' VB
Dim aButton As New Button()
' Adds the Button to the next available cell
TableLayoutPanel1.Controls.Add(aButton)
' Adds the Button to a cell at (2,2)
TableLayoutPanel1.Controls.Add(aButton, 2, 2)
```

```
// C#
Button aButton = new Button();
// Adds the Button to the next available cell
TableLayoutPanel1.Controls.Add(aButton);
// Adds the Button to a cell at (2,2)
TableLayoutPanel1.Controls.Add(aButton, 2, 2);
```

Table 1-7 lists important properties and methods of the *TableLayoutPanel* control.

Table 1-7   Important Members of the *TableLayoutPanel* Control

Property/Method	Description
AutoScroll	Property. Determines if the *TableLayoutPanel* will display scroll bars when controls are hosted outside the visible bounds of the *Panel*. Scroll bars are displayed when this property is set to *True* and are not displayed when it is set to *False*.
CellBorderStyle	Property. Determines the style of the cell borders. This property can be set to *None*, which indicates no cell borders, or to a variety of different visual styles.
ColumnCount	Property. Indicates the number of columns. You can add or remove columns by incrementing or decrementing the *ColumnCount* property.
Columns	Property. Represents the collection of columns. Available only at design time; accessing this property launches the Columns And Rows Styles editor.
ColumnStyles	Property. Represents the collection of column styles. Available only at run time.

Table 1-7   Important Members of the *TableLayoutPanel* Control

Property/Method	Description
GrowStyle	Property. Represents how the *TableLayoutPanel* grows when new controls are added to it. This property can be set to *AddColumns*, *AddRows*, or *FixedSize*.
RowCount	Property. Indicates the number of rows. You can add or remove rows by incrementing or decrementing the *RowCount* property.
Rows	Property. Represents the collection of rows. Available only at design time; accessing this property launches the Columns And Rows Styles editor.
RowStyles	Property. Represents the collection of row styles. Available only at run time.
Controls.Add	Method of the *Controls* collection. Can be used to add a control, either to the next available cell or to a specific cell identified by its column and row coordinates.

The *TabControl* Control

The *TabControl* control enables you to group sets of controls on tabs, rather like files in a filing cabinet or dividers in a notebook. For example, you might create property pages for an application in which each page represents the properties of a specific component. The *TabControl* serves as a host for one or more *TabPage* controls, which themselves contain controls. The user can switch between tab pages (and the controls contained therein) by clicking the tabs on the *TabControl*.

The most important property of the *TabControl* is the *TabPages* property. *TabPage* controls are specialized container controls that are hosted only inside *TabControl* controls. Each *TabPage* has its own set of properties, and you can access these properties by editing the *TabPages* property at design time. This launches the TabPage Collection Editor as shown in Figure 1-9.

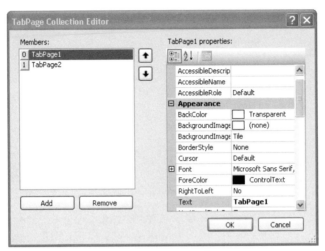

Figure 1-9   The TabPage Collection Editor

Individual *TabPage* controls are a lot like *Panel* controls. They are scrollable controls and will generate scroll bars as needed if the *AutoScroll* property is set to *True*. Individual *TabPage* controls also have a *Text* property, which represents the text that is shown on the tab that represents this page in the *TabControl*. Also like *Panel* controls, TabPages have a *BorderStyle* property that can be set to *None*, *FixedSingle*, or *Fixed3D*, with results similar to those in the the *Panel* control.

The *TabControl* has several properties that can be used to customize the look and feel of the control. The *Appearance* property controls how the tabs look. This property can be set to *Normal*, *Buttons*, or *FlatButtons*, each of which generates a different visual style. The *Alignment* property determines whether the tabs appear on the *Top*, *Bottom*, *Left*, or *Right* of the *TabControl*. The *TabControl* also has a property called *Multiline*, which indicates if more than one row of tabs is allowed. When set to *True*, multiple rows of tabs are supported. When *False*, only a single row of tabs is allowed. Important properties of the *TabControl* control and *TabPage* control are shown in Table 1-8 and Table 1-9, respectively.

Table 1-8   Important Properties of the *TabControl* Control

Property	Description
Appearance	Determines the visual style of the *TabControl*.
Alignment	Determines whether the tabs appear on the *Top*, *Bottom*, *Left*, or *Right* of the *TabControl*.

Table 1-8   Important Properties of the *TabControl* Control

Property	Description
Multiline	Determines whether more than one row of tabs is allowed on the *TabControl.*
TabPages	Represents the collection of *TabPage* controls hosted by the *TabControl.*

Table 1-9   Important Properties of the *TabPage* Control

Property	Description
AutoScroll	Determines if the *TabPage* will display scroll bars when controls are hosted outside the visible bounds of the Panel. Scroll bars are displayed when set to *True* and are not displayed when set to *False*.
BorderStyle	Represents the visual appearance of the *TabPage* border. It can be set to *None*, which indicates no border; *FixedSingle*, which creates a single-line border; or *Fixed3D*, which creates a border with a three-dimensional appearance.
Text	Represents the text displayed on the tab in the *TabControl* that represents this *TabPage*.

The *SplitContainer* Control

The *SplitContainer* control creates a subsection of the form where a *Splitter* divides the *SplitContainer* into two *SplitterPanel* controls that function similarly to *Panel* controls. The user can grab the *Splitter* with the mouse and move its location, thus changing the relative size of each *SplitterPanel*. The *SplitContainer.Dock* property is set to *Fill* by default because the most common use for *SplitContainers* is to create divided Windows Forms.

The *SplitContainer* exposes its two child *SplitterPanel* controls through its *Panel1* and *Panel2* properties. These properties allow you to access the properties of the contained *SplitterPanel* controls.

Each *SplitterPanel* contained by the *SplitContainer* control functions in basically the same way as a *Panel* control. They can host controls and are distinct from the rest of the form. They can display scroll bars when the *AutoScroll* property is set to *True*. The individual *SplitterPanel* controls of a *SplitContainer* do not have individual borders, so they expose no *BorderStyle* property like standalone *Panel* controls do, but the *SplitContainer* control itself does have a *BorderStyle* property. Like the *BorderStyle* property of the *Panel* control, this property can be set to *None*, *FixedSingle*, or *Fixed3D*. When the *BorderStyle* property is set, it affects the appearance of the *Splitter* also.

The orientation of the *Splitter* is determined by the *Orientation* property. When set to *Vertical*, the *Splitter* stretches from the top to the bottom of the *SplitContainer*. When set to *Horizontal*, the Splitter stretches from left to right.

The *FixedPanel* property allows you to designate a panel in the *SplitContainer* that will remain constant in size if the control is resized. This property can be set to Panel1 so that only Panel2 will be resized, to Panel2 so that only Panel1 will be resized, or to *None* so that both panels will be resized proportionally when the control is resized. Note that a panel is fixed by the *FixedPanel* property only in instances when the *SplitContainter* control is resized. The user is still able to resize the panels by grabbing and moving the Splitter with the mouse.

You can disable the ability of the user to move the *Splitter* by setting the *IsSplitterFixed* property. When set to *True*, the *Splitter* is fixed in its location and cannot be moved by the user. You can manually move the *Splitter* in code by changing the *SplitterDistance* property in code. This property represents the distance, in pixels, of the *Splitter* from the left edge (when *Orientation* is *Horizontal*) or the top edge (when *Orientation* is *Vertical*). You can change the thickness of the *Splitter* by setting the *SplitterWidth* property, which is also represented in pixels.

You can hide one of the panels in a *SplitContainer* by setting either the *Panel1Collapsed* or *Panel2Collapsed* properties to *True*. When one of these properties is set to *True*, the corresponding panel is collapsed and the other panel expands to fill the *SplitContainer*. Note that you cannot set both of these controls to *False*. For example, if you set *Panel1Collapsed* to *False* when the *Panel2Collapsed* is already set to *False*, *Panel2Collapsed* will be set to *True*.

You can set a minimum size for individual panels by setting the *Panel1MinSize* and *Panel2MinSize* properties. These properties represent the minimum number of pixels to which a panel can be sized. Important properties of the *SplitContainer* control are shown in Table 1-10.

Table 1-10   Important Properties of the *SplitContainer* Control

Property	Description
BorderStyle	Represents the visual appearance of the TabPage border. It can be set to *None*, which indicates no border; *FixedSingle*, which creates a single-line border; or *Fixed3D*, which creates a border with a three-dimensional appearance.
FixedPanel	Represents the panel of the *SplitContainer* that is fixed in size. This property can be set to *Panel1*, *Panel2*, or *None*, in which case, no panel has a fixed size.
IsSplitterFixed	Determines whether the location of the Splitter is fixed and cannot be moved by the user.
Orientation	Determines whether the Splitter is oriented horizontally or vertically in the *SplitContainer*. It can be set to *Horizontal* or *Vertical*.
Panel1	Exposes the properties of the *SplitContainer* control's SplitterPanel1.
Panel1Collapsed	Determines whether SplitterPanel1 is collapsed or regular size. The panel is collapsed when this property is set to *True*.
Panel1MinSize	Gets or sets the minimum size for Panel1.
Panel2	Exposes the properties of the *SplitContainer* control's SplitterPanel2.
Panel2Collapsed	Determines whether SplitterPanel2 is collapsed or regular size. *Panel* is collapsed when this property is set to *True*.
Panel2MinSize	Gets or sets the minimum size for Panel2.
SplitterDistance	Represents the distance of the Splitter from either the top or left edge of the form, depending on the value of the *Orientation* property.
SplitterWidth	Gets or sets the width of the Splitter in pixels.

Quick Check

1. What is the purpose of the *Dock* property?

2. What are Containers and what are they used for?

Quick Check Answers

1. The *Dock* property allows you to attach a control to one of the sides of the form, or to fill all available space in the form.

2. Containers are specialized controls that can be used to host other controls. They can be used to provide a variety of different control-display layouts.

Lab: Practice with Container Controls

In this lab, you will practice using container controls by creating a Windows Form with a variety of Container controls.

▶ **Exercise: Practice with Container Controls**

1. Open Visual Studio and create a new Windows Forms project.

2. From the Toolbox, drag a TabControl to the surface of the Form. In the Property Grid, set the *Dock* property to *Fill*.

3. In the Property Grid, choose the *TabPages* property to open the TabPages Collection Editor. Add tab pages until there is a total of four pages. Set the *Text* properties of these four *TabPage* controls to *GroupBox*, *FlowLayoutPanel*, *TableLayoutPanel*, and *SplitContainer*, respectively. Click OK.

4. In the form, select the tab labeled GroupBox. From the Toolbox, drag a *Group-Box* control onto the surface of the *TabPage* control.

5. Drag two *RadioButton* controls into the *GroupBox*.

6. In the form, select the tab labeled FlowLayoutPanel. From the Toolbox, drag a *FlowLayoutPanel* control onto the surface of the *TabPage* control. Set the *Dock* property of the *FlowLayoutPanel* to *Fill*.

7. From the Toolbox, add four *Button* controls to the *FlowLayoutPanel*.

8. Double-click Button1 and add the following code to the *Button1_Click* event handler:

```vb
' VB
FlowLayoutPanel1.SetFlowBreak(Button3, True)
```

```
// C#
flowLayoutPanel1.SetFlowBreak(button3, true);
```

9. Select the Designer for the form. In the form, select the tab labeled *TableLayout-Panel*. From the Toolbox, add a *TableLayoutPanel* control to the *TabPage*. Set the *CellBorderStyle* property to *Inset* and *AutoScroll* to *True*.

10. From the Toolbox, add a *Button* control to the upper left cell of the *TableLayout-Panel*.

11. Double-click the Button and add the following code to the *Button5_Click* event handler:

```
' VB
Dim aButton As New Button
TableLayoutPanel1.Controls.Add(aButton, 1, 1)
```

```
// C#
Button aButton = new Button();
tableLayoutPanel1.Controls.Add(aButton, 1, 1);
```

12. In the Designer, choose the SplitContainer tab. From the Toolbox, add a *Split-Container* control to this *TabPage*. Set the *BorderStyle* property to *Fixed3d*.

13. From the Toolbox, add two *Button* controls to *Panel1* of the *SplitContainer*. Set the *Text* properties of these buttons to *Fix/Unfix Panel1* and *Fix/Unfix Splitter*. Resize the buttons as necessary to display the text.

14. Add a Button to Panel2 and set the *Text* property to *Collapse/Uncollapse Panel1*. Resize the button as necessary to display the text.

15. Double-click the button labeled Fix/Unfix Panel1 and add the following code to the *Click* event handler:

```
' VB
If SplitContainer1.FixedPanel = FixedPanel.Panel1 Then
     SplitContainer1.FixedPanel = FixedPanel.None
Else
     SplitContainer1.FixedPanel = FixedPanel.Panel1
End If
```

```
// C#
if (splitContainer1.FixedPanel == FixedPanel.Panel1)
{
     splitContainer1.FixedPanel = FixedPanel.None;
}
     else splitContainer1.FixedPanel = FixedPanel.Panel1;
```

16. Double-click the button labeled Fix/Unfix Splitter and add the following code to the *Click* event handler:

```
' VB
SplitContainer1.IsSplitterFixed = Not SplitContainer1.IsSplitterFixed
```

```
// C#
splitContainer1.IsSplitterFixed = !(splitContainer1.IsSplitterFixed);
```

17. Double-click the button labeled Collapse/Uncollapse Panel1 and add the following code to the *Click* event handler:

```
' VB
SplitContainer1.Panel1Collapsed = Not SplitContainer1.Panel1Collapsed
```

```
// C#
splitContainer1.Panel1Collapsed = !(splitContainer1.Panel1Collapsed);
```

18. Press F5 to run the application.

19. On the GroupBox tab, alternately select the radio buttons and note that the radio buttons are automatically exclusive.

20. On the FlowLayoutPanel tab, resize the form with the mouse. Note the automatic change in layout that occurs. Click Button1 and note the effect of setting a flow break on Button3.

21. On the TableLayoutPanel tab, click Button5 to observe how new controls are added to the *TableLayoutPanel*.

22. On the SplitContainer tab, resize the form and resize each panel by moving the Splitter. Click each button in turn and observe the effect on the ability of the control to resize.

Lesson Summary

- Container controls can be used to group and arrange controls on a form. Container controls include *Panel*, *GroupBox*, *FlowLayoutPanel*, *TableLayoutPanel*, and *SplitContainer* controls.

- *GroupBox* controls are usually used to group *RadioButton* controls.

- *Panel* controls create distinct subsections of a form. *FlowLayoutPanel* controls and *TableLayoutPanel* controls are derivatives of the Panel that provide added layout capabilities.

- The SplitContainer encapsulates two *SplitterPanel* controls and a Splitter. The user can resize the panels by grabbing and moving the Splitter.

- The *TabControl* control maintains a collection of *TabPage* controls that each function similarly to individual panels. Each tab page can be selected at run time by choosing the corresponding tab that is displayed on the edge of the tab control.

Lesson Review

You can use the following questions to test your knowledge of the information in this lesson. The questions are also available on the companion CD if you prefer to review them in electronic form.

NOTE Answers

Answers to these questions and explanations of why each answer choice is correct or incorrect are located in the "Answers" section at the end of the book.

---

1. Which of the following code samples correctly demonstrates how to set a flow break on a control named *aButton* in a *FlowLayoutPanel* named FLPanel1?

   A.
   ```
   ' VB
   aButton.SetFlowBreak()

   // C#
   aButton.SetFlowBreak();
   ```

   B.
   ```
   ' VB
   aButton.SetFlowBreak(FLPanel1)

   // C#
   aButton.SetFlowBreak(FLPanel1);
   ```

   C.
   ```
   ' VB
   FLPanel1.SetFlowBreak(aButton)

   // C#
   FLPanel1.SetFlowBreak(aButton);
   ```

   D.
   ```
   ' VB
   FLPanel1.aButton.SetFlowBreak

   // C#
   FLPanel1.aButton.SetFlowBreak();
   ```

2. You are designing an application that includes a property page that enables the user to set properties of the application. These properties are divided into three categories: Appearance, Execution, and Memory Management. Which container control represents the best starting point for the user interface?

   A. *TableLayoutPanel*

   B. *FlowLayoutPanel*

   C. *GroupBox*

   D. *TabControl*

3. Which of the following is the correct way to add a control to a form at design time? (Choose all that apply.)

   A. Select a control in the Toolbox and double-click the form.

   B. Select a control in the Toolbox and draw the form with the mouse.

   C. Double-click the control in the Toolbox.

   D. Select the control in the Toolbox and drag it to the form.

4. Which of the following code samples demonstrates the correct way to add a *Button* control to a form named Form1 at run time?

   A. ' VB
   ```
   Form1.Controls.Add(Button)
   ```

   ```
   // C#
   Form1.Controls.Add(Button);
   ```

   B. ' VB
   ```
   Dim aButton As New Button
      Form1.Controls.Add(aButton)
   ```

   ```
   // C#
   Button aButton = new Button();
      Form1.Controls.Add(aButton);
   ```

   C. ' VB
   ```
   Dim aButton As New Button
      Form1.Add(aButton)
   ```

   ```
   // C#
   Button aButton = new Button();
      Form1.Add(aButton);
   ```

   D. ' VB
   ```
   Form1.Add(New Button)
   ```

   ```
   // C# Form1.Add(new Button);
   ```

5. Which code sample correctly demonstrates how to add a new panel to a *Split-Container* named SpC1?

   A. ' VB
   ```
   SpC1.Controls.Add(New Panel)
   ```

   ```
   // C#
   SpC1.Controls.Add(new Panel());
   ```

   B. ' VB
   ```
   SpC1.Controls.Add(New SplitterPanel)
   // C#
   SpC1.Controls.Add(new SplitterPanel());
   ```

C. ' VB
```
SpC1.Add(New SplitterPanel)
```

```
// C#
SpC1.Add(new SplitterPanel());
```

D. ' VB
```
None of the above
```

```
// C#
None of the above
```

Chapter Review

To further practice and reinforce the skills you learned in this chapter, you can perform the following tasks:

- Review the chapter summary.
- Review the list of key terms introduced in this chapter.
- Complete the case scenarios. These scenarios set up real-world situations involving the topics of this chapter and ask you to create a solution.
- Complete the suggested practices.
- Take a practice test.

Chapter Summary

- The form is the basic building block of Windows Forms applications. Forms provide a variety of properties that can be used to affect the appearance of the user interface, including *Text*, *BorderStyle*, *Size*, *Opacity*, and the behavior of the user interface, such as *WindowState* and *TopMost*.
- Forms are generally rectangular, but non-rectangular forms can be created by setting the *Region* property to a non-rectangular region.
- Container controls can host and help manage layout of individual controls.
- The *SplitContainer* control can be used to create dynamically sizable sections of a form, each of which contains its own controls.
- Controls can be added to a form at design time by selecting a control from the toolbox or dynamically at run time.

Key Terms

Do you know what these key terms mean? You can check your answers by looking up the terms in the glossary at the end of the book.

- container control
- control
- toolbox

Case Scenarios

In the following case scenario, you will apply what you've learned about Windows forms and the user interface. You can find answers to these questions in the "Answers" section at the end of this book.

Case Scenario 1: Designing a User Interface

You are a Windows Forms developer recently hired by Adventure Works to create an internal Windows Forms application. This application is to be an administrator version of a highly successful Web site that uses frames for navigational purposes and presents a complex user interface with several controls and images. Your job is to make the look and feel of the Microsoft Windows application user interface match the Web site experience as closely as possible. What are some possible strategies that could be used to design this user interface (UI)?

Case Scenario 2: Designing a Web Browser

Adventure Works has asked you be part of the team that will create a Web browser for their internal site. The .NET control WebBrowser will be used for the actual Web browsing functionality. One of the primary demands for the user interface is the ability to have only a single instance of the application running but to be able to have multiple Web pages open that the user can rapidly switch between without having to navigate back and forth. How might you use container controls to design this aspect of the user interface?

Suggested Practices

To master the "Add and Configure a Windows Form" objective, complete the following tasks.

Add a Windows Form to a Project at Design Time

For this task, complete Practice 1.

- **Practice 1** Create a custom form that appears as an ellipse at run time. This form should contain functionality that allows the user to close it at run time.

Configure a Windows Form to Control Accessibility, Appearance, Behavior, Configuration, Data, Design, Focus, Layout, Style, and Other Functionality

For this task, complete Practices 1, 2, and 3.

- **Practice 1**   Create an application that enables the user to create new instances of a form by clicking a button.

- **Practice 2**   Create an application that enables the user to resize the form and change visual properties of the form such as BorderStyle and Opacity. Set the startup form to always be on top of the user interface and to start in the upper left-hand corner of the screen.

- **Practice 3**   Create a multiform application and set the second form to be the startup form. Set the startup form to be maximized at startup.

Manage Control Layout on a Windows Form

For this task, complete Practice 1.

- **Practice 1**   Create an application that uses the *GroupBox*, *Panel*, *TabControl*, *FlowLayoutPanel*, *TableLayoutPanel*, and *SplitContainer* controls to arrange the layout of controls on a form.

Take a Practice Test

The practice tests on this book's companion CD offer many options. For example, you can test yourself on just the content covered in this chapter, or you can test yourself on all the 70-526 certification exam content. You can set up the test so that it closely simulates the experience of taking a certification exam, or you can set it up in study mode so that you can look at the correct answers and explanations after you answer each question.

MORE INFO   **Practice tests**

For details about all the practice test options available, see the "How to Use the Practice Tests" section in this book's Introduction.

Chapter 2

Configuring Controls and Creating the User Interface

This chapter explores, in depth, how to configure controls and create the user interface. Controls are graphical components that provide reproducible functionality that can be used to create a consistent user interface experience over several applications. Microsoft Visual Studio 2005 provides controls for information display, data input, user interaction, and a variety of other specialized tasks.

In this chapter, you will learn general procedures for manipulating controls in your application, and you will learn about the specific properties of command and text display controls. In Chapter 3, "Advanced Windows Forms Controls," you will learn about value-setting controls, list-based controls, and other advanced Windows Forms controls.

Exam objectives in this chapter:

- Add and configure a Windows Forms control.
    - Configure controls on a Windows Form at design time to optimize the user interface (UI).
    - Modify control properties.
    - Configure controls in a Windows Form at run time to ensure that the UI complies with best practices.
    - Create and configure command controls on a Windows Form.
    - Create and configure text edit controls on a Windows Form.
    - Create and configure text display controls on a Windows Form.
    - Use the *LinkLabel* control to add Web-style links to Windows Forms applications.

Lessons in this chapter:

Before You Begin

To complete the lessons in this chapter, you must have:

- A computer that meets or exceeds the minimum hardware requirements listed in the "Introduction" at the beginning of the book.

- Visual Studio 2005 Professional Edition installed on your computer.

- An understanding of Microsoft Visual Basic or C# syntax and familiarity with the .NET Framework.

- Completed Chapter 1, "Windows Forms and the User Interface," or have a good understanding of Windows Forms, how to add controls to forms, and how to use the Visual Studio Integrated Development Environment (IDE).

Real World

Matt Stoecker

The design of the user interface is crucial to the success of an application. I find that a user interface must be internally consistent, flow logically, and be easy for the user to use and understand. Poorly designed user interfaces have led to lost hours in training and use and, ultimately, to lost productivity.

Lesson 1: Configuring Controls in Windows Forms

This lesson describes general principles of creating and configuring controls. You will learn common properties of controls, how to change the properties of controls at design time or at run time, and how to control the layout of your controls. You will learn the various mechanisms the IDE exposes to modify controls quickly, and you will learn how to design your user interface in accordance with best practices.

After this lesson, you will be able to:

- Modify the size of a control at design time.
- Modify the location of a control at design time.
- Anchor a control within a Windows Form or other container control.
- Dock a control within a Windows Form or other container control.
- Modify control properties by using the Properties window.
- Modify control properties by using SmartTags.
- Manage the allocation of controls in a Windows Form by using the Document Outline window.
- Configure controls in a Windows Form at run time to ensure that the user interface follows best practices.

Estimated lesson time: 45 minutes

Overview of Controls

Controls are components that combine a graphical interface with pre-designed functionality. Controls are reusable units of code that are designed to fulfill particular tasks. For example, the *TextBox* control is designed to display text and receive textual input from the user, and it contains properties, methods, and events that facilitate these tasks.

All controls inherit from the base class *Control* and, as such, share a variety of properties relating to size, location, and other general aspects of controls. Table 2-1 describes some of the common properties of controls.

Table 2-1 **Common Properties of Controls**

Property	Description
Anchor	Determines how the control is anchored in its parent form or container control.

Table 2-1   **Common Properties of Controls**

Property	Description
BackColor	Gets or sets the *BackColor* of the control.
BackgroundImage	Represents the image that is painted as the background image of the control.
CausesValidation	Represents whether a control causes validation; validation enables you to verify that user input meets specific formatting and value requirements.
ContainsFocus	Indicates whether this control or one of its child controls has the focus.
Controls	Gets the collection of controls contained within this control. Used only for containers.
Cursor	Represents the cursor that is used when the mouse pointer is over this control.
Dock	Determines how the control is docked in its parent form or container control.
Enabled	Gets or sets whether the control is enabled. If a control is not enabled, it will appear grey and cannot be selected or edited.
Font	Gets or sets the font used to display text by this control.
ForeColor	Represents the color used in the foreground of this control, primarily for displaying text.
HasChildren	Gets a value that indicates if this control has any child controls.
Height	Represents the height of the control in pixels.
Location	Indicates the location of the upper left-hand corner of this control relative to the upper left-hand corner of its parent form or container control.
MaximumSize	Gets or sets the maximum size for the control.
MinimumSize	Gets or sets the minimum size for the control.

Table 2-1   Common Properties of Controls

Property	Description
Name	Represents the name used to refer to the control in code. This property can be altered only at design time and cannot be modified at run time.
Parent	Gets or sets the parent form or container control for this control. Setting this property adds the control to the new parent's controls collection.
Region	Gets or sets the window region associated with the control.
Size	Represents the size of the control in pixels.
TabOrder	Indicates in what order the control will be selected when the *Tab* key is used to navigate from control to control.
Tag	Enables the programmer to store a value or object associated with the control.
Text	Gets or sets the text associated with the control. The text might or might not be displayed, depending on the type of control and other property settings.
Visible	Indicates whether the control is visible.
Width	Represents the width of the control in pixels.

Configuring Controls at Design Time

As seen in Chapter 1, you can add a control to a form or container control at design time by dragging it from the Toolbox, selecting it in the Toolbox and clicking the form, or double-clicking the control in the Toolbox. Using any of these methods, you can add the control to the design surface. Once the control is in the Designer, you can modify its properties. Many of the properties of a control can be adjusted graphically in the designer by using the mouse. For other properties, you can modify control properties in the Properties window.

Control Size and Location

The method of modifying a control with the mouse is intuitive and allows you to adjust the control to exactly the desired size. You adjust the size of a control with the mouse by first selecting the control, usually by clicking it in the Designer. This causes the control to be outlined by white squares and a dotted line as shown in Figure 2-1.

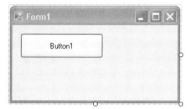

Figure 2-1   A selected control in the designer

Once the control has been selected, you can resize it in the Designer by grabbing an edge or a corner and dragging it with the mouse.

You can also resize a control in the Properties window by modifying the *Size* property. The *Size* property has two components, *Width* and *Height*, which represent the width and height of the control in pixels. You can modify these individual components by expanding the *Size* property and typing a new value for one of the components in the Property Grid, or you can modify the *Size* property directly. The control is resized accordingly.

You can choose one of two ways to resize a control.

▶ **To resize a control at design time**

  1. Select the control, and then drag a corner or an edge to the appropriate size.

  2. Modify the *Size* property in the Property Grid by either changing the *Size* property directly or expanding the *Size* property and changing the *Height* or *Width*.

The designer also provides an easy way to set the location of a control on a form or container control. The location of a control can be changed graphically by grabbing the middle of the control with the mouse and dragging it to the new location.

You can also set the location of the control by modifying the *Location* property in the Property Grid. The *Location* property represents the coordinates of the upper left-hand corner of the control relative to the upper left-hand corner of the parent form or container control. The *Location* property has two components, *X* and *Y*. You can modify the *Location* property directly in the Property Grid, or you can expand the *Location* property and individually set the *X* or *Y* values. The property will relocate to the new location.

You can choose one of two ways to change the location of a control.

▶ **To change the location of a control at design time**

1. Grab the middle of the control with the mouse and drag it to the appropriate location.

2. Set the *Location* property of the control in the Property Grid, either by setting the *Location* property directly or by expanding the *Location* property and modifying the values of *X* or *Y* as appropriate.

You can also reposition a group of controls graphically with the mouse. You must first select all of the controls that you want to move, either by outlining the appropriate controls with the mouse or by holding down the *Ctrl* key and clicking each control in turn. A group of selected controls is shown in Figure 2-2.

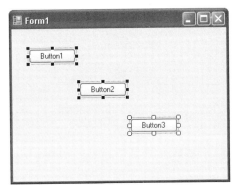

Figure 2-2   A group of selected controls in the Designer

Once the group of controls is selected, you can move the group by grabbing the middle of one of the controls and moving it with the mouse.

The Layout Toolbar

The Layout toolbar provides a quick and easy way to accomplish many of the control layout tasks required at design time. The Layout toolbar is not one of the default toolbars, so you might need to add it to the IDE. You can add the Layout toolbar by selecting the View menu, choosing Toolbars, and then selecting Layout. The Layout toolbar is shown in Figure 2-3.

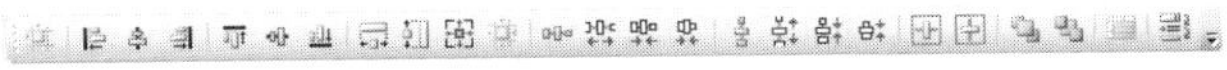

Figure 2-3   The Layout toolbar

The Layout toolbar allows you to adjust the vertical and horizontal spacing of a group of controls. The toolbar buttons associated with these tasks are shown in Figure 2-4.

Figure 2-4   Horizontal and vertical spacing buttons

You can apply any of these layout buttons to a group of controls by selecting the group of controls and then clicking the appropriate button.

▶ **To adjust control spacing with the Layout toolbar**

1. If necessary, add the Layout toolbar to the IDE by selecting the View menu, choosing Toolbars, and then selecting Layout.

2. Select the group of controls that you want to adjust.

3. Adjust the control spacing by clicking the appropriate button.

The Layout toolbar also contains buttons that allow you to align the controls in the designer. The buttons involved in alignment are shown in Figure 2-5.

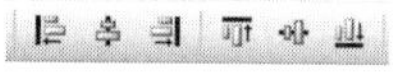

Figure 2-5   Control alignment buttons

You can apply any of these alignment buttons to a group of controls by selecting the group of controls and then clicking the appropriate button.

▶ **To adjust control alignment with the Layout toolbar**

1. If necessary, add the Layout toolbar to the IDE by selecting the View menu, choosing Toolbars, and then selecting Layout.

2. Select the group of controls that you want to adjust.

3. Adjust the control spacing by clicking the appropriate button.

Snaplines

Snaplines are new features that give you visual aid and feedback when locating controls on a form or within a container control. When a control is dragged onto a form or container control, snaplines appear, providing cues relating to control alignment.

When a control is dragged near the edge of a form, container control, or other control, a snapline appears, indicating the distance represented by the *Margin* property. Additionally, snaplines indicating vertical and horizontal alignment of control edges appear when a control that is being dragged comes into alignment with an adjacent control. When a snapline appears, you can drop the control to create an aligned user interface. Horizontal, vertical, and margin snaplines are shown in Figure 2-6.

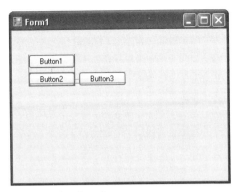

Figure 2-6   Snaplines

If snaplines are disabled, you can enable them in the Options dialog box as described in the following steps.

▶ **To enable snaplines**

1. From the Tools menu, select Options to open the Options dialog box.

2. In the left-hand pane, expand Windows Forms Designer and select General.

3. In the Property Grid, set LayoutMode to SnapLines.

4. Click OK.

Quick Check

1. What is the purpose of Snaplines?

2. What can you use the Layout Toolbar for?

Quick Check Answers

1. Snaplines appear at design time and help you align controls to the form or to each other.

2. The Layout toolbar allows you to align controls on a form and adjust their spacing.

Modifying Control Properties at Design Time

Although you can modify properties of controls such as location and size by manipulating the control in the designer, there are other mechanisms that allow you to set control properties in the designer, including the Properties window, SmartTags, and the Document Outline window.

The Properties Window

The primary interface for setting control properties is the Properties window, which exposes the properties of a form, component, or control that can be set at design time. You can set property values for most properties by selecting the property and typing a new value for the property into the Properties window. For some properties, such as the *Dock* and *Anchor* properties, the Properties window provides specialized graphical interfaces that assist in setting the property value. The Properties window is shown in Figure 2-7.

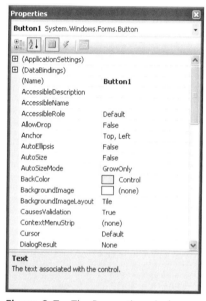

Figure 2-7   The Properties window

If the Properties window is not visible, you can open it with the following procedure.

▶ **To open the Properties window**

From the View menu, choose Properties window or press F4.

▶ **To set a property in the Properties window**

1. With the mouse, click the property you want to set.

2. Type the new value for the property, or use the specialized interface if this property provides one.

Dock and *Anchor* Properties

The *Dock* and *Anchor* properties allow you to define how a control behaves within the confines of its parent form or container control. The *Anchor* property defines a constant distance between one or more edges of a control and the corresponding edges of the control's parent form or container control. The *Dock* property allows you to attach a control to an edge of the parent form or container control or to fill the form completely.

The *Anchor* Property

The *Anchor* determines which edges of the control, if any, maintain a constant distance from the edge of its parent form or container control when the parent is resized. The default value for this property is *Top*, *Left*, which means that the top and left edges of the control will maintain a constant distance from the corresponding edges of its parent. This has the effect of the control maintaining both its position and size when the parent is resized. If opposite edges (for example, right and left) are both set in the *Anchor* property, the control will stretch when the parent is resized. If neither of opposite edges is set in the *Anchor* property, the control will float when the parent is resized.

You set the *Anchor* property in the Property Grid. The *Anchor* property has a special interface (shown in Figure 2-8) that allows you to choose the edges to anchor.

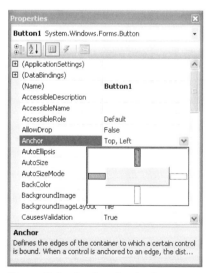

Figure 2-8 Setting the *Anchor* property

▶ **To set the *Anchor* property**

1. In the Properties window, choose Anchor and click the drop-down box. The *Anchor* property visual interface appears.

2. Click the bars indicating the edges you want to anchor. When finished, click outside of the *Anchor* property interface.

The *Dock* Property

The *Dock* property allows you to attach a control to the edge of its parent. For example, a control docked to the top edge of a form or container control will always be connected to the top edge of the parent control and will automatically resize in the left and right directions when its parent is resized. The *Dock* property can also be set to *Fill*, in which case, the control will grow to occupy all of the available space in the parent control. This setting is usually used with a container control, such as *SplitContainer* or *FlowLayoutPanel*.

Like the *Anchor* property, the *Dock* property provides a graphical interface for setting the value, as shown in Figure 2-9.

Figure 2-9   Setting the *Dock* Property

▶ **To set the *Dock* property**

1. In the Properties window, choose the *Dock* property and click the drop-down box. The *Dock* property visual interface appears.

2. Click the box indicating the value you want to set the *Dock* property to.

Smart Tags

Some controls expose their most common tasks through smart tags. When present, smart tags appear as small boxes in the upper right-hand corner of the control, as shown in Figure 2-10.

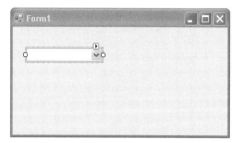

Figure 2-10   A Combo box with a smart tag

When the smart tag is clicked, a box that facilitates the most common tasks appears, as shown in Figure 2-11.

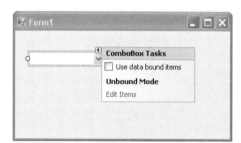

Figure 2-11   Combo box smart tag tasks

▶ **To modify control properties by using smart tags**

1. For controls that expose smart tags, click the smart tag in the designer. A control-specific Tasks box opens.

2. Use the Tasks box to perform common tasks associated with the control.

Document Outline Window

When creating forms that contain several container controls, the Document Outline window can be useful for allocating controls between the various containers. The Document Outline window graphically displays all of the controls and container controls that reside in a form. With the mouse, you can grab controls in the Document Outline window and move them from one container to another. You can also delete controls from the form by deleting them in the Document Outline window and add them by copying them from the Toolbox and pasting them into the Document Outline window. Figure 2-12 shows the Document Outline window.

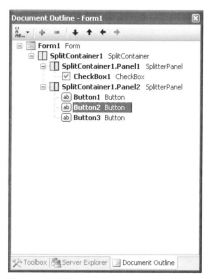

Figure 2-12   The Document Outline window

▶ **To open the Document Outline window**

From the View menu, select Other Windows, and then select Document Outline; or press Ctrl+Alt+T.

▶ **To move controls from one container to another in the Document Outline window**

1. In the Document Outline window, grab the control you want to move with the mouse.

2. Drag the control onto the name of the container control you want to add it to.

▶ **To remove a control from a project with the Document Outline window**

Select the control in the Document Outline window and press Delete. Note that, if you delete a container control in this fashion, you will also delete any contained controls.

▶ **To add a control to a project with the Document Outline window**

1. Right-click a control in the Toolbox and choose Copy.

2. In the Document Outline window, right-click the form or container control you want to add a new control to and choose Paste.

Best Practices for User Interface Design

How your user interface is composed influences how easily your application can be learned and used. Primary considerations for user interface design include:

- Simplicity
- Position of controls
- Consistency
- Aesthetics

Simplicity

Simplicity is an important aspect of a user interface. An overly complex user interface makes an application more difficult to learn, resulting in lost productivity. A user interface should allow a user to quickly complete all tasks required by the program but should expose only the functionality needed at each stage of the application.

When designing your user interface, keep program flow and execution in mind. Controls that display related data should be grouped together on the form. Container controls can be used to organize related controls into distinct subsections of a form. Controls such as list boxes, combo boxes, and check boxes can be used to display data and allow users to choose between preset options. Enable default values whenever possible. For example, if most of the intended users of an application will choose United States in a Country field, set United States as the default value for that field. Note that you should always make it easy to override a default value when necessary.

Position of Controls

The location of controls on your user interface should reflect their relative importance and frequency of use. For example, if your form collects both required and optional information, the controls that collect required information are more important and, thus, should receive greater prominence in the user interface.

Because relatedness of information is an important consideration, controls that display related information should be grouped together. For example, if you have a form that displays information about a customer, a purchase, or an employee, you can group each set of controls on a *TabControl* that allows the user to easily move back and forth between displays.

Consistency

A user interface should exhibit a consistent design across each form in your application. An inconsistent design can make your application seem disorganized or chaotic, hindering adoption by your target audience.

Consistency is created from the use of colors, fonts, size, and types of control. Before any application development takes place, decide on a visual scheme that will remain consistent throughout the application. The use of system colors and fonts can create a consistent user experience throughout the application.

Aesthetics

Whenever possible, a user interface should be inviting and pleasant. Although clarity and simplicity should not be sacrificed for the sake of attractiveness, try to create an application that will not dissuade users.

The use of color can help make your user interface attractive to the target audience, but overuse can inhibit adoption. Loud, vibrant colors might be initially appealing but can cause eyestrain and might be unappealing to some users. When possible, use muted colors with broad appeal. Never rely on color alone to convey information and, when designing for international audiences, be aware that certain colors might have cultural significance.

Usability should determine the fonts you choose for your application. You should avoid fonts that are difficult to read; stick to common, easy-to-read fonts such as Times New Roman or Arial. Use decorative fonts for special visual effects only when appropriate and never to convey important information.

Lab: Practice Configuring Controls

In this lab, you will practice configuring controls at design time. You will use the techniques described in the previous lesson to add controls to a Windows Form, set the location and size in the Property Grid, and use smart tags, the Layout toolbar, snaplines, and the Document Outline window.

▶ **Exercise 1: Practice Configuring Controls**

1. Open Visual Studio and create a new Windows Forms project.

2. From the Toolbox, drag a SplitContainer onto the form.

3. Open the SplitContainer smart tag and choose Horizontal splitter orientation. The *SplitContainer's Orientation* property is set to *Horizontal*.

4. From the Toolbox, drag three *Button* controls into the top panel of the Split-Container. Use snaplines to align them horizontally.

5. Select Button1. In the Properties window, set the *Location* property to *0, 0*.

6. Select Button2. In the Properties window, set the *Size* property to *30, 50*.

7. If the Layout toolbar is not visible, add it to the IDE by choosing View, Toolbars, and then Layout.

8. In the form, select all three controls and align their bottom edges by selecting Align Bottoms in the Layout Toolbar.

9. Press Ctrl+Alt+T to open the Document Outline window.

10. In the Document Outline window, select Button 3 and move it to *SplitContainer1.SplitterPanel2*.

11. In the form, select Button3. In the Properties window, set the *Dock* property to Bottom.

12. In the form, select Button2. In the Properties window, set the *Anchor* property to *Bottom, Right*.

13. Press F5 to run the application. Using the mouse, resize the form and observe the different behavior of the three buttons.

Lesson Summary

■ Visual Studio 2005 provides multiple mechanisms for managing the layout of controls on your form, including:

❑ The Properties window

❑ Layout toolbar

❑ Snaplines

❑ Control modification in the designer using the mouse

■ Individual properties of controls can be modified in the Properties window. Some properties provide specialized graphical interfaces to assist in setting the property value.

■ Smart tags expose the most common configuration tasks of several controls.

■ The *Anchor* and *Dock* properties allow you to set specialized behaviors for controls on your form.

■ The Document Outline window provides an easy way to manage the allocation of controls between your form and container controls.

Lesson Review

The following questions are intended to reinforce key information presented in this lesson. The questions are also available on the companion CD if you prefer to review them in an electronic form.

NOTE   Answers

Answers to these questions and explanations of why each answer choice is right or wrong are located in the "Answers" section at the end of the book.

---

1. Which of the following can be used to modify the size of a control in a form at design time? (Choose all that apply.)

   A. Grabbing and dragging the edges of the control

   B. Setting the control size in the View menu

   C. Clicking the smart tag and entering a new size for the control

   D. Editing the *Size* property in the Properties window

2. Which of the following methods can be used to modify the location of controls in a form at design time? (Choose all that apply.)

   A. Changing the *Location* property in the Properties window

   B. Grabbing the control and moving it with the mouse

   C. Using the Layout toolbar to adjust control spacing

   D. Using the Location window to graphically position controls

3. What setting of the *Anchor* property would allow controls to float freely when the form is resized?

   A. *Top*

   B. *Top, Bottom*

   C. *None*

   D. *Right, Left*

4. What setting of the *Dock* property will cause the control to fill its form or container control?

   A. *Top.*

   B. *Fill.*

   C. *Top, Left, Right, Bottom.*

   D. None, you should use the *Anchor* property.

Lesson 2: Creating and Configuring Command and Text Display Controls

This lesson details the use of command and text display controls. Text display controls such as *Label* and *LinkLabel* are most commonly used to convey read-only information to the user. Command controls such as the *Button* are used to execute tasks or proceed with the application. You will learn common properties and events of the *Button*, *Label*, and *LinkLabel* controls and how to use them in designing your user interface.

> **After this lesson, you will be able to:**
> - Configure a *Button* control that a user can click to perform actions.
> - Use a *Label* control to display text that the user cannot alter.
> - Use the *LinkLabel* control to add Web-style links to Windows Forms applications.
>
> **Estimated lesson time: 30 minutes**

The *Button* Control

One of the most familiar controls in the Toolbox is the *Button* control. The *Button* control is the primary control that enables command interaction between the user and the user interface. The *Button* can display a short string on the front and respond to user clicks. The *Button* control gives a visual cue when clicked and exposes an *event handler* that allows the user to write code that executes when the *Button* is clicked.

The *Button* control exposes several properties that enable you to customize its appearance and behavior. Table 2-2 shows important properties of the *Button* control.

Table 2-2   Important Properties of the *Button* Control

Property	Description
AutoEllipsis	Enables the automatic handling of text that extends beyond the width of the button.
DialogResult	Sets a *DialogResult* value that you can associate with the button, such as *DialogResult.OK* or *DialogResult.Cancel*.
FlatAppearance	Defines styles that govern how the button appears and behaves when the *FlatStyle* property is set to *Flat*.
FlatStyle	Sets the visual style of the button when a user moves the mouse over the button and clicks.

Table 2-2 **Important Properties of the *Button* Control**

Property	Description
Text	Sets the text that appears on the button.
TextAlign	Indicates how the text displayed on the button will be aligned.

Responding to Clicks

The primary function of a *Button* control in the user interface is to respond to user mouse clicks. *Buttons* typically cause code to be executed when clicked by the user. For example, you might have an OK button that causes the application execution to proceed after the user has provided necessary information, or you might have a Cancel button that returns execution to a previous step.

You can write code to be executed when the button is clicked by using the *Button.Click* event handler. This is a method that receives the button click and then executes appropriate code.

▶ **To write code for the *Button.Click* event handler**

1. In the Designer, double-click the button you want to write code for. Visual Studio automatically generates a method declaration named *Button_Click* and adds code behind-the-scenes to configure the method to handle the *Button.Click* event. Visual Studio displays the new *Button_Click* method that will run when the user clicks the button.

2. Write the appropriate code in this method. At run time, this code will be executed when the button is clicked. The following code shows an example of a complete *Button_Click* method.

```
' VB
Private Sub Button1_Click(ByVal sender As System.Object, ByVal e As System.EventArgs)_
   Handles Button1.Click
      MsgBox("The Button has been clicked!")
End Sub
```

```
// C#
private void button1_Click(object sender, EventArgs e)
{
    MessageBox.Show("The Button has been clicked!");
}
```

Events and event handlers will be covered in greater detail in Chapter 4, "Tool-Strips, Menus, and Events."

Responding to Other Clicks

Although the *Button.Click* event handler is useful for responding to simple clicks, you can also configure a button or other control to respond to other mouse clicks as well, such as right-clicks. You can respond to these clicks by using the *MouseDown* event.

One of the arguments for the *Button.MouseDown* event handler is an instance of *MouseClickEventArgs*. This argument contains detailed information about the location and click-state of the mouse and can be used to differentiate between left-clicks, right-clicks, double-clicks, or other mouse interactions. Table 2-3 describes the properties of the *MouseClickEventArgs* class.

Table 2-3   Properties of *MouseClickEventArgs*

Property	Description
Button	Indicates the mouse button that was pressed. Possible values are *Left, Right, Middle, None, XButton1,* or *XButton2.*
Clicks	Gets the number of times the button was pressed and released.
Delta	Gets a count of how many notches the mouse wheel has rotated.
Location	Gets the current location of the mouse pointer.
X	Gets the X coordinate of the mouse pointer.
Y	Gets the Y coordinate of the mouse pointer.

Using the values exposed by the *MouseClickEventArgs* instance, you can determine the button that was clicked and the position of the mouse wheel. Note that if any button other than the left button clicks a control, the control will not give the visual feedback (the "click" in the user interface) that is customary for a button.

▶ **To respond to various mouse clicks**

1. In the Designer, select the *Button* control you want to write code for.

2. In the Properties window, click the lightning bolt button (shown in Figure 2-13 here) to view the *Button's* events.

Figure 2-13   The lightning bolt button

3. In the Properties window, double-click the cell next to *MouseDown* to have Visual Studio generate and display an event handler for *Button.MouseDown*.

4. Write code in this event handler that responds to the desired mouse click combination. The following example demonstrates how to differentiate between the left and right buttons.

```vb
' VB
Private Sub Button1_MouseDown(ByVal sender As System.Object, ByVal e As _
  System.Windows.Forms.MouseEventArgs) Handles Button1.MouseDown
    Select Case e.Button
        Case Windows.Forms.MouseButtons.Left
            MsgBox("The left button was clicked")
        Case Windows.Forms.MouseButtons.Right
            MsgBox("The right button was clicked")
        Case Else
            MsgBox("Some other button was clicked")
    End Select
End Sub
```

```csharp
// C#
private void button1_MouseDown(object sender, MouseEventArgs e)
{
    switch (e.Button)
    {
        case MouseButtons.Left:
            MessageBox.Show("The left button was clicked");
            break;
        case MouseButtons.Right:
            MessageBox.Show("The right button was clicked");
            break;
        default:
            MessageBox.Show("Some other button was clicked");
            break;
    }
}
```

FlatStyle and *FlatAppearance*

The *FlatStyle* property governs whether the button has a three-dimensional, raised appearance, or a flat appearance. You can give a button a flat appearance by setting the *FlatStyle* property to *Flat*.

When the *FlatStyle* property is set to *Flat*, the *FlatAppearance* property determines how the button looks and behaves in the user interface. The *FlatAppearance* property is an instance of a structure that contains properties described in Table 2-4.

Table 2-4   Properties of *FlatAppearance*

Property	Description
BorderColor	This property sets the color of the button border.
BorderSize	This property sets the size of the button border.
MouseDownBackColor	This property sets the color of the button when the left mouse button clicks this button.
MouseOverBackColor	This property sets the color of the button when the mouse pointer is over the button.

When the *FlatStyle* is set to *Flat*, there are fewer built-in visual cues that allow the user to interact with the button. You can provide additional cues by setting appropriate values in the *FlatAppearance* property. The following procedure describes how to set the *BackColor* of the button when under the mouse.

▶ **To change the *BackColor* of a button when under the mouse**

1. In the Properties window, set the *FlatStyle* property to *Flat*.

2. Expand the *FlatAppearance* property.

3. In the *FlatAppearance* property, set the *MouseOverBackColor* property to the color you want the button to have when under the mouse.

Accept and Cancel Buttons

A common scenario when creating dialog forms is to create an Accept or Cancel button on the form that provides an appropriate *DialogResult* value to the form when clicked. You can use the *DialogResult* property of the *Button* to create Accept or Cancel buttons.

▶ **To create an Accept or Cancel button**

1. From the Toolbox, drag a button onto the form and set the *Text* property to an appropriate value (for example, *Accept* for an Accept button).

2. In the Properties window, set the *DialogResult* property to *OK* for an Accept button or *Cancel* for a cancel button.

3. In the Designer, double-click the button to open the code window.

4. In the *Button_Click* event handler, close the form as shown here:

```
' VB
Me.Close()
```

```
// C#
this.Close();
```

When a form is shown with the *ShowDialog* method, it will automatically return the dialog result associated with the button that was clicked. The following example demonstrates how this form might be used. The hypothetical form is called DialogForm.

```
' VB
Dim aForm As New DialogForm
Dim aResult As System.Windows.Forms.DialogResult
aResult = aForm.ShowDialog
If aResult = DialogResult.Ok Then
   ' Do something
   Else
   ' Do something else
End If
```

```
// C#
Dialog aForm = new DialogForm();
System.Window.Forms.DialogResult aResult;
aResult = aForm.ShowDialog();
if (aResult == DialogResult.Ok)
{
    // Do something
}
else
{
    // Do something else
}
```

The *Label* Control

The *Label* control is primarily used to display read-only textual information to the user. For example, labels are frequently used to display an informative string beside a control, such as "First Name" beside a *TextBox* control meant to collect the user's first name. Labels can also be used to define shortcut keys for other controls.

The text displayed in a Label is set in the Label's *Text* property. You can set the Label to resize itself automatically to the size of the text by setting the Label's *AutoSize* property to *True*. If the *AutoSize* property is set to *False*, you can set the size of the *Label* by grabbing and dragging the control edges in the designer.

Label controls can be used to define access keys for other controls. *Access keys* are keys that, when pressed in combination with the *Alt* key, move the focus to the desired control. The following procedure describes how to use a *Label* control to define an access key for another control.

▶ **To define an access key**

1. From the Toolbox, drag a *Label* control onto the form, near the control for which you want to define the access key (for example, a *TextBox* control).

2. In the Properties window, set the *Text* property to a descriptive name for the control. Precede the letter that you want to use for the access key with an ampersand (&) character. For example, to use F as the access key, you might set the Label's *Text* property to *&First Name*.

3. In the Properties window, set the *UseMnemonic* property to *True* (the default).

4. In the Properties window, set the *TabIndex* property to one less than the *TabIndex* property of the control for which you are defining an access key. Verify that two controls do not have the same *TabIndex* value.

The *LinkLabel* Control

The *LinkLabel* control allows you to create a Web-style link in your form that opens a Web page or performs some other action when clicked. The *LinkLabel* control contains a variety of properties that allow you to configure the *LinkLabel* control. Table 2-5 shows important properties of the *LinkLabel* control.

Table 2-5   Important Properties of the *LinkLabel* Control

Property	Description
ActiveLinkColor	Sets the color of active links.
LinkArea	Indicates the area of the *LinkLabel* that functions as a link.
LinkBehavior	Indicates the behavior of the link.
LinkColor	Sets the color of the link.
LinkVisited	Indicates whether the link has been visited.
VisitedLinkColor	Sets the color of visited links.

Specifying Link Color

You can specify the color of the link that is displayed in the *LinkLabel* control by setting the properties of the *LinkLabel* control. The *LinkColor* indicates the color of the link before being clicked. The *ActiveLinkColor* represents the color of the link when the link is being clicked, and the *VisitedLinkColor* is the color of a link that has been visited. Note that you must set the *LinkVisited* property of the *LinkLabel* control to *True* for the link to appear in the color indicated by the *VisitedLinkColor* property. All of these properties can be set at design time in the Properties window.

Specifying Link Behavior

The underlying behavior of the link is determined by the *LinkBehavior* property. The *LinkBehavior* property has four possible values: *SystemDefault*, *AlwaysUnderline*, *HoverUnderline*, and *NeverUnderline*. The behavior that each of these values defines is fairly self-explanatory. When set to *SystemDefault*, the *LinkLabel* will display the same default link behavior as is specified by the system. When set to *AlwaysUnderline*, the link will always be underlined. Similarly, when set to *NeverUnderline*, the link will never be underlined, and when set to *HoverUnderline*, the link will be underlined only when the mouse hovers over the link. The *LinkBehavior* property is generally set at design time in the Properties window.

Opening a Form or Web Page with *LinkLabel*

You use the *LinkLabel.LinkClicked* event handler to open a new form or Web page. You can also use this technique to set the *LinkVisited* property to *True*, which will cause the link to appear in the color of the *VisitedLinkColor* property. The following procedure demonstrates how to open a new form or Web page with the *LinkLabel* control.

▶ **To open a form or Web Page with the *LinkLabel* control**

1. Set the *Text* property of the *LinkLabel* control to an appropriate value that indicates the link destination (for example, *Shipping Form* or *Microsoft Web Site*).

2. In the Designer, double-click the *LinkLabel* to create a *LinkLabel.LinkClicked* event handler.

3. Write the appropriate code to open a new Web page or to display a new form. Set the *LinkVisited* property of the *LinkLabel* to *True*. An example is shown here. This example assumes you have a *LinkLabel* control named *LinkLabel1* and a form named *ShippingForm* in your project.

```
' VB
' Opens a new Form
ShippingForm.Show()
' Opens a new web site in Internet Explorer
System.Diagnostics.Process.Start("www.microsoft.com")
' Set the LinkVisited property to True
LinkLabel1.LinkVisited = True
```

```
// C#
// Opens a new Form
ShippingForm.Show();
// Opens a new web site in Internet Explorer
System.Diagnostics.Process.Start("www.microsoft.com");
// Set the LinkVisited property to true
linkLabel1.LinkVisited = true;
```

Quick Check

1. What events of the *Button* control can be used to respond to mouse clicks?

2. When would you use a *LinkLabel* control instead of a *Label* control?

Quick Check Answers

1. The *Click* event responds to the right button click, and the *MouseDown* event can be used to respond to other button clicks.

2. The *Label* control is designed primarily to label other controls on a form. The *LinkLabel* control can label other controls but also exposes a link to the user that can open a new form or Web page.

Lab: Practice with *Command* and *Text Display* Controls

In this lab, you will practice some of the techniques covered in this lesson. You will add a *LinkLabel* to a form and configure it to open a dialog form that asks the user to input his name.

▶ **Exercise 1: Creating a Dialog Form**

1. From the Toolbox, drag a *LinkLabel* control onto the form.

2. In the Property Grid, set the *Text* property to *Open Form*.

3. From the Project menu, choose Add Windows Form and add a new Windows Form to your project named Form2.

4. In the Designer, drag two *Button* controls onto Form2. Set the *Text* property of these buttons to *Accept* and *Cancel*.

5. Set the *DialogResult* property of the AcceptButton to *OK* and the *DialogResult* property of the Cancel button to *Cancel*.

6. From the Toolbox, drag two *TextBox* controls onto the form.

7. *C# only*: Set the *Modifiers* property of each *TextBox* control to *Internal*.

8. From the Toolbox, drag two *Label* controls onto the form and place each near a *TextBox* control.

9. Set the *Text* properties of the *Label* controls to *&First Name* and *&Last Name*.

10. Set the *UseMnemonic* property for each label to *True*.

11. In the Properties window, set the *TabIndex* property as shown.

Control	Tab Index Setting
Label1	0
TextBox1	1
Label2	2
TextBox2	3
Button1	4
Button2	5

12. In the Designer, choose the tab for Form1. Double-click the *LinkLabel* control to create a *LinkLabel.LinkClicked* event handler. Add the following code:

```
' VB
Dim aResult As DialogResult
aResult = Form2.ShowDialog()
If aResult = Windows.Forms.DialogResult.OK Then
    MsgBox("Your name is " & Form2.TextBox1.Text & " " & _
        Form2.TextBox2.Text)
End If
LinkLabel1.LinkVisited = True
```

```
// C#
DialogResult aResult;
Form2 aForm = new Form2();
aResult = aForm.ShowDialog();
if (aResult == System.Windows.Forms.DialogResult.OK)
{
    MessageBox.Show("Your name is " + aForm.textBox1.Text + " " +
        aForm.textBox2.Text);
}
linkLabel1.LinkVisited = true;
```

13. Press F5 to run the application. Click the *LinkLabel* to open the form. Test the access keys and both the Accept and the Cancel buttons.

Lesson Summary

- The *Button* control is the primary command control for the user interface. The *Button_Click* event handler is the method that is executed when the button is clicked. The button can respond to other mouse button clicks via the *Mouse-Down* event.

- The *FlatAppearance* property governs how a *Button* looks and behaves when the *FlatStyle* property is set to *Flat*.

- By setting the *DialogResult* value of a *Button* control, you can create a Cancel or Accept button. You can then examine the result of the form as you would a standard dialog box.

- The *Label* control conveys read-only information to the user. You can use the Label to define an access key by setting the *Text*, *TabOrder*, and *UseMnemonic* properties.

- The *LinkLabel* control allows you to create Web-style links in your user interface. The *LinkColor*, *ActiveLinkColor*, and *VisitedLinkColor* properties control the color of the link in the *LinkLabel* control. You write code to open new forms or Web pages in the *LinkLabel.LinkClicked* event handler.

Lesson Review

The following questions are intended to reinforce key information presented in this lesson. The questions are also available on the companion CD if you prefer to review them in electronic form.

NOTE Answers

Answers to these questions and explanations of why each answer choice is right or wrong are located in the "Answers" section at the end of the book.

---

1. Which Button events can be used to respond to mouse clicks? (Choose all that apply.)

   A. *Button.Click*

   B. *Button.LinkClicked*

   C. *Button.MouseDown*

   D. *Button.MouseOver*

2. Which property does not control how a Button looks or behaves when the *Flat-Style* property is set to *Flat*?

    A. *FlatAppearance.MouseOverBackColor*

    B. *FlatAppearance.MouseDownBackColor*

    C. *FlatAppearance.BorderSize*

    D. *FlatAppearance.Text*

3. Which is necessary to define an access key using a *Label* control? (Choose all that apply.)

    A. Set the TabOrder so that the control for the access key is immediately after the Label.

    B. Set the *UseMnemonic* property to *True*.

    C. Set the *Text* property with an ampersand to indicate the access key.

    D. Set the *CausesValidation* property to *True*.

4. Which properties can be used to define the color behavior of the *LinkLabel* control? (Choose all that apply.)

    A. *ActiveLinkColor*

    B. *LinkLabel_LinkClicked*

    C. *VisitedLinkColor*

    D. *LinkBehavior*

Lesson 3: Creating and Configuring Text Edit Controls

This lesson describes how to create and configure text edit controls. *TextBox* controls are used to both display text to the user and receive textual input. The *MaskedTextBox* allows you to display text in a preset format and validate user input against a format. In this lesson, you will learn how to configure the *TextBox* and *MaskedTextBox* controls to receive and display user input.

After this lesson, you will be able to:

- Configure the *TextBox* control to receive editable, multiline input from the user.
- Configure the *MaskedTextBox* control for formatted text and data entry.

Estimated lesson time: 30 minutes

The *TextBox* Control

The *TextBox* control is the primary control used to receive textual input from the user. The *TextBox* allows you to receive text from and display text to the user. You can create text boxes that can display multiline text, and you can create text boxes that display a password character instead of the actual text.

The *TextBox* control exposes several properties that allow you to configure its behavior. Important properties of the *TextBox* control are shown in Table 2-6.

Table 2-6   Important Properties of the *TextBox* Control

Property	Description
AutoCompleteCustomSource	Holds a string collection that contains auto-complete data when the *AutoCompleteMode* is set to a value other than *None* and the *AutoCompleteSource* is set to *Custom*.
AutoCompleteMode	Sets the *AutoComplete* mode of the control. Possible values are *None*, *Append*, *Suggest*, or *Suggest-Append*.
AutoCompleteSource	Sets the source for auto-complete data. Can be set to any of a variety of system sources or to a custom source provided by the *AutoCompleteCustomSource* property.

Table 2-6   Important Properties of the *TextBox* Control

Property	Description
CharacterCasing	Indicates the casing of the characters in the *TextBox* control. Possible values are *Normal*, *Upper*, or *Lower*.
Lines	Returns a string array representing the individual lines of the text box. This property is most useful when *MultiLine* is set to *True*. Note that a line is defined as a string that is terminated by a carriage return character and does not refer to visible lines in the UI as might be seen when the *WordWrap* property is set to *True*.
MaxLength	Specifies the maximum number of characters that can be entered into the *TextBox*.
MultiLine	Indicates whether the *TextBox* can contain only a single line of text or multiple lines.
PasswordChar	Sets the password character to be displayed in the *Textbox* instead of the actual characters of the text.
ReadOnly	Indicates whether the text in the *TextBox* can be edited.
ScrollBars	Indicates the scroll bars that will be displayed in the *TextBox* when the *MultiLine* property is set to *True*.
Text	Gets or sets the text contained in the *TextBox*.
UseSystemPasswordChar	Indicates whether to use the system password instead of the actual text character in the *TextBox*.
WordWrap	Indicates whether words automatically wrap from one line to the next when the *MultiLine* property is set to *True*.

The main purpose of the *TextBox* control is to provide a container for editable text. Users can input text into text boxes or edit textual data the application displays. The text held by the *TextBox* property is accessible via the *Text* property. The text in the *TextBox* is editable if the *ReadOnly* property is set to *False*, which is the default. If the *ReadOnly* property is set to *True*, the user cannot edit the text displayed.

Creating a MultiLine *TextBox* Control

TextBox controls are single-line by default, but you can create a multiline *TextBox* by setting the *MultiLine* property to *True*. This allows you to resize the *TextBox* vertically as well as horizontally.

When the *MultiLine* property is set to *True*, several other properties become important. The *Lines* property exposes a string array that contains the individual lines of the *TextBox*. The *ScrollBars* property indicates whether scroll bars will be displayed for the *TextBox* and, if so, whether *Horizontal*, *Vertical*, or both will be displayed. The *Word-Wrap* property indicates whether words will automatically wrap from one line to the next. Note that if the *WordWrap* property is set to *True*, horizontal scroll bars will never appear, even if the *ScrollBars* property is set to *Horizontal*.

Creating a Password *TextBox* Control

You can use the *PasswordChar* or *UseSystemPasswordChar* properties to create a text box that can receive text input but display a masking character instead of the actual text, rendering the user input unreadable by observers. This is most commonly used to create a text box for entering a password. If the *PasswordChar* property is set to a character (for example, an asterisk ["*"]), that character will be displayed whenever the user types a character into the text box. Note that the actual characters the user types will be stored in the *Text* property—only the rendering of these characters in the UI will change. You can also set the *UseSystemPasswordChar* property to *True*, which will display the password character defined by the system for each character typed in the text box. If *UseSystemPasswordChar* is set to *True* and *PasswordChar* is set to a character, the system password character will be used.

The *MaskedTextBox* Control

The *MaskedTextBox* control is a modified *TextBox* that allows you to define a preset pattern for accepting or rejecting user input. The *Mask* property allows you to specify required or optional characters, or specify whether input characters are letters or numbers, and apply formatting for the display of strings. Important properties of the *MaskedTextBox* are shown in Table 2-7.

Table 2-7   Important Properties of the *MaskedTextBox* Control

Property	Description
AllowPromptAsInput	Indicates whether the prompt character is valid as input.
AsciiOnly	Indicates if only ASCII characters are valid as input. When set to *True*, only *A–Z* and *a–z* are accepted as input.
BeepOnError	Indicates whether the *MaskedTextBox* sends a system beep for every input character it rejects.
CutCopyMaskFormat	Determines whether literals and prompt characters are included when the text is cut or copied.
HidePromptOnLeave	Indicates whether prompt characters are hidden when the *MaskedTextBox* loses the focus.
InsertKeyMode	Gets or sets the text insertion mode for the *MaskedTextBox*.
Mask	Defines the input mask for the *MaskedTextBox* (explained in detail in the following text).
PromptChar	Gets or sets the character used for the prompt.
RejectInputOnFirstFailure	Gets or sets a value indicating whether parsing of user input stops after the first invalid character is reached.
ResetOnPrompt	Indicates how an input character that matches the prompt character should be handled.
ResetOnSpace	Determines how a space input character should be handled.
SkipLiterals	Indicates whether literals in the mask should be reentered or skipped.
TextMaskFormat	Indicates whether prompt characters and literal characters are included in the text returned by the *Text* property.

The *Mask* Property

The most important property of the *MaskedTextBox* is the *Mask* property. This property allows you to define a string that represents the required format of an input string in the *MaskedTextBox*. The *MaskedTextProvider* associated with the *MaskedTextBox* provides the parsing engine that parses the *Mask* format. The code characters used by the default *MaskedTextProvider* are shown in Table 2-10.

Table 2-8   Elements of the Default *MaskedTextProvider*

Masking Element	Description
0	Represents a required digit between 0 and 9.
9	Represents an optional digit between 0 and 9.
#	Represents an optional digit between 0 and 9, or a space. Plus (+) and minus (−) signs are also accepted.
L	Represents a required letter, either uppercase or lowercase (A–Z, a–z).
?	Represents an optional letter, uppercase or lowercase (A–Z, a–z).
&	Represents a required character. If *AsciiOnly* is set to *True*, this element behaves like the *L* element.
C	Represents an optional character. If *AsciiOnly* is set to *True*, this element behaves like the [?] element.
A, a	Represents an optional alphanumeric character. If *AsciiOnly* is set to *True*, it will accept only A–Z and a–z.
.	Decimal placeholder. Represents a decimal character. The actual character used will be the decimal character that is set by the control's *FormatProvider*.
,	Thousands placeholder. Represents a thousands separator. The actual character used will be the thousands separator that is set by the control's *FormatProvider*.

Table 2-8   Elements of the Default *MaskedTextProvider*

Masking Element	Description
:	Time separator. Represents a time separator. The actual character used will be the time separator character that is set by the control's *FormatProvider*.
/	Date separator. Represents a date separator. The actual character used will be the date separator that is set by the control's *FormatProvider*.
$	Currency symbol. Represents a currency symbol. The actual character used will be the currency symbol that is set by the control's *FormatProvider*.
<	Shift down. Converts all following characters to lowercase.
>	Shift up. Converts all following characters to uppercase.
|	Disables a previous shift up or shift down.
\	Escapes a mask character, turning it into a literal character. The double slash (\\) is the escape sequence for a backslash.
All other characters	All other characters appear as themselves in the *MaskedTextBox* and cannot be moved or deleted by the user.

You can design a mask for the masked text box by creating a string made of characters described in Table 2-8. Setting the *Mask* property of the *MaskedEditBox* restricts the input that is allowed to the format determined by the mask string. Some examples of mask strings, together with input strings and the output string that is displayed in the control, are shown in Table 2-9.

Table 2-9   Examples of Mask Strings

Mask String	Input Text	Displayed Text
(999)-000-0000	1234567890	(123)-456-7890
00/00/0000	07141969	07/14/1969 – Note that the actual date separator displayed will be determined by the control's *FormatProvider*.

Table 2-9   Examples of Mask Strings

Mask String	Input Text	Displayed Text
$99,999.00	1234567	$12,345.00 – Note that the actual currency symbol, thousands separator, and decimal separator will be determined by the control's *FormatProvider*.
LL>L|LLL<LL	abcdABCD	abCdABcd

Configuring the *MaskedTextBox* for User Input

In addition to the *Mask* property, the *MaskedTextBox* control has several properties that affect how the control behaves when receiving user input. The *AsciiOnly* property determines if only ASCII characters are allowed as input; when set to *True*, it restricts input to A–Z and a–z. Other inputs are rejected. You can set the control to notify users when an error has been committed by setting the *BeepOnError* property to *True*. The *SkipLiterals* property determines whether literal characters should be reentered by the user (if set to *False*) or skipped over in the *MaskedTextBox* (when set to *True*).

The *RejectInputOnFirstFailure* property governs how text that is pasted into the *MaskedTextBox* is handled. If a string that does not match the *Mask* format is pasted into the *MaskedTextBox*, the *MaskedTextBox* will reject the entire string if the *RejectInputOnFirstFailure* is set to *True*. If set to *False*, the *MaskedTextBox* will accept all the characters that match the *Mask* format.

The *Prompt* property sets the character that is displayed in the *MaskedTextBox* when there is no input for a given position. The default value for the *Prompt* character is the underscore character (_). The *AllowPromptAsInput* and *ResetOnPrompt* properties govern how the prompt character is treated when entered as input. If the *ResetOnPrompt* property is set to *True*, prompt characters will be accepted, the *Mask* will be reset for that character position, and the cursor will advance to the next position. If the *ResetOnPrompt* property is set to *False* and the *AllowPromptAsInput* property is set to *True*, then the prompt character will be processed as regular input. If both properties are set to *False*, the prompt character will be rejected. The *ResetOnSpace* property governs the treatment of spaces in the same way that *ResetOnPrompt* governs the treatment of prompt characters.

Manipulating Text in the *MaskedTextBox*

The text shown in the *MaskedTextBox* is not necessarily the text that is available to the user when cutting and pasting or to the application when text is manipulated programmatically. The *CutCopyMaskFormat* determines how the text in the *MaskedTextBox* is treated when it is cut or copied by the user. The default value for this property is *IncludeLiterals*, in which case, literals from the *Mask* are included when text is cut or copied, but prompt characters are not. You can also set this property to *ExcludePromptAndLiterals*, which excludes both literals and prompts; *IncludePrompt*, which includes prompt characters but excludes literals; and *IncludePromptAndLiterals*, which includes both prompts and literals. The *TextMaskFormat* property has the same possible values and functions in the same way with respect to the text returned by the *Text* property.

Quick Check

1. How can you create a *TextBox* with more than one line?
2. What is the purpose of the *MaskedTextBox*?

Quick Check Answers

1. You can create a multiline *TextBox* by setting the *MultiLine* property to *True*.
2. The *MaskedTextBox* control is used to display a format to the user for data entry or display, and to validate that data is input in the correct format.

Lab: Practice with Text Display Controls

In this lab, you will add additional controls to the project you created in Lesson 2. You will add a multi-line textbox to prompt the user for an address, and you will add a *MaskedTextBox* to collect a phone number.

▶ **Exercise 1: Adding Text Display Controls**

1. In Visual Studio, load the solution you completed in Lesson 2 or the completed Lesson 2 solution located on the companion CD in the code folder.
2. In the Solution Explorer, double-click Form2 to open the Designer for Form2.
3. From the Toolbox, drag a *TextBox* onto the form. Drag a *Label* onto the form next to the *TextBox*.
4. Set the *Text* property of the *Label* to *Address*.

5. Set the *Multiline* property of the *TextBox* to *True* and set the *WordWrap* property to *False*. Set the *ScrollBars* property to *Both*. Resize the *TextBoxt* to make it large enough to hold an address. From the Toolbox, drag a *MaskedTextBox* and a *Label* onto the form.

6. Set the *Text* property of the *Label* to *Phone Number*.

7. Set the *Mask* property of the *MaskedTextBox* to (999)-000-0000.

8. *C# only.* Set the *Modifiers* property of the *TextBox* and *MaskedTextBox* to *Internal*.

9. In the Solution Explorer, right-click Form1 and choose View Code.

10. In the *LinkLabel1_LinkClicked* event handler, add the following code to the If block beneath the code you added in Lesson 2.

```
' VB
MsgBox("Your address is " & Form2.TextBox3.Text)
MsgBox("Your phone number is " & Form2.MaskedTextBox1.Text)
```

```
// C#
MessageBox.Show("Your address is " + aForm.textBox3.Text);
MessageBox.Show("Your phone number is " + aForm.maskedTextBox1.Text);
```

11. Press F5 to run and test your application.

Lesson Summary

- The *TextBox* control allows the user to enter text. The text that is entered can be accessed through the *Text* property.

- *TextBox* controls can be single-line or multiline, depending on the value of the *MultiLine* property.

- The *MaskedTextBox* control can be configured for formatted text display and entry.

- The *Mask* property determines the formatting for text in *MaskedTextBox* controls.

Lesson Review

The following questions are intended to reinforce key information presented in this lesson. The questions are also available on the companion CD if you prefer to review them in electronic form.

NOTE Answers

Answers to these questions and explanations of why each answer choice is right or wrong are located in the "Answers" section at the end of the book.

1. Which of the following properties of the *TextBox* control should be set to the value indicated to ensure that the *TextBox* can accommodate a string 10,000 characters in length?

   A. *MultiLine = True*

   B. *WordWrap = True*

   C. *ScrollBars = True*

   D. *MaxLength = 10000*

2. Which of the following *Mask* property settings will configure a *MaskedTextBox* for the entry of a social security number, which is displayed as three digits, followed by a hyphen, then two digits, followed by another hyphen and then finally four digits?

   A. *999-99-9999*

   B. *999/00/0000*

   C. *000-00-0000*

   D. *000/00/0000*

3. You have a *MaskedTextBox* with the *Mask* property set to *000-0000* to indicate a 7-digit phone number. You want users to be able to cut and paste the entire string, including the '-' character, but when the program accesses the *Masked-TextBox* you want to exclude the '-' character. Which of the following will configure the *MaskedTextBox* to provide this functionality?

   A. Set the *CutCopyMaskFormat* property to *ExcludePromptAndLiterals* and *TextMaskFormat* to *IncludeLiterals*.

   B. Set the *CutCopyMaskFormat* property to *IncludeLiterals* and *TextMaskFormat* to *ExcludePromptAndLiterals*.

   C. Set the *CutCopyMaskFormat* property to *ExcludePromptAndLiterals* and *TextMaskFormat* to *IncludePrompt*.

   D. Set the *CutCopyMaskFormat* property to *IncludeLiterals* and *TextMaskFormat* to *IncludeLiterals*.

Chapter Review

To further practice and reinforce the skills you learned in this chapter, you can perfom the following tasks:

- Review the chapter summary.
- Review the list of key terms introduced in this chapter.
- Complete the case scenarios. These scenarios set up real-world situations involving the topics of this chapter and ask you to create a solution.
- Complete the suggested practices.
- Take a practice test.

Chapter Summary

- Controls are visual components that contain functionality designed to enable common tasks. You can add controls to the designer by dragging them from the Toolbox.
- The Visual Studio IDE contains several mechanisms for managing the layout of controls on your form, including:
  - The Properties window.
  - Layout toolbar.
  - Snaplines.
  - Control modification in the designer using the mouse.
  - *Anchor* and *Dock* properties.
- The *Button* control is designed to accept user commands and execute code when clicked. You can use the *Button_Click* and *Button_MouseDown* events to respond to user clicks.
- Label controls are primarily used to display read-only text and can be used to create access keys for other controls.
- The *LinkLabel* control allows you to create Web-style links that open Web pages or other forms when clicked.
- The *TextBox* control is used to receive user input as well as to display text. *TextBox* controls can be either single-line or multiline.

- The *MaskedTextBox* enables you to specify a format for text display or user input. It enables you to configure how that format restricts user input and how the format is treated during user cut and copy operations.

Key Terms

Do you know what these key terms mean? You can check your answers by looking up the times in the glossary at the end of the book.

- access key
- event handler
- mask
- snaplines

Case Scenarios

In the following case scenarios, you will apply what you've learned about how to use controls to design user interfaces. You can find answers to these questions in the "Answers" section at the end of this book.

Case Scenario 1: Designing a Simple User Interface

Your organization, Humongous Insurance, is creating an application to help customers calculate the future value of bonds and other investments that will be held for a number of years. As a new employee, you are assigned a simple task: create the front-end interface and prepare the user input to be processed by the calculation engine that will be supplied by another development team. You begin by reviewing the technical requirements.

Technical Requirements

Create a user interface that accepts the following information from users in a simple, straightforward way:

- Current investment value
- Assumed interest rate
- Time span in years

Questions

Answer the following questions for your manager:

1. How can you provide an easy-to-understand interface that provides visual cues to the user, clearly indicates currency when appropriate, and accepts user input for all three of the aforementioned factors?

2. How can you provide a keyboard-based system of navigation as an alternative to mouse use?

Case Scenario 2: Designing a User Interface

Your company has been contracted to design and implement a reservation system for a ski resort and chalet. You have been handed the job of creating a page that is used to enter and display client data. You begin by reviewing the technical requirements.

Technical Requirements

Create a user interface that accepts the following information from users in a simple, straightforward way:

- First and Last Name.
- Address.
- City, state, and Zip Code.
- Credit card number.
- A general area for comments about the client.
- At the bottom of the technical requirements section is a note from the head of security that reads, "We need to be extra careful about our customer credit card information. Make sure it isn't displayed with the rest of the data."

Questions

Answer the following questions for your manager:

1. What controls are most appropriate for the design of the user interface?

2. How can you keep customer credit card data from being displayed but still enable its entry?

Suggested Practices

To master the Add and configure a Windows Forms control objective, you must complete the following practices, as well as the practices in Chapter 3.

Add and Configure a Windows Forms Control

For this task, complete practices 1, 2, and 3.

- **Practice 1**   Build an application that performs simple arithmetic calculation and displays the result to the user.
- **Practice 2**   Create a front-end for a hotel reservation system that collects relevant data about the customer.
- **Practice 3**   Design *MaskedTextBox* masks that create formats appropriate for apartment numbers, monthly bank deposits, dates and times, and other real-world examples.

Take a Practice Test

The practice tests on this book's companion CD offer many options. For example, you can test yourself on just the content covered in this chapter, or you can test yourself on all the 70-526 certification exam content. You can set up the test so that it closely simulates the experience of taking a certification exam, or you can set it up in study mode so that you can look at the correct answers and explanations after you answer each question.

MORE INFO   Practice tests

For details about all the practice test options available, see the "How to Use the Practice Tests" section in this book's Introduction.

Chapter 3
Advanced Windows Forms Controls

This chapter continues where Chapter 2, "Configuring Controls and Creating the User Interface," left off with an in-depth examination of Windows Forms controls. In this chapter, you will learn how to create and configure controls for displaying lists, setting values and dates, displaying images, browsing the Web, and notifying the user of background processes. You will also learn how to create access keys for controls without using the *Label* control as shown in Chapter 2.

Exam objectives in this chapter:
- Add and configure a Windows Forms control.
  - ❑ Provide a list of options on a Windows Form by using a *ListBox* control, a *ComboBox* control, or a *CheckedListBox* control.
  - ❑ Configure the layout and functionality of a Windows Form to display a list of items.
  - ❑ Implement value-setting controls on a Windows Form.
  - ❑ Configure a *WebBrowser* control.
  - ❑ Add and configure date-setting controls on a Windows Form.
  - ❑ Display images by using Windows Forms controls.
  - ❑ Configure the *NotifyIcon* component.
  - ❑ Create access keys for Windows Forms controls.

Lessons in this chapter:

Before You Begin

To complete the lessons in this chapter, you must have:

- A computer that meets or exceeds the minimum hardware requirements listed in the "Introduction" at the beginning of the book.

- Microsoft Visual Studio 2005 Professional Edition installed on your computer.

- An understanding of Microsoft Visual Basic or C# syntax and familiarity with the .NET Framework.

- Completed Chapter 1, "Windows Forms and the User Interface," or have a good understanding of Windows Forms, how to add controls to forms, and how to use the Visual Studio Integrated Development Interface (IDE).

Real World

Matt Stoecker

When I am creating a user interface (UI), the large variety of Windows controls that are available for use dramatically streamlines the UI creation process. Built-in controls for displaying lists and images and setting dates and other values allow me to spend less time on UI coding tasks and more time developing the application's custom functionality.

Lesson 1: Creating and Configuring *List-Display* Controls

A common scenario in user interface design is to present lists of data to users and to allow them to select items from that list. Visual Studio provides several list-based controls that allow a variety of presentation options. In this lesson, you will learn about the basic list-based controls, such as the *ListBox*, *ComboBox*, and *CheckedList-Box*, as well as more specialized list-based controls such as *ListView*, *TreeView*, *NumericUpDown*, and *DomainUpDown*. You will learn how to display lists and select items from lists.

After this lesson, you will be able to:

- Programmatically determine which item in a list appears in a given position.
- Add or remove items from a list of items in a list-based control.
- Bind a list-based control to a data source.
- Sort list data.
- Display data in a drop-down combo box.
- Select one or more items from a pre-defined list.
- Use the *ListView* control to display a list of items with icons.
- Use the *TreeView* control to display a list of items in a hierarchical view.
- Configure the *DomainUpDown* control to display a list of strings.
- Configure the *NumericUpDown* control to display a list of numbers.

Estimated lesson time: 60 minutes

Overview of List-Based Controls

The basic list-based controls are the *ListBox*, *ComboBox*, and *CheckedListBox* controls. Although differing somewhat in appearance and functionality, each of these controls organizes and presents lists of data in the same way, and each contains an *Items* collection that organizes the items contained in one of these controls.

The *Items* collection is basically a collection of objects. Although these objects are often strings, they do not have to be. If a collection does contain a string, however, the string representation of the object will be displayed in the control.

ListBox Control

The *ListBox* control is the simplest of the list-based controls. It serves primarily to display a simple list of items in an easy-to-navigate user interface. Users can select one or more items. Table 3-1 describes the important properties of the *ListBox* control.

Table 3-1   Important Properties of the *ListBox* Control

Property	Description
DataSource	Sets the source for data binding in this control.
DisplayMember	Represents the data member that is displayed in this control.
FormatString	Specifies a formatting string that will be used to format the entries in the control if *FormattingEnabled* is set to *True*.
FormattingEnabled	Determines whether the entries in the control are formatted using the *FormatString*.
Items	Returns the collection of items contained in this control.
MultiColumn	Indicates whether this item shows multiple columns of items or only a single item.
SelectedIndex	Gets the index of the selected item or, if the *SelectionMode* property is set to *MultiSimple* or *MultiSelect*, returns any selected index.
SelectedIndices	Returns a collection of all selected indexes.
SelectedItem	Returns the selected item or, if the *SelectionMode* property is set to *MultiSimple* or *MultiSelect*, returns any selected item.
SelectedItems	Returns a collection of all selected items.
SelectedValue	In a data-bound control, returns the value associated with the selected item. If the control is not data bound, or, if the *ValueMember* is not set, this property returns the *ToString* value of the selected item.

Table 3-1 Important Properties of the *ListBox* Control

Property	Description
SelectionMode	Determines how many items can be selected in a *ListBox*. Can be set to *None*, *Single*, *MultiSimple*, or *MultiExtended*. *MultiSimple* allows the selection of multiple objects, and *MultiExtend* allows the use of the *Shift* and *Ctrl* keys when making multiple selections.
ValueMember	Indicates the data member that will provide the values for the *ListBox*.

ComboBox Control

The *ComboBox* control is similar to the *ListBox* control, but, in addition to allowing the user to select items from a list, it provides a space for a user to type an entry as well as select items from a list. Additionally, the *ComboBox* can be configured to either display a list of options or provide a drop-down list of options. Table 3-2 details the important properties of the *ComboBox* control.

Table 3-2 Important Properties of the *ComboBox* Control

Property	Description
DataSource	Sets the source for data binding in this control.
DisplayMember	Represents the data member that is displayed in this control.
DropDownHeight	Sets the maximum height for the drop-down box.
DropDownStyle	Determines the style of the combo box. Can be set to *Simple*, which is similar to a *ListBox*; *DropDown*, which is the default; or *DropDownList*, which is similar to *DropDown*, but does not allow the user to type a new value.
DropDownWidth	Sets the width of the drop-down section of the combo box.
FormatString	Specifies a formatting string that will be used to format the entries in the control if *FormattingEnabled* is set to *True*.

Table 3-2   Important Properties of the *ComboBox* Control

Property	Description
FormattingEnabled	Determines whether the entries in the control are formatted using the *FormatString*.
Items	Returns the collection of items contained in this control.
SelectedIndex	Gets the index of the selected item, or, if the *SelectionMode* property is set to *MultiSimple* or *MultiSelect*, returns any selected index.
SelectedItem	Returns the selected item, or, if the *SelectionMode* property is set to *MultiSimple* or *MultiSelect*, returns any selected item.
SelectedValue	In a data-bound control, returns the value associated with the selected item. If the control is not data bound, or, if the *ValueMember* is not set, this property returns the *ToString* value of the selected item.
ValueMember	Indicates the data member that will provide the values for the *ListBox*.

CheckedListBox Control

The *CheckedListBox* displays a list of items to users and allows them to select multiple items by checking boxes that are displayed next to the items. Any number of items can be checked, but only one item can be selected at a time. You can retrieve a collection that represents the checked items by accessing the *CheckedItems* collection, and you can get a collection of the checked indexes by accessing the *CheckedIndices* collection. Table 3-3 details the important properties of the *CheckedListBox* control.

Table 3-3   Important Properties of the *CheckedListBox* Control

Property	Description
CheckedIndices	Returns a collection that represents all of the checked indexes.
CheckedItems	Returns a collection that exposes all of the checked items in the control.

Table 3-3 Important Properties of the *CheckedListBox* Control

Property	Description
FormatString	Specifies a formatting string that will be used to format the entries in the control if *FormattingEnabled* is set to *True*.
FormattingEnabled	Determines whether the entries in the control are formatted using the *FormatString*.
Items	Returns the collection of items contained in this control.
MultiColumn	Indicates whether this control shows multiple columns of items or only a single item.
SelectedIndex	Gets the index of the selected item, or, if the *SelectionMode* property is set to *MultiSimple* or *MultiSelect*, it can return any selected index.
SelectedItem	Returns the selected item, or, if the *SelectionMode* property is set to *MultiSimple* or *MultiSelect*, it can return any selected item.

You can set an item to be checked or unchecked by calling the *SetItemChecked* method as shown below:

```
' VB
CheckedListBox.SetItemChecked(0, True)
```

```
// C#
checkedListBox.SetItemChecked(0, true);
```

Likewise, you can use the *SetItemCheckState* method to set the *CheckState* of an item:

```
' VB
CheckedListBox.SetItemCheckState(0, CheckState.Indeterminate)
```

```
// C#
checkedListBox.SetItemCheckState(0, CheckState.Indeterminate);
```

Adding Items to and Removing Items from a List-Based Control

You can add or remove items to a list-based control through either the designer at design time or code at run time.

To add items to a list-based control at design time, you select the control in the designer and then, in the Properties window, select the *Items* property. The String Collection Editor (shown in Figure 3-1) opens. All of the items currently contained in the control are shown. Items can then be added to or removed from this list.

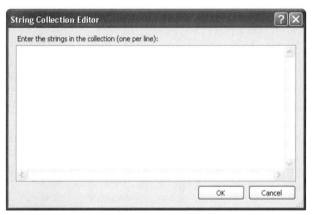

Figure 3-1   The String Collection Editor

You can also use code to programmatically add and remove items from the control at run time. To add an item, you use the *Items.Add* method as shown in the following code example:

```
' VB
ListBox1.Items.Add("This string will be added to the list")
```

```
// C#
listBox1.Items.Add("This string will be added to the list");
```

If you have several items to add at once, you can use the *AddRange* method to add an array of items to the control, as shown here:

```
' VB
ListBox1.Items.AddRange(New String() {"Item1", "Item2", "Item3"})
```

```
// C#
listBox1.Items.AddRange(new String[] {"Item1", "Item2", "Item3"});
```

You can use the *Items.Insert* method to add an item to a specific index in the list. The index of items is a zero-based index, so the first item in the control is at index 0. When you add an item to an index that is already occupied by an item, that item and any items beneath it are shifted down one index. The following code shows how to insert an item to be third in the displayed list, assuming that the *ListBox1* control is already populated with several items.

```
' VB
ListBox1.Items.Insert(2, "This item will be third")
```

```
// C#
listBox1.Items.Insert(2, "This item will be third");
```

You can use the *Items.Remove* method to remove an item from the list. This method requires a reference to the object that you want to remove from the items collection. Note that if your control contains a collection of objects that are not strings, you will need to pass a reference to the object itself to remove it, not just to the string representation that appears in the control. The following example demonstrates the *Items.Remove* method.

```
' VB
ListBox1.Items.Remove("This string will be removed")
```

```
// C#
listbox1.Items.Remove("This string will be removed");
```

If you do not know the actual item that you want to remove at run time but have the index of the item you want to remove, you can use the *Items.RemoveAt* method. This method removes the item at a given index and adjusts the indexes of the other items accordingly. The *Items.RemoveAt* method is demonstrated in the following code example:

```
' VB
' Removes the third item in the list
ListBox1.Items.RemoveAt(2)
```

```
// C#
// Removes the third item in the list
listBox1.Items.RemoveAt(2);
```

To remove all items from a list-based control, you can use the *Items.Clear* method, as shown here:

```
' VB
ListBox1.Items.Clear()
```

```
// C#
listbox1.Items.Clear();
```

Determining Where an Item Appears in a List

If you want to determine where an item appears in a list programmatically, you can do so by using the *Items.IndexOf* method. This method takes the item you want to find as an argument and returns an integer that represents the index of that item. If the item is not found in the *Items* collection, the *IndexOf* method returns -1. An example of the *IndexOf* method is shown here:

```
' VB
Dim anIndex As Integer
anIndex = ListBox1.IndexOf("A String")
```

```
// C#
int anIndex;
anIndex = listBox1.IndexOf("A String");
```

You can also programmatically determine the index of an item that has been selected by the user by using the *SelectedIndex* property. The *SelectedIndex* property returns the item that has been selected in the user interface at run time. If more than one item has been selected, the *SelectedIndex* property can return any of the selected items. The *SelectedIndex* property is demonstrated here:

```
' VB
Dim anIndex As Integer
anIndex = ListBox1.SelectedIndex
```

```
// C#
int anIndex;
anIndex = listBox1.SelectedIndex;
```

In controls where the *SelectionMode* property is set to *MultiSimple* or *MultiExtended*, you can return all of the selected indexes by using the *SelectedIndices* property, as shown in the following example:

```
' VB
For Each i As Integer In ListBox1.SelectedIndices
    Console.WriteLine(ListBox1.Items(i).ToString)
Next
```

```
// C#
foreach (int i in listBox1.SelectedIndices)
{
    Console.WriteLine(listBox1.Items[i].ToString());
}
```

Binding List-Based Controls to Data Sources

You will frequently want to expose data to the user in list-based controls. You can bind *ListBox* controls and *ComboBox* controls (but not *CheckedListBox* controls) to a data source by using the *DataSource*, *DisplayMember*, and *ValueMember* properties to bind a list-based control to a column of data in a data table.

Add a data source to your project. Adding data sources to your project is covered in detail in Chapter 5, "Configuring Connections and Connecting to Data."

▶ **To bind a list-based control to a data source**

1. In the Designer, select the list-based control that you want to bind to a data source.

2. In the Properties window, click the *DataSource* property to open the data source configuration interface, as shown in Figure 3-2. Set the *DataSource* property to a table contained in one of the data sources in your project.

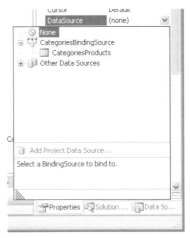

Figure 3-2   Setting the *DataSource* property

3. In the Properties window, click the *DisplayMember* property. Visual Studio displays the columns in the selected table. This is the column whose rows will be displayed in the control.

4. In the Properties window, click the *ValueMember* property. Choose a column name in the interface to bind the control to. This is the column whose members will provide the value that is returned from the selected index in the control.

The *DataSource* property indicates the data source (usually a data table) that the data in the control is drawn from. The *DisplayMember* property represents the column of data in the data source that is displayed to the user in the control. The *ValueMember* property allows you to designate an additional column of values to be represented in the control. For example, you might set the *DisplayMember* property to the Products column to indicate a list of products to the user but set the *ValueMember* to a Products-Code column that returned a numeric code for each product. In this instance, whenever an item was selected, the *SelectedItem* property would return the item displayed in the *ListBox*, and the *SelectedValue* property would return the corresponding item from the ProductsCode column.

Sorting in List-Based Controls

You can sort the objects displayed in a list-based control by setting the *Sorted* property to *True*, as shown here:

```
' VB
ListBox1.Sorted = True
```

```
// C#
listBox1.Sorted = true;
```

Sorting data at the data source will be covered in Chapter 7, "Create, Add, Delete, and Edit Data in a Disconnected Environment."

Setting a Format for Items Displayed in a List-Based Control

You can format the items that you display in a list-based control. For example, if you are displaying a list of monetary values, you can format them all as currency, and they will be displayed in the currency format that is appropriate to the culture the application is running under.

You can set a format for a list-based control by setting the *FormatString* property at design time. Selecting and clicking the *FormatString* property in the Properties window launches the Format String Dialog dialog box, shown in Figure 3-3.

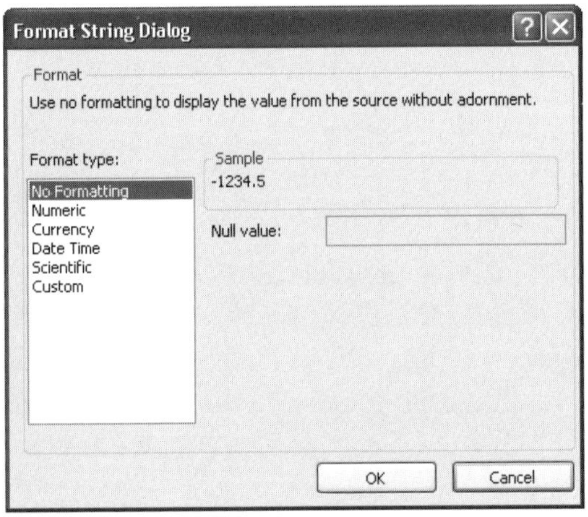

Figure 3-3 The Format String Dialog dialog box

The *FormattingEnabled* property determines whether to use the formatting indicated by the *FormatString*. When the *FormattingEnabled* property is set to *True*, the entries in the control will be displayed in the format indicated by *FormatString* property.

Custom Format Strings If the preset format strings do not provide the correct format for an item, you can create a custom format string. Table 3-4 describes the characters that can be used to create a custom format string.

Table 3-4 Custom Format String Characters

Character	Description
0	Zero placeholder. If the value being formatted has a digit in the position where the '0' appears in the format string, then that digit is copied to the result string. The position of the left-most '0' before the decimal point and the right-most '0' after the decimal point determines the range of digits that are always present in the result string. Note that the "00" specifier causes the value to be rounded to the nearest digit preceding the decimal, where rounding away from zero is always used. For example, formatting 34.5 with "00" would result in the value 35.
#	Digit placeholder. If the value being formatted has a digit in the position where the '#' appears in the format string, then that digit is copied to the result string. Otherwise, nothing is stored in that position in the result string. Note that this specifier never displays the '0' character if it is not a significant digit, even if '0' is the only digit in the string. It will display the '0' character if it is a significant digit in the number being displayed. The "##" format string causes the value to be rounded to the nearest digit preceding the decimal, where rounding away from zero is always used. For example, formatting 34.5 with "##" would result in the value 35.
.	Decimal separator. The first '.' character determines the location of the first decimal separator in the formatted value. Additional '.' characters are ignored. Note that the actual character used will be the decimal separator determined by the current locale.

Table 3-4 Custom Format String Characters

Character	Description
,	Thousands separator and scaling. First, if the format string contains a ',' character between two digit placeholders (0 or #) and to the left of the decimal point if one is present, then the output will have thousand separators inserted between each group of three digits to the left of the decimal separator. The actual character used as the decimal separator in the result string is determined by the *NumberGroupSeparator* property of the current *NumberFormatInfo* that controls formatting.
	If the format string contains one or more ',' characters immediately to the left of the decimal point, then the number will be divided by the number of ',' characters multiplied by 1000 before it is formatted. For example, the format string "0,," will represent 100 million as simply 100.
%	Percentage placeholder. The presence of the % symbol causes the number represented to be multiplied by 100 before formatting. The % symbol appears in the place that it occurs in the format string.
E0, E+0, E-0, e0, e+0, e-0	Scientific notation. If any of the strings "E", "E+", "E-", "e", "e+", or "e-" are present in the format string and are followed immediately by at least one '0' character, then the number is formatted using scientific notation with an 'E' or 'e' inserted between the number and the exponent. The number of '0' characters following the scientific notation indicator determines the minimum number of digits to output for the exponent. The "E+" and "e+" formats indicate that a sign character (plus or minus) should always precede the exponent. The "E", "E-", "e", or "e-" formats indicate that a sign character should only precede negative exponents.
\	Escape character. In C#, this character is used to indicate that the character immediately following the '\' is to be interpreted as an escape sequence. In Visual Basic this character has no effect.

Table 3-4 Custom Format String Characters

Character	Description
"ABC", 'ABC'	Literal strings. Characters enclosed in "" or '' are displayed as literal strings in the formatted string.
;	Section separator. The ';' character is used to separate sections for positive, negative, and zero numbers in the format string. You can provide up to three sections in a format string, each containing its own format. These sections should be separated by ';' characters and will be applied to positive, negative, and zero numbers respectively.
Other Characters	Other characters in the format string are represented as literal strings.

Selecting Items in a List-Based Control

You can programmatically select items in a list-based control by using the *SelectedItem* or *SelectedIndex* property. You can select an item in a list-based control as shown in the following example:

```
' VB
ListBox1.SelectedItem = "This item will be selected"
```

```
// C#
listBox1.SelectedItem = "This item will be selected";
```

If the *SelectedItem* property is set to an item that is not contained in the control, there will be no effect, and no item will be selected.

If the control allows multiple selections, you can select multiple items by setting the *SelectedItem* property multiple times if the *SelectionMode* property is set to *MultiSimple* or *MultiExtended* (which is only supported by the *ListBox* control). Once selected, an item will remain selected until unselected by the user. An example is shown here:

```
' VB
ListBox1.SelectedItem = "This item will be selected"
ListBox1.SelectedItem = "This item will be selected too"
```

```
// C#
listBox1.SelectedItem = "This item will be selected";
listBox1.SelectedItem = "This item will be selected too";
```

The *SelectedIndex* property functions in a way similar to the *SelectedItem* property, except that it is an Integer type that corresponds to the sequential item in the list. You can select an item in the control by setting the *SelectedIndex* property to the corresponding index, and you can select multiple items by setting the property multiple times in succession. The main difference between the behavior of the *SelectedItem* property and the *SelectedIndex* property is that the *SelectedIndex* property will throw an exception if an attempt is made to set it to a nonexistent index.

The *ListView* Control

The *ListView* control allows you to view lists of items with optional associated icons in the manner of Windows Explorer. Using the *ListView* control, you can display items with large associated icons, small associated icons, or additional details about the item. Table 3-5 shows important properties of the *ListView* control.

Table 3-5   Important Properties of the *ListView* Control

Property	Description
Columns	Contains the collection of columns to be displayed when the *View* property is set to *Details*.
Groups	Contains an optional collection of groups that can be used to categorize the items contained in the *Items* collection.
Items	A collection of *ListViewItems* that is displayed in the *ListView* control.
LargeImageList	The *ImageList* component from which images for *ListViewItems* are drawn when the *View* property is set to *LargeIcon*.
ShowGroups	Determines whether the groups contained in the *Groups* collection are shown.
SmallImageList	The *ImageList* component from which images for *ListViewItems* are drawn when the *View* property is set to *SmallIcon*.
View	Indicates the manner in which *ListView* items are displayed.

The most important property in the *ListView* control is the *Items* property. This property contains a collection of *ListViewItem* objects. Unlike the list-based controls examined earlier, *ListViewItems* are specific objects that contain additional information about the item being displayed such as icons that are shown in the control. Table 3-6 shows important properties of the *ListViewItem* class.

Table 3-6   Important Properties of the *ListViewItem* Class

Property	Description
Group	The group, if any, in the *ListView* control's *Groups* collection that this *ListViewItem* belongs to.
ImageIndex	The index, if any, of the Image to be used for this item when the *View* property is set to *LargeIcon* or *SmallIcon*. If the *ImageIndex* property is set, the *ImageKey* property is set to "".
ImageKey	The key of the Image, if any, to be used for this item when the *View* property is set to *LargeIcon* or *SmallIcon*. If the *ImageKey* property is set, the *ImageIndex* property is set to *null*.
SubItems	Contains the sub-items that will be shown when the *View* property is set to *Details*. These items should correspond to the columns in the *ListView* control's *Columns* collection.
Text	The text that is shown in the *ListView* property.

You can add *ListViewItems* to the *ListView* and edit the properties of individual *ListViewItems* by clicking the *Items* property of the *ListView* control to open the ListViewItem Collection Editor, shown in Figure 3-4.

The *ListView* control organizes the images associated with the *ListViewItems* in *ImageList* objects that are exposed in the *SmallImageList* and *LargeImageList* properties. The *ImageList* class will be discussed in greater detail in Lesson 2, "Creating and Configuring Value-Setting Controls," of this chapter. You can set the images associated with a particular *ListViewItem* by setting either the *ImageIndex* or *ImageKey* property of each *ListViewItem*. The *View* property determines if the *ListView* items are shown with large images, small images, or in a view that exposes the sub-items of the *ListViewItems*.

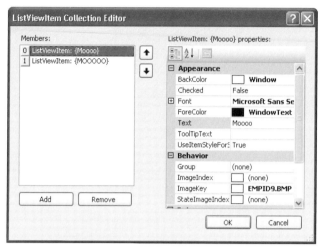

Figure 3-4   The ListView Collection Editor

▶ **To display a list of items with icons in the *ListView* control**

1. In the Designer, drag an *ImageList* control from the Toolbox to the design surface.

2. In the Properties window, click the *Images* property of the *ImageList* to add images to the *Images* collection.

3. In the Designer, select the *ListView* control. In the Properties window, set the *SmallImageList*, *LargeImageList*, or both to the *ImageList* object.

4. In the Properties window, click Items to add *ListViewItems* to the *ListView*.

5. In the ListViewItem Collection Editor, set either the *ImageIndex* or the *ImageKey* property for each *ListViewItem* to the appropriate image in the *ImageList*. Also, set any other properties, such as *Text*, at this point.

6. In the Designer, select the *ListView* control. In the Properties window, set the *View* property to either *LargeIcon* or *SmallIcon*.

TreeView Control

The *TreeView* control allows you to display a list of objects in a hierarchical manner. Each object in the *TreeView* control represents an instance of the *TreeNode* class, which contains information about the location of the node within the *TreeView* control. Nodes containing child nodes in the *TreeView* control can be collapsed and expanded. Figure 3-5 shows a *TreeView* control in a form.

Figure 3-5   The *TreeView* control

The primary property of the *TreeView* control is the *Nodes* property. This property contains the collection of *TreeNodes* that comprise the root objects in the *TreeView*. Each individual *TreeNode* object contains its own collection of *TreeNodes* that represent child nodes of that node. Table 3-7 describes some of the important properties of the *TreeNode* class.

Table 3-7   Important Properties of the *TreeNode* Class

Property	Description
FirstNode	Returns the first node in the current group of child nodes.
LastNode	Returns the last node in the current group of child nodes.
NextNode	Returns the next sibling tree node.
NextVisibleNode	Returns the next visible node.
Nodes	Returns the collection of child nodes belonging to this node.
Parent	Returns the parent node of the current node. If the current node is a root node in the *TreeView*, accessing this property will throw a *NullReferenceException*.
PrevNode	Returns the previous node.
PrevVisibleNode	Returns the previous visible node.
TreeView	Returns a reference to the *TreeView* control that the *TreeNode* is contained in.

Adding and Removing Nodes from the *TreeView* Controls

At design time, you can add nodes to a *TreeView* control by clicking the *Nodes* property in the Properties window to display the TreeNode Editor (shown in Figure 3-6). You can add new root nodes or new child nodes and set the properties of each *TreeNode*.

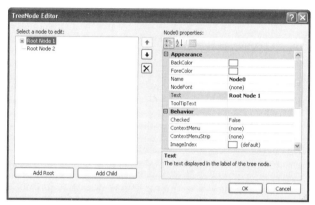

Figure 3-6   The TreeNode Editor

At run time, you can create new *TreeNode* objects and add them as root nodes to the *TreeView* control or add them as child nodes to another *TreeNode*. For both of these procedures, you use the *Nodes.Add* method, as shown here:

```
' VB
Dim aNode As New TreeNode("New Node")
' Add a child node to the new node
aNode.Nodes.Add(New TreeNode("New Child"))
' Adds aNode and its child As a new root node in a TreeView control named TreeView1
TreeView1.Nodes.Add(aNode)
' Adds a second child node to the first node in TreeView1
TreeView1.Nodes(0).Nodes.Add(New TreeNode("Second Child"))
```

```
// C#
TreeNode aNode = new TreeNode("New Node");
// Add a child node to the new node
aNode.Nodes.Add(new TreeNode("New Child"));
// Adds aNode and its child as a new root node in a TreeView control named TreeView1
treeView1.Nodes.Add(aNode);
// Adds a second child node to the first node in TreeView1
treeView1.Nodes[0].Nodes.Add(new TreeNode("Second Child"));
```

You can remove nodes from the *Nodes* collection by using the *Remove* and *RemoveAt* methods. The *Remove* method takes a reference to a particular node as a parameter and removes it from the collection if it exists in the collection. If the specified node does not exist in the collection, this method call is ignored. The *RemoveAt* method removes the node at a specified index. If the specified index is not present in the nodes collection, an ArgumentOutOfRange exception is thrown. The following example demonstrates the *Remove* and *RemoveAt* methods.

```
' VB
' Removes the node named aNode from the collection
TreeView1.Nodes.Remove(aNode)
' Removes the node at index 3 from the collection.
TreeView1.Nodes.RemoveAt(3)
```

```
// C#
// Removes the node named aNode from the collection
treeView1.Nodes.Remove(aNode);
// Removes the node at index 3 from the collection.
treeView1.Nodes.RemoveAt(3);
```

Expanding and Collapsing Nodes

The *TreeView* control presents a hierarchical view of nodes that can be expanded or collapsed to reveal or hide the child nodes as appropriate. You can expand or collapse child nodes programmatically at run time by using the *Expand* and *Collapse* methods as shown in the following example:

```
' VB
' Expands the child nodes of a TreeNode named aNode
aNode.Expand()
' Collapses the child nodes of a TreeNode named aNode
aNode.Collapse()
```

```
// C#
// Expands the child nodes of a TreeNode named aNode
aNode.Expand();
// Collapses the child nodes of a TreeNode named aNode
aNode.Collapse();
```

NumericUpDown Control

The *NumericUpDown* control allows you to set a range of numbers that a user can browse and select. A range of numbers is presented in the control, and the user can click the up and down arrows to increase or decrease the number as necessary. Table 3-8 shows important properties of the *NumericUpDown* control.

Table 3-8   Important Properties of the *NumericUpDown* Control

Property	Description
Hexadecimal	Indicates whether the numeric value will be shown in hexadecimal.

Table 3-8   Important Properties of the *NumericUpDown* Control

Property	Description
Increment	Gets or sets the amount to increment or decrement with each button click.
Maximum	Indicates the maximum value for the control.
Minimum	Indicates the minimum value for the control.
ThousandsSeparator	Indicates whether the culture-appropriate thousands separator will be used when displaying values greater than 1,000.
Value	Gets or sets the current value of the control.

▶ **To configure the *NumericUpDown* control**

1. Set the *Minimum* property to the minimum numeric value for the control.

2. Set the *Maximum* property to the maximum numeric value for the control.

3. Set the *Increment* property to the amount you want to increment and decrement with each arrow button click.

4. If desired, set the *Value* property to a default value.

DomainUpDown Control

The *DomainUpDown* control is similar to the *NumericUpDown* control in that it allows users to browse a specified series of data and set a value for the control. Instead of browsing numeric values, however, the *DomainUpDown* control allows the user to browse a collection of preset strings. Table 3-9 describes the important properties of the *DomainUpDown* control.

Table 3-9   Important Properties of the *DomainUpDown* Control

Property	Description
Items	Contains the collection of strings that are displayed in the *DomainUpDown* control.
ReadOnly	Indicates whether the *Text* of the control can be altered by the user.
Text	Gets or sets the text of the control.

The *Items* collection contains the strings that are displayed in the *DomainUpDown* control and can be added by clicking the *Items* property in the Properties window and adding it in the String Collection Editor. When *ReadOnly* is set to *False*, the user can choose to type a string in the *DomainUpDown* control instead of choosing one of the strings. Note that strings typed by the user are not added to the *Items* collection. Also note that the *Text* property defines the default value for the control, not the *Items* collection.

Quick Check

1. What is the purpose of the *TreeView* control?

2. What is the purpose of a *ListView* control and when would you use one?

Quick Check Answers

1. The *TreeView* control allows you to display a list of data in a hierarchically related manner.

2. The *ListView* control provides a highly configurable control that allows you to display lists of data in a variety of different ways. You can use a *ListView* control when you want to provide different options to the user for the display of list data, such as providing icons or details about the data.

Lab: The Adventure Works Ski Instructor Reservation Form

Over the next two labs, you will use what you have learned in this lesson and the next to add functionality to a simple application designed to reserve ski instructors. In this lab, you will add a *ComboBox* that allows the user to select the mountain they want to ski on, a *ListView* control to select a ski instructor, and a *NumericUpDown* control to select the length of the lesson.

▶ **Exercise 1: The Ski Instructor Reservation Form**

1. In Visual Studio, open the partial solution for Chapter 3, Lesson 1, "Creating and Configuring List-Display Controls." This solution is located on the companion CD in the Code folder.

2. In Form1, beneath the Name TextBox, add a *Label* control and a *ComboBox* control. Set the *Text* of the *Label* control to **Choose Ski Run**.

3. Set the *DropDownStyle* property of the *ComboBox* to *DropDownList*.

4. Add the following items to the *ComboBox Items* property: **Camelback**, **Powder Point**, and **The Plunge**.

5. Add a *Label* control and a *NumericUpDown* control to the form. Set the *Text* property of the *Label* to **Lesson Length**.

6. Set the *Minimum* property of the *NumericUpDown* control to **1** and the *Maximum* property to **3**.

7. Add a *Label* control and a *ListView* control to the form. Set the *Text* property of the *Label* control to **Choose Instructor**.

8. In the Properties window, set the *View* property of the *ListView* control to **Small-Icon**. In Lesson 2 you will associate the items in this list with images.

9. In the Properties window, add four *ListViewItems* to the *Items* property of the *List-View*. Set their *Text* properties to **Sandy**, **Jack**, **Libby**, and **Christa**.

10. Add a *Button* control to the form and set the *Text* property to **Make Reservation**.

11. In the Designer, double-click the Button and add the following code to the *Button_Click* event handler.

```
' VB
If  ListView1.SelectedItems.Count > 0 Then
    MsgBox("Your reservation with " &  listView1.SelectedItems(0).Text & _" is
confirmed.")
End If

// C#
if (listView1.SelectedItems.Count > 0)
{
    MessageBox.Show("Your reservation with " + listView1.SelectedItems[0].Text + " is
confirmed.");
}
```

12. Press F5 to test your application.

Lesson Summary

■ List-based controls are used to organize and present lists of information to the user. The *ListBox*, *ComboBox*, and *CheckedListBox* controls organize items through the *Items* property and share many common methods and properties.

■ The *ListBox* control allows you to display a selection of items to the user and enables the user to select one or more items from that list.

■ The *ComboBox* control can appear similar to a *ListBox* control or as a drop-down list. You can require the user to select from a list or choose to allow them to type an entry that is not present in the list.

- The *CheckedListBox* control allows you to display a list of items with a check box beside each one, enabling the user to check as many items as desired. Although multiple items can be checked, only one item can be selected in the *CheckedList-Box* at any time.

- The *ListView* control allows specialized displays of lists of items. Items can be displayed in association with icons that are provided by an *ImageList* component or with additional columns of sub-items.

- The *TreeView* control allows you to display lists of items in a hierarchical format. Each node contains a collection of child nodes, which can themselves have child nodes. Nodes can be expanded or collapsed.

- The *NumericUpDown* control allows the user to click up or down arrows to select a numeric value. The *DomainUpDown* control allows the user to click up or down arrows to select from a pre-selected set of options.

Lesson Review

You can use the following questions to test your knowledge of the information in this lesson. The questions are also available on the companion CD if you prefer to review them in electronic form.

NOTE Answers

Answers to these questions and explanations of why each answer choice is right or wrong are located in the "Answers" section at the end of the book.

---

1. Which of the following properties and methods can be used to find the index of a selected item in a *ListBox* control? (Choose all that apply.)

   A. *ListBox.IndexOf*

   B. *ListBox.SelectedIndex*

   C. *ListBox.SelectedIndices*

   D. *ListBox.Select*

2. Which of the following methods cannot be used to add an item to the *Items* collection of a *ComboBox*, *ListBox*, or *CheckedListBox* control?

   A. *Items.Add*

   B. *Items.Insert*

   C. *Items.AddRange*

   D. *Items.Contains*

3. Which of the following is NOT a valid setting for the *View* property of the *List-View* control?

    A. *LargeIcon*

    B. *Details*

    C. *Tree*

    D. *SmallIcon*

Lesson 2: Creating and Configuring Value-Setting, Date-Setting, and Image-Display Controls

Allowing users to select or choose from a set of options, set dates, and work with images are common scenarios for user interface design. In this lesson, you will learn to use value-setting controls such as *CheckBox*, *RadioButton*, and *TrackBar* and date-setting controls such as *DateTimePicker* and *MonthCalendar*; and you will learn to work with images using the *ImageList* component and the *PictureBox* control.

After this lesson, you will be able to:

- Set two or more mutually exclusive options in the user interface using a *RadioButton*.
- Use the *CheckBox* control to indicate whether a condition is on or off.
- Allow navigation through a large amount of information or visually adjust a numeric setting using a *TrackBar*.
- Allow the user to select a single item from a list of dates or times using the *DateTimePicker* control.
- Present an intuitive graphical interface for users to view and set date information using the *MonthCalendar*.
- Add images to or remove images from the *ImageList* component.
- Display graphics using the *PictureBox* control.

Estimated lesson time: 45 minutes

Value-Setting Controls

Value-setting controls allow the user to set values or pick options from a preset list in the user interface. The *CheckBox* control allows a user to select or deselect particular options in a non-exclusive manner, while the *RadioButton* allows you to present a range of options to the user, only one of which can be selected. The *TrackBar* control allows the user to rapidly set a value in a graphical interface.

The *CheckBox* Control

The *CheckBox* control is a very familiar control to users. It allows the user to mark a check box next to a label to indicate acceptance or rejection of the option presented. *CheckBox* controls function in a non-exclusive manner—you can have multiple *CheckBox* controls on a single form, and any combination of them can be checked or unchecked at a single time. Table 3-10 shows important properties of the *CheckBox* control.

Table 3-10 Important Properties of the *CheckBox* Control

Property	Description
AutoCheck	Determines whether the *CheckBox* is automatically checked when the text is clicked.
Checked	Gets or sets whether the *CheckBox* is checked.
CheckState	Returns the *CheckState* of the control. Possible values for this property are *Checked*, *Unchecked*, and *Indeterminate*.
Text	The text displayed next to the check box.
ThreeState	Determines whether the *CheckBox* control allows two check states or three.

The most common usage for the *CheckBox* control is to allow the user to make a binary decision about an option by either checking the box or not checking it. Typically, the check box is used for non-exclusive options; that is, checking a particular check box usually does not affect the state of other text boxes. Figure 3-7 shows an example of a hypothetical pizza order form. Radio buttons are used to choose between the exclusive options Pizza or Calzone, and *CheckBox* controls are used to select toppings for the pizza or calzone that is selected.

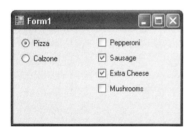

Figure 3-7 Example of *CheckBox* and *RadioButton* controls

You can programmatically determine if a *CheckBox* control is checked by accessing the *Checked* property. This property will return *True* if the control is checked and *False* if the control is unchecked or indeterminate.

A less common use for the *CheckBox* is to allow the user to choose between three settings: *Checked*, *Unchecked*, or *Indeterminate*. This can be useful to indicate to the user that a conscious decision must be made for each option rather than simply setting a default option. You enable three-state *CheckBox* controls by setting the *ThreeState* property to *True*. This allows the user to cycle through the three states, rather than just the two, for the check box. You can determine the state of the check box by accessing the *CheckState* property.

Note that you can set the *CheckState* property to *Indeterminate* at design time even if you set the *ThreeState* property to *False*. This causes the *CheckBox* controls to start in the indeterminate state, but once the user makes a selection, they must be either checked or unchecked; in this case, the user is not allowed to reset the check box to indeterminate.

The *RadioButton* Control

The *RadioButton* control is used to present exclusive options to the user. The hypothetical pizza order form in Figure 3-7 demonstrates the use of *RadioButton* controls, allowing the user to choose either a pizza or a calzone but not both. Table 3-11 shows important properties of the *RadioButton* control.

Table 3-11   Important Properties of the *RadioButton* Control

Property	Description
Checked	Indicates whether the *RadioButton* is selected.
Text	The text displayed next to the radio button.

You can determine if a particular *RadioButton* is selected by accessing the *Checked* property, which returns *True* if selected.

All *RadioButton* controls in a given container control are exclusive of each other. That means that if one *RadioButton* control is selected, the others will all be deselected. This has the net effect of allowing the user to choose only one of a group of options.

If you want to have several exclusive groups of *RadioButton* controls, the most common method is to group them in a *GroupBox* control. Each group of *RadioButton* controls in a particular *GroupBox* will be exclusive of each other but unaffected by other *RadioButton* controls in other *GroupBox* containers. An example of *RadioButton* controls in *GroupBox* containers is shown in Figure 3-8.

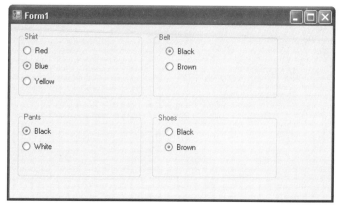

Figure 3-8   Example of Grouped *RadioButton* controls

The *TrackBar* Control

The *TrackBar* control provides a simple interface that allows the user to set a value from a predetermined range of values by graphically manipulating a slider with the mouse or keyboard commands. This allows the user to rapidly set a value from a potentially very large range. Table 3-12 shows important properties of the *TrackBar* control.

Table 3-12   Important Properties of the *TrackBar* Control

Property	Description
LargeChange	The number of positions the slider moves in response to mouse clicks or the *Page Up* and *Page Down* keys.
Maximum	The maximum value for the *TrackBar*.
Minimum	The minimum value for the *TrackBar*.
SmallChange	The number of positions the slider moves in response to arrow key keystrokes.
TickFrequency	The number of positions between tick marks on the *TrackBar*.
TickStyle	Indicates where ticks appear on the *TrackBar*.
Value	The value returned by the *TrackBar*.

The *Trackbar* control is shown in Figure 3.9.

Figure 3-9   The *TrackBar* control

The *TrackBar* control can return an integer value in any range between the values of the *Minimum* and *Maximum* properties. The user can set this value by manipulating the graphical slider on the track bar. Clicking the control or using the *Page Up* and *Page Down* keys while the control is selected will cause the value to change by the increment set in the *LargeChange* property. Using the arrow keys while the control is selected will cause the value to change by the increment set in the *SmallChange* property. The user can also grab the slider with the mouse and adjust it to whatever value is needed. The *Value* property indicates the current value of the track bar.

Choosing Dates and Times

User interfaces frequently require that the user be allowed to set a date or time. For example, an application that allowed a user to make a reservation would require that a date for the reservation be entered. Visual Studio provides two controls that enable Date and Time choosing: the *DateTimePicker* and the *MonthCalendar*.

DateTimePicker Control

The *DateTimePicker* control allows the user to set a date, a time, or both in an easy-to-understand graphical interface. The interface is similar to a *ComboBox* control. The user can click the drop-down box to display a calendar interface that allows the user to choose a day from a calendar or type a time into the text area in the *DateTimePicker*. The chosen day or time is then displayed in the text area of the *DateTimePicker*, and the *Value* property is set to the chosen *DateTime*. Table 3-13 shows important properties of the *DateTimePicker* control.

Table 3-13   Important Properties of the *DateTimePicker* Control

Property	Description
CustomFormat	The custom DateTime format to be used when the *Format* property is set to *Custom*.

Table 3-13   Important Properties of the *DateTimePicker* Control

Property	Description
Format	Sets the format for the DateTime format that is displayed in the *DateTimePicker*. Can be set to *Long*, which displays the value in long date format; *Short*, which displays the value in short date format; *Time*, which displays the time only; or *Custom*, which uses the custom DateTime format indicated by the *CustomFormat* property.
MaxDate	The maximum *DateTime* value the *DateTimePicker* will accept.
MinDate	The minimum *DateTime* value the *DateTimePicker* will accept.
Value	The *DateTime* value that the *DateTimePicker* is currently set to.

When the *Format* property is set to *Long* or *Short*, only the date is displayed, and the date can be set only through the graphical interface. When the *Format* property is set to *Time*, the user can type a new time value into the text area of the *DateTimePicker*. The user can still choose a day through the drop-down interface. Although this day will be reflected in the *Value* property, it will not be displayed when the *Format* property is set to *Time*.

MonthCalendar

The *MonthCalendar* control is a highly configurable control that allows the user to select a range of dates in a highly intuitive interface. Table 3-14 shows the important properties of the *MonthCalendar* control.

Table 3-14   Important Properties of the *MonthCalendar* Control

Property	Description
AnnuallyBoldedDates	Contains an array of dates and times that will appear bolded every year.
BoldedDates	Contains an array of dates and times that will appear bolded.
FirstDayOfWeek	Determines which day of the week is set as the first day of the week in the *MonthCalendar* control.

Table 3-14   Important Properties of the *MonthCalendar* Control

Property	Description
MaxDate	Sets the maximum date that can be chosen in the *MonthCalendar*.
MinDate	Sets the minimum date that can be chosen in the *MonthCalendar*.
MaxSelectionCount	Sets the maximum number of days that can be selected in the *MonthCalendar*.
MonthlyBoldedDates	Contains an array of dates and times that will appear bolded every month in the *MonthCalendar*.
SelectionEnd	Indicates the ending date and time of the *Selection-Range* property.
SelectionRange	Contains the range of dates selected by the user.
SelectionStart	Indicates the starting date and time of the *Selection-Range* property.

The user can select a single date by clicking a date in the *MonthCalendar*, or a continuous range of dates, by holding down the *Shift* key while clicking the starting date and the ending date. The range of dates selected cannot be a greater number of days than is indicated by the *MaxSelectionCount* property.

At run time, you can retrieve the selected dates by accessing the *SelectionStart* and *SelectionEnd* properties, which expose the *Start* and *End* properties of the *Selection-Range* property. The following example demonstrates how to access the *SelectionStart* and *SelectionEnd* properties.

```vb
' VB
MsgBox("Your vacation starts on " & _
    MonthCalendar1.SelectionStart.ToLongDateString & _
    " and ends on " & MonthCalendar1.SelectionEnd.ToLongDateString)
```

```csharp
// C#
MessageBox.Show("Your vacation starts on " +
    monthCalendar1.SelectionStart.ToLongDateString() + " and ends on " +
    monthCalendar1.SelectionEnd.ToLongDateString());
```

Working with Images

Images allow you to liven up your user interface as well as provide important information to the user. Visual Studio contains several components and controls that facilitate the display of images. The *PictureBox* control is an all-around control that displays pictures in several different formats. The *ImageList* manages and organizes a collection of images and can be used to display images in *ListView* or to organize images for other controls.

PictureBox Control

The *PictureBox* control is the basic control used for displaying images in the user interface. The *PictureBox* control can display pictures in a variety of formats, including .bmp, .jpg, .gif, metafiles, and icons. You can display images that are present in application resource files or compiled into the application, or you can load images from a Web or disk address. Table 3-15 details important properties of the *PictureBox* control.

Table 3-15   Important Properties of the *PictureBox* Control

Property	Description
ErrorImage	The image that will be displayed if the selected image fails to load.
Image	The image to be loaded in the *PictureBox*.
ImageLocation	A Web or disk address to load the image from.
InitialImage	The image to be displayed in the *PictureBox* while the image is loading.
SizeMode	Determines how the control handles image placement and sizing.

You can set the *Image* property at design time by clicking it in the Properties window, which opens the Select Resource dialog box, shown in Figure 3-10.

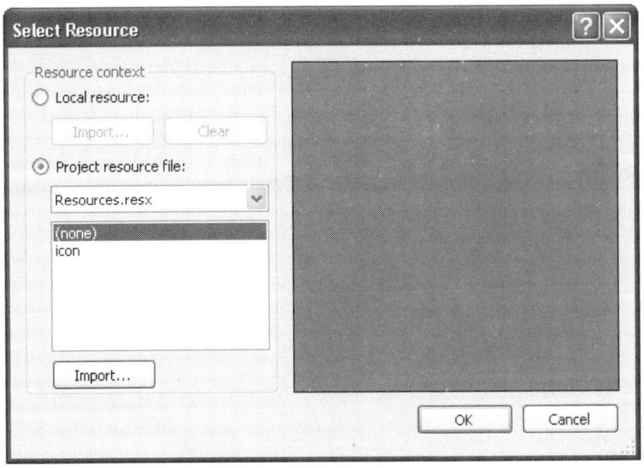

Figure 3-10   The Select Resource dialog box

You can select an image resource that is already present in a project resource file by selecting the Project Resource File radio button and selecting the .resx file that contains the image, or you can import a new image into a resource file by clicking the Import button and navigating to the image you want to import. The selected image will be added to the selected .resx file. You can also import the image as a local resource by selecting the Local Resource radio button and clicking the Import button to browse to the image you want to import. Importing an image as a local resource will make it available only to the *PictureBox* control and unavailable to the rest of the application.

Instead of loading an image from a resource, you can specify a URL from which to load an image by setting the *ImageLocation* property. When the *ImageLocation* property is set, the image is loaded from the specified address, and the *Image* property is set to that image.

At run time, you can set the *Image* property to an instance of an image, as shown in the following example:

```vb
' VB
Dim anImage As New System.Drawing.Bitmap("C:\anImage.bmp")
PictureBox1.Image = anImage
```

```csharp
// C#
System.Drawing.Bitmap anImage = new
    System.Drawing.Bitmap(@"C:\anImage.bmp");
pictureBox1.Image = anImage;
```

ImageList Component

The *ImageList* component is not a control as such, but it is a component that allows you to organize groups of images. Although it has no visual representation itself, it can supply images to other controls, such as *ListView*, or serve as a repository for images to be loaded into a picture box. You can set the size and color depth for the images and iterate through them as you would a collection. Table 3-15 shows important properties of the *ImageList* component.

Table 3-16   Important Properties of the ImageList Component

Property	Description
ColorDepth	Sets the color depth for the images contained in the *ImageList* component.
Images	The collection of images organized by the *ImageList* component.
ImageSize	Sets the size for the images contained in the *ImageList* control.

You can add new items to the *ImageList* control by clicking the *Images* property in the Properties window. This opens the Images Collection Editor, as shown in Figure 3-11.

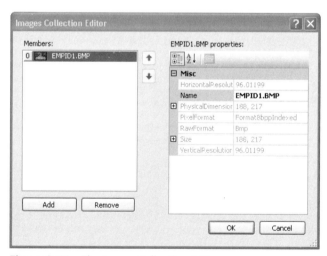

Figure 3-11   The Image Collection Editor

The Images Collection Editor images can be added, removed, or their order in the collection changed via the Images Collection editor. Once images have been added to the *ImageList* component, you can set the color depth for each image by setting the

ColorDepth property, and you can set all of the images to a specified size by setting the *ImageSize* property.

At run time, you can access the images contained in the *ImageList* component via the *Images* collection, as shown in the following example:

```
' VB
PictureBox1.Image = ImageList1.Images(0)
```

```
// C#
pictureBox1.Image = imageList1.Images[0];
```

ImageList components can be used to provide images to other controls in your user interface. Several controls, such as *Button*, *CheckBox*, *RadioButton*, and others, host *ImageList*, *ImageKey*, and *ImageIndex* properties. You can provide images from an *ImageList* component to these controls by setting these properties.

▶ **To provide an image to a control from an *ImageList* component**

1. Set the *ImageList* property of the control to the *ImageList* component that hosts the image you want to provide.

2. Set either the *ImageIndex* property or the *ImageKey* property to the appropriate image in the *ImageList*.

Quick Check

1. What is the difference between how a *RadioButton* control and a *CheckBox* control are used?

2. What is the purpose of an *ImageList* control and how is it used?

Quick Check Answers

1. Radio buttons are used to allow the user to choose a single option from a set of exclusive options. *Checkbox* controls allow the user to select multiple options, usually without regard to whether any other options in the group are selected.

2. An *ImageList* control is used to organize a set of related images. An *ImageList* is generally used to provide images to the controls on a form. You can set the *ImageList* property of the controls on a form to an instance of the *Image-List* and then set either the *ImageIndex* or the *IndexKey* property to specify the image.

Lab: Adventure Works Ski Instructor Reservation Form

In this lab, you will build on the solution you created in the lab in Chapter 1. You will add a group of *CheckBox* controls to allow the user to indicate required ski rental equipment, a group of *RadioButton* controls to allow the user to indicate his ski skill level, and an *ImageList* component to integrate with the *ListView* control so the user will be able to see faces to go with the names.

▶ **Exercise 1: Adding to the Ski Instructor Reservation Form**

1. Open the solution you completed in Lesson 1, or open the Lesson 1 completed solution from the CD.

2. Open Form1 in designer view. Drag a *GroupBox* onto the form. Set the *Text* property of the *GroupBox* to **Rental Equipment**.

3. Drag three *CheckBox* controls into the *GroupBox*. Set the *Text* properties of the *CheckBox* controls to **Skis**, **Poles**, and **Boots**.

4. Drag a *GroupBox* onto the form. Set the *Text* property of the *GroupBox* to **Skill Level**.

5. Drag three *RadioButton* controls into the *GroupBox*. Set the *Text* properties of the *RadioButton* controls to **Beginner**, **Intermediate**, and **Advanced**.

6. Drag a *Label* control and a *DateTimePicker* control onto the form. Set the *Text* property of the *Label* to **Select Lesson Time**.

7. Set the *Format* property of the *DateTimePicker* to **Time**.

8. Drag an *ImageList* component from the *Toolbox* onto the Form.

9. In the Properties window, set the *ImageSize* property of the *ImageList* component to **32,32**, and set the *ColorDepth* property to **Depth16Bit**.

10. In the Properties window, add four images to the *ImageList* component. You will find sample images on the Companion CD in the Images sub-folder of the Code folder.

11. In the Designer, select the *ListView* control. In the Properties window, set the *SmallImageList* property to **ImageList1**.

12. In the Properties window, click Items to open the ListViewItem Collection Editor. In the ListViewItem Collection Editor, set the *ImageIndex* property for *ListViewItems* **0,1,2**, and **3** to **0,1,2**, and **3**, respectively. Images should now display next to the icons in the *ListView* control.

13. Press F5 to build and test your application.

Lesson Summary

- The *CheckBox* control allows users to select options non-exclusively. You can use groups of *CheckBox* controls to allow the user to select multiple options.

- The *RadioButton* control allows you to present a group of exclusive options to the user. You can use groups of *RadioButton* controls to present a list of options, only one of which can be chosen.

- The *TrackBar* control allows the user to rapidly and graphically set a numeric value by adjusting a slider with mouse or keyboard commands.

- The *DateTimePicker* control allows the user to set a date or time. When set to Time format, times can be typed into the *DateTimePicker*. Days can be chosen from the drop-down calendar interface.

- The *MonthCalendar* control is a highly configurable control that allows the user to select a range of dates from an intuitive user interface. You can configure bolded dates and set the maximum length of the date range to be selected by the user.

- The *PictureBox* control is an all-purpose control for displaying images in the user interface and can display images in a variety of formats. The *ImageList* component organizes a collection of images and can set images to a common size and color depth.

Lesson Review

The following questions are intended to reinforce key information presented in this lesson. The questions are also available on the companion CD if you prefer to review them in electronic form.

NOTE   Answers

Answers to these questions and explanations of why each answer choice is right or wrong are located in the "Answers" section at the end of the book.

---

1. Which of the following are possible values for the *Checked* property of a *Check-Box* control? (Choose all that apply.)

    A. *Checked*

    B. *False*

    C. *Indeterminate*

    D. *Unchecked*

    E. *True*

    F. *NotChecked*

2. You are designing an application that asks the user to select a period ranging from one day to seven days in a given month. Which of the following configurations for a *MonthCalendar* control are best choices to facilitate this functionality? (Choose all that apply.)

    A. Set the *MaxSelectionCount* property to 7.

    B. Set the *SelectionRange* property to the first and last days of the month in question.

    C. Set the *MaxDate* property to the last day of the month in question.

    D. Set the *MinDate* property to the first day of the month in question.

3. Which of the following code examples correctly associates an image from an *ImageList* component with a *Button* control? Assume an *ImageList* component named *ImageList1* and a *Button* control named *Button1*. (Choose all that apply.)

    A.
```
' VB
Button1.Image = ImageList1

// C#
button1.Image = imageList1;
```

    B.
```
' VB
Button1.ImageList = ImageList1
Button1.ImageKey = ImageList1.Images(0)

// C#
button1.ImageList1 = imageList1;
button1.ImageKey = imageList1.Images(0);
```

    C.
```
' VB
Button1.ImageList = ImageList1
Button1.ImageIndex = 0

// C#
button1.ImageList = imageList1;
button1.ImageIndex = 0;
```

    D.
```
' VB
Button1.ImageList = ImageList1
Button1.ImageKey = "myImage"

// C#
button1.ImageIndex = imageList1;
button1.ImageKey = "myImage";
```

Lesson 3: Configuring the *WebBrowser* Control and the *NotifyIcon* Component and Creating Access Keys

Visual Studio provides several ways to extend the user interface. The *WebBrowser* control provides an all-purpose control for viewing HTML files and loading content from the World Wide Web. The *NotifyIcon* component allows you to notify users when processes are running in the background, and access keys provide additional options to the user for navigating between controls.

> **After this lesson, you will be able to:**
> - Configure properties and use methods of the *WebBrowser* control.
> - Add application icons to the task bar with *NotifyIcon*.
> - Associate a context menu with a *NotifyIcon* component.
> - Create an access key for a control.
>
> **Estimated lesson time: 30 minutes**

The *WebBrowser* Control

The *WebBrowser* control provides all of the functionality required to load and display HTML pages and other file types, as well as the functionality needed to navigate to locations on the World Wide Web. You can configure the *WebBrowser* to expose online help for your application, to load and print documents, or to display files in a variety of formats. Table 3-17 shows important properties of the *WebBrowser* control.

Table 3-17   Important Properties of the *WebBrowser* Control

Property	Description
AllowWebBrowserDrop	Determines if documents dropped into the *WebBrowser* control are automatically opened.
CanGoBack	Returns whether the *WebBrowser* control is able to navigate backward.
CanGoForward	Returns whether the *WebBrowser* control is able to navigate forward.
Document	Returns the current HTML document in the *WebBrowser* control.

Table 3-17 Important Properties of the *WebBrowser* Control

Property	Description
DocumentStream	Returns the stream associated with the current document.
DocumentText	Returns a string representation of the current document.
DocumentTitle	Returns the title of the current document.
DocumentType	Returns the type of the current document.
IsOffline	Returns whether the system is offline.
IsWebBrowserContext-MenuEnabled	Determines if the standard Microsoft Internet Explorer context menu is enabled for the *WebBrowser*.
ScriptErrorsSuppressed	Determines whether script errors that occur in the document are suppressed or shown in a dialog box.
ScrollBarsEnabled	Determines whether scrollbars are enabled for the control.
URL	Gets or sets the URL for the current document.
WebBrowserShortcuts-Enabled	Gets or sets whether standard Internet Explorer keyboard shortcuts are enabled for the *WebBrowser*.

The *WebBrowser* control also contains a variety of methods that enable navigation within the *WebBrowser*. Table 3-18 details important methods of the *WebBrowser* control.

Table 3-18 Important Methods of the *WebBrowser* Control

Method	Description
GoBack	Navigates to the previous page in the navigation history if one is available.
GoForward	Navigates to the next page in the navigation history if one is available.
GoHome	Navigates to the browser's home page.

Table 3-18   Important Methods of the *WebBrowser* Control

Method	Description
GoSearch	Navigates to the browser's search page.
Navigate	Navigates to the specified URL.
Print	Prints the current document.
ShowPageSetupDialog	Displays the Internet Explorer page setup dialog box.
ShowPrintDialog	Displays the Internet Explorer print dialog box.
ShowPrintPreviewDialog	Displays the Internet Explorer print preview dialog box.
ShowPropertiesDialog	Displays the Internet Explorer properties dialog box.
ShowSaveAsDialog	Displays the Internet Explorer Save As dialog box if the document is of a type other than an HTML page.
Stop	Cancels any pending navigation and stops any dynamic page elements.

Navigating the Web with the *WebBrowser* Control

The *WebBrowser* control provides methods that enable navigation of the Web in your application. The primary method for navigation is the *Navigate* method. This method takes a string argument that indicates the URL for the document to be loaded into the *WebBrowser* control. The following example demonstrates the Navigate method.

```vb
' VB
WebBrowser1.Navigate("www.microsoft.com")
```

```csharp
// C#
webBrowser1.Navigate("www.microsoft.com");
```

Once navigation is complete, the *WebBrowser* control raises the *DocumentCompleted* event. By handling this event, you can execute code after the document has loaded.

You can use other methods of the *WebBrowser* control to access your document history. The *GoBack* method navigates to the previous page in the document history, and the *GoForward* method navigates to the next page in the document history. If no page is available in the document history, there is no effect.

Working with Documents in the *WebBrowser* Control

You can also use the *Navigate* method to load other documents into the *WebBrowser* control. The following example demonstrates how to load a Microsoft Office Word document into the *WebBrowser* control.

```vb
' VB
WebBrowser1.Navigate("C:\Test.doc")
```

```csharp
// C#
webBrowser1.Navigate(@"C:\Test.doc");
```

When working with documents in the *WebBrowser* control, you can allow the user to save the document by using the *ShowSaveAsDialog* method. This method displays the Save As dialog box and allows the user to choose a format to save the document.

You can also use the *WebBrowser* control for printing documents. You can call the *ShowPrintDialog* and *ShowPrintPreview* methods to enable printing of the document. These methods show the Print dialog box and the Print Preview dialog box, respectively, and allow the user to continue on to printing the document.

The *NotifyIcon* Component

The *NotifyIcon* component is not a control but, rather, a component that represents an icon that appears in the system tray. The *NotifyIcon* component is usually used with applications that run in the background. They can provide information about the program execution by displaying balloon tips, and you can associate a *ContextMenuStrip* with the *NotifyIcon* to allow the user to execute commands from a context menu. Table 3-19 shows important properties of the *NotifyIcon* component.

Table 3-19   Important Properties of the *NotifyIcon* Component

Property	Description
BallonTipIcon	The icon that will be shown in the balloon tip. This property can be set to *None*, which displays no icon, or to *Info*, *Warning*, or *Error*.
BalloonTipText	Sets the text that is displayed in the balloon tip.
BalloonTipTitle	Sets the title of the balloon tip.
ContextMenuStrip	Gets or sets the *ContextMenuStrip* associated with the *NotifyIcon*.

Table 3-19   Important Properties of the *NotifyIcon* Component

Property	Description
Icon	The icon that is shown in the system tray.
Text	The text that is shown when the user's mouse rests on the icon in the system tray.
Visible	Indicates whether the icon is visible in the system tray.

To display a *NotifyIcon* in the system tray, you must set the *Icon* property to the icon you want to display and set the *Visible* property to *True*. You can add icons to your project by creating a new instance of the *System.Drawing.Icon* class, or by adding existing icon files to your project from the Project>Add Existing Item menu option.

The *NotifyIcon* component contains properties that govern the display of the balloon tip. The balloon tip can be used to display information to the user. You can set the *Icon*, *Text*, and *Title* of the balloon tip by setting the *BalloonTipIcon*, *BalloonTipText*, and *BalloonTipTitle* properties, respectively. After the appropriate properties are set, you can display the balloon tip by calling the *ShowBalloonTip* method. The *ShowBalloonTip* method takes a parameter that indicates the number of seconds that the balloon tip is shown. Following is an example of the *ShowBalloonTip* method:

```
' VB
NotifyIcon1.ShowBalloonTip(12)
```

```
// C#
notifyIcon1.ShowBalloonTip(12);
```

You can associate a *ContextMenuStrip* with the *NotifyIcon* component to allow users to execute commands from the menu by right-clicking the icon. You can associate a *ContextMenuStrip* with the *NotifyIcon* component by clicking the *ContextMenuStrip* property in the Properties window and setting the property to a *ContextMenuStrip* in your solution. Creating *ContextMenuStrips* will be discussed in detail in Chapter 4, "ToolStrips, Menus, and Events."

Creating Access Keys

Access keys enable the user to move the focus to a particular control by pressing the *Alt* key and the access key you have defined for a particular control. In Chapter 2, you learned how to use a *Label* control to create an access key for another control. The following procedure describes how to create access keys for individual controls.

NOTE   Creating an access key for a control

To create an access key for a control with this procedure, the control must be capable of receiving the focus, it must have a *Text* property, and it must have a *UseMnemonic* property. If the control you want to create an access key for does not have a *UseMnemonic* property, use the procedure described in Chapter 2. If the control cannot receive the focus, you cannot create an access key for it by any procedure.

▶ **To create an access key for a control**

1. Set the *Text* property to the text you want the control to display.

2. In the *Text* property, prepend the letter that you want to make the access key with the ampersand (**&**) symbol.

3. In the Properties window, set the *UseMnemonic* property to *True*. The letter preceded by the ampersand symbol will appear underlined, and, at run time, the user will be able to shift the focus to the control by pressing the *Alt* key along with the underlined key.

Quick Check

- What is the purpose of access keys?

Quick Check Answers

- Access keys allow you to provide keyboard shortcuts that move the focus to the control that the access key is associated with.

Lab: Creating a WebBrowser

In this lab, you will create a limited but functional Web browser. You will add controls to facilitate backward and forward navigation, as well as allowing a user to type a URL and navigate to the specified location.

▶ **Exercise 1: Creating a Web Browser**

1. In Visual Studio, start a new Windows Forms project.

2. In the Properties window for Form1, set the *Size* property to *600,400*.

3. From the Toolbox, drag a *SplitContainer* onto the Form.

4. From the Toolbox, drag a *WebBrowser* control onto Panel2.

5. From the Toolbox, drag three *Button* controls and a *TextBox* control onto Panel1.

6. Set the *Text* property of the *Button* controls to *&Back*, *&Forward*, and *&Navigate*.

7. Set the *UseMnemonic* property of each *Button* control to *True*.

8. Select the *SplitContainer*. In the Properties window, set the *Orientation* property to *Horizontal* and adjust the size of Panel1 so that just the buttons are showing. Set the *FixedPanel* property to Panel1.

9. In the Designer, double-click the Back button to open the *Button_Click* event handler for this button. Add the following line of code:

```
' VB
WebBrowser1.GoBack()
```

```
// C#
webBrowser1.GoBack();
```

10. In the Designer, double-click the Forward button to open the *Button_Click* event handler for this button. Add the following line of code:

```
' VB
WebBrowser1.GoForward()
```

```
// C#
webBrowser1.GoForward();
```

11. In the Designer, double-click the Navigate button to open the *Button_Click* event handler for this button. Add the following line of code:

```
' VB
WebBrowser1.Navigate(TextBox1.Text)
```

```
// C#
webBrowser1.Navigate(textBox1.Text);
```

12. Press F5 to build and test your application.

Lesson Summary

■ The *WebBrowser* control encapsulates all of the functionality necessary to access the Internet and load a variety of document types. It contains methods that facilitate navigation of the World Wide Web and the file system.

■ The *NotifyIcon* component allows you to set an icon in the system tray and provide notifications to users regarding processes running in the background. You can display messages to the user via balloon tips and can enable commands by associating a *ContextMenuStrip* with the *NotifyIcon*.

■ You can use the *Text* and *UseMnemonic* properties to define access keys for controls that can receive the focus. Only controls that are capable of receiving the focus can have access keys defined for them. If a control can receive the focus but does not have *Text* or *UseMnemonic* properties, you can define an access key with a *Label* control, as described in Chapter 2.

Lesson Review

The following questions are intended to reinforce key information presented in this lesson. The questions are also available on the companion CD if you prefer to review them in electronic form.

NOTE   Answers

Answers to these questions and explanations of why each answer choice is right or wrong are located in the "Answers" section at the end of the book.

---

1. Which of the following methods can be used to print the current document in a *WebBrowser* control? (Choose all that apply.)

    A. *WebBrowser.Print*

    B. *WebBrowser.ShowPrintDialog*

    C. *WebBrowser.ShowPrintPreviewDialog*

    D. *WebBrowser.ShowPropertiesDialog*

2. You are designing an application that runs in the background and want to enable the application to notify the user when a severe error occurs. Which of the following properties of the *NotifyIcon* component can facilitate this functionality? (Choose all that apply.)

    A. *BalloonTipIcon*

    B. *BalloonTipText*

    C. *BalloonTipTitle*

    D. *Text*

3. Which of the following are required to create an access key for a control without using an associated label? (Choose all that apply.)

    A. The *Enabled* property must be set to *True*.

    B. The control must have a *Text* property.

    C. The *UseMnemonic* property must be set to *True*.

    D. The control must be of a type that is able to receive the focus.

Chapter Review

To further practice and reinforce the skills you learned in this chapter, you can perform the following tasks:

- Review the chapter summary.
- Review the list of key terms introduced in this chapter.
- Complete the case scenarios. These scenarios set up real-world situations involving the topics of this chapter and ask you to create a solution.
- Complete the suggested practices.
- Take a practice test.

Chapter Summary

- List-based controls are used to organize and present lists of information to the user. Basic list-based controls such as *ListBox*, *ComboBox*, and *CheckedListBox* organize their contents in the *Items* property, which exposes common methods for adding, removing, and otherwise manipulating contained items.

- Specialized list-based controls, such as *ListView* and *TreeView*, are designed to fill specific roles. The *ListView* control allows you to display icons and other information about its contained members. The *TreeView* control displays contained members in a hierarchical tree display that the user can expand or collapse as needed.

- Value-setting controls allow the user to set a value that can later be read by the program through the user interface. *CheckBox* and *RadioButton* controls set Boolean values for their *Checked* property, allowing the user to choose yes or no to a set of presented options.

- The *ImageList* component organizes images and makes them available to controls in the application. Controls that expose an *ImageList* property can reference a given image list and display contained images.

- The *WebBrowser* control is an all-purpose control for browsing the Web and file system. It allows you to work with a variety of document types and contains methods that facilitate navigation, printing, and saving documents.

- The *NotifyIcon* component can display information about a process that is running in the background. You can display information by setting the *BalloonTip* properties and showing the balloon tip. You can expose commands to the user by associating a *ContextMenuStrip* with the *NotifyIcon* component.

- You can use the *Text* and *UseMnemonic* properties to designate access keys for a control. Any control that can receive the focus and has *Text* and *UseMnemonic* properties can define its own access key. If a control can receive the focus but does not have *Text* or *UseMnemonic* properties, you can define an access key using a *Label* control as shown in Chapter 2.

Key Terms

Do you know the what these key terms mean? You can check your answers by looking up the terms in the glossary at the end of the book.

- access keys
- list
- list-based control
- value-setting control

Case Scenarios

In the following case scenarios, you will apply what you've learned about how to use controls to design user interfaces. You can find answers to these questions in the "Answers" section at the end of this book.

Case Scenario 1: Incorporating List-Based Controls into the User Interface

Humongous Insurance has grown so large that they need some help keeping track of their employees. You have been put on the team that will design the new human resources application. Other developers will supply a programmatic representation of the organization chart and a database of information about the employees. Your job is to create a user interface that allows the organization chart to be browsed by the user and allows additional information about each employee to be displayed in the user interface.

Questions

Answer the following questions for your manager:

1. What is your suggested control layout for the user interface? How will you be able to display the organization chart in a compact, easy-to-browse format?

2. How can we display photos of our employees as part of this application?

Case Scenario 2: Working with Files and Background Processes

As part of their document backup plan, Humongous Insurance has created an automated program that reads their electronic documents in a variety of different formats (such as .doc, .txt, and .htm), saves them to a backup location, and prints a hard copy on a high-throughput printer. For the most part, this application works fine without user interaction and displays no user interface. Occasionally, however, a problem occurs with a document that requires user intervention. You have been put in charge of designing the user interface for the rare occasions that do arise.

Technical Requirements

- The user interface must display only when there is a problem, and cannot be launched without action by a user.

- The user must be able to examine the document and manually save and print it.

Questions

Answer the following questions for your manager:

1. How can we warn the user of a problem without displaying the user interface at all times? How will we allow the user to launch a user interface when there is a problem?

2. When there is a problem, how can we design the user interface so that the user is able to examine, print, and save individual files?

Suggested Practices

To successfully master the Add and Configure a Windows Forms Control exam objective, complete the following practices, as well as the practices in Chapter 2.

- **Practice 1** Build an application that duplicates the functionality of Windows Explorer. You should be able to display a directory tree in one pane and files in a particular directory in another pane.

- **Practice 2** Build an application that acts like an appointment book. It should allow the user to choose a date and time, add information about the appointment, track and display details about the appointment, and visually display to the user on a *MonthCalendar* control what days have appointments set.

■ **Practice 3**   Expand the Web browser you created in Lesson 3 to disable the Back and Forward buttons if *webBrowser1.CanGoBack* or *webBrowser1.CanGoForward* are False. You can do this by handling the *WebBrowser.CanGoBackChanged* and *WebBrowser.CanGoForwardChanged* events. Also, allow the user to navigate to a page by typing an address in the *TextBox* control and pressing Enter.

Take a Practice Test

The practice tests on this book's companion CD offer many options. For example, you can test yourself on just the content covered in this chapter, or you can test yourself on all the 70-526 certification exam content. You can set up the test so that it closely simulates the experience of taking a certification exam, or you can set it up in study mode so that you can look at the correct answers and explanations after you answer each question.

MORE INFO   Practice tests

For details about all the practice test options available, see the "How to Use the Practice Tests" section in this book's Introduction.

Chapter 4
Tool Strips, Menus, and Events

This chapter describes additional ways to extend the user interface. Tool strips allow you to create useful toolbars in a manner consistent with the look and feel of Microsoft Office. Menus allow you to define custom commands that can be executed by the user. Events are raised by controls in response to changes in application conditions or user interaction, and, by handling events, you can write code that executes in response to events.

Exam objectives in this chapter:
- Add and configure a Windows Forms control.
  - Display images by using Windows Forms controls.
- Create and configure menus.
  - Create and configure a *MenuStrip* component on a Windows Form.
  - Change the displayed menu structure programmatically.
  - Create and configure the *ContextMenuStrip* on a Windows Form.
- Create event handlers for Windows Forms and controls.
  - Use the Windows Forms Designer to create event handlers.
  - Manage mouse and keyboard events within Windows Forms applications.
  - Program a Windows Forms application to recognize modifier keys.
  - Use the Windows Forms Designer to create default event handlers.
  - Create event handlers at run time to respond to system or user events dynamically.
  - Connect multiple events to a single event handler.
  - Use the Code Editor to override methods defined in the base class.

Lessons in this chapter:

Before You Begin

To complete the lessons in this chapter, you must have:

- A computer that meets or exceeds the minimum hardware requirements listed in the "Introduction" at the beginning of the book.

- Microsoft Visual Studio 2005 Professional Edition installed on your computer.

- An understanding of Microsoft Visual Basic or C# syntax and familiarity with the Microsoft .NET Framework.

- Completed Chapter 3, "Advanced Windows Forms Controls," or have a good understanding of Windows Forms controls and the Visual Studio IDE.

Real World

Matt Stoecker

The new *ToolStrip* and *MenuStrip* controls in the .NET Framework 2.0 have dramatically improved the speed with which I can develop a user interface. The *ToolStrip* control allows me to create user interfaces that are consistent with Microsoft Office applications and to create a more familiar experience for the user, which leads to more rapid adoption and, ultimately, increased productivity.

Lesson 1: Configuring Tool Strips

The *ToolStrip* control is a new control in the .NET Framework version 2.0 that was designed to facilitate the creation of custom toolbars that have the look and feel of Microsoft Office and Microsoft Internet Explorer toolbars. Using the *ToolStrip* control, you can rapidly develop highly configurable, professional-looking toolbars that expose your custom functionality.

After this lesson, you will be able to:

- Configure a tool strip to create a tool bar.
- Configure a status strip to create a status bar.
- Add various tool strip items to a *ToolStrip* control.
- Add an image to a tool strip item.
- Enable repositioning of tool strip items by the user.
- Add a *ToolStrip* control to a ToolStripContainer.
- Merge two tool strips.

Estimated lesson time: 30 minutes

Overview of the *ToolStrip* Control

The *ToolStrip* control enables you to create toolbars that have a professional and consistent look and feel. *ToolStrip* controls are containers for *ToolStripItems*, which are controls that are designed to be hosted inside a tool strip. *ToolStripItems* can be used to provide a wide variety of options and functionality to the user.

ToolStrip controls encapsulate much of the functionality required for management of a toolbar. They manage the layout and positioning of their contained tool strip controls, enable reordering of the tool strip items by the user, manage rendering, and create overflow buttons when more tool strip items are hosted on a tool strip than can be displayed. Table 4-1 shows some of the important properties of the *ToolStrip* control.

Table 4-1   Important Properties of the *ToolStrip* Control

Property	Description
AllowItemReorder	Indicates whether items can be reordered by the user. When set to *True*, contained tool strip items can be reordered when the user holds down the *Alt* key and grabs the item with the mouse.

Table 4-1   Important Properties of the *ToolStrip* Control

Property	Description
AllowMerge	Indicates whether this tool strip can be merged with another tool strip.
CanOverflow	Indicates whether tool strip items can be automatically moved to the overflow button when needed.
Dock	Indicates how the tool strip is docked. Although *ToolStrip* controls can be free in the form, they are most commonly docked to one of the form edges.
LayoutStyle	Indicates how the controls on the tool strip are laid out. A value of *HorizontalStackWithOverFlow* indicates that items are stacked horizontally and overflow as needed. *VerticalStackWithOverFlow* stacks items vertically and overflows as needed. *StackWithOverflow* determines the stack model appropriate to the *Dock* property of the tool strip. *Flow* allows the items to stack horizontally or vertically as needed, and *Table* arranges all of the items flush left.
RenderMode	Determines how the tool strip items are rendered. System uses system settings, Professional indicates a Microsoft Office–style appearance, and ManagerRenderMode gets the setting automatically.
ShowItemToolTips	Indicates whether tooltips for individual tool strip items are displayed.
Stretch	When hosted in a ToolStripContainer, indicates whether the tool strip will stretch to the full length of the ToolStripPanel.
TextDirection	Indicates the direction of the text in controls hosted in the tool strip.

The *StatusStrip* control is very similar to the *ToolStrip* control and can host the same controls that a *ToolStrip* control can. The primary differences are in the default setting for the properties. *StatusStrip* controls are designed to dock at the bottom of the form and provide status updates to the user and have default properties set to values that facilitate this functionality. *ToolStrip* controls are designed for a variety of tool-based roles and have default values for properties that indicate a more generalized role.

Adding Tool Strip Items to a Tool Strip

At design time, you can add tool strip items to a tool strip by choosing appropriate items from the drop-down menu in the Designer as shown in Figure 4-1.

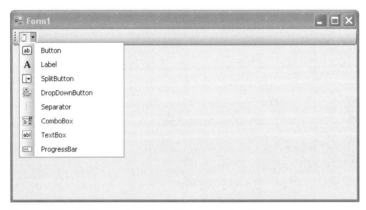

Figure 4-1   Adding a tool strip item at design time

The item you choose from the menu will be added to the tool strip, and an instance of it will be added to your application. You can set properties for the item in the Properties window and refer to the item in code.

At run time, you can dynamically add items to a tool strip by using the *ToolStrip.Items .Add* method. This method allows you to specify a reference to an existing tool strip item and add it to the toolbar, or it will create and add a new tool strip item when you specify text or an image. An example is shown here:

```
' VB
Dim aToolStripItem As ToolStripItem
Dim bToolStripItem As ToolStripItem
aToolStripItem = myToolStrip.Items.Add("New Item")
bToolStripItem = myToolStrip.Items.Add(anImage)
```

```
// C#
ToolStripItem aToolStripItem;
ToolStripItem bToolStripItem;
aToolStripItem = myToolStrip.Items.Add("New Item");
bToolStripItem = myToolStrip.Items.Add(anImage);
```

In this example, a new tool strip item is added when text or an image is specified. When items are added in this way, the resulting item is always a *ToolStripButton* object. The

ToolStrip.Items.Add method returns a reference to the new item so you can set properties and events for it at run time.

You can also create a new tool strip item and then add it directly, as shown here:

```
' VB
Dim aComboBox As New ToolStripComboBox()
myToolStrip.Items.Add(aComboBox)
```

```
// C#
ToolStripComboBox aComboBox = new ToolStripComboBox();
myToolStrip.Items.Add(aComboBox);
```

By following this example, you can create a tool strip item of any kind and add it to a tool strip at run time.

Tool Strip Items

The .NET Framework 2.0 provides several items designed to be hosted in tool strips. Items such as the *ToolStripLabel*, *ToolStripButton*, *ToolStripTextBox*, *ToolStripComboBox* and *ToolStripProgressBar* controls are similar to the *Label*, *Button*, *TextBox*, *ComboBox*, and *ProgressBar* controls, but are designed to be hosted in tool strips. *ToolStripSplitButton*, *ToolStripDropDownButton*, and *ToolStripSeparator* are new controls designed to provide functionality specific to tool strips.

Common Properties of Tool Strip Items

Tool strip items have several common properties that govern their behavior in the tool strip. Table 4-2 demonstrates the most important properties that all tool strip items share.

Table 4-2   Important Properties of Tool Strip Items

Property	Description
MergeAction	This property determines how a tool strip item behaves with the tool strip that contains it when it is merged with another tool strip. Possible values are *Append*, *Insert*, *MatchOnly*, *Remove*, and *Replace*. Merging tool strips will be discussed later in this lesson.
MergeIndex	This property indicates where a tool strip item will appear in a merged tool strip if the *MergeAction* property is set to *Insert*.

Table 4-2   Important Properties of Tool Strip Items

Property	Description
ToolTipText	Gets or sets the text that will be shown in a tooltip when the mouse hovers over the tool strip item if the *ToolStrip.ShowItem-ToolTips* property is set to *True*. Note that the *ToolStripSeparator* control does not have this property.

ToolStripLabel

The *ToolStripLabel* control combines the functionality of the *Label* control and the *LinkLabel* control. When the *IsLink* property is set to *False*, the *ToolStripLabel* displays the text contained in its *Text* property in the tool strip and acts similarly to a basic *Label* control. When the *IsLink* property is set to *True*, the control behaves like a *LinkLabel* control. You can program actions to be taken when the label is clicked in the *ToolStripLabel.Click* event handler.

ToolStripButton

The *ToolStripButton* control is analogous to the familiar *Button* control. It appears on the tool strip as a button, usually displaying an icon that indicates what function it contains. The user can click the button to execute an action. Clicking the button executes code in the *ToolStripButton.Click* event handler.

ToolStripSeparator

The *ToolStripSeparator* control is basically a visual cue that separates items in a tool strip from other items in a tool strip. Although it can respond to mouse clicks via the *ToolStripSeparator.Click* event handler, it is primarily used to provide visual feedback.

ToolStripComboBox

The *ToolStripComboBox* control is similar to the *ComboBox* control, but it is hosted in a tool strip. Like the *ComboBox*, it can be set to styles of *Simple*, *DropDown*, or *DropDownList*, and the items are found in the *Items* collection. When an item is selected or typed into the *ToolStripComboBox*, that item is then exposed via the *Text* property.

ToolStripTextBox

The *ToolStripTextBox* is very similar to the basic *TextBox* control. The user can type a string into the text box, and this string will be programmatically accessible via the

ToolStripTextBox.Text property. The main difference in functionality is that the *Tool-StripTextBox* does not have a *MultiLine* property and, thus, can have only one line.

ToolStripProgressBar

The *ToolStripProgressBar* is a control that is designed to provide feedback to the user when progress is made on a time-consuming task, and it functions very similarly to the standard *ProgressBar* control. The *Minimum* and *Maximum* properties set the minimum and maximum values for the *ToolStripProgressBar*, and the *Value* property determines the current setting. The visual appearance is set by the *Style* property, and when *Style* is set to *Blocks* or *Continuous*, the *Value* property is reflected in the visual interface as a percentage of the maximum that is filled in the progress bar. When set to *Marquee*, blocks continuously move across the progress bar at the rate specified by the *Marquee-AnimationSpeed* property. At run time, you can advance the value of the *ToolStrip-ProgressBar* either by setting the *Value* property directly or by using the *Increment* and *PerformStep* methods.

ToolStripDropDownButton

The *ToolStripDropDownButton* allows you to create a drop-down menu that appears when the button is clicked. At design time, you can create the menu by typing text for menu items in the menu designer, as shown in Figure 4-2.

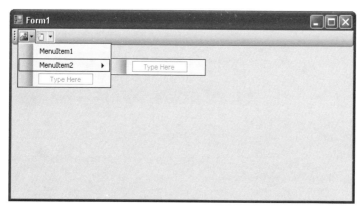

Figure 4-2   Creating a menu with the *ToolStripDropDownButton*

Each menu item has its own *ToolStripMenuItem.Click* event that you can respond to.

ToolStripSplitButton

The *ToolStripSplitButton* control combines the functionality of the *ToolStripButton* and *ToolStripDropDownButton* controls. This control exposes a button that a user can click to execute code, but it also exposes a drop-down menu in the style of the *ToolStripDropDownButton* control. You can handle the *ToolStripSplitButton.Click* event to write code for the button clicks, or you can write code that is executed for each *ToolStripMenuItem.Click* event.

Displaying Images on Tool Strip Items

The *ToolStripButton*, *ToolStripDropDownButton*, and *ToolStripSplitButton* controls can display text, images, or a combination of both. Table 4-3 shows how the properties of these controls govern how images are displayed.

Table 4-3   Image Display Properties of *ToolStripButton* Controls

Property	Description
DisplayStyle	Determines whether the control is displayed with text, image, or both.
Image	Gets or sets the image that associates with this control.
ImageAlign	Indicates how the image is aligned in the control.
ImageScaling	Specifies whether the image will be resized to fit the control.
ImageTransparent-Color	Indicates the color in the image that will appear as transparent when rendered in the user interface.

Add a *ToolStripButton*, *ToolStripSplitButton*, or *ToolStripDropDownButton* to the toolbar.

▶ **To display an image on a tool strip**

1. Select the control. In the Properties window, ensure that the *DisplayStyle* property is set to *Image* or *ImageAndText*.

2. In the Properties window, select the image for the control by clicking the *Image* property and selecting or browsing to the appropriate image in the Select Resource dialog box.

The *ToolStripContainer*

The *ToolStripContainer* class is a specialized container control designed specifically for containing tool strips and enabling rafting, which is the process by which a user can grab a tool strip and move it from one edge of the container to another.

The *ToolStripContainer* contains five panels: four *ToolStripPanels* (one on each edge of the form) and one *ContentPanel*. The most common scenario for the *ToolStripContainer* is to add it to a form and set the *Dock* property to *Fill*. This results in the *ToolStripContainer* filling the entire form and having tool strip containers available on all sides.

At design time, you can add a tool strip to a tool strip container by dragging it from the Toolbox onto one of the tool strip panels. You can control which tool strip panels are available to the user by setting the *TopToolStripPanelVisible*, *BottomToolStripPanelVisible*, *LeftToolStripPanelVisible*, and *RightToolStripPanelVisible* properties. When these properties are set to *True*, the corresponding panel is available for tool strip rafting at run time. When set to *False*, the panel is not available.

Merging Tool Strips

ToolStrip controls can be merged at run time and their items incorporated into a single tool strip. Merging tool strips is accomplished by invoking the *ToolStripManager.Merge* method as shown here:

```
' VB
ToolStripManager.Merge(sourceToolStrip, targetToolStrip)
```

```
// C#
ToolStripManager.Merge(sourceToolStrip, targetToolStrip);
```

The *ToolStripManager* is a static class that manages the display and layout of the tool strips on a form. Because it is a static class, there is no need to instantiate it—you can invoke the methods directly.

The preceding example takes the first tool strip, *sourceToolStrip*, and merges it with the second tool strip (*targetToolStrip*). The tool strip items on *sourceToolStrip* are then merged with the items on *targetToolStrip* as is determined by their *MergeAction* property value. Table 4-4 summarizes the merge action taken by the *MergeAction* property value.

Table 4-4   *ToolStripItem MergeAction* Property Values and Merge Actions

MergeAction Value	Action Taken
Append	Appends the item at the end of the list of items.
Insert	Inserts the item at the location specified by the *MergeIndex* property.
MatchOnly	Looks for a match but takes no action.
Remove	If a matching tool strip item is found, it is removed from the resulting tool strip.
Replace	If a matching tool strip item is found, it is replaced with this tool strip.

When tool strips are merged, each tool strip item in the source tool strip is compared to each tool strip item in the target tool strip. The comparison is based on the *Text* property of each tool strip item. Thus, if any two tool strip items have the same *Text* property, they will be considered a match, even if they are different types (for example, a *ToolStripLabel* and a *ToolStripButton* that both have a *Text* property that is set to *Execute* will be considered a match). If a match is found, and the source tool strip item has the *MergeAction* property set to *MatchOnly*, *Remove*, or *Replace*, then the appropriate action will be taken. Otherwise, the tool strip item will be appended or inserted as determined by the *MergeAction* property.

For tool strips to be merged successfully, they must have their *AllowMerge* property set to *True*.

Quick Check

1. What is the purpose of the *ToolStrip* control?
2. What kinds of *ToolStripItems* can be hosted in a *ToolStrip* control?

Quick Check Answers

1. The *ToolStrip* control is used to host *ToolStripItems* which can be used to expose commonly used commands or provide frequently used functionality in an environment that is highly configurable at run time.
2. The *ToolStrip* can host any kind of *ToolStripItem*, including *ToolStripMenuItem* controls.

Lab 1: Creating a *ToolStrip*–Based Web Browser

In this lab, you will explore the functionality of *ToolStrip* and *ToolStripItem* controls by creating a simple Web browser that uses *ToolStripItem* controls to enable its functionality. In the first exercise, you will add a tool strip that implements basic Web browser functionality. In the second exercise, you will add a tool strip that allows the user to search the Web.

▶ **Exercise 1: Creating a Web Browser**

1. Start a new Windows Forms Project.

2. From the Toolbox, drag a *ToolStripContainer* onto the form. Set the *Dock* property to *Fill*.

3. Enlarge the form to a comfortable size for a Web browser.

4. From the Toolbox, drag a *WebBrowser* control into the center panel of the *ToolStripContainer*.

5. From the Toolbox, drag a *ToolStrip* control to the top panel of the *ToolStripContainer*.

6. Using the ToolStrip designer, add the following controls to the tool strip in this order: two *ToolStripButton* controls, a *ToolStripComboBox*, and two more *ToolStripButton* controls.

7. In the Properties window, set the *Name*, *Image*, and *ToolTipText* properties of the *ToolStripButton* controls as shown in the following table. The image files can be found in the code folder on the CD.

Default Name	New Name	Image	ToolTipText
ToolStripButton1	BackButton	Back.bmp	Navigate Back
ToolStripButton2	ForwardButton	Forward.bmp	Navigate Forward
ToolStripButton3	GoButton	Go.bmp	Navigate
ToolStripButton4	StopButton	Stop.bmp	Stop Navigation

8. Double-click BackButton and add the following code to the *BackButton_Click* event handler:

```
' VB
WebBrowser1.GoBack()
```

```
// C#
webBrowser1.GoBack();
```

9. Double-click ForwardButton and add the following code to the *ForwardButton-_Click* event handler:

```
' VB
WebBrowser1.GoForward()
```

```
// C#
webBrowser1.GoForward();
```

10. Double-click GoButton and add the following code to the *StopButton.Click* event handler:

```
' VB
If Not ToolStripComboBox1.Text = "" Then
    WebBrowser1.Navigate(ToolStripComboBox1.Text)
    ToolStripComboBox1.Items.Add(ToolStripComboBox1.Text)
    If ToolStripComboBox1.Items.Count = 11 Then
        ToolStripComboBox1.Items.RemoveAt(0)
    End If
End If
```

```
// C#
if (!(toolStripComboBox1.Text == ""))
{
    webBrowser1.Navigate(toolStripComboBox1.Text);
    toolStripComboBox1.Items.Add(toolStripComboBox1.Text);
    if (toolStripComboBox1.Items.Count == 11)
    {
        toolStripComboBox1.Items.RemoveAt(0);
    }
}
```

11. Double-click StopButton and add the following code to the *StopButton_Click* event handler:

```
' VB
WebBrowser1.Stop()
```

```
// C#
webBrowser1.Stop();
```

12. Press F5 to test your application.

▶ **Exercise 2: Adding a Search Tool Strip**

1. From the Toolbox, drag a second *ToolStrip* onto the *Top* panel of the *ToolStrip-Container*.

2. In the ToolStrip designer, add a *ToolStripTextBox* and a *ToolStripButton* to the new tool strip.

3. In the Properties window, set the *Text* property of the *ToolStripButton* to Search MSN and the *DisplayStyle* property to Text.

4. Double-click the tool strip button and add the following code to its event handler:

```
' VB
WebBrowser1.Navigate("http://search.msn.com/results.aspx?q=" & ToolStripTextBox1.Text)
```

```
// C#
webBrowser1.Navigate(@"http://search.msn.com/results.aspx?q=" +
toolStripTextBox1.Text);
```

5. Press F5 to test your application. Note that the two tool strips can be individually positioned and moved to other panels in the *ToolStripContainer*.

Lesson Summary

- The *ToolStrip* control is a host for *ToolStripMenuItem* controls that can be used to create toolbar-style functionality for your forms. Toolbars provide support for item reordering, rafting, and overflow of items onto the overflow button.

- Many tool strip items duplicate functionality of full-size Windows Forms controls such as *ToolStripLabel*, *ToolStripButton*, *ToolStripTextBox*, *ToolStripComboBox*, and *ToolStripProgressBar*. Tool strip controls that do not have analogous Windows Forms controls include *ToolStripSeparator*, *ToolStripDropDownButton*, and *ToolStripSplitButton*.

- You can display images on the *ToolStripItems* control with the *Image* property.

- The *ToolStripContainer* control allows you to create forms that include support for rafting toolbars.

- The *ToolStripManager* class is a static class that exposes methods for tool strip management. You can use the *ToolStripManager.Merge* method to merge tool strips.

Lesson Review

You can use the following questions to test your knowledge of the information in this lesson. The questions are also available on the companion CD if you prefer to review them in electronic form.

NOTE Answers

Answers to these questions and explanations of why each choice is right or wrong are located in the "Answers" section at the end of the book.

---

1. Which of the following code snippets will correctly merge two tool strips named aToolStrip and bToolStrip?

   A. ' VB
   ```
   aToolStrip.Merge(bToolStrip)
   ```

   // C#
   ```
   aToolStrip.Merge(bToolStrip);
   ```

   B. ' VB
   ```
   ToolStripManager.Merge(aToolStrip, bToolStrip)
   ```

   // C#
   ```
   ToolStripManager.Merge(aToolStrip, bToolStrip);
   ```

   C. ' VB
   ```
   Dim aManager As New ToolStripManager()
   aManager.Merge(aToolStrip, bToolStrip)
   ```

   // C#
   ```
   ToolStripManager aManager = new ToolStripManager();
   aManager.Merge(aToolStrip, bToolStrip);
   ```

   D. ' VB
   ```
   ToolStrip.Merge(aToolStrip, bToolStrip)
   ```

   // C#
   ```
   ToolStrip.Merge(aToolStrip, bToolStrip);
   ```

2. Which of the following code snippets will add a new *ToolStripButton* to a tool strip named aToolStrip?

   A. ' VB
   ```
   aToolStrip.Items.Add(New ToolStripButton("Click me"))
   ```

   // C#
   ```
   aToolStrip1.Items.Add(new ToolStripButton("Click me"));
   ```

   B. ' VB
   ```
   ToolStripManager.Add(aToolStrip, New ToolStripButton("Click me"))
   ```

   // C#
   ```
   ToolStripManager.Add(aToolStrip, new ToolStripButton("Click me"));
   ```

   C.

   ' VB
   ```
   aToolStrip.Buttons.Add(New ToolStripButton("Click me"))
   ```

```
// C#
aToolStrip.Buttons.Add(new ToolStripButton("Click me"));
```

D. ' VB
```
aToolStrip.Items.NewItem(Items.ToolStripButton("Click me"))
```

```
// C#
aToolStrip.Items.NewItem(Items.ToolStripButton("Click me"));
```

Lesson 2: Creating and Configuring Menus

Menus have always been a part of Windows Forms applications. They give the user quick and easy access to important application commands in an easy-to-understand, easy-to-browse interface. The .NET Framework version 2.0 introduced MenuStrips, which allow the rapid creation of Forms menus as well as context menus (also known as shortcut menus, which appear when the user right-clicks an object). In this lesson, you will learn how to create menus and context menus and configure them for use in your application.

> **After this lesson, you will be able to:**
> - Create and configure a *MenuStrip* component on a Windows Form.
> - Change the Displayed menu structure programmatically.
> - Create and configure the *ContextMenuStrip* component on a Windows Form.
>
> **Estimated lesson time: 30 minutes**

Overview of the *MenuStrip* Control

The *MenuStrip* control is essentially a *ToolStrip* control that is optimized for the display of *ToolStripMenuItems*. The *MenuStrip* control derives from *ToolStrip* and can host all of the tool strip items described in the previous lesson. Its primary function, however, is to host *ToolStripMenuItems*.

ToolStripMenuItems are the controls that provide the visual representation for items on a menu. They can appear as text, an image, or both, and can execute code found in their *ToolStripMenuItem.Click* event handlers when clicked. Each *ToolStripMenuItem* can contain its own set of menu items, allowing for the creation of nested menus.

The menu strip exposes many properties that affect the behavior of its hosted *ToolStripMenuItems*. Important properties of the *MenuStrip* control are shown in Table 4-5.

Table 4-5   Important Properties of the *MenuStrip* Control

Property	Description
AllowItemReorder	Indicates whether items can be reordered by the user. When set to *True*, contained items can be reordered when the user holds down the *Alt* key and grabs the item with the mouse.

Table 4-5 Important Properties of the *MenuStrip* Control

Property	Description
AllowMerge	Indicates whether this menu strip can be merged with another tool strip.
Dock	Indicates how the menu strip is docked. Although *Menu-Strip* controls can be free in the form, they are most commonly docked to one of the form edges.
LayoutStyle	Indicates how the controls on the tool strip are laid out. A value of *HorizontalStackWithOverFlow* indicates that items are stacked horizontally and overflow as needed. *Vertical-StackWithOverFlow* stacks items vertically and overflows as needed. *StackWithOverflow* determines the stack model appropriate to the Dock property of the tool strip. *Flow* allows the items to stack horizontally or vertically as needed, and *Table* arranges all of the items flush left.
RenderMode	Determines how the tool strip items are rendered. System uses system settings, Professional indicates a Microsoft Office–style appearance, and ManagerRenderMode gets the setting automatically.
ShowItemToolTips	Indicates whether tooltips for individual tool strip items are displayed.
Stretch	When hosted in a ToolStripContainer, it indicates whether the tool strip will stretch to the full length of the ToolStrip-Panel.
TextDirection	Indicates the direction of the text in controls hosted in the tool strip.

Note that the properties of the *MenuStrip* control are very similar to the properties of the *ToolStrip* control. Because *MenuStrip* derives from *ToolStrip*, it exposes most of the same properties as the *ToolStrip* control and encapsulates most of the same functionality.

ToolStripMenuItems provide all of the functionality that is expected of menus. Table 4-6 explains some of the important properties of the *ToolStripMenuItem* control.

Table 4-6 Important Properties of the *ToolStripMenuItem* Control

Property	Description
AutoSize	Determines whether the menu item is automatically sized to fit the text.
Checked	Determines whether the menu item appears as checked.
CheckOnClick	Determines whether the menu item is automatically checked when clicked.
CheckState	Returns the CheckState of the menu item. The CheckState can be Checked, Unchecked, or Indeterminate.
DisplayStyle	Determines how the tool strip menu item is displayed. This property can be set to *None*, which provides no visual representation; *Text*, which shows only text; *Image*, which displays the item only with an image; or *ImageAndText*, which displays the image next to the text.
DoubleClickEnabled	Determines whether the *DoubleClick* event will fire.
DropDownItems	Contains a collection of tool strip items (usually tool strip menu items but not necessarily) that appear in the drop-down list when this item is chosen.
Enabled	Determines whether the tool strip menu item is enabled.
Image	Sets the image to be associated with this tool strip menu item.
MergeAction	Determines the action taken by this tool strip menu item when menus are merged.
MergeIndex	Determines the order of items in the resultant menu after menus are merged.
ShortcutKeyDisplay-String	Sets a custom string for the shortcut key that is displayed next to the menu item. If shortcut keys are enabled and this property is left blank, the actual key combination will be displayed.

Table 4-6   Important Properties of the *ToolStripMenuItem* Control

Property	Description
ShortcutKeys	Defines the key combination that will act as a shortcut to execute the menu command.
ShowShortcutKeys	Indicates whether shortcut keys are enabled.
Text	Gets or sets the text displayed in the menu item.
TextImageRelation	Determines how the text and image are displayed together when the *DisplayStyle* property is set to *ImageAndText*.

Creating Menu Strips and Tool Strip Menu Items

You can create a *MenuStrip* at design time in the same way that you create any control: by dragging it from the Toolbox onto the design surface. Once added to the design surface, an interface for creating tool strip menu items appears. You can type a string into the box in the menu strip to create a new tool strip menu item. After a new item has been created, additional boxes appear to the right and beneath the newly created tool strip menu item to allow you to create more items or sub-items of the first item. This interface disappears if you move the focus elsewhere in the designer, but you can make it reappear by clicking the tool strip menu item. The *ToolStripMenuItem* control design interface is shown in Figure 4-3.

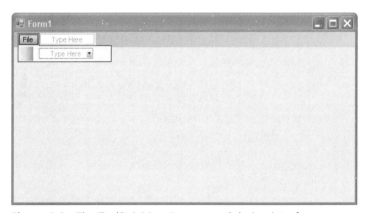

Figure 4-3   The *ToolStripMenuItem* control design interface

Note that the default naming scheme for the *ToolStripMenuItem* control is different from the default naming scheme for other controls. Although controls such as *Button* are appended with a number when added to the form (such as Button1), tool strip menu items are prepended with the text of the menu item. For example, if you created a File menu item, the default name would be *FileToolStripMenuItem*. You can rename a menu item by changing the *Name* property in the Properties window.

Changing Properties for Multiple Tool Strip Menu Items at Once

At times, you might want to edit properties for several menu items (or any control) at the same time. This is generally done to ensure that all controls have the same setting for a particular property. If you edit properties for different types of controls, the Properties window displays only those properties and events that all controls have in common.

▶ **To change multiple menu item properties at once**

1. While holding down the *Ctrl* key, click each menu item you want to edit to select it.

2. Make the appropriate changes in the Properties window. Changes you make will be made to all selected menu items.

You can also add tool strip menu items to menu strips programmatically at run time. You can either add a pre-existing menu item (for example, an item on another menu strip) or create a brand new menu item and add it to the menu strip. The following code example demonstrates each of these techniques.

```
' VB
' Adds an existing ToolStripMenuItem to the MenuStrip
MenuStrip1.Items.Add(OpenToolStripMenuItem)
' Creates a new ToolStripMenuItem and adds it to the MenuStrip
Dim HelpToolStripMenuItem As New ToolStripMenuItem("Help")
MenuStrip1.Items.Add(HelpToolStripMenuItem)
```

```
// C#
// Adds an existing ToolStripMenuItem to the MenuStrip
menuStrip1.Items.Add(OpenToolStripMenuItem);
// Creates a new ToolStripMenuItem and adds it to the MenuStrip
ToolStripMenuItem HelpToolStripMenuItem = new
    ToolStripMenuItem("Help");
menuStrip1.Items.Add(HelpToolStripMenuItem);
```

You can also use the *MenuStrip.Items.Add* method to add new tool strip menu items even if you don't have a reference to an existing tool strip menu item. The following example shows how you can specify text or an image to create a tool strip menu item and get a reference to it.

```
' VB
Dim newMenuItem1 As ToolStripMenuItem
Dim newMenuItem2 As ToolStripMenuItem
```

```
' Adds a new menu item by specifying text
newMenuItem1 = MenuStrip1.Items.Add("File")
' Adds a new menu item by specifying an image
newMenuItem2 = MenuStrip1.Items.Add(anImage)
```

// C#
```
ToolStripMenuItem newMenuItem1;
ToolStripMenuItem newMenuItem2;
// Adds a new menu item by specifying text
newMenuItem1 = MenuStrip1.Items.Add("File");
// Adds a new menu item by specifying an image
newMenuItem2 = MenuStrip1.Items.Add(anImage);
```

You can use similar techniques to add new or existing tool strip menu items to the drop-down items of an existing tool strip menu item. This has the effect of creating new items in a sub-menu. The following example demonstrates programmatically adding a tool strip menu item to the *DropDownItems* collection of an existing tool strip menu item:

' VB
```
Dim newMenuItem1 As ToolStripMenuItem
Dim newMenuItem2 As ToolStripMenuItem
' Adds an existing ToolStripMenuItem to another existing ToolStripMenuItem
FileToolStripMenuItem.DropDownItems.Add(OpenToolStripMenuItem)
' Creates a new ToolStripMenuItem and adds it to the MenuStrip
Dim HelpToolStripMenuItem As New ToolStripMenuItem("Help")
FileToolStripMenuItem.DropDownItems.Add(HelpToolStripMenuItem)
' Adds a new menu item by specifying text
newMenuItem1 = FileToolStripMenuItem.DropDownItems.Add("Open")
' Adds a new menu item by specifying an image
newMenuItem2 = FileToolStripMenuItem.DropDownItems.Add(anImage)
```

// C#
```
ToolStripMenuItem newMenuItem1;
ToolStripMenuItem newMenuItem2;
// Adds an existing ToolStripMenuItem to another existing ToolStripMenuItem
FileToolStripMenuItem.DropDownItems.Add(OpenToolStripMenuItem);
// Creates a new ToolStripMenuItem and adds it to the MenuStrip
ToolStripMenuItem HelpToolStripMenuItem = new ToolStripMenuItem("Help");
FileToolStripMenuItem.DropDownItems.Add(HelpToolStripMenuItem);
// Adds a new menu item by specifying text
newMenuItem1 = (ToolStripMenuItem)FileToolStripMenuItem.DropDownItems.Add("Open");
// Adds a new menu item by specifying an image
newMenuItem2 = (ToolStripMenuItem)FileToolStripMenuItem.DropDownItems.Add(anImage);
```

Copying Menu Items at Design Time

At times, you might want to copy menu items from one location to another. For example, if you are creating different menus but you want to have a common set of options between them, you can easily copy menu items by copying and pasting in the designer.

▶ **To copy menu items at design time**

1. In the Designer, right-click the menu item you want to copy and choose Copy from the context menu.

2. In the Designer, right-click the menu item that is the intended location of the copied menu and choose Paste from the context menu. The menu item is copied into the new location.

Note that you can copy top-level items to sub-level items, sub-level items to top-level items, top-level items to top-level items, or sub-level items to sub-level items with this procedure.

Adding Enhancements to Menus

Menus are capable of displaying a variety of enhancements that streamline the user experience and enhance usability. This section will cover how to create check marks, access keys, separator bars, and shortcut keys on menu items.

Adding Check Marks to Menu Items

You can display check marks next to any menu item except a top-level menu item. This is useful when you want to indicate to the user that a menu option is selected or enabled. You can display a check mark beside a menu item by setting the *Checked* property to *True*, as shown here:

```
' VB
OptionToolStripMenuItem.Checked = True
```

```
// C#
optionToolStripMenuItem.Checked = true;
```

Alternatively, you can define whether the menu item is selected by setting the *CheckState* property to *Checked*, as shown here:

```
' VB
OptionToolStripMenuItem.CheckState = CheckState.Checked
```

```
// C#
optionToolStripMenuItem.CheckState = CheckState.Checked;
```

The *Checked* property is a *Boolean* property that returns whether an item is checked. If the item is checked, the *Checked* property returns *True*. If the item is in any other state, the *Checked* property returns *False*. The *CheckState* property on the other hand, indicates the actual state of the menu item and will return either *CheckState.Checked*, *CheckState.UnChecked*, or *Checkstate.Indeterminate*.

If you want a menu item to appear checked when the user clicks the item, you can set the *CheckOnClick* property to *True*. This will cause the check mark on the menu item to toggle between checked and unchecked each time the user clicks the menu item. You can programmatically change the check state or determine if the menu item is checked using the *ToolStripMenuItem.CheckState* or *ToolStripMenuItem.Checked* properties.

Adding Separator Bars to Menus

It can be useful to add separator bars to menus to set groups of menu options apart from each other. You can add a separator to any sub-menu at design time by choosing Separator from the drop-down box in the menu item design interface, as shown in Figure 4-4.

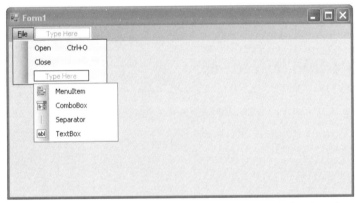

Figure 4-4   Choosing a separator in the menu item design interface

Note that if you want to add a separator to a top-level menu, you must do so programmatically by creating a new instance of the *ToolStripSeparator* control and inserting it into the correct location in the *MenuStrip.Items* collection, as shown here:

```
' VB
Dim aSeparator As New ToolStripSeparator
MenuStrip1.Items.Insert(1, aSeparator)
```

```
// C#
ToolStripSeparator aSeparator = new ToolStripSeparator();
menuStrip1.Items.Insert(1, aSeparator);
```

Creating Access Keys

Access keys enable you to access menu items by defining keys that, when pressed in combination with the *Alt* key, will execute the menu command. For example, if a File menu defines the *F* key as an access key, when *Alt+F* is pressed, the File menu will open. Menus that contain sub-menus open when the access key combination is pressed, and menus that invoke commands will invoke those commands. Note that the menu item must be visible for the access key to function. Thus, if you define an access key for an Open menu item that exists in the File sub-menu, the File menu must be opened first for the access key combination to function.

You can create an access key for a menu by preceding the letter you want to define the access key for with an ampersand (&) symbol. For example, to create an *Alt+F* access key combination for the File menu, you would set the *FileToolStripMenuItem*'s *Text* property to *&File*.

Creating Shortcut Keys

Unlike access keys, shortcut keys are a combination of keystrokes that allow direct invocation of a menu item whether the menu item is visible or not. For example, you might define the *Ctrl+E* key combination to be a shortcut key for the Exit menu command in the File menu. Even if the File menu is not open, *Ctrl+E* will cause the Exit menu command to be executed. Also, unlike access keys, you cannot create shortcut keys for top-level menus—you can create them only for items in sub-menus.

You can create a shortcut key at design time by setting the *ShortcutKeys* property in the Properties window. Clicking the *ShortcutKeys* property launches a visual interface than enables you to define a key combination. This interface is shown in Figure 4-5.

If you want to display the shortcut key combination next to the menu item, you can set the *ShowShortcutKeys* property of the *ToolStripMenuItem* control to *True*. You can also define a custom text to be shown instead of the key combination. If you want to define a custom text, you can set it in the *ShortcutKeyDisplayString* property.

Figure 4-5   The *ShortcutKeys* property user interface

Moving Items Between Menus

You can move items from one menu to another at run time. This allows you to dynamically customize menus for special purposes. You can move a menu item to a new menu strip by using the *MenuStrip.Items.Add* method to add it to the new menu strip. It will be removed from the previous menu strip automatically. If you want to add the menu item to a particular location in the new menu strip, you can use the *Insert* method to add it at a particular index. Examples are shown here:

```
' VB
' Adds the FileToolStripMenuItem
MenuStrip2.Items.Add(FileToolStripMenuItem)
' Inserts FileToolStripMenuItem to the location corresponding to index 1
MenuStrip2.Items.Insert(1, FileToolStripMenuItem)
```

```
// C#
// Adds the FileToolStripMenuItem
menuStrip2.Items.Add(FileToolStripMenuItem);
// Inserts FileToolStripMenuItem to the location corresponding to index 1
menuStrip2.Items.Insert(1, FileToolStripMenuItem);
```

You can also use the analogous methods of the *ToolStripMenuItem.DropDownItems* property to move items from one menu to another. Examples are shown here:

```vbnet
' VB
' Adds the FileToolStripMenuItem
AppToolStripMenuItem.DropDownItems.Add(FileToolStripMenuItem)
' Inserts FileToolStripMenuItem to the location corresponding to index 1
AppToolStripMenuItem.DropDownItems.Insert(1, FileToolStripMenuItem)
```

```csharp
// C#
// Adds the FileToolStripMenuItem
AppToolStripMenuItem.DropDownItems.Add(FileToolStripMenuItem);
// Inserts FileToolStripMenuItem to the location corresponding to index 1
AppToolStripMenuItem.DropDownItems.Insert(1, FileToolStripMenuItem);
```

Disabling, Hiding, and Deleting Menu Items

At times, it makes sense to remove certain options from a menu. You might want a menu item to be disabled when conditions aren't appropriate for it to be invoked or to hide a menu item that shouldn't be displayed. In some cases, you might want to delete a menu item completely from a menu.

You can disable a menu item by setting the *Enabled* property to *False*. This will cause the menu item to appear dimmed. It will still be visible to the user, but it cannot be invoked by mouse clicks or keystrokes.

You can hide a menu item by setting the *Visible* property to *False*. This will keep the menu item from appearing in the menu. Note, however, that it does not disable the menu item, and if the *Enabled* property is set to *True*, the menu item can still be invoked through shortcut keys if they have been defined for this menu item. Hide menu items sparingly; if a user is looking for a specific menu item, it is typically better for them to see it dimmed because the *Enabled* property has been set to *False*. Otherwise, they might continue looking for the hidden menu item on other menus.

If you need to delete a menu item from a menu entirely, you can do so by using the *MenuStrip.Items.Remove* and *MenuStrip.Items.RemoveAt* methods to remove an item from a top-level menu or the *ToolStripMenuItem.DropDownItems.Remove* and *ToolStripMenuItem.DropDownItems.RemoveAt* methods to remove an item from a sub-menu, as shown in the following examples:

```vbnet
' VB
'Removes FileToolStripMenuItem from MenuStrip1
MenuStrip1.Items.Remove(FileToolStripMenuItem)
' Removes FileToolStripMenuItem from AppToolStripMenuItem
AppToolStripMenuItem.DropDownItems.Remove(FileToolStripMenuItem)
' Removes the ToolStripMenuItem at index 4 from MenuStrip1
MenuStrip1.Items.RemoveAt(4)
' Removes the ToolStripMenuItem at index 4 from AppToolStripMenuItem
```

```
AppToolStripMenuItem.DropDownItems.RemoveAt(4)
```

```
// C#
// Removes FileToolStripMenuItem from menuStrip1
menuStrip1.Items.Remove(FileToolStripMenuItem);
// Removes FileToolStripMenuItem from AppToolStripMenuItem
AppToolStripMenuItem.DropDownItems.Remove(FileToolStripMenuItem);
// Removes the ToolStripMenuItem at index 4 from menuStrip1
menuStrip1.Items.RemoveAt(4);
// Removes the ToolStripMenuItem at index 4 from AppToolStripMenuItem
AppToolStripMenuItem.DropDownItems.RemoveAt(4);
```

Merging Menus

Menus can be merged at run time and their items incorporated into a single menu. You can merge *MenuStrips*, *ContextMenuStrips* (which are covered in greater detail later in this lesson), or both. In fact, you can even merge *MenuStrip* controls with *ToolStrip* controls. Like merging tool strips, merging menu strips is accomplished by invoking the *ToolStripManager.Merge* method on the static *ToolStripManager* class, as shown here:

```
' VB
ToolStripManager.Merge(sourceMenuStrip, targetMenuStrip)
```

```
// C#
ToolStripManager.Merge(sourceMenuStrip, targetMenuStrip);
```

The preceding example takes the first menu strip, *sourceMenuStrip*, and merges it with the second menu strip (*targetMenuStrip*). The tool strip menu items on *sourceMenuStrip* are then merged with the items on *targetMenuStrip* as determined by their *MergeAction* property value. Table 4-7 summarizes the merge action taken by *MergeAction* property value.

Table 4-7 *ToolStripItem MergeAction* **Property Values and Merge Actions**

MergeAction Value	Action Taken
Append	Appends the item at the end of the list of items.
Insert	Inserts the item at the location specified by the *MergeIndex* property.
MatchOnly	Looks for a match but takes no action.
Remove	If a matching tool strip item is found, it is removed from the resulting tool strip.

Table 4-7 *ToolStripItem MergeAction* Property Values and Merge Actions

MergeAction Value	Action Taken
Replace	If a matching tool strip item is found, it is replaced with this tool strip.

When menu strips are merged, each tool strip menu item in the source menu strip is compared to each menu item in the target menu strip. The comparison is based on the *Text* property of each menu item. Thus, if any two tool strip menu items have the same *Text* property, they will be considered a match. If a match is found, and the source tool strip menu item has the *MergeAction* property set to *MatchOnly*, *Remove*, or *Replace*, the appropriate action will be taken. Otherwise, the tool strip menu item will be appended or inserted as determined by the *MergeAction* property.

For menu strips to be merged successfully, they must have their *AllowMerge* property set to *True*.

Switching Between *MenuStrip* Controls Programmatically

As application conditions change, adding and removing menu items might not be sufficient to meet the needs of your application, and you might opt to completely replace a menu strip with another menu strip. You can remove a *MenuStrip* control from the form entirely by removing it from the form's *Controls* collection, and you can likewise add a new *MenuStrip* control by adding it to the form's *Controls* collection. The following example demonstrates how to remove MenuStrip1 from the form and replace it with MenuStrip2 at run time.

```
' VB
Me.Controls.Remove(MenuStrip1)
Me.Controls.Add(MenuStrip2)
```

```
// C#
this.Controls.Remove(MenuStrip1);
this.Controls.Add(MenuStrip2);
```

Note that the menu strip you add should not already be a member of the form's *Controls* collection.

Context Menus and the *ContextMenuStrip* Control

Context menus are familiar to all users of Windows Forms applications. These shortcut menus are displayed when the user right-clicks an object. The *ContextMenuStrip* control allows you to create context menus and associate them with a selected object.

The *ContextMenuStrip* control is similar to the *MenuStrip* control. Both controls have an intuitive design interface that allows you to create tool strip menu items quickly, and both expose a collection of tool strip menu items in the *Items* property. The main difference between the *ContextMenuStrip* and the *MenuStrip* controls is that the *ContextMenuStrip* control does not have a top-level menu and is not visible at run time unless invoked by right-clicking the control that it is associated with.

Adding and Removing Context Menu Items

You can easily add and remove items from a context menu strip by using the *Context-MenuStrip.Items.Add* and *ContextMenuStrip.Items.Remove* methods, as shown in the following example:

```
' VB
' Adds an item to the ContextMenuStrip
ContextMenuStrip1.Items.Add(ExitToolStripMenuItem)
' Removes an item from the ContextMenuStrip
ContextMenuStrip1.Items.Remove(ExitToolStripMenuItem)
```

```
// C#
// Adds an item to the ContextMenuStrip
contextMenuStrip1.Items.Add(ExitToolStripMenuItem);
// Removes an item from the ContextMenuStrip
contextMenuStrip1.Items.Remove(ExitToolStripMenuItem);
```

Associating a *ContextMenuStrip* Property with a Control

All controls that can display a context menu expose a *ContextMenuStrip* property that represents the context menu associated with that control. When this property is set to a valid *ContextMenuStrip* control, the context menu will appear when the user right-clicks the control at run time. You can set this property at design time in the Properties window.

You can also set the *ContextMenuStrip* property for a control at run time. The following example demonstrates how to create a context menu dynamically from pre-existing menu items and then associate it with a control:

```
' VB
ContextMenuStrip1.Items.Add(ExitToolStripMenuItem)
ContextMenuStrip1.Items.Add(OpenToolStripMenuItem)
Button1.ContextMenuStrip = ContextMenuStrip1
```

```
// C#
contextMenuStrip1.Items.Add(ExitToolStripMenuItem);
contextMenuStrip1.Items.Add(OpenToolStripMenuItem);
button1.ContextMenuStrip = contextMenuStrip1;
```

Copying Menu Items from Existing Menu Strips at Run Time

You will frequently want to create context menus that also expose the same menu items as items in regular menus. Although a single tool strip menu item can belong to only one menu strip at a time, it is a simple task to create an exact copy of a menu item at run time. The *ToolStripMenuItem* constructor has several overloads that allow you to specify the text, image, and click event handler. The following example demonstrates how to make a copy of an existing tool strip menu item named *ExitToolStrip-MenuItem* and add it to a *ContextMenuStrip* control named *ContextMenuStrip1*. This example assumes the existence of a method named *ExitToolStripMenuItem_Click*, which is the event handler for the *ExitToolStripMenuItem.Click* event.

```vb
' VB
Dim anItem As ToolStripMenuItem
anItem = New ToolStripMenuItem(ExitToolStripMenuItem.Text, _
   ExitToolStripMenuItem.Image, New EventHandler(addressof _
   ExitToolStripMenuItem_Click))
ContextMenuStrip1.Items.Add(anItem)
```

```csharp
// C#
ToolStripMenuItem anItem;
anItem = new ToolStripMenuItem(ExitToolStripMenuItem.Text, _
   ExitToolStripMenuItem.Image, new
   EventHandler(ExitToolStripMenuItem_Click));
ContextMenuStrip1.Items.Add(anItem);
```

Quick Check

1. What is the difference between a *MenuStrip* and a *ContextMenuStrip*?
2. How do you associate a *ContextMenuStrip* with a control?

Quick Check Answers

1. A *ContextMenuStrip* is designed to be shown when the user right-clicks on a control. Thus it contains no top-level elements and has no visual presence on the form until a control is right-clicked.
2. You can associate a *ContextMenuStrip* with a control by setting that control's *ContextMenuStrip* property.

Lab 2: Adding File Browsing Capability to Your Web Browser

In this lab, you will extend the capabilities of the Web browser you created in Lesson 1, "Configuring Tool Strips." You will add a menu, with menu items that allow you to browse, print, or save a file.

▶ **Exercise 1: Extending the Capabilities of Your Web Browser**

1. Open your completed lab from Lesson 1 or load the Lab 1 solution from the folder on the companion CD.

2. Open Form1. In the Designer, drag a *MenuStrip* control from the Toolbox to the top panel of the *ToolStripContainer*.

3. Add a top-level tool strip menu item named &File to the menu strip.

4. Add the following sub-menu items to the File tool strip menu item: &Open, &Print, P&rint Preview, &Save, and &Exit.

5. From the Toolbox, drag an *OpenFileDialog* component onto the form.

6. In the Designer, double-click *OpenToolStripMenuItem* to open the code window to the *OpenToolStripMenuItem_Click* event handler. Add the following code to this method:

```vb
' VB
Dim result As DialogResult
result = OpenFileDialog1.ShowDialog()
If result = System.Windows.Forms.DialogResult.OK Then
    WebBrowser1.Navigate(OpenFileDialog1.FileName)
End If
```

```csharp
// C#
DialogResult result;
result = openFileDialog1.ShowDialog();
if (result == System.Windows.Forms.DialogResult.OK)
    webBrowser1.Navigate(openFileDialog1.FileName);
```

7. Double-click the PrintToolStripMenuItem to open its *Click* event handler and add the following code:

```vb
' VB
WebBrowser1.ShowPrintDialog()
```

```csharp
// C#
webBrowser1.ShowPrintDialog();
```

8. Double-click the *PrintPreviewToolStripMenuItem* and add the following line to its *Click* event handler:

```vb
' VB
WebBrowser1.ShowPrintPreviewDialog()
```

```
// C#
webBrowser1.ShowPrintPreviewDialog();
```

9. Double-click the *SaveToolStripMenuItem* and add the following line to its *Click* event handler:

```
' VB
WebBrowser1.ShowSaveAsDialog()
```

```
// C#
webBrowser1.ShowSaveAsDialog();
```

10. Double-click the *ExitToolStripMenuItem* and add the following line to its *Click* event handler:

```
' VB
Application.Exit()
```

```
// C#
Application.Exit();
```

11. In the Properties window, set the *ShortCutKeys* property of *ExitToolStripMenuItem* to *Ctrl+E*.

12. Press F5 to test your application.

Lesson Summary

- The *MenuStrip* control is the host for *ToolStripMenuItems*, which represent individual menu items. The top-level menu items in a menu strip are contained in the *Items* collection.

- Individual tool strip menu items can host their own sub-menus, which are contained in the *DropDownItems* collection.

- Individual menu items can be displayed with check marks next to the menu items and can have access keys and shortcut keys to allow keyboard-based navigation.

- Menus can be merged by using the *ToolStripManager.Merge* method. The configuration of the menu resulting from a merge is determined by the individual *ToolStripMenuItem MergeAction* and *MergeIndex* properties.

- *ContextMenuStrip* allows you to create context menus for your application. Menus created with the *ContextMenuStrip* control are not visible at run time and do not host a top-level menu but behave like *MenuStrip* controls otherwise. You can associate a *ContextMenuStrip* with a control by setting the control's *ContextMenuStrip* property.

Lesson Review

You can use the following questions to test your knowledge of the information in this lesson. The questions are also available on the companion CD if you prefer to review them in electronic form.

NOTE Answers

Answers to these questions and explanations of why each choice is right or wrong are located in the "Answers" section at the end of the book.

---

1. Which of the following are required to create an access key for a menu item?

    A. The *UseMnemonic* property for the *ToolStripMenuItem* must be set to *True*.

    B. The *AccessKeys* property must be set to the correct key.

    C. The letter for the access key in the *Text* property must be preceded by an ampersand (&) symbol.

    D. The *ShortCutKeys* property must be set to *Ctrl* + the letter for the access key.

2. Which of the following code snippets will add a new menu named Menu1 to a form at run time?

    A. ' VB
       ```
       ToolStripManager.Menus.Add(Menu1)
       ```

       // C#
       ```
       ToolStripManager.Menus.Add(Menu1);
       ```

    B. ' VB
       ```
       ToolStripManager.Merge(Form1, Menu1)
       ```

       // C#
       ```
       ToolStripManager.Merge(Form1, Menu1);
       ```

    C. ' VB
       ```
       ToolStripManager.Controls.Add(Menu1)
       ```

       // C#
       ```
       ToolStripManager.Controls.Add(Menu1);
       ```

    D. ' VB
       ```
       Me.Controls.Add(Menu1)
       ```

       // C#
       ```
       this.Controls.Add(Menu1);
       ```

3. Which of the following are required to associate and enable a context menu strip named ContextMenu1 with a button named Button1?

    A. The *ContextMenuStrip* property for *Button1* must be set to *ContextMenu1.*

    B. The *ShowPopUp* property for *Button1* must be set to *True.*

    C. Button1 must call the *ContextMenu1.ShowPopUp* method in its *RightClick* event handler.

    D. The *ContextMenu1.Control* property must be set to *Button1.*

Lesson 3: Using Events and Event Handlers

Events are messages that represent something interesting happening in your application. When an event is raised, other parts of your application are given an opportunity to respond to those events by executing methods called *event handlers*. In this lesson, you will learn how to work with form and control events, how to assign event handlers at design time, and how to assign event handlers at run time. You will also learn how to use the code editor to override methods that are defined in your base class.

> **After this lesson, you will be able to:**
> - Use the Windows Forms Designer to create default event handlers.
> - Use the Windows Forms Designer to create event handlers.
> - Manage mouse and keyboard events within Windows Forms applications.
> - Program a Windows Forms application to recognize modifier keys.
> - Create event handlers at run time to respond to system or user events dynamically.
> - Connect multiple events to a single event handler.
> - Use the Code Editor to override methods defined in the base class.
>
> **Estimated lesson time: 30 minutes**

Overview of Events

Events are members of the class or control that raises them. You've been using events throughout the labs in this book. Whenever you create an *OnClick* method, you are responding to that control's *Click* event. An event represents a message that is sent to the rest of the application. When something noteworthy happens, a control or class can raise an event, which sends out the message. This message can wrap any arguments that contain information about the event and send them out to the rest of the application. A method that has the same signature as the event (i.e., it has the same number and types of parameters) can handle the event, which means that the method is executed when the event occurs. An event can be handled by more than one method, and a given method can handle more than one event.

Controls and forms can raise a variety of events in response to user input. The most familiar event is the *Click* event, which is raised by almost all controls when the mouse is positioned on the control and the left mouse button is clicked. Other common events exposed by controls include events that respond to mouse and keyboard input. Some common events raised by controls are shown in Table 4-8.

Table 4-8 Common Events Raised by Controls

Event	Description
Click	Occurs when the left mouse button is clicked. Depending on the control, it can also occur with certain keyboard input, for example, when the control is selected and the *Enter* key is pressed.
DoubleClick	Occurs when the left mouse button is clicked twice rapidly. Not all controls respond to the *DoubleClick* event.
KeyDown	Occurs when a key is pressed when a control has the focus. Contains different information from the *KeyPress* event.
KeyPress	Occurs when a key is pressed when a control has the focus. Contains different information from the *KeyDown* event.
KeyUp	Occurs when a key is released while the control has the focus.
MouseClick	Occurs when a control is clicked by the mouse.
MouseDoubleClick	Occurs when a control is double-clicked by the mouse.
MouseDown	Occurs when the mouse pointer is over a control and the mouse button is pressed.
MouseEnter	Occurs when the mouse pointer enters the control.
MouseHover	Occurs when the mouse pointer rests on the control.
MouseLeave	Occurs when the mouse pointer exits the control.
MouseMove	Occurs when the mouse moves over the control.
MouseUp	Occurs when a mouse button is released over the control.
MouseWheel	Occurs when the mouse wheel moves while the control has the focus.

Each event carries some information about itself to the method that handles it. Events raised by controls usually contain two parameters: a parameter that carries an object reference to the control that raised it and a parameter that derives from the *EventArgs* class that carries event arguments. In some events, such as the *Click* event, the *EventArgs* argument carries practically no information. In others, such as the *MouseClick* event, a great deal of information about the state of the mouse is carried in the *MouseClickEventArgs* argument.

Creating Event Handlers in the Designer

You can create event handlers in the Designer by using the Properties window. By pressing the "lightning bolt" button in the Properties window (shown in Figure 4-6),

Figure 4-6   The Events button in the Properties window

The Properties window displays the events that can be raised by the control, as shown in Figure 4-7.

Figure 4-7   The Properties window configured to display events

Creating Default Event Handlers

You can create default event handlers for an event through the Properties window. A default event handler is a method that handles a given event for a control and has a descriptive name. For example, the default event handler for the *Click* event of a button named Button1 would be called *Button1_Click*. The following procedure describes how to create a default event handler.

▶ **To create a default event handler**

1. In the Designer, select the control. In the Properties window, click the "lightning bolt" button to list events for that control.

2. Double-click the entry for the event for which you want to create the default event handler. The method is created with the proper signature and the Code Editor opens to the new method.

3. Add the code that you want to execute when the event is raised.

Creating Event Handlers in the Designer

In addition to default event handlers, you can use the designer to assign other methods to handle events raised by controls. The following procedure describes how to create an event handler other than the default event handler.

1. In the Code Editor, create a method whose signature matches the signature of the event that you want to handle. For example, if you wanted to handle the *Button.Click* event, you would create a *Sub* (void) method with *Object* and *EventArgs* parameters.

2. In the Designer, select the control for which you want to create an event handler. In the Properties window, click the lightning bolt to list the events for this control.

3. Single-click the cell next to the event you want to create a handler for. A drop-down arrow appears.

4. Click the drop-down arrow to display a list of methods that match the signature of the event. Choose the event you created in the Code Editor.

Assigning Multiple Events to the Same Event Handler

You can assign multiple events to the same event handler. All that is required is that the signature of the method matches the signature of the event. You can assign multiple events in a single control to a single event handler, or you can assign events from several controls to a single event handler. An example of when this might be useful would be in an application such as a calculator. You might have the *Button* controls that are used to input numbers all share the same *Click* event handler, programming logic into the event handler to distinguish between the buttons that are clicked.

You can assign multiple events to the same event handler in the same way that you assign an individual event. Select the control and then, in the Properties window, select the event for which you want to assign a handler. Choose the method for the event handler from the drop-down menu. Repeat the process for each event you want to assign a handler to.

Managing Mouse and Keyboard Events

Most of the events involved in interacting with the user are mouse and keyboard events. Controls can raise events in response to mouse clicks or a variety of keystrokes and can detect whether modifier keys such as *Ctrl*, *Alt*, or *Shift* are pressed. This section describes how to respond to mouse and keyboard events.

Mouse Events

Controls can interact with the mouse in several ways. Controls raise events when the mouse enters the control, leaves the control, moves over the control, clicks, hovers over the control, or when the mouse wheel moves while the pointer is over a control.

Click and DoubleClick   The most familiar mouse events are the *Click* and *DoubleClick* events. The *Click* event is raised by a control when the mouse pointer is over the control and the left button is pressed and released. This event is also raised when the control has the focus and the *Enter* key is pressed. The *DoubleClick* event is raised when the left mouse button is clicked twice in rapid succession. Note that not all controls respond to the *DoubleClick* event.

The *Click* and *DoubleClick* events have a fairly simple signature. They return an *Object* reference to the control that raised the event (the parameter that Visual Studio names *Sender* when it generates a handler) and an instance of the *EventArgs* class that carries no useful information about the event. The following code example demonstrates the appropriate signature for an event handler that handles the *Click* or *DoubleClick* event.

```
' VB
Private Sub ClickHandler(ByVal sender As System. Object, ByVal e As _
    System.EventArgs)
    ' Insert code to be executed when the event is raised
End Sub
```

```
// C#
private void ClickHander(object sender, EventArgs e)
{
    //   Insert code to be executed when the event is raised
}
```

You can assign any method with this signature to handle the *Click* or *DoubleClick* events.

Mouse Movement Events   Controls raise events that track the movement of the mouse pointer into and out of the bounds of the control. These events are detailed in Table 4-9.

Table 4-9   Mouse Movement Events

Event	Description
MouseEnter	This event is raised when the mouse pointer enters a control.
MouseHover	This event is raised when the mouse pointer hovers over the control.
MouseLeave	This event is raised when the mouse pointer exits the control.

Like the *Click* event, these events pass relatively little information to the methods that handle them. Their event handlers also require an *Object* parameter representing the sender of the event and an *EventArgs* parameter.

Other Mouse Events   Although the events described previously are useful for tracking mouse movement and clicks, they provide practically no information about the event itself. If you want to retrieve more information about the event, such as the position of the mouse, use one of the mouse events that pass an instance of *MouseEventArgs* in its signature. These events are shown in table 4-10.

Table 4-10   Mouse Events That Pass *MouseEventArgs*

Event	Description
MouseClick	This event is raised when a mouse button is pressed and released on a control.
MouseDoubleClick	This event is raised when a mouse button is clicked twice on a control.
MouseDown	This event is raised when a mouse button is pressed over a control.
MouseMove	This event is raised when the mouse moves over the control.
MouseUp	This event is raised when a mouse button is released over a control.

Table 4-10   Mouse Events That Pass *MouseEventArgs*

Event	Description
MouseWheel	This event is raised when the mouse wheel is moved.

All of the events shown in Table 4-10 require a handler with two parameters: an object parameter that represents the control that raised the event and an instance of *Mouse-EventArgs*. The following example demonstrates an event handler for any of these methods.

```vb
' VB
Private Sub MouseHandler(ByVal sender As System.Object, ByVal e As _
   System.MouseEventArgs)
   ' Insert code to handle your event here
End Sub
```

```csharp
// C#
private void MouseHandler(object sender, MouseEventArgs e)
{
   // Insert code to handle your event here
}
```

The instance of *MouseEventArgs* that is passed to the event handler contains a large amount of information about the event. It contains properties that describe what buttons were clicked, how many times they were clicked, the location of the mouse, and how far the mouse wheel has been turned. Table 4-11 shows the *MouseEvent-Args* properties.

Table 4-11   *MouseEventArgs* Properties

Property	Description
Button	Indicates which button was pressed.
Clicks	Indicates how many times the button was pressed.
Delta	Indicates the number of clicks the mouse wheel has moved.
Location	Indicates the current location of the mouse.
X	Indicates the X coordinate of the mouse.
Y	Indicates the Y coordinate of the mouse.

Keyboard Events

Controls that can receive keyboard input can raise three keyboard events:

- *KeyDown*
- *KeyPress*
- *KeyUp*

KeyDown and KeyUp The *KeyDown* and *KeyUp* events are raised when a key is pressed and a key is released respectively. The control that has the focus raises the event. When these events are raised, they package information about which key or combination of keys were pressed or released in an instance of *KeyEventArgs* that is passed to the method that handles the event. Table 4-12 describes the properties of *KeyEventArgs*.

Table 4-12 *KeyEventArgs* Properties

Property	Description
Alt	Gets a value indicating whether the *Alt* key was pressed.
Control	Gets a value indicating whether the *Ctrl* key was pressed.
Handled	Gets or sets a value indicating whether the event was handled.
KeyCode	Returns an *enum* value representing which key was pressed.
KeyData	Returns data representing the key that was pressed, together with whether the *Alt*, *Ctrl*, or *Shift* key was pressed.
KeyValue	Returns an integer representation of the *KeyData* property.
Modifiers	Gets the modifier flags for the event, indicating what combination of *Alt*, *Ctrl*, or *Shift* key was pressed.
Shift	Gets a value indicating whether the *Shift* key was pressed.
SuppressKeyPress	Gets or sets a value indicating whether the key event should be passed on to the underlying control.

The *KeyUp* and *KeyDown* events determine what key and what modifier keys, if any, were pressed. This information is exposed through properties in the *KeyEventArgs* reference that is passed to the event handler.

Determining When Modifier Keys Have Been Pressed   The *KeyEventArgs* properties *Alt*, *Control*, and *Shift* return a Boolean value that indicates if the *Alt*, *Ctrl*, and *Shift* keys are pressed, respectively. A value of *True* is returned if the key is pressed, and *False* is returned if the key is not pressed. The following code demonstrates a *KeyUp* event handler that checks whether the *Ctrl* key is pressed.

```vb
' VB
Private Sub TextBox1_KeyUp(ByVal sender As System.Object, ByVal e As _
   System.Windows.Forms.KeyEventArgs) Handles TextBox1.KeyUp
   If e.Control = True Then
      MsgBox("The CTRL key is still down")
   End If
End Sub
```

```csharp
// C#
private void textBox1_KeyUp(object sender,
   e System.Windows.Forms.KeyEventArgs)
{
   if (e.Control == true)
      MessageBox.Show("The CTRL key is still down");
}
```

KeyPress   When a user presses a key that has a corresponding *ASCII* value, the *KeyPress* event is raised. Keys with a corresponding *ASCII* value include any alphabetic or numeric characters (alphanumeric a–z, A–Z, and 0–9) as well as some special keyboard characters such as the *Enter* and *Backspace* keys. If a key or key combination does not produce an ASCII value, such as the *Alt*, *Ctrl*, or *Shift* key, it will not raise the *KeyPress* event.

This event is most useful for intercepting keystrokes and evaluating them. When this event is raised, an instance of *KeyPressEventArgs* is passed to the event handler as a parameter. The *KeyPressEventArgs* exposes the character representation of the key(s) pressed through the *KeyPressEventArgs.KeyChar* property. You can use this property to evaluate keystrokes received by your application.

Creating Event Handlers at Run Time

You can create event handlers for events and add them in code at run time by associating an existing event with an existing method. You might want to create an event handler at run time to modify the way an application responds to events. Visual Basic and Microsoft Visual C# have somewhat different methods for creating event handlers at run time, so this section presents separate procedures for each.

▶ **To create or remove an event handler at run time in Visual Basic**

1. Create a Sub whose signature matches the signature for the event. Use the *AddHandler* keyword to associate the event handler with the event. The *AddressOf* operator must be used to create a delegate at run time. An example is shown here:

```
' VB
AddHandler Button1.Click, AddressOf myEventHandler
```

2. You can remove an event handler at run time by using the *RemoveHandler* keyword, as shown here:

```
' VB
RemoveHandler Button1.Click, AddressOf myEventHandler
```

▶ **Creating or Removing an Event Handler at Run Time in C#**

1. Create a method whose signature matches the signature for the event. Unlike Visual Basic, this method can return a value. Use the += operator to associate the method with the event. Here is an example:

```
// C#
button1.Click += myMethod;
```

2. You can remove an event handler at run time by using the =- operator, as shown here:

```
// C#
button1.Click -= myMethod;
```

Overriding Methods in the Code Editor

When you inherit from a base class, your class automatically gains all of the implementation and functionality of that base class. At times, you will want to override a method that has been defined in a base class. For example, if you want to create a new visual representation for a control that inherits from a standard Windows Forms control, you must override the *Paint* method. You must also override virtual (*MustOverride*) methods in abstract classes, and you can override methods to provide functionality that is different from what might be provided by the base class.

The Code Editor allows you to override methods easily in your base class. In the Code Editor, inside the class body but outside of a method, type *Overrides* (Visual Basic) or *override* (C#). An Intellisense window showing all of the overridable methods in the base class appears. Choose the method you want to override from the window and the rest of the method is stubbed out for you automatically. All you have to do then is add the implementation. The Code Editor and Intellisense window are shown in Figures 4-8 and 4-9.

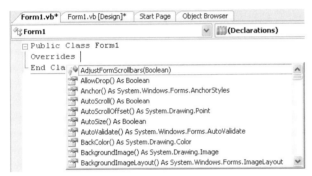

Figure 4-8   Overriding a method in Visual Basic

Figure 4-9   Overriding a method in C#

> ### Quick Check
> - Briefly explain what an event is and how it works in the application's execution cycle.
>
> ### Quick Check Answer
> - An event is a notification that is sent from a control or component to the rest of the application. When an event is fired, any methods that are register to handle that event will execute.

Lab 3: Practice with Mouse Events

In this lab, you will create a simple application that tracks the mouse events that happen to a particular control.

▶ **Exercise 1: Creating the Event Monitor**

In Visual Studio, create a new Windows Forms application.

1. From the Toolbox, drag a *Label* control and a *ListBox* control onto the form.

2. In the Properties window, set the *Label1.Text* property to Mouse Here!

3. Select Label1. In the Properties window, generate default event handlers for *Click, DoubleClick, MouseClick, MouseDoubleClick, MouseDown, MouseEnter, MouseHover, MouseLeave, MouseMove,* and *MouseUp*.

4. In the Code Editor, add code to each of the default event handlers as shown in the Table 4-13.

Table 4-13   Code for default event handlers

Event Handler	Visual Basic	C#
Click	ListBox1.Items.Add ("Click")	listBox1.Items.Add ("Click");
DoubleClick	ListBox1.Items.Add ("DoubleClick")	listBox1.Items.Add ("DoubleClick");
MouseClick	ListBox1.Items.Add ("MouseClick")	listBox1.Items.Add ("MouseClick");
MouseDoubleClick	ListBox1.Items.Add ("MouseDoubleClick")	listBox1.Items.Add ("MouseDoubleClick");
MouseDown	ListBox1.Items.Add ("MouseDown")	listBox1.Items.Add ("MouseDown");

Table 4-13 Code for default event handlers

Event Handler	Visual Basic	C#
MouseEnter	ListBox1.Items.Add ("MouseEnter")	listBox1.Items.Add ("MouseEnter");
MouseHover	ListBox1.Items.Add ("MouseHover")	listBox1.Items.Add ("MouseHover");
MouseLeave	ListBox1.Items.Add ("MouseLeave")	listBox1.Items.Add ("MouseLeave");
MouseMove	ListBox1.Items.Add ("MouseMove")	listBox1.Items.Add ("MouseMove");
MouseUp	ListBox1.Items.Add ("MouseUp")	listBox1.Items.Add ("MouseUp");

5. Press F5 to test your application. Move the mouse pointer over the label and perform various mouse operations. Note that each mouse event is recorded in the *ListBox*, and note the order in which events occur.

Lesson Summary

- Events represent a programmatic notification that something interesting has happened in the application. You can assign methods called event handlers to execute in response to an event. Event handlers must have a signature that matches the event that they handle.

- You can create event handlers in the Designer through the Properties window. You can create a default event handler or assign the event to any method or methods that have the correct signature.

- Controls can respond to events that are raised by the mouse and keyboard. *MouseEventArgs*, *KeyEventArgs*, and *KeyPressEventArgs* provide detailed information regarding the state of the mouse or keyboard to their respective events.

- You can add and remove event handlers at run time by using the *AddHandler* and *RemoveHandler* keywords for Visual Basic and the += and -= operators for c#.

- You can override methods that can be overridden in the base class in the Visual Studio Code Editor. The Intellisense window provides a list of available methods and can automatically stub overridden methods in the Code Editor.

Lesson Review

You can use the following questions to test your knowledge of the information in this lesson. The questions are also available on the companion CD if you prefer to review them in electronic form.

NOTE Answers

Answers to these questions and explanations of why each choice is right or wrong are located in the "Answers" section at the end of the book.

---

1. Which of the following properties of an instance e of the *KeyEventArgs* class can be used in a *KeyDown* event handler to determine if the *Ctrl* key has been pressed? (Choose all that apply.)

   A. *e.Control*

   B. *e.KeyCode*

   C. *e.KeyData*

   D. *e.Modifiers*

2. Which of the following code examples will add a new event handler named *ClickHandler* to the *Button1.Click* event at run time?

   A.
   ```
   ' VB
   Button1.Click.AddHandler(ClickHandler)

   // C#
   ClickHandler += Button1.Click;
   ```

   B.
   ```
   ' VB
   AddHandler(Button1.Click, ClickHandler)

   // C#
   AddHandler(Button1.Click, ClickHandler);
   ```

   C.
   ```
   ' VB
   AddHandler Button1.Click, AddressOf ClickHandler

   // C#
   Button1.Click += ClickHandler;
   ```

   D.
   ```
   ' VB
   Button1.Click += AddressOf ClickHandler

   // C#
   Button1.Click ++ ClickHandler;
   ```

Chapter Review

To further practice and reinforce the skills you learned in this chapter, you can perform the following tasks:

■ Review the chapter summary.

■ Review the list of key terms introduced in this chapter.

■ Complete the case scenarios. These scenarios set up real-world situations involving the topics of this chapter and ask you to create a solution.

■ Complete the suggested practices.

■ Take a practice test.

Chapter Summary

■ *ToolStrip* controls can host a wide range of functionality. *ToolStripItems* duplicate the functionality of several other Windows Forms controls as well as combine some Windows Forms functionality with menu functionality.

■ Tool strips support rafting, merging, rearrangement of controls, and overflow of controls.

■ *MenuStrip* controls are used to create menus for forms and host *ToolStripMenuItem* controls, which represent menu entries and commands.

■ *MenuStrip* controls derive from *ToolStrip* and expose similar functionality. Menus can be merged using the *ToolStripManager* class.

■ The *ContextMenuStrip* control is used for creating context menus. You can associate a context menu with a control by setting the *ContextMenuStrip* property.

■ The Properties window can be used to create default event handlers or to assign preexisting methods to handle events.

■ A variety of mouse and keyboard events are raised in response to user actions. The *MouseEventArgs* parameter in many of the mouse events provides detailed information regarding the state of the mouse, and the *KeyEventArgs* and *KeyPressEventArgs* parameters provide information regarding the state of the keyboard.

■ Event handlers can be created at run time and used to dynamically associate events with methods.

Key Terms

Do you know what these key terms mean? You can check your answers by looking up the terms in the glossary at the end of the book.

- event
- event handler
- MenuStrip
- ToolStrip
- ToolStripItem
- ToolStripMenuItem

Case Scenarios

In the following case scenarios, you will apply what you've learned about how to use controls to design user interfaces. You can find answers to these questions in the "Answers" section at the end of this book.

Case Scenario 1: Designing a Complex User Interface

Well, you've been moving up in the world at Trey Research, your current employer. You've been tasked with the design of the front end of an insurance application for Humongous Insurance, one of your clients. True to their name, they want a humongous front end, with an enormous amount of options and commands available to the user. Your task is to provide full functionality for your client while at the same time creating an application that is intuitive and easy to use.

Questions

Answer the following questions for your manager:

1. How can we make all of these commands available without making the user interface (UI) completely impossible to use?

2. How can we make all of these commands intuitive and easy to learn?

Case Scenario 2: More Humongous Requirements

Now that you've successfully implemented menus and toolbars for Humongous Insurance, you must implement a series of keyboard commands.

Technical Requirements

- All main menu items must have access keys.

- Key menu items must have shortcut keys that are accessible by the user.

- Certain *TextBox* controls on the form must auto-fill when *Ctrl* key combinations are pressed.

Questions

1. How can this functionality be implemented?

Suggested Practices

- Create toolbars with similar members and practice merging them together, changing the *MergeIndex* and *MergeItem* properties of each tool strip item.

- Build an application similar to the application from Lab 3, "Practice with Mouse Events," that monitors keyboard events.

- Build an application that consists of a form with a single button that the user can chase around the form with the mouse but can never actually click.

Take a Practice Test

The practice tests on this book's companion CD offer many options. For example, you can test yourself on just the content covered in this chapter, or you can test yourself on all the 70-526 certification exam content. You can set up the test so that it closely simulates the experience of taking a certification exam, or you can set it up in study mode so that you can look at the correct answers and explanations after you answer each question.

MORE INFO   Practice tests

For details about all the practice test options available, see the "How to Use the Practice Tests" section in this book's Introduction.

Chapter 5

Configuring Connections and Connecting to Data

Typically, most real-world applications use databases as a store for the data in that application. For example, inventory systems, contact management systems, and airline reservation systems store data in a database and then retrieve the necessary records into the application as needed. In other words, the data used by an application is stored in a database external to the actual application, and it is retrieved into the application as required by the program.

When creating applications that work with data, the Microsoft .NET Framework provides many classes that aid in the process. The classes that you use for common data tasks such as communicating, storing, fetching, and updating data are all located in the *System.Data* namespace. The classes in the *System.Data* namespace make up the core data access objects in the .NET Framework. These data access classes are collectively known as ADO.NET.

Before you can begin working with data in an application, you must first establish and open a connection and communicate with the desired data source. This chapter describes how to create the various connection objects that are used to connect applications to different data sources and sets the basis for working with data in the following chapters. After learning to establish connections to databases in this chapter, we will move on to Chapter 6, "Working with Data in a Connected Environment," which provides instructions for running queries, saving data, and creating database objects directly between your application and a database. Chapter 7, "Create, Add, Delete, and Edit Data in a Disconnected Environment," describes how to create *DataSet* and *DataTable* objects that allow you to temporarily store data while it is being used in a running application. Finally, Chapter 8, "Implementing Data-Bound Controls," provides information on binding data to be displayed and worked with in Windows Forms controls.

Typically, data sources are relational databases such as Microsoft SQL Server and Oracle, but, additionally, you can connect to data in files such as Microsoft Office Access (.mdb) and SQL Server (.mdf) database files. The connection object you use is based on the type of data source your application needs to communicate with.

Exam objectives in this chapter:

- Manage connections and transactions.

    - ❏ Configure a connection to a database using the Data Source Configuration Wizard.

    - ❏ Configure a connection to a database using the Server Explorer.

    - ❏ Configure a connection to a database using the *Connection* class.

    - ❏ Connect to a database using specific database *Connection* objects.

    - ❏ Enumerate through instances of SQL Server.

    - ❏ Open an ADO.NET connection to a database.

    - ❏ Close an ADO.NET connection to a database by using the *Close* method of the *Connection* object.

    - ❏ Protect access to the connection details of a data source.

    - ❏ Create a connection designed for reuse in a connection pool.

    - ❏ Control a connection pool by configuring *ConnectionString* values based on database type.

    - ❏ Use the *Connection* events to detect database information.

    - ❏ Handle exceptions when connecting to a database.

Lessons in this chapter:

Before You Begin

To complete the lessons in this chapter, you must have:

- A computer that meets or exceeds the minimum hardware requirements listed in the "Introduction" at the beginning of the book.

- Microsoft Visual Studio 2005 Professional Edition installed on your computer.

- An understanding of Microsoft Visual Basic or C# syntax and familiarity with the .NET Framework.

- A basic understanding of relational databases.

- Available data sources, including SQL Server 2005 (SQL Server 2005 Express Edition is acceptable), the *Northwind* sample database for SQL Server, and the Nwind.mdb Access database file. Directions for setting up the sample databases are located in the Setting up Sample Databases Read Me file on the companion CD.

Real World

Steve Stein

At a previous employer, I was responsible for extracting data from an arcane proprietary database that was virtually impossible to connect to directly. As a result, time-consuming reports were periodically generated that were then imported into a workable database management system for further processing. Thinking back, I realize how much easier life would have been if I had been able to spin up a connection object and communicate directly with the data source without the need for the intermediary process of creating reports and exporting and importing data.

Lesson 1: Creating and Configuring Connection Objects

This lesson describes the two ways to create and configure *connection objects*: visually, using the Add Connection dialog box, and programmatically, by handcrafting the objects in code. Whether you choose to create connections visually or programmatically, the end result is the same—a configured connection object ready to open a connection and communicate with your data source. For this lesson, we will focus only on creating connection objects as opposed to actually connecting and communicating with a data source. In Lesson 2, "Connecting to Data Using Connection Objects," we will move on to the next level to open the connection and retrieve information from the data source.

After this lesson, you will be able to:

- Configure a connection to a database using the Server Explorer.
- Configure a connection to a database using the Data Source Configuration Wizard.
- Configure a connection to a database using the *Connection* class.
- Connect to a database using specific database connection objects.

Estimated lesson time: 30 minutes

What Is a Connection Object?

A connection object is simply a representation of an open connection to a data source. The easiest way to describe a connection object is, first, to explain what a connection object is not! A connection object does not fetch or update data, it does not execute queries, and it does not contain the results of queries; it is merely the pipeline that commands and queries use to send their SQL statements and receive results. Although connection objects typically can be thought of as the place where you set your *connection string*, they also have additional methods for working with the connection, such as methods that open and close connections as well as methods for working with *connection pools* and transactions. Essentially, connection objects provide a conduit for sending commands to a database and retrieving data and information into your application, as shown in Figure 5-1.

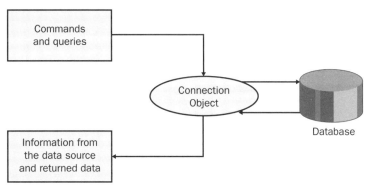

Figure 5-1 Connection objects are your application's communication pipeline to a database

Creating Connections in Server Explorer

To simplify the process of creating applications that access data, Visual Studio provides the Server Explorer window as a central location to manage data connections
independent of any actual projects. In other words, you can create data connections in
Server Explorer and access them in any project. Data connections created in Server
Explorer are user-specific settings in Visual Studio that display the connections each
time you open Visual Studio (instead of creating connections as part of developing a
specific application that stores them in that application). Of course, you can create
data connections as part of the development process from within an open project, but
we will cover that in the next section.

Creating Connections Using Data Wizards

Visual Studio provides a few wizards that simplify the process of creating applications
that access data and that create data connections as a result of completing the wizards. The main wizard for bringing data into an application is the Data Source Configuration Wizard. When you run the Data Source Configuration Wizard and select
the Database path, you end up with a configured connection object ready to use in
your application. In addition to creating a configured connection object, the Data
Source Configuration Wizard also allows you to select the database objects you want
to use in your application.

Creating Connection Objects Programmatically

In situations where you do not want to use the visual tools previously described and
need to create your connections manually, it is an easy process to create connection
objects in code programmatically. The first step is to decide which type of connection

object to create. The choice is fairly simple because it is dependant on the back-end data source your application needs to communicate with.

Table 5-1 lists the primary connection objects available in ADO.NET and the data sources they are designed to access.

Table 5-1   Connection Objects

Name	Target Data Source
SqlConnection	SQL Server 2000 and SQL Server 2005 databases
OleDbConnection	OLE DB data sources (such as Office Access databases via Jet 4.0)
OdbcConnection	Open database connectivity (ODBC) data sources such as a Data Source Name (DSN) as defined in the ODBC Data Source Administrator dialog
OracleConnection	Oracle 7.3, 8i, or 9i databases

The properties, methods, and events associated with the connection objects in the preceding table vary because each connection object is designed to efficiently connect and interact with its respective data sources, but each connection object contains the same base properties, methods, and events that are inherited from the *System.Data .Common.DbConnection* class.

Table 5-2 lists the properties common to all connection objects.

Table 5-2   Connection Properties

Name	Description
ConnectionString	Gets or sets the string used to open the connection.
ConnectionTimeout	Read only. Gets the time to wait while establishing a connection before terminating the attempt and generating an error.
Database	Read only. Gets the name of the current database after a connection is opened or the database name specified in the connection string before the connection is opened.
DataSource	Read only. Gets the name of the database server to which it is connected.

Table 5-2   Connection Properties

Name	Description
ServerVersion	Read only. Gets a string that represents the version of the server to which the object is connected.
State	Read only. Gets a string that describes the state of the connection.

Table 5-3 lists the methods common to all connection objects.

Table 5-3   Connection Methods

Name	Description
BeginDbTransaction	Starts a database transaction.
BeginTransaction	Starts a database transaction.
ChangeDatabase	Changes the current database for an open connection.
Close	Closes the connection to the database. This is the preferred method of closing any open connection.
CreateCommand	Creates and returns a *System.Data.Common.DbCommand* object associated with the current connection.
CreateDbCommand	Creates and returns a *System.Data.Common.DbCommand* object associated with the current connection.
EnlistTransaction	Enlists in the specified transaction as a distributed transaction.
GetSchema	Returns schema information for the data source of this *System.Data.Common.DbConnection* class.
New	Initializes a new instance of the *System.Data.Common-.DbConnection* class.
OnStateChange	Raises the *System.Data.Common.DbConnection.StateChange* event.
Open	Opens a database connection with the settings specified by the *System.Data.Common.DbConnection.ConnectionString*.

Table 5-4 lists the events common to all connection objects.

Table 5-4   Connection Events

Name	Description
StateChange	Occurs when the state of the connection changes.
InfoMessage	Occurs when the server returns a warning or informational message.

To create connections programmatically using the four primary data providers, you start by instantiating a new connection object and setting its *ConnectionString* property that you will use to open the connection.

NOTE   *System.Data.OracleClient* reference

By default, Microsoft Windows applications in Visual Studio are created with references to the *System.Data.SqlClient*, *System.Data.OleDb*, and *System.Data.Odbc* namespaces, so these are immediately available to be coded against and appear in IntelliSense with no further action. By default, a reference to the *System.Data.OracleClient* namespace is not included and must be added to your application to create *OracleConnection* objects.

Creating SQL Server Connection Objects in Code

Create *SqlConnection* objects with the *New* keyword. You can instantiate the connection and set the connection string in the same call, or you can assign the connection string to the *SqlConnection.ConnectionString* property after instantiating the connection. Be sure to replace *ServerName* and *DatabaseName* with valid values for your environment. To eliminate the need to qualify the objects fully in code, add an Imports System.Data.SqlClient statement (Visual Basic) or using System.Data.SqlClient; statement (C#) to the top of your code file. Use the *WithEvents* keyword (in Visual Basic) or create event handlers in C# if your application needs to respond to the connection objects events.

```vb
' VB
Private WithEvents ConnectionToSql As New SqlConnection _
    ("Data Source=ServerName;Initial Catalog=DatabaseName;Integrated Security=True")
```

```csharp
// C#
SqlConnection ConnectionToSql = new SqlConnection
    ("Data Source=ServerName;Initial Catalog=DatabaseName;Integrated Security=True");
```

Creating OLE DB Connection Objects in Code

Create *OleDbConnection* objects with the *New* keyword. You can instantiate the connection and set the connection string in the same call, or you can assign the connection string to the *OleDbConnection.ConnectionString* property after instantiating the connection. Be sure to replace the data source with a valid path if you are connecting to an *Office Access* database, or replace the connection string with a valid connection string for the OLE DB data source you want to connect to. To eliminate the need to fully qualify the objects in code, add an Imports System.Data.OleDb statement (Visual Basic) or using System.Data.OleDb; statement (C#) to the top of your code file.

```
' VB
Private WithEvents ConnectionToOleDb As New System.Data.OleDb.OleDbConnection _
  ("Provider=Microsoft.Jet.OLEDB.4.0;Data Source=""Nwind.mdb"";Persist Security Info=False")
```

```
// C#
System.Data.OleDb.OleDbConnection ConnectionToOleDb = new System.Data.OleDb.OleDbConnection
  ("Provider=Microsoft.Jet.OLEDB.4.0;Data Source=\"Nwind.mdb";Persist Security Info=False");
```

Creating ODBC Connection Objects in Code

Create *OdbcConnection* objects with the *New* keyword. You can instantiate the connection and set the connection string in the same call, or you can assign the connection string to the *OdbcConnection.ConnectionString* property after instantiating the connection. Be sure to replace the connection string with a valid connection string for the ODBC data source you want to connect to. To eliminate the need to qualify the objects fully in code, add an *Imports System.Data.Odbc* statement (Visual Basic) or *using System.Data.Odbc;* statement (C#) to the top of your code file.

```
' VB
Private WithEvents ConnectionToOdbc As New OdbcConnection _
    ("Dsn=MS Access Database;dbq=C:\Nwind.mdb;defaultdir=C:\DataSources;" & _
    "driverid=281;fil=MS Access;maxbuffersize=2048;pagetimeout=5;uid=admin")
```

```
// C#
OdbcConnection ConnectionToOdbc = new OdbcConnection
    ("Dsn=MS Access Database;dbq=C:\\DataSources;" +
    "driverid=281;fil=MS Access;maxbuffersize=2048;pagetimeout=5;uid=admin");
```

Creating Oracle Connection Objects in Code

Create *OracleConnection* objects with the *New* keyword. You can instantiate the connection and set the connection string in the same call, or you can assign the connection string to the *OracleConnection.ConnectionString* property after instantiating the connection. Be sure to replace the connection string with a valid one for the *Oracle* database you want to connect to. To eliminate the need to qualify the objects fully in code, add an Imports System.Data.OracleClient statement (Visual Basic) or using System.Data.OracleClient; statement (C#) to the top of your code file.

```
' VB
Private WithEvents ConnectionToOracle As New OracleConnection _
    ("Data Source=Oracle8i;Integrated Security=yes")
```

```
// C#
private OracleConnection ConnectionToOracle = new OracleConnection
    ("Data Source=Oracle8i;Integrated Security=yes;
```

Lab: Creating New Data Connections

In this lab you will practice creating new Data Connections in Server Explorer and using the Data Source Configuration Wizard.

▶ **Exercise 1: Creating Connections in Server Explorer**

The following steps describe how to create a Data Connection (a connection to a database) in Server Explorer.

1. If the Server Explorer window is not visible, select Server Explorer from the View menu.

2. Right-click the Data Connections node and select Add Connection.

   The first time you add a connection in Visual Studio, the Choose Data Source dialog box opens.

NOTE   Add Connection dialog box

If the Add Connection dialog box opens instead of the Choose Data Source dialog box, click the Change button located at the top of the Add Connection dialog box.

The Choose Data Source dialog box (or the similar Change Data Source dialog box) is where you select the data source you want to connect to, as well as the data provider to use for the connection. Notice how the proper data provider is automatically populated when you select different data sources. You can choose any valid provider you want for any selected data source, but Visual Studio automatically selects the most appropriate data provider based on the selected data source.

For our first connection, we'll create a connection to the *Northwind Traders* sample database in SQL Server.

3. Select Microsoft SQL Server for the data source and click OK.

   The Add Connection dialog box now appears with Microsoft SQL Server as the selected data source.

   NOTE **.NET Framework Data Providers**

   The .NET Framework Data Provider for SQL Server is designed to connect to SQL Server 7 and later versions. When connecting to SQL Server 6 or earlier, highlight the <other> data source and select the .NET Framework Data Provider for OLE DB. Then, in the Add Connection dialog box, select the Microsoft OLE DB Provider for SQL Server.

4. Type the name of your SQL Server in the server name area.

5. Select the appropriate method of authentication to access your SQL Server.

6. Choose Select or enter a database name option and select the *Northwind* database from the drop-down list.

7. You can verify the connection is valid by clicking Test Connection and then clicking OK to close the dialog box and create the connection in Server Explorer.

   After creating the connection, the Properties window provides information related to the connection as well as information related to the actual database you are connected to.

8. Select the connection you just created in the Server Explorer window to view the available information in the properties window.

   NOTE **Connection properties**

   The available properties are based on the type of data source you are connected to as well as the state of the connection. If the connection is closed, you might see only a small list of properties made up of the connection string used to connect to the database, the specific .NET Framework data provider used by the connection, and the state of the connection. To view additional properties, it is necessary to open the connection by expanding the connection node in Server Explorer. Once open, the connection provides additional properties such as the database owner, whether the database is case sensitive, and the type of database and version number.

▶ **Exercise 2: Creating Connections using the Data Source Configuration Wizard**

To create data connections using the Data Source Configuration Wizard, perform the following steps:

1. Create a Windows Forms application.

2. Select Add New Data Source from the Data menu.

3. The default data source type is Database, so just click Next.

4. The Choose Your Data Connection page of the wizard is where you create your connection object.

NOTE   Available connections

The drop-down list is populated with the connections already available in Server Explorer. If you completed the previous section and created a data connection to the *Northwind* database, it will be available in this drop-down list.

---

5. For this exercise, we will create a new connection, so click the New Connection button to open the Add Connection dialog box.

NOTE   Add Connection dialog box

Just like adding a new connection to Server Explorer, you use the Add Connection dialog box to create the connection. Basically, when creating new connections visually, whether using one of the data wizards or Server Explorer, the Add Connection dialog box is always used.

---

6. Type the name of your SQL server in the server name area.

7. Select the appropriate method of authentication to access your SQL server.

8. Choose Select or enter a database name option and select the *Northwind* database from the drop-down list.

9. You can verify that the connection is valid by clicking Test Connection, and then clicking OK to close the dialog box.

NOTE   Including sensitive data

If your connection uses SQL authentication and requires a user name and password to connect to your database, the option to include or exclude sensitive data in the connection string is enabled. By default, the connection string will not include sensitive data, and you will need to provide this information in your application when you attempt to open the connection and connect to the database. You can select the option to include sensitive data in the connection string, but this is not considered best practice because users who have access to the connection string might be able to view the password. Using *integrated security* is the recommended option.

At this point in the wizard, you have successfully created your data connection and can view the connection string by expanding the Connection string node.

To add the connection to your project, finish the wizard by completing the following steps.

10. Click Next. You are presented with the option of saving the Connection string in the application configuration file as well as providing a name for the connection. By default, the selection is set to save the connection; this is probably a good idea for most applications. Saving your connection in the application configuration file would be advantageous if, after deployment, you wanted to point at a different data source. Then you (or a systems administrator) could easily modify the configuration setting rather than having to change the connection string in code and recompile and redeploy the application. Once a connection string is saved to the application configuration file it can be accessed and modified using the Project Designer. Open the Project Designer by double-clicking the My Project icon (VB) or the Properties icon (C#) in Solution Explorer. After the Project Designer opens, click the Settings tab to access the connection strings stored in your application.

11. The Choose Your Database Objects page of the wizard allows you to select the Tables, Views, Stored Procedures, and so on to be used in your application. For this lesson, expand the *Tables* node and select the Customers and Orders tables.

12. Click Finish. A typed dataset with the connection object defined in the wizard is added to your project.

Now that you've completed the wizard, let's take a look at where the connection is and what it contains. The connection created as a result of running the wizard is located within the designer-generated dataset code file. To view the actual connection object, open the dataset in the Dataset Designer by double-clicking the dataset object in Solution Explorer. (The *Dataset* object is the *NorthwindDataSet.xsd* node.) Select the title bar of a TableAdapter on the design surface (for example, select Customers-TableAdapter). The connection information is available in the Properties window, where you can expand the node and see the name, modifier, and connection string.

NOTE *ConnectionString* property

The *ConnectionString* property displays the connection string saved in the application configuration file. Modifying the connection string here in the Properties window is the same as editing the connection string in the Settings file and affects all connections that reference that setting.

> **Quick Check**
>
> 1. How do I decide which connection object I need to create?
> 2. What is the minimum information required to create a connection object?
>
> **Quick Check Answers**
>
> 1. Choose a connection object by selecting the .NET Framework Data Provider that is designed to work best with your particular data source.
> 2. At the least, you need to know the valid connection string that you can use to connect to your data source.

Lesson Summary

- Connection objects provide two-way communication between your application and a data source.

- Connection objects can be added to Server Explorer, where they can then be easily incorporated into future projects.

- To create connection objects, you must have a valid connection string and the proper credentials to access the data source.

- Connection objects can be created either visually or programmatically, depending on user preference and development style.

- There are four primary connection objects, one for each of the .NET Framework Data Providers.

Lesson Review

The following questions are intended to reinforce key information presented in this lesson. The questions are also available on the companion CD if you prefer to review them in electronic form.

NOTE   Answers

Answers to these questions and explanations of why each choice is right or wrong are located in the "Answers" section at the end of the book.

---

1. Where is the connection object located that was created as a result of running the Data Source Configuration Wizard?

    A. In the application configuration file

    B. In the Data Sources window

    C. In the designer-generated dataset code file

    D. In the generated form code

2. When should you use the *OleDbConnection* object? (Choose all that apply.)

    A. When connecting to an *Oracle* database

    B. When connecting to an *Office Access* database

    C. When connecting to SQL Server 6.x.

    D. When connecting to SQL Server 2000

3. What user interface component is used to create connections?

    A. The Data Source Configuration Wizard

    B. The Server Explorer window

    C. The Add Connection dialog box

    D. The Properties window

Lesson 2: Connecting to Data Using Connection Objects

Now that you have learned how to create connection objects using the primary .NET data providers, let's start using them and actually connect to some data sources. This lesson will explain how to use a connection object and open a connection to a data source. After opening the connection, we will verify that the connection is opened by examining the *ConnectionState* property. Once we verify that the connection state is opened, we will also cause the *InfoMessage* event to fire and display the message returned by the data source.

After this lesson, you will be able to:

- Open an ADO.NET connection to a database.
- Close an ADO.NET connection to a database by using the *Close* method of the connection object.
- Use the *Connection* events to detect database information.

Estimated lesson time: 45 minutes

Opening and Closing Data Connections

Open and close connections using the appropriately named *Open* and *Close* methods. To open a connection to a database, the connection object must contain a connection string that points to a valid data source as well as enough information to pass the appropriate credentials to the data source. When connections are opened and closed, you can keep an eye on the state of the connection by responding to the *StateChange* event. The following example will show how to open and close connections and will also update the text in a label in reaction to the *StateChange* event. We will also demonstrate how the *InfoMessage* event can be used to provide informational messages from a data source to the application. And, finally, we will demonstrate how the connection object can provide information about the data source by retrieving metadata (for example, the server version number) from an open connection.

Connection Events

Connection objects provide the *StateChanged* and *InfoMessage* events to provide information to your application regarding the status of the database and information pertaining to commands executed using a specific connection object.

- **StateChanged** Event   This event is raised when the current state of the database changes from Open to Closed.

- **InfoMessage** Event   In addition to monitoring the state of a connection, each connection object provides an *InfoMessage* event that is raised when warnings or messages are returned from the server. Informational messages are typically provided when low-severity errors are returned by the data source that the connection object is connected to. For example, SQL Server errors with a severity of 10 or less are provided to the *InfoMessage* event.

NOTE Severity levels

Each error message in SQL Server has an associated severity level. The severity level, as its name implies, provides a clue as to the type of error being returned. Severity levels range from 0 thru 25. Errors with severity levels between 0 and 19 can typically be handled without user intervention, whereas errors with severity level between 20 and 25 will typically cause your connection to close. For more information on SQL Server errors and severity levels see the Error Message Severity Levels topic in the *SQL Books Online*.

Lab: Practice Opening and Closing Data Connections

In this lab you will practice working with connection objects by opening and closing the connections and displaying connection information back to the user.

▶ **Exercise 1: Opening and Closing Data Connections**

To demonstrate working with connection objects, perform the following steps:

1. Create a new Windows application and name it **DataConnections**.

2. Because Windows applications are not created with a reference to the *System .Data.OracleClient* namespace, from the Project menu select the *Add Reference* command and locate the *System.Data.OracleClient* component and click OK.

3. Add twelve buttons to the form, setting the *Name* and *Text* properties as shown in Table 5-5.

NOTE Similar Connections

No matter which connection objects you use, the methods for opening and closing, handling events, and so on, is the same. Feel free to only set up the example using the connection object for the provider you are interested in working with.

Table 5-5   **Button Settings for Data Connections Form**

Name property	Text property
OpenSqlButton	Open SQL
OpenOleDbButton	Open OLE DB
OpenOdbcButton	Open ODBC
OpenOracleButton	Open Oracle
CloseSqlButton	Close SQL
CloseOleDbButton	Close OLE DB
CloseOdbcButton	Close ODBC
CloseOracleButton	Close Oracle
GetSqlInfoButton	Get SQL Info
GetOleDbInfoButton	Get OLE DB Info
GetOdbcInfoButton	Get ODBC Info
GetOracleInfoButton	Get Oracle Info

4. Add four labels to the form, setting the *Name* and *Text* properties as shown in Table 5-6.

Table 5-6   **Label Settings for Data Connections Form**

Name property	Text property
SqlConnectionStateLabel	Closed
OleDbConnectionStateLabel	Closed
OdbcConnectionStateLabel	Closed
OracleConnectionStateLabel	Closed

Arrange the controls so the form layout looks similar to Figure 5-2.

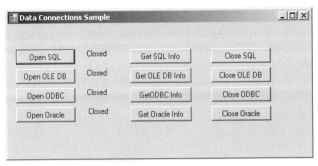

Figure 5-2   Form with controls arranged in preparation for creating connection objects

To create the connection objects for this lesson, we will take the code examples from Lesson 1, "Creating and Configuring Connection Objects," and add them to our form as follows.

5. Open the form you just created in code view.

6. Add the code to create all four connection objects so that you end up with code that looks like the following.

IMPORTANT Connection strings

Be sure to modify the connection strings to point to your specific server and database for each provider.

```vb
' VB
Imports System.Data.SqlClient
Imports System.Data.OleDb
Imports System.Data.Odbc
Imports System.Data.OracleClient

Public Class Form1
    ' Declare the connection objects for the four data providers
    Private WithEvents ConnectionToSql As New SqlConnection( _
        "Data Source=.\sqlexpress;Initial Catalog=Northwind;Integrated Security=True")
    Private WithEvents ConnectionToOleDb As New System.Data.OleDb.OleDbConnection( _
        "Provider=Microsoft.Jet.OLEDB.4.0;Data Source=""C:\DataSources\Nwind.mdb"";" & _
        "Persist Security Info=False")
    Private WithEvents ConnectionToOdbc As New OdbcConnection( _
        "Dsn=MS Access Database;dbq=C:DataSources\Nwind.mdb;defaultdir=C:\DataSources;"
& _
        "driverid=281;fil=MS Access;maxbuffersize=2048;pagetimeout=5;uid=admin")
    Private WithEvents ConnectionToOracle As New OracleConnection("Data
Source=MyOracleDB;Integrated Security=yes;")
End Class
```

```csharp
// C#
using System;
using System.Collections.Generic;
using System.ComponentModel;
using System.Data;
using System.Drawing;
using System.Text;
using System.Windows.Forms;
using System.Data.SqlClient;
using System.Data.OleDb;
using System.Data.Odbc;
using System.Data.OracleClient;

namespace DataConnections
{
    public partial class Form1 : Form
    {
        public Form1()
        {
            InitializeComponent();
        }

        // Declare the connection objects for the four data providers
        private SqlConnection ConnectionToSql = new SqlConnection(
            "Data Source=.\\sqlexpress;Initial Catalog=Northwind;Integrated
Security=True");
        private OleDbConnection ConnectionToOleDb = new
System.Data.OleDb.OleDbConnection(
            "Provider=Microsoft.Jet.OLEDB.4.0;Data Source=C:\\DataSources\\Nwind.mdb");
        private OdbcConnection ConnectionToOdbc = new OdbcConnection(
            "Dsn=MS Access Database;dbq=C:\\DataSources\\Nwind.mdb;" +
          "defaultdir=C:\\DataSources;driverid=281;fil=MS Access;maxbuffersize=2048;" +
            "pagetimeout=5;uid=admin");
        private OracleConnection ConnectionToOracle = new OracleConnection("Data
Source=MyOracleDB;Integrated Security=yes;");

    }
}
```

To open connections to a database, use the connection object's *Open* method. To demonstrate this, we will call the *Open* method for each connection when the open buttons are clicked.

7. Create event handlers for the open buttons for each provider and add the following code, which will open the connection to the database when the open buttons are clicked.

```vbnet
' VB
Private Sub OpenSqlServerButton_Click(ByVal sender As System.Object, _
        ByVal e As System.EventArgs) Handles OpenSqlServerButton.Click
```

```
    ConnectionToSql.Open()
End Sub

Private Sub OpenOleDbButton_Click(ByVal sender As System.Object, _
    ByVal e As System.EventArgs) Handles OpenOleDbButton.Click
    ConnectionToOleDb.Open()
End Sub

Private Sub OpenOdbcButton_Click(ByVal sender As System.Object, _
    ByVal e As System.EventArgs) Handles OpenOdbcButton.Click
    ConnectionToOdbc.Open()
End Sub

Private Sub OpenOracleButton_Click(ByVal sender As System.Object, _
    ByVal e As System.EventArgs) Handles OpenOracleButton.Click
    ConnectionToOracle.Open()
End Sub

// C#
private void OpenSqlServerButton_Click(object sender, EventArgs e)
{
    ConnectionToSql.Open();
}
private void OpenOleDbButton_Click(object sender, EventArgs e)
{
    ConnectionToOleDb.Open();
}
private void OpenOdbcButton_Click(object sender, EventArgs e)
{
    ConnectionToOdbc.Open();
}
private void OpenOracleButton_Click(object sender, EventArgs e)
{
    ConnectionToOracle.Open();
}
```

To close database connections, use the connection object's *Close* method. Technically, you can also call the *Dispose* method of the connection object to close the connection, but the preferred technique is to call the *Close* method. Worth noting is that calling the *Close* method also rolls back all pending transactions and releases the connection back to the connection pool. To implement this, create event handlers for the close buttons for each provider and add code to call the *Close* method to the body of the handler.

8. Add the *Close* methods into the event handlers to close the connection to the database when the close buttons are clicked.

```
' VB
Private Sub CloseSqlButton_Click(ByVal sender As System.Object, _
```

```
        ByVal e As System.EventArgs) Handles CloseSqlButton.Click
        ConnectionToSql.Close()
    End Sub

    Private Sub CloseOleDbButton_Click(ByVal sender As System.Object, _
        ByVal e As System.EventArgs) Handles CloseOleDbButton.Click
        ConnectionToOleDb.Close()
    End Sub

    Private Sub CloseOdbcButton_Click(ByVal sender As System.Object, _
        ByVal e As System.EventArgs) Handles CloseOdbcButton.Click
        ConnectionToOdbc.Close()
    End Sub

    Private Sub CloseOracleButton_Click(ByVal sender As System.Object, _
        ByVal e As System.EventArgs) Handles CloseOracleButton.Click
        ConnectionToOracle.Close()
    End Sub

    // C#
    private void CloseSqlButton_Click(object sender, EventArgs e)
    {
        ConnectionToSql.Close();
    }

    private void CloseOleDbButton_Click(object sender, EventArgs e)
    {
        ConnectionToOleDb.Close();
    }

    private void CloseOdbcButton_Click(object sender, EventArgs e)
    {
        ConnectionToOdbc.Close();
    }

    private void CloseOracleButton_Click(object sender, EventArgs e)
    {
        ConnectionToOracle.Close();
    }
```

When the state of a connection changes, the value in the *CurrentState* property of the connection object is updated to reflect the connection's current state. When opening and closing a connection, we can inspect the value in this property to verify that the connection is actually opening and closing. Each connection object raises a *StateChange* event that can be responded to in order to monitor the state of the connection. To populate the connection-state labels, we need to create event handlers for the *StateChange* events for each provider. Inside the *StateChange* event handlers, add code that updates the connection-state labels with the value of the connection's *CurrentState* property, which is provided as an event argument.

9. Add the following code to the form, which updates the connection-state label values whenever the current state of a connection changes. Create the form load handler for C# so you can add the *StateChange* event handlers.

```vb
' VB
Private Sub ConnectionToSql_StateChange(ByVal sender As Object, _
    ByVal e As System.Data.StateChangeEventArgs) Handles ConnectionToSql.StateChange
    SqlConnectionStateLabel.Text = e.CurrentState.ToString
End Sub

Private Sub ConnectionToOleDb_StateChange(ByVal sender As Object, _
    ByVal e As System.Data.StateChangeEventArgs) Handles ConnectionToOleDb.StateChange
    OleDbConnectionStateLabel.Text = e.CurrentState.ToString
End Sub

Private Sub ConnectionToOdbc_StateChange(ByVal sender As Object, _
    ByVal e As System.Data.StateChangeEventArgs) Handles ConnectionToOdbc.StateChange
    OdbcConnectionStateLabel.Text = e.CurrentState.ToString
End Sub

Private Sub ConnectionToOracle_StateChange(ByVal sender As Object, _
    ByVal e As System.Data.StateChangeEventArgs) Handles ConnectionToOracle.StateChange
    OracleConnectionStateLabel.Text = e.CurrentState.ToString
End Sub

// C#
private void Form1_Load(object sender, EventArgs e)
{
    ConnectionToSql.StateChange += new
System.Data.StateChangeEventHandler(this.ConnectionToSql_StateChange);
    ConnectionToOleDb.StateChange += new
System.Data.StateChangeEventHandler(this.ConnectionToOleDb_StateChange);
    ConnectionToOdbc.StateChange += new
System.Data.StateChangeEventHandler(this.ConnectionToOdbc_StateChange);
    ConnectionToOracle.StateChange += new
System.Data.StateChangeEventHandler(this.ConnectionToOracle_StateChange);
}

private void ConnectionToSql_StateChange(object sender, StateChangeEventArgs e)
{
    SqlConnectionStateLabel.Text = e.CurrentState.ToString();
}

private void ConnectionToOleDb_StateChange(object sender, StateChangeEventArgs e)
{
    OleDbConnectionStateLabel.Text = e.CurrentState.ToString();
}
```

```
private void ConnectionToOdbc_StateChange(object sender, StateChangeEventArgs e)
{
    OdbcConnectionStateLabel.Text = e.CurrentState.ToString();
}

private void ConnectionToOracle_StateChange(object sender, StateChangeEventArgs e)
{
    OracleConnectionStateLabel.Text = e.CurrentState.ToString();
}
```

10. Press F5 to run the application and test the form to see the functionality we have so far.

11. When the form opens, click the Open SQL button and verify that the connection-state label changes to show that the connection is now open.

12. Click the Close SQL button and verify that the connection-state label changes to reflect the current state of the connection, which is now closed.

To demonstrate use of the *InfoMessage* event, you need to create an event handler to process the message. To eliminate the need to create a database object that throws an error with a low severity, we are going to take advantage of a feature built into the *SqlConnection* object that allows us to capture errors with severities up to severity level 16 by setting the connection object's *FireInfoMessageEvent-OnUserErrors* property to *True* before executing a method that will force an error to be thrown.

13. Add the following code, which will handle the GetSqlInfo button's click event and the *SqlConnection* object's *InfoMessage* event.

Upon examination of the code in the button-click event, you can see we are going to change the database on the connection to an invalid name, which will raise an error with severity level 11 and cause the *InfoMessage* event to fire. When the event fires, the code in the *InfoMessage* event handler will open a message box displaying the error.

```
' VB
Private Sub GetSqlInfoButton_Click(ByVal sender As System.Object, _
    ByVal e As System.EventArgs) Handles GetSqlInfoButton.Click
    ConnectionToSql.FireInfoMessageEventOnUserErrors = True
    ConnectionToSql.ChangeDatabase("Northwind1")
End Sub

Private Sub ConnectionToSql_InfoMessage(ByVal sender As Object, _
    ByVal e As System.Data.SqlClient.SqlInfoMessageEventArgs) Handles
ConnectionToSql.InfoMessage
    MsgBox(e.Message)
End Sub
```

```csharp
// C#
// Add this line of code into the form load handler to hook up the InfoMessage handler.
ConnectionToSql.InfoMessage += new
System.Data.SqlClient.SqlInfoMessageEventHandler(this.ConnectionToSql_InfoMessage);

private void GetSqlInfoButton_Click(object sender, EventArgs e)
{
    ConnectionToSql.FireInfoMessageEventOnUserErrors = True;
    ConnectionToSql.ChangeDatabase("Northwind1");
}

private void ConnectionToSql_InfoMessage(object sender, SqlInfoMessageEventArgs e)
{
    MessageBox.Show(e.Message);
}
```

In addition to the previous types of information available from connection objects, you can also return some meta data from the data source you are connected to. In Lesson 1, we examined the connection properties in the Properties window for the connections available in Server Explorer. This information is available at run time from the connection object as well. As an example, let's add a few more lines of code to our application and implement the Get Info buttons of the remaining connections to return the server versions of the data sources they are connected to.

Quick Check

1. How do you open a connection to a data source?
2. How do you close a connection to a data source?
3. How do you know when warnings and information are returned from a data source?

Quick Check Answers

1. Call the *Open* method of a connection object.
2. Call the *Close* method of a connection object.
3. Monitor and process the *InfoMessage* event.

---

14. Add the following code to the bottom of the form.

```vb
' VB
Private Sub GetOleDbInfoButton_Click(ByVal sender As System.Object, ByVal e As
System.EventArgs) Handles GetOleDbInfoButton.Click
   MsgBox(ConnectionToOleDb.ServerVersion.ToString, "Server Version")
```

```
End Sub

Private Sub GetOdbcInfoButton_Click(ByVal sender As System.Object, ByVal e As
System.EventArgs) Handles GetOdbcInfoButton.Click
    MsgBox(ConnectionToOdbc.ServerVersion.ToString, "Server Version")
End Sub

Private Sub GetOracleInfoButton_Click(ByVal sender As System.Object, ByVal e As
System.EventArgs) Handles GetOracleInfoButton.Click
    MsgBox(ConnectionToOracle.ServerVersion.ToString, "Server Version")
End Sub

// C#
private void GetOleDbInfoButton_Click(object sender, EventArgs e)
{
    MessageBox.Show(ConnectionToOleDb.ServerVersion.ToString(), "Server Version");
}

private void GetOdbcInfoButton_Click(object sender, EventArgs e)
{
    MessageBox.Show(ConnectionToOdbc.ServerVersion.ToString(), "Server Version");
}

private void GetOracleInfoButton_Click(object sender, EventArgs e)
{
    MessageBox.Show(ConnectionToOracle.ServerVersion.ToString(), "Server Version");
}
```

Now let's run the application one more time to check out the additional functionality and verify that the info message and meta data is available from our connection objects.

15. Press F5 to run the application.

16. Click the Open SQL button to open the connection to the SQL server and update the connection-state label.

17. Press the Get SQL Info button to change the database to the invalid *Northwind1* database and raise the *InfoMessage* event that will display in the message box.

IMPORTANT   Possible invalid operation exception

The connection must be open, or an Invalid Operation exception will be thrown and the *InfoMessage* event will not fire.

---

18. Click the Close SQL button to close the connection to SQL Server and update the connection-state label.

19. Click the Open OLE DB button to open the connection to the OLE DB data source and update the connection-state label.

20. Click the Get OLE DB Info button to retrieve the server version of the OLE DB data source.

21. Click the Close OLE DB button to close the connection and update the connection-state label.

22. Save the application.

IMPORTANT   Save the application

Save this application because we will use it in Lesson 4, "Handling Connection Errors."

Lesson Summary

- Open connections by calling the *Open* method of a connection object.

- Close connections by calling the *Close* method of a connection object.

- Determine whether a connection is opened or closed by monitoring the *State-Changed* event.

- Use the *InfoMessage* event to process any warnings or informational messages that are returned from the server.

Lesson Review

The following questions are intended to reinforce key information presented in this lesson. The questions are also available on the companion CD if you prefer to review them in electronic form.

NOTE   Answers

Answers to these questions and explanations of why each choice is right or wrong are located in the "Answers" section at the end of the book.

---

1. What is the minimal information needed by a connection string to open a connection to a SQL Server 2000 or SQL Server 2005 database? (Choose all that apply.)

   A. A valid data source

   B. A valid provider name

   C. A valid filepath

   D. Appropriate credentials or Integrated Security settings

2. What happens when you call the *Close* method of a connection object? (Choose all that apply.)

    A. The connection is destroyed.

    B. The connection is returned to the connection pool.

    C. The *StateChange* event is fired.

    D. All non-committed pending transactions are rolled back.

3. What types of information are typically exposed by the *InfoMessage* event?

    A. Information regarding the current state of a connection

    B. High-severity SQL Server errors (severity 17 and above)

    C. Low-severity SQL Server errors (severity 10 and below)

    D. Network errors that are encountered when attempting to open a connection

Lesson 3: Working with Connection Pools

This lesson explains what connection pooling is and how to control connection pooling options when creating and configuring connection objects.

After this lesson, you will be able to:

■ Configure a connection for connection pooling by configuring connection string values.

Estimated lesson time: 30 minutes

What Is Connection Pooling?

Connection pooling enables the reuse of existing connections to reduce the overhead of continuously creating and disposing of connections that have the same configuration. In other words, opening and closing connections that use the same connection string and credentials can reuse a connection that is available in the pool. Typical applications use the same connection objects to continuously fetch and update data from a database. Connection pooling provides a much higher level of performance by eliminating the need for the database to constantly create and dispose of connections.

Connection pools are separated by process, application domain, and connection string. For connection strings that use integrated security, a separate pool is created for each unique identity.

Controlling Connection Pooling Options

Connection pooling is enabled by default when creating ADO.NET connection objects. You can control connection pooling behavior (or disable pooling altogether) by setting connection string keywords specific to connection pooling. For example, to specifically disable connection pooling, you set *Pooling=False* in your connection string. Table 5-7 provides a list of connection string keywords that can be used to control how a specific connection interacts with the connection pool. Not all keywords are available for every provider. For example the OLE DB provider controls connection pooling (also known as resource or session pooling) based on the value set for the *OLE DB Services* keyword in the connection string.

Table 5-7   **Connection Pooling Connection String Keywords**

Name	Default	Description
Connection Lifetime	*0*	When a connection is returned to the pool, if its creation time was longer than *x* seconds ago, with *x* being the value of this property, then the connection is destroyed. Values are in seconds, and a value of *0* indicates the maximum connection timeout.
Connection Reset	*True*	Determines whether the database connection is reset when being drawn from the pool. For SQL Server 7.0, setting to *False* avoids making an additional server round trip when obtaining a connection, but the connection state, such as database context, is not being reset.
Enlist	*True*	If you want to use a connection as part of a transaction you can set this to *True* and the pooler will automatically enlist the connection in the creation thread's current transaction context.
Load Balance Timeout	*0*	The minimum number of seconds for the connection to live in the connection pool before being destroyed.
Max Pool Size	*100*	The maximum number of connections allowed in the pool for this specific connection string. In other words if your application continuously connects to the database you might need to increase the Max Pool Size. For example, if your application has many users that all use the same connection string and there is the possibility of needing more than 100 connections you would want to increase the Max Pool Size, this may occur when many users are accessing the database server using a common client or Web page.

Table 5-7   Connection Pooling Connection String Keywords

Name	Default	Description
Min Pool Size	*0*	The minimum number of connections allowed in the pool.
Pooling	*True*	When true, the *SqlConnection* object is drawn from the appropriate pool or, if it is required, is created and added to the appropriate pool. Recognized values are *True*, *False*, *Yes*, and *No*.

In addition to connection string properties that control connection pooling behavior, there are also methods available on connection objects that can affect the pool as well. The available methods are typically used when you are closing connections in your application and you know they will not be used again. This clears the connection pool by disposing of the connections instead of returning them to the pool when they are closed. Any connections that are already in the pool and open will be disposed of the next time they are closed. Table 5-8 lists the available methods for interacting with connection pools.

Table 5-8   Connection Pooling Specific Methods

Name	Object	Description
ClearAllPools	*SqlConnection* and *OracleConnection*	Empties all connection pools for a specific provider.
ClearPool	*SqlConnection* and *OracleConnection*	Empties the connection pool associated with the specified connection.
ReleaseObject-Pool	*OleDbConnection* and *OdbcConnection*	Indicates that the object pool can be released when the last underlying connection is released.

Configuring Connections to Use Connection Pooling

By default, all .NET Framework Data Providers available in ADO.NET have connection pooling turned on, but the level of control available for working with connection pooling varies based on the provider being used.

Configuring Connection Pooling with SQL Server Connections

By default, the *SqlConnection* object automatically uses connection pooling. Each time you call *SqlConnection.Open* with a unique connection string, a new pool is created. Control connection pooling behavior by setting the connection pool keywords in the connection string as described earlier in Table 5-7. For example, consider a connection where you want to set the minimum pool size. By assigning a value greater than zero to the *Min Pool Size* keyword you ensure the pool will not be destroyed until after the application ends. To set the minimum pool size to 5, use a connection string similar to the following:

```
Data Source=SqlServerName;Initial Catalog=DatabaseName;
    Integrated Security=True;Min Pool Size=5
```

The minimum pool size is 0 by default, which means each connection needs to be created and initialized as they are requested, by increasing the minimum pool size in the connection string the indicated number of connec tions are created and ready to use, which can reduce the time it takes to establish the connection on those initial connections.

Configuring Connection Pooling with OLE DB Connections

The OLE DB connection object (*OleDbConnection*) automatically pools connections through the use of OLE DB session pooling. You control how OLE DB connections use pooling by adding an *OLE DB Services* keyword to the connection string and setting its value based on the combination of services you want to enable or disable for the connection.

The following connection strings explicitly enable connection pooling by setting the *OLE DB Services* keyword to *-1*.

OLE DB connection string for an Office Access database (assumes the Nwind.mdb file exists in the following path: C:\DataSources\Nwind.mdb):

```
Provider=Microsoft.Jet.OLEDB.4.0;Data Source=C:\DataSources\Nwind.mdb;
    OLE DB Services=-1
```

OLE DB Connection for a SQL Server database (replace *ServerName* and *Database-Name* with valid values for your data source):

```
Provider=SQLOLEDB;Data Source=ServerName;OLE DB Services=-1;
    Integrated Security=SSPI;Initial Catalog=DatabaseName
```

The following connection strings disable connection pooling and automatic transaction enlistment by setting the *OLE DB Services* keyword to *-4*.

```
Provider=Microsoft.Jet.OLEDB.4.0;Data Source=C:\DataSources\Nwind.mdb;OLE DB Services=-4
```

Table 5-9 lists the OLE DB Services values to set in an OLE DB connection string.

Table 5-9   Table 5-9 OLE DB Connection String Settings for OLE DB Services

OLE DB Service	Connection String Keyword/Value
All services on	"OLE DB Services = -1;"
All services except *Pooling* and *AutoEnlistment* of transactions	"OLE DB Services = -4;"
All services except *Client Cursor*	"OLE DB Services = -5;"
All services except *Pooling, AutoEnlistment*, and *Client Cursor*	"OLE DB Services = -8;"
No services (all services disabled)	"OLE DB Services = 0;"

Configuring Connection Pooling with ODBC Connections

To enable or disable connection pooling for connections that use the ODBC connection object (*OdbcConnnection*), you must use the ODBC Data Source Administrator dialog box in Windows.

Access the ODBC Data Source Administrator dialog box by performing the following steps:

1. In the Administrative Tools folder on your Start menu, open Data Sources (ODBC).
2. Select the Connection Pooling tab.
3. Double-click the driver from the list of available ODBC drivers that you want to set connection pooling options for.
4. In the Set Connection Pooling Attributes dialog box, select the option to either pool connections or not pool connections. If you select the option to pool connections, you can also set the number of seconds for unused connections to remain in the pool (the connection lifetime).
5. Click OK to save the settings and repeat for other drivers if desired.

IMPORTANT   ODBC settings

The settings for a particular ODBC driver are in effect for all applications/connections that use that particular driver.

Configuring Connection Pooling with Oracle Connections

Connections that use the .NET Framework Data Provider for Oracle automatically use connection pooling by default. You can control how the connection uses pooling by setting connection string keywords.

Table 5-10 details the connection string keywords available for altering connection pooling activities.

Table 5-10   Table 5-10 Oracle Connection String Settings for Connection Pooling

Name	Default	Description
Connection Lifetime	*0*	When a connection is returned to the pool, its creation time is compared with the current time, and the connection is destroyed if that time span exceeds the value specified. Values are in seconds and a value of *0* indicates the maximum connection timeout.
Enlist	*True*	When true, the pooler automatically enlists the connection in the creation thread's current transaction context. Recognized values are *True*, *False*, *Yes*, and *No*.
Max Pool Size	*100*	The maximum number of connections allowed in the pool.
Min Pool Size	*0*	The minimum number of connections allowed in the pool.
Pooling	*True*	When true, the *OracleConnection* object is drawn from the appropriate pool or, if it is required, is created and added to the appropriate pool.

Lesson Summary

- Connection pooling is enabled by default.
- Connection pooling options are set in the connection string except for the ODBC provider, which uses the ODBC Data Source Administrator dialog box in Windows.

Lesson Review

The following questions are intended to reinforce key information presented in this lesson. The questions are also available on the companion CD if you prefer to review them in electronic form.

NOTE Answers

Answers to these questions and explanations of why each choice is right or wrong are located in the "Answers" section at the end of this book.

---

1. What determines the connection pool that a connection should use? (Choose all that apply.)

    A. A connection string

    B. The identity or credentials of the user opening the connection

    C. The database being connected to

    D. The connection object used to connect to the database

2. What are the recommended techniques for enabling connection pooling on for a SQL Server 2000 or SQL Server 2005 database? (Choose all that apply.)

    A. Setting the *OLE DB Services* connection string keyword to *-4*

    B. Opening a connection and not explicitly disabling pooling

    C. Setting the connection string keyword *Pooling = True* in the connection string

    D. Using the Connection Pooling tab of the ODBC Data Source Administrator dialog box

3. How do I explicitly turn on connection pooling for an OLE DB data source?

    A. By setting the *OLE DB Services* connection string keyword to *0*

    B. By setting the *OLE DB Services* connection string keyword to *-4*

    C. By setting the *OLE DB Services* connection string keyword to *-1*

    D. By setting the *OLE DB Services* connection string keyword to *-7*

Lesson 4: Handling Connection Errors

This lesson explains how to handle errors that are thrown while working with SQL Server. ADO.NET provides two classes specifically for processing errors: the *SqlException* class and the *SqlError* class. Let's see how to work with these classes and how to catch and handle errors that may be returned from the data source.

After this lesson, you will be able to:

- Handle exceptions when connecting to a database.
- Use the *SqlException* class to detect connection errors.
- Use the *SqlError* class to detect connection errors.

Estimated lesson time: 20 minutes

When SQL Server returns a warning or an error, the .NET Framework Data Provider for SQL Server creates and throws a *SqlException* that you can catch in your application to deal with the problem. When *SqlException* is thrown, inspect the *SqlException* *.Errors* property to access the collection of errors that are returned from the SQL server. The *SqlException.Errors* property is a *SqlErrorCollection* class (a collection of *SqlError* classes) that always contains at least one *SqlError* object.

MORE INFO   SQL Server errors

SqlConnection will remain open for messages with a severity level of 19 and below, but it will typically close automatically when the severity is 20 or greater.

Lab: Handling Database Connection Errors

In this lab you will practice catching a *SqlException* in your application.

▶ **Exercise 1: Handling Database Connection Errors**

In this lab you will practice working with database connection errors (specifically, the SqlException and SqlError objects) in your application. To do this let's create a Windows application.

1. Create a new Windows application and name it **HandlingConnectionErrors**.

2. Add 3 Buttons to the form and set the following properties:

    Button1:

    - *Name* = GoodConnectButton
    - *Text* = Connect (valid connection string)

Button2:

❏ *Name* = ConnectToInvalidUserButton

❏ *Text* = Connect to invalid user

Button3:

❏ *<Name* = ConnectToInvalidDatabaseButton

❏ *<Text* = Connect to invalid database

3. Double click each button to create the button click event handlers and switch to code view.

4. Add an Imports statement (using in C#) for the *System.Data.SqlClient* namespace.

5. The following code creates a new connection based on the connection string passed into it, attempts to open the connection, and then displays any errors it encounters. Add this code below the button click event handlers:

```vb
' VB
Private Sub ConnectToDatabase(ByVal connectionString As String)

    Dim connection As New SqlConnection(connectionString)

    Try
        connection.Open()
    Catch ex As SqlException
        Dim errorMessage As String = ""

        ' Iterate through all errors returned
        ' You can check the error numbers to handle specific errors
        For Each ConnectionError As SqlError In ex.Errors
            errorMessage += ConnectionError.Message & " (error: " & _
                ConnectionError.Number.ToString & ")" & Environment.NewLine
            If ConnectionError.Number = 18452 Then
                MessageBox.Show("Invalid Login Detected, please provide valid
credentials!")
            End If
        Next
        MessageBox.Show(errorMessage)
    Finally
        connection.Close()
    End Try
End Sub

// C#
private void ConnectToDatabase(string connectionString)
{
    SqlConnection connection = new SqlConnection(connectionString);

    try
```

```
    {
        connection.Open();
    }
    catch (SqlException ex)
    {
        string errorMessage = "";
        // Iterate through all errors returned
        // You can check the error numbers to handle specific errors
        foreach (SqlError ConnectionError in ex.Errors)
        {
            errorMessage += ConnectionError.Message + " (error: " +
                ConnectionError.Number.ToString() + ")" + Environment.NewLine;
            if (ConnectionError.Number == 18452)
            {
                MessageBox.Show("Invalid Login Detected, please provide valid
credentials!");
            }
        }
        MessageBox.Show(errorMessage);
    }
    finally
    {
        connection.Close();
    }
}
```

6. Add the following code so the three button click event handlers look like the following:

```
' VB
Private Sub GoodConnectButton_Click _
    (ByVal sender As System.Object, ByVal e As System.EventArgs) _
    Handles GoodConnectButton.Click
    ' This is a valid connection string
    Dim GoodConnection As String = _
        "Data Source=.\sqlexpress;Initial Catalog=Northwind;Integrated Security=True;"
    ConnectToDatabase(GoodConnection)
End Sub

Private Sub ConnectToInvalidUserButton_Click _
    (ByVal sender As System.Object, ByVal e As System.EventArgs) _
    Handles ConnectToInvalidUserButton.Click
    ' This connection string has invalid credentials
    Dim InvalidUserConnection As String = _
        "Data Source=.\sqlexpress;Initial Catalog=Northwind;User ID = InvalidUser"
    ConnectToDatabase(InvalidUserConnection)
End Sub

Private Sub ConnectToInvalidDatabaseButton_Click _
    (ByVal sender As System.Object, ByVal e As System.EventArgs) _
    Handles ConnectToInvalidDatabaseButton.Click
```

```
        ' This connection string has an invalid/unavailable database
        Dim InvalidDatabaseConnection As String = _
            "Data Source=.\sqlexpress;Initial Catalog=InvalidDatabase;Integrated
Security=True"
        ConnectToDatabase(InvalidDatabaseConnection)
    End Sub

    // C#
    private void GoodConnectButton_Click(object sender, EventArgs e)
    {
        // This is a valid connection string
        String GoodConnection =
            "Data Source=.\\sqlexpress;Initial Catalog=Northwind;Integrated Security=True;";
        ConnectToDatabase(GoodConnection);
    }

    private void ConnectToInvalidUserButton_Click(object sender, EventArgs e)
    {
        // This connection string has invalid credentials
        String InvalidUserConnection =
            "Data Source=.\\sqlexpress;Initial Catalog=Northwind;User ID = InvalidUser";
        ConnectToDatabase(InvalidUserConnection);
    }

    private void ConnectToInvalidDatabaseButton_Click(object sender, EventArgs e)
    {
        // This connection string has an invalid/unavailable database
        String InvalidDatabaseConnection =
            "Data Source=.\\sqlexpress;Initial Catalog=InvalidDatabase;Integrated
Security=True";
        ConnectToDatabase(InvalidDatabaseConnection);
    }
```

7. Run the application.

8. Click the Connect (valid connection string) button and no errors should be raised.

9. Click the Connect To Invalid User button and the code to catch the specific login error (error 18452) is executed.

10. Click the Connect To Invalid Database button and you can see that an error was raised and is displayed in the MessageBox.

Lesson Summary

■ A *SqlException* object is created when an error is detected on the SQL server.

■ Every instance of a SqlException exception contains at least one SqlError warning that contains the actual error information from the server.

Lesson Review

The following questions are intended to reinforce key information presented in this lesson. The questions are also available on the companion CD if you prefer to review them in electronic form.

NOTE Answers

Answers to these questions and explanations of why each choice is right or wrong are located in the "Answers" section at the end of the book.

1. What types of errors will cause a *SqlConnection* object to close? (Choose all that apply.)

   A. Errors wth a severity level of 1 through 9

   B. Errors wth a severity level of 10 through 19

   C. Errors wth a severity level of 20 through 29

   D. Errors wth a severity level of 30 or greater

2. What property contains the actual error message returned by SQL Server? (Choose all that apply.)

   A. *SqlException.Source*

   B. *SqlException.Message*

   C. *SqlError.Class*

   D. *SqlError.Message*

Lesson 5: Enumerating the Available SQL Servers on a Network

This lesson describes how to return a list of visible SQL Server instances on a network comparable to the Server name drop-down list in the Add Connection dialog box.

> **After this lesson, you will be able to:**
> - Enumerate through instances of SQL Server.
>
> **Estimated lesson time: 20 minutes**

The .NET Framework offers applications a way to discover SQL Server instances on a network so your programs can process this information when necessary. To retrieve the list of available SQL Servers, use the *Instance* property of the *SqlDataSourceEnumerator* class and call the *GetDataSources* method. The *GetDataSources* method returns a *Data-Table* that contains information for each SQL server that is visible on the network. The returned data table contains the columns listed in Table 5-11.

Table 5-11   Table 5-11 *DataTable* Schema Returned by the *GetDataSources* Method

Column Name	Description
ServerName	Name of the SQL server containing the visible instance
InstanceName	Name of the server instance or empty for servers running default instances
IsClustered	Indicates whether the server is part of a cluster
Version	The version number of the SQL server

Why Do Only Some or No SQL Servers Appear in My Grid?

Depending on how your network or even single machine is set up, the list of available servers may or may not be complete. In addition to things such as network traffic and timeout issues, the way your network implements security can cause servers to be hidden from the returned list as well. If you are running SQL Server 2005, there is a service named SQL Browser that needs to be running to see SQL Server instances. And even if your SQL Browser service is running, your firewall may be blocking the request for SQL information; the firewall is likely to be blocking communication requests through port 1433, which is the default port that SQL Server default instances are set up to use. There are obvious security implications concerning turning on the SQL Browser service, as well as enabling communications through specific ports through your firewall, but these are beyond the scope of this book. A good resource is the "SQL Browser service" section of *SQL Books Online*, and I encourage you to read that before changing any settings on your firewall or SQL Server configuration.

Lab: Returning the List of Visible SQL Servers

In this lab you will practice enumerating the SQL Servers on your network.

▶ **Exercise 1: Enumerating the SQL Servers on a Network**

To demonstrate how to retrieve the list of visible SQL servers, let's create a small application to display the information returned from the *GetDataSources* method in a *DataGridView*.

1. Create a new Windows application named **SqlServerEnumerator**.

2. Add a DataGridView to the form and name it **VisibleSqlServers**.

NOTE   Note DataGridView

The *DataGridView* is the control typically used for displaying data. The *DataGridView* is discussed in more detail in Chapter 8.

---

3. Add a *Button* control below the grid and set its *Name* property to GetDataSources-Button.

4. Set the Button's *Text* property to Get Visible Servers.

5. Double-click the Get Visible Servers button to create the *Click* handler and switch to code view.

6. Add code so that the handler looks like the following:

```
' VB
Dim instance As System.Data.Sql.SqlDataSourceEnumerator = _
    System.Data.Sql.SqlDataSourceEnumerator.Instance
isibleSqlServers.DataSource = instance.GetDataSources
```

```
// C#
System.Data.Sql.SqlDataSourceEnumerator instance =
    System.Data.Sql.SqlDataSourceEnumerator.Instance;
VisibleSqlServers.DataSource = instance.GetDataSources();
```

Now run the application and click the Get Visible Servers button. All visible SQL servers on your network will appear in the grid, looking similar to Figure 5-3.

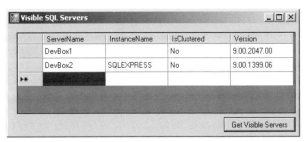

Figure 5-3   Grid showing all visible SQL Servers on your network

Lesson Summary

- You can use the *SqlDataSourceEnumerator* object to return a list of visible SQL servers on a network.

- The list of servers returned may not be complete due to factors such as firewall settings and protocol configurations on the SQL Server services.

Lesson Review

The following questions are intended to reinforce key information presented in this lesson. The questions are also available on the companion CD if you prefer to review them in electronic form.

NOTE   Answers

Answers to these questions and explanations of why each choice is right or wrong are located in the "Answers" section at the end of this book.

1. What object is used to return the list of visible SQL Servers?

   A. *VisibleSqlServers*

   B. *GetDataSources*

   C. *SqlDataSourceEnumerator*

   D. *ServerName*

2. What factors can cause SQL servers to be invisible on the network? (Choose all that apply.)

   A. The computer's firewall settings

   B. The amount of network traffic

   C. The availability of the SQL Browser service

   D.   The *Visible* property of the SQL Server

 3. Which of the following pieces of information is available through the *SqlServer-Enumerator* object? (Choose all that apply.)

   A.   The name of the SQL server

   B.   The number of databases currently on the server

   C.   The version number of the server

   D.   The instance name for servers that are not running default instances

Lesson 6: Securing Sensitive Connection String Data

Because of the sensitive nature of most data in real-world scenarios, it is extremely important to protect your servers and databases from unauthorized access. To ensure limited access to your data source, it is a best practice to secure information such as user IDs, data source names, and, of course, passwords. Storing this type of information as plain text is not recommended because of the obvious security risk. It is also worth noting that plain text saved in compiled applications is easily decompiled, rendering your data accessible by persons with questionable intent.

After this lesson, you will be able to:

■ Protect access to a data source's connection details.

Estimated lesson time: 45 minutes

Real World

Steve Stein

In another of my previous jobs (okay, I've had a few!), I took a position as a system administrator for a local mortgage company. My first task was to get familiar with the infrastructure of their company network. I immediately realized that basically every employee was set up with an administrator account and had access to the entire network. Although this story isn't specific to securing connection strings, it does provide insight into how important it is to lock down your sensitive data!

The suggested method of implementing security in applications that access data is to use Windows Authentication (also known as Integrated Security). To further protect sensitive connection information when using Integrated Security, it is also recommended that you set the *Persist Security Information* keyword to *False* in the connection string. This ensures that the credentials used to open the connection are discarded and not stored where someone might be able to retrieve them.

Table 5-12 provides the key/value pairs to set in the connection string for implementing integrated security in the four .NET Framework Data Providers.

Table 5-12   Table 5-12 Connection String Keywords for Turning on Integrated Security

Data Provider	Key/Value pair
SqlClient	Integrated Security=*True*
SqlClient and OleDb	Integrated Security=*SSPI*
Odbc	Trusted_Connection=*Yes*
OracleClient	Integrated Security=*Yes*

As stated earlier, if you absolutely must use a connection string that contains sensitive information, do not store the connection string in the compiled application. As an alternative, you can use the application configuration file (app.config). The app.config file stores connection strings as XML, and your application gets its connection information by querying this file at run time (as opposed to compiling the connection string into the application itself). By default the application configuration file stores it's information unencrypted, as shown in Figure 5-4.

Figure 5-4   An unencrypted configuration file

Securing Data in Configuration Files

Now that you've moved your sensitive connection string data out of the compiled application and into the application's configuration file, the connection string is still unencrypted and can be read by anyone with permission to open the configuration file. Therefore, you still need a way to prevent unauthorized personnel from viewing the connection information if they somehow gain access to your configuration file. The suggested method of securing configuration files is to encrypt the sections that contain sensitive information, as shown in Figure 5-5.

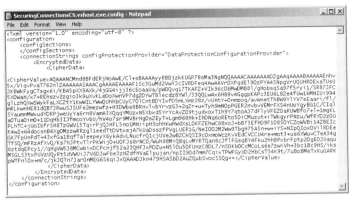

Figure 5-5   An encrypted configuration file

The suggested approach to encrypting configuration data is to use a protected-configuration provider. There are two protected-configuration providers available in the .NET Framework as well as a base class you can use to implement your own if the two available providers are not sufficient for your application.

Lab: Securing a Configuration File

In this lab you will practice encrypting and decrypting a configuration file.

▶ **Exercise 1: Encrypting and Decrypting a Configuration File**

In this lesson, you will see how to use the DpapiProtectedConfigurationProvider to encrypt and decrypt the ConnectionStrings section of the app.config file.

1. Create a new Windows Application and name it *SecuringConnectionStrings*.

2. Add a reference to the *System.Configuration* namespace.

3. Add two buttons to the form, setting the *Name* and *Text* properties to the following:

Name property	*Text* property
EncryptButton	Encrypt
DecryptButton	Decrypt

4. Create a data source and add a connection string to the application configuration file by running the Data Source Configuration Wizard.

5. Create event handlers for the button-click events.

6. Switch to code view and paste the following code into the editor:

The following code locates the connection string setting in the application's configuration file. The connection string setting is marked for *encryption* by calling the *ProtectSection* method. Setting the *ForceSave* property to *True* ensures the configuration file is saved whether changes are made or not; and the *Configuration .Save* call saves the file once it has been encrypted.

```vb
' VB
Imports System
Imports System.Configuration

Public Class Form1
    Private Sub EncryptConnectionString()
        ' Get the configuration file
        Dim config As System.Configuration.Configuration = _
        ConfigurationManager.OpenExeConfiguration(ConfigurationUserLevel.None)

        ' Create the provider name
        Dim provider As String = _
            "DataProtectionConfigurationProvider"

        ' Encrypt the ConnectionStrings
        Dim connStrings As ConfigurationSection = _
        config.ConnectionStrings
        connStrings.SectionInformation.ProtectSection(provider)
        connStrings.SectionInformation.ForceSave = True
        config.Save(ConfigurationSaveMode.Full)
    End Sub

    Private Sub DecryptConnectionString()
        ' Get the configuration file
        Dim config As System.Configuration.Configuration = _
        ConfigurationManager.OpenExeConfiguration(ConfigurationUserLevel.None)

        ' Decrypt the ConnectionStrings
        Dim connStrings As ConfigurationSection = _
        config.ConnectionStrings
        connStrings.SectionInformation.UnprotectSection()
        connStrings.SectionInformation.ForceSave = True
        config.Save(ConfigurationSaveMode.Full)
    End Sub

    Private Sub EncryptButton_Click(ByVal sender As System.Object, ByVal e As
System.EventArgs) Handles EncryptButton.Click
        EncryptConnectionString()
    End Sub

    Private Sub DecryptButton_Click(ByVal sender As System.Object, ByVal e As
System.EventArgs) Handles DecryptButton.Click
        DecryptConnectionString()
```

```
    End Sub
End Class

// C#
using System;
using System.Collections.Generic;
using System.ComponentModel;
using System.Data;
using System.Drawing;
using System.Text;
using System.Windows.Forms;
using System.Configuration;

namespace SecuringConnectionsCS
{
    public partial class Form1 : Form
    {
        public Form1()
        {
            InitializeComponent();
        }

        private void EncryptConnectionString()
        {
            // Get the configuration file
            System.Configuration.Configuration config =
ConfigurationManager.OpenExeConfiguration(ConfigurationUserLevel.None);

            // Create the provider name
            string provider = "DataProtectionConfigurationProvider";

            //Encrypt the connectionStrings
            ConfigurationSection connstrings = config.ConnectionStrings;
            connstrings.SectionInformation.ProtectSection(provider);
            connstrings.SectionInformation.ForceSave = true;
            config.Save(ConfigurationSaveMode.Full);
        }

        private void DecryptConnectionString()
        {
            //Get the configuration file
            System.Configuration.Configuration config =
ConfigurationManager.OpenExeConfiguration(ConfigurationUserLevel.None);

            // Decrypt the connectionStrings
            ConfigurationSection connstrings = config.ConnectionStrings;
            connstrings.SectionInformation.UnprotectSection();
            connstrings.SectionInformation.ForceSave = True;
            config.Save(ConfigurationSaveMode.Full);
        }

        private void EncryptButton_Click(object sender, EventArgs e)
        {
```

```
            EncryptConnectionString();
        }

        private void DecryptButton_Click(object sender, EventArgs e)
        {
            DecryptConnectionString();
        }
    }
}
```

7. Run the application and click the Encrypt button.

8. While the application is running, navigate to the project's folder and locate the configuration file (SecuringConnectionStrings.vshost.exe.config).

9. Open the file and verify that the *ConnectionStrings* section is encrypted.

10. Now go back to the form and click the Decrypt button.

11. Reopen the .config file and notice that the connection string has reverted back to plain text.

Lesson Summary

■ Windows Authentication (also called Integrated Security) is the suggested method for connecting to data securely.

■ Store connection strings that contain sensitive information in the application configuration file and encrypt all settings that contain confidential information.

Lesson Review

The following questions are intended to reinforce key information presented in this lesson. The questions are also available on the companion CD if you prefer to review them in electronic form.

NOTE Answers

Answers to these questions and explanations of why each choice is right or wrong are located in the "Answers" section at the end of this book.

---

1. What is the connection string's key/value pair for using Windows Authentication in SQL Server 2000 and SQL Server 2005? (Choose all that apply.)

    A. *Integrated security = yes*

    B. *Integrated Security =SSPI*

    C. *Integrated Security = True*

    D. *Trusted_Connection = Yes*

2. If you must use a user name and password to connect to a database, where should you store the sensitive information?

    A. Compiled in the application

    B. In an encrypted application configuration file

    C. In a resource file deployed with the application

    D. In the registry

3. What is the recommended method for securing sensitive connection string information?

    A. Encrypting the data in the application configuration file

    B. Using a code obfuscator

    C. Using integrated security (Windows Authentication)

    D. Querying the user for his or her credentials at run time

Chapter Review

To further practice and reinforce the skills you learned in this chapter, you can perform the following tasks:

- Review the chapter summary.
- Complete the case scenarios. These scenarios set up real-world situations involving the topics of this chapter and ask you to create a solution.
- Complete the additional practices.
- Take a practice test.

Chapter Summary

- Connection objects are created by setting a valid connection string and enabling communication between your application and a data source. ADO.NET provides four primary connection objects that can be used to connect to almost any standard database.
- Connection objects contain several properties, methods, and events that are used for opening and closing connections to a data source, providing information regarding the current state of the connection and surfacing warnings and informational messages from a data source.
- Connection objects enable connection pooling by default. By setting connection–pooling specific connection string keywords, you can control how connections interact with the connection pool.
- By wrapping connection calls in a try-catch block, you can process errors returned from SQL Server by using the *SqlException* and *SqlError* classes.
- By using Windows Authentication and application configuration files, you can protect sensitive information such as passwords in your programs.

Key Terms

Do you know what these key terms mean? You can check your answers by looking up the terms in the glossary at the end of the book.

- connection object
- connection string

- connection pool
- encryption
- integrated security

Case Scenarios

In the following case scenarios, you will apply what you've learned about configuring connections and connecting to data. You can find answers to these questions in the "Answers" section at the end of this book.

Case Scenario 1: Troubleshooting a SQL Connection

You just landed a sweet job at the Alpine Ski House and have been assigned to maintain the application that keeps track of inventory in the ski rental hut. The client application connects to a SQL Server database where the inventory data is stored. You decide to test the application before the season begins, and the first time you run the application and try to check inventory, you get an unhandled exception originating from the SQL server.

How can you modify the application so that users can better identify and troubleshoot connection problems?

Case Scenario 2: Securing Sensitive Data

You are working as an application developer at Contoso Pharmaceuticals and have been tasked with rewriting their in-house research and development application. The first thing you notice is that they store user name and password information in plain text within the application code base.

Create a list of suggested remedies to present to upper management.

Suggested Practices

To gain further knowledge on the subject of working with connections, complete the following practices.

- **Practice 1**   Create an application that targets different databases, which can be selected when the application starts.
- **Practice 2**   Design a reusable block of code that can be used to handle SQL Server errors of any severity.

■ **Practice 3**   Create a component that writes to a log every time a connection to a database is opened.

Take a Practice Test

The practice tests on this book's companion CD offer many options. For example, you can test yourself on just the content covered in this chapter, or you can test yourself on all the 70-526 certification exam content. You can set up the test so that it closely simulates the experience of taking a certification exam, or you can set it up in study mode so that you can look at the correct answers and explanations after you answer each question.

MORE INFO   **Practice tests**

For details about all the practice test options available, see the "How to Use the Practice Tests" section in this book's Introduction.

Chapter 6
Working with Data in a Connected Environment

This chapter describes how to use *Command* objects to execute SQL statements, call stored procedures, and perform catalog operations against a database from within your applications. In addition to describing how to execute commands, we will provide details about using the *DataReader* object that provides access to the data returned from the database when executing commands.

Exam objectives in this chapter:

- Create, add, delete, and edit data in a connected environment.
    - ❏ Retrieve data by using a *DataReader* object.
    - ❏ Build SQL commands in Server Explorer.
    - ❏ Build SQL commands in code.
    - ❏ Create parameters for a *Command* object.
    - ❏ Perform database operations by using a *Command* object.
    - ❏ Retrieve data from a database by using a *Command* object.
    - ❏ Perform asynchronous operations by using a *Command* object.
    - ❏ Perform bulk copy operations.
    - ❏ Store and retrieve binary large object (BLOB) data types in a database.
- Manage connections and transactions.
    - ❏ Perform transactions by using the *Transaction* object.

Lessons in this chapter:

Before You Begin

To complete the lessons in this chapter, you must have:

■ A computer that meets or exceeds the minimum hardware requirements listed in the "Introduction" at the beginning of the book.

■ Microsoft Visual Studio 2005 Professional Edition installed on your computer.

■ An understanding of Microsoft Visual Basic or C# syntax and familiarity with the Microsoft .NET Framework.

■ Available data sources, including Microsoft SQL Server (SQL Server Express Edition is acceptable), the Northwind Traders sample database for SQL Server, and the Nwind.mdb Microsoft Office Access database file.

■ A basic understanding of relational databases.

■ Completed the exercises or understood the concepts presented in Chapter 5, "Configuring Connections and Connecting to Data."

Real World

Steve Stein

When I originally set out to learn how to program data access applications in the first version of ADO.NET, I struggled to understand the relationships between the many different objects in the *System.Data* namespace. I later realized that I was trying to understand the more complex *DataSet* and *DataAdapter* objects without establishing a foundation of knowledge regarding the underlying objects that the *DataSet* and *DataAdapter* are made up of—specifically, the *Connection*, *Command*, and *Parameter* objects. A solid understanding of working with these data infrastructure objects allowed me to truly understand the inner workings of the more complex objects that you typically use in most Microsoft Windows applications.

Lesson 1: Creating and Executing *Command* Objects

This lesson describes how to execute SQL statements, call stored procedures, and perform catalog operations (for example, creating database objects such as tables and stored procedures) against a database using *Command* objects. This lesson will also explain how to use the *DataReader* object that will contain the data returned from executing commands and how to iterate through the *DataReader* and access the returned data.

After this lesson, you will be able to:

- Build SQL commands in code.
- Perform database operations by using the *Command* object.
- Perform asynchronous operations using the *Command* object.
- Retrieve data from a database by using a *Command* object.
- Retrieve data by using a *DataReader* object.

Estimated lesson time: 60 minutes

What Are *Command* Objects?

To execute SQL statements and stored procedures against a database (from your application), you use *Command* objects. *Command* objects contain the necessary information to execute SQL statements, stored procedures, functions, and so on against a data source; return data to your application; and perform database catalog operations such as creating, altering, and deleting database objects. In other words, you can use *Command* objects to execute any valid SQL statement.

NOTE   SQL Statements and Stored Procedures

SQL (which means Structured Query Language) statements are the actual commands that are sent to a SQL Server when executing commands. Commands can be run that manipulate data or change the definition of the database itself. Stored procedures are SQL statements that are saved in the database and can be reused and executed when necessary. If you find yourself continuously running the same SQL command (or the same set or batch of SQL commands) you might want to consider creating some stored procedures to simplify your data access logic.

Just like *Connection* objects, there are *Command* objects for each of the .NET Framework Data Providers. Select the specific *Command* object that coincides with the .NET Framework Data Provider being used to communicate with your data source. If you are using the .NET Framework Data Provider for SQL Server, you would use a *SqlCommand* object; similarly, if you are using the .NET Framework Data Provider for OLE DB, you would use an *OleDbCommand* object.

The primary properties of a *Command* object are the *CommandText*, *CommandType*, and *Connection* properties. Set the *CommandType* property to a value representing the command you want to execute against the data source. For example, to execute a standard SQL statement, set the *CommandType* property to *Text* (*SqlCommand.CommandType* = *CommandType.Text*) and then set the *CommandText* property to a string representing the SQL statement you want to run. To execute a stored procedure, set the *CommandType* property to *StoredProcedure* (*SqlCommand.CommandType* = *CommandType.StoredProcedure*) and then set the *CommandText* property to the name of the stored procedure. Additionally, you can configure *Command* objects to execute asynchronously or within a specific transaction context.

Table 6-1 lists the primary .NET Framework Data Provider *Command* objects available in ADO.NET and the data sources they are designed to access.

Table 6-1   *Command* Objects

Name	Data Target Source
SqlCommand	SQL Server 2000 and SQL Server 2005 databases
OleDbCommand	OLE DB data sources (such as Access databases via Jet 4.0)
OdbcCommand	Open database connectivity (ODBC) data sources such as a Data Source Name (DSN) as defined in the ODBC Data Source Administrator dialog box
OracleCommand	Oracle 7.3, 8i, or 9i databases

Table 6-2 lists the common properties for the .NET Framework Data Provider *Command* objects.

Table 6-2   Common *Command* Object Properties

Name	Description
CommandText	Set this to any valid SQL statement or the name of any valid stored procedure. The *CommandType* value determines the manner of execution (see the following).

Table 6-2 Common *Command* Object Properties

Name	Description
CommandTimeout	The time in seconds before terminating the attempt to execute a command.
CommandType	Typically set to either *Text* (execute the *CommandText* as a SQL statement) or *StoredProcedure* (execute the stored procedure set in the *CommandText* property).
Connection	Set this to the connection object this command should use.
Parameters	The commands parameters collection. When running parameterized queries or stored procedures, you must add parameter objects to this collection.
Transaction	The *SqlTransaction* within which the *SqlCommand* executes.

Table 6-3 lists the common methods for the .NET Framework Data Provider *Command* objects.

Table 6-3 Common *Command* Object Methods

Name	Description
Cancel	Tries to cancel the execution of the command.
ExecuteNonQuery	Executes SQL statements or stored procedures that do not return data.
ExecuteReader	Executes commands that return tabular (or rows) of data.
ExecuteScalar	Executes SQL statements or stored procedures that return a single value. If you call *ExecuteScalar* with a statement that returns rows of data, the query executes but returns only the first column of the first row returned by the query. Additional columns or rows are ignored.
ExecuteXMLReader	Returns XML formatted data. Returns a *System.Xml.XmlReader* object.

Table 6-4 lists the common events for .NET Framework Data Provider *Command* objects.

Table 6-4 Common *Command* Object Events

Name	Description
Disposed	Fires when the command is disposed.
StatementCompleted (*SqlCommand* only)	Occurs when a SQL statement completes.

Creating and Configuring *Command* Objects

Create *Command* objects by declaring an instance of the desired *Command* object and setting the *CommandType* and *CommandText* properties. To execute the command, you must also set the command's *Connection* property to a valid *Connection* object.

Creating a *Command* Object That Executes a SQL Statement

To execute commands that run SQL statements against a database, set the *CommandType* property to *Text* and set the *CommandText* property to the SQL statement you want to execute.

The following code shows how to instantiate a *Command* object that executes a SELECT query that returns all customers in the Northwind Traders sample database:

```
' VB
Dim CustomersCommand As New SqlCommand
CustomersCommand.Connection = NorthwindConnection
CustomersCommand.CommandType = CommandType.Text
CustomersCommand.CommandText = "SELECT CustomerID, CompanyName FROM Customers"
```

```
// C#
SqlCommand CustomersCommand = new SqlCommand();
CustomersCommand.Connection = NorthwindConnection;
CustomersCommand.CommandType = CommandType.Text;
CustomersCommand.CommandText = "SELECT CustomerID, CompanyName FROM Customers";
```

Creating a *Command* Object That Executes a Stored Procedure

To execute commands that run existing stored procedures in a database, set the *CommandType* property to *StoredProcedure* and set the *CommandText* property to the name of the stored procedure you want to execute.

The following code shows how to instantiate a *Command* object that executes a stored procedure named "Ten Most Expensive Products" in the Northwind Traders sample database:

```vb
' VB
Dim TopTenCommand As New SqlCommand
TopTenCommand.Connection = NorthwindConnection
TopTenCommand.CommandType = CommandType.StoredProcedure
TopTenCommand.CommandText = "Ten Most Expensive Products"
```

```csharp
// C#
SqlCommand TopTenCommand = new SqlCommand();
TopTenCommand.Connection = NorthwindConnection;
TopTenCommand.CommandType = CommandType.StoredProcedure;
TopTenCommand.CommandText = "Ten Most Expensive Products";
```

Creating a *Command* Object That Performs Catalog Operations

To execute commands that run DML actions (Data Manipulation Language), create commands that run SQL statements and call the *ExecuteNonQuery* method of the command. For example, to create a new table in a database using a *Command* object, you can use code similar to the following:

```vb
' VB
Dim CreateTableCommand As New SqlCommand

CreateTableCommand.Connection = NorthwindConnection
CreateTableCommand.CommandType = CommandType.Text
CreateTableCommand.CommandText = "CREATE TABLE SalesPersons (" & _
            "[SalesPersonID] [int] IDENTITY(1,1) NOT NULL, " & _
            "[FirstName] [nvarchar](50)  NULL, " & _
            "[LastName] [nvarchar](50)  NULL)"
```

```csharp
// C#
SqlCommand CreateTableCommand = new SqlCommand();

CreateTableCommand.Connection = NorthwindConnection;
CreateTableCommand.CommandType = CommandType.Text;
CreateTableCommand.CommandText = "CREATE TABLE SalesPersons (" +
            "[SalesPersonID] [int] IDENTITY(1,1) NOT NULL, " +
            "[FirstName] [nvarchar](50)  NULL, " +
            "[LastName] [nvarchar](50)  NULL)";
```

Creating a *Command* Object That Returns a Single Value

To execute commands that return single values (scalar values), create commands that run SQL statements or stored procedures that return a single value (as opposed to commands that return rows or tabular data). Set the *CommandText* property to a SQL statement or stored procedure that returns a single value and call the *ExecuteScalar* method of the command. Declare a variable with the data type of the single value being returned from the database and cast the results of the *ExecuteScalar* call to the expected data type. (The *ExecuteScalar* method returns an *Object*, so you must cast the *ExecuteScalar* method to the equivalent of the returned data type.) In the following example, the SQL statement returns an Integer, so you cast the *ExecuteScalar* call to an Integer, but you must cast the *ExecuteScalar* call to the specific type that your command returns.

For example, to return the results of a SQL statement that runs an aggregate function (such as the count of customers), use code similar to the following:

```vb
' VB
Dim ExecuteScalarCommand As New SqlCommand
ExecuteScalarCommand.Connection = NorthwindConnection
ExecuteScalarCommand.CommandType = CommandType.Text
ExecuteScalarCommand.CommandText = "SELECT Count(*) FROM Customers"

' Open the connection and execute the command
ExecuteScalarCommand.Connection.Open()
Dim CustomerCount As Integer = CInt(ExecuteScalarCommand.ExecuteScalar)
MessageBox.Show("There are " & CustomerCount.ToString & " customers")
ExecuteScalarCommand.Connection.Close()
```

```csharp
// C#
SqlCommand ExecuteScalarCommand = new SqlCommand();
ExecuteScalarCommand.Connection = NorthwindConnection;
ExecuteScalarCommand.CommandType = CommandType.Text;
ExecuteScalarCommand.CommandText = "SELECT Count(*) FROM Customers";

// Open the connection and execute the command
ExecuteScalarCommand.Connection.Open();
int CustomerCount = (int)ExecuteScalarCommand.ExecuteScalar();
MessageBox.Show("There are " + CustomerCount.ToString() + " customers");
ExecuteScalarCommand.Connection.Close();
```

In the preceding example, when the command is executed, the value returned from the database is assigned to the *CustomerCount* variable and displayed in a message box for verification.

Creating a *Command* Object that Returns XML Data

You can also execute commands that return data formatted as XML. To execute commands that return XML data, create commands that run SQL statements that return

XML or retrieve existing XML-formatted data from your database. Set the *CommandText* property to a SQL statement that returns XML and call the *ExecuteXMLReader* method of the command. Calling the *ExecuteXMLReader* method returns a *System.Xml.XmlReader* object, which is similar to a data reader except that it is specifically for accessing XML-formatted data.

For example, to return the results of a SQL statement as well-formed XML, use code similar to the following:

```vb
' VB
Dim ExecuteXMLCommand As New SqlCommand
ExecuteXMLCommand.Connection = NorthwindConnection
ExecuteXMLCommand.CommandType = CommandType.Text

' Add the For XML Auto clause to return the data As well formed XML
ExecuteXMLCommand.CommandText = "SELECT CustomerID FROM Customers For XML Auto"

ExecuteXMLCommand.Connection.Open()
Dim reader As System.Xml.XmlReader = ExecuteXMLCommand.ExecuteXmlReader
' Add code here to iterate through the XMLReader
reader.Close()
ExecuteXMLCommand.Connection.Close()
```

```csharp
// C#
SqlCommand ExecuteXMLCommand = new SqlCommand();
ExecuteXMLCommand.Connection = NorthwindConnection;
ExecuteXMLCommand.CommandType = CommandType.Text;

// Add the For XML Auto clause to return the data as well formed XML
ExecuteXMLCommand.CommandText = "SELECT CustomerID FROM Customers For XML Auto";

ExecuteXMLCommand.Connection.Open();
System.Xml.XmlReader reader = ExecuteXMLCommand.ExecuteXmlReader();
// Add code here to iterate through the XMLReader;
reader.Close();
ExecuteXMLCommand.Connection.Close();
```

Creating SQL Commands (SQL Statements) with the Query Designer

When configuring command objects, you can use the Query Designer to assist in creating SQL statements for your *Command* objects to execute against the database.

To create queries with the Query Designer select a database in Server Explorer and select New Query from the Data menu. The Query Designer opens, presenting a list of available objects (tables, views, etc.) in the database to which you can add your query.

After adding the tables and selecting columns, you can customize the query by adding sorting and filtering for desired columns. Additional commands as well as the command to run the query are available on the QueryDesigner menu.

Performing Database Operations Using *Command* Objects

After configuring a *Command* object with the SQL statement or stored procedure you want to run, you must then explicitly execute the command to return data from the database. A couple of the preceding code examples showed a glimpse of how to call some of the available execute methods of a command. Let's look in a bit more depth at all the available methods of executing commands.

Each .NET Framework Data Provider *Command* object exposes three main execution methods that can be used to return data, update data, call stored procedures and functions, and so on, or perform catalog operations such as executing data definition language (DDL) commands against a data source.

Table 6-5 describes the available execution methods for the .NET Framework Data Providers.

NOTE   Asynchronous methods

Additional methods for executing asynchronous commands will be explained later in this chapter.

Table 6-5   *Command* Object Execution Methods

Method	Description
ExecuteReader	Use this method when running SQL statements or stored procedures that return tabular data (rows of data).
ExecuteScalar	Use this method when running SQL statements that return a single value.
ExecuteNonQuery	Use this method when performing catalog operations such as creating database objects, running stored procedures that do not return data, or performing Insert, Update, and Delete statements when you do not need to return data.
ExecuteXmlReader (*SqlCommand* only)	Use this method to run SQL statements or stored procedures that return data formatted as XML.

Quick Check

1. What *CommandType* setting do you use to execute a SQL statement that creates a new table in a database?

2. What data type is returned when calling the *ExecuteScalar* method of a command?

3. What are the three main properties you must set to execute a *Command* object?

Quick Check Answers

1. You set the *CommandType* to *CommandType.Text* because you set the *CommandText* property to a standard CREATE TABLE SQL statement.

2. *ExecuteScalar* returns an object, which is why you must cast the return value to the type of the data returned.

3. *Connection*, *CommandType*, and *CommandText.*

Executing Commands Asynchronously

In addition to the execution commands listed in Figure 6-2, an additional set of commands are specifically used for asynchronous calls to a database. Executing commands asynchronously is the process of having the command execute on a separate thread from the rest of your application so users do not have to wait for the command to complete before continuing work in other parts of the application. For example, commands that are not executed asynchronously can cause your form to "freeze" until the command has completed. You might want to execute commands asynchronously when you know the execution will take some time and you need to perform other tasks in your application while waiting for the command to complete.

Table 6-6 provides a list of *Command* object methods that are used for asynchronous execution.

Table 6-6   Asynchronous Specific *Command* Object Methods

Method	Description
BeginExecuteNonQuery	Starts the asynchronous version of the *ExecuteNonQuery* method.

Table 6-6 Asynchronous Specific *Command* Object Methods

Method	Description
BeginExecuteReader	Starts the asynchronous version of the *ExecuteReader* method.
BeginExecuteXmlReader	Starts the asynchronous version of the *ExecuteXmlReader* method.
EndExecuteNonQuery	Call this method after the *StatementComplete* event fires to complete execution of the command.
EndExecuteReader	Call this method after the *StatementComplete* event fires to return the *DataReader* with the data returned by the command.
EndExecuteXMLReader	Call this method after the *StatementComplete* event fires to return the *XmlReader* with the data returned by the command.

When executing commands asynchronously, you explicitly call the *Begin* and *End* methods of the selected *Command* object. Calling the *Begin* method sends the command (SQL statement or stored procedure call) to the database, and then you can perform other operations in your application. When the command finishes executing, the *StatementCompleted* event fires, notifying the application that it can call the *End* method of the command and access the data for further processing.

The following code shows how you can continue processing even while a command is in the process of executing:

```
'VB
Dim results As New System.Text.StringBuilder

Dim NorthWindConnection As New SqlConnection("Data Source=.\;Initial Catalog=Northwind;" & _
    Integrated Security=True; asynchronous processing = true")
Dim command1 As New SqlCommand("WAITFOR DELAY '00:00:05'; " & _
    Select * From [Order Details]", NorthWindConnection)

NorthWindConnection.Open()
Dim r As IAsyncResult = command1.BeginExecuteReader

MessageBox.Show("The command has been executed but processing is free to display" & _
    " this message before the results have been returned!")

Dim reader As SqlDataReader = command1.EndExecuteReader(r)
```

```
While reader.Read
    For i As Integer = 0 To reader.FieldCount - 1
        results.Append(reader(i).ToString & vbTab)
    Next
    results.Append(Environment.NewLine)
End While

reader.Close()
command1.Connection.Close()
MessageBox.Show(results.ToString)

// C#
System.Text.StringBuilder results = new System.Text.StringBuilder();
SqlConnection NorthWindConnection = new SqlConnection("Data Source=.\\;Initial
Catalog=Northwind;" +
    "Integrated Security=True; asynchronous processing = true");
SqlCommand command1 = new SqlCommand("WAITFOR DELAY '00:00:05'; " +
    Select * From [Order Details]", NorthWindConnection);
NorthWindConnection.Open();
IAsyncResult r  = command1.BeginExecuteReader();

MessageBox.Show("The command has been executed but processing is free " +
    "to display this message before the results have been returned!");

SqlDataReader reader =  command1.EndExecuteReader(r);
while (reader.Read())
{
    for (int i = 0; i< reader.FieldCount - 1; i++)
    {
        results.Append(reader[i].ToString() + "\t");
    }
    results.Append(Environment.NewLine);
}

reader.Close();
command1.Connection.Close();
MessageBox.Show(results.ToString());
```

Executing Multiple SQL Statements Using a *DataReader*

In addition to returning the results from a single SQL statement, you can use a *Command* object and *DataReader* to return the results of multiple SQL statements. To execute more than one SQL statement, set the *CommandText* property of a *Command* object to multiple SQL statements separated by semicolons (;). After calling the *ExecuteReader* method, the *DataReader* will hold the number of result sets equal to the number of SQL statements executed. To access the data returned by the additional statements, call the *NextResult* method of the *DataReader*.

For example, the following code creates a *SqlCommand* and sets it to call two separate SQL statements that return data from different tables. To access the additional data, check the value of the *DataReader.NextResult* method. If it returns *True*, there is another result set in the reader; if it returns *False*, the reader is done.

NOTE   Updating a Previous Exercise

You can modify the code in the *ExecuteSqlButton* event handler with the following example to try out returning multiple result sets.

```vb
' VB
ExecuteSqlCommand.CommandText = "SELECT CustomerID, CompanyName" _
    & "FROM Customers; SELECT ProductName, UnitsInStock FROM Products"
Dim reader As SqlDataReader = ExecuteSqlCommand.ExecuteReader

Dim MoreResults As Boolean = True

Do While MoreResults
    While reader.Read
        For i As Integer = 0 To reader.FieldCount - 1
            results.Append(reader(i).ToString & vbTab)
        Next
        results.Append(Environment.NewLine)
    End While
    MoreResults = reader.NextResult()
Loop
```

```csharp
// C#
ExecuteSqlCommand.CommandText = "SELECT CustomerID, CompanyName FROM " +
    "Customers; SELECT ProductName, UnitsInStock FROM Products";
SqlDataReader reader = ExecuteSqlCommand.ExecuteReader();

bool MoreResults = false;

do
{
    while (reader.Read())
    {
        for (int i = 0; i < reader.FieldCount; i++)
        {
            results.Append(reader[i].ToString() + "\t");
        }
        results.Append(Environment.NewLine);
    }
    MoreResults = reader.NextResult();
} while (MoreResults);
```

Lab: Executing SQL Statements and Calling Stored Procedures

In this lab you will use *Command* objects to execute SQL statements and stored procedures as well as using *DataReaders* to iterate through the returned data.

▶ **Exercise 1: Executing SQL Statements and Calling Stored Procedures**

Let's create a Windows application and demonstrate creating commands and executing the many types of queries, stored procedures, and functions that would be used in a real-world data application.

1. Create a Windows application and name it **ExecutingCommands**.

2. Add a TextBox to Form1 and set the following properties:

   ❏ *Name* = ResultsTextBox

   ❏ *MultiLine* = True

   ❏ *ScrollBars* = Both

3. Add a button below the TextBox and set the following properties:

   ❏ *Name* = ExecuteSqlButton

   ❏ *Text* = Execute SQL

4. Add a second button and set the following properties:

   ❏ *Name* = ExecuteSprocButton

   ❏ *Text* = Execute Sproc

5. Add a third button and set the following properties:

   ❏ *Name* = CreateTableButton

   ❏ *Text* = Create Table

   Arrange the controls so they appear similar to Figure 6-1.

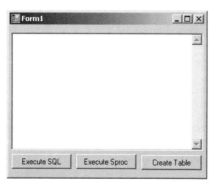

Figure 6-1   Form with controls arranged in preparation for executing command objects

Now let's write some code and implement functionality to execute a command that runs a simple SQL SELECT statement and populates the textbox with a list of *CustomerID* and *CompanyName* values from the Northwind Traders customers table. Remember from the preceding table that, when running SQL statements, you need to call the *ExecuteReader* method of the *Command* object. Calling the *ExecuteReader* method returns a *DataReader* object to access the data returned by the SQL statement. The *DataReader* represents a read-only stream of rows that must be read sequentially while moving through the reader. In other words, once the reader is returned, all you can do is read the data out of it until the reader is empty, and then you close and dispose of the reader.

6. Double-click the Execute SQL button to create the button-click event handler and switch to code view.

7. Add the following code to the *Form1* class to set *Option Strict* on, add a reference to the *SqlClient* namespace, and create a form-scoped connection to the Northwind Traders database.

NOTE   Northwind Connection String

Replace the *NorthwindConnection* with a valid connection string to the Northwind Traders database.

```vb
' VB
Imports System.Data
Imports System.Data.SqlClient

Public Class Form1
    Private NorthwindConnection As New SqlConnection _
        ("Data Source=<ValidServerName>;Initial Catalog=Northwind;Integrated
Security=True")

    Private Sub ExecuteSqlButton_Click _
        (ByVal sender As System.Object, ByVal e As System.EventArgs) _
        Handles ExecuteSqlButton.Click
    End Sub
End Class

// C#
using System;
using System.Collections.Generic;
using System.ComponentModel;
using System.Data;
using System.Drawing;
using System.Text;
using System.Windows.Forms;
using System.Data.SqlClient;
```

```
namespace ExecutingCommands
{
    public partial class Form1 : Form
    {
        private SqlConnection NorthwindConnection = new SqlConnection
            ("Data Source=.\\sqlexpress;Initial Catalog=Northwind;Integrated
Security=True");
    }
}
```

8. Add the following code to the *ExecuteSqlButton_Click* event handler:

```vb
' VB
' Create a StringBuilder to store the results of the query
Dim results As New System.Text.StringBuilder

' Create an instance of the Command object
Dim ExecuteSqlCommand As New SqlCommand

' Set the command's connection to the Northwind database
ExecuteSqlCommand.Connection = NorthwindConnection

' Executing SQL statements uses CommandType = Text
ExecuteSqlCommand.CommandType = CommandType.Text

' The CommandText is set to the SQL statement we want to run
ExecuteSqlCommand.CommandText = "SELECT CustomerID, CompanyName FROM Customers"

' You must open the connection before executing the command
ExecuteSqlCommand.Connection.Open()

' Assign the results of the SQL statement to a data reader
Dim reader As SqlDataReader = ExecuteSqlCommand.ExecuteReader

While reader.Read
    For i As Integer = 0 To reader.FieldCount - 1
        results.Append(reader(i).ToString & vbTab)
    Next
    results.Append(Environment.NewLine)
End While

' Close the data reader and the connection
reader.Close()
ExecuteSqlCommand.Connection.Close()

ResultsTextBox.Text = results.ToString
```

```csharp
// C#
//Create a StringBuilder to store the results of the query
System.Text.StringBuilder results = new System.Text.StringBuilder();

// Create an instance of the Command object
SqlCommand ExecuteSqlCommand = new SqlCommand();
```

```
// Set the command's connection to the Northwind database
ExecuteSqlCommand.Connection = NorthwindConnection;

// Executing SQL statements uses CommandType = Text
ExecuteSqlCommand.CommandType = CommandType.Text;

// The CommandText is set to the SQL statement we want to run
ExecuteSqlCommand.CommandText = "SELECT CustomerID, CompanyName FROM Customers";

// You must open the connection before executing the command
ExecuteSqlCommand.Connection.Open();

// Assign the results of the SQL statement to a data reader
SqlDataReader reader = ExecuteSqlCommand.ExecuteReader();

while (reader.Read())
{
    for (int i = 0; i < reader.FieldCount; i++)
    {
        results.Append(reader[i].ToString() + "\t");
    }
    results.Append(Environment.NewLine);
}

// Close the data reader and the connection
reader.Close();
ExecuteSqlCommand.Connection.Close();

ResultsTextBox.Text = results.ToString();
```

9. Run the application and click the Execute SQL button (see Figure 6-2).

Figure 6-2 Form displaying data after executing the SQL command

Now write some code and implement functionality to execute a command that runs a stored procedure. Notice that the execution methods in the preceding table show that when running stored procedures that return rows, you still call the *ExecuteReader* method of the *Command* object.

10. Double-click the Execute Sproc button to create the button-click event handler and switch to code view.

    For this handler, you will copy and reuse much of the code from the foregoing example. Typically, in an efficient production application, you would refactor similar code out into its own method but, for the sake of clarity in this demonstration, just copy the code you want to reuse into the additional button-click event handlers.

    The main difference between calling a standard SQL command and calling a stored procedure is that when calling a stored procedure you set the *CommandType* property to *StoredProcedure* and set the *CommandText* property to the name of the stored procedure. Then you call the *ExecuteReader* method just like executing a SQL statement and iterate through the reader exactly as before.

11. Add the following code to the *ExecuteSprocButton_Click* event handler:

```vb
' VB
Dim results As New System.Text.StringBuilder
Dim ExecuteSprocCommand As New SqlCommand

ExecuteSprocCommand.Connection = NorthwindConnection
ExecuteSprocCommand.CommandType = CommandType.StoredProcedure
ExecuteSprocCommand.CommandText = "Ten Most Expensive Products"

ExecuteSprocCommand.Connection.Open()
Dim reader As SqlDataReader = ExecuteSprocCommand.ExecuteReader

While reader.Read
    For i As Integer = 0 To reader.FieldCount - 1
        results.Append(reader(i).ToString & vbTab)
    Next
    results.Append(Environment.NewLine)
End While

reader.Close()
ExecuteSprocCommand.Connection.Close()

ResultsTextBox.Text = results.ToString
```

```csharp
// C#
System.Text.StringBuilder results = new System.Text.StringBuilder();

SqlCommand ExecuteSprocCommand = new SqlCommand();

ExecuteSprocCommand.Connection = NorthwindConnection;
ExecuteSprocCommand.CommandType = CommandType.StoredProcedure;
ExecuteSprocCommand.CommandText = "Ten Most Expensive Products";

ExecuteSprocCommand.Connection.Open();
```

```
SqlDataReader reader = ExecuteSprocCommand.ExecuteReader();

while (reader.Read())
{
    for (int i = 0; i<reader.FieldCount;i++)
    {
        results.Append(reader[i].ToString() + "\t");
    }
    results.Append(Environment.NewLine);
}
reader.Close();
ExecuteSprocCommand.Connection.Close();

ResultsTextBox.Text = results.ToString();
```

Let's add some more functionality by writing some code to perform a catalog operation and execute a command that creates a new table in the database. The execution methods in the preceding table show that performing catalog operations requires the use of the *ExecuteNonQuery* method of the *Command* object. For this method, you do not use a data reader because no data will be returned by the command. After creating the table, simply inspect the database in Server Explorer and verify that the command executed successfully.

12. Double-click the Create Table button to create the button-click event handler and switch to code view.

13. Add the following code to the *CreateTableButton_Click* event handler:

```
' VB
Dim CreateTableCommand As New SqlCommand

CreateTableCommand.Connection = NorthwindConnection
CreateTableCommand.CommandType = CommandType.Text
CreateTableCommand.CommandText = "CREATE TABLE SalesPersons (" & _
            "[SalesPersonID] [int] IDENTITY(1,1) NOT NULL, " & _
            "[FirstName] [nvarchar](50)  NULL, " & _
            "[LastName] [nvarchar](50)  NULL)"

CreateTableCommand.Connection.Open()
CreateTableCommand.ExecuteNonQuery()
CreateTableCommand.Connection.Close()

// C#
SqlCommand CreateTableCommand = new SqlCommand();

CreateTableCommand.Connection = NorthwindConnection;
CreateTableCommand.CommandType = CommandType.Text;
CreateTableCommand.CommandText = "CREATE TABLE SalesPersons (" +
"[SalesPersonID] [int] IDENTITY(1,1) NOT NULL, " +
"[FirstName] [nvarchar](50)  NULL, " +
"[LastName] [nvarchar](50)  NULL)";
```

```
CreateTableCommand.Connection.Open();
CreateTableCommand.ExecuteNonQuery();
CreateTableCommand.Connection.Close();
```

14. Run the application and click the Create Table button. Navigate to Server Explorer and refresh the *Tables* node of the Northwind Traders database. Verify the existence of the new SalesPersons table.

Lesson Summary

- *Command* objects are used to execute SQL statements and stored procedures against a database.

- There are specific *Command* objects for each of the .NET Framework Data Providers.

- The *CommandType* property determines whether a command executes a SQL statement or stored procedure.

- Commands can also be used to perform catalog operations on a database.

- Commands can be executed asynchronously.

- *DataReader* objects are created when command execution returns tabular data.

Lesson Review

The following questions are intended to reinforce key information presented in this lesson. The questions are also available on the companion CD if you prefer to review them in electronic form.

NOTE   Answers

Answers to these questions and explanations of why each choice is right or wrong are located in the "Answers" section at the end of the book.

---

1. What are the *Command* object property settings to execute a stored procedure? (Choose all that apply.)

   A. *CommandType* = Text, *CommandText* = stored procedure name

   B. *CommandType* = Text, *CommandText* = SQL syntax to execute the stored procedure

   C. *CommandType* = *StoredProcedure*, *CommandText* = SQL syntax to execute the stored procedure

   D. *CommandType* = *StoredProcedure*, *CommandText* = stored procedure name

2. What should you do to access the returned tabular data after starting execution of a command that runs asynchronously? (Choose all that apply.)

   A. Call the *EndExecuteNonQuery* method.

   B. Call the *EndExecuteReader* method.

   C. Wait for the *StatementCompleted* event to fire and iterate through the *DataReader*.

   D. Wait for the *StatementCompleted* event to fire, call the *EndExecuteReader* method, and then iterate through the *DataReader*.

3. How do you execute multiple SQL statements using a *DataReader*?

   A. Call the *ExecuteReader* method of two *Command* objects and assign the results to the same instance of a *DataReader*.

   B. Call the *ExecuteReader* method of a single *Command* object twice.

   C. Set the *Command.CommandText* property to multiple SQL statements delimited by a semicolon.

   D. Set the *Command.CommandType* property to multiple result sets.

Lesson 2: Working with Parameters in SQL Commands

This lesson describes how to create parameters in *Command* objects. It explains how to add parameters to SQL statements and stored procedures, and it explains how to assign values to parameters that are passed to the data source as well as how to read parameter values that are returned from the data source.

After this lesson, you will be able to:

■ Create parameters for a *Command* object.

Estimated lesson time: 60 minutes

What Is a Parameter and Why Should I Use Them?

A parameter can be thought of as a type of variable that you can use to pass and return values between your application and a database. Just like a variable in your application, parameters are created to contain a certain data type. Parameter data types are assigned using the types defined in the *System.Data.SqlDbType* enumeration. The *SqlDbType* enumeration contains a list of the types available in SQL Server as opposed to application variables that are typically assigned one of the .NET Framework base data types.

You pass parameter values to SQL statements (and stored procedures) when you want to change the criteria of your queries quickly. A typical use of a parameter is in the WHERE clause of a SQL query. Parameters also allow you to control how user input is entered into a query and virtually eliminates potential SQL injection attacks.

MORE INFO **SQL Parameter Syntax**

SQL Server uses the @ symbol as a prefix to denote named parameters, so syntax like @City in a SQL statement represents a parameter. Other databases (for example, Microsoft Office Access and OLE DB data sources) do not use named parameters but, instead, represent parameters with a question mark (?) symbol. When working with these types of data sources, the order of parameters is used to track what parameter values are used for each parameter.

For example, you can use a parameter to pass in the value for the City column and quickly change the results of your query by changing the value of the parameter. In other words, assigning different values to the parameter and running the query determines the result set that the query will return. The following SQL statements illustrate this:

```
--SQL statement with named parameter
SELECT  CustomerID, CompanyName, City
FROM Customers
WHERE City = @City

--SQL statement with 'unnamed' parameter
SELECT  CustomerID, CompanyName, City
FROM Customers
WHERE City = ?
```

Types of Parameters

When executing *Command* objects, you typically use parameters to send data to the database. This type of parameter is referred to as an *Input* parameter. In addition to *Input* parameters, you might also want to use a parameter to retrieve information coming out of the database; this type of parameter is called an *Output* parameter. There is also a third type of parameter, which is referred to as an *InputOutput* parameter. *InputOutput* parameters are used to both send and receive data when executing a command. The type of parameter is designated in the *Direction* property of the parameter and is assigned a value from the *ParameterDirection* enumeration. In other words, when creating a parameter, you can set its *Direction* property to *Input*, *Output*, *InputOutput*, or *ReturnValue*.

NOTE Default Parameter Direction

Parameters are *Input* parameters by default.

Creating Parameters

Create parameters by declaring an instance of the *Parameter* class and setting its name and data type to coincide with the parameter name and data type expected by the data source. You can also set the parameter's *ParameterDirection* property to choose the type of parameter to create.

The following code creates an *Input* parameter:

```
' VB
Dim TotalCostParameter as New SqlParameter
TotalCostParameter.ParameterName = "@TotalCost"
TotalCostParameter.SqlDbType = SqlDbType.Money

// C#
SqlParameter TotalCostParameter = new SqlParameter();
TotalCostParameter.ParameterName = "@TotalCost";
TotalCostParameter.SqlDbType = SqlDbType.Money;
```

The following code creates an *Output* parameter:

```vb
' VB
Dim TotalCostParameter As New SqlParameter("@TotalCost", SqlDbType.Money)
TotalCostParameter.Direction = ParameterDirection.Output
```

```csharp
// C#
SqlParameter TotalCostParameter = new SqlParameter("@TotalCost", SqlDbType.Money);
TotalCostParameter.Direction = ParameterDirection.Output;
```

Adding Parameters to *Command* Objects

Command objects have a *Parameters* property that represents a collection of parameters for that command (for example, the *SqlParameter.Parameters* property). After you create a parameter, you must add it to the *Parameters* collection of the *Command* object that will execute the SQL statement or stored procedure that uses the parameter.

The following code illustrates how to add a parameter to a *Command* object (assuming the *GetCostCommand* already exists):

```vb
' VB
GetCostCommand.Parameters.Add(TotalCostParameter)
```

```csharp
// C#
GetCostCommand.Parameters.Add(TotalCostParameter);
```

Lab: Working with Parameters

In this lab you practice using parameters in *Command* objects. You will pass parameters to stored procedures as well as SQL statements.

▶ **Exercise 1: Creating and Executing a Parameterized SQL Statement**

For this exercise, create a form that executes a parameterized query by allowing the user to enter a value into a TextBox that will be passed to the database as the parameter in a query.

1. Create a new Windows application and name it **ParameterizedQueries**.

2. Add a TextBox to the form and set the following properties:
   - ❑ *Name* = CityTextBox
   - ❑ *Text* = London

3. Add a second TextBox and set the following properties:
   - ❑ *Name* = ResultsTextBox
   - ❑ *MultiLine* = True

4. Add a button and set the following properties. Now, the form should resemble Figure 6-3:

     ❑ *Name* = ExecuteSqlButton
     ❑ *Text* = Execute SQL

Figure 6-3   Form with controls in preparation for executing the parameterized SQL statement

5. Double-click the Execute SQL button to create the button-click event handler and switch the form to code view.

6. Add references to the *System.Data* and *System.Data.SqlClient* namespaces.

7. Add code to create a connection on the form.

     At this point, your form code should look like the following (substitute a valid connection string for the *NorthwindConnection*):

```vb
' VB
Imports System.Data
Imports System.Data.SqlClient

Public Class Form1
    Private NorthwindConnection As New SqlConnection _
        ("Data Source=<ValidServerName>;Initial Catalog=Northwind;Integrated
Security=True")

    Private Sub ExecuteSqlButton_Click _
        (ByVal sender As System.Object, ByVal e As System.EventArgs) _
        Handles ExecuteSqlButton.Click
    End Sub
End Class
```

```csharp
// C#
using System;
using System.Collections.Generic;
```

```
using System.ComponentModel;
using System.Data;
using System.Drawing;
using System.Text;
using System.Windows.Forms;
using System.Data.SqlClient;

namespace ParameterizedQueries
{
    public partial class Form1 : Form
    {
    private SqlConnection NorthwindConnection = new SqlConnection
      ("Data Source=.\\sqlexpress;Initial Catalog=Northwind;Integrated Security=True");
        public Form1()
        {
            InitializeComponent();
        }

        private void ExecuteSqlButton_Click(object sender, EventArgs e)
        {

        }
    }
}
```

8. Add the following code to the *ExecuteSqlButton_Click* method to create a new command object and set it to the parameterized query:

```
' VB
' Create a new Command object
Dim CustomersByCityCommand As New SqlCommand

' Set the command properties
CustomersByCityCommand.Connection = NorthwindConnection
CustomersByCityCommand.CommandType = CommandType.Text
CustomersByCityCommand.CommandText = & _
"SELECT CustomerID, CompanyName, City " & _
"FROM Customers " & _
"WHERE City = @City"
```

```
// C#
// Create a new Command object
SqlCommand CustomersByCityCommand = new SqlCommand();

// Set the command properties
CustomersByCityCommand.Connection = NorthwindConnection;
CustomersByCityCommand.CommandType = CommandType.Text;
CustomersByCityCommand.CommandText = "SELECT CustomerID, CompanyName, City " +
                                "FROM Customers " +
                                "WHERE City = @City";
```

9. Add the following code below the previous code (but still within the event han-
    dler) to create the parameter and assign it to the command:

```vb
' VB
' Create the @City parameter
Dim CityParameter As New SqlParameter

' Set its name and data type
CityParameter.ParameterName = "@City"
CityParameter.SqlDbType = SqlDbType.NVarChar

' Since the city column in the database allows
' null values we can set the IsNullable property
' to allow null values.
CityParameter.IsNullable = True

' Add the parameter to the Commmand object
CustomersByCityCommand.Parameters.Add(CityParameter)
```

```csharp
// C#
// Create the @City parameter
SqlParameter CityParameter = new SqlParameter();

// Set its name and data type
CityParameter.ParameterName = "@City";
CityParameter.SqlDbType = SqlDbType.NVarChar;

// Since the city column in the database allows
// null values we can set the IsNullable property
// to allow null values.
CityParameter.IsNullable = true;

// Add the parameter to the Commmand object
CustomersByCityCommand.Parameters.Add(CityParameter);
```

10. Now add the following code that will set the value of the parameter to whatever
    is typed into the text box, set the code to run the query, and display the results
    in the ResultsTextBox. (Add this code below the previously added code but con-
    tinue to keep it within the event handler.)

```vb
' VB
' Set the parameters value to the
' the text in the CityTextBox
CityParameter.Value = CityTextBox.Text

' Create a StringBuilder to store the results of the query
Dim results As New System.Text.StringBuilder

' You must open the connection before executing the command
CustomersByCityCommand.Connection.Open()
```

```
' Assign the results of the SQL statement to a data reader
Dim reader As SqlDataReader = CustomersByCityCommand.ExecuteReader

While reader.Read
    For i As Integer = 0 To reader.FieldCount - 1
        results.Append(reader(i).ToString & vbTab)
    Next
    results.Append(Environment.NewLine)
End While

' Close the data reader and the connection
reader.Close()
CustomersByCityCommand.Connection.Close()

ResultsTextBox.Text = results.ToString
```

// C#
```
// Set the parameters value to the
// text in the CityTextBox
CityParameter.Value = CityTextBox.Text;

// Create a StringBuilder to store the results of the query
System.Text.StringBuilder results =new System.Text.StringBuilder();

// You must open the connection before executing the command
CustomersByCityCommand.Connection.Open();

// Assign the results of the SQL statement to a data reader
SqlDataReader reader = CustomersByCityCommand.ExecuteReader();

while (reader.Read())
{
    for (int i=0; i< reader.FieldCount; i++)
    {
        results.Append(reader[i].ToString() + "\t");
    }
    results.Append(Environment.NewLine);
}

// Close the data reader and the connection
reader.Close();
CustomersByCityCommand.Connection.Close();

ResultsTextBox.Text = results.ToString();
```

11. Run the application and click the Execute SQL button. As shown in Figure 6-4, the application displays the command results.

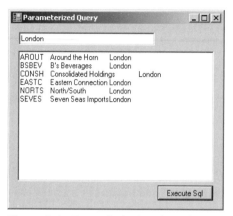

Figure 6-4   Form displaying data after executing the parameterized SQL statement

12. Type Madrid and rerun the query (click the *Execute SQL* button).

13. Verify that the results show only customers from the *City* value passed in to the parameter.

▶ **Exercise 2: Creating and Executing a Parameterized Stored Procedure**

1. Create a new Windows application and name it **ParameterizedStoredProcedure**.

2. Add a TextBox to the form and set the following properties:

   ❑ *Name* = CategoryNameTextBox

   ❑ *Text* = Beverages

3. Add a second TextBox and set the following properties:

   ❑ *Name* = OrdYearTextBox

   ❑ *Text* = 1997

4. Add a third TextBox and set the following properties:

   ❑ *Name* = ResultsTextBox

   ❑ *MultiLine* = True

   ❑ *ScrollBars* = Both

5. Add a button and set the following properties. The form should now resemble Figure 6-5:

   ❑ *Name* = ExecuteStoredProcedureButton

   ❑ *Text* = Execute Stored Procedure

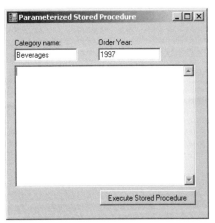

Figure 6-5 Form with controls in preparation for executing the parameterized stored procedure

6. Double-click the Execute Stored Procedure button to create the button-click event handler and switch the form to code view.

7. Add references to the *System.Data* and *System.Data.SqlClient* namespaces.

8. Add code to create a connection on the form.

   At this point, your form code should look like the following (substitute a valid connection string for the *NorthwindConnection*):

```
' VB
Imports System.Data
Imports System.Data.SqlClient

Public Class Form1
    Private NorthwindConnection As New SqlConnection _
        ("Data Source=<ValidServerName>;Initial Catalog=Northwind;Integrated
Security=True")

    Private Sub ExecuteStoredProcedureButton_Click _
        (ByVal sender As System.Object, ByVal e As System.EventArgs) _
        Handles ExecuteStoredProcedureButton.Click

    End Sub
End Class

// C#
using System;
using System.Collections.Generic;
using System.ComponentModel;
using System.Data;
using System.Drawing;
using System.Text;
using System.Windows.Forms;
```

```
using System.Data.SqlClient;

namespace ParameterizedStoredProcedureCS
{
    public partial class Form1 : Form
    {
        public Form1()
        {
            InitializeComponent();
        }
        private SqlConnection NorthwindConnection = new SqlConnection
            ("Data Source=<ValidServerName>;Initial Catalog=Northwind;" +
             "Integrated Security=True");

        private void ExecuteStoredProcedureButton_Click(object sender, EventArgs e)
        {

        }
    }
}
```

9. Add the following code to the *ExecuteStoredProcedureButton_Click* method to create a new *Command* object and set it to the SalesByCategory stored procedure:

```
' VB
' Create a new Command object
Dim SalesByCategoryCommand As New SqlCommand

' Set the command properties
SalesByCategoryCommand.Connection = NorthwindConnection
SalesByCategoryCommand.CommandType = CommandType.StoredProcedure
SalesByCategoryCommand.CommandText = "SalesByCategory"
```

```
// C#
// Create a new Command object
SqlCommand SalesByCategoryCommand = new SqlCommand();

// Set the command properties
SalesByCategoryCommand.Connection = NorthwindConnection;
SalesByCategoryCommand.CommandType = CommandType.StoredProcedure;
SalesByCategoryCommand.CommandText = "SalesByCategory";
```

10. This stored procedure takes two parameters, so add the following code below the previous code to create the parameters and assign them to the command:

```
' VB
' Create the @CategoryName parameter
Dim CategoryNameParameter As New SqlParameter

' Set its name and data type
CategoryNameParameter.ParameterName = "@CategoryName"
CategoryNameParameter.SqlDbType = SqlDbType.NVarChar
```

```
' Create the OrdYear parameter
Dim OrdYearParameter As New SqlParameter("@OrdYear", SqlDbType.NVarChar)

' Add the parameters to the Commmand object
SalesByCategoryCommand.Parameters.Add(CategoryNameParameter)
SalesByCategoryCommand.Parameters.Add(OrdYearParameter)
```

```
// C#
// Create the @CategoryName parameter
SqlParameter CategoryNameParameter = new SqlParameter();

// Set its name and data type
CategoryNameParameter.ParameterName = "@CategoryName";
CategoryNameParameter.SqlDbType = SqlDbType.NVarChar;

// Create the OrdYear parameter
SqlParameter OrdYearParameter =new SqlParameter("@OrdYear", SqlDbType.NVarChar);

// Add the parameters to the Commmand object
SalesByCategoryCommand.Parameters.Add(CategoryNameParameter);
SalesByCategoryCommand.Parameters.Add(OrdYearParameter);
```

11. Now add the code that will set the value of the parameters to whatever is typed into the two text boxes, set the code to run the query, and display the results in the ResultsTextBox.

```
' VB
' Set the parameter values to the
' text in the CategoryNameTextBox
' and the OrdYearTextBox

CategoryNameParameter.Value = CategoryNameTextBox.Text
OrdYearParameter.Value = OrdYearTextBox.Text

' Create a StringBuilder to store the results of the query
Dim results As New System.Text.StringBuilder

' Open the connection before executing the command
SalesByCategoryCommand.Connection.Open()

' Assign the results of the SQL statement to a data reader
Dim reader As SqlDataReader = SalesByCategoryCommand.ExecuteReader

While reader.Read
    For i As Integer = 0 To reader.FieldCount - 1
        results.Append(reader(i).ToString & vbTab)
    Next
    results.Append(Environment.NewLine)
End While

' Close the data reader and the connection
reader.Close()
SalesByCategoryCommand.Connection.Close()
```

```
ResultsTextBox.Text = results.ToString

// C#
// Set the parameter values to the
// text in the CategoryNameTextBox
// and the OrdYearTextBox

CategoryNameParameter.Value = CategoryNameTextBox.Text;
OrdYearParameter.Value = OrdYearTextBox.Text;

// Create a StringBuilder to store the results of the query
System.Text.StringBuilder results = new System.Text.StringBuilder();

// Open the connection before executing the command
SalesByCategoryCommand.Connection.Open();

// Assign the results of the SQL statement to a data reader
SqlDataReader reader = SalesByCategoryCommand.ExecuteReader();

while (reader.Read())
{
    for(int i = 0; i< reader.FieldCount; i++)
    {
    results.Append(reader[i].ToString() + "\t");
    }
    results.Append(Environment.NewLine);
}
// Close the data reader and the connection
reader.Close();
SalesByCategoryCommand.Connection.Close();

ResultsTextBox.Text = results.ToString();
```

12. Run the application and click the Execute Stored Procedure button (see Figure 6-6).

Figure 6-6   Form displaying data after executing the parameterized stored procedure

13. Now try typing another category name and executing the stored procedure, verifying that the results are now displaying a list of products from the selected category. (For example, type Condiments, Seafood, or Produce.)

▶ **Exercise 3: Using *InputOutput* and *Output* Parameters**

1. Create a new Windows application and name it **InputOutputParameters**.

2. Add a TextBox to the form and set the following properties:

   ❑ *Name* = OrderIDTextBox

   ❑ *Text* = 10250

3. Add a second TextBox and set its *Name* property to FreightCostTextBox.

4. Add a button and set the following properties:

   ❑ *Name* = GetFreightCostButton

   ❑ *Text* = Get Freight Cost

   Below the button, add a second set of controls.

5. Add a TextBox and set the following properties:

   ❑ *Name* = CompanyNameTextBox

   ❑ *Text* = Alfreds Futterkiste

6. Add another TextBox and set its *Name* property to ContactNameTextBox.

7. Add a button and set the following properties. The form should now resemble Figure 6-7:

   ❑ *Name* = GetContactNameButton

   ❑ *Text* = Get Contact Name

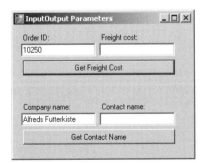

Figure 6-7   Form with controls in preparation for demonstrating *InputOutput* parameters

8. Double-click the Get Freight Cost button to create an event handler.

9. Add references to the *System.Data* and *System.Data.SqlClient* namespaces.

10. Add code to create a connection on the form.

At this point, your form code should look like the following (substitute a valid connection string for the *NorthwindConnection*):

```vb
' VB
Imports System.Data
Imports System.Data.SqlClient

Public Class Form1
    Private NorthwindConnection As New SqlConnection _
        ("Data Source=<ValidServerName>;Initial Catalog=Northwind;Integrated
Security=True")

    Private Sub GetFreightCostButton_Click _
        (ByVal sender As System.Object, ByVal e As System.EventArgs) _
        Handles GetFreightCostButton.Click

    End Sub
End Class
```

```csharp
// C#
using System;
using System.Collections.Generic;
using System.ComponentModel;
using System.Data;
using System.Drawing;
using System.Text;
using System.Windows.Forms;
using System.Data.SqlClient;

namespace InputOutputParametersCS
{
    public partial class Form1 : Form
    {
        public Form1()
        {
            InitializeComponent();
        }

        private SqlConnection NorthwindConnection = new SqlConnection
            ("Data Source=<ValidServerName>;Initial Catalog=Northwind;" +
             "Integrated Security=True");

        private void GetFreightCostButton_Click(object sender, EventArgs e)
        {

        }
    }
}
```

11. Add the following code to the *GetFreightCostButton* event handler:

```vb
' VB
' Create a new Command object
Dim GetFreightCost As New SqlCommand

' Set the command properties
GetFreightCost.Connection = NorthwindConnection
GetFreightCost.CommandType = CommandType.StoredProcedure
GetFreightCost.CommandText = "GetFreightCost"

' Create the Output parameter to receive the freight cost
Dim FreightCostParameter As New SqlParameter
FreightCostParameter.Direction = ParameterDirection.Output

' Set its name and data type
FreightCostParameter.ParameterName = "@Freight"
FreightCostParameter.SqlDbType = SqlDbType.Money

' Create the OrderID parameter and set its value
Dim OrderIDParameter As New SqlParameter("@OrderID", SqlDbType.Int)
OrderIDParameter.Value = OrderIDTextBox.Text

' Add both parameters to the Commmand object
GetFreightCost.Parameters.Add(FreightCostParameter)
GetFreightCost.Parameters.Add(OrderIDParameter)

' open the connection before executing the command
GetFreightCost.Connection.Open()

' Execute the sproc; because we are using parameters
' to access the data we call ExecuteNonQuery instead of
' ExecuteReader.
GetFreightCost.ExecuteNonQuery()
GetFreightCost.Connection.Close()
FreightCostTextBox.Text = Format(FreightCostParameter.Value, "c")
```

```csharp
// C#
// Create a new Command object
SqlCommand GetFreightCost = new SqlCommand();

// Set the command properties
GetFreightCost.Connection = NorthwindConnection;
GetFreightCost.CommandType = CommandType.StoredProcedure;
GetFreightCost.CommandText = "GetFreightCost";

// Create the Output parameter to receive the freight cost
SqlParameter FreightCostParameter = new SqlParameter();
FreightCostParameter.Direction = ParameterDirection.Output;

// Set its name and data type
FreightCostParameter.ParameterName = "@Freight";
FreightCostParameter.SqlDbType = SqlDbType.Money;
```

```
// Create the OrderID parameter and set its value
SqlParameter OrderIDParameter =new SqlParameter("@OrderID", SqlDbType.Int);
OrderIDParameter.Value = OrderIDTextBox.Text;

// Add both parameters to the Commmand object
GetFreightCost.Parameters.Add(FreightCostParameter);
GetFreightCost.Parameters.Add(OrderIDParameter);

// open the connection before executing the command
GetFreightCost.Connection.Open();

// Execute the sproc; because we are using parameters
// to access the data we call ExecuteNonQuery instead of
// ExecuteReader.
GetFreightCost.ExecuteNonQuery();
GetFreightCost.Connection.Close();
FreightCostTextBox.Text = FreightCostParameter.Value.ToString();
```

12. Run the application and click the Get Freight Cost button.

   The Freight Cost TextBox displays 65.83, the cost of freight for order number 10250. Type other valid OrderID numbers into the Order Id TextBox and run the stored procedure to verify that the output parameter contains the correct freight cost for those orders.

   Now that you've seen how to use output parameters that return data from the database, let's implement the Get Contact name functionality and see how to use *InputOutput* parameters to both send data into the database as well as return data from the database.

13. Double-click the GetContactName button to create an event handler.

14. Add the following code to the *GetContactName* handler:

```
' VB
' Create a new Command object
Dim GetContactNameCommand As New SqlCommand

' Set the command properties
GetContactNameCommand.Connection = NorthwindConnection
GetContactNameCommand.CommandType = CommandType.StoredProcedure
GetContactNameCommand.CommandText = "GetContactName"

' Create the InputOutput parameter to send and receive data
Dim NameParameter As New SqlParameter
NameParameter.Direction = ParameterDirection.InputOutput

' Set its name, data type, and value
NameParameter.ParameterName = "@Name"
NameParameter.SqlDbType = SqlDbType.NVarChar
NameParameter.Value = CompanyNameTextBox.Text

' Add the parameters to the Commmand object
```

```
GetContactNameCommand.Parameters.Add(NameParameter)

' Open the connection before executing the command
GetContactNameCommand.Connection.Open()

' Execute the sproc
GetContactNameCommand.ExecuteNonQuery()
GetContactNameCommand.Connection.Close()
ContactNameTextBox.Text = NameParameter.Value.ToString

// C#
// Create a new Command object
SqlCommand GetContactNameCommand = new SqlCommand();

// Set the command properties
GetContactNameCommand.Connection = NorthwindConnection;
GetContactNameCommand.CommandType = CommandType.StoredProcedure;
GetContactNameCommand.CommandText = "GetContactName";

// Create the InputOutput parameter to send and receive data
SqlParameter NameParameter = new SqlParameter();
NameParameter.Direction = ParameterDirection.InputOutput;

// Set its name, data type, and value
NameParameter.ParameterName = "@Name";
NameParameter.SqlDbType = SqlDbType.NVarChar;
NameParameter.Value = CompanyNameTextBox.Text;

// Add the parameters to the Commmand object
GetContactNameCommand.Parameters.Add(NameParameter);

// Open the connection before executing the command
GetContactNameCommand.Connection.Open();

// Execute the sproc
GetContactNameCommand.ExecuteNonQuery();
GetContactNameCommand.Connection.Close();
ContactNameTextBox.Text = NameParameter.Value.ToString();
```

15. Run the application and click the Get Contact Name button.

    The Contact name TextBox displays the contact name record for Alfreds Futterkiste, Maria Anders. Type other valid company names from the Customers table and the Contact name TextBox will display their contacts.

Lesson Summary

- *Command* objects contain collections of *Parameter* objects that move data back and forth between the application and the database.

- Parameters can be *Input* parameters, *Output* parameters, or *Input/Output* parameters.

■ Parameters are assigned data types consistent with the database data types (as opposed to the .NET Framework data types).

■ To facilitate passing user input to a SQL statement using parameters, a parameter can be assigned the value in a control at run time, such as a TextBox.

Lesson Review

The following questions are intended to reinforce key information presented in this lesson. The questions are also available on the companion CD if you prefer to review them in electronic form.

NOTE   Answers

Answers to these questions and explanations of why each choice is correct or incorrect are located in the "Answers" section at the end of the book.

---

1. When would you typically use an *Input* parameter? (Choose all that apply.)

   A. When the parameter value is created based on user input

   B. When the parameter is used to send data from the application to the database

   C. When the command is set to execute a statement with a Where clause

   D. When the parameter value is passed to an Insert statement

2. Where are the three primary kinds of parameters?

   A. *Input, Integer, String*

   B. *Integer, String, DateTime*

   C. *int, varchar, nvarchar*

   D. *Input, Output, InputOutput*

3. How do you determine the actual SQL datatype of a *SqlParameter* (the type expected by the SQL Server)?

   A. It is the .NET Framework data type in your application that the parameter represents.

   B. It is the type of column or data in SQL Server that the command expects.

   C. It is the type of column in a *DataTable* that it represents.

   D. It is any type defined in the *SqlDbDataType* enumeration.

Lesson 3: Saving and Retrieving BLOB Values in a Database

This lesson describes how to work with BLOBs (binary large objects) using *Command* objects. BLOBs in a database are more complex than simple strings containing names and addresses or numeric values containing integers or money values. BLOBs are things like graphics and photos, documents saved in binary formats, and even complete assemblies or executables that you want to store in a database. Unlike running queries or stored procedures that return "simple" data types, working with binary objects is a little more complex.

> **After this lesson, you will be able to:**
> - Obtain BLOB values from a database using a *DataReader* object.
>
> **Estimated lesson time: 45 minutes**

Working with BLOBs

Saving and fetching binary data presents interesting problems that are typically not encountered when querying standard rows of data. The problems arise because you will probably not want to move the entire BLOB in one piece but will likely need to break it up into smaller portions. For example, consider having to move a large binary that is several megabytes in size. Loading the entire BLOB into a variable consumes a lot of memory and can seriously affect the performance of your application. Having to work with a table of these BLOBs, you can quickly see the dilemma.

The good thing is that the .NET Framework provides classes that are specifically designed for moving large amounts of binary data. Specifically, access to these classes—for example, the *BinaryReader* and *BinaryWriter* classes, the *FileStream* and *MemoryStream* classes, and so on—is enabled in the *System.IO* namespace. Although this lesson does not use all the available stream objects, it should provide enough of a starting point to understand the basics of saving and fetching binary data from a database.

BLOBs and the *DataReader*

In previous lessons, you have seen that the main ADO.NET object for accessing retrieved data is the *DataReader*. Although the *DataReader* provides an easy model for working with records where the number of columns and layout of the data are known, (meaning you have been able to easily iterate through the reader and display the data), it also provides a means for returning BLOB data. By setting its *CommandBehavior* to *SequentialAccess,* you can then call the *GetBytes* method, which allows you to read the data in smaller, user-definable amounts. The bytes that make up a BLOB are transported in and out of the database to your application using byte arrays.

The following exercise demonstrates how to read and write binary data to the database, providing two distinctly different models. In the first model, you know how big your data is and you save it in one action. This is illustrated in the *SaveBlobToDatabase* method. In the *FetchBlobFromDatabase* method, you read the bits into a file, but you do it in small chunks defined by the *BufferSize* variable.

▶ **Exercise 1: Saving and Retrieving BLOB Values**

This sample application demonstrates several of the concepts explained in this chapter. In addition to just saving and fetching BLOB values, it also sets up some infrastructure for the application that uses *Command* objects to create a new table in the database (to hold the BLOB values) and executes parameterized queries to populate the list of available BLOBs and retrieve the BLOB value. The code has been compartmentalized, so it should be very easy to parse the routines that are important to you.

1. Create a new Windows application and name it **BLOBSample**.

2. Add a ComboBox to the form and set its *Name* property to BlobList.

3. Add a button below the ComboBox and set the following properties:
   - ❏ *Name* = RefreshBlobListButton
   - ❏ *Text* = Refresh List

4. Add a second button and set the following properties:
   - ❏ *Name* = SaveBlobButton
   - ❏ *Text* = Save BLOB to Database

5. Add a third button and set the following properties (see Figure 6-8):
   - ❏ *Name* = FetchBlobButton
   - ❏ *Text* = Fetch BLOB from Database

Figure 6-8   Form with controls in preparation for manipulating BLOB data

6. Double-click the form to create a *Form_Load* event handler.

   Because this lesson's objective is to explain working with BLOB values, let's just add all the infrastructure code at once and get the form set up. You can analyze this code at your leisure!

7. Replace the Form1 code with the following:

```vb
' VB
Imports System.Data
Imports System.Data.SqlClient
Imports System.IO

Public Class Form1

    Private NorthwindConnection As New SqlConnection _
        ("Data Source=.\sqlexpress;Initial Catalog=Northwind;Integrated Security=True")
    Private CompleteFilePath As String = ""
    Private SavePath As String = ""
Private Sub GetCompleteFilePath()
    Dim OpenDialog As New OpenFileDialog
    OpenDialog.Title = "Select Document File to Save"
    OpenDialog.ShowDialog()
    CompleteFilePath = OpenDialog.FileName
End Sub

Private Sub GetSavePath()
    Dim SavePathDialog As New FolderBrowserDialog
    SavePathDialog.Description = "Select a folder to restore BLOB file to"
    SavePathDialog.ShowDialog()
    SavePath = SavePathDialog.SelectedPath
End Sub

' Create a table to hold our BLOB values
Private Sub CreateDocumentStorageTable()
    Dim CreateTableCommand As New SqlCommand

    CreateTableCommand.Connection = NorthwindConnection
    CreateTableCommand.CommandType = CommandType.Text
```

```vb
        CreateTableCommand.CommandText = "IF OBJECT_ID ( 'DocumentStorage' ) IS NOT NULL " & _
                              "DROP TABLE DocumentStorage; " & _
                              "CREATE TABLE DocumentStorage(" & _
                              "DocumentID int IDENTITY(1,1) NOT NULL, " & _
                              "FileName nvarchar(255) NOT NULL, " & _
                              "DocumentFile varbinary(max) NOT NULL)"

    CreateTableCommand.Connection.Open()
    CreateTableCommand.ExecuteNonQuery()
    CreateTableCommand.Connection.Close()
End Sub

Private Sub Form1_Load(ByVal sender As System.Object, ByVal e As System.EventArgs)
Handles MyBase.Load
    Dim response As DialogResult = MessageBox.Show("Create the Document Storage Table?"
& _
        Environment.NewLine & "Click Yes to create a new DocumentStorage table. Click No
if you already have one!", _
        "Create DocumentStorage table", MessageBoxButtons.YesNo, _
        MessageBoxIcon.Question, MessageBoxDefaultButton.Button2)
    Select Case response
        Case Is = Windows.Forms.DialogResult.Yes
            CreateDocumentStorageTable()
        Case Is = Windows.Forms.DialogResult.No
            refreshBlobList()
        End Select
End Sub

Private Sub refreshBlobList()
    Dim GetBlobListCommand As New SqlCommand _
        ("SELECT FileName FROM DocumentStorage", NorthwindConnection)
    Dim reader As SqlDataReader

    GetBlobListCommand.Connection.Open()
    reader = GetBlobListCommand.ExecuteReader
    While reader.Read
        BlobList.Items.Add(reader(0))
    End While

    reader.Close()
    GetBlobListCommand.Connection.Close()

    BlobList.SelectedIndex = 0
End Sub
End Class

// C#
using System;
using System.Collections.Generic;
using System.ComponentModel;
using System.Data;
using System.Drawing;
using System.Text;
```

```csharp
using System.Windows.Forms;
using System.Data.SqlClient;
using System.IO;

namespace BlobSampleCS
{
    public partial class Form1 : Form
    {
        public Form1()
        {
            InitializeComponent();
        }

        private SqlConnection NorthwindConnection = new SqlConnection
    ("Data Source=.\\sqlexpress;Initial Catalog=Northwind;Integrated Security=True");
        private String CompleteFilePath = "";
        private String SavePath = "";

        private void GetCompleteFilePath()
        {
            OpenFileDialog OpenDialog = new OpenFileDialog();
            OpenDialog.Title = "Select Document to Save";
            OpenDialog.ShowDialog();
            CompleteFilePath = OpenDialog.FileName;
        }

        private void GetSavePath()
        {
            FolderBrowserDialog SavePathDialog = new FolderBrowserDialog();
            SavePathDialog.Description = "Select a folder to restore BLOB file to";
            SavePathDialog.ShowDialog();
            SavePath = SavePathDialog.SelectedPath;
        }

        // Create a table to hold our BLOB values.
        private void CreateDocumentStorageTable()
        {
            SqlCommand CreateTableCommand = new SqlCommand();
            CreateTableCommand.Connection = NorthwindConnection;
            CreateTableCommand.CommandType = CommandType.Text;
            CreateTableCommand.CommandText =
                        "IF OBJECT_ID ( 'DocumentStorage' ) IS NOT NULL " +
                        "DROP TABLE DocumentStorage; " +
                        "CREATE TABLE DocumentStorage(" +
                        "DocumentID int IDENTITY(1,1) NOT NULL, " +
                        "FileName nvarchar(255) NOT NULL, " +
                        "DocumentFile varbinary(max) NOT NULL)";

            CreateTableCommand.Connection.Open();
            CreateTableCommand.ExecuteNonQuery();
            CreateTableCommand.Connection.Close();
        }
```

```csharp
private void Form1_Load(object sender, EventArgs e)
{
  DialogResult response = MessageBox.Show("Create the Document Storage Table?" +
  Environment.NewLine +
  "Click Yes to create a new DocumentStorage table." +
  "Click No if you already have one!",
  "Create DocumentStorage table", MessageBoxButtons.YesNo,
  MessageBoxIcon.Question,
  MessageBoxDefaultButton.Button2);
    switch (response)
    {
        case DialogResult.Yes:
            CreateDocumentStorageTable();
            break;
        case DialogResult.No:
            RefreshBlobList();
            break;
    }

}

private void RefreshBlobList()
{
    SqlCommand GetBlobListCommand = new SqlCommand
        ("SELECT FileName FROM DocumentStorage", NorthwindConnection);
    SqlDataReader reader;

    GetBlobListCommand.Connection.Open();
    reader = GetBlobListCommand.ExecuteReader();
    while (reader.Read())
    {
        BlobList.Items.Add(reader[0]);
    }
    reader.Close();
    GetBlobListCommand.Connection.Close();
    BlobList.SelectedIndex = 0;
}

    }
}
```

8. Add the following code to save the BLOB to the database:

```vb
' VB
Private Sub SaveBlobToDatabase()

    ' This call lets you select the
    ' binary file to save As a BLOB
    ' in the database.
    GetCompleteFilePath()

    ' The BLOB holds the byte array to save.
    Dim BLOB() As Byte
```

```vb
    ' The FileStream is the stream of bytes
    ' that represent the binary file.
    Dim FileStream As New IO.FileStream _
        (CompleteFilePath, IO.FileMode.Open, IO.FileAccess.Read)
    ' The reader reads the binary data from the FileStream.
    Dim reader As New IO.BinaryReader(FileStream)

    ' The BLOB is asigned the bytes from the reader.
    ' The file length is passed to the ReadBytes method
    ' telling it how many bytes to read.
    BLOB=
reader.ReadBytes(CInt(My.Computer.FileSystem.GetFileInfo(CompleteFilePath).Length))

    FileStream.Close()
    reader.Close()

    ' Create a command object to save
    ' the BLOB value.
    Dim SaveDocCommand As New SqlCommand
    SaveDocCommand.Connection = NorthwindConnection
    SaveDocCommand.CommandText = "INSERT INTO DocumentStorage" & _
                                 "(FileName, DocumentFile)" & _
                                 "VALUES (@FileName, @DocumentFile)"

    ' Create parameters to store the filename and BLOB data.
    Dim FileNameParameter As New SqlParameter("@FileName", SqlDbType.NChar)
    Dim DocumentFileParameter As New SqlParameter("@DocumentFile", SqlDbType.Binary)
    SaveDocCommand.Parameters.Add(FileNameParameter)
    SaveDocCommand.Parameters.Add(DocumentFileParameter)

    ' Parse the filename out of the complete path
    ' and assign it to the parameter.
    FileNameParameter.Value = _
        CompleteFilePath.Substring(CompleteFilePath.LastIndexOf("\") + 1)

    ' Set the DocumentFile parameteter to the BLOB Value.
    DocumentFileParameter.Value = BLOB

    ' Execute the command and save the BLOB to the database.
    Try
        SaveDocCommand.Connection.Open()
        SaveDocCommand.ExecuteNonQuery()
        MessageBox.Show(FileNameParameter.Value.ToString & _
            " saved to database.", "BLOB Saved!", MessageBoxButtons.OK, _
            MessageBoxIcon.Information)
    Catch ex As Exception
        MessageBox.Show(ex.Message, "Save Failed", _
            MessageBoxButtons.OK, MessageBoxIcon.Error)
    Finally
        SaveDocCommand.Connection.Close()
    End Try
End Sub
```

```csharp
// C#
private void SaveBlobToDatabase()
{
    // This call lets you select the
    // binary file to save As a BLOB
    // in the database.
    GetCompleteFilePath();

    // The BLOB holds the byte array to save.
    byte[] BLOB;

    // The FileStream is the stream of bytes
    // that represent the binary file.
    System.IO.FileStream FileStream = new System.IO.FileStream _
        (CompleteFilePath, System.IO.FileMode.Open, System.IO.FileAccess.Read);

    // The reader reads the binary data from the FileStream.
    System.IO.BinaryReader reader = new System.IO.BinaryReader(FileStream);

    // The BLOB is asigned the bytes from the reader.
    // The file length is passed to the ReadBytes method
    // telling it how many bytes to read.

    System.IO.FileInfo file = new FileInfo(CompleteFilePath);

    BLOB = reader.ReadBytes((int)(file.Length));

    FileStream.Close();
    reader.Close();

    // Create a command object to save
    // the BLOB value.
    SqlCommand SaveDocCommand = new SqlCommand();
    SaveDocCommand.Connection = NorthwindConnection;
    SaveDocCommand.CommandText = "INSERT INTO DocumentStorage" +
                    "(FileName, DocumentFile)" +
                    "VALUES (@FileName, @DocumentFile)";

    // Create parameters to store the filename and BLOB data.
    SqlParameter FileNameParameter = new SqlParameter("@FileName", SqlDbType.NChar);
    SqlParameter DocumentFileParameter = new SqlParameter _
        ("@DocumentFile", SqlDbType.Binary);
    SaveDocCommand.Parameters.Add(FileNameParameter);
    SaveDocCommand.Parameters.Add(DocumentFileParameter);

    // Parse the filename out of the complete path
    // and assign it to the parameter.
    FileNameParameter.Value = CompleteFilePath.Substring _
        (CompleteFilePath.LastIndexOf("\\")+ 1);

    // Set the DocumentFile parameteter to the BLOB Value.
    DocumentFileParameter.Value = BLOB;
```

```csharp
// Execute the command and save the BLOB to the database.
try
{
    SaveDocCommand.Connection.Open();
    SaveDocCommand.ExecuteNonQuery();
    MessageBox.Show(FileNameParameter.Value.ToString() + " saved to database.", _
        "BLOB Saved!", MessageBoxButtons.OK, MessageBoxIcon.Information);
}
catch (Exception ex)
{
    MessageBox.Show(ex.Message, "Save Failed", MessageBoxButtons.OK, _
        MessageBoxIcon.Error);
}
finally
{
    SaveDocCommand.Connection.Close();
}
}
```

9. Add the following code to retrieve the BLOB from the database and write it back out as a file:

```vb
' VB
Private Sub FetchBlobFromDatabase()

    ' Verify there is a BLOB selected to retrieve.
    If BlobList.Text = "" Then
        MessageBox.Show("Select a BLOB to fetch from the ComboBox")
        Exit Sub
    End If

    ' Get the path to save the BLOB to.
    GetSavePath()

    ' Create the Command object to fetch the selected BLOB.
    Dim GetBlobCommand As New SqlCommand("SELECT FileName, DocumentFile " & _
        "FROM DocumentStorage " & _
        "WHERE FileName = @DocName", NorthwindConnection)
    GetBlobCommand.Parameters.Add("@DocName", SqlDbType.NVarChar).Value = _
        BlobList.Text


    ' Current index to write the bytes to
    Dim CurrentIndex As Long = 0

    ' number of bytes to store in the BLOB.
    Dim BufferSize As Integer = 100

    ' Actual number of bytes returned when calling GetBytes.
    Dim BytesReturned As Long

    ' The Byte array used to hold the buffer.
    Dim Blob(BufferSize - 1) As Byte
```

```vbnet
        GetBlobCommand.Connection.Open()

        Dim reader As SqlDataReader = _
            GetBlobCommand.ExecuteReader(CommandBehavior.SequentialAccess)

        Do While reader.Read
            ' Create or open the selected file.
            Dim FileStream As New IO.FileStream(SavePath & "\" & _
                reader("FileName").ToString, IO.FileMode.OpenOrCreate, IO.FileAccess.Write)

            ' Set the writer to write the BLOB to the file.
            Dim writer As New IO.BinaryWriter(FileStream)

            ' Reset the index to the beginning of the file.
            CurrentIndex = 0

            ' Set the BytesReturned to the actual number of bytes returned
            by the GetBytes call.
                BytesReturned = reader.GetBytes(1, CurrentIndex, Blob, 0, BufferSize)

            ' If the BytesReturned fills the buffer keep appending to the file.
            Do While BytesReturned = BufferSize
                writer.Write(Blob)
                writer.Flush()

                CurrentIndex += BufferSize
                BytesReturned = reader.GetBytes(1, CurrentIndex, Blob, 0, BufferSize)
            Loop

            ' When the BytesReturned no longer fills the buffer, write the remaining bytes.
            writer.Write(Blob, 0, CInt(BytesReturned - 1))
            writer.Flush()

            writer.Close()
            FileStream.Close()
        Loop

        reader.Close()
        GetBlobCommand.Connection.Close()
    End Sub
```

```csharp
// C#
private void FetchBlobFromDatabase()
{
    // Verify there is a BLOB selected to retrieve.
    if (BlobList.Text == "")
    {
        MessageBox.Show("Select a BLOB to fetch from the ComboBox");
        return;
    }


    // Get the path to save the BLOB to.
```

```csharp
GetSavePath();

// Create the Command object to fetch the selected BLOB.
SqlCommand GetBlobCommand = new SqlCommand("SELECT FileName, DocumentFile " +
    "FROM DocumentStorage " + "WHERE FileName = @DocName", NorthwindConnection);

GetBlobCommand.Parameters.Add("@DocName", SqlDbType.NVarChar).Value = BlobList.Text;

// Current index to write the bytes to.
long CurrentIndex = 0;

// number of bytes to store in the BLOB.
int BufferSize = 100;

// Actual number of bytes returned when calling GetBytes.
long BytesReturned ;

// The Byte array used to hold the buffer.
byte[] Blob = new byte[BufferSize];

GetBlobCommand.Connection.Open();

SqlDataReader reader =
GetBlobCommand.ExecuteReader(CommandBehavior.SequentialAccess);

while(reader.Read())
{
    // Create or open the selected file.
    System.IO.FileStream FileStream = new System.IO.FileStream(SavePath + "\\" + _
        reader["FileName"].ToString(), System.IO.FileMode.OpenOrCreate, _
        System.IO.FileAccess.Write);

    // Set the writer to write the BLOB to the file.
    System.IO.BinaryWriter writer= new System.IO.BinaryWriter(FileStream);

    // Reset the index to the beginning of the file.
    CurrentIndex = 0;

    // Set the BytesReturned to the actual number
    // of bytes returned by the GetBytes call.
    BytesReturned = reader.GetBytes(1, CurrentIndex, Blob, 0, BufferSize);

    // If the BytesReturned fills the buffer keep appending to the file.
    while (BytesReturned == BufferSize)
    {
        writer.Write(Blob);
        writer.Flush();

        CurrentIndex += BufferSize;
        BytesReturned = reader.GetBytes(1, CurrentIndex, Blob, 0, BufferSize);
    }
```

```
        // When the BytesReturned no longer fills the buffer, write the remaining bytes.
        writer.Write(Blob, 0, (int)(BytesReturned));
        writer.Flush();

        writer.Close();
        FileStream.Close();
    }
    reader.Close();
    GetBlobCommand.Connection.Close();
}
```

10. Double-click each of the three buttons to create the button-click event handlers
    and add the following code to the form:

```vb
' VB
Private Sub SaveBlobButton_Click(ByVal sender As System.Object, ByVal e As
System.EventArgs)_
    Handles SaveBlobButton.Click
        SaveBlobToDatabase()
End Sub

Private Sub FetchBlobButton_Click(ByVal sender As System.Object, _
    ByVal e As System.EventArgs)_
    Handles FetchBlobButton.Click
        FetchBlobFromDatabase()
End Sub

Private Sub RefreshBlobListButton_Click(ByVal sender As System.Object, _
    ByVal e As System.EventArgs) Handles RefreshBlobListButton.Click
        refreshBlobList()
End Sub
```

```csharp
// C#
private void RefreshBlobListButton_Click(object sender, EventArgs e)
{
    RefreshBlobList();
}

private void SaveBlobButton_Click(object sender, EventArgs e)
{
    SaveBlobToDatabase();
}

private void FetchBlobButton_Click(object sender, EventArgs e)
{
    FetchBlobFromDatabase();
}
```

11. Run the application. When the application starts, you have the option of creating
    the table that stores the BLOB values. If you select *Yes*, the table is created, replac-
    ing any existing DocumentStorage table with a new one.

CAUTION   Existing DocumentStorage Table in your database

If you already have a DocumentStorage table in your database and select *Yes* to create one, the existing table is dropped along with any records it may contain.

---

12. Click the Save BLOB to Database button and navigate to any Microsoft Office Word document on your hard drive. As soon as you select a file, it is saved to the database and a confirmation message appears.

13. Click the Refresh List button, and the file you just saved appears in the combo box.

14. Now click the Fetch BLOB from Database button and select a folder to save the file (BLOB data) out to.

NOTE   Save location

Select a different folder than the one containing the original file.

---

15. Click OK and the BLOB is retrieved from the database and written out to the file location specified. Navigate to the folder you selected and verify that the file is there.

NOTE   Binary file types

Even though the sample indicates that you should save a document, you can actually select and save any binary file into the database.

Lesson Summary

- BLOBs are large binary objects that may need to be saved and retrieved from a database.

- BLOBs typically need to be transferred in sections rather than as one big piece.

- *DataReaders* can read large binary objects as well as standard data types.

Lesson Review

The following questions are intended to reinforce key information presented in this lesson. The questions are also available on the companion CD if you prefer to review them in electronic form.

NOTE Answers

Answers to these questions and explanations of why each choice is correct or incorrect are located in the "Answers" section at the end of the book.

---

1. Why is moving BLOB data to and from a database more complex than manipulating standard data types? (Choose all that apply.)

    A. Because BLOB data typically is transferred with a "stream" object

    B. Because BLOB data is not in a readable format

    C. Because BLOB data tends to be large and typically needs to be transferred in smaller pieces

    D. Because BLOB data cannot be read into a *DataReader*

2. How do you configure a command to return binary large objects?

    A. By setting its *Connection* property to read binary data

    B. By calling the *ExecuteNonQuery* method and reading the results into a *BinaryReader*

    C. By calling the *ExecuteReader* method and casting the *DataReader* to a *BufferedStream*

    D. By setting the *CommandBehavior* to *SequentialAccess* in the *ExecuteReader* methods constructor

3. How do you transfer the individual chunks of binary data returned in a *DataReader* into a byte array?

    A. Call the *DataReader.GetData* method and add the results to the byte array.

    B. Call *DataReader.Read* and access the bytes through a column ordinal.

    C. Call the *DataReader.GetBytes* method and add the results to the byte array.

    D. Call the *DataReader.GetSqlByte* method and add the results to the byte array.

Lesson 4: Performing Bulk Copy Operations

This lesson describes how to copy large amounts of data quickly, using the *SqlBulkCopy* object provided by the *System.Data.SqlClient* namespace and the BULK INSERT SQL statement in SQL Server. In addition to performing an individual bulk copy operation, you will also learn how to perform a set of bulk copy operations wrapped within a transaction.

After this lesson, you will be able to:

- Perform bulk copy operations to copy data to SQL Server (4.1.19.1).
- Perform bulk copy operations in transactions (4.1.19.2).
- Execute the SQL Server Transact-SQL BULK INSERT statement by using the *SqlCommand* object (4.1.19.3).

Estimated lesson time: 45 minutes

Why Perform Bulk Copies?

Copying large amounts of data from one database table to another (or from a file to a database table) can take a lot of time and resources if you simply create an application that reads individual rows out of the original data source and then insert the individual rows into the destination data source. To accomplish the task of moving many records (or entire tables) of data, use the .NET Framework and SQL Server bulk copy features, which perform the transfer of the bulk copies more efficiently than transferring individual records.

Lab: Bulk Copying

In this lab you will bulk copy data from one table to another.

Creating Tables to Copy Data into

To demonstrate how to perform a bulk copy operation, you need tables to copy data into. A quick way to create the tables is to use Server Explorer and the Visual Database Tools to do some cutting and pasting! Use the following steps to create CustomerHistory and OrderHistory tables, which you will use to bulk copy the Customer and Order table data into.

1. In Server Explorer, expand the *Tables* node for the Northwind database.
2. Right-click the Customers table and select Open Table Definition.

3. Select the first row by clicking the box with the key icon.

4. Press Ctrl+A to select all the rows.

5. Press Ctrl+C to copy them to the clipboard.

6. Right-click the *Tables* node in Server Explorer and select Add New Table.

7. Select the empty row (not a cell but the entire row) and press Ctrl+V to paste the table definition into the row.

8. Select only the CustomerID row. Right-click the CustomerID row and select Set Primary Key.

9. Save the table and name it **CustomerHistory**.

10. Repeat these steps with the Orders table, set the OrderID as the primary key, and save the table with the name **OrderHistory**.

▶ **Exercise 1: Perform Bulk Copy Operations to Copy Data to SQL Server**

In this first bulk copy exercise, you will load all the records from the Customers table into a *DataReader* and then copy them into the *CustomerHistory* table using the *SqlBulkCopy* object.

1. Create a new Windows application and name it **BulkCopySample**.

2. Add a button to the form and set the following properties:
   - ❑ *Name* = CopyCustomersButton
   - ❑ *Text* = Copy Customers

3. Add a second button to the form and set the following properties:
   - ❑ *Name* = CopyOrdersButton
   - ❑ *Text* = Copy Orders

4. Double-click the Copy Customers button to create an event handler.

5. Add references to the *System.Data* and *System.Data.SqlClient* namespaces.

6. Add code to create *two* connections on the form, a *SourceConnection* and a *DestinationConnection*. For this example, you can use two connections to the same Northwind database.

   At this point, your form code should look like the following (substitute a valid connection string for the *SourceConnection* and *DestinationConnection* objects):

```
' VB
Imports System.Data
Imports System.Data.SqlClient
```

```
Public Class Form1
    Private SourceConnection As New SqlConnection _
        ("Data Source=<ServerName>;Initial Catalog=Northwind;Integrated Security=True")
    Private DestinationConnection As New SqlConnection _
        ("Data Source=<ServerName>;Initial Catalog=Northwind;Integrated Security=True")
    Private Sub CopyCustomersButton_Click(ByVal sender As System.Object, _
        ByVal e As System.EventArgs) Handles CopyCustomersButton.Click
    End Sub
End Class
```

```
// C#
using System;
using System.Collections.Generic;
using System.ComponentModel;
using System.Data;
using System.Drawing;
using System.Text;
using System.Windows.Forms;
using System.Data.SqlClient;

namespace BulkCopySampleCS
{
    public partial class Form1 : Form
    {
        public Form1()
        {
            InitializeComponent();
        }

        private SqlConnection SourceConnection = new SqlConnection _
            ("Data Source=.\\sqlexpress;Initial Catalog=Northwind;Integrated
Security=True");
        private SqlConnection DestinationConnection = new SqlConnection _
            ("Data Source=.\\sqlexpress;Initial Catalog=Northwind;Integrated
Security=True");

        private void CopyCustomersButton_Click(object sender, EventArgs e)
        {
        }
    }
}
```

7. Add code to bulk copy the data from the Customers table into the CustomerHistory table. Add the following code below the *CopyCustomerButton_Click* event
   handler:

```
' VB
Private Sub BulkCopyCustomers()
    Dim GetCustomersCommand As New SqlCommand("SELECT * FROM Customers", _
        SourceConnection)

    SourceConnection.Open()
```

```vb
            Dim reader As SqlDataReader = GetCustomersCommand.ExecuteReader

            Dim BulkCopier As New SqlBulkCopy(DestinationConnection)

            DestinationConnection.Open()
            BulkCopier.DestinationTableName = "CustomerHistory"
            BulkCopier.WriteToServer(reader)

            reader.Close()
            SourceConnection.Close()
            DestinationConnection.Close()
        End Sub
```

```csharp
// C#
|private void BulkCopyCustomers()
{
    SqlCommand GetCustomersCommand = new SqlCommand _
        ("SELECT * FROM Customers", SourceConnection);

    SourceConnection.Open();
    SqlDataReader reader = GetCustomersCommand.ExecuteReader();

    SqlBulkCopy BulkCopier = new SqlBulkCopy(DestinationConnection);

    DestinationConnection.Open();
    BulkCopier.DestinationTableName = "CustomerHistory";
    BulkCopier.WriteToServer(reader);

    reader.Close();
    SourceConnection.Close();
    DestinationConnection.Close();
}
```

8. Add a line to the *CopyCustomerButton_Click* event handler to call the *BulkCopy-Customers* method.

9. Add code to bulk copy the data from the Orders table into the OrderHistory table. Add the following code below the *BulkCopyCustomers* method:

```vb
' VB
Private Sub BulkCopyOrders()
    Dim GetOrdersCommand As New SqlCommand("SELECT * FROM Orders", SourceConnection)

    SourceConnection.Open()
    Dim reader As SqlDataReader = GetOrdersCommand.ExecuteReader

    Dim BulkCopier As New SqlBulkCopy(DestinationConnection)

    DestinationConnection.Open()
    BulkCopier.DestinationTableName = "OrderHistory"
    BulkCopier.WriteToServer(reader)

    reader.Close()
```

```vb
    SourceConnection.Close()
    DestinationConnection.Close()
End Sub
```

```csharp
// C#
private void BulkCopyOrders()
{
    SqlCommand GetOrdersCommand = new SqlCommand _
        ("SELECT * FROM Orders", SourceConnection);

    SourceConnection.Open();
    SqlDataReader reader = GetOrdersCommand.ExecuteReader();

    SqlBulkCopy BulkCopier = new SqlBulkCopy(DestinationConnection);

    DestinationConnection.Open();
    BulkCopier.DestinationTableName = "OrderHistory";
    BulkCopier.WriteToServer(reader);

    reader.Close();
    SourceConnection.Close();
    DestinationConnection.Close();
}
```

10. Double-click the Copy Orders button and add a line to the *CopyOrdersButton_Click* event handler to call the *BulkCopyOrders* method.

11. Run the application.

12. Click the Copy Customers button.

13. Click the Copy Orders button.

14. Close the form and navigate to Server Explorer.

15. Right-click the CustomerHistory and OrderHistory tables and select Show Table Data.

Verify that the data from the Customers and Orders tables were successfully copied into the CustomerHistory and OrderHistory tables.

IMPORTANT Save the application!

The next section builds on this example, so do not discard the application.

Add Functionality to Demonstrate Executing the SQL BULK INSERT Statement

In addition to copying a large amount of data with the *SqlBulkCopy* object, you can also configure *Command* objects to take advantage of SQL Server features that perform efficient bulk copying. SQL Server provides a BULK INSERT statement for copying data from data files into SQL tables. Create data files with the .bcp utility provided by SQL Server. Although creating data and format files is beyond the scope of this book, they are included on the CD for this example.

Copy the Customers.fmt and NorthwindCustomers.txt files from the CD to the C:\DataSources directory. (You can actually copy these anywhere on your hard drive as long as you point to the correct path in the code example.)

NOTE   Data file location

When executing the BulkInsertStatement in the example below, keep in mind the path being passed to the statement is relative to the database server so be sure the file exists at the indicated path on the server before executing the command.

The NorthwindCustomers.txt file contains all 91 records from the Customers table and the SQL BULK INSERT statement will populate the CustomerHistory table created in the previous section.

1. Delete all the records from the CustomerHistory table so that it is empty.

2. Add a button to the form (below the Copy Orders button) and set the following properties:

   ❑ *Name* = ExecuteBulkInsertButton

   ❑ *Text* = BULK INSERT

3. Double-click the BULK INSERT button and add the following code into the button click event handler (modify the path if necessary):

```vb
' VB
Dim BulkInsertStatement As String = "BULK INSERT CustomerHistory " & _
    "FROM 'C:\Datasources\NorthwindCustomers.txt'"

Dim BulkInsertCommand As New SqlCommand(BulkInsertStatement, SourceConnection)

Try
    SourceConnection.Open()
    BulkInsertCommand.ExecuteNonQuery()
Catch ex As Exception
    MessageBox.Show(ex.Message)
Finally
    SourceConnection.Close()
End Try
```

```csharp
// C#
string BulkInsertStatement = "BULK INSERT CustomerHistory " +
```

```
    "FROM 'C:\\Datasources\\NorthwindCustomers.txt'";

SqlCommand BulkInsertCommand = new SqlCommand(BulkInsertStatement, SourceConnection);

try
{
    SourceConnection.Open();
    BulkInsertCommand.ExecuteNonQuery();
}
catch (Exception ex)
{
    MessageBox.Show(ex.Message);
}
finally
{
    SourceConnection.Close();
}
```

4. Run the application.

5. Click the BULK INSERT button.

6. Inspect the CustomerHistory table's data and verify that the data was success-fully inserted. You may need to refresh the table if it is already opened in the doc-ument window.

▶ **Exercise 2: Perform Bulk Copy Operations in a Transaction**

In this next bulk copy exercise, you will perform basically the same bulk copy action as you did in the last exercise, using only the Customers data, but this time, you will wrap the copy operation in a transaction. You will set the batch size to copy 50 records at a time, causing two separate sets of rows to copy because the Customers table contains 91 records.

1. Create a new Windows application and name it **BulkCopyTransaction**.

2. Add a button to the form and set the following properties:
   - ❏ *Name* = PrepareTableButton
   - ❏ *Text* = Prepare Table

3. Add a second button to the form and set the following properties:
   - ❏ *Name* = BulkCopyButton
   - ❏ *Text* = Execute Bulk Copy

4. Double-click the Execute Bulk Copy button to create an event handler.

5. Add references to the *System.Data* and *System.Data.SqlClient* namespaces.

6. This example needs only one connection, so add a *SourceConnection* to the form. When using an internal transaction, the *SqlBulkCopy* object creates the destination connection when it is instantiated.

At this point, your form code should look like the following (substitute a valid connection string for the *SourceConnection* object):

```vb
' VB
Imports System.Data
Imports System.Data.SqlClient


Public Class Form1

    Private SourceConnection As New SqlConnection _
        ("Data Source=.\sqlexpress;Initial Catalog=Northwind;Integrated Security=True")

    Private Sub BulkCopyButton _Click(ByVal sender As System.Object, _
        ByVal e As System.EventArgs) Handles BulkCopyButton.Click

    End Sub
End Class
```

```csharp
// C#
using System;
using System.Collections.Generic;
using System.ComponentModel;
using System.Data;
using System.Drawing;
using System.Text;
using System.Windows.Forms;
using System.Data.SqlClient;

namespace BulkCopyTransactionCS
{
    public partial class Form1 : Form
    {
        public Form1()
        {
            InitializeComponent();
        }

        private SqlConnection SourceConnection = new SqlConnection _
            ("Data Source=.\\SqlExpress;Initial Catalog=Northwind;Integrated
Security=True");

        private void BulkCopyButton_Click(object sender, EventArgs e)
        {

        }
    }
}
```

To verify that the transaction performs as expected, you actually want part of the bulk copy operation to fail. To accomplish this, leave a single record in the CustomerHistory table to force a primary key violation and cause the transaction to roll back the active batch and without updating any records. To leave this "spoiler" record, you'll create a *PrepareTable* method that deletes all records in the CustomerHistory table except for the record for White Clover Markets (WHITC).

7. Double-click the Prepare Table button and add the following code to the event handler:

```vb
' VB
Dim GetCustomersCommand As New SqlCommand _
    ("DELETE FROM CustomerHistory WHERE CustomerID <> 'WHITC'", SourceConnection)
SourceConnection.Open()
GetCustomersCommand.ExecuteNonQuery()
SourceConnection.Close()
```

```csharp
// C#
SqlCommand GetCustomersCommand = new SqlCommand _
    ("DELETE FROM CustomerHistory WHERE CustomerID <> 'WHITC'", SourceConnection);
SourceConnection.Open();
GetCustomersCommand.ExecuteNonQuery();
SourceConnection.Close();
```

8. Add the following code to the form:

These methods are the code that performs the actual Bulk Copy operation using the *SqlBulkCopy* object. The source and destination connections are used to transfer the data, 50 records at a time (*BatchSize* property). The *DestinationTableName* is where the data is copied to.

```vb
' VB
Private Sub BulkCopyCustomers()
    Dim GetCustomersCommand As New SqlCommand _
        ("SELECT * FROM Customers", SourceConnection)

    SourceConnection.Open()
    Dim reader As SqlDataReader = GetCustomersCommand.ExecuteReader

    Dim BulkCopier As New SqlBulkCopy _
        (SourceConnection.ConnectionString, SqlBulkCopyOptions.UseInternalTransaction)
    BulkCopier.BatchSize = 50

    BulkCopier.DestinationTableName = "CustomerHistory"
    Try
        BulkCopier.WriteToServer(reader)
    Catch ex As Exception
        MessageBox.Show(ex.Message)
    Finally
```

```
        BulkCopier.Close()
        reader.Close()
        SourceConnection.Close()
    End Try
End Sub

// C#
private void BulkCopyCustomers()
{
    SqlCommand GetCustomersCommand = new SqlCommand _
        ("SELECT * FROM Customers", SourceConnection);

    SourceConnection.Open();
    SqlDataReader reader = GetCustomersCommand.ExecuteReader();

    SqlBulkCopy BulkCopier = new SqlBulkCopy _
(SourceConnection.ConnectionString, SqlBulkCopyOptions.UseInternalTransaction);
    BulkCopier.BatchSize = 50;
    BulkCopier.DestinationTableName = "CustomerHistory";

    try
    {
        BulkCopier.WriteToServer(reader);
    }
    catch (Exception ex)
    {
        MessageBox.Show(ex.Message);
    }
    finally
    {
        BulkCopier.Close();
        reader.Close();
        SourceConnection.Close();
    }
}
```

9. Add the *BulkCopyCustomers* method call into the *BulkCopyButton.Click* event handler.

10. Run the application and click the Prepare Table button.

11. With the application running, navigate to Server Explorer, right-click the CustomerHistory table, and select Show Table Data.

12. If the CustomerHistory table was filled with data from the last exercise, you should now see only the record for White Clover Markets. *Select this record and delete it!* (If you didn't complete the last exercise and your table is already empty, that is fine.)

13. Navigate back to the running application and click the Execute Bulk Copy button. The operation should complete successfully and copy the entire Customers table into the CustomerHistory table.

14. Go back to Server Explorer and look at the data in the CustomerHistory table; it should contain all 91 records.

15. Go back to the running form and, once again, click the Prepare Table button.

16. Inspect the table data; now there should be only the White Clover Markets record.

17. Go back to the running form and click the Execute Bulk Copy button.

    This time, you should get a message box to appear, indicating a primary key violation. This is due to the attempted insertion of the existing White Clover Markets record.

18. Click OK in the message box and inspect the table data again.

    What you see are 51 records—the first bulk copy batch of 50 (the batch size you set in code) and the original WHITC record. Notice that the records between the fiftieth and WHITC (which is actually the eighty-ninth record in the table) did not get inserted; the transaction rolled those inserts back because they were all part of the same batch that was part of the internal transaction.

Lesson Summary

- Bulk copying provides an efficient way to copy large amounts of data.

- The *SqlBulkCopy* object provides a .NET Framework class to perform bulk copy operations in your application.

- The SQL BULK INSERT statement provides a way to perform bulk copy operations using the resources in SQL Server.

- Bulk copy operations can be performed from within a transaction.

Lesson Review

The following questions are intended to reinforce key information presented in this lesson. The questions are also available on the companion CD if you prefer to review them in electronic form.

NOTE   Answers

Answers to these questions and explanations of why each choice is correct or incorrect are located in the "Answers" section at the end of the book.

1. How many connection objects are needed to perform a bulk copy operation using the *SqlBulkCopy* object? (Choose all that apply.)

    A. One connection for each database the application needs to connect to

    B. Two connections for each database the application needs to connect to

    C. Two connections total, one connection for the source database, and one connection for the destination database

2. Where does the SQL BULK INSERT statement usually get the data to copy?

    A. From a data file created with the .bcp utility

    B. From a query executed by a *Command* object

    C. From a *DataReader*

    D. From a database table in either the same or another database

3. How many records are copied when performing a bulk copy operation in an internal transaction that fails?

    A. All records up until the transaction fails.

    B. It depends on the batch size and how many successful batches were copied before the transaction failed.

    C. All records from all batches except for the batch where the transaction failed.

    D. No records are copied because the transaction failed.

Lesson 5: Performing Transactions by Using the *Transaction* Object

This lesson describes how to perform transactions while running database operations using the *Transaction* object.

After this lesson, you will be able to:

■ Perform transactions by using the *Transaction* object.

Estimated lesson time: 30 minutes

What Is a Transaction?

Transactions are commands that are executed as a group with the premise that if any command in the group fails, the entire transaction can be aborted and any changes already made by any commands in the group can be rolled back as if none of the commands were ever executed. Transactions are crucial to maintaining the integrity of the data in a database.

Real World

Steve Stein

I used to work with a proprietary inventory application that would allow purchase orders to be received into the system and closed out even in situations when the vendor database was unavailable. Basically this caused the accounts payable system to deny payment when the bills came in for the items on the "disconnected" purchase orders. This was a rare occurrence and only manifested itself when several events happened at the right time but was obviously a flaw in the transaction that flagged the goods as received into inventory and ready for payment.

How to Create Transactions

Just like *Connection* and *Command* objects, each .NET Framework Data Provider offers a *Transaction* object for performing transactions. Create transactions by instantiating the provider-specific *Transaction* object and assigning it the transaction returned from calling the *BeginTransaction* method on connection objects.

The following code illustrates creating a transaction:

```vb
' VB
Dim transaction As SqlTransaction
transaction = NorthwindConnection.BeginTransaction()
```

```csharp
// C#
SqlTransaction transaction;
transaction = NorthwindConnection.BeginTransaction();
```

Setting the Isolation Level of a Transaction

Isolation levels in a transaction control whether other threads can access the data while it is being accessed by the processes within your transaction. Because of the nature of transactions, the modification of several records in related tables is a typical action. Setting isolation levels provides a way to balance the level of data integrity issues and concurrent access to the data accessed by a transaction.

The *Transaction* object's *IsolationProperty* is set by passing one of the values in Table 6-7 when calling the connection's *BeginTransaction* method. For example, if you wanted to set the isolation level to *Snapshot* isolation in the previous example, you could have used the following line of code to begin the transaction.

NOTE Isolation levels

Not every database supports all available isolation levels, so this line of code may not be applicable with the database server you are using.

```vb
' VB
transaction = NorthwindConnection.BeginTransaction(IsolationLevel.Snapshot)
```

```csharp
// C#
transaction = NorthwindConnection.BeginTransaction(IsolationLevel.Snapshot);
```

Table 6-7 lists the possible values for the *Transaction* object's *IsolationLevel* property.

Table 6-7   Isolation Levels

Name	Description
Chaos	Pending changes from highly isolated transactions cannot be overwritten.
ReadCommitted	Shared locks are held while the data is being read to avoid dirty reads, but the data can be changed before the end of the transaction, resulting in non-repeatable reads or phantom data.

Table 6-7 Isolation Levels

Name	Description
ReadUncommitted	A dirty read is possible, meaning that no shared locks are issued and no exclusive locks are honored.
RepeatableRead	Locks are placed on all data that is used in a query, preventing other users from updating the data. Prevents non-repeatable reads but phantom rows are still possible.
Serializable	Locks are placed on all data that is used in a query, preventing other users from updating the data. Prevents non-repeatable reads but phantom rows are still possible.
Snapshot	Reduces blocking by storing a version of data that one application can read while another is modifying the same data. Indicates that from one transaction you cannot see changes made in other transactions, even if you re-query.
Unspecified	A different isolation level than the one specified is being used, but the level cannot be determined.
	When using *OdbcTransaction*, if you do not set *IsolationLevel* or you set *IsolationLevel* to *Unspecified*, the transaction executes according to the default isolation level of the underlying ODBC driver.

Enlisting in a Distributed Transaction

In addition to starting new transactions and setting isolation levels of a transaction, you can configure your connection to enlist in an existing distributed transaction. A distributed transaction is a transaction that spans many resources, such as multiple SQL Server databases (as opposed to a local transaction that typically uses a single database).

The following code shows how to enlist in a distributed transaction and assumes that the *activeTransaction* variable is set to an existing distributed transaction:

```
' VB
NorthwindConnection.EnlistTransaction(activeTransaction)
```

```
// C#
NorthwindConnection.EnlistTransaction(activeTransaction);
```

Lab: Performing Transactions

In this lab you will practice working with the *Transaction* object using the *Commit* and *Rollback* methods.

▶ **Exercise 1: Performing Transactions with the *Transaction* Object**

To demonstrate using a transaction, the following example will attempt to execute two separate commands that will insert records into two different tables. In an effort to provide clarity to the example, the transaction will be committed or rolled back based on user input. In a real-world scenario, you would likely execute the *Commit* and *Rollback* methods based on error conditions or business logic in your application, but the process to accept or abort the transaction is exactly the same.

1. Create a new Windows application named **PerformingTransactions**.

2. Add a button to the form and set the following properties:

   ❑ Name = PerformTransactionButton

   ❑ Text = Perform Transaction

3. Double-click the Perform Transaction button.

4. Add references to the *System.Data* and *System.Data.SqlClient* namespaces.

5. Add code to create a Northwind connection on the form.

6. At this point, the form code should look similar to the following:

```vb
' VB
Imports System.Data
Imports System.Data.SqlClient

Public Class Form1
    Private NorthwindConnection As New SqlConnection _
        ("Data Source=.\sqlexpress;Initial Catalog=Northwind;Integrated Security=True")

    Private Sub PerformTransactionButton_Click(ByVal sender As System.Object, _
        ByVal e As System.EventArgs) Handles PerformTransactionButton.Click

    End Sub
End Class
```

```csharp
// C#
using System;
using System.Collections.Generic;
using System.ComponentModel;
using System.Data;
using System.Drawing;
using System.Text;
using System.Windows.Forms;
```

```
using System.Data.SqlClient;

namespace PerormingTransactionsCS
{
    public partial class Form1 : Form
    {
        public Form1()
        {
            InitializeComponent();
        }

        private SqlConnection NorthwindConnection = new SqlConnection _
            ("Data Source=.\\sqlexpress;Initial Catalog=Northwind;Integrated
Security=True");

        private void PerformTransactionButton_Click(object sender, EventArgs e)
        {

        }
    }
}
```

7. Add the following code to the form to allow the application to work every time the button is clicked:

```
' VB
Private Sub DeleteExtraRecords()
    ' If you have already ran the application
    ' delete the 2 records to prevent a primary
    ' key violation.
    Dim Command1 As New SqlCommand("DELETE FROM Territories WHERE TerritoryID = 98012; " _
        & "DELETE FROM Region WHERE RegionID = 10", NorthwindConnection)
    NorthwindConnection.Open()
    Command1.ExecuteNonQuery()
    NorthwindConnection.Close()
End Sub
```

```
// C#
private void DeleteExtraRecords()
{
    // If you have already ran the application
    // delete the 2 records to prevent a primary
    // key violation.
    SqlCommand Command1 = new SqlCommand("DELETE FROM Territories WHERE TerritoryID =
98012; " +
        "DELETE FROM Region WHERE RegionID = 10", NorthwindConnection);
    NorthwindConnection.Open();
    Command1.ExecuteNonQuery();
    NorthwindConnection.Close();
}
```

8. The following code creates the *Transaction* object and the commands and executes them within the transaction. Add this code to the form:

```vb
' VB
Private Sub PerformTransaction()
    ' Remove the records from this example
    ' so it works each time the button is clicked!
    DeleteExtraRecords()

    ' Create the transaction
    Dim transaction As SqlTransaction

    ' Create 2 commands to execute in the transaction
    Dim Command1 As New SqlCommand("INSERT INTO Region" & _
        "(RegionID, RegionDescription)" & _
        "VALUES (10,'Northwest')", NorthwindConnection)
    Dim Command2 As New SqlCommand("INSERT INTO Territories" & _
        "(TerritoryID, TerritoryDescription, RegionID)" & _
        "VALUES (98012, 'Bothell', 10)", NorthwindConnection)

    ' Open the connection and begin the transaction
    NorthwindConnection.Open()
    transaction = NorthwindConnection.BeginTransaction

    ' Set the commands to execute within the transaction
    Command1.Transaction = transaction
    Command2.Transaction = transaction

    ' Execute the commands
    Command1.ExecuteNonQuery()
    Command2.ExecuteNonQuery()

    ' After executing the commands display a dialog
    ' that allows the user to complete or abort the
    ' transaction.
    Dim response As DialogResult = MessageBox.Show("Commands have already been executed." & _
        Environment.NewLine & "Proceed with transaction?", _
        "Performing Transaction", MessageBoxButtons.YesNo)

    ' Process the response and either
    ' Commit or Rollback.
    Select Case response
        Case Windows.Forms.DialogResult.Yes
            transaction.Commit()
        Case Windows.Forms.DialogResult.No
            transaction.Rollback()
    End Select

    NorthwindConnection.Close()
End Sub
```

```csharp
// C#
private void PerformTransaction()
{
    // Remove the records from this example
    // so it works each time the button is clicked!
    DeleteExtraRecords();

    // Create the transaction
    SqlTransaction transaction;

    // Create 2 commands to execute in the transaction
    SqlCommand Command1 = new SqlCommand("INSERT INTO Region" +
        "(RegionID, RegionDescription)" +
        "VALUES (10,'Northwest')", NorthwindConnection);
    SqlCommand Command2 = new SqlCommand("INSERT INTO Territories" +
        "(TerritoryID, TerritoryDescription, RegionID)" +
        "VALUES (98012, 'Bothell', 10)", NorthwindConnection);


    // Open the connection and begin the transaction
    NorthwindConnection.Open();
    transaction = NorthwindConnection.BeginTransaction();

    // Set the commands to execute within the transaction
    Command1.Transaction = transaction;
    Command2.Transaction = transaction;

    // Execute the commands
    Command1.ExecuteNonQuery();
    Command2.ExecuteNonQuery();

    // After executing the commands display a dialog
    // that allows the user to complete or abort the
    // transaction.
    DialogResult response = MessageBox.Show("Commands have already been executed." +
        Environment.NewLine + "Proceed with transaction?", "Performing Transaction",
        MessageBoxButtons.YesNo);

    // Process the response and either
    // Commit or Rollback.
    switch (response)
    {
        case DialogResult.Yes:
            transaction.Commit();
            break;
        case DialogResult.No:
            transaction.Rollback();
            break;
    }

    NorthwindConnection.Close();
}
```

9. Add code to the Perform Transaction button's click event to call the *Perform-Transaction* method.

10. Run the application and click the Perform Transaction button.

11. Select Yes to commit the transaction.

12. Inspect the Region and Territories tables and verify that the new records for Northwest and Bothell were inserted.

13. Click the Perform Transaction button again (which initially deletes the records that were added in the preceding step 11) but, this time, select No in the dialog box to roll back the transaction.

14. Inspect the Region and Territories table once more and verify that the records were *not* inserted. If you still see the records, you might have to refresh the data in the Show Data windows.

Lesson Summary

- Transactions provide a way to maintain the integrity of your data by allowing a set of commands to be rolled back if one of them does not complete successfully.

- Transactions are provider specific.

- Transactions are created with the *BeginTransaction* method of a *Connection* object.

- The availability of data (that is being modified by a transaction) can be controlled by setting the isolation level of a transaction.

- Commands can be set to enlist in existing distributed transactions as well as in local transactions.

Lesson Review

The following questions are intended to reinforce key information presented in this lesson. The questions are also available on the companion CD if you prefer to review them in electronic form.

NOTE   Answers

Answers to these questions and explanations of why each choice is correct or incorrect are located in the "Answers" section at the end of the book.

---

1. How do you create a new transaction?

   A. Assign a transaction variable the return value of the *Connection.BeginTransaction* method.

   B. Declare a new instance of the *Transaction* class.

   C. Call the *Command.CreateTransaction* method.

   D. Declare a new *Command.Transaction* object.

2. What is the main purpose of a transaction?

   A. To validate that multiple commands complete successfully

   B. To handle exceptions that may occur on the database during command execution

   C. To abort the outcome of an executed command and return data to the state it was in prior to the transaction

   D. To provide an option to abort the outcome of executed commands and return data to the state it was in prior to the transaction

3. What is the difference between a local transaction and a distributed transaction?

   A. Local transactions are performed on a single database table, whereas distributed transactions are performed on multiple database tables.

   B. Local transactions are performed on a single database, whereas distributed transactions are performed on multiple databases on the same server.

   C. Local transactions are performed on a single database server, whereas distributed transactions can be performed across multiple database servers.

   D. Local transactions are performed on a database on the local machine, whereas distributed transactions are performed on a database on a remote machine.

Chapter Review

To further practice and reinforce the skills you learned in this chapter, you can perform the following tasks:

- Review the chapter summary.
- Complete the case scenarios. These scenarios set up real-world situations involving the topics of this chapter and ask you to create a solution.
- Complete the additional practices.
- Take a practice test.

Chapter Summary

- SQL statements and stored procedures can be run using provider-specific *Command* objects.
- Data returned by *Command* objects can be accessed through provider-specific *DataReader* objects.
- *Command* objects have parameter collections that can contain one or more parameters for executing parameterized queries and stored procedures.
- BLOB data can be saved and retrieved from a database using *DataReaders* and *Stream* objects.
- Bulk copy operations can be performed using the *SqlBulkCopy* object as well as by executing a SQL BULK INSERT statement.
- Commands can be executed within the context of a local transaction, or a command can be enlisted in a distributed transaction.

Key Terms

- BLOB
- parameter
- transaction

Case Scenarios

In the following case scenarios, you will apply what you've learned about working with data in a connected environment. You can find answers to these questions in the "Answers" section at the end of this book.

Case Scenario 1: Troubleshooting a Non-Performing Application

You've been contracted by The Phone Company to investigate why their Customer Relationship Management (CRM) application is running slow, causing support techs to spend an unreasonable amount of time waiting for queries to execute. After several days of analyzing their code base and backend database, you come to the conclusion that the lack of performance is due to the exponential increase of their customer base, which is causing too many records to be fetched when running queries that were not designed with scalability in mind. You also notice the archiving utility is constantly running, moving individual records from current to history.

List the potential improvements you can make to the application.

Case Scenario 2: Preventing the Inventory System from Selling Unavailable Products

Your biggest customer, Wide World Importers, is now selling items from many new manufacturers around the globe. Their system is set up to forward orders to the correct manufacturers if local warehouses are out of stock so items can be drop-shipped to the proper customers. The main problem this poses is that they seem to be forwarding orders for items that are not in stock or have longer than acceptable lead times, and it's causing customers to become extremely upset.

Given that each manufacturer exposes its inventory information and projected manufacture date for new inventory, what modifications can you make to the Wide World Importers sales application to remedy this problem?

Suggested Practices

To gain further knowledge on the subject of working with data in a connected environment, complete the following practices:

- **Practice 1**   Create an application that saves data to the Northwind Employees table and allows you to select a picture from your hard drive to save in the Photo column.
- **Practice 2**   Create an application that queries the Northwind Customers table and has separate commands to return data based on *CompanyName*, *City*, or *PostalCode*.
- **Practice 3**   Create an application that bulk copies all Northwind Orders, which have already shipped, into a ShippedOrders table.

Take a Practice Test

The practice tests on this book's companion CD offer many options. For example, you can test yourself on just the content covered in this chapter, or you can test yourself on all the 70-526 certification exam content. You can set up the test so that it closely simulates the experience of taking a certification exam, or you can set it up in study mode so that you can look at the correct answers and explanations after you answer each question.

MORE INFO   **Practice tests**

For details about all the practice test options available, see the "How to Use the Practice Tests" section in this book's Introduction.

Chapter 7

Create, Add, Delete, and Edit Data in a Disconnected Environment

This chapter describes how to work with data loaded from a database or XML document into your application. ADO.NET provides several objects, such as *DataSet* and *DataTable* objects, for caching data in applications so that you can disconnect from the database and work with the data in your application and then reconnect when you are ready to save your updates back to the data source.

Exam objectives in this chapter:

- Create, add, delete, and edit data in a disconnected environment.
  - ❏ Create a *DataSet* graphically.
  - ❏ Create a *DataSet* programmatically.
  - ❏ Add a *DataTable* to a *DataSet*.
  - ❏ Add a relationship between tables within a *DataSet*.
  - ❏ Navigate a relationship between tables.
  - ❏ Merge *DataSet* contents.
  - ❏ Copy *DataSet* contents.
  - ❏ Create a typed *DataSet*.
  - ❏ Create *DataTables*.
  - ❏ Manage data within a *DataTable*.
  - ❏ Create and use *DataViews*.
  - ❏ Represent data in a *DataSet* by using XML.
  - ❏ Use the *OleDbDataAdapter* object to access an ADO Recordset or Record.
  - ❏ Generate *DataAdapter* commands automatically by using the *Command-Builder* object.

❑ Generate *DataAdapter* commands programmatically.

❑ Populate a *DataSet* by using a *DataAdapter*.

❑ Update a database by using a *DataAdapter*.

❑ Resolve conflicts between a *DataSet* and a database by using a *DataAdapter*.

❑ Respond to changes made to data at the data source by using *DataAdapter* events.

❑ Perform batch operations by using *DataAdapters*.

Lessons in this chapter:

Before You Begin

To complete the lessons in this chapter, you must have:

■ A computer that meets or exceeds the minimum hardware requirements listed in the "Introduction" at the beginning of the book.

■ Microsoft Visual Studio 2005 Professional Edition installed on your computer.

■ An understanding of Microsoft Visual Basic or C# syntax and familiarity with the Microsoft .NET Framework.

■ Available data sources, including Microsoft SQL Server (SQL Server Express Edition is acceptable), the Northwind sample database for SQL Server, and the Nwind.mdb Microsoft Office Access database file.

■ A basic understanding of relational databases.

■ Completed the exercises or understood the concepts presented in Chapter 5, "Configuring Connections and Connecting to Data," and Chapter 6, "Working with Data in a Connected Environment."

Real World

Steve Stein

I always spent way too much time whenever I needed to create objects to cache data in my applications. With *DataSet* objects, the standard database structures are already there, so quickly creating a representative object model for my data is really easy.

Lesson 1: Creating *DataSet* Objects

DataSet objects are available in the *System.Data* namespace and are used as an in-memory cache of the data being used in your application. *DataSet* objects contain *DataTable* objects that can be related with *DataRelation* objects much like the structure of a relational database.

After this lesson, you will be able to:
- Create a *DataSet* graphically.
- Create a typed *DataSet*.
- Create a *DataSet* programmatically.
- Add a *DataTable* to a *DataSet*.
- Add a relationship between tables within a *DataSet*.
- Navigate a relationship between tables.

Estimated lesson time: 45 minutes

DataSet Objects

Datasets are objects that you use to temporarily store the data that is used in your application. There are basically two distinct kinds of *DataSet* objects: typed, and untyped. Untyped *DataSets* are the standard generic instances of the *DataSet* class where you manually build up the *DataSet* definition (schema) by creating *DataTable* objects (untyped *DataTables*) and adding them to the *Tables* collection in the *DataSet*. You can access untyped *DataTable* and *DataColumn* objects through their collection indices. Typed *DataSet* objects derive their schema from an .xsd file and contain explicitly typed collections (such as a specific *CustomersTable* object).

There are three distinct ways to create *DataSet* objects in Visual Studio:

- Declare a new *DataSet* object programmatically in the code editor, which results in an empty *DataSet* that requires creating *DataTable* and optional *DataRelation* objects to be added to the *DataSet*.

- Use design-time tools such as the DataSet Designer and the Data Source Configuration Wizard which assists in the creation of typed *DataSet* objects by stepping you through the process of selecting or creating a data connection and then allowing you to select database objects available from that connection to build up a typed *DataSet* and have most, if not all, of the necessary code generated for you.

- Drag a *DataSet* object from the Toolbox onto a form and use the Table and Column Collection editors to build up the schema of your *DataSet*.

This lesson describes how to create *DataSet* objects using each of these methods.

NOTE   Generating *DataSet* objects

You can also create *DataSet* objects based on configured *DataAdapter* objects. This will be covered in Lesson 3, "Creating *DataAdapter* Objects," of this chapter.

Creating *DataSet* Objects Programmatically

Create *DataSet* objects by declaring instances of them. You can optionally provide the name of the *DataSet*. For example, the following code example creates a new *DataSet* named *NorthwindDataSet*:

```
' VB
   Dim NorthwindDataset As New DataSet ("NorthwindDataset")
```

```
// C#
   DataSet NorthwindDataset = new DataSet ("NorthwindDataset");
```

Adding *DataTable* Objects to a *DataSet*

After declaring a new *DataSet*, you need to add *DataTable* objects to it to actually hold the data in your application. The following code sample shows how to add a *CustomersTable* and *OrdersDataTable* to the *NorthwindDataset*:

```
' VB
' Create some DataTables
Dim CustomersTable As New DataTable
Dim OrdersDataTable As New DataTable

' Add DataTables to the Dataset's Tables collection.
NorthwindDataset.Tables.Add(CustomersTable)
NorthwindDataset.Tables.Add(OrdersDataTable)

// C#
// Create some DataTables
DataTable CustomersTable = new DataTable ();
DataTable OrdersDataTable = new DataTable ();

// Add DataTables to the Dataset's Tables collection.
NorthwindDataset.Tables.Add(CustomersTable);
NorthwindDataset.Tables.Add(OrdersDataTable);
```

Adding a Relationship Between Tables in a *DataSet*

After adding tables to a *DataSet*, you can use *DataRelation* objects to represent the relation between *DataTable* objects just like the relationships between tables in a database. Create relationships in *DataSet* objects by declaring *DataRelation* objects and providing the columns from the parent and child tables to the *DataRelation* constructor. After creating the relationship, you must add it to the *Relations* collection of the *DataSet*.

The following code sample creates a relationship in the *NorthwindDataSet* and assumes the *Customers* and *Orders DataTable* objects each have a CustomerID column that is used to relate the table's data together:

```vb
' VB
' Create the new relationship.
Dim CustomersOrders As New DataRelation ("CustomersOrders", _
    CustomersTable.Columns("CustomerID"), OrdersTable.Columns("CustomerID"))

' Add the relationship to the DataSet.
NorthwindDataset.Relations.Add(CustomersOrders)
```

```csharp
// C#
// Create the new relationship.
DataRelation CustomersOrders = new DataRelation ("CustomersOrders",
    CustomersTable.Columns["CustomerID"], OrdersTable.Columns["CustomerID"]);

// Add the relationship to the DataSet.
NorthwindDataset.Relations.Add(CustomersOrders);
```

Navigate a Relationship Between Tables

To access related records in *DataTable* objects, you must first select a *DataRow* from either the parent or child table and then call either the *GetParentRow* or *GetChildRows* method of the *DataRow*. Calling the *GetParentRow* method returns a single *DataRow* representing the parent record, whereas calling the *GetChildRows* method returns an array of *DataRows* representing all rows that are related to the selected parent.

Returning the Parent Row of a Selected Child Record   The following example returns the *Customer* of a selected *Order*:

```vb
' VB
Dim Customer As DataRow = SelectedOrdersRow.GetParentRow("FK_Orders_Customers")
```

```csharp
// C#
DataRow Customer = SelectedOrdersRow.GetParentRow("FK_Orders_Customers");
```

Returning the Related Child Rows of a Selected Parent Row   The following example returns the *Orders* of a selected *Customer*:

```
' VB
Dim Orders() As DataRow = SelectedCustomersRow.GetChildRows("FK_Orders_Customers")
```

```
// C#
DataRow Orders() = SelectedCustomersRow.GetChildRows("FK_Orders_Customers");
```

Merging *DataSet* Contents

You can take the contents from one *DataSet* (the source dataset) and merge it with the contents of another *DataSet* (the target dataset) using the *DataSet.Merge* method.

When merging datasets, the actual data is combined depending on whether a similar record exists in the *DataSet* into which it will be merged. For example, if you merge two datasets that both contain a record with the same primary key, the values in the target *DataSet* will be overwritten with the new values in the source *DataSet*. You can control this behavior and restrict changes from being made in the target *DataSet* by passing in a true or false value to the *PreserveChanges* flag in the *Merge* method. In addition to merging the actual data, when you merge two *DataSet*s that have tables with differing schema, you can pass an optional MissingSchemaAction parameter to the *Merge* method that controls the behavior of the merge when the source *DataSet* has objects that are not currently in the target *DataSet*. The following are valid values for the MissingSchemaAction parameter:

- **Add (default)**   All schema items in the source *DataSet* are added to the target DataSet and populated.
- **AddWithKey**   All schema items and primary key settings are added to the target *DataSet*.
- **Error**   An exception will be thrown when the schemas in the source and target *DataSet*s do not match.
- **Ignore**   All schema inconsistencies between the source and target *DataSet*s are ignored.

In the following code example, the contents of the OldSalesDataSet are merged into the contents of the SalesHistoryDataSet. The PreserveChanges parameter is set to *True* and any schema differences will be ignored.

```
' VB
SalesHistoryDataSet.Merge(OldSalesDataSet, True, MissingSchemaAction.Ignore)
```

```
// C#
SalesHistoryDataSet.Merge(OldSalesDataSet, true, MissingSchemaAction.Ignore);
```

Copying DataSet Contents

In some situations you may need to create a copy of the data in a *DataSet*. For example, you might need to manipulate a copy of the data and perform some processing, but you might not want to modify the original data. To create a copy of a *DataSet*, you simply create a new *DataSet* object and assign it the return value of the *DataSet*. Copy method. The following code example demonstrates this:

```
' VB
Dim CopyOfDataSet As New DataSet
CopyOfDataSet = OriginalDataSet.Copy
```

```
// C#
DataSet CopyOfDataSet = new DataSet();
CopyOfDataSet = OriginalDataSet.Copy();
```

Lab: Creating *DataSet* Objects

In this lab you will create typed and untyped *DataSet* objects.

▶ **Exercise 1: Creating a *DataSet* with the DataSet Designer**

The DataSet Designer is a design-time tool that assists in the creation of typed *DataSet* objects by allowing you to drag and drop database tables from Server Explorer onto the design surface. As you drop tables on the surface, they are added to the *DataSet* as typed objects that make programming as simple as writing the table and column names you want to access.

1. Create a Windows application and name it **DataSetDesignerExample**.

2. From the Project menu, select Add New Item.

3. Select the *DataSet* template and name it **NorthwindDataSet.xsd**.

4. Navigate to the Customers table in Server Explorer and drag it onto the design surface.

5. Navigate to the Orders table in Server Explorer and drag it onto the design surface.

After dropping the Customers and Orders tables onto the *DataSet* Designer, the design surface should look similar to Figure 7-1.

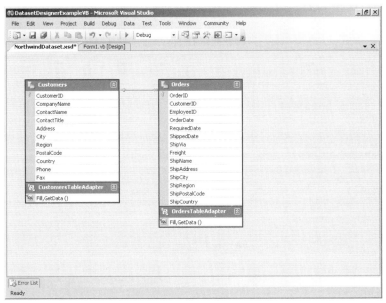

Figure 7-1 *Customers* and *Orders DataTable* objects and *TableAdapter* objects as seen in the DataSet Designer

6. Build the project before moving on to the next step.

7. Drag a *ListBox* onto Form1 and name it **CustomersListBox**.

8. Drag a button onto Form1 and set the following properties:

   ❑ *Name* = GetCustomersButton

   ❑ *Text* = Get Customers

9. Double-click the Get Customers button and add the following code to the *GetCustomersButton_Click* event handler:

```
' VB
' Instantiate a Northwind typed dataset.
Dim NorthwindDataSet1 As New NorthwindDataSet

' Instantiate a CustomersTableAdapter.
Dim CustomersTableAdapter1 As New NorthwindDataSetTableAdapters.CustomersTableAdapter

' Call the default Fill method to load all customers into the Customers DataTable.
CustomersTableAdapter1.Fill(NorthwindDataSet1.Customers)

' Loop through the rows in the Customers table and add the value from the CompanyName
column
```

```
' to the ListBox.
For Each NWCustomer As NorthwindDataSet.CustomersRow In NorthwindDataSet1.Customers.Rows
    CustomersListBox.Items.Add(NWCustomer.CompanyName)
Next

// C#
// Instantiate a Northwind typed dataset.
NorthwindDataSet NorthwindDataSet1 = new NorthwindDataSet ();

// Instantiate a CustomersTableAdapter.
NorthwindDataSetTableAdapters.CustomersTableAdapter CustomersTableAdapter1 =
    new NorthwindDataSetTableAdapters.CustomersTableAdapter();

// Call the default Fill method to load all customers into the Customers DataTable.
CustomersTableAdapter1.Fill(NorthwindDataSet1.Customers);

// Loop through the rows in the Customers table and add the value from the CompanyName
column
// to the ListBox.
foreach (NorthwindDataSet.CustomersRow NWCustomer in NorthwindDataSet1.Customers.Rows)
{
    CustomersListBox.Items.Add(NWCustomer.CompanyName);
}
```

10. Run the application and click the Get Customers button. Verify that the *Company-Name* from each customer is displayed in the *CustomersListBox* similar to Figure 7-2.

Figure 7-2   The *CompanyName* from all customers appearing in the *CustomersListBox* after clicking the Get Customers button

▶ **Exercise 2: Creating a Typed *DataSet* with the Data Source Configuration Wizard**

This exercise provides instructions for creating a strongly typed *DataSet* using the Data Source Configuration Wizard.

1. Create a Windows application and name it **DataSourceWizardExample**.

2. Start the Data Source Configuration Wizard by selecting Add New Data Source from the Data menu.

NOTE Data menu

If the Data menu is not available, open the form in Design view.

3. Leave the default selection of Database on the Choose A Data Source Type page, as shown in Figure 7-3. Then, click Next.

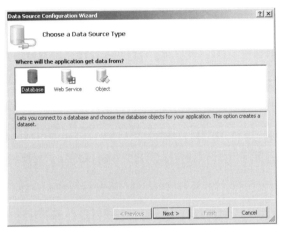

Figure 7-3   The Choose a Data Source Type page of the Data Source Configuration Wizard

4. The list box displays the available data connections from Server Explorer. Select a connection to the Northwind sample database or create a new data connection on the Choose Your Data Connection page, as shown in Figure 7-4. Then, click Next. If prompted, click Yes to add the database to your project.

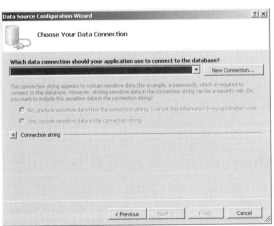

Figure 7-4   The Choose Your Data Connection page of the Data Source Configuration Wizard

5. After selecting the desired data connection, you are given the option of saving it to the application configuration file. Leave the default option selected, as shown in Figure 7-5. Then, click Next.

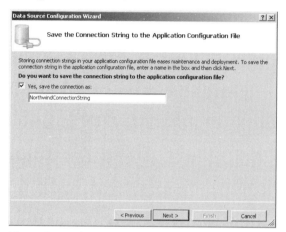

Figure 7-5   The Save the Connection String to the Application Configuration File page of the Data Source Configuration Wizard

6. Expand the *Tables* node and select the Customers table on the Choose Your Database Objects page, as shown in Figure 7-6.

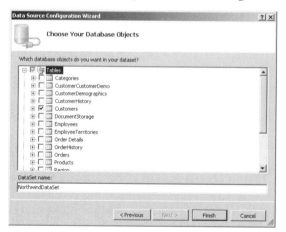

Figure 7-6   The Choose Your Database Objects page of the Data Source Configuration Wizard

7. Click Finish to complete the wizard and add the typed *DataSet* to your project.

After completing the wizard, the data source is available in the Data Sources window, which enables the quick construction of data-bound forms.

8. With Form1 in Design view, select Show Data Sources from the Data menu.

9. Drag the *Customers* node from the Data Sources window onto Form1, as shown in Figure 7-7.

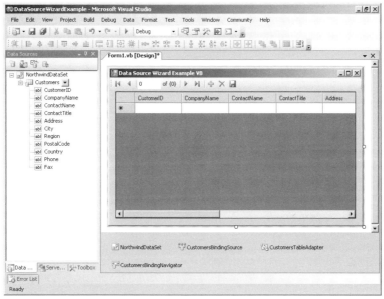

Figure 7-7   Form1 in the Visual Studio IDE after dropping the *Customers* node from the Data Sources window

Visual Studio adds code to fill the Customers DataTable to the form as a result of dropping the Customers table from the Data Sources window.

10. Run the application and verify that the Customers table data appears on the form, as shown in Figure 7-8.

	CustomerID	CompanyName	ContactName	ContactTitle	Address
▶	ALFKI	Alfreds Futterkiste	Maria Anders	Sales Represent...	Obere Str. !
	ANATR	Ana Trujillo Empa...	Ana Trujillo	Owner	Avda. de la
	ANTON	Antonio Moreno ...	Antonio Moreno	Owner	Mataderos
	AROUT	Around the Horn	Thomas Hardy	Sales Represent...	120 Hanov
	BERGS	Berglunds snabb...	Christina Berglund	Order Administrator	Berguvsvä
	BLAUS	Blauer See Delik...	Hanna Moos	Sales Represent...	Forsterstr. 5
	BLONP	Blondesddsl père...	Frédérique Citeaux	Marketing Manager	24, place K
	BOLID	Bólido Comidas p...	Martín Sommer	Owner	C/ Araquil,
	BONAP	Bon app'	Laurence Lebihan	Owner	12, rue des
	BOTTM	Bottom-Dollar Ma...	Elizabeth Lincoln	Accounting Man...	23 Tsawas

Figure 7-8   The Customers data displayed on Form1

▶ **Exercise 3: Configuring Untyped *DataSet* Objects**

Create untyped *DataSet* objects by dragging *DataSet* objects from the Toolbox onto a form.

1. Create a Windows application and name it **UntypedDataSet**.

2. From the Data section of the Toolbox, drag a *DataSet* object onto Form1.

3. In the Add DataSet dialog box, select Untyped DataSet and click OK.

4. Drag a *DataGridView* onto the form.

5. Select the DataSet1 instance in the component tray and navigate to the Tables property in the Properties window. Click the ellipsis in the *Tables* property to open the Tables Collection Editor.

6. Add a table and set its *Name* and *TableName* properties to *Categories*.

7. Select the *Columns* property and click the ellipsis to open the Columns Collection Editor.

8. Add a column and set the following properties:
    ❑ *AllowDBNull* = False
    ❑ *AutoIncrement* = True
    ❑ *ColumnName* = CategoryID
    ❑ *DataType* = System.Int32
    ❑ *Name* = CategoryID

9. Add a second column and set the following properties:
    ❑ *AllowDBNull* = False
    ❑ *ColumnName* = CategoryName
    ❑ *Name* = CategoryName

10. Close the Columns Collection Editor, select the *Constraints* property, and add a Unique constraint.

11. Select the CategoryID column and the Primary key check box and click OK.

12. Close the Constraints Collection Editor and the Tables Collection Editor.

13. Add a button to the form and set the following properties:
    ❑ *Name* = FillDataSetButton
    ❑ *Text* = Fill DataSet

14. Create a *Form1_Load* event handler and add the following code:

```
' VB
DataGridView1.DataSource = DataSet1.Tables("Categories")
DataGridView1.SelectionMode = DataGridViewSelectionMode.FullRowSelect

// C#
dataGridView1.DataSource = dataSet1.Tables["Categories"];
dataGridView1.SelectionMode = DataGridViewSelectionMode.FullRowSelect;
```

15. Create a *FillDatasetButton_Click* event handler and add the following code to it:

```
' VB
Dim newRow As DataRow = DataSet1.Tables("Categories").NewRow()
newRow.Item("CategoryName") = "Beverages"
DataSet1.Tables("Categories").Rows.Add(newRow)

Dim newRow2 As DataRow = DataSet1.Tables("Categories").NewRow()
newRow2.Item("CategoryName") = "Condiments"
DataSet1.Tables("Categories").Rows.Add(newRow2)

Dim newRow3 As DataRow = DataSet1.Tables("Categories").NewRow()
newRow3.Item("CategoryName") = "Seafood"
DataSet1.Tables("Categories").Rows.Add(newRow3)

// C#
DataRow newRow  = dataSet1.Tables["Categories"].NewRow();
newRow["CategoryName"] = "Beverages";
dataSet1.Tables["Categories"].Rows.Add(newRow);

DataRow newRow2 = dataSet1.Tables["Categories"].NewRow();
newRow2["CategoryName"] = "Condiments";
dataSet1.Tables["Categories"].Rows.Add(newRow2);

DataRow newRow3 = dataSet1.Tables["Categories"].NewRow();
newRow3["CategoryName"] = "Seafood";
dataSet1.Tables["Categories"].Rows.Add(newRow3);
```

16. With Form1 in Design view, select *DataSet1* in the component tray.

17. From the *Tables* property in the Property window, open the Tables Collection Editor and add another table to the *DataSet*.

18. Set its *Name* and *TableName* properties to *Products*.

19. Add a column and set the following properties:

   ❑ *AllowDBNull* = False

   ❑ *AutoIncrement* = True

   ❑ *ColumnName* = ProductID

- ❏ *DataType* = System.Int32
- ❏ *Name* = ProductID

20. Add a column and set the following properties:
    - ❏ *AllowDBNull* = False
    - ❏ *ColumnName* = ProductName
    - ❏ *DataType* = System.String
    - ❏ *Name* = ProductName

21. Add a column and set the following properties:
    - ❏ *AllowDBNull* = False
    - ❏ *ColumnName* = CategoryID
    - ❏ *DataType* = System.Int32
    - ❏ *Name* = CatID

22. Click Close. Select the *Constraints* property for the Products table and add a *Unique* constraint.

23. Select the ProductID column and the Primary key check box and click OK.

24. Add a Foreign Key Constraint and set the following:
    - ❏ *Parent table* = Categories
    - ❏ *Child table* = Products
    - ❏ *Key columns* = CategoryID
    - ❏ *Foreign Key columns* = CategoryID

25. Click OK.

26. Close the Collection Editors, and then close the Table Collection Editor.

27. Select *DataSet1* in the component tray and add a *DataRelation* by clicking the ellipsis in the *Relations* property of *DataSet1*.

28. Click Add in the Relations Collection Editor. Set the following in the Relations dialog box:
    - ❏ *Name* = CategoriesProducts
    - ❏ *Parent table* = Categories
    - ❏ *Child table* = Products
    - ❏ *Key columns* = CategoryID
    - ❏ *Foreign Key columns* = CategoryID

29. Close the dialog boxes.

30. Add the following code to the bottom of the *FilllDatasetButton_Click* event handler:

```vb
' VB
Dim newRow4 As DataRow = DataSet1.Tables("Products").NewRow()
newRow4.Item("CategoryID") = 1
newRow4.Item("ProductName") = "Chai"
DataSet1.Tables("Products").Rows.Add(newRow4)

Dim newRow5 As DataRow = DataSet1.Tables("Products").NewRow()
newRow5.Item("CategoryID") = 2
newRow5.Item("ProductName") = "Aniseed Syrup"
DataSet1.Tables("Products").Rows.Add(newRow5)

Dim newRow6 As DataRow = DataSet1.Tables("Products").NewRow()
newRow6.Item("CategoryID") = 3
newRow6.Item("ProductName") = "Ikura"
DataSet1.Tables("Products").Rows.Add(newRow6)

Dim newRow7 As DataRow = DataSet1.Tables("Products").NewRow()
newRow7.Item("CategoryID") = 1
newRow7.Item("ProductName") = "Chang"
DataSet1.Tables("Products").Rows.Add(newRow7)

Dim newRow8 As DataRow = DataSet1.Tables("Products").NewRow()
newRow8.Item("CategoryID") = 2
newRow8.Item("ProductName") = "Chef Anton's Gumbo Mix"
DataSet1.Tables("Products").Rows.Add(newRow8)

Dim newRow9 As DataRow = DataSet1.Tables("Products").NewRow()
newRow9.Item("CategoryID") = 3
newRow9.Item("ProductName") = "Boston Crab Meat"
DataSet1.Tables("Products").Rows.Add(newRow9)

// C#
DataRow newRow4 = dataSet1.Tables["Products"].NewRow();
newRow4["CategoryID"] = 1;
newRow4["ProductName"] = "Chai";
dataSet1.Tables["Products"].Rows.Add(newRow4);

DataRow newRow5  = dataSet1.Tables["Products"].NewRow();
newRow5["CategoryID"] = 2;
newRow5["ProductName"] = "Aniseed Syrup";
dataSet1.Tables["Products"].Rows.Add(newRow5);

DataRow newRow6 = dataSet1.Tables["Products"].NewRow();
newRow6["CategoryID"] = 3;
newRow6["ProductName"] = "Ikura";
dataSet1.Tables["Products"].Rows.Add(newRow6);

DataRow newRow7 = dataSet1.Tables["Products"].NewRow();
newRow7["CategoryID"] = 1;
```

```
newRow7["ProductName"] = "Chang";
dataSet1.Tables["Products"].Rows.Add(newRow7);

DataRow newRow8 = dataSet1.Tables["Products"].NewRow();
newRow8["CategoryID"] = 2;
newRow8["ProductName"] = "Chef Anton's Gumbo Mix";
dataSet1.Tables["Products"].Rows.Add(newRow8);

DataRow newRow9 = dataSet1.Tables["Products"].NewRow();
newRow9["CategoryID"] = 3;
newRow9["ProductName"] = "Boston Crab Meat";
dataSet1.Tables["Products"].Rows.Add(newRow9);
```

31. Create an event handler for the *DataGridView1_CellDoubleClick* event and add the following code:

```
' VB
' Get the CategoryID of the selected row
Dim Category As Integer = CInt(DataGridView1.SelectedRows(0).Cells("CategoryID").Value)

' Get the underlying DataRow that is selected
Dim rows() As DataRow = DataSet1.Tables("Categories").Select("CategoryID = " & Category)

' Use the GetChildRows method to navigate the relationship and return the related records
Dim ProductList As String = ""
For Each r As DataRow In rows(0).GetChildRows("CategoriesProducts")
    ProductList += r.Item("ProductName").ToString & Environment.NewLine
Next

' Display the products in a message box
MessageBox.Show(ProductList)
```

```
// C#
// Get the CategoryID of the selected row
int Category  = (int)dataGridView1.SelectedRows[0].Cells["CategoryID"].Value;

// Get the underlying DataRow that is selected
DataRow[] rows = dataSet1.Tables["Categories"].Select("CategoryID = " + Category);

// Use the GetChildRows method to navigate the relationship
// and return the related records
string ProductList = "";
foreach (DataRow r in rows[0].GetChildRows("CategoriesProducts"))
{
ProductList += r["ProductName"].ToString() + Environment.NewLine;
}

// Display the products in a message box
MessageBox.Show(ProductList);
```

32. Run the application and click the Fill Dataset button.

33. Now double-click one of the categories in the grid to open a message box displaying the related products.

Lesson Summary

- Create *DataSet* objects programmatically by instantiating new *DataSet* objects in code and adding *DataTable* and *DataRelation* objects, much like tables and relationships in a database.

- Create typed *DataSet* objects with the DataSet Designer and the Data Source Configuration Wizard.

- Typed *DataSet* objects are automatically created with *TableAdapter* objects that have methods that fill and update the data in the data tables of the *DataSet*.

- Untyped and typed *DataSet* objects can be created by dragging a *DataSet* object from the data Toolbox onto a form.

Lesson Review

The following questions are intended to reinforce key information presented in this lesson. The questions are also available on the companion CD if you prefer to review them in electronic form.

NOTE Answers

Answers to these questions and explanations of why each choice is correct or incorrect are located in the "Answers" section at the end of the book.

---

1. What is a *DataSet*? (Choose all that apply.)
   A. A pointer to a remote database
   B. A collection of *DataTable* and *DataRelation* objects
   C. An in-memory cache of data
   D. A collection of records from a database

2. What are the three main objects when working with a *DataSet*?
   A. *DataTable*, *DataRelation*, and *DataAdapter*
   B. *DataTable*, *DataColumn*, and *DataRelation*
   C. *DataTable*, *DataRelation*, and *Constraint*
   D. *DataTable*, *DataColumn*, and type

3. How do you programmatically access related records in a *DataSet*?
    A. By calling the *GetParentRow* and *GetChildRows* methods of a *DataSet*
    B. By calling the *GetParentRow* and *GetChildRows* methods of a *DataTable*
    C. By calling the *GetParentRow* and *GetChildRows* methods of a *DataRow*
    D. By accessing the *ParentColumns* and *ChildColumns* of a *DataRelation*

Lesson 2: Creating *DataTable* Objects

This lesson describes how to create *DataTable* objects, which are ADO.NET objects in the *System.Data* namespace that provide in-memory storage for the data in your application similar to a table in a database. *DataTable* objects can be added to *DataSet* objects and related to other *DataTable* objects using a *DataRelation* object, or you can use *DataTable* objects as standalone objects independent of *DataSet* objects.

Once a *DataTable* object is created, define the schema of the table by creating and adding columns and constraints similar to tables in a database. This lesson will focus on creating and configuring the *DataTable*, preparing it to receive data. The process of filling the *DataTable* with data, as well as manipulating the data in the table, will be covered later in this chapter.

After this lesson, you will be able to:

■ Create *DataTable* objects.

   ❑ Create a *DataTable*.

   ❑ Add a *DataTable* to a *DataSet*.

   ❑ Define the schema of a *DataTable*.

   ❑ Add columns to a table.

   ❑ Create expression columns.

   ❑ Create AutoIncrementing columns.

   ❑ Define a primary key for a table.

   ❑ Add constraints to a table.

Estimated lesson time: 45 minutes

How to Create *DataTable* Objects

Create *DataTable* objects by declaring an instance of the *DataTable* object. You can optionally provide the name of the *DataTable* as well as the *Namespace* that will be used when rendering the data in XML. For example, the following code example creates a new *DataTable* named *SalesData*:

```
' VB
Private SalesDataTable As New DataTable ("SalesData")
```

```
// C#
Private DataTable SalesDataTable = new DataTable("SalesData");
```

How to Add a *DataTable* to a *DataSet*

DataTable objects can be used as standalone objects but, when representing relational data in your application, it is much more useful to work with *DataTable* objects as part of *DataSet* objects where you can relate them together with *DataRelation* objects and access related records, much like working with a database. For example, the following code sample creates a new *DataTable* and adds it to a *DataSet*:

```
' VB
' Create a new Dataset.
Dim NorthwindDataset As New DataSet("NorthwindData")

' Create a new DataTable.
Dim CustomersTable As New DataTable("Customers")

' Add the Datatable to the Dataset's Tables collection.
   NorthwindDataset.Tables.Add(CustomersTable)
```

```
// C#
// Create a new DataSet.
DataSet NorthwindDataset = new DataSet("NorthwindData");

// Create a new DataTable.
DataTable CustomersTable = new DataTable("Customers");

// Add the DataTable to the Dataset's Tables collection.
NorthwindDataset.Tables.Add(CustomersTable);
```

How to Create Expression Columns in *DataTable* Objects

Expression columns can be added to a *DataTable* when you want to store the results of a calculation between existing columns as an additional column in the table. In other words, you can perform a calculation on existing columns and store the results in an additional column (the expression column). For example, consider the Order Details table in the Northwind database. The table contains a UnitPrice column and a Quantity column. What the table does not have is a TotalPrice (also called an ExtendedPrice) column. If you wanted to add a column that displayed (or stored) the total price of a row in the Order Details table, you could accomplish this by adding an expression column. The following code example shows how to create an expression column and add it to the NorthwindDataSet.Order_Details table.

```
' VB
' Create a new DataColumn and set its name and data type.
Dim TotalPriceColumn As New DataColumn("TotalPrice", GetType(System.Double))

' Set the column's Expression property to the desired expression,
' in this case the UnitPrice x Quantity, which is the total price
```

```
' of this record.
TotalPriceColumn.Expression = ("UnitPrice * Quantity")

' Now add the column to the DataTable
  NorthwindDataSet.Order_Details.Columns.Add(TotalPriceColumn)
```

```
// C#
// Create a new DataColumn and set its name and data type.
DataColumn TotalPriceColumn = new DataColumn
    ("TotalPrice", System.Type.GetType("System.Double"));

// Set the column's Expression property to the desired expression,
// in this case the UnitPrice x Quantity, which is the total price of this record.
TotalPriceColumn.Expression = ("UnitPrice * Quantity");

// Now add the column to the DataTable
northwindDataSet.Order_Details.Columns.Add(TotalPriceColumn);
```

How to Create Auto-Incrementing Columns in *DataTable* Objects

The *DataTable* itself assigns values to an auto-incrementing column in the table. This is typical of a table that contains information such as order information where it is desirable to have a unique OrderID, but the actual value of the OrderID column isn't important other than that it needs to be unique. *DataColumn* objects provide specific properties to create auto-incrementing columns where you can set the starting value, called the *AutoIncrementSeed*, as well as the increment, or number added to the last value, which is called the *AutoIncrementStep*.

The following code sample shows how to create an auto-increment column that creates records with a *SalesOrderID* value starting at *100*, and adds 5 to the previous value with each new row added. In other words, the first record created will have a value of *100* in the SalesOrderID column, and the next row will have a value of *105*, the next row *110*, and so on.

```
' VB
' Create the SalesOrderID column and set its data type to an integer.
SalesTable.Columns.Add("SalesOrderID", Type.GetType("System.Int32"))

' Set the AutoIncrement property to true makes this an
' auto increment column!
SalesTable.Columns("SalesOrderID").AutoIncrement = True

' Provide the starting value in the AutoIncrementSeed property.
SalesTable.Columns("SalesOrderID").AutoIncrementSeed = 100

' The amount added to the previous row's value is determined by the
' AutoIncrementStep value.
SalesTable.Columns("SalesOrderID").AutoIncrementStep = 5
```

```csharp
// C#
// Create the SalesOrderID column and set its data type to an integer.
SalesTable.Columns.Add("SalesOrderID", Type.GetType("System.Int32"));

// Set the AutoIncrement property to true makes this an
// auto increment column!
SalesTable.Columns["SalesOrderID"].AutoIncrement = true;

// Provide the starting value in the AutoIncrementSeed property.
SalesTable.Columns["SalesOrderID"].AutoIncrementSeed = 100;

// The amount added to the previous row's value is determined by the
// AutoIncrementStep value.
SalesTable.Columns["SalesOrderID"].AutoIncrementStep = 5;
```

How to Add Constraints to a *DataTable*

DataTable objects can be created with constraints similar to tables in databases. For example, you can designate columns in a *DataTable* to be foreign keys, or you can designate columns to contain unique values when it is inappropriate for a table to contain records with duplicate values in a column.

How to Create a Foreign Key Constraint

Create foreign key constraints by creating an instance of the *ForeignKey* class and assigning the desired column or columns from the parent and child tables to the constraint. For example, the following bit of code creates a new foreign key constraint between the OrderID columns from the Orders and OrderDetails tables in Northwind:

```vb
' VB
Dim ForeignKey As New ForeignKeyConstraint("FK_Orders_OrderDetails", _
    NorthwindDataset.Orders.Columns("OrderID"), _
    NorthwindDataset.Order_Details.Columns("OrderID"))
NorthwindDataset.Orders.Constraints.Add(ForeignKey)
```

```csharp
// C#
ForeignKeyConstraint ForeignKey = new ForeignKeyConstraint("FK_Orders_OrderDetails",
    NorthwindDataset.Orders.Columns["OrderID"],
    NorthwindDataset.Order_Details.Columns["OrderID"]);
NorthwindDataset.Orders.Constraints.Add(ForeignKey);
```

How to Create a Unique Constraint

Create unique constraints by creating an instance of the *UniqueConstraint* class and assigning the column to contain unique values to the constructor. For example, the following bit of code places a unique constraint on the OrderID column in the Orders table in Northwind:

```
' VB
Dim Unique As New UniqueConstraint(NorthwindDataSet.Orders.OrderIDColumn)
NorthwindDataSet.Orders.Constraints.Add(Unique)
```

```
// C#
UniqueConstraint unique = new UniqueConstraint(NorthwindDataSet.Orders.OrderIDColumn);
northwindDataSet.Orders.Constraints.Add(unique);
```

Quick Check

1. How do you add *DataTables* to a *DataSet*?
2. How do you display the computation of existing columns in a table?

Quick Check Answers

1. Add the table to the *DataSet.Tables* collection.
2. By creating an expression column.

Lab: Creating *DataTable* Objects

In this lab you will create *DataTable* objects.

▶ **Exercise 1: Creating a *DataTable***

The following example describes how to create a *DataTable* as well as how to create a new row of data and add it to the table. For demonstration purposes, the *DataTable* is displayed in a *DataGridView*.

1. Create a Windows application and name it **CreatingDataTables**.
2. Add a *DataGridView* to Form1 and name it **TableGrid**.
3. Add a button to the form and set the following properties:
   - ❑ *Name* = CreateTableButton
   - ❑ *Text* = Create Table
4. Add a second button to the form and set the following properties:
   - ❑ *Name* = AddRowButton
   - ❑ *Text* = Add Row
5. Double-click each button to create the button click event handlers.
6. Add the following code to the form (global to the form, outside any methods):

```
' VB
' Instantiate a new table (global to the form).
```

```
Private CustomersTable As New DataTable("Customers")
```

```
// C#
// Instantiate a new table (global to the form).
private DataTable CustomersTable = new DataTable("Customers");
```

7. Add the following code to the *CreateTableButton_Click* event handler:

```
' VB
' Set the DataGridView to display the table
TableGrid.DataSource = CustomersTable

' Define the schema of the table by adding DataColumn objects to
' the table's Columns collection.
CustomersTable.Columns.Add("CustomerID", Type.GetType("System.String"))
CustomersTable.Columns.Add("CompanyName", Type.GetType("System.String"))
CustomersTable.Columns.Add("ContactName", Type.GetType("System.String"))
CustomersTable.Columns.Add("ContactTitle", Type.GetType("System.String"))
CustomersTable.Columns.Add("Address", Type.GetType("System.String"))
CustomersTable.Columns.Add("City", Type.GetType("System.String"))
CustomersTable.Columns.Add("Region", Type.GetType("System.String"))
CustomersTable.Columns.Add("PostalCode", Type.GetType("System.String"))
CustomersTable.Columns.Add("Country", Type.GetType("System.String"))
CustomersTable.Columns.Add("Phone", Type.GetType("System.String"))
CustomersTable.Columns.Add("Fax", Type.GetType("System.String"))

' Set the CustomerID column As the primary key
Dim KeyColumns(1) As DataColumn
KeyColumns(0) = CustomersTable.Columns("CustomerID")
CustomersTable.PrimaryKey = KeyColumns

' Set the CustomerID and CompanyName columns
' to disallow Null values.
CustomersTable.Columns("CustomerID").AllowDBNull = False
CustomersTable.Columns("CompanyName").AllowDBNull = False
```

```
// C#
// Set the DataGridView to display the table
TableGrid.DataSource = CustomersTable;

// Define the schema of the table
// by adding DataColumn objects to
// the table's Columns collection.
CustomersTable.Columns.Add("CustomerID", Type.GetType("System.String"));
CustomersTable.Columns.Add("CompanyName", Type.GetType("System.String"));
CustomersTable.Columns.Add("ContactName", Type.GetType("System.String"));
CustomersTable.Columns.Add("ContactTitle", Type.GetType("System.String"));
CustomersTable.Columns.Add("Address", Type.GetType("System.String"));
CustomersTable.Columns.Add("City", Type.GetType("System.String"));
CustomersTable.Columns.Add("Region", Type.GetType("System.String"));
CustomersTable.Columns.Add("PostalCode", Type.GetType("System.String"));
CustomersTable.Columns.Add("Country", Type.GetType("System.String"));
CustomersTable.Columns.Add("Phone", Type.GetType("System.String"));
```

```
CustomersTable.Columns.Add("Fax", Type.GetType("System.String"));

// Set the CustomerID column as the primary key
DataColumn[] KeyColumns = new DataColumn[1];
KeyColumns[0] = CustomersTable.Columns["CustomerID"];
CustomersTable.PrimaryKey = KeyColumns;

// Set the CustomerID and CompanyName columns
// to disallow Null values.
CustomersTable.Columns["CustomerID"].AllowDBNull = false;
CustomersTable.Columns["CompanyName"].AllowDBNull = false;
```

8. Add the following code to the *AddRowButton_Click* event handler:

```
' VB
' Create a record (DataRow) to add to the table.
Dim CustRow As DataRow = CustomersTable.NewRow
With CustRow
    .Item("CustomerID") = "ALFKI"
    .Item("CompanyName") = "Alfreds Futterkiste"
    .Item("ContactName") = "Maria Anders"
    .Item("ContactTitle") = "Sales Representative"
    .Item("Address") = "Obere Str. 57"
    .Item("City") = "Berlin"
    .Item("Region") = Nothing
    .Item("PostalCode") = "12209"
    .Item("Country") = "Germany"
    .Item("Phone") = "030-0074321"
    .Item("Fax") = "030-0076545"
End With

' Add the record to the table.
CustomersTable.Rows.Add(CustRow)
```

```
// C#
// Create a record (DataRow) to add to the table.
DataRow CustRow = CustomersTable.NewRow();
Object[] CustRecord =  {"ALFKI", "Alfreds Futterkiste", "Maria Anders",
    "Sales Representative", "Obere Str. 57", "Berlin",
      null, "12209", "Germany", "030-0074321","030-0076545"};
CustRow.ItemArray = CustRecord;

// Add the record to the table.
CustomersTable.Rows.Add(CustRow);
```

9. Run the application and click the Create Table button.

   The grid displays an empty data table with the columns as shown in Figure 7-9.

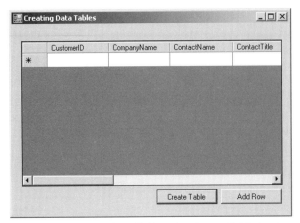

Figure 7-9 Form after clicking the Create Table button

10. Click the Add Row button, and a new record is added to the table, as shown in Figure 7-10.

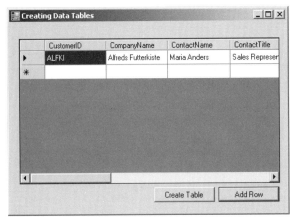

Figure 7-10 Form after clicking the Add Row button

11. Click the Add Row button again, and note the exception that occurs.

Lesson Summary

■ *DataTable* objects contain columns (*DataColumn* objects) and constraints just like tables in a database.

■ *DataColumn* and *Constraint* objects define the schema of a *DataTable*.

■ Constraints are created and added to the *DataTable.Constraints* collection.

Lesson Review

The following questions are intended to reinforce key information presented in this lesson. The questions are also available on the companion CD if you prefer to review them in electronic form.

NOTE Answers

Answers to these questions and explanations of why each choice is correct or incorrect are located in the "Answers" section at the end of the book.

---

1. What are the steps to create a *DataTable* programmatically?

   A. Run the Data Source Configuration Wizard.

   B. Instantiate a new *DataTable* and add *DataColumn* objects to the *Data-Table.Columns* collection.

   C. Add a new *DataSet* object to your project.

   D. Instantiate a new *DataSet* object.

2. What object would you set the properties on to create a primary key for a *DataTable*?

   A. *DataSet*

   B. *DataTable*

   C. *DataColumn*

   D. *DataRelation*

3. How do you specify that a *DataColumn* in a *DataTable* is part of a foreign key?

   A. Set the *DataColumn.ForeignKey* property to *True*.

   B. Set the *DataTable.ForeignKey* property to the desired *DataColumn*.

   C. Instantiate a new *ForeignKey* class and add it to the *DataTable.Constraints* collection.

   D. Define the foreign key in the *DataRelation* object.

Lesson 3: Creating *DataAdapter* Objects

DataAdapter objects contain the connection information as well as the Select, Update, Insert, and Delete commands needed to fetch and update data from a database and populate *DataTable* and *DataSet* objects. This lesson describes how to create and work with *DataAdapter* objects in ADO.NET.

After this lesson, you will be able to:

- Generate a strongly typed *DataSet*.
- Use the *OleDbDataAdapter* object to access an ADO Recordset or record.
- Generate *DataAdapter* commands automatically, using the *CommandBuilder* object.
- Generate *DataAdapter* commands programmatically.
- Populate a *DataSet* with a *DataAdapter*.
- Update the database with a *DataAdapter*.
- Resolve conflicts between a *DataSet* and a database, using the *DataAdapter*.
- Respond to changes made to data at the data source by using *DataAdapter* events.
  - ❑ Detect and respond to the *RowUpdating* event.
  - ❑ Detect and respond to the *RowUpdated* event.
  - ❑ Detect and respond to the *FillError* event.
- Perform batch operations using *DataAdapter* objects.
  - ❑ Perform batch updates with a *DataAdapter*.
  - ❑ Handle batch update-related events and errors.

Estimated lesson time: 45 minutes

What Is a *DataAdapter*?

DataAdapter objects are provider-specific objects (meaning there are specific data adapters for each provider, for example, *SqlDataAdapter* and *OleDbDataAdapter* objects) that contain information such as a data connection and commands, that enable your application to communicate with a database and fill a *DataSet* object's *DataTable* objects with data, as well as send updated data back to the database after changes are made to the data in your application's *DataTable* objects.

How to Create *DataAdapter* Objects

You can create *DataAdapter* objects visually, using the Data Adapter Configuration Wizard, or programmatically, by instantiating an instance of the desired provider-specific adapter and passing in a SELECT statement and a valid *Connection* object to the constructor. The practices in this lesson provide detailed instructions for creating adapters both visually and programmatically.

The following code shows how to instantiate a new *DataAdapter* by passing in the initial SELECT statement and a valid *Connection* object to the constructor.

```
' VB
' Create the SqlDataAdapter
Dim SqlDataAdapter1 as New SqlDataAdapter("SELECT * FROM Shippers", NorthwindConnection)
```

```
// C#
// Create the SqlDataAdapter
private SqlDataAdapter SqlDataAdapter1 = new SqlDataAdapter
    ("SELECT * FROM Shippers", NorthwindConnection);
```

DataAdapter Commands

DataAdapter objects are typically configured by specifying a single SELECT statement, which is used by the *DataAdapter* to fetch data and populate a *DataTable* in a *DataSet*. It's important to understand how the *DataAdapter* uses that SELECT statement as the basis for automatically generating the Insert, Update, and Delete statements that are needed to save changes made in the *DataSet* back to the database when calling the *Update* method of the *DataAdapter*. The *DataAdapter* generates these additional commands for you as part of the DataAdapter Configuration Wizard, (or DataSource Configuration Wizard, depending on your method of configuring data objects).

When creating *DataAdapters* programmatically, you may want to create the commands manually, or when using complex queries you may need to manually configure the commands used for updating. There are two ways to configure commands for a *DataAdapter*: you can create *Command* objects and assign them to their corresponding *DataAdapter* properties, or you can use a *CommandBuilder* object.

Creating *Command* Objects for a *DataAdapter*

Create the Select, Insert, Update, and Delete commands for the *DataAdapter* by coding individual valid commands for your particular database and assigning them to the corresponding *DataAdapter* command property. For example, the following code shows how to create the individual commands for a *DataAdapter* named *SqlDataAdapter1*.

This example assumes a valid *NorthwindConnection* object, as well as valid SQL statements for each command. (See the *CreatingDataAdapterCommands* sample on the CD.)

```
' VB
' Create the SqlDataAdapter
Dim SqlDataAdapter1 As New SqlDataAdapter("SELECT * FROM Shippers", NorthwindConnection)

Dim InsertCommand As New SqlCommand("Valid SQL Insert statement", NorthwindConnection)
' configure any necessary parameters for your command

Dim UpdateCommand As New SqlCommand("Valid SQL Update statement", NorthwindConnection)
' configure any necessary parameters for your command

Dim DeleteCommand As New SqlCommand("Valid SQL Delete statement", NorthwindConnection)
' configure any necessary parameters for your command

' Add the commands to the DataAdapter
SqlDataAdapter1.InsertCommand = InsertCommand
SqlDataAdapter1.UpdateCommand = UpdateCommand
SqlDataAdapter1.DeleteCommand = DeleteCommand
```

```
// C#
// Create the SqlDataAdapter
private SqlDataAdapter SqlDataAdapter1 = new SqlDataAdapter
    ("SELECT * FROM Shippers", NorthwindConnection);

SqlCommand InsertCommand =new SqlCommand("Valid SQL Insert statement", NorthWindConnection);
// configure any necessary parameters for your command

SqlCommand UpdateCommand =new SqlCommand("Valid SQL Update statement", NorthWindConnection);
// configure any necessary parameters for your command

SqlCommand DeleteCommand =new SqlCommand("Valid SQL Delete statement", NorthWindConnection);
// configure any necessary parameters for your command

// Add the commands to the DataAdapter
SqlDataAdapter1.InsertCommand = InsertCommand;
Sql1.UpdateCommand = UpdateCommand;
SqlDataAdapter1.DeleteCommand = DeleteCommand;
```

Using a *CommandBuilder* to Generate Commands for a *DataAdapter*

If your *DataAdapter* uses a Select statement that fetches data from a single table, you can use a *CommandBuilder* to automatically generate the Insert, Update, and Delete statements for the adapter. Another requirement to use a *CommandBuilder* is that your Select statement must return at least one primary key or unique column from the table.

To generate commands automatically using a *CommandBuilder*, instantiate a new *CommandBuilder* object in code and pass the *DataAdapter* that you want to generate the commands for into the constructor.

The following code shows how to generate commands for a *DataAdapter* named *SqlDataAdapter1* using a *CommandBuilder*:

```vb
' VB
' Instantiate a DataAdapter with a valid Select statement
Dim SqlDataAdapter1 As New SqlDataAdapter("Valid Single Table Select Statement")
' Instantiate a CommandBuilder for SqlDataAdapter1
Dim commands As New SqlCommandBuilder(SqlDataAdapter1)
```

```csharp
// C#
// Instantiate a DataAdapter with a valid Select statement
SqlDataAdapter SqlDataAdapter1 = new SqlDataAdapter("Valid Single Table Select Statement");
// Instantiate a CommandBuilder for SqlDataAdapter1
SqlCommandBuilder commands = new SqlCommandBuilder(SqlDataAdapter1);
```

Generating Typed *DataSet* Objects from *DataAdapter* Objects

You can generate strongly typed *DataSet* objects based on the information contained in a configured *DataAdapter* by selecting the Generate DataSet command on the Data menu. You need an existing *DataAdapter* configured with a *SelectCommand* to successfully generate a typed *DataSet* using the Generate DataSet command.

Resolving Conflicts Between a *DataSet* and a Database Using the *DataAdapter*

DataAdapter objects provide two specific properties that assist in resolving conflicts that may occur when attempting to fill a *DataSet* with a *DataAdapter*: the *MissingMapping-Action* property and the *MissingSchemaAction* property. These conflicts typically occur when changes have been made to the database schema or to the DataSet schema. For example, if columns are added to a table in the database and you attempt to perform a SELECT * from that table, the adapter uses these properties to decide what to do with the extra column and data.

MissingMappingAction

The *MissingMappingAction* property determines what your application should do when it attempts to fill data into a *DataSet* and the *DataSet* does not contain any matching table or column mappings that the *DataAdapter* is trying to fill. Set the

MissingMappingAction property to one of the values in the *MissingMappingAction* enumeration shown in Table 7-1.

Table 7-1 *MissingMappingAction* **Enumerations**

Name	Description
Error	Setting the *MissingMappingAction* to *Error* will throw an InvalidOperationException if the *DataAdapter* attempts to fill data in a column or table that does not exist.
Ignore	No action is taken. Any data that is targeted to a column or table that does not exist is discarded.
Passthrough	The column or table is created in the *DataSet* and populated with the available data.

MissingSchemaAction

The *MissingSchemaAction* property determines what your application should do when it attempts to fill data into a *DataSet* and the *DataSet* does not contain the expected schema that the *DataAdapter* is trying to fill. Set the *MissingSchemaAction* property to one of the values in the *MissingSchemaAction* enumeration shown in Table 7-2.

Table 7-2 *MissingSchemaAction* **Enumeration**

Name	Description
Add	The column or table is created in the DataSet and populated with the available data.
AddWithKey	The column is created (including any primary key information associated with the column) in the DataSet and populated with the available data.
Error	Setting the *MissingMappingAction* to *Error* will throw an InvalidOperationException if the *DataAdapter* attempts to fill data in a column or table that does not exist.
Ignore	No action is taken. Any data that is targeted to a column or table that does not exist is discarded.

Perform Batch Operations Using *DataAdapter* Objects

DataAdapter objects provide the opportunity to execute commands in batches through the *DataAdapter.UpdateBatchSize* property. Execute commands in batches when you are updating large numbers of records and want to reduce round trips to the database.

Perform Batch Updates with a *DataAdapter*

Set the *UpdateBatchSize* property of the *DataAdapter* to an integer representing the number of statements to execute as a batch. For example, to send batches of five statements at a time, you would set *UpdateBatchSize* = 5. Setting *UpdateBatchSize* = 0 causes the batch size to default to the largest batch size the server can process.

Handle Batch Update-Related Events and Errors

When performing batch updates, the *DataAdapter* fires a *RowUpdating* event for each row being updated but fires only one *RowUpdated* event for the entire batch.

> **Real World**
>
> *Steve Stein*
>
> One of the first applications I ever worked on had a back end database that contained about 20 or so tables. The number of custom objects that were used to perform queries and updates to the data in all these different tables was ridiculous! *DataAdapters* would have provided me with a more organized infrastructure and taken care of creating most, if not all of the actual update logic for me.

Lab: Working with *DataAdapter* Objects

In this lab you will create *DataAdapters*.

▶ **Exercise 1: Creating a *DataAdapter* with the Data Adapter Configuration Wizard**

1. Create a Windows application and name it **DataAdapterWizardExample**.

   In this version of Visual Studio, *DataAdapter* objects have been removed from the Toolbox in lieu of using the Designer-generated *TableAdapters*, so first add the *SqlDataAdapter* back into the Toolbox for this example.

2. Right-click the Data section of the Toolbox and select Choose Items.

3. In the Choose Toolbox Items dialog box, select the *SqlDataAdapter* item on the .NET Framework Components tab and click OK.

    This adds the *SqlDataAdapter* item into the Toolbox.

4. Drag the *SqlDataAdapter* object onto Form1 to start the Data Adapter Configuration Wizard.

5. On the Choose Your Data Connection page, select a connection to the Northwind database (or create a new connection if necessary).

6. On the Choose A Command Type page, leave the default setting of Use SQL Statements and click Next.

7. On the Generate the SQL statements page, type the following SQL statement:

    ```
    SELECT * FROM Customers
    ```

8. Click Finish to complete the wizard and add an instance of the configured *SqlDataAdapter* to the form.

9. Generate a strongly typed *DataSet* based on the configured adapter by selecting Generate DataSet on the Data menu and then clicking OK completing the Generate DataSet dialog box.

    You will notice that SqlDataAdapter1 is selected in the dialog box; this is the information that will be used to generate the strongly typed *DataSet*.

10. Replace the name of *DataSet1* with *NorthwindDataSet1* in the Generate DataSet dialog box; click OK to create a new *DataSet* and add it to the project.

11. Drag a *DataGridView* onto Form1.

12. Double-click an empty area of the form to create a *Form_Load* event handler.

13. Add the following code to the *Form_Load* event handler:

    ```vb
    ' VB
    ' Set the grid to display the customers table
    DataGridView1.DataSource = NorthwindDataSet1.Customers

    ' Call the Fill method of the DataAdapter to load the customers table with data.
    SqlDataAdapter1.Fill(NorthwindDataSet1.Customers)
    ```

    ```csharp
    // C#
    // Set the grid to display the customers table
    dataGridView.DataSource = NorthwindDataSet1.Customers;

    // Call the Fill method of the DataAdapter to load the customers table with data.
    sqlDataAdapter1.Fill(NorthwindDataSet1.Customers);
    ```

14. Run the application and verify that the Customers table appears in the grid.

15. Add a button to the form and set the following properties:

    ❑ *Name* = UpdateButton

    ❑ *Text* = "Save Changes"

16. Double-click the Save Changes button to create the button-click event handler.

17. Add the following code to the *UpdateButton_Click* event handler:

```
' VB
' Call the Update method of the data adapter to save the changes to the database.
SqlDataAdapter1.Update(NorthwindDataSet1)
```

```
// C#
// Call the Update method of the data adapter to save the changes to the database.
sqlDataAdapter1.Update(northwindDataSet1);
```

18. *DataAdapter* objects expose events that can be used when performing operations against a data source, for example, the *RowUpdating*, *RowUpdated*, and *FillError* events. The following steps add code and logic to the example that demonstrates working with these events.

19. In the Class Name drop-down list (the left-side *ComboBox* on top of the code editor), select SqlDataAdapter1. (For C# projects, select the SqlDataAdapter in the component tray and use the Events button in the Properties window to create events.)

20. Create an event handler for the *RowUpdating* event by selecting RowUpdating from the Method Name drop-down list.

21. Add the following code to the *RowUpdating* event handler:

```
' VB
' Create a Customer Row and assign it the row being changed
Dim CustRow As NorthwindDataset.CustomersRow = CType(e.Row,
NorthwindDataset.CustomersRow)

' Display a dialog to confirm the update
Dim response As DialogResult = MessageBox.Show("Continue updating " & _
    CustRow.CustomerID.ToString & "?", "Continue Update?", MessageBoxButtons.YesNo)

' Cancel the update if user selects No
If response = Windows.Forms.DialogResult.No Then
    e.Status = UpdateStatus.SkipCurrentRow
End If
```

```
// C#
// Create a Customer Row and assign it the row being changed
NorthwindDataset.CustomersRow CustRow = (NorthwindDataset.CustomersRow)e.Row;

// Display a dialog to confirm the update
```

```
DialogResult response = MessageBox.Show("Continue updating " +
    CustRow.CustomerID.ToString() + "?", "Continue Update?", MessageBoxButtons.YesNo);

// Cancel the update if user selects No
if (response == DialogResult.No)
{
    e.Status = UpdateStatus.SkipCurrentRow;
}
```

22. Create an event handler for the *RowUpdated* event by selecting RowUpdated from the Method Name drop-down list. (For C# projects, select the SqlData-Adapter in the component tray and use the Events button in the Properties window to create events.)

23. Add the following code to the *RowUpdated* event handler:

```
' VB
' Create a Customer Row and assign it the row being changed
Dim CustRow As NorthwindDataSet.CustomersRow = CType(e.Row,
NorthwindDataSet.CustomersRow)
MessageBox.Show(CustRow.CustomerID.ToString & " has been updated")

' After the row is updated reset the table to reflect the changes
NorthwindDataSet1.Customers.Clear()
SqlDataAdapter1.Fill(NorthwindDataSet1.Customers)
```

```
// C#
// Create a Customer Row and assign it the row being changed
northwindDataSet.CustomersRow CustRow = (northwindDataSet.CustomersRow)e.Row;
MessageBox.Show(CustRow.CustomerID.ToString() + " has been updated");

// After the row is updated reset the table to reflect the changes
northwindDataSet1.Customers.Clear();
sqlDataAdapter1.Fill(northwindDataSet1.Customers);
```

24. Create an event handler for the *FillError* event by selecting FillError from the Method Name drop-down list. (For C# projects, select the SqlDataAdapter in the component tray and use the Events button in the Properties window to create events.)

25. Add the following code to the *FillError* event handler:

```
' VB
' Display a dialog to respond to the error
Dim response As DialogResult = MessageBox.Show _
    ("The following error occurred while Filling the DataSet: " _
    & e.Errors.Message.ToString & " Continue attempting to fill?", _
    "FillError Encountered", MessageBoxButtons.YesNo)

' Attempt to continue if user selects Yes
If response = Windows.Forms.DialogResult.Yes Then
    e.Continue = True
```

```
Else
    e.Continue = False
End If
```

```
// C#
// Display a dialog to respond to the error
DialogResult response = MessageBox.Show
    ("The following error occurred while Filling the DataSet: " +
    e.Errors.Message.ToString() + " Continue attempting to fill?",
    "FillError Encountered", MessageBoxButtons.YesNo);

// Attempt to continue if user selects Yes
if (response == DialogResult.Yes)
{
  e.Continue = true;
}
else
{
    e.Continue = false;
}
```

26. Run the application and change some values in at least two different records.

27. Click the Save Changes button.

    At this point, the data adapter events allow you to respond to the dialog box asking whether to continue the update. Notice how you can individually handle each specific row the adapter is attempting to update.

▶ **Exercise 2: Creating *DataAdapters* in Code**

1. Create a Windows application and name it **ProgrammingDataAdapters**.

2. Add a *DataGridView* to the form.

3. Add the *System.Data.SqlClient* namespace to the form.

4. Add a *Connection* object for the Northwind database.

5. At this point, your form code should look like the following:

```
' VB
Imports System.Data.SqlClient

Public Class Form1
    Private NorthwindConnection As New SqlConnection( _
    "Data Source=.\sqlexpress;Initial Catalog=Northwind;Integrated Security=True")

End Class
```

```
// C#
using System;
using System.Collections.Generic;
using System.ComponentModel;
```

```
using System.Data;
using System.Drawing;
using System.Text;
using System.Windows.Forms;
using System.Data.SqlClient;

namespace ProgrammingDataAdaptersCS
{
    public partial class Form1 : Form
    {
        public Form1()
        {
            InitializeComponent();
        }

        private SqlConnection NorthwindConnection = new SqlConnection( _
            "Data Source=.\\sqlexpress;Initial Catalog=Northwind;Integrated
Security=True");
    }
}
```

6. Add code to create a *DataAdapter* below the *NorthwindConnection*.

' **VB**
```
Private SqlDataAdapter1 As New SqlDataAdapter("SELECT * FROM Customers",
NorthwindConnection)
```

// **C#**
```
private SqlDataAdapter SqlDataAdapter1;
```

7. Because *DataAdapters* are used to fill *DataSets*, add code below the preceding lines to create a new *NorthwindDataSet* with a Customers table:

' **VB**
```
Private NorthwindDataSet As New DataSet("Northwind")
Private CustomersTable As New DataTable("Customers")
```

// **C#**
```
private DataSet NorthwindDataSet = new DataSet("Northwind");
private DataTable CustomersTable = new DataTable("Customers");
```

8. Create a *Form_Load* event handler and add the following code to it:

' **VB**
```
NorthwindDataset.Tables.Add(CustomersTable)
SqlDataAdapter1.Fill(NorthwindDataset.Tables("Customers"))
DataGridView1.DataSource = NorthwindDataset.Tables("Customers")
```

// **C#**
```
SqlDataAdapter1 = new SqlDataAdapter("SELECT * FROM Customers", NorthwindConnection);
NorthwindDataset.Tables.Add(CustomersTable);
SqlDataAdapter1.Fill(NorthwindDataset.Tables["Customers"]);
dataGridView1.DataSource = NorthwindDataset.Tables["Customers"];
```

At this point, the *DataAdapter* contains only a Select command. Create a *CommandBuilder* that will provide the additional Insert, Update, and Delete commands required for updating the database with changes when the *DataAdapter.Update* method is called.

9. Add the following code beneath the previously added lines in the *Form_Load* event handler:

```vb
' VB
Dim commands As New SqlCommandBuilder(SqlDataAdapter)
```

```csharp
// C#
SqlCommandBuilder commands = new SqlCommandBuilder(SqlDataAdapter);
```

10. Add a button to the form and set the following properties:

   ❑ *Name* = UpdateButton

   ❑ *Text* = Save Changes

11. Double-click the Save Changes button and add the following code to the *UpdateButton_Click* event handler:

```vb
' VB
NorthwindDataset.EndInit()
SqlDataAdapter1.Update(NorthwindDataset.Tables("Customers"))
```

```csharp
// C#
NorthwindDataset.EndInit();
SqlDataAdapter1.Update(NorthwindDataset.Tables["Customers"]);
```

12. Run the application and change a value in one of the records in the grid.

13. Click the Save Changes button to send the updated value to the database.

14. Verify that the changes were saved to the database.

▶ **Exercise 3: Access an ADO Recordset or Record with a Data Adapter**

1. Create a new Windows application and name it **AccessingRecordsets**.

   Add a reference to the ADO objects:

2. From the Project menu, select Add Reference.

3. Select the COM tab.

4. Select Microsoft ActiveX Data Objects 2.8 Library and click OK.

5. Add a *DataGridView* to the form.

6. Add a button to the form and set the following properties:

   ❑ *Name* = FillRecordSetButton

   ❑ *Text* = Fill Recordset

7. Switch to code view and add the following method to the form:

```vb
' VB
    Private Function GetRecordset() As ADODB.Recordset
        ' Set to a valid OleDb connection string to the
        ' Northwind database.
        Dim NorthwindOleDbConnection As String = _
            "Provider=SQLOLEDB;Data Source=.\sqlexpress;" & _
            "Integrated Security=SSPI;Initial Catalog=Northwind"

        ' Create the New Recordset
        Dim rs As New ADODB.Recordset()
        rs.Open("SELECT * FROM Customers", NorthwindOleDbConnection, " & _
          "ADODB.CursorTypeEnum.adOpenStatic, ADODB.LockTypeEnum.adLockBatchOptimistic)

        Return rs
    End Function
```

```csharp
// C#
private ADODB.Recordset GetRecordset()
{
    // Set to a valid OleDb connection string to the
    // Northwind database.
    String NorthwindOleDbConnection = "Provider=SQLOLEDB;Data Source=.\\sqlexpress;" +
        "Integrated Security=SSPI;Initial Catalog=Northwind";

    // Create the New Recordset
    ADODB.Recordset rs = new ADODB.Recordset();
    rs.Open("SELECT * FROM Customers", NorthwindOleDbConnection, " +
      ADODB.CursorTypeEnum.adOpenStatic, ADODB.LockTypeEnum.adLockBatchOptimistic, 0);
    return rs;
}
```

8. Double-click the Fill Recordset button and add the following code to the button-click event handler:

```vb
' VB
' Create a new DataTable to hold our data
Dim CustomersTable As New DataTable("Customers")

' Create a new DataAdapter to fill the DataTable
Dim Adapter As New OleDb.OleDbDataAdapter

' Fill the Customers DataTable with the
' ADO Recordset.
Adapter.Fill(CustomersTable, GetRecordset())

' Display the Customers table in the DataGridView.
DataGridView1.DataSource = CustomersTable
```

```csharp
// C#
// Create a new DataTable to hold our data
DataTable CustomersTable = new DataTable("Customers");
```

```
// Create a new DataAdapter to fill the DataTable
System.Data.OleDb.OleDbDataAdapter Adapter = new System.Data.OleDb.OleDbDataAdapter();

// Fill the Customers DataTable with the
// ADO Recordset.
Adapter.Fill(CustomersTable, GetRecordset());

// Display the Customers table in the DataGridView.
dataGridView1.DataSource = CustomersTable;
```

9. Run the application and click the Fill Recordset button.

10. The customers table is filled by the *OleDbDataAdapter* filling the *DataTable* with the Recordset.

Lesson Summary

- *DataAdapter* objects contain a *Connection* object.

- *DataAdapter* objects contain individual Insert, Update, and Delete commands (in addition to the Select command) to save changes back to the database.

- You can generate a typed *DataSet* based on the Select command of a configured *DataAdapter*.

- A *CommandBuilder* object can be used to automatically generate the Insert, Update, and Delete commands of a *DataAdapter* based on a valid (single table) Select command.

- Resolve conflicts when filling data using the *MissingSchemaAction* and *Missing-MappingAction* properties.

- You can use an *OleDbDataAdapter* to fill *DataSet* objects using ADO Recordsets.

Lesson Review

The following questions are intended to reinforce key information presented in this lesson. The questions are also available on the companion CD if you prefer to review them in electronic form.

NOTE Answers

Answers to these questions and explanations of why each choice is correct or incorrect are located in the "Answers" section at the end of the book.

---

1. What are the main objects that make up a *DataAdapter*?

    A. *Connection* and *DataTable* objects

    B. *Connection* and *Command* objects

    C. *DataTable* and *DataSet* objects

    D. *Command* and *DataSet* objects

2. How do you configure a *DataAdapter* to save changes back to a database? (Choose all that apply.)

    A. Instantiate a *CommandBuilder* object and pass it a *DataAdapter* with a configured Select command.

    B. Call the *DataAdapter.Update* method.

    C. Assign a valid *Command* object to the *DataAdapter* object's *InsertCommand*, *UpdateCommand*, and *DeleteCommand* properties.

    D. Call the *DataAdapter.Fill* method.

3. How do you use a *DataAdapter* to access an ADO Recordset?

    A. Create a Recordset and call the *DataSet.Fill* method.

    B. Create a *DataSet* and set its *DataSource* property to the Recordset.

    C. Call the *DataAdapter.Fill* method and pass the Recordset as an argument.

    D. Set the *DataAdapter* command's CommandText to the name of the Recordset.

Lesson 4: Working with Data in *DataTable* Objects

This lesson describes how to load data into a *DataTable* as well as insert, update, and delete rows in a *DataTable*. In addition to modifying the data in a *DataTable*, we will also explain how to inspect the row state and row version of a record to determine what changes have been made to the data since the last update.

After this lesson, you will be able to:

- ■ Manage data within a *DataTable*.
  - ❑ Add data to a table.
  - ❑ View data in a table.
  - ❑ Edit data in a row.
  - ❑ Use row states and row versions.
  - ❑ Add a row to a table.
  - ❑ Delete a row from a table.
  - ❑ Add and read row error information.
  - ❑ Accept or reject changes to rows in a *DataTable*.
- ■ Handle *DataTable* events.

Estimated lesson time: 30 minutes

Adding Data to a *DataTable*

To add data to a *DataTable*, you create a new *DataRow*. For typed *DataSet* objects, create a row of the typed table; for example, create a new *CustomersRow*. After creating a new row, set the individual columns to the desired values. After creating the row and setting the values, you must add the row to the *DataTable* by adding it to the *Data-Table.Rows* collection.

The following example creates a new row, sets a couple of column values, and adds the row to the Customers table. Because the *NewRow* method returns an untyped *DataRow*, it is cast to a typed *CustomersRow*.

```vb
' VB
Dim NewRow As NorthwindDataset.CustomersRow = _
    CType(NorthwindDataset1.Customers.NewRow, NorthwindDataset.CustomersRow)
NewRow.CustomerID = "WINGT"
NewRow.CompanyName = "Wingtip Toys"
NewRow.ContactName = "Steve Lasker"
```

```
NorthwindDataset1.Customers.Rows.Add(NewRow)

// C#
NorthwindDataset.CustomersRow NewRow =
    (NorthwindDataset.CustomersRow)NorthwindDataset1.Customers.NewRow;
NewRow.CustomerID = "WINGT";
NewRow.CompanyName = "Wingtip Toys";
NewRow.ContactName = "Steve Lasker";
…
NorthwindDataset1.Customers.Rows.Add(NewRow);
```

Editing Data in a *DataTable*

Modify values in individual columns of a *DataTable* by selecting the *DataRow* you want to edit and assigning a new value to the desired column.

For example, the following code changes the CompanyName column of the *Selected-Row* to the value assigned, in this case, "Contoso":

```
' VB
SelectedRow("CompanyName") = "Contoso"
```

```
// C#
SelectedRow["CompanyName"] = "Contoso";
```

Deleting Data in a *DataTable*

To delete rows from a *DataTable*, call the *DataRow.Delete* method, which sets the row's *RowState* to *Deleted*, which allows you to iterate through the deleted rows prior to committing the deletion (by calling the *DataAdapter.Update* method or calling *AcceptChanges*).

The following code sample marks the selected row for deletion from the *DataTable*. The row will be permanently removed from the table the next time *AcceptChanges* is called.

```
' VB
SelectedRow.Delete
```

```
// C#
SelectedRow.Delete();
```

Maintaining Changes to *DataRow* Objects

Changes to *DataRow* objects that have not yet been accepted or rejected are maintained by the *RowState* and *DataRowVersion* enumerations.

The *RowState* is used to determine the state of a row. When first populated, the rows in a *DataTable* have a *RowState* of *Unchanged*. Table 7-3 details the different values of the *RowState* enumeration.

Table 7-3 *RowState* Enumeration

Value	Description
Unchanged	No changes have been made since the last *AcceptChanges* call or since the initial filling of the *DataTable*.
Added	This row has been added since the last *AcceptChanges* call.
Modified	This row has been updated since the last *AcceptChanges* call.
Deleted	This row has been deleted from the *DataTable* since the last *AcceptChanges* call.
Detached	This row has not yet been added to any *DataTable.Rows* collection.

In addition to *RowState*, each row also maintains different versions after changes are made. These differing versions are accessed by passing a value from the *DataRow-Version* enumeration as an argument in addition to the column index when accessing the data in a row. For example, you can access the current and original values of a column in a specific *DataRow* to perform processing prior to calling *AcceptChanges*.

Accepting and Rejecting Changes to a *DataTable*

When all changes to a row are deemed valid, you can accept the modifications by calling the *DataRow.AcceptChanges* method. Calling the *AcceptChanges* method sets the *RowState* of the row to *Unchanged* and commits all current values to original. You can call *AcceptChanges* on the *DataRow*, *DataTable*, or entire *DataSet*. If you decide to abort changes instead of accepting them, call the *RejectChanges* method of the *DataRow*, *DataTable*, or *DataSet*.

DataTable Events

DataTable objects expose several events that are raised when changes are being made to the data in the table.

The main events available when working with *DataTable* objects are listed in Table 7-4.

Table 7-4   *DataTable* Events

Event	Desription
ColumnChanged	Raised after a value is inserted into a column
ColumnChanging	Raised when a value is submitted to change a column
RowChanged	Raised after a row in the table has been edited
RowChanging	Raised when a row in the table is edited
RowDeleted	Raised after a row is marked for deletion
RowDeleting	Raised when a row is marked for deletion

Row Errors

When errors are encountered during the processing of *DataRows*, a value is added to the *RowError* property. The *RowError* property is a string that is typically set to an error message describing the error, but it can be set to any string and used as needed in your application. Once a *DataRow.RowError* property is assigned, the *DataTable.HasErrors* property is automatically set to *True*, indicating errors exist in the *DataTable*. When it is determined that errors exist, you can use the *DataTable.GetErrors* method to return an array of *DataRows* containing all rows that have errors or, more specifically, all rows with a *RowError* value other than null (nothing, or the empty string).

To remove an error, set the *DataRow.RowError* property to an empty string.

Quick Check

1. How do you add data to a *DataTable*?
2. How do you commit pending modifications to the data in a *DataTable*?

Quick Check Answers

1. Create a new *DataRow* and add it to the *DataTable.Rows* collection.
2. By calling *AcceptChanges* on the *DataRow*, *DataTable*, or *DataSet*.

Lab: Working with Data in a *DataTable*

In this lab you will manipulate the data in a *DataTable*.

▶ **Exercise 1: Working with *DataTable* Objects**

This practice will provide code examples that demonstrate adding data to a table, deleting rows in a table, and editing existing values in a data row and how to view the *RowState* and *DataRowVersion* information for records in a *DataTable*. After modifying records, the *AcceptChanges* and *RejectChanges* methods will be demonstrated as well.

1. Create a Windows application and name it **WorkingWithDataTables**.

2. Add a *DataGridView* to the form and change its *Name* property to *Customers-DataGridView*.

3. Add a button to the form and set the following properties:

    ❑ *Name* = FillTableButton

    ❑ *Text* = Fill Table

4. Drop a *SqlDataAdapter* from the Toolbox onto the form to start the Data Adapter Configuration Wizard.

NOTE *SqlDataAdapter Toolbox item*

If the *SqlDataAdapter* is not in the Toolbox, right-click the Data section of the Toolbox, select Choose Items, and then select the *SqlDataAdapter* item on the .NET Framework Components tab. Click OK.

---

5. Select or create a new connection to the Northwind database and click Next.

6. Leave the default option to Use SQL Statements, and then click Next.

7. Type **SELECT * FROM Customers** on the Generate The SQL Statements page and click Finish.

    The adapter and related *Connection* object are added to the form and appear in the component tray.

8. Right-click *SqlDataAdapter1* in the component tray and select Generate DataSet.

9. In the Generate DataSet dialog box, replace *DataSet1* with NorthwindDataSet and click OK.

    An instance of the *NorthwindDataSet* is added to the form and appears in the component tray.

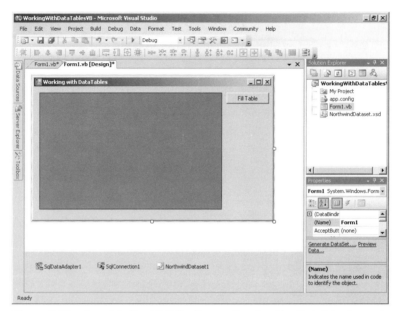

Figure 7-11 Form1 in the VS IDE after configuring the *DataAdapter* and generating the *DataSet*

10. Add the *System.Data.SqlClient* namespace to your form.

11. Create a *Form Load* event handler and add the following code to the *Form1_Load* event handler:

```
' VB
CustomersDataGridView.DataSource = NorthwindDataset1.Customers
' For this example we will turn off the ability to edit directly in a cell.
CustomersDataGridView.MultiSelect = False
CustomersDataGridView.SelectionMode = DataGridViewSelectionMode.CellSelect
CustomersDataGridView.EditMode = DataGridViewEditMode.EditProgrammatically
```

```
// C#
CustomersDataGridView.DataSource = NorthwindDataset1.Customers;
// For this example we will turn off the ability to edit directly in a cell.
CustomersDataGridView.MultiSelect = false;
CustomersDataGridView.SelectionMode = DataGridViewSelectionMode.CellSelect;
CustomersDataGridView.EditMode = DataGridViewEditMode.EditProgrammatically;
```

12. Create a button-click event handler for the *FillTableButton* and add the following code:

```
' VB
SqlDataAdapter1.Fill(NorthwindDataset1.Customers)
```

```
// C#
sqlDataAdapter1.Fill(NorthwindDataset1.Customers);
```

```
Add a button to the form and set the following properties:
```

❑ *Name* = AddRowButton

❑ *Text* = Add Row

13. Create a button-click event handler for the *AddRowButton* and add the following code:

```vb
' VB
' Create a new instance of a Customers row.
Dim NewRow As NorthwindDataset.CustomersRow = _
    CType(NorthwindDataset1.Customers.NewRow, NorthwindDataset.CustomersRow)

' Set the values for each column in the row.
With NewRow
    .CustomerID = "WINGT"
    .CompanyName = "Wingtip Toys"
    .ContactName = "Steve Lasker"
    .ContactTitle = "CEO"
    .Address = "1234 Main Street"
    .City = "Buffalo"
    ._Region = "NY"
    .PostalCode = "98052"
    .Country = "USA"
    .Phone = "206-555-0111"
    .Fax = "206-555-0112"
End With

' Add the new row to the Rows collection of the Customers table.
Try
    NorthwindDataset1.Customers.Rows.Add(NewRow)
Catch ex As Exception
    MessageBox.Show(ex.Message, "Add Row Failed")
End Try
```

```csharp
// C#
// Create a new instance of a Customers row.
NorthwindDataset.CustomersRow NewRow =
    (NorthwindDataset.CustomersRow)NorthwindDataset1.Customers.NewRow();

// Set the values for each column in the row.
NewRow.CustomerID = "WINGT";
NewRow.CompanyName = "Wingtip Toys";
NewRow.ContactName = "Steve Lasker";
NewRow.ContactTitle = "CEO";
NewRow.Address = "1234 Main Street";
NewRow.City = "Buffalo";
NewRow.Region = "NY";
NewRow.PostalCode = "98052";
NewRow.Country = "USA";
NewRow.Phone = "206-555-0111";
NewRow.Fax = "206-555-0112";

// Add the new row to the Rows collection of the Customers table.
```

```
try
{
    NorthwindDataset1.Customers.Rows.Add(NewRow);
}
catch (Exception ex)
{
    MessageBox.Show(ex.Message, "Add Row Failed");}
```

14. Add the following code to the form class that creates a function to return the *CustomersRow* selected in the grid:

```vb
' VB
Private Function GetSelectedRow() As NorthwindDataset.CustomersRow
    ' Get the selected DataRow
    Dim SelectedCustomerID As String = _
        CustomersDataGridView.CurrentRow.Cells("CustomerID").Value.ToString
    ' Using the SelectedCustomerID get the selected row.
    Dim SelectedRow As NorthwindDataset.CustomersRow = _
        NorthwindDataset1.Customers.FindByCustomerID(SelectedCustomerID)

    Return SelectedRow
End Function
```

```csharp
// C#
private NorthwindDataset.CustomersRow  GetSelectedRow()
{
    // Get the selected DataRow
    String SelectedCustomerID  =
        CustomersDataGridView.CurrentRow.Cells["CustomerID"].Value.ToString();
    // Using the SelectedCustomerID get the selected row.
    NorthwindDataset.CustomersRow SelectedRow  =
        NorthwindDataset1.Customers.FindByCustomerID(SelectedCustomerID);

    return SelectedRow;
}
```

15. Add a button to the form and set the following properties:

   ❑ *Name* = DeleteRowButton

   ❑ *Text* = Delete Row

16. Create a button-click event handler for the *DeleteRowButton* and add the following code:

```vb
' VB
' Call the Delete method of the selected row to mark it as deleted in the DataTable
GetSelectedRow.Delete()
```

```csharp
// C#
// Call the Delete method of the selected row to mark it as deleted in the DataTable
GetSelectedRow().Delete();
```

17. Add three buttons to the form and set the following properties:
    - ❑ *Name* = UpdateValueButton
    - ❑ *Text* = Update Value
    - ❑ *Name* = AcceptChangesButton
    - ❑ *Text* = Accept Changes
    - ❑ *Name* = RejectChangesButton
    - ❑ *Text* = Reject Changes

18. Add a *TextBox* next to the *UpdateValueButton* and set its *Name* property to Cell-ValueTextBox.

19. Add three more *TextBox* objects and set the *Name* properties to the following:
    - ❑ *OriginalDRVTextBox*
    - ❑ *CurrentDRVTextBox*
    - ❑ *RowStateTextBox*

    The Form layout should appear similar to Figure 7-12.

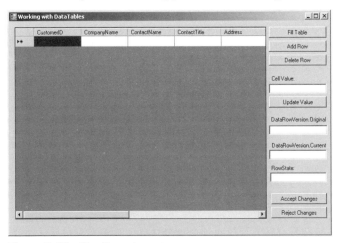

Figure 7-12   The Form layout

20. Add the following code to the form class that updates the text boxes with the row versions and row state:

```
' VB
Private Sub UpdateRowVersionDisplay()
    ' Display the Original and Current DataRowVersion of the selected Cell
    Try
        CurrentDRVTextBox.Text = GetSelectedRow.Item _
```

```vb
                    (CustomersDataGridView.CurrentCell.OwningColumn.Name, _
                    DataRowVersion.Current).ToString
        Catch ex As Exception
            CurrentDRVTextBox.Text = ex.Message
        End Try

        Try
            OriginalDRVTextBox.Text = GetSelectedRow.Item _
                (CustomersDataGridView.CurrentCell.OwningColumn.Name, _
                DataRowVersion.Original).ToString
        Catch ex As Exception
            OriginalDRVTextBox.Text = ex.Message
        End Try

        ' Display the current RowState of the selected row
        RowStateTextBox.Text = GetSelectedRow.RowState.ToString
    End Sub
```

```csharp
// C#
private void UpdateRowVersionDisplay()
{
    // Display the Original and Current DataRowVersion of the selected Cell
    try
    {
        CurrentDRVTextBox.Text = GetSelectedRow()
            [CustomersDataGridView.CurrentCell.OwningColumn.Name,
            DataRowVersion.Current].ToString();
    }
    catch (Exception ex)
    {
        CurrentDRVTextBox.Text = ex.Message;
    }

    try
    {
        OriginalDRVTextBox.Text = GetSelectedRow()
            [CustomersDataGridView.CurrentCell.OwningColumn.Name,
            DataRowVersion.Original].ToString();
    }
    catch (Exception ex)
    {
        OriginalDRVTextBox.Text = ex.Message;
    }

    // Display the current RowState of the selected row
    RowStateTextBox.Text = GetSelectedRow().RowState.ToString();
}
```

21. Create an event handler for the *UpdateValueButton_Click* event and add the following code:

```vb
' VB
GetSelectedRow(CustomersDataGridView.CurrentCell.OwningColumn.Name) =
CellValueTextBox.Text
UpdateRowVersionDisplay()
```

```csharp
// C#
GetSelectedRow()[CustomersDataGridView.CurrentCell.OwningColumn.Name] =
    CellValueTextBox.Text;
UpdateRowVersionDisplay();
```

22. Create an event handler for the *CustomersDataGridView_CellClick* event and add the following code:

```vb
' VB
' Populate the CellValueTextBox with the selected cell
CellValueTextBox.Text = CustomersDataGridView.CurrentCell.Value.ToString
' Refresh the other text boxes
UpdateRowVersionDisplay()
```

```csharp
// C#
// Populate the CellValueTextBox with the selected cell
CellValueTextBox.Text = CustomersDataGridView.CurrentCell.Value.ToString();
// Refresh the other text boxes
UpdateRowVersionDisplay();
```

23. Create an event handler for the *AcceptChangesButton.*Click event and add the following code:

```vb
' VB
GetSelectedRow().AcceptChanges()
UpdateRowVersionDisplay()
```

```csharp
// C#
GetSelectedRow().AcceptChanges();
UpdateRowVersionDisplay();
```

24. Create an event handler for the *RejectChangesButton* and add the following code:

```vb
' VB
GetSelectedRow().RejectChanges()
UpdateRowVersionDisplay()
```

```csharp
// C#
GetSelectedRow().RejectChanges();
UpdateRowVersionDisplay();
```

25. Run the application and click the Fill Table button.

26. Click around the grid and notice that the *Original* and *Current* values show as the same, and the *RowState* display is *Unchanged*.

27. Now click the cell that contains Maria Anders (in the first row) and type **Maria AndersEdited** in the CellValueTextBox.

28. Click the UpdateValue button and notice that the value is updated in the grid, the Current and Original text boxes display the different versions of the record, and the *RowState* has been changed to read *Modified*.

29. Now click the Add Row button.

30. Scroll down to the bottom of the grid and select one of the cells in the new record (WINGT).

    Notice that the *RowState* is *Added* to reflect that this is a new row, and the Original text box shows that there is no original data, again because this is a new row.

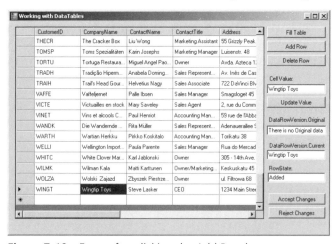

Figure 7-13   Form after clicking the Add Row button

31. Scroll back to the row with the *MariaAndersEdited* field and select it.

32. Click the RejectChanges button and inspect the row version and row state values.

33. Scroll to the WINGT record and select it.

34. Click the Accept Changes button and inspect the row version and row state values.

Lesson Summary

- Add data to a *DataTable* by creating a new *DataRow* and adding it to the *Data-Table.Rows* collection.

- Edit data in a *DataTable* by setting the values of the individual *DataColumn* objects in a *DataRow*.

- Delete rows in a *DataTable* by calling the *Delete* method of a *DataRow*.

- Monitor and keep track of changes to *DataRow* objects by using the *RowState* and *RowVersion* enumerations.

- *DataTable* events are raised as data is changed in specific *DataColumn* objects or entire *DataRow* objects.

- Set the *RowError* property of a *DataRow* to indicate a row with an error.

Lesson Review

The following questions are intended to reinforce key information presented in this lesson. The questions are also available on the companion CD if you prefer to review them in electronic form.

NOTE Answers

Answers to these questions and explanations of why each choice is correct or incorrect are located in the "Answers" section at the end of the book.

---

1. When adding a new row to a *DataTable*:

   A. Create an instance of a *DataRow* and call the *Update* method of the *Data-Adapter*.

   B. Create an instance of a *DataRow* (or typed row), and add it to the *Rows* collection of the *DataTable*.

   C. Call the *DataTable.NewRow* method.

   D. Create an instance of a *DataRow*.

2. How do you access the original value in the CustomerId column?

   A. OriginalValue = DataRow("CustomerID").DataRowVersion.Original

   B. OriginalValue = DataColumn("CustomerID").Original

   C. OriginalValue = DataRow("CustomerID", DataRowVersion.Original)

   D. OriginalValue = DataRow("CustomerID")

3. What *DataTable* event would you handle to validate for an acceptable value in a column? (Choose all that apply.)

   A. *ColumnChanged*

   B. *ColumnChanging*

   C. *RowChanged*

   D. *RowChanging*

Lesson 5: Working with XML in *DataSet* Objects

This lesson describes how to use *DataSet* objects when working with data formatted as XML. *DataSet* objects can be filled from an XML document or an XML stream, and they can load or write out their schema information. *DataSet* objects have several methods for working with XML data that will be described in the following examples.

After this lesson, you will be able to:

■ Represent data in a *DataSet* using XML.

❑ Load a *DataSet* from an XML stream or document.

❑ Write a *DataSet* as XML data.

❑ Load *DataSet* schema information from an XML stream or document.

❑ Write *DataSet* schema information as XML schema (XSD).

❑ Synchronize a *DataSet* with an *XmlDataDocument*.

❑ Perform an XPath query on a *DataSet*.

❑ Apply an XSLT transform to a *DataSet*.

❑ Create nested *DataRelation* objects in a *DataSet* to represent XML data.

❑ Generate *DataSet* relational structures from XML schema (XSD).

❑ Map XML schema (XSD) constraints to *DataSet* constraints.

❑ Infer *DataSet* structures from an XML stream or document.

Estimated lesson time: 60 minutes

Writing a *DataSet* as XML Data

To save the data in a *DataSet* as XML-formatted data, use the *WriteXml* method of the *DataSet*. You can save the XML data directly to a file, or you can write it to a stream. Call the *WriteXml* method of a *DataSet* to save the contents of all tables in the *DataSet* as XML or call the *WriteXml* method of an individual *DataTable* to write the data from only that table.

The following code example saves the data in the *NorthwindDataSet* to a file named Northwind.xml.

```
' VB
NorthwindDataset.WriteXml("Northwind.xml")
```

```
// C#
NorthwindDataset.WriteXml("Northwind.xml");
```

Writing *DataSet* Schema Information as XML Schema

To save a *DataSet* object's schema information, use the *WriteXmlSchema* method of the *DataSet*. You can save the XML schema information directly to a file, or you can write it to a stream. Call the *WriteXmSchema* method of a *DataSet* to save the schema of the entire *DataSet* or call the *WriteXmlSchema* method of an individual *DataTable* to write the schema from only that table.

The following code example saves the data in the *NorthwindDataSet* object's schema information to a file named Northwind.xsd.

```
' VB
NorthwindDataset.WriteXmlSchema("Northwind.xsd")
```

```
// C#
NorthwindDataset.WriteXmlSchema("Northwind.xsd");
```

Loading a *DataSet* from an XML Stream or Document

To load XML data into a *DataSet*, use the *ReadXml* method of the *DataSet*. You can read the XML data directly from a file, or you can read it from a stream. Call the *ReadXml* method of a *DataSet* to load the entire *DataSet* or call the *ReadXml* method of an individual *DataTable* to load only the data for that table.

The following code example loads the *NorthwindDataSet* from the contents of a file named Northwind.xml.

```
' VB
NorthwindDataset.ReadXml("Northwind.xml")
```

```
// C#
NorthwindDataset.ReadXml("Northwind.xml");
```

Loading *DataSet* Schema Information from an XML Stream or Document

To load schema information into a *DataSet*, use the *ReadXmlSchema* method of the *DataSet*. Load the XML schema information directly from an .xsd file or read it from a stream. Call the *ReadXmlSchema* method of a *DataSet* to load the entire *DataSet* or call the *ReadXmlSchema* method of an individual *DataTable* to load the schema for only that table.

The following code example reads the schema information into the *NorthwindDataSet* from a file named Northwind.xsd.

```vb
' VB
NorthwindDataset.ReadXmlSchema("Northwind.xsd")
```

```csharp
// C#
NorthwindDataset.ReadXmlSchema("Northwind.xsd");
```

Synchronizing a *DataSet* with an *XmlDataDocument*

When working with XML data and *DataSet* objects, you will typically need to manipulate data through the *DataSet* classes as well as XML classes available in the .NET Framework. Keeping your *DataSet* and *XmlDataDocument* in synch allows you to process the data using whichever method of access you prefer while working on the same data source.

The following code example shows how to create a new *XmlDataDocument* and synchronize it with the *NorthwindDataSet*.

```vb
' VB
Dim NwDataDocument As New XmlDataDocument(NorthwindDataset)
```

```csharp
// C#
XmlDataDocument NwDataDocument = new XmlDataDocument(NorthwindDataset);
```

Perfoming an XPath Query on a *DataSet*

You can perform XPath queries against data in a *DataSet* after synchronizing a *DataSet* with an *XmlDataDocument*. Pass an XPath query to the *XmlDataDocument.DocumentElement.SelectNodes* method. The *SelectNodes* method returns the data as a collection of *Xml.XmlNode* objects.

The following code example shows how to execute an XPath query and iterate through the results:

```vb
' VB
Dim row As DataRow
Dim NwDataDocument As New Xml.XmlDataDocument(NorthwindDataset)
Dim CustomerNodes As Xml.XmlNodeList = NwDataDocument.DocumentElement.SelectNodes("*")
For Each xmlNode As Xml.XmlNode In CustomerNodes
    row = NwDataDocument.GetRowFromElement(CType(xmlNode, Xml.XmlElement))
    If row IsNot Nothing Then
```

```
        ' access data through row indices for example:
        MessageBox.Show(row(1).ToString())
    End If
Next
```

```csharp
// C#
 DataRow row;
Xml.XmlDataDocument NwDataDocument = new Xml.XmlDataDocument(NorthwindDataset)
Xml.XmlNodeList CustomerNodes = NwDataDocument.DocumentElement.SelectNodes("*");
foreach (Xml.XmlNode xmlNode In CustomerNodes)
{
    row = NwDataDocument.GetRowFromElement(Xml.XmlElement)xmlNode;
    if (row != null)
    {
        // access data through row indices for example:
        MessageBox.Show(row[1].ToString());
    }
}
```

Lab: Working with XML in *DataSets*

In this lab you will load and save XML Data to a *Dataset*.

▶ **Exercise 1: Saving a *DataSet* Objects as XML**

This example takes the data from a *DataSet* and saves it as formatted XML in a file named Northwind.xml.

1. Create a Windows application and name it **SavingDataSetsAsXml**.

2. Drag a *SqlDataAdapter* onto the form to start the Data Adapter Configuration Wizard.

3. Select a connection to the Northwind sample database.

4. On the Choose A Command Type page, select the default value of Use SQL Statements. Then, click Next.

5. On the Generate The SQL Statements page, type **SELECT * FROM Customers**. Then, click Finish.

6. Change the name from SqlDataAdapter1 to CustomersAdapter.

7. Drag a second *SqlDataAdapter* onto the form to start the Data Adapter Configuration Wizard again.

8. On the Choose A Command Type page, select the default value of Use SQL Statements. Then, click Next.

9. Type **SELECT * FROM Orders** in the Generate the SQL statements page. Then, click Finish.

10. Change the name from SqlDataAdapter1 to OrdersAdapter.

11. Right-click the *CustomersAdapter* in the component tray and select Generate DataSet.

12. Name the new *DataSet NorthwindDataSet* (replacing DataSet1). Select both the Customers and Orders tables and click OK.

13. Drag a *DataGridView* onto the form and set its *Name* property to *CustomersGrid*.

14. Drag a button onto the form and set the following properties:
    - ❑ *Name* = FillDataSetButton
    - ❑ *Text* = Fill DataSet

15. Drag a second button onto the form and set the following properties:
    - ❑ *Name* = SaveXmlDataButton
    - ❑ *Text* = Save XML Data

16. Drag a third button onto the form and set the following properties:
    - ❑ *Name* = SaveXmlSchemaButton
    - ❑ *Text* = Save XML Schema

17. Double-click the Fill DataSet button to create the button-click event handler.

18. Add the following code to the *FillDataSetButton_Click* event handler:

```
' VB
' Fill the Customers and Orders tables.
CustomersAdapter.Fill(NorthwindDataSet1.Customers)
OrdersAdapter.Fill(NorthwindDataSet1.Orders)

' Bind the grid to the Customers table.
CustomersGrid.DataSource = NorthwindDataSet1.Customers

// C#
// Fill the Customers and Orders tables.
CustomersAdapter.Fill(northwindDataSet1.Customers);
OrdersAdapter.Fill(northwindDataSet1.Orders);

// Bind the grid to the Customers table.
CustomersGrid.DataSource = northwindDataSet1.Customers;
```

19. Double-click the Save Xml Data button to create the button-click event handler.

20. Add the following code to the *SaveXmlDataButton_Click* event handler:

```
' VB
Try
    NorthwindDataset1.WriteXml("C:\DataSources\Northwind.xml")
```

```
        MessageBox.Show("Data saved As Northwind.xml")
    Catch ex As Exception
        MessageBox.Show(ex.Message)
    End Try
```

```
// C#
try
{
    northwindDataSet1.WriteXml(@"C:\DataSources\Northwind.xml");
    MessageBox.Show("Data saved as Northwind.xml");
}
catch (Exception ex)
{
    MessageBox.Show(ex.Message);
}
```

21. Double-click the Save Xml Schema button to create the button-click event handler.

22. Add the following code to the *SaveXmlSchemaButton_Click* event handler:

```
' VB
Try
    NorthwindDataset1.WriteXmlSchema("C:\DataSources\Northwind.xsd")
    MessageBox.Show("Schema saved As Northwind.xsd")
Catch ex As Exception
    MessageBox.Show(ex.Message)
End Try
```

```
// C#
try
{
    NorthwindDataset1.WriteXmlSchema(@"C:\DataSources\Northwind.xsd");
    MessageBox.Show("Schema saved as Northwind.xsd");
}
catch (Exception ex)
{
    MessageBox.Show(ex.Message);
}
```

23. Run the application and click the Fill DataSet button.

   The *NorthwindDataSet* is filled with data and the Customers table is displayed in the grid.

24. Click the Save Xml Data button.

   The Northwind.xml file is saved to the C:\Datasources directory.

25. Click the Save Xml Schema button.

   The Northwind.xsd file is saved to the C:\Datasources directory.

26. Navigate to the C:\Datasources directory and open the Northwind.xml and Northwind.xsd files to verify that the data and schema information was saved to the files.

The Northwind.xml and Northwind.xsd files are required for the next practice.

▶ **Exercise 2: Loading *DataSet* Objects with XML Data**

This example creates an untyped *DataSet* and defines its schema based on the contents of the Northwind.xsd file. After loading the schema information, you will load the *DataSet* with the contents of the Northwind.xml file and display it in a grid. This practice expects the Northwind.xml and Northwind.xsd files to be available in the C:\Datasources directory.

1. Create a Windows application and name it **LoadDataSetsWithXml**.

2. Add a *DataGridView* to the Form and name it **CustomersGrid**.

3. Add another *DataGridView* to the form and name it **OrdersGrid**.

4. Drag a button onto the form and set the following properties:
   - ❏ *Name* = LoadSchemaButton
   - ❏ *Text* = Load Schema

5. Drag a button onto the form and set the following properties:
   - ❏ *Name* = LoadDataButton
   - ❏ *Text* = Load Data

6. Create an event handler for the *LoadSchemaButton_Click* event (double-click the Load Schema button) and add the following code:

```
' VB
' Read the schema information (.xsd file) into the dataset.
NorthwindDataset.ReadXmlSchema("C:\Datasources\Northwind.xsd")

' Bind the CustomersGrid and OrdersGrid to display the data.
CustomersGrid.DataSource = NorthwindDataset.Tables("Customers")
OrdersGrid.DataSource = NorthwindDataset.Tables("Orders")

// C#
// Read the schema information (.xsd file) into the dataset.
NorthwindDataset.ReadXmlSchema(@"C:\Datasources\Northwind.xsd");

// Bind the CustomersGrid and OrdersGrid to display the data.
CustomersGrid.DataSource = NorthwindDataset.Tables["Customers"];
OrdersGrid.DataSource = NorthwindDataset.Tables["Orders"];
```

7. Create an event handler for the *LoadDataButton_Click* event (double-click the
    Load Data button) and add the following code:

    ```vb
    ' VB
    ' Read the xml data into the dataset.
    NorthwindDataset.ReadXml ("C:\Datasources\Northwind.xml")
    ```

    ```csharp
    // C#
    // Read the schema xml data into the dataset
    NorthwindDataset.ReadXml(@"C:\Datasources\Northwind.xml");
    ```

8. Run the application and click the Load Schema button.

    The grids display the columns for the Customers and Orders tables based on the
    schema information loaded from the Northwind.xsd file.

9. Click the Load Data button.

    The contents of the Northwind.xml file are loaded into the *DataSet* and dis-
    played in their respective grids on the form.

Lesson Summary

- The data in a *DataSet* can be written out as XML data.

- The schema of a *DataSet* can be written out as XML Schema (an .xsd file).

- The data in an XML file or document can be loaded into a *DataSet*.

- The schema information in an .xsd file can be loaded into a *DataSet*.

- A *DataSet* and an *XMLDataDocument* can be kept in synch so you can manipulate the data and have it be reflected in both objects.

- XPath queries can be performed on *DataSet* data.

Lesson Review

The following questions are intended to reinforce key information presented in this
lesson. The questions are also available on the companion CD if you prefer to review
them in electronic form.

NOTE Answers

Answers to these questions and explanations of why each choice is correct or incorrect are located
in the "Answers" section at the end of the book.

1. How do you load the schema information from an .xsd file into a *DataSet*?

    A. Call the *GetXmlSchema* method passing in the path to the .xsd file to the method.

    B. Call the *ReadXml* method passing in the path to the .xsd file to the method.

    C. Call the *ReadXmlSchema* method passing in the path to the .xsd file to the method.

    D. Set the *DataSet*'s *Name* property to the .xsd filename.

2. How do you synchronize a *DataSet* with an *XmlDataDocument*?

    A. By passing the *XmlDataDocument* to the *DataSet.GetXml* method

    B. By declaring a new instance of an *XmlDataDocument* and passing in the name of the *DataSet* you want to synchronize with

    C. By calling the *XmlDataDocument.Load* method

    D. By calling the *XmlDataDocument.Synch* method

3. How do you execute an XPath query on a *DataSet*?

    A. Synchronize with an XML document and perform the XPath query on the raw XML.

    B. Pass the XPath query as a string to the *DataTable.Select* method.

    C. Pass the XPath query as a string to the *DocumentElement.SelectNodes* method of a synchronized *XmlDataDocument*.

    D. Pass the XPath query as a string to the *DataTable.Find* method.

Lesson 6: Creating and Using *DataView* Objects

This lesson describes how to work with *DataView* objects (*System.Data.DataView*). *DataView* objects provide a way to work with *DataTable* objects and can be displayed in data-bindable controls such as a *DataGridView*. *DataView* objects provide sorting and filtering capabilities as well as the ability to modify the data in the related *DataTable*.

After this lesson, you will be able to:

■ Create and use *DataView* objects.

❑ Create a *DataView*.

❑ Sort and filter data using a *DataView*.

❑ View data using a *DataView*.

❑ Search for data within a *DataView*.

❑ Navigate relationships using a *DataView*.

❑ Modify data using a *DataView*.

❑ Handle *DataView* events.

❑ Set default table views using a *DataViewManager*.

Estimated lesson time: 45 minutes

Creating *DataView* Objects

You can create new *DataView* objects or reference an existing *DataView*. Create new *DataView* objects by generating a new instance of a *DataView* and passing in the name of the *DataTable* for the view to represent or display. *DataTable* objects actually have a *DefaultView* property that contains the *DataView* the table uses by default. Reference this existing *DataView* by assigning an instance of a *DataView* to the *DataTable.DefaultView* property. *DataView* objects offer the advantage of allowing you to bind multiple controls to the same data source and to display different records or different sort orders.

The following code samples show how to create *DataView* objects as previously described.

```
' VB
' Create a new DataView
Dim CustomersDataView As New DataView(NorthwindDataset.Customers)
```

```
' Create a reference to the DataTable's default DataView
Dim CustomersDataView As DataView = Northwind.Customers.DefaultView

// C#
// Create a new DataView
DataView CustomersDataView = new DataView(NorthwindDataset.Customers);

// Create a reference to the DataTable's default DataView
DataView CustomersDataView = Northwind.Customers.DefaultView;
```

Sorting and Filtering Data Using a *DataView*

Sort data in a *DataView* by setting the *DataView.Sort* property to the column name you want to sort on. To sort on multiple columns, separate column names with a comma (,). Complete the Sort expression with ASC to sort in ascending order, or DESC to sort in descending order. (ASC is the default behavior.)

The following code sample sorts the *DataView* in descending order on the Contact-Name column:

```
' VB
CustomersDataView.Sort = "ContactName DESC"

// C#
CustomersDataView.Sort = "ContactName DESC";
```

Viewing Data Using a *DataView*

In most cases, you will probably bind *DataView* objects to controls such as the *Data-GridView* or, maybe, data bind each column in a *DataRowView* to individual controls such as *TextBox* objects. For situations in which you need to programmatically access the data in a *DataView*, it is important to note that a *DataView* contains a collection of *DataRowView* objects that represent the rows in the related *DataTable*. Each *DataRow-View* contains an array representing the columns in the row. To access the individual values in each column, iterate over the *DataRowView* objects and read the column through the index or column name.

The following code example assigns the values of the first and second columns to the *RowValues* variable:

```
' VB
' Access column values by passing the column name to access the DataRowView column
Dim FullName As String = DataRowView("FirstName").ToString() & " " & _
    DataRowView("LastName").ToString()
```

```
' Access column values by passing the column index to access the DataRowView column
Dim FullName As String = DataRowView(0).ToString() & " " & DataRowView(1).ToString()
```

```
// C#
// Access column values by passing the column name to access the DataRowView column
string FullName = DataRowView("FirstName").ToString() + " " +
DataRowView("LastName").ToString();
```

```
// Access column values by passing the column index to access the DataRowView column
string FullName = DataRowView(0).ToString() + " " + DataRowView(1).ToString();
```

Modifying the Data in a *DataView*

You can edit values in a row by accessing the individual column values in a *DataRow-View* and assigning the new value to the column (item array of the *DataRowView*).

The following code sample assigns a value of *Steve* to the FirstName column of the selected *DataRowView*:

```
' VB
' Edit column values by passing the column name
' to access the DataRowView column and assigning the new value
DataRowView("FirstName") = "Steve"
```

```
' Edit column values by passing the column index
' to access the DataRowView column and assigning the new value
DataRowView(0) = "Steve"
```

```
// C#
// Edit column values by passing the column name
// to access the DataRowView column and assigning the new value
DataRowView("FirstName") = "Steve"
```

```
// Edit column values by passing the column index
// to access the DataRowView column and assigning the new value
DataRowView(0) = "Steve"
```

Searching Data in a *DataView*

Search for records in a *DataView* using the *Find* and *FindRows* methods. Pass a value to the *Find* or *FindRows* method and both methods search for that value in the column set in the *Sort* property. In other words, if the *DataView.Sort* is set to *CustomerID*, pass *CustomerID* values to the *Find* and *FindRows* methods; if the *DataView.Sort* property is set to *ContactName*, pass *ContactName* to the *Find* and *FindRows* methods.

The following code example sets the sort key to the CustomerID column, and then it calls the *Find* method and passes in ALFKI (the CustomerID) as the search string.

```
' VB
CustomersDataView.Sort = "CustomerID"
Dim FoundRow As Integer
FoundRow = CustomersDataView.Find("ALFKI")
Dim s As String = CustomersDataView.Item(FoundRow)("CompanyName").ToString

// C#
CustomersDataView.Sort = "CustomerID";
int FoundRow;
FoundRow = CustomersDataView.Find("ALFKI");
string s = CustomersDataView.Item[FoundRow]["CompanyName"].ToString();
```

Navigating Related Data in a *DataView*

You can retrieve records from related tables using *DataView*s as long as the *DataTable* associated with the *DataView* is related to another *DataTable* through a *DataRelation* object. To display the related records, call the *CreateChildView* method of a *DataRow-View* and pass in the name of the *DataRelation* that relates the *DataTable* objects. This creates a new *DataView* containing only the related records.

The following code creates a *DataView* made up of orders for a selected customer.

```
' VB
OrdersDataView = CustomersDataRowView.CreateChildView("FK_Orders_Customers")
OrdersDataGridView.DataSource = OrdersDataView

// C#
OrdersDataView = CustomersDataRowView.CreateChildView("FK_Orders_Customers");
OrdersDataGridView.DataSource = OrdersDataView;
```

Working with *DataView* Events

The main event to program against for a *DataView* is the *ListChanged* event. The *ListChanged* event is raised when data or schema changes occur in the underlying *DataTable*, or if changes are made to a *DataRelation* attached to the *DataView* object's table.

Setting the *DataTable* Object's Default Table Views Using a *DataViewManager*

A *DataViewManager* is basically a collection of *DataViewSetting* objects that are used to set the default sorting and filtering behavior of each *DataTable* in a *DataSet*.

You can use a *DataViewManager* as a data source for data-bound controls. For example, if you create a *DataViewManager* to manage several tables from the Northwind *DataSet*, you can use code similar to the following to bind it to the individual tables:

```vb
' VB
Dim dvm As New DataViewManager(NorthwindDataSet1)
OrdersDataGridView.DataSource = dvm.DataViewSettings("Customers").Table
```

```csharp
// C#
DataViewManager dvm = new DataViewManager(NorthwindDataSet1);
OrdersDataGridView.DataSource = dvm.DataViewSettings("Customers").Table;
```

Lab: Working with *DataView* Objects

In this lab you will use *DataView* objects to sort and filter the data displayed from a *DataTable*.

▶ **Exercise 1: Working with *DataView* Objects**

This example demonstrates sorting and filtering using a *DataView*.

1. Create a Windows application and name it **DataViewExample**.

2. Add a *DataGridView* to the form and set its *Name* property to *CustomersGrid*.

3. Add a *TextBox* and set the following properties:
   - ❏ *Name* = SortTextBox
   - ❏ *Text* = CustomerID

4. Add a second *TextBox* and set the following properties:
   - ❏ *Name* = FilterTextBox
   - ❏ *Text* = City = 'London'

5. Add a button to the form and set the following properties:
   - ❏ *Name* = SetDataViewPropertiesButton
   - ❏ *Text* = Set DataView Properties

6. Add a second button and set the following properties. Your form should resemble Figure 7-14.
   - ❏ *Name* = AddRowButton
   - ❏ *Text* = Add Row

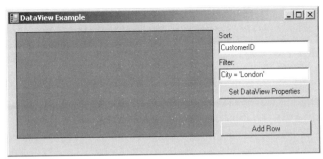

Figure 7-14 Suggested initial control layout for a *DataView* example

7. Create a new Data Source by selecting Add New Data Source from the Data menu.

8. Select Database and click Next.

9. Select a valid data connection to the Northwind sample database.

10. Select the defaults until the Choose Your Database Objects page appears.

11. Select the Customers and Orders tables and click Finish.

12. Build the project.

13. Locate the *CustomersTableAdapter* in the Toolbox and drag it onto the form.

14. Locate the *OrdersTableAdapter* in the Toolbox and drag it onto the form.

15. Locate the *NorthwindDataSet* in the Toolbox and drag it onto the form.

16. Double-click an empty area on the form to create the *Form1_Load* event handler.

17. Add the following code within the *Form1* class. (Paste this code outside of the *Form1_Load* event handler.)

```
' VB
' Create a DataView for the Customers and
' Orders tables.
Private WithEvents CustomersDataView As DataView
Private WithEvents OrdersDataView As DataView
```

```
// C#
// Create a DataView for the Customers and
// Orders tables.
DataView customersDataView;
DataView ordersDataView;
```

18. Add the following code to the *Form1_Load* event handler:

```
' VB
' Load the Customers and Orders tables with data
CustomersTableAdapter1.Fill(NorthwindDataSet1.Customers)
OrdersTableAdapter1.Fill(NorthwindDataSet1.Orders)
```

```
' Set the DataViews to use the Customers and Orders tables
CustomersDataView = New DataView (NorthwindDataSet1.Customers)
OrdersDataView = New DataView (NorthwindDataSet1.Orders)

' Set the initial Sort order of the DataView
CustomersDataView.Sort = "CustomerID"

' Set the CustomersGrid to display the CustomersDataView
CustomersGrid.DataSource = Customers

// C#
// Load the Customers and Orders tables with data
customersTableAdapter1.Fill(northwindDataSet1.Customers);
ordersTableAdapter1.Fill(northwindDataSet1.Orders);

// Set the DataViews to use the Customers and Orders tables
customersDataView = new DataView (northwindDataSet1.Customers);
ordersDataView = new DataView (northwindDataSet1.Orders);

// Set the initial Sort order of the DataView
customersDataView.Sort = "CustomerID";

// Set the CustomersGrid to display the CustomersDataView
CustomersGrid.DataSource = customersDataView;
```

19. Run the application.

    The form opens, displaying the *CustomersDataView* in the grid, as shown in
    Figure 7-15.

Figure 7-15   CustomersGrid displaying the *CustomersDataView*

20. Close the application.

21. Double-click the Set DataView Properties button and add the following code to
    the button-click event handler:

```
' VB
CustomersDataView.Sort = SortTextBox.Text
CustomersDataView.RowFilter = FilterTextBox.Text
```

```csharp
// C#
customersDataView.Sort = SortTextBox.Text;
customersDataView.RowFilter = FilterTextBox.Text;
```

22. Run the application and notice that all customers appear in the grid.

23. Click the Set DataView Properties button and notice that only customers with a value of *London* in their City column appear in the grid.

24. Change the *FilterTexBox.Text* to City = 'Madrid'.

25. Click the Set DataView Properties button and now only customers from Madrid appear in the grid.

26. Close the application.

27. Double-click the Add Row button and add the following code to the button-click event handler:

```vb
' VB
' Create a new row
Dim newCustomerRow As DataRowView = CustomersDataView.AddNew()

' Set a couple of column values
newCustomerRow("CustomerID") = "WINGT"
newCustomerRow("CompanyName") = "Wing Tip Toys"

' Commit the row by explicitly ending the edit
newCustomerRow.EndEdit()
```

```csharp
// C#
// Create a new row
DataRowView newCustomerRow = customersDataView.AddNew();

// Set a couple of column values
newCustomerRow["CustomerID"] = "WINGT";
newCustomerRow["CompanyName"] = "Wing Tip Toys";

// Commit the row by explicitly ending the edit
newCustomerRow.EndEdit();
```

28. Add another button (under the Add Row button) and set the following properties:
    - *Name* = GetOrdersButton
    - *Text* = Get Orders

29. Add another *DataGridView* below the Customers grid and set its *Name* property to OrdersGrid.

30. Double-click the Get Orders button and add the following code to the button-click event handler:

```vb
' VB
' Get the CustomerID for the row selected in the CustomersGrid
Dim selectedCustomerID As String = _
    CStr(CustomersGrid.SelectedCells(0).OwningRow.Cells("CustomerID").Value)

' Create a DataRowView and assign it the selected row.
Dim selectedRow As DataRowView = CustomersDataView _
    (CustomersDataView.Find(selectedCustomerID))

' Call the CreateChildView method to navigate the relationship and create a
' new DataView based on the related records.
OrdersDataView = selectedRow.CreateChildView(NorthwindDataSet1.Relations _
    ("FK_Orders_Customers"))

' Set the OrdersGrid to display the related Dataview
OrdersGrid.DataSource = OrdersDataView
```

```csharp
// C#
// Get the CustomerID for the row selected in the CustomersGrid
string selectedCustomerID =
    (string)CustomersGrid.SelectedCells[0].OwningRow.Cells["CustomerID"].Value;

// Create a DataRowView and assign it the selected row.
DataRowView selectedRow = customersDataView
[customersDataView.Find(selectedCustomerID)];

// Call the CreateChildView method to
// navigate the relationship and create a
// new DataView based on the related records.
ordersDataView = selectedRow.CreateChildView
    (northwindDataSet1.Relations["FK_Orders_Customers"]);

// Set the OrdersGrid to display the related Dataview
OrdersGrid.DataSource = ordersDataView;
```

31. Run the application and click the Get Orders button.

32. Select a different customer and click the Get Orders button to display the orders of the selected customer.

Lesson Summary

- *DataView* objects provide access to *DataTable* objects with easy sorting and filtering capabilities.

- Sort and filter *DataView* objects, using the *Sort* and *RowFilter* properties.

- A *DataView* contains a *DataRowView*, representing each *DataRow* in a *DataTable*.

- Search for specific records in a *DataView* with the *Find* and *FindRows* methods.

- *DataView* objects can navigate relationships and can retrieve related records.
- *DataView* objects raise a *ListChanged* event when modifications are made to the data in a *DataTable*.

Lesson Review

The following questions are intended to reinforce key information presented in this lesson. The questions are also available on the companion CD if you prefer to review them in electronic form.

NOTE   Answers

Answers to these questions and explanations of why each choice is correct or incorrect are located in the "Answers" section at the end of the book.

---

1. How do you access the individual columns in the rows of a *DataView*? (Choose all that apply.)

   A. Through the *DataColumn* in the *DataTable*

   B. Through the associated *DataTable* object's *DataRow*

   C. Through the indexer of a *DataRowView*

   D. Through the associated *DataTable* object's *DataColumn*

2. What is returned when calling the *DataView.Find* method?

   A. An individual *DataRow*

   B. The index of the "found" row in the *DataView*

   C. An individual *DataRowView*

   D. A collection of *DataRow* objects

3. How do you access an order for a selected customer?

   A. Call the *GetChildRows* method of the *DataView*.

   B. Call the *CreateChildView* method of the *DataView*.

   C. Call the *CreateChildView* method of the *DataRowView*.

   D. Call the *GetParentRow* method of the *DataView*.

Chapter Review

To further practice and reinforce the skills you learned in this chapter, you can perform the following tasks:

- Review the chapter summary.
- Complete the case scenarios. These scenarios set up real-world situations involving the topics of this chapter and ask you to create a solution.
- Complete the additional practices.
- Take a practice test.

Chapter Summary

- Create *DataSet* objects programmatically by instantiating new *DataSet* objects in code and adding *DataTable* and *DataRelation* subjects, much like tables and relationships in a database.
- Create typed *DataSet* objects with the DataSet Designer and the Data Source Configuration Wizard.
- *DataTable* objects contain columns (*DataColumn* objects) and constraints just like tables in a database.
- *DataAdapter* objects contain a *Connection* object.
- *DataAdapters* contain individual Insert, Update, and Delete commands (in addition to the Select command) to save changes back to the database.
- You can use an *OleDbDataAdapter* to fill *DataSet* objects using ADO Recordsets.
- Add data to a *DataTable* by creating a new *DataRow* and adding it to the *DataTable.Rows* collection.
- Edit data in a *DataTable* by setting the values of the individual *DataColumns* in a *DataRow*.
- Delete rows in a *DataTable* by calling the *Delete* method of a *DataRow*.
- Set the *RowError* property of a *DataRow* to indicate a row with an error.
- The data in a *DataSet* can be written out as XML data.
- The schema of a *DataSet* can be written out as XML schema (an .xsd file).
- A *DataSet* and an *XMLDataDocument* can be kept in synch so you can manipulate the data and have it be reflected in both objects.

- XPath queries can be performed on *DataSet* data.
- *DataView* objects provide access to *DataTable* objects with easy sorting and filtering capabilities.
- A *DataView* contains a *DataRowView*, representing each *DataRow* in a *DataTable*.
- Search for specific records in a *DataView* with the *Find* and *FindRows* methods.
- *DataView* objects can navigate relationships and can retrieve related records.

Key Terms

Do you know what the key terms mean? You can check your answers by looking up the terms in the gloassary at the end of the book.

- *DataAdapter*
- *DataColumn*
- *DataSet*
- *DataTable*
- *DataView*

Case Scenarios

In the following case scenarios, apply what you've learned about working with data in a disconnected environment. You can find answers to these questions in the "Answers" section at the end of this book.

Case Scenario 1: Upgrading an Old Application

You just landed a huge contract with Humongous Insurance and have been tasked with updating their pending-claims database. Their system is old, and the amount of data is astronomical. Upon initial investigation, you verify the use of many temporary comma-delimited files as well as an outdated object model being used to represent their application's in-memory data.

List the potential improvements you can make to the application.

Case Scenario 2: Slow System Performance

Your technology-challenged brother-in-law just inherited five Southridge Video locations. Somehow, it has become your job to troubleshoot the application used to charge customers for renting videos. After examining the system, you realize that every transaction processes the store's entire inventory of movies.

List the potential improvements you can make to the application.

Suggested Practices

To gain further knowledge on the subject of working with data in a connected environment, complete the following practices.

- **Practice 1**   Create a new SQL Server database and then create a *DataSet* and *DataTable* object based on this new database.

- **Practice 2**   Create an application that writes a single XML file for the Northwind Customers, Orders, and OrderDetails tables. Then create a second application that uses these three XML files as the data source to fill the project's *DataSet*.

- **Practice 3**   Create an application that uses the *DataViewManager* object to display the data from several *DataTable* objects on a form.

Take a Practice Test

The practice tests on this book's companion CD offer many options. For example, you can test yourself on just the content covered in this chapter, or you can test yourself on all the 70-526 certification exam content. You can set up the test so that it closely simulates the experience of taking a certification exam, or you can set it up in study mode so that you can look at the correct answers and explanations after you answer each question.

MORE INFO   Practice tests

For details about all the practice test options available, see the "How to Use the Practice Tests" section in this book's Introduction.

Chapter 8

Implementing Data-Bound Controls

This chapter describes how to display data on Windows Forms. When controls on a form are data-bound, the underlying data source stays in synch with the values in the controls. Windows Forms provide classes for binding data between a Windows Form control, such as a *TextBox*, and data from a data source. Data binding allows you to bring data into your application, typically into a dataset, then allows users to modify that data by editing values in controls bound to that data and sending the changes back to the database. The data-binding infrastructure handles most of the behind-the-scenes tasks such as keeping the control in synch with the *DataTable*.

Exam objectives in this chapter:

- Implement data-bound controls.
    - ❏ Use the *DataGridView* control to display and update the tabular data contained in a data source.
    - ❏ Use a simple data-bound control to display a single data element on a Windows Form.
    - ❏ Implement complex data binding to integrate data from multiple sources.
    - ❏ Navigate forward and backward through records in a dataset in Windows Forms.
    - ❏ Enhance navigation through a dataset by using the *DataNavigator* component.
    - ❏ Define a data source by using a *DataConnector* component.
    - ❏ Create data forms by using the Data Source Configuration Wizard and Data Sources window.

Lessons in this chapter:

Before You Begin

To complete the lessons in this chapter, you must have:

- A computer that meets or exceeds the minimum hardware requirements listed in the "Introduction" at the beginning of the book.

- Microsoft Visual Studio 2005 Professional Edition installed on your computer.

- An understanding of Microsoft Visual Basic or C# syntax and familiarity with the Microsoft .NET Framework.

- Available data sources, including Microsoft SQL Server (SQL Server Express Edition is acceptable), the Northwind Traders sample database for SQL Server, and the Nwind.mdb Microsoft Office Access database file.

- A basic understanding of relational databases.

- Completed the exercises or understood the concepts presented in Chapter 5, "Configuring Connections and Connecting to Data."

Real World

Steve Stein

Some of my first applications that accessed data had more code written to move data in and out of the user interface than the code to load, validate, and update data combined. If you consider the maintenance nightmare of such an application paired together with the flawed logic I was typically guilty of introducing into applications back then, you can imagine the countless hours involved. Using Windows Forms data binding is an excellent way to present data to users.

Lesson 1: Creating a Data-Bound Form with the Data Sources Wizard

This lesson describes how to create a Windows Form that displays data in a *DataGrid-View* using the Data Source Configuration Wizard and the Data Sources window.

After this lesson, you will be able to:

- Create data forms by using the Data Form Wizard.
- How to run the Data Source Configuration Wizard to create data-bound Windows Forms and see what options you can choose and what the wizard generates.

Estimated lesson time: 20 minutes

What Does the Wizard Create?

Running the Data Source Configuration Wizard creates a typed *DataSet* in your application and populates the Data Sources window with the objects selected while running the wizard. After running the wizard, you still need to drag items onto your form to create the instances of the objects needed to access the data.

Lab 1: Creating a Data-Bound Windows Form

In this lab you will create a Windows Form with controls bound to data.

▶ **Exercise 1: Create a Data-Bound Form with the Data Sources Wizard**

Let's now create a Windows application and demonstrate creating a data source and binding controls to data by dragging and dropping items from the Data Sources window.

1. Create a Windows application and name it DataSourcesWizardExample.

2. Start the Data Source Configuration Wizard by selecting Add New Data Source from the Data menu.

3. On the Choose a Data Source Type page, leave the default selection of Database and click Next.

4. On the Choose Your Data Connection page, select a connection to the Northwind sample database or create a new connection if needed.

5. Click Next, keeping the default values until you get to the Choose Your Database Objects page, and select the following from the *Tables* node:

    ❑ *Customers*

    ❑ *Orders*

❑ *Order Details*

6. Click Finish to add the dataset to your project.

7. On the Data menu, select Show Data Sources to display the Data Sources window. The Data Sources window should appear similar to Figure 8-1.

Figure 8-1   Data Sources window displaying the Customers, Orders, and Order Details tables from the *NorthwindDataSet*

8. Drag the *Customers* node from the Data Sources window onto Form1.

A *DataGridView* and *BindingNavigator* are added to the form, and several data-related objects appear in the component tray, as shown in Figure 8-2.

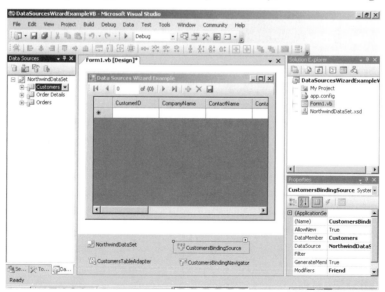

Figure 8-2   Form1 and additional components after dragging *Customers* node from the Data Sources window

9. Run the application.

    At this point, you have a working application with a *DataGridView* data-bound to the Customers table. If you switch to code view in the Integrated Development Environment (IDE), you can see that code has been added to fill the Customers table with data in the form load event, and code has been added to the save button of the BindingNavigator to send updates back to the database.

    The running application should display the Customers data as shown in Figure 8-3.

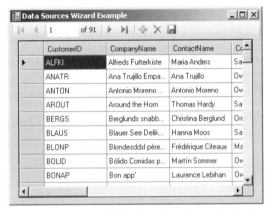

Figure 8-3   Form displaying data from the Customers table

10. Stop the application and open the form in Design view.

11. Expand the *Customers* node in the Data Sources window.

12. Drag the *Orders* node (nested within the *Customers* node) onto the form.

    Notice the *OrdersBindingSource* and *OrdersTableAdapter* added to the component tray.

13. Run the application.

    Click a row in the Customers table. Notice that the *Orders DataGridView* displays all orders for the selected customer, as shown in Figure 8-4.

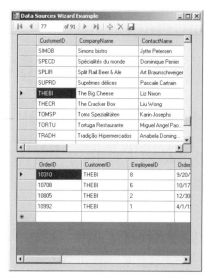

Figure 8-4   Form displaying Orders data for the selected customer

Lesson Summary

- Populate the Data Sources window by running the Data Source Configuration Wizard.

- Drag items from the Data Sources window to create data-bound controls on a form.

- Code to fill the table with data and to save changes back to the database is automatically added to the form.

- In the Data Sources window, related records are displayed as nested nodes in the tree view.

Lesson Review

The following questions are intended to reinforce key information presented in this lesson. The questions are also available on the companion CD if you prefer to review them in electronic form.

NOTE   Answers

Answers to these questions and explanations of why each choice is right or wrong are located in the "Answers" section at the end of the book.

1. How do you add items to the Data Sources window? (Choose all that apply.)

    A. Select Add New Data Source from the Data Sources window.

    B. Drag a *DataSet* from the Toolbox onto a form.

    C. Select Add New Data Source from the Data menu.

    D. Run the Data Source Configuration Wizard.

2. How do you create data-bound controls on a Windows Form?

    A. Drag items from Server Explorer onto the Dataset Designer.

    B. Drag items from the Data Sources window onto a form.

    C. Drag items from the Toolbox onto a form.

    D. Set data related *Form* properties in the Properties window.

3. How do you bind controls to display data from related tables on a Windows Form?

    A. By selecting the main node of the related table in the Data Sources window and dragging it onto a form

    B. By selecting the child node in the Data Sources window and dragging it onto a form

    C. By dragging a *Relation* object onto the Dataset Designer

    D. By binding to the child *DataTable* in the *DataSet*

Lesson 2: Implementing Data-Bound Controls

This lesson describes how to bind Windows Forms controls to data and navigate forward and back through the bound data. You can bind simple controls such as a *TextBox* or a *Label*, or even a *MonthCalendar* to a single element of data, or you can bind more-complex controls such as the *DataGridView* and *ComboBox* to multiple elements of data. This lesson will also describe how to use a *BindingSource* as the source of your data. With *BindingSource* components, you can easily redirect the underlying source of your data.

After this lesson, you will be able to:

■ Use a simple data-bound control to display a single data element on a Windows Form.

■ Implement complex data binding to integrate data from multiple sources.

■ Navigate forward and backward through records in a dataset in Windows Forms.

■ Enhance navigation through a dataset by using the *DataNavigator* component.

■ Define a data source by using a *DataConnector* component.

Estimated lesson time: 45 minutes

Binding Controls to Data

Binding controls to data is simply describing the process of displaying data (such as data from a database) in Windows Forms controls.

Simple *data binding* describes the process of displaying a single element of data in a control, for example, a *TextBox* displaying the value from a single column in a table such as a company name.

Complex data binding describes the process of binding a control to more than one source of data. For example, consider a combo box that displays a list of category names. What if the table you are displaying has only a category ID such as the Products and Categories tables in the Northwind sample database? You can use complex data binding to display the value from a column in one *DataTable* based on a foreign key value in another *DataTable*.

Simple Data Binding

Simple data binding is binding a single element of data to a single control property such as a *TextBox* displaying the *ProductName* column from a table (in its *Text* property).

The following code shows how to bind the *ProductName* column from a *DataTable* to a *TextBox* named *TextBox1*.

```
' VB
TextBox1.DataBindings.Add("Text", productsBindingSource, "ProductName")
```

```
// C#
TextBox1.DataBindings.Add("Text", productsBindingSource, "ProductName");
```

Complex Data Binding

Complex data binding is binding more than one element of data to more than one property of a control, for example, a *DataGridView* control that displays an entire table or a *List* control that displays multiple columns of data.

Controls that enable complex data binding typically contain a *DataSource* property and a *DataMember* property. The *DataSource* property typically will be a *BindingSource* or *DataSet* object. The *DataMember* property typically will be the table or collection to actually display.

The following code shows how to bind a *DataGridView* to the Northwind Customers table using a *BindingSource* component:

```
' VB
Dim customersBindingSource As New BindingSource(NorthwindDataSet1, "Customers")
DataGridView1.DataSource = customersBindingSource
```

```
// C#
BindingSource customersBindingSource = new BindingSource(northwindDataSet1, "Customers");
DataGridView1.DataSource = customersBindingSource;
```

The following code shows how to bind a *DataGridView* to the Northwind Customers table using a dataset:

```
' VB
DataGridView1.DataSource = NorthwindDataSet1
DataGridView1.DataMember = "Customers"
```

```
// C#
DataGridView1.DataSource = northwindDataSet1;
DataGridView1.DataMember = "Customers";
```

Real World

Steve Stein

During the initial release of the .NET Framework, one of my projects was to create a client form to display data. Because my specific task did not suit itself to using a grid, I designed the form with individual controls. Trying to work out my data binding and navigation logic was quite difficult due to the complexity of working with the *CurrencyManager* and other data binding objects. The introduction of the *BindingSource* and *BindingNavigator* components simplified the process of navigating through my data down to a couple of button clicks!

Navigating Records in a *DataSet*

To navigate the records in a data source, use a *BindingNavigator* component. Assign the *BindingNavigator.BindingSource* property a valid *BindingSource* component, and the *BindingNavigator* can be used to move back and forth through the records in that data source.

The *BindingNavigator* uses the navigational methods available on the *BindingSource* to navigate records. For example, *MoveNext* and *MovePrevious* methods are available on the *BindingSource*.

Defining a Data Source Using a *BindingSource* Component

The *BindingSource* component contains the information needed by controls to bind to a *BindingSource* by passing it a reference to a *DataTable* in a *DataSet*. By binding to the *BindingSource* instead of to the *DataSet*, you can easily redirect your application to another source of data without having to redirect all the data binding code to point to the new data source.

The following code shows how to create a *BindingSource* and assign it a reference to the Northwind Customers table.

```
' VB
customersBindingSource = New BindingSource(NorthwindDataSet1, "Customers")
```

```
// C#
customersBindingSource = New BindingSource(northwindDataSet1, "Customers");
```

Quick Check

1. What is the difference between simple and complex binding?
2. How do you navigate back and forth through the records in a *DataTable*?

Quick Check Answers
1. Simple binding binds an individual bit of data (field, column, etc.) to a single property of the control to bind to, whereas complex binding binds multiple bits of data to multiple properties of a control.
2. By calling the *Move* methods of a *BindingSource* component, or by using a *BindingNavigator*.

Lab: Data Binding Controls

In this lab you will bind data to Windows Forms Controls.

▶ **Exercise 1: Simple Data Binding**

This practice creates a Windows application and shows how to implement simple data-bound controls. This example will configure the data binding in code (as opposed to dragging items from the Data Sources window).

1. Create a Windows Application and name it **SimpleDataBindingExample**.
2. From the Data Sources window, click Add New Data Source (creates a new typed dataset by running the Data Source Configuration Wizard).
3. Leave the default selection of Database (on the Choose a Data Source Type page) and click Next.
4. On the Choose Your Data Connection page, select a connection to the Northwind sample database or create a new connection if needed.
5. Click Next, keeping the default values until you get to the Choose Your Database Objects page and select Products from the *Tables* node.
6. Click Finish to add the dataset to your project.
7. Build the project.
8. Drag a *NorthwindDataSet* object from the Toolbox onto the form. (You must build the project for the *NorthwindDataSet* to appear in the Toolbox.)
9. Drag a *ProductsTableAdapter* object from the Toolbox onto the form.

    Now that we have a dataset (and *TableAdapter* to fill it), we can create some controls to display and navigate the data in the dataset (*NorthwindDataSet*).
10. Add a *TextBox* control to the form and set its *Name* property to **ProductIDTextBox**.

11. Add another *TextBox* to the form and set its *Name* property to **ProductName-TextBox**.

    Add a couple of buttons for navigating the records.

12. Add another *Button* control and set the following properties:

    ❏ *Name* = **PreviousButton**

    ❏ *Text* = **Previous**

13. Add a *Button* control and set the following properties:

    ❏ *Name* = **NextButton**

    ❏ *Text* = **Next**

14. Double-click an empty area on the form and create a *Form1_Load* event handler.

15. Add code to create a *BindingSource* global to the form and then add the code to configure the data binding to the *Form1_Load* event handler so your form code looks like the following:

```
' VB
' Create a BindingSource for the Products table
Private productsBindingSource As BindingSource

Private Sub Form1_Load(ByVal sender As System.Object, ByVal e As System.EventArgs) _
    Handles MyBase.Load
    ' Load the products table with data
    ProductsTableAdapter1.Fill(NorthwindDataSet1.Products)

    ' Create a BindingSource to the Products table
    productsBindingSource = New BindingSource(NorthwindDataSet1, "Products")

    ' Configure the bindings of the TextBoxes
    ProductIDTextBox.DataBindings.Add("Text", productsBindingSource, "ProductID")
    ProductNameTextBox.DataBindings.Add("Text", productsBindingSource, "ProductName")
End Sub

// C#
//Create a BindingSource for the Products table
private BindingSource productsBindingSource;

private void Form1_Load(object sender, EventArgs e)
{
    // Load the products table with data
    productsTableAdapter1.Fill(northwindDataSet1.Products);

    // Create a BindingSource to the Products table
    productsBindingSource = new BindingSource(northwindDataSet1, "Products");

    // Configure the bindings of the TextBoxes
```

```
        ProductIDTextBox.DataBindings.Add("Text", productsBindingSource, "ProductID");
        ProductNameTextBox.DataBindings.Add("Text", productsBindingSource, "ProductName");
    }
```

16. Double-click the Previous button and add the following code, which navigates back to the previous record in the data source of *BindingSource*.

    ' **VB**
    ```
    productsBindingSource.MovePrevious()
    ```

    // **C#**
    ```
    productsBindingSource.MovePrevious();
    ```

17. Double-click the Next button and add the following code, which navigates to the next record in the data source of *BindingSource*.

    ' **VB**
    ```
    productsBindingSource.MoveNext()
    ```

    // **C#**
    ```
    productsBindingSource.MoveNext();
    ```

18. Run the application.

    Click the Next and Previous buttons to move back and forth through the data in the Products table. Each text box is bound to a single column in the data table, and the *BindingSource* object handles the low-level maintenance.

▶ **Exercise 2: Complex Data Binding**

This practice creates a Windows application and shows how to implement a complex data-bound control (*DataGridView*). This example will configure the data binding in code (as opposed to dragging items from the Data Sources window).

1. Create a Windows application and name it **ComplexDataBindingExample**.

2. From the Data Sources window, click Add New Data Source (creates a new typed dataset by running the Data Source Configuration Wizard).

3. Leave the default selection of Database (on the Choose a Data Source Type page) and click Next.

4. On the Choose Your Data Connection page, select a connection to the Northwind sample database or create a new connection if needed.

5. Click Next, keeping the default values until you get to the Choose Your Database Objects page and select Products from the *Tables* node.

6. Click Finish to add the dataset to your project.

7. Build the project.

8. Drag a *NorthwindDataSet* object from the Toolbox onto the form. (You must build the project for the *NorthwindDataSet* to appear in the Toolbox.)

9. Drag a *ProductsTableAdapter* from the Toolbox onto the form.

10. Drag a *DataGridView* onto the form and set its *Name* property to *ProductsGrid*.

11. Drag a *Button* control onto the form and set the following properties:

    ❑ *Name* = **BindGridButton**

    ❑ *Text* = **Bind Grid**

12. Double-click the button and add the following code to the *Button Click* event handler:

```vb
' VB
' Load the products table with data from the database
ProductsTableAdapter1.Fill(NorthwindDataSet1.Products)

' Create a new BindingSource component
Dim ProductsBindingSource As New BindingSource(NorthwindDataSet1, "Products")

' Bind the grid to the BindingSource component
ProductsGrid.DataSource = ProductsBindingSource
```

```csharp
// C#
// Load the products table with data from the database
productsTableAdapter1.Fill(northwindDataSet1.Products);

// Create a new BindingSource component
BindingSource productsBindingSource = new BindingSource(northwindDataSet1, "Products");

// Bind the grid to the BindingSource component
ProductsGrid.DataSource = productsBindingSource;
```

13. Drag a *BindingNavigator* onto the form.

14. Add the following line of code to the end of the *Button Click* event code added previously.

```vb
' VB
' Hook the navigator to the BindingSource
BindingNavigator1.BindingSource = ProductsBindingSource
```

```csharp
// C#
// Hook the navigator to the BindingSource
bindingNavigator1.BindingSource = productsBindingSource;
```

15. Run the application.

16. Click the Bind Grid button and the Products table data is loaded into the *Data-GridView* control. You can navigate back and forth using the *BindingNavigator* because it is configured to use the same *BindingSource* object as the grid. Because

the *BindingSource* object already was configured to use the Products table, the *DataGridView.DataSource* property needed only to be set to the *ProductsBinding-Source* object without setting the *DataMember* property.

Lesson Summary

■ Simple data binding displays a single element of data in a control.

■ Complex data binding binds multiple elements of data to multiple properties of a control.

■ Navigate data in a *DataSet* using a *BindingNavigator* component.

■ Use *BindingSource* components as a way to abstract the actual data source in code.

Lesson Review

The following questions are intended to reinforce key information presented in this lesson. The questions are also available on the companion CD if you prefer to review them in electronic form.

NOTE Answers

Answers to these questions and explanations of why each choice is right or wrong are located in the "Answers" section at the end of the book.

---

1. What does it mean for a control to implement "simple" data binding?

    A. The control displays only a single column of data.

    B. The control displays data only as strings such as in *TextBox* or *ListBox* controls.

    C. The control can display only native data types.

    D. The control has a single property bound to a single column of data.

2. What two main pieces of information do you need when binding to a complex data bound control?

    A. The name of the database and the name of the data table

    B. The name of the database and the name of the dataset

    C. The object data source, such as a *BindingSource* or a *DataSet*, and the list to display, such as a *DataTable*

    D. The name of the *DataSet* and the name of the control

3. Why use a *BindingSource* component? (Choose all that apply.)

A. The *BindingSource* component provides a level of abstraction between bound controls and a data source, simplifying the process of redirecting 1your application to use a different data source.

B. The *BindingSource* component provides methods to navigate back and forth through a *DataTable*.

C. The *BindingSource* component contains the methods necessary for sending updates back and forth between the application and the database.

D. The *BindingSource* provides events through which you can add validation logic to your code.

Lesson 3: Working with the *DataGridView*

This lesson describes how to configure and work with data in a *DataGridView* control. The *DataGridView* can display many types of data but typically is used to display the contents of a *DataTable* in a *DataSet*.

After this lesson, you will be able to:

- Use the *DataGridView* control to display and update the tabular data contained in a data source.
- Bind a *DataGridView* control to a data source.
- Configure a *DataGridView* to use multiple data sources.
- Manage columns in a *DataGridView* control by using the Edit Columns dialog box.
- Format a *DataGridView* control by using styles.
- Format a *DataGridView* control by using custom painting.
- Configure the column and cell types of a *DataGridView* control.
- Add tables and columns to a *DataGridView* control.
- Delete columns in a *DataGridView* control.
- Respond to clicks in a *DataGridView* control.
- Validate input with a *DataGridView* control.
- Change displayed data at run time in a *DataGridView* control.

Estimated lesson time: 60 minutes

Displaying a Dataset in the *DataGridView* Control

To display a dataset in a *DataGridView* control or, more specifically, to display a *DataTable* in a *DataGridView*, set the *DataSource* property of the *DataGridView* to the *DataSet* and set the *DataMember* property of the *DataGridView* to the name of the *DataTable*. For example, the following code displays the Northwind Customers table in a *DataGridView*:

```
' VB
DataGridView1.DataSource = NorthwindDataSet1
DataGridView1.DataMember = "Customers"
```

```
//C#
DataGridView1.DataSource = northwindDataSet1;
DataGridView1.DataMember = "Customers";
```

You can also set a *DataGridView* control to display a dataset using the smart tag available on a *DataGridView* control by selecting the *DataSet* in the Choose Data Source ComboBox available on the smart tag. The Choose Data Source command allows you to select a *DataSet* and *DataTable* to display from the *DataSet* list already defined in your project, or you can create a new *DataSet* to display by selecting Add Project Data Source on the smart tag, which will start the Data Source Configuration Wizard.

Configuring *DataGridView* Columns

There are six built-in types of columns you can use in a *DataGridView*, as outlined in Table 8-1. When adding columns to a *DataGridView*, select the type of column based on the data you plan to display in it.

Table 8-1 *DataGridView* Column Types

Column Type	Description
DataGridViewTextBoxColumn	Use this column type to display text and numeric values. A data-bound *DataGridView* automatically generates this type of column when binding to strings and numeric values.
DataGridViewCheckBoxColumn	Use this column to display Boolean values. A *DataGridView* automatically generates this type of column when binding to Boolean values.
DataGridViewImageColumn	Use this column to display images. A *DataGrid-View* automatically generates this type of column when binding to *Image* and *Icon* objects. You can also bind a *DataGridViewImage* column to a byte array.
DataGridViewButtonColumn	Use this column to provide users with a button control.
DataGridViewComboBoxColumn	Use this column type to present lists of choices. This would typically be used for lookups to other tables.
DataGridViewLinkColumn	Use this column type to display links to other data.

Table 8-1 *DataGridView* Column Types

Column Type	Description
Custom Column	If none of the preceding column types provides the specific functionality you require, you can always create a custom column type. To create a custom column, define your class to inherit from *DataGridViewColumn* or any class with a base class of *DataGridViewColumn*. (For example, inherit from *DataGridViewTextBoxColumn* to extend the functionality of that type.)

Adding Tables and Columns to a *DataGridView*

To display a table in a *DataGridView*, you add and define the columns to the *DataGridView* that make up the schema of the table. You can add columns to a *DataGridView* with Designers using the Add Column dialog box or programmatically in code.

First, decide which type of column to use (refer to Table 8-1, shown previously), and then use one of the following procedures to add the column to your *DataGridView*.

Adding Columns to a *DataGridView* Using the Designer

To add columns to a *DataGridView* in the Designer, perform the following procedures:

1. Select the *DataGridView* on your form.
2. Display the smart tag of the *DataGridView*.
3. Select Add Column.
4. In the Add Column dialog box, define the column by setting the appropriate values in the dialog box.

Adding Columns to a *DataGridView* Programmatically

To add columns to a *DataGridView* in code, create an instance of the type of DataGridView column to create, define the column by setting the appropriate properties, and then add the column to the *DataGridView.Columns* collection.

For example, the following code sample creates a new text box column named *Product-Name*:

```
' VB
Dim ProductNameColumn As New DataGridViewTextBoxColumn
ProductNameColumn.Name = "ProductName"
ProductNameColumn.HeaderText = "Product Name"
ProductNameColumn.ValueType = System.Type.GetType("System.String")
DataGridView1.Columns.Add(ProductNameColumn)
```

```
// C#
DataGridViewTextBoxColumn ProductNameColumn = new DataGridViewTextBoxColumn();
ProductNameColumn.Name = "ProductName";
ProductNameColumn.HeaderText = "Product Name";
ProductNameColumn.ValueType = System.Type.GetType("System.String");
DataGridView1.Columns.Add(ProductNameColumn); .
```

Deleting Columns in the *DataGridView*

Deleting columns in a *DataGridView* can be accomplished using the designers in Visual Studio, or programmatically in code.

Deleting Columns in a *DataGridView* Using the Designer

To delete columns in a *DataGridView* using the Designer, perform the following procedures:

1. Select the *DataGridView* on your form.
2. Display the smart tag for the *DataGridView*.
3. Select Edit Columns.
4. In the Edit Columns dialog box, select the column you want to remove from the *DataGridView*.
5. Click the Remove button.

Deleting Columns in a *DataGridView* Programmatically

To delete columns in a *DataGridView* in code, call the *Remove* method and provide the name of the column you want to delete. For example, the following code example deletes a column named *ProductName* from *DataGridView1*:

```
' VB
DataGridView1.Columns.Remove("ProductName")
```

```
// C#
DataGridView1.Columns.Remove["ProductName"];
```

Determining the Clicked Cell in a *DataGridView*

To determine the clicked cell, use the *DataGridView.CurrentCell* property. The *Current-Cell* provides a reference to the currently selected cell and provides properties to access the value of the data in the cell as well as the row and column index of the cell's current location in the *DataGridView*.

```vb
' VB
Dim CurrentCellValue As String
CurrentCellValue = CustomersDataGridView.CurrentCell.Value.ToString
```

```csharp
// C#
String CurrentCellValue;
CurrentCellValue = CustomersDataGridView.CurrentCell.Value.ToString();
```

Validating Input in the *DataGridView*

To validate input in an individual cell in a *DataGridView*, handle the *DataGridView.CellValidating* event and cancel the edit if the value fails validation. The *CellValidating* event is raised when a cell loses focus. Add code to the event handler for the *CellValidating* event to verify that the values in specific columns conform to your business rules and application logic. The event arguments contain the proposed value in the cell as well as the row and column index of the cell being edited.

For example, the following code validates that the *ProductName* column does not contain an empty string (use this sample for a *DataGridView* that is not bound to data):

```vb
' VB
If DataGridView1.Columns(e.ColumnIndex).Name = "ProductName" Then
    If e.FormattedValue.ToString = "" Then
        dataGridView1.Rows(e.RowIndex).ErrorText = "Product Name is a required field"
        e.Cancel = True
    Else
        dataGridView1.Rows(e.RowIndex).ErrorText = ""
    End If
End If
```

```csharp
// C#
if (DataGridView1.Columns[e.ColumnIndex].Name == "ProductName")
{
    if (e.FormattedValue.ToString() == "")
    {
        DataGridView1.Rows[e.RowIndex].ErrorText = "Product Name is a required field";
        e.Cancel = true;
    }
    else
    {
```

```
            DataGridView1.Rows[e.RowIndex].ErrorText = "";
    }
}
```

The following code validates that the *ProductName* column does not contain an empty string (use this example for a *DataGridView* that *is* bound to data):

```vb
' VB
If DataGridView1.Columns(e.ColumnIndex).DataPropertyName = "ProductName" Then
    If e.FormattedValue.ToString = "" Then
        dataGridView1.Rows(e.RowIndex).ErrorText = "Product Name is a required field"
        e.Cancel = True
    Else
        dataGridView1.Rows(e.RowIndex).ErrorText = ""
    End If
End If
```

```csharp
// C#
if (DataGridView1.Columns[e.ColumnIndex].DataPropertyName == "ProductName")
{
    if (e.FormattedValue.ToString() == "")
    {
        DataGridView1.Rows[e.RowIndex].ErrorText = "Product Name is a required field";
        e.Cancel = true;
    }
    else
    {
        DataGridView1.Rows[e.RowIndex].ErrorText = "";
    }
}
```

Format a *DataGridView* Using Styles

Format the look of a *DataGridView* by setting the grid's cell styles. Although each cell can have a specific style applied to it, many cells typically share the same style.

The *DataGridView* provides several built-in default cell styles that you can customize and use, or you can create new cell styles and apply them to your *DataGridView* cells. The following example demonstrates how to apply the alternating rows style.

Format a *DataGridView* Control by Using Custom Painting

To format a *DataGridView* using custom painting, you can handle the *CellPainting* event and insert your own custom painting code. When you handle the *CellPainting* event, the *DataGridViewCellPaintingEventArgs* provide access to many properties that simplify custom painting. When you handle the *CellPainting* event, be sure to set *e.Handled* to *True* so the grid will not call its own cell painting routine.

Place the following code in the *CellPainting* event handler to paint all cells *LightSkyBlue*:

```vb
' VB
' Paint the cell background color LightSkyBlue
e.Graphics.FillRectangle(Brushes.LightSkyBlue, e.CellBounds)

' Draw the contents of the cell
If Not (e.Value Is Nothing) Then
    e.Graphics.DrawString(e.Value.ToString, e.CellStyle.Font, _
        Brushes.Black, e.CellBounds.X, e.CellBounds.Y)
End If
e.Handled = True
```

```csharp
// C#
// Paint the cell background color LightSkyBlue
e.Graphics.FillRectangle(Brushes.LightSkyBlue, e.CellBounds);
// Draw the contents of the cell
if (e.Value != null)
{
    e.Graphics.DrawString(e.Value.ToString(), e.CellStyle.Font,
        Brushes.Black, e.CellBounds.X, e.CellBounds.Y);
}
e.Handled = true;
```

> ## Quick Check
> 1. What properties do you set on a *DataGridView* to display a specific *DataTable*?
> 2. How do you determine what cell is clicked in a *DataGridView*?
>
> ### Quick Check Answers
> 1. Set the *DataSource* property to the *DataSet*, and the *DataMember* property to the name of the *DataTable*.
> 2. Inspect the *DataGridView.CurrentCell* property.

Lab: Working with the *DataGridView*

In this lab you will work with data in a *DataGridView* control.

▶ **Exercise 1: Working with the *DataGridView***

Now let's create a Windows application and demonstrate how to manipulate the definition as well as the columns and data in a *DataGridView* control.

1. Create a Windows application and name it **DataGridViewExample**.
2. Open the Data Sources window (on the Data menu, select Show Data Sources).

3. Click Add New Data Source to start the Data Source Configuration Wizard.

4. Leave the default of Database and click Next.

5. Select (or create) a connection to the Northwind sample database and click Next.

6. Expand the *Tables* node. Select the Customers table, and then click Finish.

7. Drag the *Customers* node from the Data Sources window onto the form.

    At this point, you can actually run the application, and the form appears with the Customers table loaded into the *DataGridView*.

8. Drag two buttons onto the form below the *DataGridView* and set the following properties:

    Button1:

    ❑ *Name* = **AddColumnButton**

    ❑ *Text* = **Add Column**

    Button2:

    ❑ *Name* = **DeleteColumnButton**

    ❑ *Text* = **Delete Column**

9. Double-click the Add Column Button to create the button-click event handler and to open the form in code view.

10. Add the following code to Form1, which adds some additional code to the *Form1_Load* event that creates a new column on the *DataTable* and the code to add a new column to the *DataGridView* in the *AddColumnButton_Click* event.

```vb
' VB
Private Sub Form1_Load(ByVal sender As System.Object, ByVal e As System.EventArgs) _
    Handles MyBase.Load
    'TODO: This line of code loads data into the 'NorthwindDataSet.Customers' table. You
can move, or remove it, As needed.
    Me.CustomersTableAdapter.Fill(Me.NorthwindDataSet.Customers)

    ' Add a new column to the Customers DataTable
    ' to be used to demonstrate adding and removing
    ' columns in a DataGridView in the methods below
    Dim Location As New DataColumn("Location")
    Location.Expression = "City + ', ' + Country"
    NorthwindDataSet.Customers.Columns.Add(Location)
End Sub

Private Sub AddColumnButton_Click(ByVal sender As System.Object, ByVal e As
System.EventArgs) _
    Handles AddColumnButton.Click
```

```vb
        Dim LocationColumn As New DataGridViewTextBoxColumn
        LocationColumn.Name = "LocationColumn"
        LocationColumn.HeaderText = "Location"
        LocationColumn.DataPropertyName = "Location"
        CustomersDataGridView.Columns.Add(LocationColumn)
    End Sub
```

```csharp
// C#
private void Form1_Load(object sender, EventArgs e)
{
    // TODO: This line of code loads data into the 'northwindDataSet.Customers' table.
You can move, or remove it, as needed.
        this.customersTableAdapter.Fill(this.northwindDataSet.Customers);
        // Add a new column to the Customers DataTable
        // to be used to demonstrate adding and removing
        // columns in a DataGridView in the methods below
        DataColumn Location = new DataColumn("Location");
        Location.Expression = "City + ', ' + Country";
        northwindDataSet.Customers.Columns.Add(Location);
}

private void AddColumnButton_Click(object sender, EventArgs e)
{
    DataGridViewTextBoxColumn LocationColumn = new DataGridViewTextBoxColumn();
    LocationColumn.Name = "LocationColumn";
    LocationColumn.HeaderText = "Location";
    LocationColumn.DataPropertyName = "Location";
    customersDataGridView.Columns.Add(LocationColumn);
}
```

11. Double-click the Delete Column Button to create the *DeleteColumnButton_Click* event handler. Add the following code to the *DeleteColumnButton_Click* event handler:

```vb
' VB
Try
        CustomersDataGridView.Columns.Remove("LocationColumn")
Catch ex As Exception
    MessageBox.Show(ex.Message)
End Try
```

```csharp
// C#
try
{
    customersDataGridView.Columns.Remove("LocationColumn");
}
catch (Exception ex)
{
    MessageBox.Show(ex.Message);
}
```

12. Drag another button onto the form and set the following properties:

❑ *Name* = **GetClickedCellButton**

❑ *Text* = **Get Clicked Cell**

13. Drag a label onto the form and place it next to the GetClickedCell button.

14. Double-click the GetClickedCell button and add the following code to the *Get-ClickedCellButton_Click* event handler:

```vb
' VB
Dim CurrentCellInfo As String
CurrentCellInfo = CustomersDataGridView.CurrentCell.Value.ToString &
Environment.NewLine
CurrentCellInfo += "Column: " &
CustomersDataGridView.CurrentCell.OwningColumn.DataPropertyName & Environment.NewLine
CurrentCellInfo += "Column Index: " &
CustomersDataGridView.CurrentCell.ColumnIndex.ToString & Environment.NewLine
CurrentCellInfo += "Row Index: " & CustomersDataGridView.CurrentCell.RowIndex.ToString

Label1.Text = CurrentCellInfo
```

```csharp
// C#
string CurrentCellInfo;
CurrentCellInfo = customersDataGridView.CurrentCell.Value.ToString() +
Environment.NewLine;
CurrentCellInfo += "Column: " +
customersDataGridView.CurrentCell.OwningColumn.DataPropertyName + Environment.NewLine;
CurrentCellInfo += "Column Index: " +
customersDataGridView.CurrentCell.ColumnIndex.ToString() + Environment.NewLine;
CurrentCellInfo += "Row Index: " +
customersDataGridView.CurrentCell.RowIndex.ToString();

label1.Text = CurrentCellInfo;
```

15. Create an event handler for the *CustomersDataGridView.CellValidating* event. (Select *CustomersDataGridView* on the form, click the Events button in the Properties window, and double-click the *CellValidating* event.)

16. Add the following code to the *CellValidating* event handler:

```vb
' VB
If CustomersDataGridView.Columns(e.ColumnIndex).DataPropertyName = "ContactName" Then
    If e.FormattedValue.ToString = "" Then
        CustomersDataGridView.Rows(e.RowIndex).ErrorText = _
            "ContactName is a required field"
        e.Cancel = True
    Else
        CustomersDataGridView.Rows(e.RowIndex).ErrorText = ""
    End If
End If
```

```csharp
// C#
if (customersDataGridView.Columns[e.ColumnIndex].DataPropertyName == "ContactName")
{
```

```
if (e.FormattedValue.ToString() == "")
{
    customersDataGridView.Rows[e.RowIndex].ErrorText =
    "ContactName is a required field";
    e.Cancel = true;
}
else
{
    customersDataGridView.Rows[e.RowIndex].ErrorText = "";
{
}
```

17. Drag another button onto the form and set the following properties:
    - ❑ *Name* = **ApplyStyleButton**
    - ❑ *Text* = **Apply Style**

18. Double-click the Apply Style button and add the following code to the *Apply-StyleButton_Click* event handler:

```
' VB
CustomersDataGridView.AlternatingRowsDefaultCellStyle.BackColor = Color.LightGray
```

```
// C#
customersDataGridView.AlternatingRowsDefaultCellStyle.BackColor = Color.LightGray;
```

19. Run the application.

20. Click the Add Column button, and then scroll to the end of the columns to verify that the new Location column is there.

21. Click the Delete Column button and verify that the Location column is deleted from the *DataGridView*.

22. Select any cell in the grid and then click the Get Clicked Cell button. The *Label* displays the contents of the cell, the name of the column the cell is in, and the column and row index of the cell.

23. And, finally, click the Apply Style button, and the *AlternatingRowCellStyle* is set up to display alternating rows with a light gray background.

Lesson Summary

- The *DataGridView* is the preferred control for displaying tabular data such as a *DataTable*.

- You can add and remove columns to a *DataGridView* in the Designer, using the Add Column and Edit Column dialog boxes available from the smart tag of the *DataGridView*.

- The *DataGridView.CurrentCell* property provides access to the currently selected cell in a *DataGridView*.

- The *DataGridView* raises a *CellValidating* event through which you can add code that verifies that the value in a column conforms to your business rules and application logic.

- You can format the look of a *DataGridView* using styles and custom painting.

Lesson Review

The following questions are intended to reinforce key information presented in this lesson. The questions are also available on the companion CD if you prefer to review them in electronic form.

NOTE   Answers

Answers to these questions and explanations of why each choice is right or wrong are located in the "Answers" section at the end of the book.

---

1. What is the best way to determine what cell a user clicks in a *DataGridView*?

    A. Use the column and row index of the selected cell.

    B. Use the *DataGridView.CurrentCell* property.

    C. Use the cursor position's *x* and *y* coordinates.

    D. Use the currently selected column and row in the bound *DataTable* to determine the clicked cell.

2. What is the preferred method of validating input in a *DataGridView*?

    A. By adding validation code to the *CellPainting* event handler

    B. By adding validation code to the *DataGridView.CellClick* event handler

    C. By adding validation code to the *DataGridView.CellValidating* event handler

    D. By adding code to the *DataGridView* partial class file

3. What is the best way to display a Boolean value in a *DataGridView*?

    A. Configure a *DataGridViewTextBoxColumn* and display *True* or *False*.

    B. Configure a *DataGridViewCheckBoxColumn* to display a check box that indicates checked or unchecked.

    C. Configure a *DataGridViewButtonColumn* to display a button that indicates pressed or unpressed.

    D. Configure a custom column to display yes or no.

Chapter Review

To further practice and reinforce the skills you learned in this chapter, you can perform the following tasks:

- Review the chapter summary.
- Complete the case scenarios. These scenarios set up real-world situations involving the topics of this chapter and ask you to create a solution.
- Complete the additional practices.
- Take a practice test.

Chapter Summary

- Populate the Data Sources window by running the Data Source Configuration Wizard.
- Drag items from the Data Sources window to create data-bound controls on a form.
- Code to fill the table with data and to save changes back to the database is automatically added to the form.
- In the Data Sources window, related records are displayed as nested nodes in the tree view.
- Simple data binding displays a single element of data in a control.
- Complex data binding binds multiple elements of data to multiple properties of a control.
- Navigate data in a *DataSet* using a *BindingNavigator* component.
- Use *BindingSource* components as a way to abstract the actual data source in code.
- The *DataGridView* is the preferred control for displaying tabular data such as a *DataTable*.
- You can add and remove columns to a *DataGridView* in the Designer using the Add Column and Edit Column dialog boxes available from the smart tag of the *DataGridView*.
- The *DataGridView.CurrentCell* property provides access to the currently selected cell in a *DataGridView*.

- The *DataGridView* raises a *CellValidating* event through which you can add code that verifies that the value in a column conforms to your business rules and application logic.

- You can format the look of a *DataGridView* using styles and custom painting.

Key Terms

Do you know what these key terms mean? You can check your answers by looking up the terms in the glossary at the end of the book.

- *BindingSource*
- data binding

Case Scenarios

In the following case scenarios, you will apply what you've learned about implementing data-bound controls. You can find answers to these questions in the "Answers" section at the end of this book.

Case Scenario 1: Upgrading an Old Application

You have been tasked with upgrading the software that keeps track of donations at the Baldwin Museum of Science. Upon initial inspection, you see that each record is displayed on a separate form so that you must navigate sequentially to go from one museum record to the next. In addition to the many forms, the application has a separate component that is specifically for keeping the database and the forms in synch.

List the potential improvements you can make to the application.

Case Scenario 2: Preventing Recompilation of a Large Application

You just landed a developer's dream job at City Power and Light. Your next big project is writing the next-generation software that runs the power grid for the entire city!

You know you are going to be working on this application for quite some time before it ever goes live, so the main database won't be available until the application is actually deployed. You will to need to design this application to easily switch between the test and production databases.

What would you do to facilitate this architecture?

Suggested Practices

To gain further knowledge on the subject of working with data in a connected environment, complete the following practices.

- **Practice 1**   Create an application that displays data from the Categories and Products tables using the Data Sources window.

- **Practice 2**   Create an application that displays data from the Customers table in a *DataGridView* and then displays that customer's orders in the same *DataGridView* when a button is clicked.

- **Practice 3**   Create an application that displays the data from the Products table and format the cells that contain discontinued products with grayed-out text.

Take a Practice Test

The practice tests on this book's companion CD offer many options. For example, you can test yourself on just the content covered in this chapter, or you can test yourself on all the 70-526 certification exam content. You can set up the test so that it closely simulates the experience of taking a certification exam, or you can set it up in study mode so that you can look at the correct answers and explanations after you answer each question.

MORE INFO   **Practice tests**

For details about all the practice test options available, see the "How to Use the Practice Tests" section in this book's Introduction.

Chapter 9

Working with XML

XML is a universally used format for communication and storage of information. XML is extensible, platform-independent, and, since it is a text-based format, can be read and written with standard text-editing tools. This chapter describes how to use the Microsoft .NET Framework to read and write XML.

Exam objectives in this chapter:

- Read, write, and validate XML by using the *XmlReader* class and the *XmlWriter* class.
  - ❏ Read XML data by using the *XmlReader*.
  - ❏ Read all XML element and attribute content.
  - ❏ Read specific element and attribute content.
  - ❏ Read XML data by using the *XmlTextReader* class.
  - ❏ Read node trees by using the *XmlNodeReader* class.
  - ❏ Validate XML data by using the *XmlValidatingReader*.
  - ❏ Write XML data by using the *XmlWriter* class.
  - ❏ Manage XML with the XML Document Object Model (DOM).
  - ❏ Read XML data into the DOM.
  - ❏ Modify an XML document by adding and removing nodes.
  - ❏ Modify nodes within an XML document.
  - ❏ Write data in XML format from the DOM.
  - ❏ Work with nodes in the XML DOM.
  - ❏ Handle DOM events.
  - ❏ Modify the XML declaration.

Lessons in this chapter:

Before You Begin

To complete the lessons in this chapter, you must have:

- A computer that meets or exceeds the minimum hardware requirements listed in the "Introduction" at the beginning of the book.

- Microsoft Visual Studio 2005 Professional Edition installed on your computer.

- An understanding of Microsoft Visual Basic or C# syntax and familiarity with the Microsoft .NET Framework.

- An understanding of basic XML structure.

Real World

Matt Stoecker

The rise of XML use in the computing world has been meteoric. When writing applications to parse information from a variety of sources, I invariably need to process XML. The .NET Framework XML classes make it easy to incorporate XML into your applications.

Lesson 1: Reading and Writing XML with the *XmlReader* and *XmlWriter* Classes

The *System.XML* namespace supplies the *XmlReader* and *XmlWriter* classes for rapid reading and writing XML. The *XmlReader* and *XmlWriter* classes are abstract classes that provide the basic interface for parsing XML and are implemented in a variety of classes. This lesson will discuss how to use the *XmlReader* and *XmlWriter* classes, as well as some of their most common implementations.

After this lesson, you will be able to:

- ■ Read XML data by using the *XmlReader*.
- ■ Read all XML element and attribute content.
- ■ Read specific element and attribute content.
- ■ Read XML data by using the *XmlTextReader* class.
- ■ Read node trees by using the *XmlNodeReader* class.
- ■ Validate XML data by using the *XmlValidatingReader*.
- ■ Write XML data by using the *XmlWriter* class.

Estimated lesson time: 45 minutes

The *XmlReader* Class

The *XmlReader* class is an abstract class that provides the base implementation for the different XML reader classes in the *System.Xml* namespace. *XmlReader* and its derivative classes provide rapid, noncached, forward-only access to an XML document. Simply put, this means that you can use an instance of a class derived from *XmlReader* to start at the beginning of an XML document and read through it from start to finish. Once content has been read, however, it cannot be returned to and is lost unless it has been saved or otherwise used by your application. Table 9-1 describes some of the important methods of *XmlReader*, and Table 9-2 explains some of the important properties of it.

Table 9-1   Important Methods of *XmlReader*

Method	Description
Create	Returns a new instance of an implementation of the *Xml-Reader* class.

Table 9-1   Important Methods of *XmlReader*

Method	Description
GetAttribute	Gets the value of the attribute with the specified index or name.
IsStartElement	Calls *MoveToContent* and tests if the current node is a start element or an empty element tag.
MoveToAttribute	Moves to the attribute with the specified index or name.
MoveToContent	Checks to see if the current node is a content node; if not, moves to the next content node or end of file.
MoveToElement	Moves the reader to the element containing the current attribute. This method can be used to move the reader back to the node when it is positioned on an attribute.
MoveToFirstAttribute	Moves the reader to the first attribute in the node.
MoveToNextAttribute	Moves the reader to the next attribute in the node.
Read	Reads the next node in the stream.
ReadInnerXml	Returns all the XML content in the current node and all of its children. The start and end nodes are excluded.
ReadOuterXml	Returns all XML content of the current node and all of its children.
Skip	Skips the children of the current node.

Table 9-2   Important Properties of *XmlReader*

Property	Description
AttributeCount	Gets the number of attributes on a current node.
EOF	Returns *True* if the reader is at the end of the file. Otherwise, it returns *False*.
HasAttributes	Determines whether the current node has attributes.
HasValue	Determines whether the current node can have a value.

Table 9-2   Important Properties of *XmlReader*

Property	Description
Item	Exposes the collection of attributes for the current node. You can get the value of an attribute by specifying the index or name.
Name	Gets the qualified name of the current node.
NodeType	Gets the type of the current node.
Value	Gets the value of the current node.

These members are found in all implementations of *XmlReader*, including *XmlText-Reader*, *XmlNodeReader*, and the default implementations of *XmlReader* returned by *XmlReader.Create* of *XmlReader*.

Creating an *XmlReader* Implementation

Although *XmlReader* is an abstract class, it exposes a static method called *Create* that returns a default implementation of *XmlReader* that will read an existing XML stream or an XML file. The following example demonstrates how to create a new implementation of *XmlReader*.

```
' VB
Dim aReader As XmlReader
' Creates a reader that reads a stream called XmlStream
aReader = XmlReader.Create(XmlStream)
' Creates a reader that reads a file located at C:\SampleXml.xml
aReader = XmlReader.Create("C:\SampleXml.xml")
```

```
// C#
XmlReader aReader;
// Creates a reader that reads a stream called XmlStream
aReader = XmlReader.Create(XmlStream);
// Creates a reader that reads a file located at C:\SampleXml.xml
aReader = XmlReader.Create(@"C:\SampleXml.xml");
```

Reading XML Content

The primary method for reading XML content in an XML file is the *Read* method, which reads the current XML node and advances the reader to the next node in the file or stream. The *Read* method returns a Boolean value that indicates whether the read was successful. You can use this method to read all nodes in an XML file sequentially, as shown in the following example:

```vb
' VB
' Assumes an XmlReader named myReader
While myReader.Read()
    ' Do something with the nodes here
End While
```

```csharp
// C#
// Assumes an XmlReader named myReader
while (myReader.Read())
{
    // Do something with the nodes here
}
```

When a node is being read, the name and value of the current node is available via the *Name* and *Value* properties of *XmlReader*. Tables 9-3 and 9-4 describe what is returned by these properties depending on the type of node being read.

Table 9-3   Return Values of the *Name* Property

Node Type	What Is Returned
Attribute	The name of the attribute
DocumentType	The document type name
Element	The tag name
EntityReference	The name of the entity referenced
ProcessingInstruction	The target of the processing instruction
XmlDeclaration	The literal string XML
All other nodes	Empty string

Table 9-4   Return Values of the *Value* Property

Node Type	What Is Returned
Attribute	The value of the attribute
CDATA	The content of the CDATA section
Comment	The content of the comment
DocumentType	The internal subset

Table 9-4 Return Values of the *Value* Property

Node Type	What Is Returned
ProcessingInstruction	The entire content, excluding the target
SignificantWhitespace	The white space between markups in a mixed-content model
Text	The content of the text node
Whitespace	The white space between markups
XmlDeclaration	The content of the declaration
All other nodes	An empty string

The following example demonstrates how these properties can be used.

```vb
' VB
While myReader.Read()
    If myReader.NodeType = Xml.XmlNodeType.Element Then
        MsgBox(myReader.Name)
    ElseIf myReader.NodeType = Xml.XmlNodeType.Text Then
        MsgBox(myReader.Value)
    End If
End While
```

```csharp
// C#
while (myReader.Read())
{
    if (myReader.NodeType == Xml.XmlNodeType.Element)
        MessageBox.Show(myReader.Name);
    else if (myReader.NodeType == Xml.XmlNodeType.Text)
        MessageBox.Show(myReader.Value);
}
```

Reading Attribute Content

XmlReader can also be used to read the attributes of a given node and the values of those attributes. The *MoveToAttribute*, *MoveToFirstAttribute* and *MoveToNextAttribute* methods control navigation through the attributes of a given node. When one of these methods is called, the *Name* property of *XmlReader* exposes the name of the attribute, and the *Value* property of *XmlReader* exposes the value of the attribute.

Moving within attributes is the only time *XmlReader* can move backward. You could, for example, read the fifth attribute of a node and then move back to the first attribute.

Once a new node has been visited, however, you cannot revisit the attributes of a previous node.

The *MoveToAttribute* Method   You can use the *MoveToAttribute* method to move the reader to a specific attribute in an XML node. This method allows you to specify the name of an attribute or the index of an attribute and move directly to it, and it returns a Boolean value that indicates whether the move is successful. If the specified attribute or index is not found, the method returns *False* and the position of the reader does not change. The following example demonstrates how to use the *MoveToAttribute* method given this XML node:

```
<Flowers Name="Rose" Varietal="Shiraz" Color="Red" Thorns="Yes">
```

```
' VB
' Assumes an XmlReader named myReader that is positioned on the node shown above
If myReader.MoveToAttribute("Color")
   MsgBox(myReader.Value)
End If
```

```
// C#
// Assumes an XmlReader named myReader that is positioned on the node shown above
if (myReader.MoveToAttribute("Color"))
   MessageBox.Show(myReader.Value);
```

ReadInnerXml and *ReadOuterXml*

You can use the *ReadInnerXml* and *ReadOuterXml* methods to return portions of the XML file as strings. The *ReadInnerXml* method returns the contents of the current XML node, including child nodes but excluding the opening and closing nodes themselves. The *ReadOuterXml* method returns the contents of the current XML node, including child nodes as well as the opening and closing nodes. For example, consider the following XML fragment:

```
<text1>mytext<subtext1>mysubtext</subtext1></text1><text2></text2>
```

If *XmlReader* is positioned on <text1>, *ReadInnerXml* returns the following string:

```
mytext<subtext1>mysubtext</subtext1>
```

and moves the position of *XmlReader* to <text2>. Given the same XML fragment, *ReadOuterXml* returns the following string:

```
<text1>mytext<subtext1>mysubtext</subtext1></text1>
```

and moves the reader position to <text2>.

Reading Attributes with *ReadInnerXml* and *ReadOuterXml*   If *XmlReader* has been positioned on an attribute, you can use *ReadInnerXml* and *ReadOuterXml* to return strings based on the attribute content. For example, consider the following XML fragment:

```
<text1 length="12" color="blue">moo</text1>
```

If the *XmlReader* is positioned on the length attribute, *ReadInnerXml* returns the following string:

```
12
```

and does not advance the position of the reader. Likewise, given the same fragment and starting position, *ReadOuterXml* returns the following string:

```
length="12"
```

Again, the position of the reader is not changed.

MoveToContent

You can use the *MoveToContent* method to skip over nodes that do not contain content, such as white space, comments, or processing instructions. The *MoveToContent* method checks to see if the current node is a content node. If it is, no action is taken. If the current node is not a content node, it moves the position of the reader to the next content-containing node. *MoveToContent* considers the following node types to be content nodes: *CDATA*, *Element*, *EndElement*, *EntityReference*, *EndEntity*, or any nonwhite space text. When *MoveToContent* is called, the reader will stop at the first of any of these nodes that it encounters. It will skip over any of the following types of nodes: *ProcessingInstruction*, *DocumentType*, *Comment*, *Whitespace*, or *SignificantWhitespace*. The following demonstrates how to call *MoveToContent*:

```vb
' VB
' Assumes an XmlReader named myReader
myReader.MoveToContent()
```

```csharp
// C#
// Assumes an XmlReader named myReader
myReader.MoveToContent();
```

Skip

Calling the *Skip* method causes *XmlReader* to skip all of the child nodes of the current node and proceed to the next node at the same level. For example, consider the following XML fragment:

```
<text1>
    <text2>
    </text2>
</text1>
<text3>
</text3>
```

If the reader is positioned on <text1> and the *Skip* method is called, the reader is advanced to the <text3> node. The following example demonstrates the use of the *Skip* method:

```
' VB
myReader.Skip()
```

```
// C#
myReader.Skip();
```

The *XmlTextReader* Class

The *XmlTextReader* class is an implementation of the *XmlReader* class. You can use all of the methods previously described in this lesson for the *XmlReader* class for the *XmlTextReader* class as well. The *XmlTextReader* is designed to read text either in a file or in a stream. You can create an *XmlTextReader* object that will read a specific stream or file by specifying the appropriate stream or file at instantiation, as shown in the following code:

```
' VB
Dim aReader As XmlTextReader
' Creates an XmlTextReader that reads a stream called XmlStream
aReader = New XmlTextReader(XmlStream)
' Creates a reader that reads a file located at C:\SampleXml.xml
aReader = New XmlTextReader("C:\SampleXml.xml")
```

```
// C#
XmlTextReader aReader;
// Creates an XmlTextReader that reads a stream called XmlStream
aReader = new XmlTextReader(XmlStream);
// Creates a reader that reads a file located at C:\SampleXml.xml
aReader = new XmlTextReader("C:\\SampleXml.xml");
```

XmlNodeReader

XmlNodeReader is another derivative class of *XmlReader* and is designed to read the XML content of an *XmlNode* object, which is generally part of an XML data object model (DOM) subtree. You can create an *XmlNodeReader* by specifying the appropriate *XmlNode*, as shown here:

```vb
' VB
Dim aReader As XmlNodeReader
' Creates an XmlNodeReader that reads an XmlNode named Node
aReader = New XmlNodeReader(Node)
```

```csharp
// C#
XmlNodeReader aReader;
// Creates an XmlNodeReader that reads an XmlNode named Node
aReader = new XmlNodeReader(Node);
```

Validating XML with *XmlValidatingReader*

The *XmlValidatingReader* allows you to validate XML against a given schema. As the document is read, it is checked for validity against the schema that are indicated. *XmlValidatingReader* wraps an existing *XmlReader* instance. You can create an *XmlValidatingReader* instance, as shown here:

```vb
' VB
' Assumes the existence of an XmlReader named aReader
Dim aValReader As XmlValidatingReader
aValReader = New XmlValidatingReader(aReader)
```

```csharp
// C#
// Assumes the existence of an XmlReader named aReader
XmlValidatingReader aValReader;
aValReader = new XmlValidatingReader(aReader);
```

NOTE *XmlValidatingReader*: Obsolete

The 70-526 exam objectives were created while the version 2.0 of the .NET Framework was still under development. Between the time the objectives were released and the .NET Framework was released, *XmlValidatingReader* was made obsolete and was replaced by validating functionality built into the *XmlReader* class. To provide coverage for the exam, this book covers both classes. In the real world, you should always use *XmlReader* to validate XML documents.

XmlValidatingReader scans the XML for any schema, detecting both inline schema and referenced schema. Referenced schema are loaded, or they can be preloaded by adding them to the *Schemas* property.

The type of schema validation is determined by the *ValidationType* property. The possible values for the *ValidationType* property are shown in Table 9-5

Table 9-5 *ValidationType* Property Values

Value	Description
None	No validation type. Setting the property to this value creates a non-validating reader.
Auto	Examines the contents of the document and determines the most appropriate validation type.
DTD	Validates according to the indicated document type definition (DTD).
Schema	Validates according to inline or referenced extensible schema definition (XSD) schema.
XDR	Validates according to inline or referenced XML-Data Reduced (XDR) schema.

The XML is validated by calling the *Read* method. This calls the *Read* method on the wrapped *XmlReader* instance and advances the reader to the next node. It also validates the new node according to the specified validation type and schema. If a validation error is encountered, it raises a *ValidationEvent*. If the *ValidationEvent* is handled, execution continues. If no event handler for the *ValidationEvent* is found, an *XmlSchemaException* is thrown. A *ValidationEvent* is also raised in the case of validation warnings, but in this case, no exception will be thrown if the event is not handled.

Handling Validation Errors When validating XML documents, you can create an event handler for the *ValidationEvent* to take appropriate action when a validation error is detected. The *ValidationEventArgs* parameter of the *ValidationEvent* contains a variety of information about the validation error or warning. This information is summarized in Table 9-6.

Table 9-6 Properties of the *ValidationEventArgs* Class

Property	Description
Exception	Contains the exception associated with the event if it exists. If there is an exception and this event is not handled, this exception will be thrown.

Table 9-6 Properties of the *ValidationEventArgs* Class

Property	Description
Message	Contains an informative message about the validation event.
Severity	Describes the severity of the event, either *Warning* or *Error*. If the severity is *Error*, an exception will be thrown if this event is not handled.

A *ValidationEvent* handler requires a signature that contains an object parameter that represents the sender of the event and a *ValidationEventArgs* parameter. The following code shows an example of a *ValidationEvent* handler.

```vb
' VB
Private Sub ValidationHandler(ByVal sender As Object, ByVal e As _
   Xml.Schema.ValidationEventArgs)
   ' Code to handle the event goes here
End Sub
```

```csharp
// C#
private void ValidationHandler(object sender,
   Xml.Schema.ValidationEventArgs e)
 {
  // Code to handle the event goes here
}
```

After creating the method, you need to add the method as a handler for the *Validation-Event*, as shown in the following code:

```vb
' VB
AddHandler aReader.ValidationEventHandler, Addressof myHandler
```

```csharp
// C#
aReader.ValidationEventHandler += myHandler;
```

Validating XML with *XmlReader*

With the introduction of the .NET Framework 2.0, you can also use the *XmlReader .Create* method to create an instance of *XmlReader* that can validate XML. The *Xml-Reader.Create* method can accept an instance of the *XmlReaderSettings* class which allows you to specify the validation type by setting the *XmlReaderSettings.Validation-Type* property. The available validation types are the same as the types shown in Table 9-5. You can specify a method to handle *ValidationEvents* by adding a handler to the *ValidationEventHandler*. The behavior is identical to the behavior of the

XmlValidatingReader. The following example demonstrates how to create an instance of *XmlReader* that validates the specified file using an event handler shown afterwards.

```vb
' VB
Dim aReader As Xml.XmlReader
Dim settings As New Xml.XmlReaderSettings()
settings.ValidationType = Xml.ValidationType.Schema
AddHandler settings.ValidationEventHandler, AddressOf settings_ValidationEventHandler
aReader = Xml.XmlReader.Create("C:\myfile.xml", settings)
```

```csharp
// C#
System.Xml.XmlReader aReader;
System.Xml.XmlReaderSettings settings = new System.Xml.XmlReaderSettings();
settings.ValidationType = System.Xml.ValidationType.Schema;
settings.ValidationEventHandler += new
    System.Xml.Schema.ValidationEventHandler(settings_ValidationEventHandler);
aReader = System.Xml.XmlReader.Create(@"C:\myfile.xml", settings);
```

And the event handler must have a signature matching the following methods:

```vb
' VB
Sub settings_ValidationEventHandler _
    (ByVal sender As Object, ByVal e As System.Xml.Schema.ValidationEventArgs)
    ' TODO: Add validation event handler
End Sub
```

```csharp
// C#
void settings_ValidationEventHandler(object sender, System.Xml.Schema.ValidationEventArgs e)
{
    // TODO: Add validation event handler
}
```

You can also create a reader that validates by wrapping a preexisting XML reader. To do this, you specify the reader instead of a URI that specifies a file. The following example replaces the last line in the previous example, and demonstrates how to specify a preexisting *XmlReader* instance named theReader.

```vb
' VB
aReader = Xml.XmlReader.Create(theReader, settings)
```

```csharp
// C#
aReader = System.Xml.XmlReader.Create(theReader, settings);
```

Writing XML with the *XmlWriter* Class

The *XmlWriter* class allows you to write XML to a file, console, stream, or other output types. It is an abstract class that can be implemented in descendant classes, but you can also create an instance of a default implementation of the *XmlWriter* class by calling the static *XmlWriter.Create* method as shown here:

```vb
' VB
' The parameter can be a stream, a file, StringBuilder, TextWriter, or XmlWriter.
Dim aWriter As XmlWriter
aWriter = XmlWriter.Create(parameter)
```

```csharp
// C#
// The parameter can be a stream, a file, StringBuilder, TextWriter, or XmlWriter.
XmlWriter aWriter;
aWriter = XmlWriter.Create(parameter);
```

You can also specify an instance of *XmlWriterSettings* when you create an instance of *XmlWriter*. The *XmlWriterSettings* instance determines, among other things, the format of the XML that is written by *XmlWriter*. The following example demonstrates how to create an implementation of *XmlWriter* with an *XmlWriterSettings* instance.

```vb
' VB
' The parameter can be a stream, a file, StringBuilder, TextWriter, or XmlWriter.
Dim aWriter As XmlWriter
Dim mySettings As New XmlWriterSettings()
' Configures the writer to indent elements
mySettings.Indent = True
aWriter = XmlWriter.Create(parameter, mySettings)
```

```csharp
// C#
// The parameter can be a stream, a file, StringBuilder, TextWriter, or XmlWriter.
XmlWriter aWriter;
XmlWriterSettings mySettings = new XmlWriterSettings();
// Configures the writer to indent elements
mySettings.Indent = true;
aWriter = XmlWriter.Create(parameter, mySettings);
```

Formatting XML Output

When you create an *XmlWriter* implementation using an instance of *XmlWriterSettings*, you can specify a number of properties that control the format of the XML output. Table 9-7 describes the formatting properties of the *XmlWriterSettings* class.

Table 9-7 Formatting Properties of *XmlWriterSettings*

Property	Description
Indent	Determines whether to indent elements.

Table 9-7   Formatting Properties of *XmlWriterSettings*

Property	Description
IndentChars	Contains the character string used for indenting. By default, this string is two spaces. If *Indent* is set to *False*, this property has no effect.
NewLineChars	Indicates the character used to create a new line.
NewLineHandling	Indicates whether to normalize line breaks in the output.
NewLineOnAttributes	Indicates whether to write attributes on a new line.

To control the output formatting for *XmlWriter,* you create a new instance of *XmlWriter-Settings*, set the properties to the correct settings for the output format you desire, and then use the appropriate form of *XmlWriter.Create* to create the writer.

Writing Elements

The *XmlWriter* class contains methods that allow you to write elements to the output file or stream. Table 9-8 describes methods of the *XmlWriter* class that are used for writing elements.

Table 9-8   Element-Writing Methods of *XmlWriter*

Method	Description
WriteComment	Writes an XML comment to the output.
WriteElementString	Writes a complete element string, including opening and closing tags.
WriteEndElement	Writes the end element for an element. If the element contains no content, a short tag ("/>") is written. Otherwise, the full end tag is written.
WriteFullEndElement	Always writes the full end tag whether the element contains content or not.
WriteStartDocument	Writes the starting element for an XML document.
WriteStartElement	Writes a start element.

Writing a Simple Element   You can use the *WriteElementString* method to write a complete element with content. This method should be used when you do not need to write attribute content into a node. You specify the name of the node and the text value to be contained in the node. The following example demonstrates the use of this method.

```
' VB
myWriter.WriteElementString("Name", "Libby")
```

```
// C#
myWriter.WriteElementString("Name", "Libby");
```

The output of this method is the following element:

```
<Name>Libby</Name>
```

Writing Complicated Elements   For writing more complicated elements, you can use the *WriteStartElement* and *WriteEndElement* methods. These methods allow you to begin a node, write any special content (such as child nodes or attributes, which will be discussed later in this chapter), and then close the node. The following example demonstrates how to use the *WriteStartElement* and *WriteEndElement* methods.

```
' VB
myWriter.WriteStartElement("FirstNames")
myWriter.WriteElementString("Name", "Libby")
myWriter.WriteEndElement()
```

```
// C#
myWriter.WriteStartElement("FirstNames");
myWriter.WriteElementString("Name", "Libby");
myWriter.WriteEndElement();
```

This code example creates the following output:

```
<FirstNames>
    <Name>Libby</Name
</FirstNames>
```

Writing Attributes

The *WriteAttributeString* method allows you to write attributes to the elements created with *WriteStartElement*. You can specify the name and the value for the attribute in the method. The following example demonstrates the use of the *WriteAttributeString* method.

```
' VB
myReader.WriteStartElement("FirstNames")
```

```
myReader.WriteAttributeString("Nicknames", "Ok")
myWriter.WriteElementString("Name", "Libby")
myReader.WriteEndElement()
```

```
// C#
myReader.WriteStartElement("FirstNames");
myReader.WriteAttributeString("Nicknames", "Ok");
myWriter.WriteElementString("Name", "Libby");
myReader.WriteEndElement();
```

```
This example generates the following output:
<FirstNames Nicknames="Ok">
   <Name>Libby</Name>
</FirstNames>
```

Quick Check

1. Briefly describe the *XmlReader* class.

2. What are two classes that can be used to validate XML against a preexisting schema?

Quick Check Answers

1. The *XmlReader* class provides rapid, forward-only access to data contained in an XML format. The *XmlReader* class can read strings, streams, or other forms of XML.

2. You can use both the *XmlValidatingReader* and the *XmlReader* classes to validate XML against a schema. If *XmlReader* is used, you must configure it appropriately using an instance of *XmlReaderSettings*.

Lab: Create an Application that Reads an XML File

In this lab, you will create an application that reads an XML file and displays the elements, attributes, and text of that file.

▶ **Exercise 1: Reading XML into *TreeView***

In Visual Studio, create a new Windows Forms project. Then, follow these steps:

1. From the Toolbox, drag a *TreeView*, a *Button*, and an *OpenFileDialog* control onto the form.

2. Set the properties of the Form and controls as shown here:

Control/Form	Property	Value
Form1	*Text*	*Read XML*
Button1	*Text*	*Read XML*
OpenFileDialog1	*Filter*	*XML Files	*.xml*

3. Right-click the Designer and then click View Code to open the code window.

4. In the code window, add the following line of code to the top of the code editor:

```
' VB
Imports System.Xml
```

```
// C#
using System.Xml;
```

5. In the Designer, double-click Button1 to open the *Button1_Click* event handler. Add the following code to the *Button1_Click* event handler.

```
' VB
' Clears the Treeview control
TreeView1.Nodes.Clear()
' Creates a new XmlReader and reads the XML file found in the open file dialog box.
Dim aReader As XmlReader
OpenFileDialog1.ShowDialog()
If Not OpenFileDialog1.FileName = "" Then
    aReader = XmlReader.Create(OpenFileDialog1.FileName)
End If
Dim aNode As TreeNode
Dim bNode As TreeNode
Dim parentNode As TreeNode
' Loops through the nodes of the XML file
While aReader.Read
    Select Case aReader.NodeType
        ' If an element is found, it creates a new node, reads the
        ' attributes, and Adds the name of the element and the attributes
        ' As a new node to the Treeview
        Case XmlNodeType.Element
            aNode = New TreeNode(aReader.Name)
            If aReader.AttributeCount > 0 Then
                Dim i As Integer
                aReader.MoveToFirstAttribute()
                aNode.Text &= " " & aReader.Name & "=" & aReader.Value
                For i = 1 To aReader.AttributeCount - 1
                    aReader.MoveToNextAttribute()
                    aNode.Text &= " " & aReader.Name & "=" & aReader.Value
                Next
            End If
```

```
            If parentNode Is Nothing Then
                TreeView1.Nodes.Add(aNode)
            Else
                parentNode.Nodes.Add(aNode)
            End If
            parentNode = aNode
        ' When an EndElement is encountered, the parent element is set one level up.
        Case XmlNodeType.EndElement
            parentNode = parentNode.Parent
        ' When a Text node is encountered, a new node is made As a child
        ' node containing the text is created
        Case XmlNodeType.Text
            bNode = New TreeNode(aReader.Value)
            aNode.Nodes.Add(bNode)
        Case Else
    End Select
End While


// C#
// Clears the Treeview control
treeView1.Nodes.Clear();
// Creates a new XmlReader and reads the XML file found in the open file dialog box.
XmlReader aReader;
openFileDialog1.ShowDialog();
aReader = XmlReader.Create(openFileDialog1.FileName);
TreeNode aNode = new TreeNode();
TreeNode bNode;
TreeNode parentNode = new TreeNode();
// Loops through the nodes of the XML file
while (aReader.Read())
{
    switch (aReader.NodeType)
    {
        // If an element is found, it creates a new node, reads the
        // attributes, and Adds the name of the element and the attributes
        // as a new node to the Treeview
        case XmlNodeType.Element:
            aNode = new TreeNode(aReader.Name);
            if (aReader.AttributeCount > 0)
            {
                aReader.MoveToFirstAttribute();
                aNode.Text += " " + aReader.Name + "=" + aReader.Value;
                for (int i = 1; i < aReader.AttributeCount; i++)
                {
                    aReader.MoveToNextAttribute();
                    aNode.Text += " " + aReader.Name + "=" + aReader.Value;
                }
            }
            if (parentNode.Text == "")
                treeView1.Nodes.Add(aNode);
            else
                parentNode.Nodes.Add(aNode);
            parentNode = aNode;
```

```
            // When an EndElement is encountered, the parent element is set one level up.
               break;
            case XmlNodeType.EndElement:
                parentNode = parentNode.Parent;
                break;
            // When a Text node is encountered, a new node is made as a child
            // node containing the text is created
            case XmlNodeType.Text:
                bNode = new TreeNode(aReader.Value);
                aNode.Nodes.Add(bNode);
                break;
        }
    }
```

6. Press F5 to run the application. Click the button marked Read XML and navigate to an XML file such as Bookstore.Xml in the where location on your disk. Note that the XML file is read and the nodes are translated into *TreeView*.

Lesson Summary

- The *XmlReader* class is an abstract class that provides uncached, forward-only access to XML contained in a file or stream. *XmlReader* is implemented in the *XmlTextReader*, *XmlNodeReader*, and *XmlValidatingReader* classes. You can also obtain an instance of a default implementation of *XmlReader* via the *XmlReader.Create* method.

- The *Read* method reads the current node of the XML content in *XmlReader* and advances the reader to the next node. Once a node has been read, it cannot be revisited by that instance of *XmlReader*.

- Attributes can be read with the *MoveToAttribute* method. While using the *MoveToAttribute* method, you can freely move back and forth between attributes in an element. This is the only exception to forward-only access in the *XmlReader* class.

- The *XmlReader.MoveToContent* method can be used to skip noncontent-containing nodes and move the reader to the next content-containing node.

- *XmlValidatingReader* validates the XML reader by *XmlReader* against an inline or referenced schema. When a validation error occurs, a *ValidationError* event is raised, which you can handle. The *ValidationErrorEventArgs* instance passed in that event provides information about the validation error. You can also validate XML with the *XmlReader* class.

- The *XmlWriter* class is an abstract class that provides methods for writing XML. You can obtain an instance of a default implementation of *XmlWriter* via the *XmlWriter.Create* method.

Lesson Review

The following questions are intended to reinforce key information presented in this lesson. The questions are also available on the companion CD if you prefer to review them in electronic form.

NOTE   Answers

Answers to these questions and explanations of why each choice is right or wrong are located in the "Answers" section at the end of the book.

---

1. Which of the following code samples will create a new instance of the *XmlReader* class?

   A.
   ```
   ' VB
   Dim aReader As New XmlReader()
   ```
   ```
   // C#
   XmlReader aReader = new XmlReader();
   ```

   B.
   ```
   ' VB
   Dim aReader As XmlReader
   aReader = XmlReader.Create()
   ```
   ```
   // C#
   XmlReader aReader;
   aReader = XmlReader.Create();
   ```

   C.
   ```
   ' VB
   Dim aReader As XmlReader
   aReader = XmlReader.Create("myXml.xml")
   ```
   ```
   // C#
   XmlReader aReader;
   aReader = XmlReader.Create("myXml.xml");
   ```

   D.
   ```
   ' VB
   Dim aReader As New XmlReader("myXml.xml")
   ```
   ```
   // C#
   XmlReader aReader = new XmlReader("myXml.xml");
   ```

2. Given the following XML fragment

```
<text1 length="12" color="blue">moo</text1>
```

and an instance of *XmlReader* named *myReader* that is positioned on the *text1* node, which of the following code samples can be used to display the value (but not the name) of the length attribute? (Choose all that apply.)

A. .' **VB**

```
myReader.MoveToAttribute("length")
MsgBox(myReader.Value)
```

// **C#**

```
myReader.MoveToAttribute("length");
MessageBox.Show(myReader.Value);
```

B. ' **VB**

```
myReader.MoveToAttribute(0)
MsgBox(myReader.Value)
```

// **C#**

```
myReader.MoveToAttribute(0);
MessageBox.Show(myReader.Value);
```

C. ' **VB**

```
myReader.MoveToAttribute("length")
MsgBox(myReader.InnerXml)
```

// **C#**

```
myReader.MoveToAttribute("length");
MessageBox.Show(myReader.InnerXml);
```

D. ' **VB**

```
myReader.MoveToAttribute("length")
MsgBox(myReader.OuterXml)
```

// **C#**

```
myReader.MoveToAttribute("length");
MessageBox.Show(myReader.OuterXml);
```

3. Given an instance of *XmlWriter* named *myWriter*, which of the following code samples will generate the following XML fragment?

```
<colors>
   <color>blue</color>
</colors>
```

A. ' **VB**

```
myWriter.WriteStartElement("colors")
myWriter.WriteElementString("color", "blue")
myWriter.WriteEndElement()
```

```
// C#
myWriter.WriteStartElement("colors");
myWriter.WriteElementString("color", "blue");
myWriter.WriteEndElement();
```

B. ```
' VB
myWriter.WriteStartElement("colors")
myWriter.WriteElementString("color", "blue")
myWriter.WriteEndElement("colors")
```

```
// C#
myWriter.WriteStartElement("colors");
myWriter.WriteElementString("color", "blue");
myWriter.WriteEndElement("colors");
```

C. ```
' VB
myWriter.WriteElementString("colors")
myWriter.WriteElementString("color", "blue")
myWriter.WriteElementString("/colors")
```

```
// C#
myWriter.WriteElementString("colors");
myWriter.WriteElementString("color", "blue");
myWriter.WriteElementString("/colors");
```

D. ```
' VB
myWriter.WriteStartElement("colors")
myWriter.WriteStartElement("color", "blue")
myWriter.WriteEndElement()
```

```
// C#
myWriter.WriteStartElement("colors");
myWriter.WriteStartElement("color", "blue");
myWriter.WriteEndElement();
```
```

Lesson 2: Managing XML with the XML Document Object Model

The XML document object model (DOM) is a hierarchical representation of a flat XML file. Platform-specific implementations of the XML DOM allow you to navigate the XML document, perform complicated searches, and modify the XML structure in a nonlinear fashion. The .NET Framework allows access to the XML DOM through the *XmlDocument* class.

After this lesson, you will be able to:

- Read XML data into the DOM.
- Modify an XML document by adding and removing nodes.
- Modify nodes within an XML document.
- Write data in XML format from the DOM.
- Work with nodes in the XML DOM.
- Handle DOM events.
- Modify XML declaration.

Estimated lesson time: 45 minutes

The *XmlDocument* Class

The XML DOM is exposed through the *System.Xml.XmlDocument* class. This class allows you to read an XML file into memory and then manipulate the structure through a variety of methods, as well as to perform searches and retrieve nodes.

The *XmlDocument* class exposes an XML document as a hierarchical collection of *XmlNode* objects. Because the *XmlDocument* class extends *XmlNode* itself, the *XmlDocument* can be thought of as the root node. Access to the child nodes of the *XmlDocument* is available through the *ChildNodes* property, or you can access specific elements through the *XmlDocument.Item* property.

Reading XML into the DOM

You can read an existing XML document into the DOM by creating a new instance of the *XmlDocument* class and then loading the XML from a *Stream*, *String* (containing the filename), *TextWriter*, or *XmlWriter*, as shown in the following example.

```
' VB
Dim aDocument As New XmlDocument()
' The parameter must be a String, Stream, TextWriter, or XmlWriter
aDocument.Load(parameter)
```

```
// C#
XmlDocument aDocument = new XmlDocument();
// The parameter must be a String, Stream, TextWriter, or XmlWriter
aDocument.Load(parameter);
```

The *Load* method does not validate the XML that is loaded into *XmlDocument*. To validate XML against a schema, pass it an instance of *XmlValidatingReader* in the *Load* method.

The *Load* method preserves all significant white space, and it preserves all white space if the *XmlDocument.PreserveWhiteSpace* property is set to *True*. If you do not want to preserve white space, you can use the *LoadXml* method.

Modifying an XML Document

You can add, remove, and copy XML nodes by using methods built into the *XmlDocument* class.

Creating New Nodes   The *XmlDocument* class allows you to create and insert new nodes into the XML document you are working with. The methods that create new nodes are described in Table 9-9.

Table 9-9 *XmlDocument* Methods for Creating New Nodes

Method	Description
CreateComment	Creates a comment node
CreateCDataSection	Creates a CData section
CreateDocumentFragment	Creates a new document fragment
CreateDocumentType	Creates a new *Document Type* node
CreateElement	Creates a new element
CreateProcessingInstruction	Creates a new processing instruction node
CreateTextNode	Creates a new text node
CreateXmlDeclaration	Creates a new XML declaration node

Table 9-9 *XmlDocument* **Methods for Creating New Nodes**

Method	Description
CreateWhitespace	Creates a new white space node
CreateSignificantWhitespace	Creates a new significant white space node

Each of these methods has its own constructor and requires different parameters. Once a new node is created, it must be inserted into an instance of *XmlDocument* by one of the methods shown in Table 9-10.

Table 9-10 **Node Insertion Methods of the** *XmlDocument* **Class**

Method	Description
InsertBefore	Inserts the new node into the document before a specified node
InsertAfter	Inserts the new node into the document after a specified node
AppendChild	Adds the specified node to the end of the list of child nodes of the node calling this method
PrependChild	Adds the specified node to the beginning of the list of child nodes of the node calling this method

The following code example demonstrates how to create a new element and a new text node, add the element to an instance of *XmlDocument*, and then insert the text into the newly created element:

```
' VB
' Declares the new XmlDocument, XmlElement, and XmlText
Dim aDocument As New Xml.XmlDocument
Dim anElement As Xml.XmlElement
Dim aText As Xml.XmlText
' Creates a new node
anElement = aDocument.CreateElement("TestNode")
' creates the new text node
aText = aDocument.CreateTextNode("This is the test text")
' Declares a new node to hold the reference to the new node that will be
' returned when anElement is inserted into the XmlDocument
Dim node As Xml.XmlNode
' Inserts anElement into the XmlDocument
node = aDocument.AppendChild(anElement)
```

```
' Inserts the text into the newly-created node
node.AppendChild(aText)
```

```
// C#
// Declares the new XmlDocument, XmlElement, and XmlText
Xml.XmlDocument aDocument = new Xml.XmlDocument;
Xml.XmlElement anElement;
Xml.XmlText aText;
// Creates a new node
anElement = aDocument.CreateElement("TestNode");
// creates the new text node
aText = aDocument.CreateTextNode("This is the test text");
// Declares a new node to hold the reference to the new node that will be
// returned when anElement is inserted into the XmlDocument
XmlNode node;
// Inserts anElement into the XmlDocument
node = aDocument.AppendChild(anElement);
// Inserts the text into the newly-created XmlDocumentnode
node.AppendChild(aText);
```

The following XML is generated by the above example:

```
<TestNode>This is the test text</TestNode>
```

Copying Existing Nodes   You can create a copy of an existing node by using the *Xml-Node.CloneNode* method. This method creates a copy of an existing node that can then be inserted into the instance of *XmlDocument*. The following example demonstrates the *CloneNode* method.

```
' VB
' Assumes a node called aNode
Dim bNode As Xml.XmlNode
bNode = aNode.CloneNode()
' bNode is now ready to be inserted into the XmlDocument
```

```
// C#
// Assumes a node called aNode
Xml.XmlNode bNode;
bNode = aNode.CloneNode();
// bNode is now ready to be inserted into the XmlDocument
```

Removing Existing Nodes   You can remove existing nodes by obtaining a reference to the parent of the node you want to remove and then calling *RemoveChild*. Here is an example:

```
' VB
aNode.RemoveChild(ChildNode)
```

```
// C#
aNode.RemoveChild(ChildNode);
```

Modifying Nodes Within an Instance of *XmlDocument*

You can use the methods exposed by the *XmlDocument* and *XmlNode* classes to modify existing nodes within an instance of *XmlDocument*. You can change the value of value-containing nodes, replace existing nodes, modify content, and set attribute values programmatically.

Changing the Value of Existing Nodes   For nodes that have a value (*Attribute*, *CDATA*, *Comment*, *DocumentType*, *ProcessingInstruction*, *SignificantWhitespace*, *Text*, *Whitespace*, *XmlDeclaration*), you can change the value directly by changing the *XmlNode.Value* property. The following example demonstrates how to change the value of an *XmlText* element.

```vb
' VB
Dim aText As New Xml.XmlText("Text1")
' Changes the value of the text element to 'Text2'
aText.Value = "Text2"
```

```csharp
// C#
Xml.XmlText aText = new Xml.XmlText("Text1");
// Changes the value of the text element to 'Text2'
aText.Value = "Text2";
```

Replacing an Entire Set of Child Nodes   If you want to replace all of the child nodes of one node with another set of nodes, you can do so by setting the *XmlNode.InnerXml* property. The *InnerXml* property of an *XmlNode* is a string that contains all content and child nodes of the node but excludes the starting and ending elements. By setting the *InnerXml* property, you can replace the existing child nodes with a string that contains your new child nodes. Here is an example:

```vb
' VB
' Assumes an XmlNode called aNode
Dim aString As String = "<Test>TestChildNodes</Test>"
aNode.InnerXml = aString
```

```csharp
// C#
// Assumes an XmlNode called aNode
String aString = "<Test>TestChildNodes</Test>'
aNode.InnerXml = aString;
```

Replacing Specific Nodes   You can replace individual nodes by using the *XmlNode.ReplaceChild* method. This method allows you to specify a child node of your *XmlNode* and to specify an *XmlNode* to replace it with. The following example shows how to use the *ReplaceChild* method.

```vb
' VB
' This example replaces the child node named OldNode with the node named
```

```
' NewNode. The parent node in this example is called aNode.
aNode.ReplaceChild(NewNode, OldNode)
```

```
// C#
// This example replaces the child node named OldNode with the node named
// NewNode. The parent node in this example is called aNode.
aNode.ReplaceChild(NewNode, OldNode);
```

Replacing or Removing a Range of Characters   For nodes that inherit from the *Xml-CharacterData* class (these are *XmlCDataSection*, *XmlComment*, *XmlSignificant-Whitespace*, *XmlText*, and *XmlWhitespace*) you can replace or remove characters using the *ReplaceData* method, which takes three parameters. The first parameter is the starting character in the existing character data to replace. The second parameter is the length of the characters to be replaced. The third parameter is a string that will be inserted into the character data at the point specified. The following example demonstrates the *ReplaceData* method.

```
' VB
Dim aText As New XmlText("myText")
aText.ReplaceData(0, 2, "your")
' The resulting value of aText is 'yourText'
```

```
// C#
XmlText aText = new XmlText("myText");
aText.ReplaceData(0, 2, "your");
// The resulting value of aText is 'yourText'
```

Setting or Updating an Attribute   You can add an attribute to an element or update the value of an existing attribute by using the *SetAttribute* method, as shown here:

```
' VB
anElement.SetAttribute("Color", "Blue")
```

```
// C#
anElement.SetAttribute("Color", "Blue");
```

The code shown in this example sets the *Color* attribute of *anElement* to *Blue*. If *anElement* does not have a *Color* attribute, it creates a new *Color* attribute and sets the value to *Blue*.

Writing XML with *XmlDocument*

You can write the content of an *XmlDocument* to a file, stream, console, or other output format with the *XmlDocument.WriteTo* method. This method writes all of the nodes in the *XmlDocument* to a specified *XmlWriter*. This is functionally equivalent to writing the *OuterXml* property. You can also write the content of the *XmlDocument* excluding the opening and closing nodes with the *WriteContentTo* method. This is functionally equivalent to writing the *InnerXml* property. The following example demonstrates how to write the nodes of an *XmlDocument* named *aDocument* to a file called *myFile.xml*.

```
' VB
Dim aWriter As Xml.XmlWriter
aWriter = Xml.XmlWriter.Create("myFile.xml")
aDocument.WriteTo(aWriter)
```

```
// C#
XmlWriter aWriter;
aWriter = Xml.XmlWriter.Create("myFile.xml");
aDocument.WriteTo(aWriter);
```

Working with *XmlNamedNodeMap*

The *XmlNamedNodeMap* organizes a collection of non-hierarchical XML nodes such as attributes or entities. The following three properties return an *XmlNamedNodeMap*:

- *XmlElement.Attributes*
- *XmlDocumentType.Entities*
- *XmlDocumentType.Notations*

The *XmlNamedNodeMap* class allows access to *XmlNodes* by the name of the node. Table 9-11 describes the important methods of the *XmlNamedNodeMap*.

Table 9-11 Important Methods of the *XmlNamedNodeMap*

Method	Description
GetNamedItem	Retrieves the *XmlNode* with the specified name
Item	Retrieves the node with the specified index
RemoveNamedItem	Removes the specified node from the *XmlNamedNodeMap*
SetNamedItem	Adds an existing *XmlNode* to the *XmlNamedNodeMap*

Working with *XmlNodeList*

The *XmlNodeList* class represents an ordered list of nodes. The following methods and properties return an *XmlNodeList*.

- *XmlNode.ChildNodes*

- *XmlDocument.GetElementsByTagName*
- *XmlElement.GetElementsByTagName*
- *XmlNode.SelectNodes*

The *XmlNodeList* class allows access to the nodes contained in it by the index of the node through the *Item* method. The *Count* property returns the number of nodes in the *XmlNodeList*. The following code example demonstrates how to loop through each node in an *XmlNodeList* named *xList*.

```
' VB
Dim j As Integer
For j = 0 To xList.Count - 1
   MsgBox(xList.Item(j).InnerXml)
Next
```

```
// C#
for (int j = 0; j <xList.Count; j++)
{
    MessageBox.Show(xList.Item(j).InnerXml);
}
```

Handling DOM Events

The *XmlDocument* class raises events in response to changes in the node structure. You can handle these events to execute code when the structure of the XML document changes. Table 9-12 describes the events that the *XmlDocument* class raises.

Table 9-12   Events Raised by the *XmlDocument* Class

Event	Description
NodeInserting	Raised when a node is about to be inserted into another node
NodeInserted	Raised when a node has been inserted into another node
NodeRemoving	Raised when a node is about to be removed from the document
NodeRemoved	Raised when a node has been removed from the document
NodeChanging	Raised when a node is about to be changed
NodeChanged	Raised when a node has been changed

You can create event handlers that execute code in response to these events. Event handlers for *XmlDocument* events have the following signature:

```
' VB
Sub DocHandler(ByVal source As Object, ByVal e As XmlNodeChangedEventArgs)
End Sub
```

```
// C#
void DocHander(object source, XmlNodeChangedEventArgs e)
{}
```

You can create an event handler for any of these events by the method described in Chapter 4, "ToolStrips, Menus, and Events."

The *XmlNodeChangedEventArgs* parameter in the event handler conveys information about the event that has been handled. Table 9-13 describes the properties of the *XmlNodeChangedEventArgs* class.

Table 9-13   Properties of the *XmlNodeChangedEventArgs* Class

Property	Description
Action	Gets a value that indicates what kind of node change event is occurring
NewParent	Gets the value of *ParentNode* after the operation completes
Node	Gets the node that is being added, removed, or changed
OldParent	Gets the value of *ParentNode* before the operation completes

Modifying the XML Declaration

The *XmlDeclaration* node is the first node in a complete *XmlDocument* instance. It specifies the XML version that is used, whether the *XmlDocument* is a standalone document, and the encoding used by the document.

You can create an *XmlDeclaration* node with the *XmlDocument.CreateXmlDeclaration* method. The *CreateXmlDeclaration* method requires the following parameters:

- **Version**   Currently, this parameter must always be set to "1.0". Other versions are not currently supported.

- **Encoding**   Represents the encoding used to encode characters in the *XmlDocument* class. The encoding determines the character page used to display characters in this document. Because different countries use different character sets, set the *Encoding* property to the encoding appropriate for the locale where it will be used. If this parameter is set to null or *Nothing*, the default value of UTF-8 is used, but no value is written to the declaration node.

■ **Standalone**   Indicates whether the document is independent of external resources. Property must be set to either *yes* or *no*. If this parameter is set to null or *Nothing*, no value is written to the declaration.

The following code example demonstrates how to create an instance of *XmlDeclaration* and insert it into an *XmlDocument* document.

```vb
' VB
Dim aDoc As New Xml.XmlDocument()
Dim aDecl As Xml.XmlDeclaration
' Creates a new XmlDeclaration and sets the encoding value to ISO-8859-1
aDecl = aDoc.CreateXmlDeclaration("1.0", "ISO-8859-1", "yes")
' Adds the XmlDeclaration
aDoc.AppendChild(aDecl)
```

```csharp
// C#
Xml.XmlDocument aDoc = new Xml.XmlDocument();
Xml.XmlDeclaration aDecl;
// Creates a new XmlDeclaration and sets the encoding value to ISO-8859-1
aDecl = aDoc.CreateXmlDeclaration("1.0", "ISO-8859-1", "yes");
// Adds the XmlDeclaration
aDoc.AppendChild(aDecl);
```

Note than an *XmlDeclaration* node must be inserted into the first position in an *Xml-Document* class. Any attempt to insert an *XmlDeclaration* node into a different position will result in an exception being thrown.

Quick Check

1. What is the purpose of the *XmlDocument* class?

2. How can you replace an entire set of child nodes on a given *XmlNode*?

Quick Check Answers

1. The *XmlDocument* class provides programmatic, in-memory access to the nodes and structure of an existing XML document.

2. You can replace all of the child nodes of a given *XmlNode* object by setting the *XmlNode.InnerXml* property.

Lab: Use the *XmlDocument* Class

In this lab, you will add *XmlDocument* functionality to a preexisting partial solution. You will load the content from the *BookStore.xml* file into an *XmlDocument* instance, and then you will add new elements to the *XmlDocument* instance.

▶ **Exercise 1: Add *XMLDocument* Functionality to a Partial Solution**

1. From the directory on the companion CD, load the partial solution for the language you are working in.

2. Open Form1 in the Designer. Then, double-click the Load XML button to open the *btnLoadXml_Click* event handler.

3. Beneath the content already in this method, add the following code:

```
' VB
doc.Load(OpenFileDialog1.FileName)
```

```
// C#
doc.Load(openFileDialog1.FileName);
```

4. In the Designer, double-click the View XML button to open the *btnViewXml_Click* event handler.

5. Add the following code to this method:

```
' VB
Dim aForm As New Form2
aForm.TextBox1.Text = doc.OuterXml
aForm.ShowDialog()
```

```
// C#
Form2 aForm = new Form2();
aForm.TextBox1.Text = doc.OuterXml;
aForm.ShowDialog();
```

6. In the Designer, double-click the Add Book button to open the *btnAddBook_Click* event handler.

7. Beneath the first line of code already in this method (for Visual Basic) or within the *if* block (for C#), add the following code:

```
' VB
If doc.OuterXml = "" Then
    MsgBox("Please load the XML file first")
    Exit Sub
End If
Dim aList As Xml.XmlNodeList
Dim aNode As Xml.XmlNode
Dim anElement As Xml.XmlElement
aList = doc.GetElementsByTagName("book")
```

```vbnet
    aNode = aList.Item(aList.Count - 1)

    ' Creates a new element
    anElement = doc.CreateElement("book")

    ' Sets attributes on the element
    anElement.SetAttribute("ISBN", txtISBN.Text)
    anElement.SetAttribute("Title", txtTitle.Text)
    anElement.SetAttribute("Price", txtPrice.Text)

    ' If there are chapters, creates the elements and adds them
    If Not ListView1.Items.Count = 0 Then
        For Each j As ListViewItem In ListView1.Items
            Dim bElement As Xml.XmlElement
            bElement = doc.CreateElement("chapter")
            bElement.SetAttribute("num", j.SubItems(0).Text)
            bElement.SetAttribute("name", j.SubItems(1).Text)
            Dim atext As Xml.XmlText
            atext = doc.CreateTextNode(j.SubItems(2).Text)
            bElement.AppendChild(atext)
            anElement.AppendChild(bElement)
        Next
    End If

    ' Inserts the node to the correct slot
    aNode.ParentNode.InsertAfter(anElement, aNode)

    ' clears the UI
    txtChapterName.Text = ""
    txtChapterText.Text = ""
    txtISBN.Text = ""
    txtPrice.Text = ""
    txtTitle.Text = ""
    ListView1.Clear()

    // C#
    if (doc.OuterXml == "")
    {
        MessageBox.Show("Please load the XML file first");
        return;
    }
    System.Xml.XmlNodeList aList;
    System.Xml.XmlNode aNode;
    System.Xml.XmlElement anElement;
    aList = doc.GetElementsByTagName("book");
    aNode = aList.Item(aList.Count - 1);

    // Creates a new element
    anElement = doc.CreateElement("book");

    // Sets attributes on the element
    anElement.SetAttribute("ISBN", txtISBN.Text);
```

```
anElement.SetAttribute("Title", txtTitle.Text);
anElement.SetAttribute("Price", txtPrice.Text);

// If there are chapters, creates the elements and adds them
if (!(listView1.Items.Count == 0))
{
    System.Xml.XmlElement bElement;
    System.Xml.XmlText atext;
    foreach (ListViewItem j in listView1.Items)
    {
        bElement = doc.CreateElement("chapter");
        bElement.SetAttribute("num", j.SubItems[0].Text);
        bElement.SetAttribute("name", j.SubItems[1].Text);
        atext = doc.CreateTextNode(j.SubItems[2].Text);
        bElement.AppendChild(atext);
        anElement.AppendChild(bElement);
    }
}

// Inserts the node to the correct slot
aNode.ParentNode.InsertAfter(anElement, aNode);

// clears the UI
txtChapterName.Text = "";
txtChapterText.Text = "";
txtISBN.Text = "";
txtPrice.Text = "";
txtTitle.Text = "";
listView1.Clear();
```

8. Press F5 to compile and run your application.

9. Press the Load Xml button and navigate to the Bookstore.xml file located in the directory on the companion CD. Select the file to load it into the *XmlDocument* instance.

10. Press the View Xml button to view the XML. Then, close Form2.

11. In Form1, add entries for *ISBN*, *Title*, and *Price*.

12. Add entries for *Chapter Name* and *Chapter Text* and click the Add Chapter button. Repeat this step as many times as you like.

13. Press the Add Book button to add the book data to your *XmlDocument* class.

14. Click the View Xml button to view the updated XML. Note that the book you added appears at the end of the XML file.

Lesson Summary

- The *XmlDocument* class provides an in-memory representation of XML data that can be modified in a direction-independent manner. XML data can be read into an *XmlDocument* instance through the *XmlDocument.Load* and *XmlDocument.LoadXml* methods.

- The *XmlDocument* class contains methods for creating all different kinds of XML nodes. Once a node has been created, it must be inserted into the XML represented by the *XmlDocument* class by a separate method.

- The *XmlDocument* class exposes several methods and properties that provide for the direct modification of the XML that it contains. You can change the value of existing nodes, replace specific nodes or an entire set of nodes, replace a range of characters in a value, or set attribute values.

- You can write XML from the XML document to an instance of the *XmlWriter* class by using the *XmlDocument.WriteTo* method.

- *XmlNamedNodeMap* consists of an unordered set of *XmlNode* instances that can be accessed by index or name. *XmlNodeList* represents an ordered set of *XmlNode* instances that can be accessed by index.

- The *XmlDocument* class raises events in response to changes in the XML structure. You can handle these events to execute code in response to changes in the XML.

- The XML declaration provides information about the XML version and the encoding used for the XML data. You can set the encoding property to a value appropriate for different international locales.

Lesson Review

The following questions are intended to reinforce key information presented in this lesson. The questions are also available on the companion CD if you prefer to review them in electronic form.

NOTE Answers

Answers to these questions and explanations of why each choice is right or wrong are located in the "Answers" section at the end of the book.

---

1. Given an *XmlDocument* named *myDoc* and an *XmlNode* that it contains named *myNode*, which of the following code samples will create a new element named *Test* and add it as a child of *myNode*?

    A. ```
        ' VB
        Dim anElement As XmlElement
        anElement = myDoc.CreateElement("Test")
        myNode.AppendChild(anElement)

        // C#
        XmlElement anElement;
        anElement = myDoc.CreateElement("Test");
        myNode.AppendChild(anElement);
        ```

    B.  ```
        ' VB
        anElement = myDoc.CreateElement("Test")
        myNode.AppendChild("Test")

        // C#
        anElement = myDoc.CreateElement("Test");
        myNode.AppendChild("Test");
        ```

    C. ```
        ' VB
        Dim anElement As XmlElement
        anElement = myDoc.CreateElement("Test")
        myDoc.AppendChild(anElement)

        // C#
        XmlElement anElement;
        anElement = myDoc.CreateElement("Test");
        myDoc.AppendChild(anElement);
        ```

    D.  ```
        ' VB
        Dim anElement As XmlElement
        anElement = myNode.CreateElement("Test")
        myNode.AppendChild(anElement)

        // C#
        XmlElement anElement;
        anElement = myNode.CreateElement("Test");
        myNode.AppendChild(anElement);
        ```

2. Given an instance of *XmlNode* named *Node1* that has a child node named *child-Node* and a string *aString* that contains a set of XML nodes, you want to replace the child node of *Node1* with the XML contained in *aString*. Which of the following code samples is correct for this scenario?

    A. ```
        ' VB
        Node1.ReplaceChild(childNode, aString)

        // C#
        Node1.ReplaceChild(childNode, aString);
        ```
        ```

B.   ` ' VB`
```
Node1.InnerXml = aString
```

```
// C#
Node1.InnerXml = aString;
```

C.   ` ' VB`
```
Node1.Value = aString
```

```
// C#
Node1.Value = aString;
```

D.   ` ' VB`
```
Node1.OuterXml = aString
```

```
// C#
Node1.OuterXml = aString;
```

Chapter Review

To further practice and reinforce the skills you learned in this chapter, you can perform the following tasks:

- Review the chapter summary.
- Review the list of key terms introduced in this chapter.
- Complete the case scenarios. These scenarios set up real-world situations involving the topics of this chapter and ask you to create a solution.
- Complete the suggested practices.
- Take a practice test.

Chapter Summary

- The *XmlReader* class is an abstract class. Implementations of this class provide non-cached, forward-only access to an XML file or stream. *XmlTextReader*, *XmlNodeReader*, and *XmlValidatingReader* all provide implementations of the *XmlReader* class. The *XmlReader.Read* method advances the reader to the next node of the XML and reads the name and value of that node. You can navigate the attributes of an element with the *MoveToAttribute* method.
- The *XmlWriter* class is an abstract class. Implementations of this class are used for writing XML content in a forward-based manner. You can obtain an instance of a default implementation of *XmlWriter* through the *XmlWriter.Create* method.
- The *XmlDocument* class provides an in-memory representation of XML data. It provides methods for creating XML nodes, inserting them into the XML document, copying nodes, removing nodes, and modifying nodes.
- The *XmlDocument* class raises events in response to changes in the XML structure. You can handle these events to execute code in response to these changes.

Key Terms

- *XmlDocument*
- *XmlNode*
- *XmlReader*
- *XmlWrite*

Case Scenarios

In the following case scenarios, you will apply what you've learned about working with XML. You can find answers to these questions in the "Answers" section at the end of this book.

Case Scenario 1: Report Archiving

Well, you're moving on up in the world of the Humongous Insurance company, and they've put you on another very important project. One thing that they love at Humongous Insurance is paperwork. Recently, affiliate offices all over the world have switched to sending weekly reports to the home office in an XML format. These reports all need to be stored and archived and will be compressed using a proprietary technology in-house. Your job is to make sure that reports coming in can be automatically parsed and fed into the compression API.

Questions

1. How can we automatically parse incoming reports?
2. How can we ensure that reports conform to our published schema?
3. How can we ensure that errors can be corrected by a human being when they occur?

Case Scenario 2: The Merger

Humongous Insurance has just acquired Trey Research. The main reason for the acquisition of Trey Research was a vast store of proprietary paperwork in custom XML formats. The acquisition is now complete and Humongous Insurance needs to replace the name of Trey Research with its own as well as with some other particulars. Unfortunately, due to variations in some of the content, a textual find-and-replace is out of the question, and the content must be replaced based on the element name that surrounds the content, not on the content itself.

Questions

- How can we create a simple application that can quickly replace some of the information contained in these nodes with our own information but leave the rest of the documents intact?

Suggested Practices

- Build an application that allows the user to enter data into a grid and then uses the *XmlWriter* class to write it to an XML file.

- Create a subclass of *XmlDocument* that validates the structure of the XML against an inline or referenced schema whenever the structure of the XML changes. Use the data object model (DOM) events to write the XML content of the *XmlDocument* instance to a stream that is read by *XmlValidatingReader* that raises events when an error occurs.

Take a Practice Test

The practice tests on this book's companion CD offer many options. For example, you can test yourself on just the content covered in this chapter, or you can test yourself on all the 70-526 certification exam content. You can set up the test so that it closely simulates the experience of taking a certification exam, or you can set it up in study mode so that you can look at the correct answers and explanations after you answer each question.

MORE INFO   **Practice tests**

For details about all the practice test options available, see the "How to Use the Practice Tests" section in this book's Introduction.

Chapter 10

Printing in Windows Forms

Creating printed documents is an essential task in most business environments, but it can be a complicated and confusing task to program. Microsoft Visual Studio 2005 provides several classes and dialog boxes that simplify the task of programming printing. This chapter describes the use of the various print dialog boxes, the *Print-Document* component, and the *PrintPreview* control.

Exam objectives in this chapter:

- Manage the print process by using print dialogs.
  - ❏ Configure Windows Forms print options at run time.
  - ❏ Change the printers attached to a user's computer in Windows Forms.
  - ❏ Configure the *PrintPreviewDialog* control.
  - ❏ Display a Print Preview window in Windows applications.
  - ❏ Set page details for printing using the *PageSetupDialog* component.
- Construct print documents.
  - ❏ Configure the *PrintDocument* component.
  - ❏ Print a text document in a Windows Form.
  - ❏ Print graphics in a Windows Form.
  - ❏ Print a document by using the *PrintDialog* component.
  - ❏ Alert users to the completion of a print job.
- Create a customized *PrintPreview* component.
  - ❏ Set the *Document* property to establish the document to be previewed.
  - ❏ Set the *Columns* and *Rows* properties to establish the number of pages displayed horizontally and vertically on the control.
  - ❏ Set the *UseAntiAlias* property to *True* to make the text appear smoother.
  - ❏ Set the *Zoom* property to establish the relative zoom level when the document preview appears.

❑ Set the *StartPage* property to establish which document page is displayed when the document preview appears.

❑ Set additional properties.

❑ Add custom methods and events to a *PrintPreviewControl*.

Lessons in this chapter:

Before You Begin

To complete the lessons in this chapter, you must have:

■ A computer that meets or exceeds the minimum hardware requirements listed in the "Introduction" at the beginning of the book.

■ Visual Studio 2005 Professional Edition installed on your computer.

■ An understanding of Microsoft Visual Basic or C# syntax and familiarity with the Microsoft .NET Framework.

Real World

Matt Stoecker

The process of creating print documents can be frustrating and difficult. Before the .NET Framework was introduced, I found the process of actually getting a document to the printer to be so difficult that I avoided it whenever I possibly could. With the introduction of the .NET Framework, printing is now easy to code and it is easier to create added value in the applications I create.

Lesson 1: Managing the Print Process by Using Print Dialogs

When printing a document, a user typically will want to have a high level of configurability over the printing process. Users typically want to be able to choose options such as paper orientation, margins, and paper size. The .NET Framework contains classes that allow you to expose a broad range of options to your users while still retaining control over the range of options you permit.

After this lesson, you will be able to:

- Configure Windows Forms print options at run time.
- Change the printers attached to a user's machine in Windows Forms.
- Configure the *PrintPreviewDialog* control.
- Display a Print Preview in Windows applications.
- Set page details for printing using the *PageSetupDialog* component.

Estimated lesson time: 45 minutes

The *PrinterSettings* Class

The class that contains all of the information about a print job and the page settings associated with that print job is the *PrinterSettings* class. Each *PrintDocument* component exposes an instance of the *PrinterSettings* class and accesses this instance to get the settings for the print job. Most of this is done automatically, and the developer need not worry about accessing the *PrinterSettings* class directly. When settings for a print job need to be configured by the user, you can enable the user to make appropriate selections by displaying the *PrintDialog* component and the *PageSetupDialog* component.

The *PrintDialog* Component

The *PrintDialog* component encapsulates a Print dialog box. This dialog box can be displayed to the user at run time to allow the user to configure a variety of options for printing as well as allowing the user to choose a printer. The *PrintDialog* component at run time is shown in Figure 10-1.

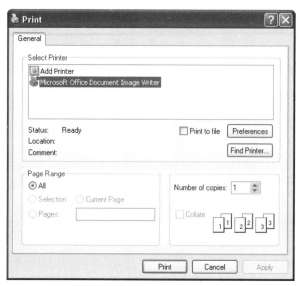

Figure 10-1 The *PrintDialog* component at run time

The *PrintDialog* component also exposes a variety of properties to the developer that allow him or her to configure the interface of the *PrintDialog* component when it is shown. The important properties of the *PrintDialog* component are described in Table 10-1.

Table 10-1 Important Properties of the *PrintDialog* Component

Property	Description
AllowCurrentPage	Indicates whether the Current Page option button is displayed.
AllowPrintToFile	Indicates whether the Print To File check box is enabled.
AllowSelection	Indicates whether the Selection option button is enabled.
AllowSomePages	Indicates whether the Pages option button is enabled.
Document	The *PrintDocument* that is associated with the PrintDialog box.
PrinterSettings	The *PrinterSettings* object associated with the selected printer. These settings are modified when the user changes settings in the dialog box.

Table 10-1 Important Properties of the *PrintDialog* Component

Property	Description
PrintToFile	Indicates whether the Print To File checkbox is selected.
ShowHelp	Indicates whether the Help button is shown.
ShowNetwork	Indicates whether the Network button is shown.

Modifying Selected Print Options with the *PrintDialog* Component

When the *PrintDialog* component is shown, the user can make changes to the configuration of the print job by setting options that are displayed in the PrintDialog box. You can restrict the options displayed by modifying the properties of the *PrintDialog* component. This generally involves setting one of the Boolean properties described in Table 10-1 to *True* to enable the option or *False* to disable the option. The following example demonstrates how to enable the user to select a range of pages to print.

```
' VB
PrintDialog1.AllowSomePages = True
```

```
// C#
printDialog1.AllowSomePages = true;
```

By setting the properties described in Table 10-1, you can configure your *PrintDialog* component to allow or restrict whatever options you desire. For example, the following code example demonstrates how to create a *PrintDialog* component that allows the user to print all pages, the current page, a selection, or a specified range of pages:

```
' VB
PrintDialog1.AllowCurrentPage = True
PrintDialog1.AllowSomePages = True
PrintDialog1.AllowSelection = True
```

```
// C#
printDialog1.AllowCurrentPage = true;
printDialog1.AllowSomePages = true;
printDialog1.AllowSelection = true;
```

Changing the Selected Printer at Run Time

The *PrintDialog* component allows the user to change the selected printer at run time by choosing a printer displayed in the Print dialog box. When the user selects a new printer, the *PrinterSettings* property is updated to reflect this.

Using the *PrintDialog* Box to Print a *PrintDocument* Component

After options have been selected, you can query the *DialogResult* returned by the *Print-Dialog.ShowDialog* method. If the *DialogResult* is OK, you can print the associated *PrintDocument* component by calling the *PrintDocument.Print* method. An example is shown here:

```
' VB
Dim aResult As DialogResult
aResult = PrintDialog1.ShowDialog()
If aResult = Windows.Forms.DialogResult.OK Then
    PrintDialog1.Document.Print()
End If
```

```
// C#
DialogResult aResult;
aResult = PrintDialog1.ShowDialog();
if (aResult == DialogResult.OK)
    PrintDialog1.Document.Print();
```

The *PageSetupDialog* Component

The *PageSetupDialog* component enables users to select options about the setup of the pages for a print job. A *PageSetupDialog* component at run time is shown in Figure 10-2.

Figure 10-2   The *PageSetupDialog* component at run time

Changes made by the user in the *PageSetupDialog* are automatically reflected in the *PrinterSettings* class of the *PrintDocument* component that is associated with the *PageSetupDialog* box. You can set the options that will be displayed to the user by setting the properties of the *PageSetupDialog* component. Important properties of the *PageSetupDialog* component are shown in Table 10-2.

Table 10-2   Important Properties of the *PageSetupDialog* Component

Property	Description
AllowMargins	Indicates whether the margins section of the dialog box is enabled.
AllowOrientation	Indicates whether the orientation section of the dialog box (landscape versus portrait) is enabled.
AllowPaper	Indicates whether the paper section of the dialog box (paper source and paper size) is enabled.
AllowPrinter	Indicates whether the printer button is enabled.
Document	The *PrintDocument* associated with this component.
EnableMetric	Indicates whether the margin settings, when displayed in millimeters, should be automatically converted to and from hundredths of an inch.
MinMargins	Indicates the minimum margins, in hundredths of an inch, the user is allowed to select.
ShowHelp	Indicates whether the Help button is visible.
ShowNetwork	Indicates whether the Network button is visible.

To show a *PageSetupDialog*, the component must be associated with an instance of the *PageSettings* class. The preferred way of doing this is to set the *Document* property to an instance of the *PrintDocument* class, which automatically sets the *PrintDocument.PrinterSettings* instance to the *PageSetupDialog.PrinterSettings* property. The following code example demonstrates how to set the *Document* property of the *PageSetupDialog* component and then display it to the user.

```
' VB
' Assumes an instance of PrintDocument named PrintDocument1 and an
' instance of PageSetupDialog named PageSetupDialog1.
```

```
PageSetupDialog1.Document = PrintDocument1
PageSetupDialog1.ShowDialog()

// C#
// Assumes an instance of PrintDocument named printDocument1 and an
// instance of PageSetupDialog named pageSetupDialog1.
pageSetupDialog1.Document = printDocument1;
pageSetupDialog1.ShowDialog();
```

The *PrintPreviewDialog* Component

The *PrintPreviewDialog* component is a self-contained dialog box that allows you to preview a print document. It does so by calling the *Print* method of the *PrintDocument* component that is specified in the component's *Document* property and redirecting the output to a graphical representation of the page contained in the dialog box. The *PrintDocumentDialog* component is shown at run time in Figure 10-3.

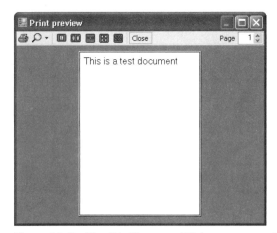

Figure 10-3   The *PrintDocumentDialog* component at run time

The dialog box allows the user to view each page before printing, adjust the number of pages displayed, and adjust the zoom factor so that pages can be viewed close up or at a distance. After viewing the preview, the user can choose to print the document by clicking the Print button, which calls the *Print* method of the *PrintDocument* component and directs the output to the printer. The following code example demonstrates how to associate a *PrintDocument* component with a *PrintPreviewDialog* component and display it to the user at run time:

```
' VB
PrintPreviewDialog1.Document = PrintDocument1
PrintPreviewDialog1.ShowDialog()
```

```
// C#
printPreviewDialog1.Document = printDocument1;
printPreviewDialog1.ShowDialog();
```

Quick Check

1. What is the purpose of the *PrintDialog* component?

2. What is the purpose of the *PrintPreview* component?

Quick Check Answers

1. The *PrintDialog* component represents a Print dialog box, and it allows you to configure print options for presentation to the user. At run time, you can call the *PrintDialog.ShowDialog* method to display the Print dialog box to the user.

2. The *PrintPreviewDialog* component represents a print preview dialog box, and allows you to configure options for displaying the document to the user prior to actually sending it to the printer.

Lab: Use Print Dialogs

In this lab, you will create a simple application that enables the user to use *PageSetup-Dialog*, *PrintDialog*, and *PrintPreviewDialog* to control the printing of a test document.

▶ **Exercise 1: Using Print Dialogs**

1. Open the partial solution for Chapter 10, Lab 1 from Open Form1. Note that it already has a *PrintDocument* component named *PrintDocument1* and that there is code in the event handler for the *PrintPage* event.

2. From the Toolbox, drag a *MenuStrip* onto the form. Add a top-level menu item named File.

3. Beneath the File menu item, add the following menu items: Page Setup, Print, Print Preview.

4. From the Toolbox, drag a *PageSetupDialog* component, a *PrintDialog* component, and a *PrintPreviewDialog* component onto the form.

5. In the Properties window, set the *Document* property of each dialog component to *PrintDocument1*.

6. In the Properties window, set the *AllowSomePages* property of *PrintDialog1* to *True*.

7. In the Designer, double-click PageSetupToolStripMenuItem and add the following code:

```
' VB
PageSetupDialog1.ShowDialog()
```

```
// C#
pageSetupDialog1.ShowDialog();
```

8. In the Designer, double-click PrintToolStripMenuItem and add the following code:

```
' VB
If PrintDialog1.ShowDialog() = Windows.Forms.DialogResult.OK Then
    PrintDocument1.Print()
End If
```

```
// C#
if (printDialog1.ShowDialog() == DialogResult.OK)
    printDocument1.Print();
```

9. In the Designer, double-click PrintPreviewToolStripMenuItem and add the following code:

```
' VB
PrintPreviewDialog1.ShowDialog()
```

```
// C#
printPreviewDialog1.ShowDialog();
```

10. Press F5 to run your application. Choose each of the menu items to demonstrate how to open the different print dialog boxes.

Lesson Summary

- The *PrintDialog* component represents a Print dialog box. By setting the *Document* property of a *PrintDialog* component, you can enable the user to change the print settings for that document. The *PrintDialog* component exposes several properties that allow you to set what options the user can configure.

- The *PageSetupDialog* component represents a Page Setup dialog box. By setting the *Document* property of a *PageSetupDialog* component, you can enable the user to change the page settings for that document. The *PageSetup* component exposes several properties that allow you to set what options the user can configure.

- The *PrintPreviewDialog* component represents a Print Preview dialog box. The *Document* property indicates the *PrintDocument* component that is currently being previewed. The *PrintPreviewDialog* component allows the user to configure the presentation of the previewed document through buttons in the user interface.

Lesson Review

The following questions are intended to reinforce key information presented in this lesson. The questions are also available on the companion CD if you prefer to review them in electronic form.

NOTE Answers

Answers to these questions and explanations of why each choice is right or wrong are located in the "Answers" section at the end of the book.

---

1. Which component would you use to allow the user to add a new printer at run time?

    A. *PrintPreviewDialog* component

    B. *PageSetupDialog* component

    C. *PrintDialog* component

    D. *PrintPreviewControl* component

2. Which of the following is required to display a *PrintDocument* in a *PrintPreviewDialog* component? (Choose all that apply.)

    A. You must set the *PrintPreviewDialog.Document* property.

    B. You must call the *PrintPreviewDialog.Print* method.

    C. You must call either the *PrintPreviewDialog.Show* or the *PrintPreviewDialog.ShowDialog* method.

    D. You must raise the *PrintPreviewDialog.PrintPages* event.

3. Which of the following can you not enable a user to do with the *PageSetupDialog* component?

    A. Set the page orientation

    B. Set the paper tray

    C. Add a printer

    D. Set the page margins

Lesson 2: Constructing Print Documents

The *PrintDocument* component represents a document that is sent to a printer. You can use the *PrintDocument* component to print text documents or graphical documents. In this lesson, you will learn to configure the *PrintDocument* component and use it to create printed documents.

After this lesson, you will be able to:

- Configure the *PrintDocument* component.
- Print a text document in a Windows Form.
- Print graphics in a Windows Form.
- Print a document by using the *PrintDialog* component.
- Alert users to the completion of a print job.

Estimated lesson time: 45 minutes

The *PrintDocument* Component

A printed document is represented by the *PrintDocument* component. It is a component that does not have a visual representation at run time but appears in the component tray at design time and can be dragged from the Toolbox to the design surface. The *PrintDocument* component encapsulates all of the information necessary to print a page.

Overview of Printing

In the .NET Framework printing model, printed content is provided directly by the application logic. A print job is initiated by the *PrintDocument.Print* method. This starts the print job and then raises one or more *PrintPage* events. If there is no client method to handle this event, printing does not take place. By providing a method to handle this event, you specify the content to be printed.

If the print job contains multiple pages, one *PrintPage* event is raised for each page in the job. This, in turn, causes the method handling the *PrintPage* event to execute multiple times. Thus, that method must implement functionality to track the print job and ensure that successive pages of a multipage document are printed. Otherwise, the first page of the document will print multiple times.

The *PrintPage* Event

The *PrintPage* event is the main event involved in printing documents. To actually send content to the printer, you must handle this event and provide code to render the content in the *PrintPage* event handler. All of the objects and information needed to send content to the printer are wrapped in the *PrintPageEventsArgs* object, which is received by the handler for this event. Table 10-3 describes the properties of the *PrintPageEventArgs* object.

Table 10-3   Properties of the *PrintPageEventArgs* Object

Property	Description
Cancel	Indicates whether a print job should be cancelled. You can cancel a pending print job by setting the *Cancel* property to *True*.
Graphics	The *Graphics* object is used to render content to the printed page. Encapsulates the drawing surface represented by the printer.
HasMorePages	Gets or sets a value that indicates whether additional pages should be printed. Set this property to *True* in the event handler to raise the event again.
MarginBounds	Gets the *Rectangle* object that represents the portion of the page within the margins.
PageBounds	Gets the *Rectangle* object that represents the total page area.
PageSettings	Gets or sets the *PageSettings* object for the current page.

Content is rendered to the printed page by the *Graphics* object provided in the *PrintPageEventArgs* object. The printed page behaves just like a form, control, or any other drawing surface that can be represented by a *Graphics* object. To render content, you use the same methods used to render content to a form. The following code example demonstrates a simple method to print a page:

```vb
' VB
' This method inscribes an ellipse inside the bounds of the page. This
' method must handle the PrintPage event in order to send content to the printer
Public Sub PrintEllipse(ByVal sender As System.Object, ByVal e As _
    System.Drawing.Printing.PrintPageEventArgs)
    e.Graphics.DrawEllipse(Pens.Black, e.MarginBounds)
End Sub
```

```
// C#
// This method inscribes an ellipse inside the bounds of the page. This
// method must handle the PrintPage event in order to send content to the printer
public void PrintEllipse(object sender, System.Drawing.Printing.PrintPageEventArgs e)
{
    e.Graphics.DrawEllipse(Pens.Black, e.MarginBounds);
}
```

The *MarginBounds* and *PageBounds* properties represent areas of the page surface. You can specify printing to occur inside the margin bounds of the page by calculating printing coordinates based on the *MarginBounds* rectangle. Printing that is to take place outside of the margin bounds, such as headers or footers, can be specified by calculating the printing coordinates based on the *PageBounds* rectangle. Print coordinates are in pixels by default.

You can specify that a print job has multiple pages by using the *HasMorePages* property. By default, this property is set to *False*. When your application logic determines that multiple pages are required to print a job, you should set this property to *True*. When the last page is printed, the property should be reset to *False*. Note that the method handling the *PrintPage* event must keep track of the number of pages in the job. Failure to do so can cause unexpected results while printing. For example, if you fail to set the *HasMorePages* property to *False* after the last page is printed, the application will continue to raise *PrintPage* events.

You can cancel a pending print job without finishing by setting the *Cancel* property to *True*. You might do this, for example, if the user clicked a Cancel button on your form.

You can end create an event handler for the *PrintPage* event by double-clicking the *PrintDocument* instance in the Designer to create a default event handler.

Printing Graphics

Printing graphics is essentially the same as rendering them to the screen. You use the *Graphics* object supplied by *PrintPageEventArgs* to render graphics to the screen. Simple shapes can be printed, or complex shapes can be created and printed using the *GraphicsPath* object. The following code example shows how to print a complex shape with a *GraphicsPath* object:

```
' VB
' This method must handle the PrintPage event
Public Sub PrintGraphics(ByVal Sender As System.Object, _
    ByVal e As System.Drawing.Printing.PrintPageEventArgs)
    Dim myPath As New System.Drawing.Drawing2D.GraphicsPath()
    myPath.AddPolygon(New Point() {New Point(1,1), New Point(12, 55), _
```

```
        New Point(34, 8), New Point(52, 53), New Point(99, 5)})
    myPath.AddRectangle(New Rectangle(33, 43, 20, 20))
    e.Graphics.DrawPath(Pens.Black, myPath)
End Sub
```

```csharp
// C#
// This method must handle the PrintPage event
public void PrintGraphics(object sender, System.Drawing.Printing.PrintPageEventArgs e)
{
    System.Drawing.Drawing2D.GraphicsPath myPath = new
        System.Drawing.Drawing2D.GraphicsPath();
    myPath.AddPolygon(new Point[] {new Point(1,1),
        new Point(12, 55), new Point(34, 8), new Point(52, 53),  new Point(99, 5)});
    myPath.AddRectangle(new Rectangle(33, 43, 20, 20));
    e.Graphics.DrawPath(Pens.Black, myPath);
}
```

To print a graphics job that has multiple pages, you must manually divide the job among pages and implement the appropriate logic. For example, the following method uses twelve pages to draw an ellipse that is six times as long as the page and two times as wide.

```
' VB
' These two variables are used to keep track of which page is printing
Private x As Integer
Private y As Integer
' This method must handle the PrintPages event
Private Sub PrintDocument1_PrintPage(ByVal sender As System.Object, _
    ByVal e As System.Drawing.Printing.PrintPageEventArgs)
    ' Draws the Ellipse at different origination points, which has the
    ' effect of sending successive page-sized pieces of the ellipse to the
    ' printer based on the value of x and y
    e.Graphics.FillEllipse(Brushes.Blue, New _
        RectangleF(-e.PageBounds.Width * x, -e.PageBounds.Height * y, _
        e.PageBounds.Width * 2, e.PageBounds.Height * 6))
    y += 1
    If y = 6 And x = 0 Then
        y = 0
        x += 1
        e.HasMorePages = True
    ElseIf y = 6 And x = 1 Then
        ' The print job is finished
        e.HasMorePages = False
    Else
        ' Fires the print event again
        e.HasMorePages = True
    End If
End Sub
```

```csharp
// C#
// These two variables are used to keep track of which page is printing
```

```
int x;
int y;
// This method must handle the PrintPages event
private void printDocument1_PrintPage(object sender,
System.Drawing.Printing.PrintPageEventArgs e)
{
    // Draws the Ellipse at different origination points, which has the
    // effect of sending successive page-sized pieces of the ellipse to the
    // printer based on the value of x and y
    e.Graphics.FillEllipse(Brushes.Blue, new RectangleF(-e.PageBounds.Width
        * x, -e.PageBounds.Height * y, e.PageBounds.Width * 2,
        e.PageBounds.Height * 6));
    y += 1;
    if (y == 6 & x == 0)
    {
        y = 0;
        x ++;
        e.HasMorePages = true;
    }
    else if (y == 6 & x == 1)
    {
        // The print job is finished
        e.HasMorePages = false;
    }
    else
    {
        // Fires the print event again
        e.HasMorePages = true;
    }
}
```

In this example, the method redraws the complete ellipse each time it is executed, but the point of origin is changed, so successive "slices" of the ellipse are printed each time the application executes.

Printing Images

You can use the *Graphics* object contained in the *PrintPageEventsArgs* to send image content to the printer with the *Graphics.DrawImage* method, as shown here:

```
' VB
' Assumes an image called myImage. This method must handle the PrintPages event
Private Sub PrintDocument1_PrintPage(ByVal sender As System.Object, _
    ByVal e As System.Drawing.Printing.PrintPageEventArgs)
    e.Graphics.DrawImage(myImage, New PointF(0,0))
End Sub
```

```
// C#
// Assumes an image called myImage. This method must handle the PrintPages event
private void PrintDocument1_PrintPage(object sender,
```

```
   System.Drawing.Printing.PrintPageEventArgs e)
{
   e.Graphics.DrawImage(myImage, new PointF(0,0));
}
```

Note that when printing an image that is larger than a single page, you must handle the paging manually, as you would for printing any other print job.

Printing Text

Printing text is similar to printing graphics. Text is printed through the *Graphics .DrawString* method, which renders a string in the specified font to the printer. As with rendering text to the screen, to print, you must specify a font for rendering the text, text to render, a *Brush* object, and coordinates at which to print. For example:

```
' VB
Dim myFont As New Font("Tahoma", 12, FontStyle.Regular, GraphicsUnit.Pixel)
Dim Hello As String = "Hello World!"
e.Graphics.DrawString(Hello, myFont, Brushes.Black, 20, 20)
```

```
// C#
Font myFont = new Font("Tahoma", 12, FontStyle.Regular, GraphicsUnit.Pixel);
string Hello  = "Hello World!";
e.Graphics.DrawString(Hello, myFont, Brushes.Black, 20, 20);
```

Note that when printing text, you must take steps in your code to ensure that you do not attempt to print outside the bounds of the page. If you do attempt to print outside the bounds of the page, content that falls outside the page bounds will not be printed.

Printing Multiple Lines

When printing multiple lines of text, such as an array of strings or lines read from a text file, you must include logic to calculate the line spacing. You can calculate the number of lines per page by dividing the height of the margin bounds by the height of the font. Similarly, you can calculate the position of each line by multiplying the line number by the height of the font. The following code example demonstrates how to print an array of strings called *myStrings*.

```
' VB
Dim ArrayCounter As Integer = 0
' This method handles a PrintDocument.PrintPage event. It assumes
' an array of strings called myStrings() has been declared and
' populated elsewhere in the application. It also assumes a font for
' printing has been initialized and called myFont
Private Sub PrintStrings(sender As Object, e As System.Drawing.Printing.PrintPageEventArgs)
' Declares the variables that will be used to keep track of spacing and paging
Dim LeftMargin As Single = e.MarginBounds.Left
```

```
Dim TopMargin As Single = e.MarginBounds.Top
Dim MyLines As Single = 0
Dim YPosition As Single = 0
Dim Counter As Integer = 0
Dim CurrentLine As String
' Calculate the number of lines per page.
MyLines = e.MarginBounds.Height / myFont.GetHeight(e.Graphics)
    ' Prints each line of the array, but stops at the end of a page
    While Counter < MyLines And ArrayCounter <= myStrings.Length -1
       CurrentLine = myStrings(ArrayCounter)
       YPosition = TopMargin + Counter * myFont.GetHeight(e.Graphics)
       e.Graphics.DrawString(CurrentLine, myFont, Brushes.Black, _
          LeftMargin, YPosition, New StringFormat())
       Counter += 1
       ArrayCounter += 1
    End While
    ' If more lines exist, print another page
    If Not (ArrayCounter = myStrings.Length -1) Then
       e.HasMorePages = True
    Else
       e.HasMorePages = False
    End If
End Sub

// C#
int ArrayCounter = 0;
private void PrintStrings(object sender, System.Drawing.Printing.PrintPageEventArgs e)
{
    // Declares the variables that will be used to keep track of spacing and paging
    float LeftMargin = e.MarginBounds.Left;
    float TopMargin = e.MarginBounds.Top;
    float MyLines = 0;
    float YPosition = 0;
    int Counter = 0;
    string CurrentLine;
    // Calculate the number of lines per page
    MyLines = e.MarginBounds.Height / myFont.GetHeight(e.Graphics);
    // Prints each line of the array, but stops at the end of a page
    while (Counter < MyLines && ArrayCounter <= myStrings.Length -1)
    {
        CurrentLine = myStrings[ArrayCounter];
        YPosition = TopMargin + Counter * myFont.GetHeight(e.Graphics);
        e.Graphics.DrawString(CurrentLine, myFont, Brushes.Black, LeftMargin,
           YPosition, new StringFormat());
        Counter ++;
        ArrayCounter++;
    }
    // If more lines exist, print another page
    if (!(ArrayCounter == myStrings.GetLength(0) -1))
       e.HasMorePages = true;
    else
       e.HasMorePages = false;
}
```

Notifying the User When Printing is Complete

Because printing can be a time-consuming process, and because the process is carried out asynchronously, it can be useful to inform the user when a print job has finished. You can create a notification of the end of printing for the user by handling the *Print-Document.EndPrint* event.

The *PrintDocument.EndPrint* event is raised after all pages of a print job have been printed. It has a signature that is the same as the *PrintPages* event—that is, it includes an object that represents the sender of the event and an instance of *System.Drawing.Printing .PrintPageEventArgs*. The following example demonstrates how to notify the user with a message box when the print job is complete:

```
' VB
Private Sub PrintDocument1_EndPrint(ByVal sender As System.Object, _
    ByVal e As System.Drawing.Printing.PrintEventArgs) Handles PrintDocument1.EndPrint
    MsgBox("Your print job is complete")
End Sub
```

```
// C#
// This method handles the PrintDocument.EndPrint method
private void PrintDocument1_EndPrint(object sender System.Drawing.Printing.PrintEventArgs e)
{
    MessageBox.Show("Your print job is complete")
}
```

Security and Printing

Printing is a secured activity, and permission to print is defined by the *PrintingPermission* class. The *PrintingPermission* class can specify four *PrintingPermissionLevel* values that detail the various secure printing environments. These levels are:

- **AllPrinting**   Provides unrestricted access to the printer.
- **DefaultPrinting**   Enables programmatic printing to the default printer and access to other printers through a printer dialog box.
- **SafePrinting**   Allows printing only through a printer dialog box.
- **NoPrinting**   Allows no access to the printers.

To protect against malicious code, applications run in the intranet or Internet security zones are granted the *DefaultPrinting* permission by default. If your application requires unrestricted printing, you can require that permission by adding an instance of the *PrintingPermission* attribute to your class or method, as shown below:

```
' VB
<Printing.PrintingPermission(Security.Permissions.SecurityAction.RequestMinimum, _
    level:=Printing.PrintingPermissionLevel.AllPrinting)> _
Public Class myPrintClass
    'Class implementation omitted
End Class
```

```
// C#
[Printing.PrintingPermission(System.Security.Permissions.SecurityAction.RequestMinimum,
    Level=System.Drawing.Printing.PrintingPermissionLevel.AllPrinting)]
public class myPrintClass
{
    // Class implementation omitted
}
```

Quick Check

1. What object represents the printer and can be used to send text, shapes, and images to the printer?

2. What method is used to print text?

Quick Check Answers

1. The *PrintPageEventArgs.Graphics* object is the *Graphics* object that represents the printed page. It encapsulates all of the methods required to draw text, shapes, and images on a printed page.

2. The *Graphics.DrawString* method is used to print text to the printer. You should use the *Graphics* object provided by the *PrintPageEventArgs* instance in the *PrintPage* event handler.

Lab: Create a Print Document

In this lab, you will expand on the solution you created in Lesson 1, "Managing the Print Process by Using Print Dialogs," and create an application that allows the user to open a text file and print the contents.

▶ **Exercise 1: Creating a Print Document**

1. From the Toolbox, drag an *OpenFileDialog* box onto the form.

2. In the Properties window, set the *Filter* property of *OpenFileDialog1* to Text Files | *.txt.

3. Beneath the *FileMenuItem*, add a menu item named Open File.

4. Double-click OpenFileToolStripMenuItem to open the code editor to the *OpenFileToolStripMenuItem_Click* event handler.

5. Outside of the *OpenFileToolStripMenuItem_Click* event handler, add the following code:

```vb
' VB
Dim s As String
Dim strings As String()
Dim ArrayCounter As Integer = 0
```

```csharp
// C#
string s;
string[] strings;
int ArrayCounter = 0;
```

6. Inside the *OpenFileToolStripMenuItem_Click* event handler, add the following code:

```vb
' VB
Dim aResult As Windows.Forms.DialogResult
aResult = OpenFileDialog1.ShowDialog
If aResult = Windows.Forms.DialogResult.OK Then
    Dim aReader As New System.IO.StreamReader(OpenFileDialog1.FileName)
    s = aReader.ReadToEnd
    aReader.Close()
    strings = s.Split(ControlChars.CrLf)
End If
```

```csharp
// C#
System.Windows.Forms.DialogResult aResult;
aResult = openFileDialog1.ShowDialog();
if (aResult == System.Windows.Forms.DialogResult.OK)
{
    System.IO.StreamReader aReader = new
        System.IO.StreamReader(openFileDialog1.FileName);
    s = aReader.ReadToEnd();
    aReader.Close();
    strings = s.Split('\n');
}
```

7. In the *PrintDocument1_PrintPage* event handler, replace the existing code with the following code:

```vb
' VB
Dim LeftMargin As Single = e.MarginBounds.Left
Dim TopMargin As Single = e.MarginBounds.Top
Dim MyLines As Single = 0
Dim YPosition As Single = 0
Dim Counter As Integer = 0
Dim CurrentLine As String
MyLines = e.MarginBounds.Height / _
```

```
    Me.Font.GetHeight(e.Graphics)
    While Counter < MyLines And ArrayCounter <= strings.Length - 1
      CurrentLine = strings(ArrayCounter)
      YPosition = TopMargin + Counter * Me.Font.GetHeight(e.Graphics)
      e.Graphics.DrawString(CurrentLine, Me.Font, Brushes.Black, _
        LeftMargin, YPosition, New StringFormat())
      Counter += 1
      ArrayCounter += 1
    End While
    If Not (ArrayCounter >= strings.Length - 1) Then
      e.HasMorePages = True
    Else
      e.HasMorePages = False
    End If

// C#
float LeftMargin = e.MarginBounds.Left;
float TopMargin = e.MarginBounds.Top;
float MyLines = 0;
float YPosition = 0;
int Counter = 0;
string CurrentLine;
MyLines = e.MarginBounds.Height /
   this.Font.GetHeight(e.Graphics);
while (Counter < MyLines && ArrayCounter <= strings.Length - 1)
{
    CurrentLine = strings[ArrayCounter];
    YPosition = TopMargin + Counter * this.Font.GetHeight(e.Graphics);
    e.Graphics.DrawString(CurrentLine, this.Font, Brushes.Black,
        LeftMargin, YPosition, new StringFormat());
    Counter++;
    ArrayCounter++;
}
if (!(ArrayCounter >= strings.GetLength(0) - 1))
    e.HasMorePages = true;
else
    e.HasMorePages = false;
```

8. Press F5 to run the application. Choose Open File from the file menu and open a text file on your computer. Choose Print Preview from the File menu to view the file in the Print Preview dialog box. Print the file. Experiment with other page and print settings.

Lesson Summary

- A printed document is represented by a *PrintDocument* component. The *Print-Document* component raises the *PrintPage* event when the *Print* method is called. Methods that handle the *PrintPage* event contain all of the logic that actually draws the shapes to be printed.

- The *PrintPageEventArgs* object that is passed as a parameter to methods handling the *PrintPage* event contains a *Graphics* object that represents the printed page. You use the methods of the *Graphics* class to draw shapes and strings to the printer.

- If multiple pages must be printed, you must set the *HasMorePages* property of the *PrintPageEventArgs* object to *True*. This will cause the *PrintPage* event to be raised again and the method(s) handling this event to be executed. You must create logic that keeps track of the page count and whether more pages remain to be printed.

- You can notify the user at the end of a print job by creating a notification in the *PrintDocument_EndPrint* event handler.

Lesson Review

The following questions are intended to reinforce key information presented in this lesson. The questions are also available on the companion CD if you prefer to review them in electronic form.

NOTE Answers

Answers to these questions and explanations of why each choice is right or wrong are located in the "Answers" section at the end of the book.

---

1. Which of the following lines of code should be used to print an additional page in the method handling the *PrintPages* event?

   A. ` ' VB`
   ```
   e.PrintPages
   ```
   ` // C#`
   ```
   e.PrintPages();
   ```

   B. ` ' VB`
   ```
   e.HasMorePages = True
   ```
   ` // C#`
   ```
   e.HasMorePages = true;
   ```

   C. ` ' VB`
   ```
   e.HasMorePages()
   ```
   ` // C#`
   ```
   e.HasMorePages();
   ```

   D. ` ' VB`
   ```
   e.Cancel = False
   ```

```
// C#
e.Cancel = false;
```

2. Which of the following lines of code will correctly calculate the number of lines that can be printed within the margins of a page in a font named myFont?

   A. ```
      ' VB
      MyLines = e.MarginBounds.Height / myFont.GetHeight(e.Graphics)
      ```

      ```
      // C#
      MyLines = e.MarginBounds.Height / myFont.GetHeight(e.Graphics);
      ```

   B. ```
      ' VB
      MyLines = e.MarginBounds.Height / myFont.GetHeight()
      ```

      ```
      // C#
      MyLines = e.MarginBounds.Height / myFont.GetHeight();
      ```

   C. ```
      ' VB
      MyLines = e.MarginBounds.Height / e.Graphics.GetHeight(myFont)
      ```

      ```
      // C#
      MyLines = e.MarginBounds.Height / e.Graphics.GetHeight(myFont);
      ```

   D. ```
      ' VB
      MyLines = e.PageBounds.Height / myFont.GetHeight(e.Graphics)
      ```

      ```
      // C#
      MyLines = e.PageBounds.Height / myFont.GetHeight(e.Graphics);
      ```

3. Which event of the *PrintDocument* component should be handled to alert the user to the completion of a print job?

   A. *BeginPrint*

   B. *EndPrint*

   C. *PrintPage*

   D. *QueryPageSettings*

Lesson 3: Creating a Customized *PrintPreview* Component

Although the *PrintPreviewDialog* component provides a simple, easy-to-use way to provide the print-preview functionality in your applications, it is difficult to customize. For custom print-preview applications, you can use the *PrintPreview* control to create a customized *PrintPreview* component.

After this lesson, you will be able to:

- Set the *Document* property to establish the document to be previewed.
- Set the *Columns* and *Rows* properties to establish the number of pages displayed horizontally and vertically on the control.
- Set the *UseAntiAlias* property to *True* to make the text appear smoother (can also make the display slower).
- Set the *Zoom* property to establish the relative zoom level when the document preview appears.
- Set the *StartPage* property to establish which document page is displayed when the document preview appears.
- Set additional properties.
- Add custom methods and events to a *PrintPreviewControl*.

Estimated lesson time: 45 minutes

The *PrintPreviewControl*

The *PrintPreviewControl* is the control at the center of the *PrintPreviewDialog* component. It encapsulates all the functionality required to preview a *PrintDocument* component by calling the *PrintDocument.Print* method and redirecting the output to the control rather than to the printer. It also contains properties that control the *Zoom* level, the page layout, and which page is displayed. Important properties of the *PrintPreviewControl* are shown in Table 10-4.

Table 10-4   Important Properties of the *PrintPreviewControl* Control

Property	Description
AutoZoom	Gets or sets a value indicating whether resizing the control or changing the number of pages shown automatically adjusts the *Zoom* property.

Table 10-4   Important Properties of the *PrintPreviewControl* Control

Property	Description
Columns	Gets or sets the number of pages that are displayed horizontally across the screen.
Document	The instance of *PrintDocument* that is associated with this *PrintPreviewControl*.
Rows	Gets or sets the number of pages that are displayed vertically on the screen.
StartPage	Gets or sets the page of the *PrintDocument* to be displayed in the first page of the control.
UseAntiAlias	Gets or sets a value indicating whether anti-aliasing is used. Anti-aliasing makes text in the control appear smoother at the cost of performance.
Zoom	Gets or sets the *Zoom* level of the document.

The *PrintPreviewControl* inherits from the *Control* class and exposes several other properties that are inherited from the *Control* class. You can set these at design time or run time, as you would any other control.

Setting the *Document* Property

The *Document* property represents the *PrintDocument* that is currently associated with the *PrintPreviewControl*. The *PrintPreviewControl* calls the *PrintDocument.Print* method and redirects the output of the *PrintPages* event handler to the *PrintPreview-Control* instead of to the printer. The following code example demonstrates how to set the *PrintPreviewControl.Document* property:

```vb
' VB
' Assumes a PrintDocument named PrintDocument1
PrintPreviewControl1.Document = PrintDocument1
```

```csharp
// C#
// Assumes a PrintDocument named printDocument1
printPreviewControl1.Document = printDocument1;
```

You can also set the *PrintPreviewControl.Document* property in the Properties window.

Setting Columns and Rows

The *Columns* property and the *Rows* property determine how many pages are shown in the *PrintPreviewControl*. The *Columns* property represents the number of pages shown across. For example, if the *Columns* property is set to 3, a maximum of 3 pages will be shown horizontally. (Although if the *PrintDocument* being previewed has fewer than 3 pages, only the pages it contains will be shown.) Likewise, if the *Rows* property is set to 3, a maximum of 3 pages will be shown vertically. The *Rows* and *Columns* properties together represent the total number of pages that will be displayed in the *PrintPreviewControl*. For example, if *Rows* is set to 3 and *Columns* is set to 4, the total number of pages that can be displayed at one time is 12. The following example demonstrates how to set the *Rows* and *Columns* properties:

```
' VB
PrintPreviewControl1.Rows = 3
PrintPreviewControl1.Columns = 4

// C#
printPreviewControl1.Rows = 3;
printPreviewControl1.Columns = 4;
```

You can also set the *Rows* and *Columns* properties in the Properties window at design time.

Anti-Aliasing

Anti-aliasing is a technology that appears to smooth the edges of drawn graphics and text to improve their appearance or readability. It does so by setting pixels on the edge of the shape being drawn to partially transparent colors. This causes the edges of the shape to appear smooth to the human eye. The tradeoff for this smoother appearance is slightly decreased performance. If you desire a smoother appearance, you can use anti-aliasing by setting the *PrintPreviewControl.UseAntiAlias* property to *True*. For better performance, you can set the *UseAntiAlias* property to *False*. The following code example demonstrates how to set the *UseAntiAlias* property:

```
' VB
PrintPreviewControl1.UseAntiAlias = True

// C#
printPreviewControl1.UseAntiAlias = true;
```

Zooming

The *Zoom* property determines how large a page appears in the *PrintPreview* control. A value of 1.0 represents full size. Larger values represent proportional increases in the size—for example, a value of 5 will display the page at 500 percent of full size. Values of less than 1 are also allowed. A value of 0.25, for example, displays the page at 25 percent. The following code example demonstrates how to set the *PrintPreview-Control.Zoom* property.

```vb
' VB
' Displays the page at 250% of normal size
PrintPreviewControl1.Zoom = 2.5
```

```csharp
// C#
// Displays the page at 250% of normal size
printPreviewControl1.Zoom = 2.5;
```

You can also zoom automatically by setting the *AutoZoom* property to *True*. When this property is set to *True*, the document displayed in the *PrintPreviewControl* is automatically resized when the *PrintPreviewControl* is resized. The following example demonstrates how to set the *AutoZoom* property to *True*.

```vb
' VB
PrintPreviewControl1.AutoZoom = True
```

```csharp
// C#
printPreviewControl1.AutoZoom = true;
```

When the *AutoZoom* property is set to *True*, the *Zoom* property is automatically changed when the control is resized.

Setting the Start Page

The *StartPage* property allows you to set the page displayed first in the *PrintPreview-Control*. When the control displays *Page*, this property indicates the page that is displayed. When more than one page is displayed in this control, this property indicates the page that is displayed in the upper left-hand corner. The *StartPage* property can be set only at run time—it cannot be set in the Properties window. The following example demonstrates how to set the *StartPage* property:

```vb
' VB
PrintPreviewControl1.StartPage = 3
```

```csharp
// C#
printPreviewControl1.StartPage = 3;
```

Note that if the *Columns* and *Rows* properties are set so that all of the pages of the *PrintDocument* can be displayed, all pages of the *PrintDocument* will be displayed and the page displayed will show in the upper left-hand corner of the *PrintPreviewControl*.

Adding Methods and Events to the *PrintPreviewControl*

Although the properties of the *PrintPreviewControl* that have been discussed in this lesson allow a considerable amount of customization, you might want to customize the *PrintPreviewControl* further by adding methods or events. For example, you might want to add a method to add columns or rows. You can create a customized *PrintPreviewControl* by creating a new class that inherits the *PrintPreviewControl* and adding additional methods or events. The following code example demonstrates a class that subclasses *PrintPreviewControl* and adds a method to add a column:

```vb
' VB
Public Class MyPrintPreviewControl
    Inherits PrintPreviewControl
    Public Sub AddColumn()
        Me.Columns += 1
    End Sub
End Class
```

```csharp
// C#
public class MyPrintPreviewControl:PrintPreviewControl
{
    public void AddColumn()
    {
        this.Columns++;
    }
}
```

Lab: Create a Customized PrintPreview Form

In this exercise, you will create a customized PrintPreview form and add it to the solution you created in Lesson 2, "Constructing Print Documents." You will add a *PrintPreviewControl* to a form and add controls that allow the user to specify the number of rows and columns, to specify the magnification, and to turn anti-aliasing on and off.

▶ **Exercise 1: Creating a Customized PrintPreview Form**

1. Open the solution you completed in Lesson 2, or open the completed Lesson 2 solution on the companion CD.

2. Add a new Form to the project.

3. From the Toolbox, drag a *SplitContainer* onto the form. The *Orientation* property should be set to vertical.

4. From the Toolbox, drag a *PrintPreviewControl* onto Panel2 and set the *Dock* property to *Fill*.

5. For C# only: Set the *Modifiers* property of *printPreviewControl1* to *Internal*.

6. From the Toolbox, add three *Label* controls, three *NumericUpDown* controls, one *Checkbox* control, and one *Button* control onto Panel1. Associate the labels with the *NumericUpDown* controls and set the properties as described in the following table:

Control	Property	Value
Label1	*Text*	*Rows*
Label2	*Text*	*Columns*
Label3	*Text*	*Magnification*
NumericUpDown1	*Minimum*	*1*
NumericUpDown2	*Minimum*	*1*
NumericUpDown3	*Minimum*	*25*
NumericUpDown1	*Maximum*	*8*
NumericUpDown2	*Maximum*	*8*
NumericUpDown3	*Maximum*	*500*
NumericUpDown3	*Increment*	*25*
CheckBox1	*Text*	*Anti-Alias*
Button1	*Text*	*Print*

7. Double-click NumericUpDown1 and add the following code to the *NumericUpDown_ValueChanged* event handler:

```vb
' VB
PrintPreviewControl1.Rows = NumericUpDown1.Value
```

```csharp
// C#
printPreviewControl1.Rows = (int)numericUpDown1.Value;
```

8. In the Designer, double-click NumericUpDown2 and add the following code to the *NumericUpDown2_ValueChanged* event handler:

    ```
    ' VB
    PrintPreviewControl1.Columns = NumericUpDown2.Value
    ```

    ```
    // C#
    printPreviewControl1.Columns = (int)numericUpDown2.Value;
    ```

9. In the Designer, double-click NumericUpDown3 and add the following code to the *NumericUpDown3_ValueChanged* event handler:

    ```
    ' VB
    PrintPreviewControl1.Zoom = NumericUpDown3.Value / 100
    ```

    ```
    // C#
    printPreviewControl1.Zoom = (double)numericUpDown3.Value / 100;
    ```

10. In the Designer, double-click CheckBox1 and add the following code to the *CheckBox1_CheckChanged* event handler:

    ```
    ' VB
    PrintPreviewControl1.UseAntiAlias = CheckBox1.Checked
    ```

    ```
    // C#
    printPreviewControl1.UseAntiAlias = checkBox1.Checked;
    ```

11. In the Designer, double-click Button1 and add the following code to the *Button1_Click* event handler:

    ```
    ' VB
    Me.DialogResult = Windows.Forms.DialogResult.OK
    ```

    ```
    // C#
    this.DialogResult = System.Windows.Forms.DialogResult.OK;
    ```

12. In the Code Editor for Form1, comment out the existing code in the *PrintPreviewToolStripMenuItem_Click* event handler and add the following code:

    ```
    ' VB
    Dim aForm As New Form2
    Dim aResult As Windows.Forms.DialogResult
    aForm.PrintPreviewControl1.Document = PrintDocument1
    aResult = aForm.ShowDialog
    If aResult = Windows.Forms.DialogResult.Ok Then
        PrintDocument1.Print
    End If
    ```

    ```
    // C#
    Form2 aForm = new Form2();
    System.Windows.Forms.DialogResult aResult;
    aForm.printPreviewControl1.Document = printDocument1;
    ```

```
aResult = aForm.ShowDialog();
if (aResult == System.Windows.Forms.DialogResult.OK)
  printDocument1.Print();
```

Press F5 to build and run your application. Select a text file with the Open File menu command and then click Print Preview to test your new PrintPreview form.

Lesson Summary

- The *PrintPreviewControl* is the control at the heart of the *PrintPreviewDialog* and contains all of the functionality required to call the *PrintPages* event and redirect the output to the control. The *Document* property represents the *PrintDocument* component that is previewed.

- The *PrintPreviewControl* exposes properties that allow you to set the number of rows, number of columns, the zoom level, whether to use anti-aliasing, and the start page. You can set these properties to configure your control.

- If you need to add additional methods or events to your *PrintPreviewControl*, you can create a class that inherits the *PrintPreviewControl* and add additional members.

Lesson Review

The following questions are intended to reinforce key information presented in this lesson. The questions are also available on the companion CD if you prefer to review them in electronic form.

NOTE   Answers

Answers to these questions and explanations of why each choice is right or wrong are located in the "Answers" section at the end of the book.

---

1. Which of the following values for the *Zoom* property will cause the document to be previewed at 250 percent of normal size?

    A. 250

    B. 25

    C. 2.5

    D. .25

2. Which of the following lines of code can be used to make previewed documents in a *PrintPreviewControl* named *PrintPreviewControl1* appear smoother?

A. ` ' VB`

```
PrintPreviewControl1.UseAntiAlias()
```

```
// C#
printPreviewControl1.UseAntiAlias();
```

B. ` ' VB`

```
PrintPreviewControl1.UseAntiAlias = True
```

```
// C#
printPreviewControl1.UseAntiAlias = true;
```

C. ` ' VB`

```
PrintPreviewControl1.Document.UseAntiAlias()
```

```
// C#
printPreviewControl1.Document.UseAntiAlias();
```

D. ` ' VB`

```
PrintPreviewControl1.Document.UseAntiAlias = True
```

```
// C#
printPreviewControl1.Document.UseAntiAlias = true;
```

Chapter Review

To further practice and reinforce the skills you learned in this chapter, you can perform the following tasks:

- Review the chapter summary.
- Review the list of key terms introduced in this chapter.
- Complete the case scenarios. These scenarios set up real-world situations involv-
  ing the topics of this chapter and ask you to create a solution.
- Complete the suggested practices.
- Take a practice test.

Chapter Summary

- The *PrintDocument* component is the primary component involved in printing
  and represents a printed page. Data is sent to the printer by handling the *Print-
  Document.PrintPages* event. Methods that handle this event receive a *PrintPage-
  EventArgs* object that contains a variety of properties useful in printing, including
  the *Graphics* object that represents the printer. Text is drawn to the printer by
  using the *Graphics.DrawString* method, and graphics are drawn to the printer by
  using the various graphics-drawing methods of the *Graphics* class. Multiple pages
  are printed by setting the *HasMorePages* property of the *PrintEventArgs* object to
  True.

- There are several dialog box components that you can use to assist the user with
  printing tasks. The *PrintDialog* component allows users to control print options
  and add new printers. The *PageSetupDialog* component allows the user to set
  options for the pages and paper. The *PrintPreviewDialog* component allows the
  user to view a representation of the printed document before it is actually
  printed.

- You can create a customized print preview form by using the *PrintPreviewControl*.
  The *PrintPreviewControl* displays a preview of the document indicated by its *Document* property and includes properties that control the look and feel of the preview, such as *Columns*, *Rows*, *UseAntiAlias*, *Zoom*, *AutoZoom*, and *StartPage*. If
  needed, you can add additional methods and events to the *PrintPreviewControl*
  class by creating a derived class.

Key Terms

- *Graphics* object
- *PrintDocument*
- *PrintPreview*

Case Scenarios

In the following case scenarios, you will apply what you've learned about printing in Windows forms. You can find answers to these questions in the "Answers" section at the end of this book.

Case Scenario 1: A Better *PrintPreview* Control

Our clients at Fabrikam, Inc., have retained us to help them implement solutions for handling their document processing needs. They need to print very large documents and would like to have a PrintPreview control that displays only one page at a time but displays each page in turn without user intervention, or can be configured to display every second page, third page, fourth page, and so on.

Questions

1. What general strategy could you use to create a component with the required functionality?

2. How could you implement the ability to display every second, third, or fourth page?

Case Scenario 2: A Simple Report Tool

Fabrikam, Inc. has also asked your company to create a tool to print simple reports. The company already uses an application to display data from their database in a Windows Form by using a group of data-bound labels and images. The form is the size of a piece of paper, and they would like the report to resemble the form as closely as possible.

Questions

1. What strategies can you use to implement a simple report tool that accurately reflects the look and feel of the preexisting form?

2. Can you automate the application so that each record in the database is printed? How would you handle printing multiple pages?

Suggested Practices

Expand the solution completed in Lesson 2 to allow the user to select a font and write logic to automatically readjust line length to fit that font.

Expand the solution completed in Lesson 2 to allow the user to create a header or a footer that will be included on each page.

Create a customized *PrintPreview* component that displays each page of a *PrintDocument* in a continually rotating fashion.

Take a Practice Test

The practice tests on this book's companion CD offer many options. For example, you can test yourself on just the content covered in this chapter, or you can test yourself on all the 70-526 certification exam content. You can set up the test so that it closely simulates the experience of taking a certification exam, or you can set it up in study mode so that you can look at the correct answers and explanations after you answer each question.

MORE INFO Practice tests

For details about all the practice test options available, see the "How to Use the Practice Tests" section in this book's Introduction.

Chapter 11

Advanced Topics in Windows Forms

Beyond using controls, data access, XML, and print support, there is additional functionality built into Windows Forms that enhances the usability and usefulness of your applications. This chapter will examine implementing drag-and-drop functionality, internationalization, and multiple document interface (MDI) forms.

Exam objectives in this chapter:
- Perform drag-and-drop operations.
    - Perform drag-and-drop operations within a Windows Forms application.
    - Perform drag-and-drop operations between applications.
    - Perform a drag-and-drop operation with a *TreeView* control.
- Implement globalization and localization for a Windows Forms application.
    - Implement globalization and localization within a Windows Forms application.
- Create and configure MDI forms.
    - Create MDI parent forms.
    - Create MDI child forms.
    - Identify the active MDI child form.
    - Send data to the active MDI child form.
    - Arrange MDI child forms.
    - Create a window list menu for an MDI application.

Lessons in this chapter:

Before You Begin

To complete the lessons in this chapter, you must have:

- A computer that meets or exceeds the minimum hardware requirements listed in the "Introduction" at the beginning of the book.

- Microsoft Visual Studio 2005 Professional Edition installed on your computer.

- An understanding of Microsoft Visual Basic or C# syntax and familiarity with the .NET Framework.

Real World

Matt Stoecker

The business world is getting smaller every day, and I find that there are increasing demands put on my application to provide support for a variety of global customers. Without Visual Studio internationalization, creating software for multiple countries would be extremely time-consuming and difficult.

Lesson 1: Implementing Drag-and-Drop Functionality

Drag-and-drop functionality refers to being able to grab data, such as a string or an object, by pressing the left mouse button, moving the mouse with the left button depressed over another control that is able to accept the data, and then releasing the mouse button to transfer the data. Drag-and-drop functionality is implemented primarily by handling events. In this lesson, you will learn to implement basic drag-and-drop functionality, implement drag-and-drop functionality between applications, and implement drag-and-drop functionality in a *TreeView* control.

After this lesson, you will be able to:

- Perform drag-and-drop operations within a Windows Forms application.
- Perform drag-and-drop operations between applications.
- Perform a drag-and-drop operation with a *TreeView* control.

Estimated lesson time: 45 minutes

Implementing Drag-and-Drop Functionality

Drag-and-drop functionality is ubiquitous in Windows Forms programming. It refers to allowing the user to grab data such as text, an image, or another object with the mouse and drag it to another control. When the mouse button is released over the other control, the data that is being dragged is dropped onto the control, and a variety of effects can then occur.

Dragging and dropping is similar to cutting and pasting. The mouse pointer is positioned over a control and the mouse button is depressed. Data is copied from a source control; when the mouse button is released, the drop action is completed. All code for copying the data from the source control and any actions taken on the target control must be explicitly coded.

The drag-and-drop process is primarily an event-driven process. There are events that occur on the source control and events that occur on the target control. The drag-and-drop events for the source control are described in Table 11-1. The drag-and-drop events for the target control are described in Table 11-2.

Table 11-1 Source Control Events Involved in Implementing Drag and Drop

Event	Description
MouseDown	Occurs when the mouse button is depressed and the pointer is over the control. In general, the *DoDragDrop* method is called in the method that handles this event.
GiveFeedBack	Provides an opportunity for the user to set a custom mouse pointer.
QueryContinueDrag	Enables the drag source to determine whether a drag event should be cancelled.

Table 11-2 Target Control Events Involved in Implementing Drag and Drop

Event	Description
DragEnter	Occurs when an object is dragged within a control's bounds. The handler for this event receives a *DragEventArgs* object.
DragOver	Occurs when an object is dragged over a target control. The handler for this event receives a *DragEventArgs* object.
DragDrop	Occurs when the mouse button is released over a target control. The handler for this event receives a *DragEventArgs* object.
DragLeave	Occurs when an object is dragged out of the control's bounds.

In addition, the *DoDragDrop* method on the source control is required to initiate the drag-and-drop process, and the target control must have the *AllowDrop* property set to *True*.

The General Sequence of a Drag-and-Drop Operation

The following is the general sequence of events that takes place in a drag-and-drop operation:

1. The drag-and-drop operation is initiated by calling the *DoDragDrop* method on the source control. This is usually done in the *MouseDown* event handler. *DoDragDrop* copies the desired data from the source control to a new instance of *DataObject* and sets flags that specify which effects are allowed with this data.

2. The *GiveFeedBack* and *QueryContinueDrag* events are raised at this point. The *GiveFeedback* event handler can set the mouse pointer to a custom shape, and the *QueryContinueDrag* event handler can be used to determine if the drag operation should be continued or aborted.

3. The mouse pointer is dragged over a target control. Any control that has the *AllowDrop* property set to *True* is a potential drop target. When the mouse pointer enters a control with the *AllowDrop* property set to *True*, the *DragEnter* event for that control is raised. The *DragEventArgs* object that the event handler receives can be examined to determine if data appropriate for the target control is present. If so, the *Effect* property of the *DragEventArgs* object can then be set to an appropriate value.

4. The user releases the mouse button over a valid target control, raising the *Drag-Drop* event. The code in the *DragDrop* event handler then obtains the dragged data and takes whatever action is appropriate in the target control.

The *DragDropEffects* Enumeration

To complete a drag-and-drop operation, the drag effect specified in the *DoDragDrop* method must match the value of the *Effect* parameter of the *DragEventArgs* object associated with the drag-and-drop event, which is generally set in the *DragDropEnter*. The *Effect* property is an instance of the *DragDropEffects* enumeration. The members of the *DragDropEffects* enumeration are described in Table 11-3.

Table 11-3 *DragDropEffects* Enumeration Members

Member	Explanation
All	Data is copied, removed from the drag source, and scrolled in the target.
Copy	The data is copied to the target.
Link	The data is linked to the target.
Move	The data is moved to the target.
None	The target does not accept the data.
Scroll	Scrolling is about to start or is currently occurring in the target.

Note that the main function of the *Effect* parameter is to change the mouse cursor when it is over the target control. The value of the *Effect* parameter has no actual effect on the action that is executed except that when the *Effect* parameter is set to *None*, no drop can take place on that control because the *DragDrop* event will not be raised.

Initiating the Drag-and-Drop Operation

The drag-and-drop operation is initiated by calling the *DoDragDrop* method on the source control. The *DoDragDrop* method takes two parameters: an *Object*, which represents the data to be copied to the *DataObject*, and an instance of *DragDropEffects*, which specifies what drag effects will be allowed with this data. The following example demonstrates how to copy the text from a text box and set the allowed effects to *Copy* or *Move*.

```vb
' VB
Private Sub TextBox1_MouseDown(ByVal sender As System.Object, ByVal e _
    As System.Windows.Forms.MouseEventArgs) Handles TextBox1.MouseDown
  TextBox1.DoDragDrop(TextBox1.Text, DragDropEffects.Copy Or DragDropEffects.Move)
End Sub
```

```csharp
// C#
private void textBox1_MouseDown(object sender, MouseEventArgs e)
{
    textBox1.DoDragDrop(textBox1.Text, DragDropEffects.Copy | DragDropEffects.Move);
}
```

Note that you can use the *Or* operator (Visual Basic) or the | operator (C#) to combine members of the *DragDropEffects* enumeration to indicate multiple effects.

Handling the *DragEnter* Event

The *DragEnter* event should be handled for every target control. This event occurs when a drag-and-drop operation is in progress and the mouse pointer enters the control. This event passes a *DragEventArgs* object to the method that handles it, and you can use the *DragEventArgs* object to query the *DataObject* associated with the drag-and-drop operation. If the data is appropriate for the target control, you can set the *Effect* property to an appropriate value for the control. The following example demonstrates how to examine the data format of the *DataObject* and set the *Effect* property.

```vb
' VB
Private Sub TextBox2_DragEnter(ByVal sender As System.Object, ByVal e As _
   System.Windows.Forms.DragEventArgs) Handles TextBox2.DragEnter
   If e.Data.GetDataPresent(DataFormats.Text) = True Then
      e.Effect = DragDropEffects.Copy
   End If
End Sub
```

```csharp
// C#
private void textBox2_DragEnter (object sender, DragEventArgs e)
{
    if (e.Data.GetDataPresent(DataFormats.Text))
    {
        e.Effect = DragDropEffects.Copy;
    }
}
```

Handling the *DragDrop* Event

When the mouse button is released over a target control during a drag-and-drop operation, the *DragDrop* event is raised. In the method that handles the *DragDrop* event, you can use the *GetData* method of the *DataObject* to retrieve the copied data from the *DataObject* and take whatever action is appropriate for the control. The following example demonstrates how to drop a *String* into a *TextBox*.

```vb
' VB
Private Sub TextBox2_DragDrop(ByVal sender As System.Object, ByVal e As _
    System.Windows.Forms.DragEventArgs) Handles TextBox2.DragDrop
    TextBox2.Text = e.Data.GetData(DataFormats.Text)
End Sub
```

```csharp
// C#
private void textBox2_DragDrop(object sender, DragEventArgs e)
{
    textBox2.Text = (string)e.Data.GetData(DataFormats.Text);
}
```

Implementing Drag and Drop Between Applications

Drag-and-drop operations between .NET Framework applications are intrinsically supported by the system. No additional steps need to be taken to enable drag-and-drop operations that take place between applications. The only conditions that must be satisfied to enable a drag-and-drop operation between applications to succeed are:

- The target control must allow one of the drag effects specified in the *DoDragDrop* method call.

- The target control must accept data in the format that was set in the *DoDragDrop* method call.

Implementing Drag and Drop in a *TreeView* Control

A common scenario for the *TreeView* control is to allow the user to rearrange the structure of the tree at run time. This can be implemented with drag and drop. Drag and drop in a *TreeView* control is slightly different than in regular controls. When a drag operation is initiated on a *TreeView* node, the *TreeView* control raises the *ItemDrag* event, which passes an instance of *ItemDragEventArgs* to the method that handles the event. The *ItemDragEventArgs* object contains a reference to the *TreeNode* that is being dragged, and this reference can be copied to the *DataObject* in the *DoDragDrop* method. The following procedure describes how to implement drag-and-drop functionality in a *TreeView* control.

▶ **To implement Drag-and-Drop functionality in a *TreeView* control**

1. Set the *AllowDrop* property of the *TreeView* to *True*. This enables the *DragEnter* and *DragDrop* events to be raised from the *TreeView* control.

2. In the *ItemDrag* of the *TreeView* event handler, call the *DoDragDrop* of the *TreeView* method, specifying the *Item* property of the *ItemDragEventArgs* object as the *Data* parameter, as shown in the following example:

```vb
' VB
Private Sub TreeView1_ItemDrag(ByVal sender As System.Object, ByVal e As _
   System.Windows.Forms.ItemDragEventArgs) Handles TreeView1.ItemDrag
   TreeView1.DoDragDrop(e.Item, DragDropEffects.Move)
End Sub
```

```csharp
// C#
private void TreeView1_ItemDrag(object sender,
   System.Windows.Forms.ItemDragEventArgs e)
{
   treeView1.DoDragDrop(e.Item, DragDropEffects.Move);
}
```

3. In the *DragEnter* event of the *TreeView* event handler, set the *Effect* property of the *DragDropEventArgs* to an appropriate value, as shown in the following example:

```vb
' VB
Private Sub TreeView1_DragEnter(ByVal sender As System.Object, ByVal e As _
   System.Windows.Forms.DragEventArgs) Handles TreeView1.DragEnter
   e.Effect = DragDropEffects.Move
End Sub
```

```csharp
// C#
private void treeView1_DragEnter(object sender, System.Windows.Forms.DragEventArgs e As)
{
   e.Effect = DragDropEffects.Move;
}
```

4. In the *DragDrop* event handler, examine the data contained in the *DataObject* of *DragDropEventArgs* to determine if a *TreeNode* is present. If a *TreeNode* is present, implement code to move the *TreeNode* to the appropriate spot. The following

code example demonstrates how to move a dropped node into the child node structure of the node under the mouse pointer:

```vb
' VB
Private Sub TreeView1_DragDrop(ByVal sender As System.Object, ByVal e As _
    System.Windows.Forms.DragEventArgs) Handles TreeView1.DragDrop
    Dim aNode As TreeNode
    ' Checks to see if a TreeNode is present
    If e.Data.GetDataPresent("System.Windows.Forms.TreeNode", False) Then
        Dim apoint As Point
        Dim TargetNode As TreeNode
        ' Gets the point under the mouse pointer
        apoint = CType(sender, TreeView).PointToClient(New Point(e.X, e.Y))
        ' Gets the node at the specified point
        TargetNode = CType(sender, TreeView).GetNodeAt(apoint)
        aNode = CType(e.Data.GetData("System.Windows.Forms.TreeNode"), _
            TreeNode)
        ' Adds the dragged node As a child to the target node
        TargetNode.Nodes.Add(aNode.Clone)
        TargetNode.Expand()
        'Removes original node
        aNode.Remove()
    End If
End Sub
```

```csharp
// C#
private void treeView1_DragDrop(object sender, System.Windows.Forms.DragEventArgs e)
{
    TreeNode aNode;
    // Checks to see if a TreeNode is present
    if (e.Data.GetDataPresent("System.Windows.Forms.TreeNode", false))
    {
        Point apoint;
        TreeNode TargetNode;
        // Gets the point under the mouse pointer
        apoint = ((TreeView)sender).PointToClient(new Point(e.X, e.Y));
        // Gets the node at the specified point
        TargetNode = ((TreeView)sender).GetNodeAt(apoint);
        aNode = (TreeNode)e.Data.GetData("System.Windows.Forms.TreeNode");
        // Adds the dragged node as a child to the target node
        TargetNode.Nodes.Add((TreeNode)aNode.Clone());
        TargetNode.Expand();
        // Removes original node
        aNode.Remove();
    }
}
```

Lab: Implement Drag and Drop

In this lab, you will implement drag-and-drop functionality between two text boxes on a form. You will implement functionality to drag the text from the first text box and copy it into the second text box when dropped.

▶ **Exercise 1: Implementing Drag and Drop**

1. In Visual Studio, create a new Windows Forms application.

2. From the Toolbox, drag two Textbox controls onto the new application.

3. Select Textbox2 and, in the Properties window, set the *AllowDrop* property to *True*.

4. In the Properties window, click the Events button to display events instead of properties. Select Textbox1 and double-click the space next to MouseDown to create the default event handler for the *Textbox1.MouseDown* event.

5. Add the following code to the *Textbox1_MouseDown* event handler:

   ```
   ' VB
   TextBox1.DoDragDrop(TextBox1.Text, DragDropEffects.Move Or DragDropEffects.Copy)
   ```

   ```
   // C#
   textBox1.DoDragDrop(textBox1.Text, DragDropEffects.Move | DragDropEffects.Copy);
   ```

6. In the Designer, select TextBox2 and double-click the space next to the *DragEnter* event in the Properties window to create the default event handler for the *TextBox2.DragEnter* event.

7. Add the following code to the *Textbox1_DragEnter* event handler:

   ```
   ' VB
   If e.Data.GetDataPresent(DataFormats.Text) = True Then
       e.Effect = DragDropEffects.Copy
   End If
   ```

   ```
   // C#
   if (e.Data.GetDataPresent(DataFormats.Text))
   {
       e.Effect = DragDropEffects.Copy;
   }
   ```

8. In the Designer, select TextBox2 and double-click the space next to the *DragDrop* event in the Properties window to create the default event handler for the *TextBox2.DragDrop* event.

9. Add the following code to the *Textbox2_DragDrop* event handler:

   ```
   ' VB
   TextBox2.Text = e.Data.GetData(DataFormats.Text)
   ```

   ```
   // C#
   textBox2.Text = (string)e.Data.GetData(DataFormats.Text);
   ```

10. Press F5 to build and run the application. Type some text into the first text box. Using the mouse, drag that text to the second text box. The text from the first text box is copied to the second text box.

Lesson Summary

- The drag-and-drop operation is initiated by calling the *DoDragDrop* method on the source control. This is usually done in the *MouseDown* event handler for the source control. The *DoDragDrop* method takes two parameters: an *Object* parameter that contains the data to be dragged and dropped and a *DragDropEffects* enumeration parameter that represents the effect or effects that are allowed for this operation.

- The *DragEnter* event on the target control is used to set the allowed effects for the target control. You can examine the data in the *e.Data* object that is present in the event parameters and determine if the data is appropriate for the control. If the data is not appropriate for the control, you can cancel the *DragDrop* operation by setting the *e.Effect* property to *None*.

- The drag-and-drop operation is completed in the *DragDrop* event on the target control. You must write code to complete the appropriate operation in this event.

- Data can be dragged and dropped between controls in different applications. No additional steps need to be taken to enable drag-and-drop operations that take place between applications.

- Drag-and-drop operations in *TreeView* controls are begun by calling the *DoDragDrop* method in the *TreeView.ItemDrag* event handler. The rest of the drag-and-drop process is generally the same as drag-and-drop operations between other controls.

Lesson Review

The following questions are intended to reinforce key information presented in this lesson. If you are unable to answer a question, review the lesson materials and try the question again.

NOTE Answers

Answers to these questions and explanations of why each choice is right or wrong are located in the "Answers" section at the end of the book.

1. Which of the following events must be handled to execute a drag-and-drop operation?

   A. *MouseDown*

   B. *MouseUp*

    C. *DragLeave*

    D. *DragDrop*

2. Which of the following is necessary to implement a drag-and-drop operation between two applications? (Choose all that apply.)

    A. You must call the *DoDragDrop* method.

    B. The target control must allow one of the drag effects specified in the *DoDragDrop* method call.

    C. The target control must accept data in the format that was set in the *DoDragDrop* method call.

    D. The target control must have the *AllowDrop* property set to *True*.

3. In which event should you initiate the drag-and-drop operation in a *TreeView* control?

    A. *TreeView.MouseDown*

    B. *TreeView.ItemDrag*

    C. *TreeView.DragEnter*

    D. *TreeView.DragDrop*

Lesson 2: Implementing Globalization and Localization for a Windows Forms Application

Applications that display data in formats appropriate to the culture and display locale-appropriate strings in the user interface are considered globally ready applications. You can create globally ready applications with Visual Studio by taking advantage of the built-in support for globalization and localization. In this lesson, you will learn how to implement localization and globalization in a Windows Forms application.

After this lesson, you will be able to:

■ Implement globalization and localization within a Windows Form.

Estimated lesson time: 30 minutes

Globalization and Localization

Globalization and *localization* are different processes of internationalization. Globalization refers to formatting existing data in formats appropriate for the current culture setting. Localization, on the other hand, refers to retrieving appropriate data based on the culture. The following examples illustrate the difference between globalization and localization:

■ **Globalization**   In some countries, currency is formatted using a period (.) as a thousand separator and a comma (,) as a decimal separator, while other countries use the opposite convention. A globalized application formats existing currency data with the appropriate thousand separator and decimal separator based on the current culture settings.

■ **Localization**   The title of a form is displayed in a given language based on the locale in which it is deployed. A localized application retrieves the appropriate string and displays it based on the current culture settings.

Culture

Culture refers to cultural information about the country or region in which the application is deployed. In the .NET Framework, cultures are represented by a culture code that represents the current language. For example, the following culture codes represent the following languages:

■ **en**   Specifies the English language

■ **eu**   Specifies the Basque language

- **tr**   Specifies the Turkish language

Culture codes can specify only the language, like the ones shown here, or they can specify both the language and the region. Culture codes that specify only the language are called neutral cultures, whereas culture codes that specify both the language and the region are called specific cultures. Examples of specific cultures are shown in the following list:

- **en-CA**   Specifies the English language and Canada as the region
- **af-ZA**   Specifies the Afrikaans language and South Africa as the region
- **kn-IN**   Specifies the Kannada language and India as the region

A complete list of culture codes can be found in the *CultureInfo* class reference topic in the .NET Framework reference documentation.

Most culture codes follow the format just described, but there are some culture codes that are exceptions. The following culture codes are examples that specify the character sets in addition to other information:

- **uz-UZ-Cyrl**   Specifies the Uzbek language, Uzbekistan as the region, and the Cyrillic alphabet
- **uz-UZ-Latn**   Specifies the Uzbek language, Uzbekistan as the region, and the Latin alphabet
- **zh-CHT**   Specifies the traditional Chinese language, no region
- **zh-CHS**   Specifies the simplified Chinese language, no region

Changing the Current Culture

Your application automatically reads the culture settings of the system and implements them. Thus, in most circumstances, you will not have to manually change the culture settings. You can, however, change the current culture of your application in code by setting the current culture to a new instance of the *CultureInfo* class. The *CultureInfo* class contains information about a particular culture and how it interacts with the application and system. For example, the *CultureInfo* class contains information about the type of calendar, date formatting, currency formatting, and so on for a specific culture. You set the current culture of an application programmatically by setting the *CurrentThread.CurrentCulture* property to a new instance of the *CultureInfo* class. The *CultureInfo* constructor requires a string that represents the appropriate culture code as a parameter. The following code example demonstrates how to set the current culture to French Canadian:

```
' VB
System.Threading.Thread.CurrentThread.CurrentCulture = New _
    System.Globalization.CultureInfo("fr-CA")

// C#
System.Threading.Thread.CurrentThread.CurrentCulture = new
    System.Globalization.CultureInfo("fr-CA");
```

Implementing Globalization

The *CurrentThread.CurrentCulture* property controls the culture that is used to format data. When *CurrentCulture* is set to a new instance of *CultureInfo*, any data formatted by the application is updated to the new format. Data that is not formatted by the application is not affected by a change in the current culture. Consider the following examples:

```
' VB
Label1.Text = "$500.00"
Label2.Text = Format(500, "Currency")

// C#
label1.Text = "$500.00";
label2.Text = (500).ToString("C");
```

When the culture is set to en-US, which represents the English language, United States as the region (which is the default culture setting for computers in the United States), both labels will display the same string; that is, "$500.00". When the current culture is set to fr-FR, which represents French language, France as the region, the text in the two labels will differ. The text in *Label1* will always read "$500.00" because it is not formatted by the application. The text in *Label2*, however, will read "500,00 £". Note that the currency symbol is changed to the appropriate symbol for the locale—in this case the Euros symbol—and the decimal separator is changed to the separator that is appropriate for the locale (in this case, the comma).

Implementing Localization

You can implement localization—that is, provide a user interface that is specific to the current locale—by using the built-in localization features of Visual Studio. Visual Studio allows you to create alternative versions of forms that are culture-specific and automatically manages retrieval of resources appropriate for the culture.

Changing the Current UI Culture

The user interface (UI) culture is represented by an instance of *CultureInfo* and is distinct from the *CultureInfo.CurrentCulture* property. The *CurrentCulture* setting determines the formatting that will be applied to system-formatted data, whereas the *CurrentUICulture* setting determines the resources that will be loaded into localized forms at run time. You can set the UI culture by setting the *CurrentThread.CurrentUICulture* property, as shown in the following example:

```
' VB
' Sets the current UI culture to Thailand
System.Threading.Thread.CurrentThread.CurrentUICulture = New _
    System.Globalization.CultureInfo("th-TH")
```

```
// C#
// Sets the current UI culture to Thailand
System.Threading.Thread.CurrentThread.CurrentUICulture = new
    System.Globalization.CultureInfo("th-TH");
```

When the current UI culture is set, the application loads resources specific to that culture if they are available. If culture-specific resources are unavailable, the user interface displays resources for the default culture.

Note that the UI culture must be set before a form that displays any localized resources is loaded. If you want to set the UI culture programmatically, you must set it before the form has been created—either in the form's constructor or in the application's *Main* method.

Creating Localized Forms

Every form exposes a *Localizable* property that determines if the form is localized. Setting this property to *True* enables localization for the form.

When the *Localizable* property of a form is set to *True*, Visual Studio .NET automatically handles the creation of appropriate resource files and manages their retrieval according to the *CurrentUICulture* setting.

At design time, you can create localized copies of a form by using the *Language* property. The *Language* property is available only at design time and assists in the creation of localized forms. When the *Language* property is set to (Default), you can edit any of the form's UI properties or controls to provide a representation for the default UI culture. To create a localized version of the form, you can set the *Language* property to any value other than (Default). Visual Studio will create a resource file for the new language and store any values you set for the UI in that file.

▶ **To create localized forms**

1. Set the *Localizable* property of your form to *True*.

2. Design the user interface of your form and translate any UI elements into the localized languages.

3. Add UI elements for the default culture. This is the culture that will be used if no other culture is specified.

4. Set the *Language* property of your form to the culture for which you want to create a localized form.

5. Add the localized UI content to your form.

6. Repeat steps 4 and 5 for each localized language.

7. Build your application.

When *CurrentUICulture* is set to a localized culture, your application will load the appropriate version of the form by reading the corresponding resource files. If no resource files exist for a specified culture, the default culture UI will be displayed.

Implementing Right-to-Left Display

Some languages are read from right to left instead of from left to right as in most Latin alphabet languages. Forms provide a *RightToLeft* property that enables implementation of a right-to-left user interface.

The *RightToLeft* property has three settings: *Yes*, *No*, and *Inherit*, with *Inherit* being the default value. When this property is set to *Inherit*, the *RightToLeft* property is determined by the value of the parent control.

Setting a control's *RightToLeft* property to *Yes* does several things, depending on the type of control. Text alignment is reversed. Thus, any text that is normally left-aligned in the control becomes right-aligned. Form captions are displayed on the right side of the form. Vertical scroll bars are displayed on the left side of scrollable controls, and horizontal scroll bars are initialized with the slider on the right side. *CheckBox* controls have their *CheckAlign* property reversed, tabs on *TabControls* are reversed, and the alignment of items in list-based controls such as list boxes and combo boxes are reversed.

The content inside a control with the *RightToLeft* property set to *Yes* is unchanged. For example, consider *TextBox* with standard left-to-right formatting, as shown in Figure 11-1.

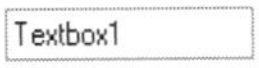

Textbox1

Figure 11-1   *TextBox* with standard left-to-right formatting

In Figure 11-2, the same *TextBox* is displayed with right-to-left formatting.

Textbox1

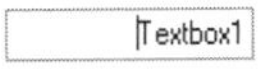

Figure 11-2   *TextBox* with right-to-left formatting

Note that only the alignment of the text has changed, not the order of the characters—the string is still read from left to right. Thus, if you create localized resources for cultures that read from right to left, you must format the strings manually.

Setting a form's *RightToLeft* property to *Yes* will cause it and any controls that have a *RightToLeft* value of *Inherit* to become right-aligned.

Creating a Mirrored Form

Forms made for cultures that read from left to right are commonly laid out to follow the writing direction. You might want to create a mirror image of your form for cultures that read from right to left. You can create a mirrored form by using the *RightToLeftLayout* property of the form. When the *RightToLeftLayout* property for a form is set to *True*, the layout of the form will appear mirrored when the *RightToLeft* property of the form is set to *True*.

Quick Check

1. What is the difference between globalization and localization?

2. What is the difference between the *CurrentCulture* and the *CurrentUICulture*?

Quick Check Answers

1. Globalization refers to formatting existing data in formats appropriate for the current culture setting. Localization refers to retrieving appropriate data based on the culture.

2. The *CurrentCulture* determines how data is formatted as appropriate for the current culture setting. The *CurrentUICulture* determines what set of resource strings should be loaded for display in the user interface.

Lab: Create Localized Forms

In this lab, you will create localized forms. You will create a form for the default culture that demonstrates date/time display and currency display as well as strings for the default culture. Then you will create a localized version of this form that includes German strings. Finally, you will create a form that allows you to choose the locale you would like to design your localized form for and sets the culture appropriately.

▶ **Exercise 1: Creating Localized Forms**

1. In Visual Studio, create a new Windows Forms application.

2. Add a new Windows Form named Form2 to your project.

3. In the Designer, select the tab for Form2. From the Toolbox, add four Label controls. Set the *Text* properties as follows:

Label	Text Property Value
Label1	*Currency Format*
Label2	*(nothing)*
Label3	*Current Date and Time*
Label4	*(nothing)*

4. Double-click Form2 to open the *Form2_Load* event handler. Add the following code to the *Form2_Load* event handler.

```
' VB
Label2.Text = Format(500, "Currency")
Label4.Text = Now.ToShortDateString
```

```
// C#
label2.Text = (500).ToString("C");
label4.Text = System.DateTime.Now.ToShortDateString();
```

5. In the Designer, set the *Form2.Localizable* property to *True* and set the *Language* property to *German (Germany)*.

6. Set the *Text* properties of *Label2* and *Label4* as follows:

Label	Text Property Value
Label2	*Währung-Format*
Label4	*Aktuelle Uhrzeit*

7. In the Designer, choose the tab for Form1.

8. From the Toolbox, add three Button controls to the form and set their *Text* properties as shown here:

Button	Button Text Property Value
Button1	United States
Button2	United Kingdom
Button3	Germany

9. In the Designer, double-click Button1 to open the *Button1_Click* default event handler and add the following code:

```vb
' VB
System.Threading.Thread.CurrentThread.CurrentCulture = New _
    System.Globalization.CultureInfo("en-US")
System.Threading.Thread.CurrentThread.CurrentUICulture = New _
    System.Globalization.CultureInfo("en-US")
Dim aform As New Form2()
aform.Show()
```

```csharp
// C#
System.Threading.Thread.CurrentThread.CurrentCulture = new
    System.Globalization.CultureInfo("en-US");
System.Threading.Thread.CurrentThread.CurrentUICulture = new
    System.Globalization.CultureInfo("en-US");
Form2 aform = new Form2();
aform.Show();
```

10. In the Designer, double-click Button2 to open the *Button2_Click* default event handler and add the following code:

```vb
' VB
System.Threading.Thread.CurrentThread.CurrentCulture = New _
    System.Globalization.CultureInfo("en-GB")
System.Threading.Thread.CurrentThread.CurrentUICulture = New _
    System.Globalization.CultureInfo("en-GB")
Dim aform As New Form2()
aform.Show()
```

```csharp
// C#
System.Threading.Thread.CurrentThread.CurrentCulture = new
    System.Globalization.CultureInfo("en-GB");
System.Threading.Thread.CurrentThread.CurrentUICulture = new
    System.Globalization.CultureInfo("en-GB");
Form2 aform = new Form2();
aform.Show();
```

11. In the Designer, double-click Button3 to open the *Button3_Click* default event handler and add the following code:

```vb
' VB
System.Threading.Thread.CurrentThread.CurrentCulture = New _
    System.Globalization.CultureInfo("de-DE")
System.Threading.Thread.CurrentThread.CurrentUICulture = New _
    System.Globalization.CultureInfo("de-DE")
Dim aform As New Form2()
aform.Show()
```

```csharp
// C#
System.Threading.Thread.CurrentThread.CurrentCulture = new
    System.Globalization.CultureInfo("de-DE");
System.Threading.Thread.CurrentThread.CurrentUICulture = new
```

```
    System.Globalization.CultureInfo("de-DE");
Form2 aform = new Form2();
aform.Show();
```

12. Press F5 to build and run your application. Click each button to see a localized form. Note that the appropriate format for currency and the date is displayed in the localized form and that the new strings are loaded for the German form.

Lesson Summary

- Culture refers to cultural information about the country or region in which the application is deployed and is represented by a culture code. Globalization refers to the process of formatting application data in formats appropriate for the locale. Localization refers to the process of loading and displaying localized strings in the user interface.

- The *CurrentCulture* setting for the thread determines the culture that will be used to format application data. The *CurrentUICulture* setting for the thread determines the culture that will be used to load localized resources.

- Localized forms can be created by setting the *Localizable* property of a form to *True* and then setting the *Language* property to a language other than *(Default)*. A new copy of the form is created for this culture, and localized resources can be added to this form.

- You can implement right-to-left display in a control by setting the *RightToLeft* property to *True*. You can reverse the control layout of an entire form by setting the *RightToLeftLayout* and *RightToLeft* properties of a Form to *True*.

Lesson Review

The following questions are intended to reinforce key information presented in this lesson. The questions are also available on the companion CD if you prefer to review them in electronic form.

NOTE Answers

Answers to these questions and explanations of why each choice is right or wrong are located in the "Answers" section at the end of the book.

1. Which of the following lines of code should be used to format data appropriately for Germany?

A. ` VB
```
System.Threading.Thread.CurrentThread.CurrentUICulture = New _
    System.Globalization.CultureInfo("de-DE")
```

// C#
```
System.Threading.Thread.CurrentThread.CurrentUICulture = New _
    System.Globalization.CultureInfo("de-DE");
```

B. ` VB
```
Me.CurrentUICulture = New System.Globalization.CultureInfo("de-DE")
```

// C#
```
this.CurrentUICulture = New System.Globalization.CultureInfo("de-DE");
```

C. ` VB
```
System.Threading.Thread.CurrentThread.CurrentCulture = New _
    System.Globalization.CultureInfo("de-DE")
```

// C#
```
System.Threading.Thread.CurrentThread.CurrentCulture = New _
    System.Globalization.CultureInfo("de-DE");
```

D. ` VB
```
Me.CurrentCulture = New System.Globalization.CultureInfo("de-DE")
```

// C#
```
this.CurrentCulture = New System.Globalization.CultureInfo("de-DE");
```

2. Given a form that contains a Label named Label1 and a Button named Button1, all with default settings, which of the following must be done to display the entire form and all controls in a right-to-left layout with right-to-left text display? Choose all that apply, and choose the fewest options necessary to accomplish the task.

   A. Set the *Label1.RightToLeft* property to *True*.

   B. Set the *Button1.RightToLeft* property to *True*.

   C. Set the *Form1.RightToLeft* property to *True*.

   D. Set the *Form1.RightToLeftLayout* property to *True*.

Lesson 3: Implementing MDI Forms

MDI applications are applications that organize child forms under a single parent form. Unlike single document interface applications, in which you can work on only one document at a time, MDI applications allow you to open, organize, and work with several documents at the same time. In this lesson, you will learn how to create and implement MDI applications.

After this lesson, you will be able to:

- Create MDI parent forms.
- Create MDI child forms.
- Identify the active MDI child.
- Send data to the active MDI child.
- Arrange MDI child forms.
- Create a window list menu for an MDI application.

Estimated lesson time: 30 minutes

MDI Applications

MDI applications follow a parent form/child form model. An MDI application generally has a single parent form (although it is possible for an application to have multiple parent forms) that contains and organizes multiple child forms. Microsoft Office Excel is an example of an MDI application—you can open multiple documents and work with them separately within the parent form. The parent form organizes and arranges all of the child documents that are currently open.

Creating an MDI Parent Form

The parent form is the main form of any MDI application. This form contains all child forms that the user interacts with and handles the layout and organization of the child forms as well. It is a simple task to create an *MDI parent* form in Visual Studio 2005.

▶ **To create an MDI parent form**

1. Create a new Windows Forms application.

2. In the Properties window for the startup form, set the *IsMDIContainer* property to *True*. This designates the form as an MDI parent form.

Creating MDI Child Forms

MDI child forms are at the center of user interaction in MDI applications. They present the data to the user and generally contain individual documents. Child forms are contained within and managed by a parent form. You can create an MDI child form by setting the *MdiParent* property of the form.

▶ **To create an MDI child form**

1. Create an MDI parent form, as described earlier.

2. In Visual Studio, add a second form to the project and add controls to implement the user interface. This is the child form.

3. In a method in the parent form, such as a menu item *Click* event handler, create a new instance of the child form and set its *MdiParent* property to *True*, as shown in the following example:

```vb
' VB
' This example takes place in a method in the parent form, and assumes a Form
' called ChildForm
Dim aChildForm As New ChildForm
' Sets the MdiParent property to the parent form
aChildForm.MdiParent = Me
aChildForm.Show
```

```csharp
// C#
//This example takes place in a method in the parent form, and assumes a Form
// called ChildForm
ChildForm aChildForm = new ChildForm();
// Sets the MdiParent property to the parent form
aChildForm.MdiParent = this;
aChildForm.Show();
```

Identifying the Active Child Form

At times, you will want to identify the active child form in an MDI application. For example, a common feature of MDI applications is a central menu on the parent form that contains commands that act upon the child form that has the focus. You can use the *ActiveMDIChild* property of the parent form to obtain a reference to the form that was last accessed. The following code example demonstrates how to obtain a reference to the active child form:

```vb
' VB
' This example demonstrates how to obtain a reference to the active child
' form from a method inside the parent form
Dim aForm As Form
aForm = Me.ActiveMDIChild
```

```
// C#
// This example demonstrates how to obtain a reference to the active child
// form from a method inside the parent form
Form aForm;
aForm = this.ActiveMDIChild;
```

Sending Data to the Active Child Form from the Clipboard

Once you have identified the active MDI form, you can use the properties of the form to send data from the clipboard to an active control on the form. You might use this functionality to implement a Paste menu item to paste data from the clipboard into a control. The following code example demonstrates how to determine if the active control is a text box and paste text from the clipboard into the text box.

```
' VB
Dim activeForm As Form = Me.ActiveMDIChild
' Checks to see if an active form exists
If Not activeForm Is Nothing Then
   If Me.ActiveControl.GetType Is GetType(TextBox) Then
      Dim aTextBox As TextBox = CType(Me.ActiveControl, TextBox)
      ' Creates a new instance of the DataObject interface.
      Dim data As IDataObject = Clipboard.GetDataObject()
      ' Checks to see of the data in the data object is text. If it is,
      ' the text of the active Textbox is set to the text in the clipboard.
      If data.GetDataPresent(DataFormats.Text) Then
         aTextBox.Text = data.GetData(DataFormats.Text).ToString()
      End If
   End If
End If
```

```
// C#
Form activeForm = this.ActiveMDIChild;
// Checks to see if an active form exists
if (activeForm != null)
{
    if (this.ActiveControl.GetType() is TextBox)
    {
       TextBox aTextBox = (TextBox)this.ActiveControl;
       // Creates a new instance of the DataObject interface.
       IDataObject data = Clipboard.GetDataObject();
       // Checks to see of the data in the data object is text. If it is,
       // the text of the active Textbox is set to the text in the clipboard.
       if (data.GetDataPresent(DataFormats.Text))
       {
          aTextBox.Text = data.GetData(DataFormats.Text).ToString();
       }
    }
}
```

Arranging MDI Child Forms

Commonly, you will want to organize the forms in an MDI application so that they are ordered. The MDI parent form can arrange the child forms that it contains by calling the *LayoutMdi* method. The *LayoutMdi* method takes a parameter that is a member of the *MdiLayout* enumeration. This method causes the forms contained by the parent form to be arranged in the manner specified by the parameter. The members of the *MdiLayout* enumeration are described in Table 11-4.

Table 11-4 *MdiLayout* Enumeration Members

Member	Description
ArrangeIcons	All MDI child icons are arranged within the client region of the MDI parent form.
Cascade	All MDI child windows are cascaded within the client region of the MDI parent form.
TileHorizontal	All MDI child windows are tiled horizontally within the client region of the MDI parent form.
TileVertical	All MDI child windows are tiled vertically within the client region of the MDI parent form.

The following example demonstrates the *LayoutMdi* method:

```
' VB
' Causes the contained forms to cascade in the parent form
Me.LayoutMdi(System.Windows.Forms.MdiLayout.Cascade)
```

```
// C#
// Causes the contained forms to cascade in the parent form
this.LayoutMdi(System.Windows.Forms.MdiLayout.Cascade);
```

Creating a Window List Menu for an MDI Application

MDI applications will frequently include a menu list of all the windows currently in an application. Users can select the appropriate window from the list and that window is activated in the MDI parent form. Visual Studio 2005 makes implementing a window list menu for an MDI application a simple task.

▶ **To create a window list menu for an MDI application**

1. From the Toolbox, drag a *MenuStrip* component onto the MDI parent form.

2. Create a top-level menu item for the window list menu. For example, you might create a menu item named WindowToolStripMenuItem.

3. In the Designer, select the *MenuStrip* component. In the Properties window, set the *MdiWindowListItem* property to the menu item you created for the window list.

   The menu will automatically be populated with entries for the child forms, and the appropriate child form will be activated when chosen from the menu.

Quick Check

1. What is an MDI application?

2. How do you create an MDI parent form?

Quick Check Answers

1. An MDI application is an application where multiple documents or forms are hosted inside a single parent form.

2. You can create an MDI parent form by setting a form's *IsMdiContainer* property to *True*.

Lab: Create a Simple MDI Application

In this lab, you will create a simple MDI application with a parent form that loads and organizes child forms. Then you will create a window list menu and another menu that allows the user to arrange the child forms inside the parent forms.

▶ **Exercise 1: Creating an MDI Application**

1. In Visual Studio, create a new Windows application.

2. In the Designer, select the form. In the Properties window, set the *IsMdiContainer* property to *True*.

3. From the Toolbox, drag a *MenuStrip* control onto the form.

4. Add three top-level menu items that read File, Windows, and Arrange.

5. Under the File menu, add a menu item that reads Add Child Form.

6. Under the Arrange menu, add three menu items that read Cascade, Horizontal, and Vertical.

7. Select MenuStrip1. In the Properties window, set the *MdiWindowListItem* property to *WindowsToolStripMenuItem*.

8. Add a second form to the project.

9. In Form1, double-click AddChildFormToolStripMenuItem to open the default event handler for its *Click* event.

10. In the Code Editor, outside of any method, add the following line of code:

```
' VB
Dim Forms As Integer
```

```
// C#
int forms;
```

11. In the *AddChildFormToolStripMenuItem_Click* event handler, add the following code:

```
' VB
forms += 1
Dim aform As New Form2
aform.MdiParent = Me
aform.Text = "Form copy " & Forms.ToString
aform.Show()
```

```
// C#
forms++;
Form2 aform = new Form2();
aform.MdiParent = this;
aform.Text = "Form copy " + forms.ToString();
aform.Show();
```

12. Double-click CascadeToolStripMenuItem to open the default *Click* event handler for this item. Add the following code:

```
' VB
Me.LayoutMdi(MdiLayout.Cascade)
```

```
// C#
this.LayoutMdi(MdiLayout.Cascade);
```

13. Double-click HorizontalToolStripMenuItem to open the default *Click* event handler for this item. Add the following code:

```
' VB
Me.LayoutMdi(MdiLayout.TileHorizontal)
```

```
// C#
this.LayoutMdi(MdiLayout.TileHorizontal);
```

14. Double-click VerticalToolStripMenuItem to open the default *Click* event handler for this item. Add the following code:

```
' VB
Me.LayoutMdi(MdiLayout.TileVertical)
```

```
// C#
this.LayoutMdi(MdiLayout.TileVertical);
```

15. Press F5 to build and run the application.

    Add new child forms by selecting the Add Child Form menu item. After you have added several, arrange them by choosing an option from the Arrange menu. Note that as new windows are added, they are automatically added to the Windows menu and can be brought to the front by selecting the appropriate menu item.

Lesson Summary

■ MDI applications follow a parent/child form model. A parent form contains and organizes multiple child forms. You can create a parent form by setting the *Form.IsMdiContainer* property to *True*. MDI child forms are created by assigning the *MdiParent* property to an appropriate MDI parent form.

■ The MDI parent form exposes methods and properties that enable the organization of its contained child forms. A reference to the active child form can be retrieved by using the *ActiveMDIChild* property of the parent form. Child forms can be arranged in the parent form by using the *LayoutMdi* method of the parent form.

■ You can create a menu list of the current MDI child forms by setting the *MdiWindowListItem* property of a *MenuStrip* control to a top-level ToolStripMenuItem. At run time, the menu will automatically be populated with the active child forms.

Lesson Review

The following questions are intended to reinforce key information presented in this lesson. The questions are also available on the companion CD if you prefer to review them in electronic form.

NOTE Answers

Answers to these questions and explanations of why each choice is right or wrong are located in the "Answers" section at the end of the book.

---

1. Which of the following is necessary to create an MDI child form and host it in a parent form? (Choose all that apply.)

    A. Set the *IsMdiParent* property of the parent form to *True*.

    B. Set the *ActiveMdiForm* property of the parent form to the child form.

    C. Set the *MdiParent* property of the child form to the parent form.

    D. Set the *MdiWindowListItem* property of the *MenuStrip* control on the parent form to an appropriate ToolStripMenuItem.

2. Which of the following lines of code can be used to obtain a reference to the active MDI child form?

    A.
```
' VB
Me.ActivateMdiChild(activeForm)

// C#
this.ActivateMdiChild(activeForm);
```

    B.
```
' VB
Me.AddOwnedForm(activeForm)

// C#
this.AddOwnedForm(activeForm);
```

    C.
```
' VB
activeForm.IsMdiChild

// C#
activeForm.IsMdiChild;
```

    D.
```
' VB
Me.ActiveMdiChild

// C#
this.ActiveMdiChild;
```

Chapter Review

To further practice and reinforce the skills you learned in this chapter, you can perform the following tasks:

- Review the chapter summary.
- Review the list of key terms introduced in this chapter.
- Complete the case scenarios. These scenarios set up real-world situations involving the topics of this chapter and ask you to create a solution.
- Complete the suggested practices.
- Take a practice test.

Chapter Summary

- The drag-and-drop operation is initiated by calling the *DoDragDrop* method on the source control. The *DoDragDrop* method takes two parameters: an *Object* parameter that contains the data to be dragged and dropped and a *DragDropEffects* enumeration parameter that represents the effect or effects that are allowed for this operation. The *DragEnter* event on the target control is used to set the allowed effects for the target control. The drag-and-drop operation is completed in the *DragDrop* event on the target control. You must write code to complete the appropriate operation in this event.

- Globalization refers to the process of formatting application data in formats appropriate for the locale. Localization refers to the process of loading and displaying localized strings in the user interface. The *CurrentCulture* setting for the thread determines the culture that will be used to format application data. The *CurrentUICulture* setting for the thread determines the culture that will be used to load localized resources. Localized forms can be created by setting the *Localizable* property of a form to *True* and then setting the *Language* property to a language other than *(Default)*. You can implement right-to-left display in a control by setting the *RightToLeft* property to *True*. You can reverse the control layout of an entire form by setting the *RightToLeftLayout* and *RightToLeft* properties of a form to *True*.

- MDI applications follow a parent form/child form model. A parent form contains and organizes multiple child forms. You can create a parent form by setting the *Form.IsMdiContainer* property to *True*. MDI child forms are created by assigning the *MdiParent* property to an appropriate MDI parent form. A reference to the active child form can be retrieved by using the *ActiveMdiChild* property of the parent form. Child forms can be arranged in the parent form by using the *LayoutMdi* method of the parent form. You can create a menu list of the current MDI child forms by setting the *MdiWindowListItem* property of a *MenuStrip* control to a top-level ToolStripMenuItem.

Key Terms

Do you know what these key terms mean? You can check you answers by looking up the terms in the glossary at the back of the book.

- drag-and-drop
- globalization
- localization
- MDI parent
- MDI child

Case Scenarios

In the following case scenarios, you will apply what you've learned about advanced topics in Windows forms. You can find answers to these questions in the "Answers" section at the end of this book.

Case Scenario 1: Still More Document Control

You have been tasked with designing a user interface for the document control system for help authors at the Fabrikam, Inc. software company. The help authors use a table of contents for their help topics that can be represented as a hierarchical set of nodes, with each node representing a topic. The users at Fabrikam would like to be able to view multiple documents at one time in this application and, after viewing them, have the option of manually rearranging the table of contents. They would like the user interface to be easy to use and mouse-driven.

Questions

1. What kind of user interface layout would allow users to view and organize more than one document at the same time?

2. How can you enable users to rearrange the table of contents in a mouse-driven application?

Case Scenario 2: Fabrikam Goes International

Fabrikam, Inc. is rocking the equities world with the introduction of their stock market tracker. This application will track the stock markets in both the United States and Europe but will be deployed all around the world. You are in charge of the globalization and localization of this application.

Key Requirements

■ Data for the European markets must be formatted for European currency and dates. Data for the U.S. markets must be formatted for U.S. currency and dates.

■ Data for European and U.S. markets must be visible simultaneously.

■ The user interface must be in a language appropriate for wherever it is deployed.

Questions

1. How can you enable users to view market data simultaneously in the appropriate formats?

2. How will you ensure that an appropriate user interface is displayed dependent on the deployed locale?

Suggested Practices

To help you successfully master the exam objectives presented in this chapter, complete the following tasks.

■ **Practice 1**   Create an application that allows the user to rearrange the nodes in a *TreeView* control but gives them the option of placing moved nodes before, after, or as a child of the target node.

■ **Practice 2**   Extend the solution in the Lesson 2 lab, "Create Localized Forms," to include a language that reads right to left. Create a localized version of the form with appropriate strings and the layout reversed.

■ **Practice 3**   Use MDI technology to create a Web browser that allows the user to open multiple Web pages at one time, organize them, and easily switch between one and another.

Take a Practice Test

The practice tests on this book's companion CD offer many options. For example, you can test yourself on just the content covered in this chapter, or you can test yourself on all the 70-526 certification exam content. You can set up the test so that it closely simulates the experience of taking a certification exam, or you can set it up in study mode so that you can look at the correct answers and explanations after you answer each question.

MORE INFO Practice tests

For details about all the practice test options available, see the "How to Use the Practice Tests" section in this book's Introduction.

Chapter 12
Enhancing Usability

Usability is a key component in designing useful Windows Forms applications. An application that takes the user into account and provides usability features will be adopted more quickly by the target audience and will improve productivity in the long run. This chapter discusses implementing accessibility, user assistance controls, and persisting application settings.

Exam objectives in this chapter:
- Implement accessibility features.
    - Implement accessibility features within a Windows Forms application.
- Create, configure, and customize user assistance controls and components.
    - Configure the *PropertyGrid* component.
    - Configure the *ProgressBar* control to indicate progress graphically.
    - Display status information by using the *StatusStrip* control.
    - Configure the *ToolTip* component.
    - Configure the *ErrorProvider* component.
    - Configure the *HelpProvider* component.
    - Play system sounds and audio files by using the SoundPlayer.
    - Configure the *Timer* component to raise an event at regular intervals.
    - Enable scrolling by using the *HScrollBar* and *VScrollBar* controls.
- Persist Windows Forms application settings between sessions.

Lessons in this chapter:

Before You Begin

To complete the lessons in this chapter, you must have:

- A computer that meets or exceeds the minimum hardware requirements listed in the "Introduction" at the beginning of the book.

- Microsoft Visual Studio 2005 Professional Edition installed on your computer.

- An understanding of Microsoft Visual Basic or C# syntax and familiarity with the Microsoft .NET Framework.

Real World

Matt Stoecker

Usable applications are used applications. In my opinion, the key to a successful application is user adoption. If using your application is difficult or a chore for your target audience, productivity will suffer. But if your target audience is excited about using your application, and your program takes the needs of your target audience into account, then adoption will increase, training time will decrease, and greater productivity will be had by all.

Lesson 1: Implementing Accessibility

Today's workforce is a diverse group of people with different talents, skills, and abilities. Many users of today's applications have difficulty using the standard user interface provided by most Windows Forms applications. You can increase the user base of your applications through *accessible design*: designing them to be accessible.

After this lesson, you will be able to:

■ Implement accessibility features in a Windows Forms application.

Estimated lesson time: 45 minutes

Implementing Accessibility

The workforce contains a significant number of people with accessibility requirements, requiring applications that meet the broad demands of today's business environment.

Microsoft Windows XP provides a variety of tools that can seamlessly provide accessibility to Windows Forms applications and create a more accessible user experience. An example of an accessibility aid is Sound Sentry, which causes the operating system to emit a visible cue whenever a sound is played. In addition, you can design accessibility principles into your application.

Designing for Accessibility

Accessible applications begin in the design phase. When accessibility is planned for in application design, you can integrate the principles of accessibility into the user interface. Some of these principles are:

■ Flexibility

■ Choice of input and output methods

■ Consistency

■ Compatibility with accessibility aids

An accessible program requires flexibility. Users must be able to customize the user interface to suit their specific needs, for example, the ability to increase font sizes if needed. A user should also have a choice of input methods such as keyboard and mouse devices. That is, the application should provide keyboard access for all important features and mouse access for all main features. A choice of output methods also renders an application more accessible, and the user should have the ability to choose among visual cues, sounds, text, and graphics. An accessible application should interact within its own operation and with other applications in a consistent manner, and it should be compatible with existing accessibility aids.

Support Standard System Settings

For your application to be accessible, it must support standard system settings for size, color, font, and input. Adopting this measure will ensure that all of a user's applications have a consistent user interface that conforms to the system settings. Users with accessibility needs can thus configure all of their applications by configuring their system settings.

You can implement standard system settings in your application by using the classes that represent the user interface options used by the system. Table 12-1 lists the classes that expose the system settings. These classes are found in the *System.Drawing* namespace.

Table 12-1   Classes That Expose System Settings

Class	Description
SystemBrushes	Exposes *Brush* objects that can be used to paint in the system colors.
SystemColors	Exposes the system colors.
SystemFonts	Exposes the fonts used by the system.
SystemIcons	Exposes the icons used by the system.
SystemPens	Exposes *Pen* objects that can be used to draw in the system colors.

These classes monitor changes to the system settings and adjust correspondingly. For example, if you build an application that uses the *SystemFonts* class to determine all of the fonts, the fonts in the application will automatically be reset when the system settings are changed.

Ensure Compatibility with the High-Contrast Option

The high-contrast option (which users can set themselves in the Control Panel) sets the Windows color scheme to provide the highest possible level of contrast in the user interface. This option is useful for users requiring a high degree of legibility.

By using only system colors and fonts, you can ensure that your application is compatible with the high-contrast settings. You should also avoid the use of background images because these tend to reduce contrast in an application.

Provide Documented Keyboard Access to All Features

Your application should provide keyboard access for all features and comprehensive documentation that describes this access. Shortcut keys for controls and menu items, as well as setting the *Tab* order for controls on the user interface, allow you to implement keyboard navigation in your user interface. Documentation of these features is likewise important. A user must have some means of discovering keyboard access to features, whether that is through user interface cues or actual documentation.

Provide Notification of the Keyboard Focus Location

The location of the keyboard focus is used by accessibility aids such as *Magnifier* and *Narrator*. Thus, it is important that the application and the user have a clear understanding of where the keyboard focus is at all times. For most purposes, this functionality is provided by the .NET Framework, but when designing your program flow, you should incorporate code to set the focus to the first control on a form when the form is initially displayed, and the *Tab* order should follow the logical program flow.

Convey No Information by Sound Alone

Whereas sound is an important cue for many users, an application should never rely on conveying information by using sound alone. When using sound to convey information, you should combine that with a visual notification such as flashing the form or displaying a message box.

Accessibility Properties of Windows Forms Controls

In addition to properties that affect the visual interface of a control, Windows Forms controls have five properties related to accessibility that determine how the control interacts with accessibility aids. These properties are summarized in Table 12-2.

Table 12-2   Accessibility Properties of Windows Controls

Property	Description
AccessibleDescription	Contains the description that is reported to accessibility aids.
AccessibleName	Contains the name that is reported to accessibility aids.
AccessibleRole	Contains the role that is reported to accessibility aids. This value is a member of the *AccessibleRole* enumeration and is used by a variety of accessibility aids to determine what kind of user interface element an object is.

Table 12-2   Accessibility Properties of Windows Controls

Property	Description
AccessibilityObject	Contains an instance of *AccessibleObject*, which provides information about the control to usability aids. This property is read-only and set by the designer.
AccessibleDefaultAction-Description	Contains a description of the default action of a control. This property cannot be set at design time and must be set in code.

These properties provide information to accessibility aids about the role of the control in the application. Accessibility aids can then present this information to the user or make decisions about how to display the control.

Quick Check

1. What is the purpose of setting accessibility properties on Windows Forms controls?

2. What are the best practices when designing for accessibility?

Quick Check Answers

1. The accessibility properties provide information about the controls in your application to accessibility aids.

2. When designing for accessibility you should support standard system settings, ensure compatibility with high-contrast mode, provide documented keyboard access for all features, provide notification for keyboard focus location, and convey no information by sound alone.

Lab: Create an Accessible User Interface

In this lab, you will create an accessible user interface. You will set the Accessibility properties for the controls in your user interface, and you will add code to your application to support high-contrast mode.

▶ **Exercise 1: Setting Accessibility Properties**

1. In Visual Studio, create a new Windows Forms application.

2. Add the following controls and set the properties as shown here.

Control	Property	Value
Label1	Text	Sign up for our mailing list!
	Font.Size	14
	BackColor	Color.Blue
	ForeColor	Color.Yellow
Label2	Text	Name
TextBox1	TabIndex	1
Label3	Text	Email Address
TextBox2	TabIndex	2
Button1	Text	Submit
	TabIndex	3
Button2	Text	Cancel
	TabOrder	4

3. Set the accessibility properties for the form and controls as shown here.

Object	Property	Setting
Form1	AccessibleName	Mailing list form
	AccessibleDescription	Mailing list form
Label1	AccessibleName	Title label
	AccessibleDescription	Sign up for our mailing list!
Label2	AccessibleName	Name label
	AccessibleDescription	Name label
TextBox1	AccessibleName	Name text box
	AccessibleDescription	Enter your name here

Object	Property	Setting
Label3	AccessibleName	E-mail label
	AccessibleDescription	E-mail label
TextBox2	AccessibleName	E-mail text box
	AccessibleDescription	Enter your e-mail address here
Button1	AccessibleName	Submit button
	AccessibleDescription	Press this button to submit the form
Button2	AccessibleName	Cancel button
	AccessibleDescription	Press this button to cancel the form

4. In the Designer, double-click the form to open the *Form1_Load* event handler. Add the following code to support high-contrast mode:

```
' VB
If SystemInformation.HighContrast
    Label1.BackColor = SystemColors.Control
    Label1.ForeColor = SystemColors.ControlText
End If

// C#
if (SystemInformation.HighContrast)
{
    label1.BackColor = SystemColors.Control;
    label1.ForeColor = SystemColors.ControlText;
}
```

5. Press F5 to run your application. Edit your computer's display properties and view the application. Note that the custom colors do not affect high-contrast mode. Also, note that the *AccessibleName* and *AccessibleDescription* properties you defined are not visible. However, they would be useful to users making use of accessibility aids.

Lesson Summary

■ Applications should be designed to support the principles of accessibility, including flexibility, a choice of input and output methods, consistency, and compatibility with accessibility aids.

- Applications should support the standard system settings. Using the system classes to access standard fonts and colors enables your application to work with accessibility aids that use system settings or the high-contrast setting.

- Accessible applications should be designed to have a variety of inputs, including documented keyboard access to all important features.

- No information should be conveyed by sound alone.

- Each control exposes several accessibility properties that are used by accessibility aids to gather and display information. You can set accessibility properties at design time in the Properties window.

Lesson Review

The following questions are intended to reinforce key information presented in this lesson. The questions are also available on the companion CD if you prefer to review them in electronic form.

NOTE Answers

Answers to these questions and explanations of why each choice is right or wrong are located in the "Answers" section at the end of the book.

---

1. Which of the following are principles of accessible design? (Choose all that apply.)

    A. Flexibility

    B. Consistency

    C. Simplicity

    D. Compatibility with accessibility aids

2. Which of the following is not a best practice for implementing accessibility?

    A. Provide audio for all important information.

    B. Support standard system settings.

    C. Ensure compatibility with high-contrast mode.

    D. Provide keyboard access to all important functionality.

Lesson 2: Using User Assistance Controls and Components

The .NET Framework contains many controls and components that can be used to enhance the usability and usefulness of your application. Controls such as the *Status-Strip* and *ProgressBar* allow you to convey information to the user in a variety of ways; the *HelpProvider*, *ErrorProvider*, and *ToolTip* components allow you to offer user assistance; and other components enable you to add a greater depth of functionality to your applications. In this lesson, you will learn how to enhance your application with user assistance controls and components.

After this lesson, you will be able to:

- Configure the *PropertyGrid* component.
- Configure the *ProgressBar* control to indicate progress graphically.
- Display status information using the *StatusStrip* control.
- Configure the *ToolTip* component.
- Configure the *ErrorProvider* component.
- Configure the *HelpProvider* component.
- Play system sounds and audio files by using the *SoundPlayer*.
- Configure the *Timer* component to raise an event at regular intervals.
- Enable scrolling by using the *HScrollBar* and *VScrollBar* controls.

Estimated lesson time: 45 minutes

User Assistance Controls and Components

The .NET Framework provides controls and components that provide a wide range of functionality when designing your user interface. In this lesson, you will learn about a variety of different controls and components that serve to enhance the user experience.

The *PropertyGrid* Control

The *PropertyGrid* control is essentially a user-configurable version of the Properties window in Visual Studio. The *PropertyGrid* control allows the user to set the properties of controls or components in a graphical interface at run time. Figure 12-1 shows the *PropertyGrid* control in a form.

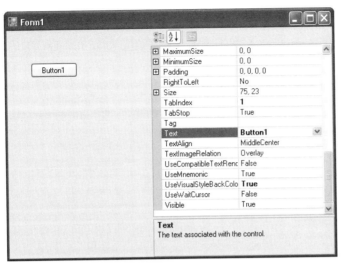

Figure 12-1   The *PropertyGrid* control in a form

The *PropertyGrid* control that is shown in Figure 12-1 is configured to access the properties of Button1. At run time, the user can change properties for Button1 by changing the appropriate value in the *PropertyGrid*. Changes to properties in the *PropertyGrid* are immediately passed on to the affected control.

The most important property for configuring the *PropertyGrid* control is the *Selected-Object* property. This property represents the control or class instance whose properties are exposed in the *PropertyGrid*. At run time, you can set the *SelectedObject* property to any object and allow the user to view its properties and set any read-write properties in the user interface. The following code example demonstrates how to set the *SelectedObject* property.

```
' VB
PropertyGrid1.SelectedObject = Button1
```

```
// C#
propertyGrid1.SelectedObject = button1;
```

The *PropertySort* property determines how the properties displayed in the *Property-Grid* are sorted and can be set to a member of the *PropertySort* enumeration. Table 12-3 displays the members of the *PropertySort* enumeration.

Table 12-3   *PropertySort* Enumeration Values

Value	Description
Alphabetical	Properties are displayed in alphabetical order.
Categorized	Properties are sorted into categories.
CategorizedAlphabetical	Properties are sorted into categories and then alphabetized.
NoSort	Properties are displayed in the order in which they are returned from the *TypeDescriptor*.

You can set the *PropertySort* property to a member of the *PropertySort* enumeration at run time, as shown in the following example.

```
' VB
PropertyGrid1.PropertySort = PropertySort.NoSort
```

```
// C#
propertyGrid1.PropertySort = PropertySort.NoSort;
```

The *ProgressBar* Control

The *ProgressBar* control allows you to visually indicate progress for a time-consuming operation. For example, you might use a *ProgressBar* control to indicate the progress of a computationally intensive operation such as copying files or printing documents. The *ProgessBar* appears as a bar that is gradually filled in from left to right as a cue to indicate the progress of a task. Important properties of the *ProgressBar* control are shown in Table 12-4.

Table 12-4   Important Properties of the *ProgressBar* Control

Property	Description
Maximum	The maximum value of the *ProgressBar* control. This property represents the value that the *Value* property will return when the *ProgressBar* is completely full.
Minimum	The minimum value of the *ProgressBar* control. This property represents the value that the *Value* property will return when the *ProgressBar* is completely empty.

Table 12-4   Important Properties of the *ProgressBar* Control

Property	Description
Step	The amount that will be added to the *Value* property when the *PerformStep* method is called.
Value	The current value of the *ProgressBar*. The *Value* property will be a value between the *Minimum* and *Maximum* properties.

You can configure the *ProgressBar* by setting the *Minimum* and *Maximum* properties to represent the range of values that you want the *ProgressBar* to represent. When the *Value* property is the same value as the *Minimum* property, the *ProgressBar* control appears completely empty. Likewise, when the *Value* property is the same value as the *Minimum* property, the *ProgressBar* control appears completely filled. When the value is between the *Minimum* and the *Maximum* properties, the *ProgressBar* appears partially filled, proportional to the value of the *Value* property.

You can increment the *ProgressBar* by using either the *PerformStep* method or the *Increment* method. The *PerformStep* method causes the *Value* property to be advanced by the value of the *Step* property. Thus, if the *Value* property is currently *100* and the *Step* property is set to *10*, calling the *PerformStep* method will advance the *Value* property to *110*, and the UI will change correspondingly. You can also use the *Increment* method to advance the value by a specified amount, as shown in the following example:

```
' VB
' Adds 5 to the Value
ProgressBar1.Increment(5)
' Adds 10 to the Value
ProgressBar1.Increment(10)
```

```
// C#
// Adds 5 to the Value
progressBar1.Increment(5);
// Adds 10 to the Value
progressBar1.Increment(10);
```

The following example demonstrates how to use the *ProgressBar* control to indicate progress to the user on a time-consuming task.

```
' VB
' Assumes a ProgressBar control named ProgressBar1 and a time-consuming
' method called CopyFiles.
ProgressBar1.Minimum = 0
ProgressBar1.Maximum = 100
ProgressBar1.Step = 1
```

```
For i As Integer = 1 to 100
   CopyFiles(i)
   ProgressBar1.PerformStep
Next
```

```
// C#
// Assumes a ProgressBar control named ProgressBar1 and a time-consuming
// method called CopyFiles.
progressBar1.Minimum = 0;
progressBar1.Maximum = 100;
progressBar1.Step = 1;
for (int i = 0; i < 101; i++)
{
   CopyFiles(i);
   progressBar1.PerformStep();
}
```

Displaying Information with the *StatusStrip* Control

The *StatusStrip* control allows you to display status information about the application. It's a subclass of the *ToolStrip* control and can host *ToolStripItems*. *ToolStrip* controls were covered in detail in Chapter 4, "ToolStrips, Menus, and Events." This section will focus on using the *StatusStrip* control to display information to the user.

The *StatusStrip* control is generally docked at the bottom edge of the form, although, like all *ToolStrip* controls, it can be docked at any edge, or it can even be undocked. You can add *ToolStripItems* to the *Status* strip either in the Designer or in code, as described in Chapter 4.

The two *ToolStripItems* that are commonly used to display information to the user in the *StatusStrip* control are the *ToolStripStatusLabel* control and the *ToolStripProgressBar* control. The *ToolStripStatusLabel* is a *ToolStripItem* control that emulates a *Label* control but resides in the *StatusStrip* control. The most important property of the *ToolStripStatusLabel* is the *Text* property, which represents the text that is displayed in the *ToolStripStatusLabel* control. You can set the text property, as shown in the following example:

```
' VB
ToolStripStatusLabel1.Text = "Meltdown Imminent"
```

```
// C#
toolStripStatusLabel1.Text = "Meltdown Imminent";
```

The *ToolStripProgressBar* is a *ToolStripItem* control that emulates a *ProgressBar* control. *ToolStripProgressBar* exposes *Minimum*, *Maximum*, *Step*, and *Value* properties like the

ProgressBar control does, and these properties function in the same way as described in the previous section. Likewise, the *ToolStripProgressBar* exposes *Increment* and *PerformStep* methods that advance the value in the same way as they do for the *ProgressBar* control.

The *ToolTip* Component

The *ToolTip* component allows you to set tooltips for controls. Tooltips appear in popup windows when the mouse hovers over the control, and they can provide short pieces of information about the control to the user. Important properties of the *ToolTip* component are described in Table 12-5.

Table 12-5 Important Properties of the *ToolTip* Component

Property	Description
Active	Indicates whether the *ToolTip* component is active.
AutomaticDelay	Gets or sets the delay for the *ToolTip* component.
AutoPopDelay	Gets or sets the period of time the tooltip remains visible if the pointer is stationary on a control with specified *ToolTip* text.
IsBalloon	Gets or sets a value indicating whether the tooltip should use a balloon window.
ReshowDelay	Gets or sets the length of time that must transpire before subsequent *ToolTip* windows appear as the pointer moves from one control to another.
ShowAlways	Gets or sets a value indicating whether a *ToolTip* window is displayed, even when its parent control is not active.
ToolTipIcon	Gets or sets a value that defines the type of icon to be displayed alongside the tooltip text.
ToolTipTitle	Gets or sets a title for the *ToolTip* window.
UseAnimation	Gets or sets a value determining whether an animation effect should be used when displaying the tooltip.
UseFading	Gets or sets a value determining whether a fade effect should be used when displaying the tooltip.

The *ToolTip* component also exposes two key methods: *GetToolTip* and *SetToolTip*. These methods are used to retrieve and set the tooltip text for a specified control.

When the *ToolTip* component is correctly configured, tooltips for controls in the form are shown automatically when the mouse hovers over the control. This requires the following:

- The *ToolTip.Active* property must be set to *True*.
- There must be a *ToolTip* set for that control.
- The control must be active, or the *ToolTip.ShowAlways* property must be set to *True*.

Setting Tooltips for Controls   You can set tooltips for controls at either design time or run time. At design time, the *ToolTip* component creates a design-time property for each control in the form. For example, if you add a *ToolTip* component named *ToolTip1* to your form, each control will gain a design-time property called *ToolTip* on *ToolTip1*. This property can be set only at design time and represents the tooltip text for that control.

▶ **To set a tooltip in the Designer**

1. In the Designer, select the property for which you want to set a tooltip.

2. In the Properties window, set the location of the property named *Tooltip* on *X*, where *X* represents the name of the *ToolTip* component.

3. Set this property to your desired tooltip text.

You can also use the *SetToolTip* method to set the tooltip text in code.

▶ **To set a tooltip in code**

Use the *SetToolTip* method to set a tooltip for the desired control, as shown in the following example:

```
' VB
ToolTip1.SetToolTip(Button1, _
    "This button activates the self-destruct sequence")
```

```
// C#
toolTip1.SetToolTip(button1,
    "This button activates the self-destruct sequence");
```

Changing the Delay Times for the *ToolTip* Component   The *ToolTip* component exposes several properties that affect the timing of tooltip display. The properties that control the timing of the tooltip display are:

- *AutoPopDelay*   This property determines the amount of time, in milliseconds, that a tooltip is shown.

- *InitialDelay*   This property determines the amount of time, in milliseconds, that the mouse pointer must hover over a control before the tooltip is shown.

- *ReshowDelay*   This property determines the amount of time, in milliseconds, that it takes for subsequent tooltips to appear as the mouse moves from one tooltip-associated control to another.

You can set these controls either in the Properties window at design time or in code, as shown in the following example:

```
' VB
ToolTip1.AutoPopDelay = 2000
ToolTip1.InitialDelay = 300
ToolTip1.ReshowDelay = 600

// C#
toolTip1.AutoPopDelay = 2000;
toolTip1.InitialDelay = 300;
toolTip1.ReshowDelay = 600;
```

You can also control all of these values by setting a single property, *AutomaticDelay*. When you set the *AutomaticDelay* property, it then sets the *AutoPopDelay*, *InitialDelay*, and *ReshowDelay* properties. The properties are set as follows: If the *AutomaticDelay* property is set to N milliseconds, the *InitialDelay* property is also set to N milliseconds. The *AutoPopDelay* property is set to $5 * N$ milliseconds, and the *ReshowDelay* property is set to $N/5$ milliseconds. You can set the *AutomaticDelay* property as shown in the following example:

```
' VB
ToolTip1.AutomaticDelay = 500

// C#
toolTip1.AutomaticDelay = 500;
```

Configuring the *ErrorProvider* Component

The *ErrorProvider* component allows you to provide feedback to the user when an error condition results for a control in the form. The *ErrorProvider* is usually used in conjunction with field validation to indicate an invalid entry. It displays an error icon next to the control that has the error condition and displays a tooltip when the mouse pointer hovers over the control.

The key method of the *ErrorProvider* component is the *SetError* method. You can use the *SetError* method to set an error on a control in the form. The following example demonstrates how to set an error with the *SetError* method:

```
' VB
' This example demonstrates how to set an error on a control named Textbox1
ErrorProvider1.SetError(TextBox1, "Value must be numeric")
```

```
// C#
// This example demonstrates how to set an error on a control named Textbox1
errorProvider1.SetError(TextBox1, "Value must be numeric");
```

Once an error is set on the control, the icon represented by the *Icon* property will flash next to the control for which the error is set, and the text set in the method will be displayed when the mouse hovers over the control. When the error condition is corrected, you can clear the error by calling the *SetError* method and setting the text to an empty string, as follows:

```
' VB
ErrorProvider1.SetError(TextBox1, "")
```

```
// C#
errorProvider1.SetError(TextBox1, "");
```

This causes the error icon to cease flashing.

The following procedure describes how to create a validation handler that uses the *ErrorProvider* component.

▶ **To validate user input with the *ErrorProvider* component**

1. Add controls, including at least one that can receive text input, to your form. Note that, for validation to function, you must have more than one control on the form.

2. Ensure that the *CausesValidation* property of each control on the form is set to *True*.

3. Add an *ErrorProvider* component to the form.

4. Select the text entry control and add code to its *Validating* event handler. Examine the contents of the text entry control and determine if they are valid. If the contents are not valid, call the *ErrorProvider.SetError* method to set the error on the control. The *Validating* event will fire as the user navigates away from the text entry control. The following example demonstrates how to validate if the text in a *TextBox* control is numeric.

```vb
' VB
Private Sub TextBox1_Validating(ByVal Sender As Object, _
    ByVal e As System.ComponentModel.CancelEventArgs) Handles TextBox1.Validating
    ' Check to see if the TextBox contains a numeric value
    If Not IsNumeric(TextBox1.Text) Then
        ErrorProvider1.SetError(TextBox1, "This value must be numeric")
    Else
        ' Set the error to an empty string to clear the error
        ErrorProvider1.SetError(TextBox1, "")
    End If
End Sub
```

```csharp
// C#
protected void textBox1_Validating (object sender,
System.ComponentModel.CancelEventArgs e)
{
    try
    {
    // Check to see if the TextBox contains a numeric value by trying to parse the string
        double x = double.Parse(textBox1.Text);
        errorProvider1.SetError(textBox1, "");
    }
    catch (System.FormatException ex)
    {
        // If the text box does not contain an numeric value, set the error on the TextBox
        errorProvider1.SetError(textBox1, "The value must be numeric");
    }
}
```

You can use the *ErrorProvider* to display errors in a dataset or any other data source. By binding the *ErrorProvider* component to the data source, you can display an error icon next to any control that is bound to the same data source. The following procedure demonstrates how to set an error in a dataset.

▶ **To view errors in a *DataSet* with the *ErrorProvider* component**

1. Bind the *ErrorProvider* component to a table in the dataset, as shown here:

```vb
' VB
' Assumes existence of DataSet1 with a Customers table
ErrorProvider1.DataSource = DataSet1
ErrorProvider1.DataMember = "Customers"
```

```csharp
// C#
// Assumes existence of DataSet1 with a Customers table
errorProvider1.DataSource = DataSet1;
errorProvider1.DataMember = "Customers";
```

2. Set the *ContainerControl* property of the *ErrorProvider* component:

```vb
' VB
ErrorProvider1.ContainerControl = Me
```

```
// C#
errorProvider1.ContainerControl = this;
```

3. Use the *SetColumnError* method to set the error on a column that contains the error and advance the binding context to the row that contains the error, as shown here:

```
' VB
DataTable1.Rows(5).SetColumnError("Name", "The data is incorrect")
Me.BindingContext(DataTable1).Position = 5
```

```
// C#
DataTable1.Rows[5].SetColumnError("Name", "The data is incorrect");
this.BindingContext[DataTable1].Position = 5;
```

Configuring the *HelpProvider* Component

An important part of any application is clear and accurate documentation. The *Help-Provider* component allows you to make help available for your application. The *HelpProvider* component enables you to associate HTML Help1.x files with your application (.chm or .htm files) and display the appropriate help topic when the F1 button is pressed.

The *Help* Namespace   The key property of the *HelpProvider* component is the *HelpNamespace* property. This property allows you to specify a .chm or .htm file that contains the help for the application. The *HelpNamespace* property is generally set at design time in the Properties window, but it can also be set in code at run time, as shown below:

```
' VB
HelpProvider1.HelpNamespace = "C:\myHelpFiles\appHelp.chm"
```

```
// C#
helpProvider1.HelpNamespace = "C:\\myHelpFiles\\appHelp.chm";
```

Methods of the *HelpProvider* Component   The *HelpProvider* component manages access to help in the *Help* namespace by setting properties for each control in the form. Table 12-6 describes the important methods of the *HelpProvider* component.

Table 12-6   Important Methods of the *HelpProvider* Component

Method	Description
SetHelpKeyword	Sets the keyword for a control, such as an index keyword or a topic keyword. This keyword will be passed to the help file when help is shown. The *HelpNavigator* setting determines how the keyword is used.
SetHelpNavigator	Sets the *HelpNavigator* for a control. This property determines how the help file is displayed.
SetHelpString	Sets the help string for a control. If the *HelpNamespace* property is not set to a file, the help string will be displayed in a popup box over the control when the F1 button is pressed.
SetShowHelp	Sets whether help is shown for a particular control.

Setting the *HelpNavigator*   The *SetHelpNavigator* method allows you to determine how help is displayed for a particular control. The *SetHelpNavigator* method requires two parameters: a control that the *HelpNavigator* will be set for, and a member of the *HelpNavigator* enumeration. The following example demonstrates how to set the *Help-Navigator* for a *Button* control named Button1:

```
' VB
HelpProvider1.SetHelpNavigator(Button1, HelpNavigator.Find)
```

```
// C#
helpProvider1.SetHelpNavigator(Button1, HelpNavigator.Find);
```

Table 12-7 describes the members of the *HelpNavigator* enumeration.

Table 12-7   Members of the *HelpNavigator* Enumeration

Member	Description
AssociateIndex	The help file opens to the index entry for the first letter of the specified keyword.
Find	The help file opens to the search page.
Index	The help file opens to the index.

Table 12-7   Members of the *HelpNavigator* Enumeration

Member	Description
KeywordIndex	The help file opens to the topic with the specified keyword if one exists; otherwise, the index entry closest to the specified keyword is displayed.
TableOfContents	The help file opens to the table of contents.
Topic	The help file opens to a specified topic if the topic exists.
TopicId	The help file opens to a topic indicated by a numeric topic identifier.

Configuring Help for a Control   The following example demonstrates how to use the *HelpProvider* component to configure help for a control named Button1.

```
' VB
' This example assumes that a help file has been compiled for your
' application and the path to that file has been set in the HelpNamespace property.
' Sets help for Button1 to be shown.
HelpProvider1.SetShowHelp(Button1, True)
' Sets the help keyword for the control
HelpProvider1.SetHelpKeyword(Button1, "Button1")
' Sets the HelpNavigator for the control
HelpProvider1.SetHelpNavigator(Button1, HelpNavigator.KeywordIndex)

// C#
// This example assumes that a help file has been compiled for your
// application and the path to that file has been set in the HelpNamespace property.
// Sets help for Button1 to be shown.
helpProvider1.SetShowHelp(button1, true);
// Sets the help keyword for the control
helpProvider1.SetHelpKeyword(button1, "button1");
// Sets the HelpNavigator for the control
helpProvider1.SetHelpNavigator(button1, HelpNavigator.KeywordIndex);
```

Playing Sound Files and System Sounds

Sound files and system sounds can be used to communicate information or alerts to your users. The *SoundPlayer* class in the *System.Media* namespace encapsulates all of the functionality required to play sound files.

▶ **To play a sound file with the *SoundPlayer* class**

1. Create an instance of the *SoundPlayer* class that specifies the sound file to be played, as shown here:

```
' VB
Dim aPlayer As New System.Media.SoundPlayer("C:\mySoundFiles\Boom.wav")
```

```
// C#
System.Media.SoundPlayer aPlayer = new
    System.Media.SoundPlayer(@"C:\mySoundFiles\Boom.wav");
```

2. Play the sound by calling the *Play* method, as shown:

```
' VB
aPlayer.Play
```

```
// C#
aPlayer.Play();
```

You can play system sounds by accessing the *System.Media.SystemSounds* class. This class contains members that represent each of the system sounds, and they can be played by calling the *Play* method.

▶ **To play a system sound**

Call the *Play* method of the appropriate system sound, as shown here:

```
' VB
System.Media.SystemSounds.Beep.Play()
```

```
// C#
System.Media.SystemSounds.Beep.Play();
```

Using the *Timer* Component to Raise an Event at Regular Intervals

The *Timer* component allows you raise the *Timer.Tick* event at regular intervals. By writing code to handle this event, you can schedule your application to call methods or take other actions at predefined intervals. For example, you might want to display the current time in a *Label* control and update it every minute.

The key property of the *Timer* component is the *Interval* property. The *Interval* property specifies the number of milliseconds between intervals of the *Tick* event. For example, if the *Interval* property is set to *2000*, the *Tick* event will be raised every two seconds. The *Interval* property can be set in the Properties window or in code, as shown in the following example:

```
' VB
Timer1.Interval = 2000
```

```
// C#
timer1.Interval = 2000;
```

Another important property of the *Timer* component is the *Enabled* property. If the *Enabled* property is set to *False*, the *Timer.Tick* event will not be raised. When the *Enabled* property is set to *True*, the *Timer.Tick* event will be raised at a frequency determined by the *Interval* property.

The *Timer.Start* and *Timer.Stop* methods allow you to start and stop the *Timer*, respectively. These methods are simply shorthand ways of setting the *Enabled* property. Calling the *Timer.Start* method sets the *Timer.Enabled* property to *True* and commences regular firing of the *Tick* event. Calling the *Timer.Stop* method sets the *Timer.Enabled* property to *False* and ceases firing of the *Tick* event.

The following example demonstrates a handler for the *Timer.Tick* event. This sample code updates the text in *Label1* with the current time every time the *Tick* event is raised.

```
' VB
Private Sub Timer1_Tick(ByVal sender As System.Object, ByVal e As _
    System.EventArgs) Handles Timer1.Tick
    Label1.Text = Now.ToLongTimeString
    End Sub
```

```
// C#
private void timer1_Tick(object sender, EventArgs e)
{
    label1.Text = DateTime.Now.ToLongTimeString;
}
```

Using the *HScrollBar* and *VScrollBar* Controls

The *HScrollBar* and *VScrollBar* controls are controls that are designed to provide easy navigation through a long list of items or values by scrolling within an application or control. The *HScrollBar* control represents a horizontal scroll bar and the *VScrollBar* control represents a vertical scroll bar, but the two controls function identically otherwise. The *ScrollBar* controls consist of two scrollbar buttons at either end of the control, a slider, and a slider track in which the slider can move. The user can position the slider and thereby change the *Value* property.

The *ScrollBar* controls are distinct from the scrollbars that appear in Forms or scrollable controls—those scroll bars are integral parts of the control or form that they function with. The *ScrollBar* controls are designed for independent operation or operation with controls that do not normally have scrollbars, such as the *PictureBox* control. The important properties of the *ScrollBar* controls are shown in Table 12-8.

Table 12-8 Important Properties of the *Scrollbar* Controls

Property	Description
LargeChange	The amount the *Value* property changes when the user presses the *PageUp* or *PageDown* keys or clicks in the *ScrollBar* track.
Maximum	The maximum value for the scrollbar. In *HScrollBar*, the *Value* property is equal to the *Maximum* property when the scrollbar slider is all the way to the right in the scroll track. In *VScrollBar*, the *Value* property is equal to the *Maximum* property when the scrollbar slider is all the way at the bottom of the scroll track.
Minimum	The minimum value for the scrollbar. In *HScrollBar*, the *Value* property is equal to the *Minimum* property when the scrollbar slider is all the way to the left in the scroll track. In *VScrollBar*, the *Value* property is equal to the *Minimum* property when the scrollbar slider is all the way at the top of the scroll track.
SmallChange	The amount the *Value* property changes when the user presses one of the arrow keys or clicks a scrollbar button.
Value	The current value of the *Scrollbar* control. This property reflects the current location of the scrollbar slider.

Persisting Application Settings Between Sessions

The .NET Framework allows you to persist property values between user sessions in the form application settings and access and change those settings at run time. You might, for example, create settings that determine the color scheme of your application or settings that "remember" user names or data connection strings.

Persisting settings is a two-step process. First, you create a setting and give it a unique name and a value. The value can be any object and should be appropriate for the property that you want to persist. Second, the property that you want to persist is bound to the setting. At run time, the settings can be accessed, changed, and saved if need be.

Creating Settings at Design Time   Visual Studio 2005 provides user interface tools that allow you to create settings quickly and easily. You can use the Settings editor (shown in Figure 12-2) to create and edit new settings.

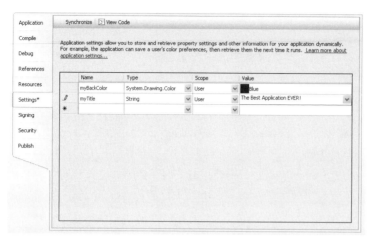

Figure 12-2 The Settings editor for creating and editing new settings

The Settings editor has four properties that must be set when they are created. The *Name* must be unique in the application. The *Type* property represents the type of setting, which should be appropriate for the property you want to bind it to. The *Scope* property must be set to either *Application* or *User*. *Settings* that are scoped for the application are read-only at run time and cannot be changed by the user. Settings that are scoped for the user are read-write at run time and can be changed and saved by the user. Finally, a value must be provided for the setting. This value must be of the type indicated by the *Type* property.

▶ **To create a setting at design time**

1. In Solution Explorer, right-click the project and choose Properties.

2. In the main window, select the Settings tab.

3. Set the Name, Type, Scope, and Value for the new setting.

4. If your application has not yet been saved, choose Save All from the File menu to save your application.

Once a setting has been created, you can bind it to a property in the Properties window.

▶ **To bind a setting to a property at design time**

1. In the Properties window for a control, expand (*ApplicationSettings*) and then click the button next to (*PropertyBinding*) to open the Application Settings window.

2. Locate the property that you want to bind to a setting. Select the appropriate setting from the drop-down box to the right of the property name. If no appropriate setting exists, you can create a new setting by clicking the (New...) link in the bottom of the drop-down box.

Accessing Settings at Run Time   You can read the values of your settings at run time and change and save the values of user-scoped settings. In Visual Basic, settings are exposed via the *My* object, and changes made to any user-scoped settings values are automatically saved. In C#, you can access settings through the *Properties.Settings.Default* object, but any changes made must be saved manually. At design time, individual settings appear in Intellisense as properties of the *Settings* object and can be treated in code as such. The following example demonstrates how to change the value of a user-scoped string setting named *TitleSetting*:

```
' VB
My.Settings.TitleSetting = "This is the new title"
```

```
// C#
Properties.Settings.DefaultSettings.TitleSetting = "This is the new Title";
Properties.Settings.DefaultSettings.Save();
```

> ## Quick Check
> 1. What is the purpose of the *Timer* component?
> 2. What is the purpose of the *ErrorProvider* component?
>
> ### Quick Check Answers
> 1. The *Timer* component is used to execute code at regular intervals.
> 2. The error provider is used to provide a visual cue to users when a validation error occurs.

Lab: Practice with User Assistance Controls

In this lab, you will create a small application that uses a timer to display and update the current time in a label, and you will use the functionality and many of the controls that have been discussed in this lesson. Although the end result of the lesson is somewhat contrived, it will allow you to practice with the different aspects of this lesson.

▶ **Exercise 1: Creating a Simple Digital Clock**

1. In Visual Studio, create a new Windows Forms application.

2. From the Toolbox, drag a *Label* control and a *Timer* component onto the form.

3. Select the *Timer* component. In the Properties window, set the *Interval* property to *1000* and the *Enabled* property to *True*.

4. In the Designer, double-click the *Timer* component to open the default event handler for the *Timer1.Tick* event. Add the following code to this method:

```
' VB
Label1.Text = Now.ToLongTimeString
```

```
// C#
label1.Text = System.DateTime.Now.ToLongTimeString();
```

5. Press F5 to compile and run your application. Note that the current time is updated in the *Label* control every second.

▶ **Exercise 2: Using the *PropertyGrid***

1. From the Toolbox, drag a *PropertyGrid* control onto the form that you created in the last exercise.

2. In the Properties window, set the *Dock* property of the *PropertyGrid* control to *Right*.

3. In the Properties window, set the *SelectedObject* property of the *PropertyGrid* control to Timer1.

4. Press F5 to compile and run the application. You can now set the properties of the *Timer* at run time via the *PropertyGrid* control.

▶ **Exercise 3: Providing Tooltips for Your Application**

1. From the Toolbox, drag a *ToolTip* component onto the form you created in Exercise 1, "Creating a Simple Digital Clock."

2. Select Label1. In the Properties window, set the tooltip on ToolTip1.

3. Press F5 to compile and run your application. Note that your label now has a tooltip associated with it.

▶ **Exercise 4: Using Settings**

1. In Solution Explorer, for the application you started in Exercise 1, right-click the project and choose Properties.

2. In the Properties pane, choose the Settings tab.

3. In the Settings window, create a setting with the following properties:

Property	Value
Name	*IntervalSetting*
Type	*Integer*
Scope	*User*
Value	*1000*

4. In the Designer, select Timer1. In the Properties window, expand (Application Settings) and then click the button next to (PropertyBinding) to open the Application Settings window.

5. In the Application Settings window, bind the *Interval* property to the *IntervalSetting* setting.

6. In the Designer, select the Form. In the Properties window, click the events button to list the events for the form. Double-click the cell next to the *FormClosing* event to open the default event handler for the *Form1.FormClosing* event. Add the following code to this event handler:

```
' VB
My.Settings.IntervalSetting = Timer1.Interval
```

```
// C#
Properties.Settings.Default.IntervalSetting = timer1.Interval;
Properties.Settings.Default.Save();
```

7. From the File menu, choose Save All.

8. Press F5 to compile and run your application. Any changes that you make to the interval property will be persisted between sessions.

Lesson Summary

- The *PropertyGrid* control allows you to set properties for controls in your application through a grid-style user interface. The *SelectedObject* property indicates the object for which the properties can be set.

- The *ProgressBar* control allows you to inform the user about progress for time-consuming processes such as file downloads. The *Minimum* and *Maximum* properties represent the minimum and maximum values for the *ProgressBar*, and the *Value* control represents the current value.

- The *StatusStrip* control is a *ToolStrip* control that is designed to display information about the status of the application. *ToolStripStatusLabel* and *ToolStripProgressBar* are *ToolStripItem* controls that are designed to work with the *StatusStrip*.

- The *ToolTip* component allows you to display tooltips for the controls on your form.

- The *ErrorProvider* component allows you to display errors in user input in your application. You can validate user input by adding code to the *Validating* event handler. If the user input is not valid, use the *SetError* method of the error provider to set the error.

- The *HelpProvider* component enables you to integrate HTML Help 1.x files (.chm and .htm) with your application. The *HelpNamespace* property represents the location of the help file that is associated with the *HelpProvider* component. You can call *SetShowHelp* to set F1 help for a control and *SetHelpKeyword* to set the keyword that will be passed on to the help file.

- The *SoundPlayer* component allows you to play sound files. You can use the *System-Sounds* class to play system sounds at run time.

- The *Timer* component allows you to execute actions at regular intervals. You can handle the *Timer.Tick* event to define code that is executed at regular intervals. The *Interval* property determines how frequently the *Timer.Tick* event is raised.

- The *HScrollBar* and *VScrollBar* controls are designed to provide a user interface that allows rapid access to a large range of values or a long list of options. The *Minimum* and *Maximum* properties represent the minimum and maximum values for the control; the *Value* property represents the current value and is tied to the current position of the slider.

- Application settings allow you to persist settings between application settings. Application-scoped settings are read-only and user-scoped settings are read-write at run time. You can access settings via the *My.Settings* object in Visual Basic or the *Properties.Settings.Default* object in C#.

Lesson Review

The following questions are intended to reinforce key information presented in this lesson. The questions are also available on the companion CD if you prefer to review them in electronic form.

NOTE   Answers

Answers to these questions and explanations of why each choice is right or wrong are located in the "Answers" section at the end of the book.

---

1. Which of the following code examples will advance the value of a progress bar named ProgressBar1 by 10? (Choose all that apply.)

   A. ' VB
   ```
   ProgressBar1.Step = 10
   ProgressBar1.PerformStep
   ```

   ```
   // C#
   progressBar1.Step = 10;
   progressBar1.PerformStep();
   ```

B.   ' VB
```
ProgressBar1.Step = 10
```

// C#
```
progressBar1.Step = 10;
```

C.   ' VB
```
ProgressBar1.Increment(10)
```

// C#
```
progressBar1.Increment(10);
```

D.   ' VB
```
ProgressBar1.Step = 10
ProgressBar1.Increment
```

// C#
```
progressBar1.Step = 10;
progressBar1.Increment();
```

2. Given a *TextBox* control, an *ErrorProvider* component, and a validation routine in the *Validating* event handler for that text box, which of the following is required to complete the validation routine and display an error icon when the user input is not valid? (Choose all that apply.)

   A. Set the *CausesValidation* property for other controls on the form to *True*.

   B. Call the *ErrorProvider.SetError* method and set the error to an informative string when user input is not valid.

   C. Call the *ErrorProvider.SetError* method and set the error to an empty value when user input is valid.

   D. Call the *ErrorProvider.Validate* method to validate the text box input.

3. Given a *TextBox* control named TextBox1 and a *HelpProvider* control named HelpProvider1 with the *HelpNamespace* property set to an appropriate help file, which of the following code samples will cause the search page for help to be displayed when the *F1* key is pressed and TextBox1 has the focus?

   A.   ' VB
```
HelpProvider1.SetShowHelp(TextBox1, True)
```

   // C#
```
helpProvider1.SetShowHelp(textBox1, true);
```

   B.   ' VB
```
HelpProvider1.SetShowHelp(TextBox1, True)
HelpProvider1.SetHelpNavigator(TextBox1, HelpNavigator.Find)
```

   // C#
```
helpProvider1.SetShowHelp(textBox1, true);
helpProvider1.SetHelpNavigator(textBox1, HelpNavigator.Find);
```

C. ' **VB**
```
HelpProvider1.SetShowHelp(TextBox1, True)
HelpProvider1.SetHelpNavigator(TextBox1, HelpNavigator.Topic)
```

// **C#**
```
helpProvider1.SetShowHelp(textBox1, true);
helpProvider1.SetHelpNavigator(textBox1, HelpNavigator.Topic);
```

D. ' **VB**
```
HelpProvider1.SetShowHelp(TextBox1, True)
HelpProvider1.SetHelpString(TextBox1, "Search")
```

// **C#**
```
helpProvider1.SetShowHelp(textBox1, true);
helpProvider1.SetHelpString(textBox1, "Search");
```

Chapter Review

To further practice and reinforce the skills you learned in this chapter, you can perform the following tasks:

- Review the chapter summary.
- Review the list of key terms introduced in this chapter.
- Complete the case scenarios. These scenarios set up real-world situations involving the topics of this chapter and ask you to create a solution.
- Complete the suggested practices.
- Take a practice test.

Chapter Summary

- Applications should be designed to support the principles of accessibility. Applications should support the standard system settings, they should be designed to have a variety of inputs, and they should convey no information solely by sound. Each control exposes several accessibility properties that are used by accessibility aids to gather and display information.

- The *PropertyGrid* control allows you to set properties for controls in your application through a grid-style user interface. The *ProgressBar* control allows you to inform the user about progress for time-consuming processes. The *StatusStrip* control is a *ToolStrip* control that is designed to display information about the status of the application.

- The *ToolTip*, *ErrorProvider*, and *HelpProvider* components provide additional design-time properties for controls on the form. The *ToolTip* component allows you to display tooltips for the controls on your form. The *ErrorProvider* component allows you to display errors in user input in your application. The *HelpProvider* component enables you to integrate HTML Help 1.x files with your application.

- The *SoundPlayer* component allows you to play sound files. The *Timer* component allows you to execute actions at regular intervals. The *HScrollBar* and *VScrollBar* controls are designed to provide a user interface that allows rapid access to a large range of values or a long list of options.

- Application settings allow you to persist settings between application settings. You can access settings via the *My.Settings* object in Visual Basic or the *Properties .Settings.Default* object in C#.

Key Terms

- accessible design
- application scope
- setting
- user scope

Case Scenarios

In the following case scenarios, you will apply what you've learned about enhancing usability. You can find answers to these questions in the "Answers" section at the end of this book.

Case Scenario 1: Putting the Final Touches on the Document Management System

Your company has created a document management application for Fabrikam, Inc., and you are in charge of putting the final touches on it. This application allows the user to browse documents from a very long list of documents stored on a central server, download and view those documents, and make any necessary changes. Most of the functionality is complete. You have been tasked with making the user interface friendlier. The following are your key requirements.

Key Requirements

- The application should provide a way to navigate the list of documents quickly and easily in the user interface.

- The application should provide feedback for the download status and provide a cue to the user when the download is complete.

- Help should be readily available to the user, and input values should be validated and provide immediate feedback if they are not valid.

Questions

What strategies can you use to implement the key requirements?

Case Scenario 2: Making the Document Management Application Accessible

The document management application is almost complete. You are now in charge of making the application accessible for all users. You have the following specific requirements:

- Application must support high-contrast mode.
- Application must be accessible to hearing-impaired users.
- Application must be accessible to users who are unable to use a mouse.
- Application must work well with all standard usability aids.

Questions

What strategies can you use to implement these requirements in this application?

Suggested Practices

- Create an application that allows you to browse sound files on your computer and play them with the *SoundPlayer* component.
- Extend the application created in the lab in Lesson 2, "Practice with User Assistance Controls," to include F1 help and validation for property values.

Take a Practice Test

The practice tests on this book's companion CD offer many options. For example, you can test yourself on just the content covered in this chapter, or you can test yourself on all the 70-526 certification exam content. You can set up the test so that it closely simulates the experience of taking a certification exam, or you can set it up in study mode so that you can look at the correct answers and explanations after you answer each question.

MORE INFO   **Practice tests**

For details about all the practice test options available, see "How to Use the Practice Tests" in this book's Introduction.

Chapter 13

Asynchronous Programming Techniques

Frequently, you will have to create applications that perform time-consuming operations such as file downloads or complex calculations. These operations can cause the user interface to lock up and become unresponsive, thus leading to an unpleasant user experience. By using asynchronous programming techniques, you can enable time-consuming operations to be run asynchronously, thus keeping the user interface responsive while the operations are run.

Exam objectives in this chapter:
- Run a background process by using the *BackgroundWorker* component.
- Announce the completion of a background process by using the *BackgroundWorker* component.
- Cancel a background process by using the *BackgroundWorker* component.
- Report the progress of a background process by using the *BackgroundWorker* component.
- Request the status of a background process by using the *BackgroundWorker* component.
- Implement advanced asynchronous techniques.
- Create an asynchronous method.
- Create a new process thread.

Lessons in this chapter:

Before You Begin

To complete the lessons in this chapter, you must have:

■ A computer that meets or exceeds the minimum hardware requirements listed in the "Introduction" at the beginning of the book.

■ Visual Studio 2005 Professional Edition installed on your computer.

■ An understanding of Visual Basic or C# syntax and familiarity with the .NET Framework.

Real World

Matt Stoecker

Even with ever increasing processor speeds, time-consuming tasks are still a central part of many of the applications I write. Before Visual Studio 2005, creating asynchronous operations was difficult and time-consuming. With the introduction of the *BackgroundWorker* component, creating simple asynchronous operations is easily accessible to programmers of all levels. For more advanced operations, delegates and threads provide the level of functionality needed.

Lesson 1: Managing a Background Process with the *BackgroundWorker* Component

Frequently you are required to perform tasks that consume fairly large amounts of time, such as file downloads. The *BackgroundWorker* component provides an easy way to run time-consuming processes in the background, thereby leaving the user interface responsive and available for user input.

After this lesson, you will be able to:

■ Run a background process by using the *BackgroundWorker* component.

■ Announce the completion of a background process by using the *BackgroundWorker* component.

■ Cancel a background process by using the *BackgroundWorker* component.

■ Report the progress of a background process by using the *BackgroundWorker* component.

■ Request the status of a background process by using the *BackgroundWorker* component.

Estimated lesson time: 45 minutes

The *BackgroundWorker* component is designed to allow you to execute time-consuming operations on a separate, dedicated thread. This allows you to run operations that take extended periods of time, such as file downloads and database transactions, asynchronously and allow the user interface to remain responsive.

The key method of the *BackgroundWorker* component is the *RunWorkerAsync* method. When this method is called, the *BackgroundWorker* component raises the *DoWork* event. The code in the *DoWork* event handler is executed on a separate, dedicated thread, allowing the user interface to remain responsive. Important members of the *BackgroundWorker* component are shown in Table 13-1.

Table 13-1   Important Members of the *BackgroundWorker* Component

Member	Description
CancellationPending	Property. Indicates whether the application has requested cancellation of a background operation.
IsBusy	Property. Indicates whether the *BackgroundWorker* is currently running an asynchronous operation.

Table 13-1   Important Members of the *BackgroundWorker* Component

Member	Description
WorkerReportsProgress	Property. Indicates whether the *BackgroundWorker* component can report progress updates.
WorkerSupportsCancellation	Property. Indicates whether the *BackgroundWorker* component supports asynchronous cancellation.
CancelAsync	Method. Requests cancellation of a pending background operation.
ReportProgress	Method. Raises the *ProgressChanged* event.
RunWorkerAsync	Method. Starts the execution of a background operation by raising the *DoWork* event.
DoWork	Event. Occurs when the *RunWorkerAsync* method is called. Code in the *DoWork* event handler is run on a separate and dedicated thread.
ProgressChanged	Event. Occurs when *ReportProgress* is called.
RunWorkerCompleted	Occurs when the background operation has been completed, cancelled, or has raised an exception.

Running a Background Process

The *RunWorkerAsync* method of the *BackgroundWorker* component starts the execution of the background process by raising the *DoWork* event. The code in the *DoWork* event handler is executed on a separate thread. The following procedure explains how to create a background process.

▶ **To create a background process with the *BackgroundWorker* component**

1. From the Toolbox, drag a *BackgroundWorker* component onto the form.

2. In the component tray, double-click the *BackgroundWorker* component to create the default event handler for the *DoWork* event. Add the code that you want to run on the separate thread. An example is shown below.

```
' VB
Private Sub BackgroundWorker1_DoWork(ByVal sender As System.Object, ByVal _
    e As System.ComponentModel.DoWorkEventArgs) Handles _
    BackgroundWorker1.DoWork
    ' Insert time-consuming operation here
```

```
End Sub
```

```
// C#
private void backgroundWorker1_DoWork(object sender, DoWorkEventArgs e)
{
    // Insert time-consuming operation here
}
```

3. Elsewhere in your code, start the time-consuming operation on a separate thread by calling the *RunWorkerAsync* method, as shown:

```
' VB
BackgroundWorker1.RunWorkerAsync()
```

```
// C#
backgroundWorker1.RunWorkerAsync();
```

Providing Parameters to the Background Process

Sometimes you will want to run a background process that requires a parameter. For example, you might want to provide the address of a file for download. You can provide a parameter in the *RunWorkerAsync* method. This parameter will be available as the *Argument* property of the instance of *DoWorkEventArgs* in the *DoWork* event handler.

▶ **To provide a parameter to a background process**

1. Include the parameter in the *RunWorkerAsync* call, as shown below:

```
' VB
RunWorkerAsync("C:\myfile.txt")
```

```
// C#
RunWorkerAsync("C:\\myfile.txt");
```

2. Retrieve the parameter from the *DoWorkEventArgs.Argument* property and cast it appropriately to use it in the background process. An example is shown below:

```
' VB
Private Sub BackgroundWorker1_DoWork(ByVal sender As System.Object, ByVal _
    e As System.ComponentModel.DoWorkEventArgs) Handles _
    BackgroundWorker1.DoWork
    Dim myPath As String
    myPath = CType(e.Argument, String)
    ' Use the argument in the process
    RunTimeConsumingProcess(myString)
End Sub
```

```
// C#
private void backgroundWorker1_DoWork(object sender, DoWorkEventArgs e)
{
```

```
    string myPath;
    myPath = (string)e.Argument;
    // Use the argument in the process
    RunTimeConsumingProcess(myString);

}
```

Announcing the Completion of a Background Process

When the background process terminates, whether because the process is completed or cancelled, the *RunWorkerCompleted* event is raised. You can alert the user to the completion of a background process by handling the *RunWorkerCompleted* event. An example is shown below:

```
' VB
Private Sub BackgroundWorker1_RunWorkerCompleted(ByVal sender As _
    System.Object, ByVal e As _
    System.ComponentModel.RunWorkerCompletedEventArgs) Handles _
    BackgroundWorker1.RunWorkerCompleted
    MsgBox("Background process completed!")
End Sub
```

```
// C#
private void backgroundWorker1_RunWorkerCompleted(object sender, RunWorkerCompletedEventArgs
e)
{
        System.Windows.Forms.MessageBox.Show("Background process completed");
}
```

You can ascertain if the background process was cancelled by reading the *e.Cancelled* property, as shown below:

```
' VB
Private Sub BackgroundWorker1_RunWorkerCompleted(ByVal sender As _
    System.Object, ByVal e As _
    System.ComponentModel.RunWorkerCompletedEventArgs) Handles _
    BackgroundWorker1.RunWorkerCompleted
    If e.Cancelled Then
        MsgBox("Process was cancelled!")
    Else
        MsgBox("Process completed")
    End If
End Sub
```

```
// C#
private void backgroundWorker1_RunWorkerCompleted(object sender, RunWorkerCompletedEventArgs
e)
{
    if (e.Cancelled)
    {
```

```
            System.Windows.Forms.MessageBox.Show ("Process was cancelled!");
    }
    else
    {
            System.Windows.Forms.MessageBox.Show("Process completed");
    }
}
```

Returning a Value from a Background Process   You might want to return a value from a background process. For example, if your process is a complex calculation you would want to return the end result. You can return a value by setting the *Result* property of the *DoWorkEventArgs* in the *DoWorkEventHandler*. This value will then be available in the *RunWorkerCompleted* event handler as the *Result* property of the *RunWorkerCompletedEventArgs* parameter, as shown in the following example:

```vb
' VB
Private Sub BackgroundWorker1_DoWork(ByVal sender As System.Object, ByVal _
    e As System.ComponentModel.DoWorkEventArgs) Handles _
    BackgroundWorker1.DoWork
    ' Assigns the return value of a method named ComplexCalculation to
    ' e.Result
    e.Result = ComplexCalculation
End Sub
Private Sub BackgroundWorker1_RunWorkerCompleted(ByVal sender As _
    System.Object, ByVal e As _
    System.ComponentModel.RunWorkerCompletedEventArgs) Handles _
    BackgroundWorker1.RunWorkerCompleted
    MsgBox("The result is " & e.Result.ToString)
End Sub
```

```csharp
// C#
private void backgroundWorker1_DoWork(object sender, DoWorkEventArgs e)
{
    // Assigns the return value of a method named ComplexCalculation to
    // e.Result
    e.Result = ComplexCalculation();
}
private void backgroundWorker1_RunWorkerCompleted(object sender, RunWorkerCompletedEventArgs e)
{
        System.Windows.Forms.MessageBox.Show("The result is " +
            e.Result.ToString());
}
```

Cancelling a Background Process

You might want to implement the ability to cancel a background process. *BackgroundWorker* supports the ability to cancel a background process, but you must implement must of the cancellation code yourself. The *WorkerSupportsCancellation* property of the *BackgroundWorker* component indicates whether the component supports cancellation. You can call the *CancelAsync* method to attempt to cancel the operation; doing so sets the *CancellationPending* property of the *BackgroundWorker* component to *True*. By polling the *CancellationPending* property of the *Background-Worker* component, you can determine whether or not to cancel the operation.

▶ **To implement cancellation for a background process**

1. In the Properties window, set the *WorkerSupportsCancellation* property to *True* to enable the *BackgroundWorker* component to support cancellation.

2. Create a method that is called to cancel the background operation. The following example demonstrates how to cancel a background operation in a *Button.Click* event handler.

```
' VB
Private Sub btnCancel_Click(ByVal sender As System.Object, ByVal e As _
    System.EventArgs) Handles btnCancel.Click
    BackgroundWorker1.CancelAsync()
End Sub
```

```
// C#
private void btnCancel_Click(object sender, EventArgs e)
{
    BackgroundWorker1.CancelAsync();
}
```

3. In the *BackgroundWorker.DoWork* event handler, poll the *BackgroundWorker.Can-cellationPending* property, and implement code to cancel the operation if it is *True*. You should also set the *e.Cancel* property to *True* as shown in the following example:

```
' VB
Private Sub BackgroundWorker1_DoWork(ByVal sender As System.Object, ByVal _
    e As System.ComponentModel.DoWorkEventArgs) Handles _
    BackgroundWorker1.DoWork
    For i As Integer = 1 to 1000000
        TimeConsumingMethod()
        If BackgroundWorker1.CancellationPending Then
            e.Cancel = True
            Exit Sub
        End If
    Next
End Sub
```

```
// C#
private void backgroundWorker1_DoWork(object sender, DoWorkEventArgs e)
{
    for (int i = 0; i < 1000000; i++)
    {
        TimeConsumingMethod();
        if (backgroundworker1.CancellationPending)
```

```
        {
            e.Cancel = true;
            return;
        }
    }
}
```

Reporting Progress of a Background Process with *BackgroundWorker*

For particularly time-consuming operations, you might want to report progress back to the primary thread. You can report progress of the background process by calling the *ReportProgress* method. This method raises the *BackgroundWorker.ProgressChanged* event and allows you to pass a parameter that indicates the percentage of progress that has been completed to the methods that handle that event. The following example demonstrates how to call the *ReportProgress* method from within the *Background-Worker.DoWork* event handler and then update a *ProgressBar* control in the *BackgroundWorker.ProgressChanged* event handler.

```vb
' VB
Private Sub BackgroundWorker1_DoWork(ByVal sender As System.Object, ByVal _
    e As System.ComponentModel.DoWorkEventArgs) Handles _
    BackgroundWorker1.DoWork
    For i As Integer = 1 to 10
        TimeConsumingProcess()
        ' Calls the Report Progress method, indicating the percentage
        ' complete
        BackgroundWorker1.ReportProgress(i*10)
    Next
End Sub
Private Sub BackgroundWorker1_ProgressChanged(ByVal sender As _
    System.Object, ByVal e As _
    System.ComponentModel.ProgressChangedEventArgs) Handles _
    BackgroundWorker1.ProgressChanged
    ProgressBar1.Value = e.ProgressPercentage
End Sub
```

```csharp
// C#
private void backgroundWorker1_DoWork(object sender, DoWorkEventArgs e)
{
    for (int i = 1;i < 11; i++)
    {
        TimeConsumingProcess();
        // Calls the Report Progress method, indicating the percentage
        // complete
        backgroundWorker1.ReportProgress(i*10);
    }

}
private void backgroundWorker1_ProgressChanged(object sender,
```

```
      ProgressChangedEventArgs e)
{
    progressBar1.Value = e.ProgressPercentage;
}
```

Note that in order to report progress with the *BackgroundWorker* component you must set the *WorkerReportsProgress* property to *True*.

Requesting the Status of a Background Process

You can determine if a *BackgroundWorker* component is executing a background process by reading the *IsBusy* property. The *IsBusy* property returns a Boolean value. If *True*, the *BackgroundWorker* component is currently running a background process. If *False*, the *BackgroundWorker* component is idle. An example follows:

```
' VB
If Not BackgroundWorker1.IsBusy
    BackgroundWorker1.RunWorkerAsync()
End If

// C#
if (!(backgroundWorker1.IsBusy))
{
    backgroundWorker1.RunWorkerAsync();
}
```

Quick Check

1. What is the purpose of the *BackgroundWorker* component?

2. Briefly describe how to implement cancellation for a background process with *BackgroundWorker*.

Quick Check Answers

1. The *BackgroundWorker* component allows you to run operations on a separate thread while allowing the user interface to remain responsive without complicated implementation or coding patterns.

2. First, you set the *WorkerSupportsCancellation* property of the *Background-Worker* component to *True*. Then create a method that calls the *Background-Worker.CancelAsync* method that is called to cancel the operation. Finally, in the background process, poll the *BackgroundWorker.CancellationPending* property and set *e.Cancel* to *True* if *CancellationPending* is *True*, and take appropriate action to halt the process.

Lab: Practice with Background Worker

In this lab you will practice using the *BackgroundWorker* component. You will add a *BackgroundWorker* component to your application and write a time-consuming method to be executed on a separate thread. You will report progress from the thread and implement functionality to cancel the background process.

▶ **Exercise 1: Practice with Background Worker**

1. Open the partial solution for this exercise from its location on the companion CD. You will find it in the Code folder in the Chapter 13 subfolder.

2. From the Toolbox, drag a *BackgroundWorker* to the form. The *BackgroundWorker* appears in the component tray.

3. In the Properties window, set the *WorkerSupportsCancellation* and *WorkerReportsProgress* properties to *True*.

4. Double-click the *BackgroundWorker* to open the default event handler for the *BackgroundWorker.DoWork* event. Add the following code to this event handler:

```vb
' VB
  Dim i As Integer
  i = CInt(e.Argument)
  For j As Integer = 1 To i
     If BackgroundWorker1.CancellationPending = True Then
        e.Cancel = True
        Exit For
     End If
     System.Threading.Thread.Sleep(1000)
     BackgroundWorker1.ReportProgress(CInt((j * 100 / i))
  Next
```

```csharp
// C#
int i;
i = int.Parse(e.Argument.ToString());
for (int j = 1; j <= i; j++)
{
   if (backgroundWorker1.CancellationPending)
   {
      e.Cancel = true;
      return;
   }
   System.Threading.Thread.Sleep(1000);
   backgroundWorker1.ReportProgress((int)((j *100/ i)));
}
```

5. In the Designer, select BackgroundWorker1 and click the Events button in the Properties window. Double-click ProgressChanged to open the Code window to the default event handler for the *ProgressChanged* event. Add the following code:

```
' VB
ProgressBar1.Value = e.ProgressPercentage
```

```
// C#
progressBar1.Value = e.ProgressPercentage;
```

6. In the Designer, select BackgroundWorker1 and click the Events button in the Properties window. Double-click RunWorkerCompleted to open the Code window to the default event handler for the *RunWorkerCompleted* event. Add the following code:

```
' VB
If Not e.Cancelled Then
   MsgBox("Run Completed!")
Else
   MsgBox("Run Cancelled")
End If
```

```
// C#
if (!(e.Cancelled))
{
    System.Windows.Forms.MessageBox.Show("Run Completed!");
}
else
{
    System.Windows.Forms.MessageBox.Show("Run Cancelled");
}
```

7. In the Designer, double-click the GO! button to open the default event handler for its *Click* event. Add the following code:

```
' VB
If Not TextBox1.Text = "" Then
   Dim i As Integer = CInt(TextBox1.Text)
   BackgroundWorker1.RunWorkerAsync(i)
End If
```

```
// C#
if (!(textBox1.Text == ""))
{
    int i = int.Parse(textBox1.Text);
    backgroundWorker1.RunWorkerAsync(i);
}
```

8. In the Designer, double-click the Cancel button to open the default event handler for its *Click* event. Add the following code:

```
' VB
BackgroundWorker1.CancelAsync()
```

```
// C#
backgroundWorker1.CancelAsync();
```

9. Press F5 to build and run your application and test all functionality.

Lesson Summary

■ The *BackgroundWorker* component allows you to execute operations on a separate thread of execution. You call the *RunWorkerAsync* method of the *Background-Worker* component to begin the background process. The event handler for the *DoWork* method contains the code that will execute on a separate thread.

■ The *BackgroundWorker.RunWorkerCompleted* event is fired when the background process is completed.

■ You can enable cancellation of a background process by setting the *Background-Worker.WorkerSupportsCancellation* property to *True*. You then signal the *BackgroundWorker* to cancel the process by calling the *CancelAsync* method, which sets the *CancellationPending* method to *True*. You must poll the *CancellationPending* property and implement cancellation code if the *CancellationPending* property registers as *True*.

■ You can report progress from the background operation. You first must set the *WorkerReportsProgress* property to *True*. You can then call the *ReportProgress* method from within the background process to report progress. This raises the *ProgressChanged* event, which you can handle to take any action.

Lesson Review

The following questions are intended to reinforce key information presented in this lesson. The questions are also available on the companion CD if you prefer to review them in electronic form.

NOTE Answers

Answers to these questions and explanations of why each choice is right or wrong are located in the "Answers" section at the end of the book.

---

1. Which of the following are required to start a background process with the *BackgroundWorker* component? (Choose all that apply.)

    A. Calling the *RunWorkerAsync* method

    B. Handling the *DoWork* event

    C. Handling the *ProgressChanged* event

    D. Setting the *WorkerSupportsCancellation* property to *True*

2. Which of the following are required to cancel a background process with the *BackgroundWorker* component? (Choose all that apply.)

    A. Set the *WorkerSupportsCancellation* property to *True*.

    B. Implement code to actually stop the process.

    C. Call the *CancelAsync* method.

    D. Set the *CancellationPending* property to *True*.

3. Which of the following are required to report the progress of a background process with the *BackgroundWorker* component? (Choose all that apply.)

    A. Call the *ReportProgress* method.

    B. Handle the *ProgressChanged* event.

    C. Poll the *IsBusy* property.

    D. Set the *WorkerReportsProgress* property to *True*.

Lesson 2: Implementing Asynchronous Methods

Although the *BackgroundWorker* component provides an excellent way to run simple tasks on a background thread, at times you might desire finer control over background processes. In this lesson you will learn to run methods asynchronously using delegates and to create new process threads.

After this lesson, you will be able to:

- Implement advanced asynchronous techniques.
- Create an asynchronous method.
- Create a new process thread.

Estimated lesson time: 45 minutes

Using Delegates

Special classes called *delegates* allow you to call methods in a variety of different ways. A delegate is essentially a type-safe function pointer. It allows you to pass a reference to an entry point for a method and invoke that method in a variety of ways without making an explicit function call. You use the *Delegate* keyword (*delegate* in C#) to declare a delegate, and you must specify the same method signature as the method that you want to call with the delegate. The following example demonstrates a sample method and the declaration of a delegate that can be used to call that method:

```
' VB
Public Function TestMethod(ByVal I As Integer) As String
   ' Insert method implementation here
End Function
Public Delegate Function myDelegate(ByVal I As Integer) As String

// C#
public string TestMethod(int I)
{
   // Insert method implementation here
}
public delegate string myDelegate(int i);
```

Once a delegate has been declared you can create an instance of it that specifies a method that has the same signature. In C# you can specify the method by simply naming the method. In Visual Basic, you must use the *AddressOf* operator to specify the method. The following example demonstrates how to create an instance of the delegate that specifies the method shown in the previous example.

```
' VB
Dim del As New myDelegate(AddressOf TestMethod)
```

```
// C#
myDelegate del = new myDelegate(TestMethod);
```

Once an instance of a delegate has been created, you can invoke the method that refers to the delegate by simply calling the delegate with the appropriate parameters or by using the delegate's *Invoke* method. Both are shown in the following example:

```
' VB
del(342)
del.Invoke(342)
```

```
// C#
del(342);
del.Invoke(342);
```

Using Delegates Asynchronously

Delegates can be used to call any method asynchronously. In addition to the *Invoke* method, every delegate exposes two methods that are used to call methods asynchronously. These methods are *BeginInvoke* and *EndInvoke*. Calling the *BeginInvoke* method on a delegate starts the method that it refers to on a separate thread. Calling *EndInvoke* retrieves the results of that method and ends the separate thread.

The *BeginInvoke* method begins the asynchronous call to the method represented by the delegate. It requires the same parameters as the method the delegate represents, as well as two additional parameters: an *AsyncCallback* delegate that references the method to be called when the asynchronous method is completed, and a user-defined object that contains information about the asynchronous call. In some cases (that will be discussed below) these parameters are not necessary and you can pass *Nothing* (*null* in C#) as parameter values. *BeginInvoke* returns an instance of *IAsyncResult*, which is used to monitor the asynchronous call.

The *EndInvoke* method retrieves the results of the asynchronous call, and can be called at any time after *BeginInvoke* has been called. The *EndInvoke* method signature requires as a parameter the instance of *IAsyncResult* returned by *BeginInvoke*, and returns the value that is returned by the method represented by the delegate. The method signature also contains any *Out* or *ByRef* parameters of the method it refers to in its signature.

You can use *BeginInvoke* and *EndInvoke* in several ways to implement asynchronous methods. Among them are:

- Calling *BeginInvoke*, doing work, and then calling *EndInvoke* on the same thread.
- Calling *BeginInvoke*, polling *IAsyncResult* until the asynchronous operation is completed, and then calling *EndInvoke*.
- Calling *BeginInvoke*, specifying a callback method to be executed when the asynchronous operation has completed, and calling *EndInvoke* on a separate thread.

Waiting for an Asynchronous Call to Return with *EndInvoke*

The simplest way to implement an asynchronous method call is to call *BeginInvoke*, do some work, and then call *EndInvoke* on the same thread that *BeginInvoke* was called on. While this approach is simplest, a potential disadvantage is that the *EndInvoke* call will block execution of the thread until the asynchronous operation is completed if it has not completed yet. Thus your main thread might still be nonresponsive if the asynchronous operation is particularly time-consuming. The *DelegateCallback* and *AsyncState* parameters are not required for this operation and so *Nothing* (*null* in C#) can be supplied for these parameters. The following example demonstrates how to implement an asynchronous call in this way, using the *TestMethod* and *myDelegate* that were defined in the examples above:

```
' VB
Dim del As New myDelegate(AddressOf TestMethod)
Dim result As IAsyncResult
result = del.BeginInvoke(342, Nothing, Nothing)
' Do some work while the asynchronous operation runs
Dim ResultString As String
ResultString = del.EndInvoke(result)
```

```
// C#
myDelegate del = new myDelegate(TestMethod);
IAsyncResult result;
result = del.BeginInvoke(342, null, null);
// Do some work while the asynchronous operation runs
string ResultString;
ResultString = del.EndInvoke(result);
```

Polling *IAsyncResult* Until Completion

Another way of executing an asynchronous operation is to call *BeginInvoke* and then poll the *IsCompleted* property of *IAsyncResult* to determine if the operation has finished. When the operation has finished, you can then call *EndInvoke*. An advantage of this approach is that you do not need to call *EndInvoke* until the operation is complete. Thus, you do not lose any time by blocking your main thread. The following example demonstrates how to poll the *IsCompleted* property.

```vb
' VB
Dim del As New myDelegate(AddressOf TestMethod)
Dim result As IAsyncResult
   result = del.BeginInvoke(342, Nothing, Nothing)
While Not result.IsCompleted
   ' Do some work
End While
Dim ResultString As String
ResultString = del.EndInvoke(result)
```

```csharp
// C#
myDelegate del = new myDelegate(TestMethod);
   IAsyncResult result;
result = del.BeginInvoke(342, null, null);
while (!(result.IsCompleted))
{
   // Do some work while the asynchronous operation runs
}
string ResultString;
ResultString = del.EndInvoke(result);
```

Executing a Callback Method When the Asynchronous Operation Returns

If you do not need to process the results of the asynchronous operation on the same thread that started the operation, you can specify a callback method to be executed when the operation is completed. This allows the operation to complete without interrupting the thread that initiated it. To execute a callback method, you must provide an instance of *AsyncCallback* that specifies the callback method. You can also supply a reference to the delegate itself so that *EndInvoke* can be called in the callback method to complete the operation. The following example demonstrates how to specify and run a callback method.

```vb
' VB
Private Sub CallAsync()
Dim del As New myDelegate(AddressOf TestMethod)
Dim result As IAsyncResult
Dim callback As New AsyncCallback(AddressOf CallbackMethod)
result = del.BeginInvoke(342, callback, del)
End Sub
Private Sub CallbackMethod(ByVal result As IAsyncResult)
Dim del As myDelegate
Dim ResultString As String
del = CType(result.AsyncState, myDelegate)
```

```
ResultString = del.EndInvoke(result)
End Sub

// C#
   private void CallAsync()
{
   myDelegate del = new myDelegate(TestMethod);
IAsyncResult result;
   AsyncCallback callback =  new AsyncCallback(CallbackMethod);
   result = del.BeginInvoke(342, callback, del);
 }
 private void CallbackMethod(IAsyncResult result)
 {
    myDelegate del;
    string ResultString;
    del = (myDelegate)result.AsyncState;
    ResultString = del.EndInvoke(result);
 }
```

Creating Process Threads

For applications that require more precise control over multiple threads, you can create new threads with the *Thread* object. The *Thread* object represents a separate thread
of execution that runs concurrently with other threads. You can create as many
Thread objects as you like, but the more threads that exist, the greater the impact on
performance and the greater the possibility of adverse threading conditions such as
deadlocks.

MORE INFO   Threading

Multithreading and the use of the *Thread* object is an extremely complex and detailed subject. The
information in this section should not be considered comprehensive. For more information, see
Managed Threading at *http://msdn2.microsoft.com/en-us/library/3e8s7xdd.aspx*.

Creating and Starting a New Thread

The *Thread* object requires a delegate to the method that will serve as the starting
point for the thread. This method must be a *Sub* (*void* in C#) method and must have
either no parameters or take a single *Object* parameter. In the latter case, the *Object*
parameter is used to pass any required parameters to the method that starts the
thread. Once a thread is created, you can start it by calling the *Thread.Start* method.
The following example demonstrates how to create and start a new thread:

```
' VB
Dim aThread As New System.Threading.Thread(Addressof aMethod)
```

```
aThread.Start()
```

```
// C#
System.Threading.Thread aThread = new
    System.Threading.Thread(aMethod);
aThread.Start();
```

For threads that accept a parameter, the procedure is similar except that the starting method can take a single *Object* as a parameter and that object must be specified as the parameter in the *Thread.Start* method. An example is shown below:

```
' VB
Dim aThread As New System.Threading.Thread(Addressof aMethod)
aThread.Start(anObject)
```

```
// C#
System.Threading.Thread aThread = new
    System.Threading.Thread(aMethod);
aThread.Start(anObject);
```

Destroying Threads

You can destroy a *Thread* object by calling the *Thread.Abort* method. This method causes the thread that it is called on to cease its current operation and raise a Thread-AbortException. If there is a *Catch* block that is capable of handling the exception it will execute along with any *Finally* blocks. The thread is then destroyed and cannot be restarted.

```
' VB
aThread.Abort()
```

```
// C#
aThread.Abort();
```

Synchronizing Threads

Two of the most common difficulties involved in multithread programming are the problems of deadlocks and race conditions. A deadlock occurs when one thread has exclusive access to a particular variable and then attempts to gain exclusive access to a second variable at the same time that a second thread has exclusive access to the second variable and attempts to gain exclusive access to the variable that is locked by the first thread. The result is that both threads wait indefinitely for the other to release the variable, and they cease operating.

A race condition occurs when two threads attempt to access the same variable at the same time. For example, consider two threads that access the same collection. The first thread might add an *Object* to the collection. The second thread might then remove an object from the collection based on the index of the object. The first thread then might attempt to access the object in the collection to find that it had been removed. Race conditions can lead to unpredictable effects that can destabilize your application.

The best way to avoid race conditions and deadlocks is by careful programming and judicious use of thread synchronization. You can use the *SyncLock* keyword in Visual Basic and the *lock* keyword in C# to obtain an exclusive lock on an object. This allows the thread that has the lock on the object to perform operations on that object without allowing any other threads to access it. Note that if any other threads attempt to access a locked object, those threads will pause until the lock is released. The following example demonstrates how to obtain a lock on an object:

```
' VB
SyncLock anObject
    ' Perform some operation
End SyncLock
```

```
// C#
lock (anObject)
{
    // Perform some operation
}
```

Some objects, such as collections, implement a synchronization object that should be used to synchronize access to the greater object. The following example demonstrates how to obtain a lock on the *SyncRoot* object of an *ArrayList* object.

```
' VB
Dim anArrayList As New System.Collections.ArrayList
SyncLock anArrayList.SyncRoot
    ' Perform some operation on the ArrayList
End SyncLock
```

```
// C#
lock (anArrayList.SyncRoot)
{
    // Perform some operation on the ArrayList
}
```

It is generally good practice when creating classes that will be accessed by multiple threads to include a synchronization object that is used for synchronized access to threads. This allows the system to lock only the synchronization object, thus conserving resources by not having to lock every single object contained in the class. A synchronization object is simply an instance of *Object* and does not need to have any functionality except to be available for locking. The following example demonstrates a class that exposes a synchronization object.

```vb
' VB
Public Class aClass
   Public SynchronizationObject As New Object()
   ' Insert additional functionality here
End Class
```

```csharp
// C#
public class aClass
{
    public object SynchronizationObject = new Object();
   // Insert additional functionality here
}
```

Special Considerations When Working with Controls

Because controls are always owned by the UI thread, it is generally unsafe to make calls to controls from a different thread. You can use the *Control.InvokeRequired* property to determine if it is safe to make a call to a control from another thread. If *InvokeRequired* returns *False*, it is safe to make the call to the control. If *InvokeRequired* returns *True*, however, you should use the *Control.Invoke* method on the owning form to supply a delegate to a method to access the control. Using *Control.Invoke* allows the control to be accessed in a thread-safe manner. The following example demonstrates setting the *Text* property of a *TextBox* control named Text1.

```vb
' VB
Public Delegate Sub SetTextDelegate(ByVal t As String)
Public Sub SetText(ByVal t As String)
   If TextBox1.InvokeRequired = True Then
      Dim del As New SetTextDelegate(AddressOf SetText)
      Me.Invoke(del, New Object() {t})
   Else
      TextBox1.Text = t
   End If
End Sub
```

```csharp
// C#
public delegate void SetTextDelegate(string t);
public void SetText(string t)
{
   if (textBox1.InvokeRequired)
   {
      SetTextDelegate del = new SetTextDelegate(SetText);
      this.Invoke(del, new object[]{t});
   }
   else
   {
```

```
        textBox1.Text = t;
    }
}
```

In the preceding example, the method tests *InvokeRequired* to determine if it is dangerous to access the control directly. In general, this will return *True* if the control is being accessed from a separate thread. If *InvokeRequired* does return *True*, the method creates a new instance of a delegate that refers to itself and calls *Control.Invoke* to set the *Text* property in a thread-safe manner.

Quick Check

1. What is a delegate? How is a delegate used?

2. What is thread synchronization and why is it important?

Quick Check Answers

1. A delegate is a type-safe function pointer. It contains a reference to the entry point of a method and can be used to invoke that method. A delegate can be used to invoke a method synchronously, or asynchronously on a separate thread.

2. When working with multiple threads of execution, problems can occur if multiple threads attempt to access the same resources. Thread synchronization is the process of ensuring that threads do not attempt to access the same resource at the same time. One way to synchronize threads is to obtain exclusive locks on the objects you wish to access, thereby prohibiting other threads from affecting them at the same time.

Lab: Practice with Delegates and Threads

In this lab, you will create an application similar to the application you created in Lesson 1. Your application will execute a time-consuming process on a separate thread that can be cancelled, reports progress, and notifies the user when finished. First, you will use delegates and asynchronous invocation to implement this functionality. After that is complete, you will modify your application to use threads.

▶ **Exercise 1: Practice with Delegates**

1. Open the partial solution for the first lab from its location on the companion CD. You will find it in the Code folder in the Chapter 13 subfolder.

2. In the Designer, right-click the form and choose View Code. Add the following method to the application:

```vb
' VB
Private Sub TimeConsumingMethod(ByVal seconds As Integer)
   For j As Integer = 1 To seconds
      System.Threading.Thread.Sleep(1000)
   Next
End Sub
```

```csharp
// C#
private void TimeConsumingMethod(int seconds)
{
   for (int j = 1; j <= seconds; j++)
   {
      System.Threading.Thread.Sleep(1000);
   }
}
```

3. Add a delegate to the application that is appropriate for TimeConsuming-Method, as shown below:

```
' VB Private Delegate Sub TimeConsumingMethodDelegate(ByVal j As Integer)
 // C# private delegate void TimeConsumingMethodDelegate(int seconds);
```

4. Add a method to report progress that sets the value of the *ProgressBar* control in a thread-safe manner and a delegate to that method, as shown below:

```vb
' VB
Public Delegate Sub SetProgressDelegate(ByVal val As Integer)
Public Sub SetProgress(ByVal val As Integer)
   If ProgressBar1.InvokeRequired = True Then
      Dim del As New SetProgressDelegate(AddressOf SetProgress)
      Me.Invoke(del, New Object() {val})
   Else
      ProgressBar1.Value = val
   End If
End Sub
```

```csharp
// C#
public delegate void SetProgressDelegate(int val);
public void SetProgress(int val)
{
   if (ProgressBar1.InvokeRequired)
   {
      SetProgressDelegate del = new SetProgressDelegate(SetProgress);
      this.Invoke(del, new object[]{val});
   }
   else
   {
      ProgressBar1.Value = val;
   }
}
```

5. Add the following line of code to the *For* loop of TimeConsumingMethod to report the progress of the method:

```
' VB
SetProgress(CInt((j * 100) / seconds))
```

```
// C#
SetProgress((int)(j * 100) / seconds);
```

6. Add a Boolean variable named *Cancel* to the application as shown below:

```
' VB
Private Cancel As Boolean
```

```
// C#
bool Cancel;
```

7. Add the following lines of code to the *For* loop of TimeConsumingMethod:

```
' VB
If Cancel Then Exit For
```

```
// C#
if (Cancel)
    break;
```

8. Add the following code after the *For* loop of TimeConsumingMethod:

```
' VB
If Cancel Then
    MsgBox("Cancelled")
    Cancel = False
Else
    MsgBox("Completed")
End If
```

```
// C#
if (Cancel)
{
    System.Windows.Forms.MessageBox.Show("Cancelled");
    Cancel = false;
}
else
{
    System.Windows.Forms.MessageBox.Show("Complete");
}
```

9. In the Designer, double-click the GO! button to open the default event handler for the button's *Click* method and add the following code:

```
' VB
Dim del As New TimeConsumingMethodDelegate(AddressOf TimeConsumingMethod)
del.BeginInvoke(CInt(TextBox1.Text), Nothing, Nothing)
```

```
// C#
TimeConsumingMethodDelegate del = new
    TimeConsumingMethodDelegate(TimeConsumingMethod);
del.BeginInvoke(int.Parse(TextBox1.Text), null, null);
```

10. In the Designer, double-click the Cancel button to open the default event handler for the button's *Click* method and add the following code:

```
' VB
Cancel = True
```

```
// C#
Cancel = true;
```

11. Press F5 to compile and test your application.

▶ **Exercise 2: Using Threads**

In this exercise you will modify the application created in the first exercise to use a *Thread* object instead of a delegate.

1. Open your completed application from Exercise 1 or the completed version on the companion CD in the Code folder in the Chapter 13 subfolder.

2. In the Code window, change the signature of TimeConsumingMethod as follows:

```
' VB
Private Sub TimeConsumingMethod(ByVal time As Object)
```

```
// C#
private void TimeConsumingMethod(object Time)
```

3. Add the following lines of code to the first lines of TimeConsumingMethod.

```
' VB
Dim seconds As Integer
seconds = CInt(Time)
```

```
// C#
int seconds;
seconds = (int)Time;
```

4. In the Designer, double-click the GO! button and replace the code that is there with the following code:

```
' VB
Dim aThread As New Threading.Thread(AddressOf TimeConsumingMethod)
aThread.Start(CInt(TextBox1.Text))
```

```
// C#
System.Threading.Thread aThread = new
    System.Threading.Thread(TimeConsumingMethod);
aThread.Start(int.Parse(textBox1.Text));
```

5. Press F5 to compile and test your application.

Lesson Summary

- Delegates are type-safe function pointers that allow you to call methods with the same signature. You can call methods synchronously by using the delegate's *Invoke* method, or asynchronously by using *BeginInvoke* and *EndInvoke*.

- When *BeginInvoke* is called, an operation specified by the delegate is started on a separate thread. You can retrieve the result of the operation by calling *EndInvoke*, which will block the calling thread until the background process is completed. You can also specify a callback method to complete the operation on the background thread if the result is not needed by the main thread.

- Thread objects represent separate threads of operation and provide for a high degree of control of background processes. You can create a new thread by specifying a method that serves as an entry point for the thread.

- You can use the *SyncLock* (Visual Basic) and *lock* (C#) keywords to restrict access to a resource to a single thread of execution.

- You must not make calls to controls from background threads. Use the *Control .InvokeRequired* property to determine if it is safe to make a direct call to a control. If invoke is required, use the *Control.Invoke* method to make a safe call to the control.

Lesson Review

The following questions are intended to reinforce key information presented in this lesson. The questions are also available on the companion CD if you prefer to review them in electronic form.

NOTE Answers

Answers to these questions and explanations of why each choice is right or wrong are located in the "Answers" section at the end of the book.

---

1. Which of the following method calls is required to execute a method asynchronously from a delegate?

    A. *Delegate.Invoke*

    B. *Delegate.BeginInvoke*

    C. *Delegate.EndInvoke*

    D. *Delegate.DynamicInvoke*

2. Which of the following are required to create and complete a background process using a *Thread* object? (Choose all that apply.)

    A. Create a new *Thread* object.

    B. Call the *Thread.Start* method to start the thread.

    C. Provide a parameter to the *Thread.Start* method.

    D. Call the *Thread.Abort* method to complete the process.

3. Which of the following can be used to make safe calls to controls from background threads? (Choose all that apply.)

    A. Nothing. Calls to controls are inherently safe.

    B. The *Control.InvokeRequired* property.

    C. The *Control.Invoke* method.

    D. The *Control.IsAccessible* property.

Chapter Review

To further practice and reinforce the skills you learned in this chapter, you can perform the following tasks:

- Review the chapter summary.
- Review the list of key terms introduced in this chapter.
- Complete the case scenarios. These scenarios set up real-world situations involving the topics of this chapter and ask you to create a solution.
- Complete the suggested practices.
- Take a practice test.

Chapter Summary

- You can maintain a responsive user interface when performing time-consuming processes by running those processes in the background. There are several ways to create a background process. Covered in this chapter were using the *BackgroundWorker* component, using delegates, and using the *Thread* class.

- The *BackgroundWorker* component allows you to specify a process to run in the background by handling the *DoWork* event. The *BackgroundWorker* process encapsulates functionality to run the background process and provide parameters to it, to indicate the completion of a background process, to cancel a background process, to report the progress of a background process, and to indicate if the process is running.

- Delegates are type-safe function pointers that allow you to call methods with the same signature. When *BeginInvoke* is called, an operation specified by the delegate is started on a separate thread. You can retrieve the result of the operation by calling *EndInvoke*, which will block the calling thread until the background process is completed.

- Thread objects represent separate threads of operation and provide for a high degree of control of background processes. You can create a new thread by specifying a method that serves as an entry point for the thread.

- You must not make calls to controls from background threads. Use the *Control .Invoke* method to make a safe call to the control.

Key Terms

- delegate
- thread

Case Scenarios

In the following case scenarios, you will apply what you've learned about asynchronous programming techniques. You can find answers to these questions in the "Answers" section at the end of this book.

Case Scenario 1: The Publishing Application

Now that the great document management application for Fabrikam, Inc. is complete, you have been asked to help design an application for distribution to their clients. This application should enable clients to download large, book-length documents from an online library while allowing the client to continue to browse the library and select other documents for download. Once download of a single document is complete, download of the next document should begin if more are selected. When download of a document is complete, the UI should be updated to reflect that.

Questions

1. What strategies can be used to coordinate document download with the UI interaction?

2. How can the UI be constantly updated without fear of deadlocks or other problems?

Case Scenario 2: Creating a Simple Game

Well, you finally have a day off from your job, so you decide to spend some time writing a nice, relaxing solitaire program. You've got the actual gameplay pretty well done and you are now just adding the bells and whistles. You would like to implement functionality that plays sounds in the background based on user interactions. These sounds are in a specialized format, and you must use a proprietary player that does not intrinsically support asynchronous play. You have a list of five possible sound files that you can play, and you would like to save time and make the coding easy on yourself.

Questions

- What is a strategy for implementing the required functionality with a minimum of complexity in your program?

Suggested Practices

To help you successfully master the exam objectives presented in this chapter, complete the following tasks.

- **Practice 1** Create an application that computes the value of pi on a separate thread and continually updates the user interface with the value in a thread-safe manner.

- **Practice 2** Create an application that uses delegates to run a process in the background that tests if a given number is a prime number and returns a Boolean value.

Take a Practice Test

The practice tests on this book's companion CD offer many options. For example, you can test yourself on just the content covered in this chapter, or you can test yourself on all the 70-526 certification exam content. You can set up the test so that it closely simulates the experience of taking a certification exam, or you can set it up in study mode so that you can look at the correct answers and explanations after you answer each question.

MORE INFO   **Practice tests**

For details about all the practice test options available, see the "How to Use the Practice Tests" section in this book's Introduction.

Chapter 14

Creating Windows Forms Controls

Controls are components that have a visible user interface presence and are capable of interacting with the user at run time. The Microsoft .NET Framework provides a variety of controls that encapsulate a wide variety of functionality. Examples of controls include the *Button* control, the *TextBox* control, and the *DateTimePicker* control. In addition to the preexisting controls, you can develop your own controls to provide specialized functionality for your applications. There are three kinds of user-created controls: composite controls, which are created by combining other Windows Forms controls; custom controls, which are created from scratch and provide their own code for drawing; and extended controls, which add functionality to a preexisting Windows Forms control. In this chapter, you will learn to create all three types of controls.

Exam objectives in this chapter:
- Create a composite Windows Forms control.
    - Create properties, methods, and events for Windows Forms controls.
    - Expose properties of constituent controls.
    - Create and use custom dialog boxes in Windows Forms applications.
    - Customize a control to paint and render.
    - Configure a control to be invisible at run time.
    - Configure a control to have a transparent background.
    - Provide a Toolbox bitmap for a control.
- Create a custom Windows Forms control by inheriting from the control class.
- Create an extended control by inheriting from an existing Windows Forms control.

Lessons in this chapter:

Before You Begin

To complete the lessons in this chapter, you must have:

- A computer that meets or exceeds the minimum hardware requirements listed in the "Introduction" at the beginning of the book.

- Microsoft Visual Studio 2005 Professional Edition installed on your computer.

- An understanding of Microsoft Visual Basic or C# syntax and familiarity with the .NET Framework.

- Completed Chapter 3, "Advanced Windows Forms Controls," or have a good understanding of Windows Forms controls and the Visual Studio IDE.

Real World

Matt Stoecker

Although the controls provided in Visual Studio 2005 cover a wide range of functionality, I find that by developing my own controls when necessary, I can create user interfaces that conform to my requirements rather than trying to bend my requirements to fit the available functionality. With custom controls, I can create exactly what I need for my user interface design.

Lesson 1: **Creating Composite Controls**

Composite controls are the simplest form of user-created controls. The composite control designer includes a graphical interface similar to a form that allows you to add preexisting controls and components, which are then bound together in a single functional unit. In this lesson, you will learn how to create a composite control as well as some general methods for control development.

After this lesson, you will be able to:

- ■ Develop a user (composite) Windows Forms control.
- ■ Create properties, methods, and events for Windows Forms controls.
- ■ Expose properties of constituent controls.
- ■ Configure a control to be invisible at run time.
- ■ Configure a control to have a transparent background.
- ■ Provide a Toolbox Bitmap for a control.

Estimated lesson time: 45 minutes

Introduction to Composite Controls

Composite controls (also known as *user controls*) are just as they sound: controls that are made up of other controls. Composite controls inherit from the *UserControl* class. The *UserControl* class provides a base level of functionality that you can build on by adding other controls as well as additional properties, methods, and events. The *UserControl* class has its own designer that allows you to use the Visual Studio Integrated Design Environment to drag additional controls from the Toolbox to the design surface and configure them. The UserControl designer is shown in Figure 14-1.

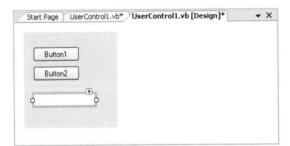

Figure 14-1 The UserControl designer

▶ **To add a composite control to a solution at design time**

1. From the Project menu, choose Add User Control. The Add New Item dialog box opens.

2. Name your control and click Add. The new control is added to the project and opened for editing in the designer.

You can create a composite control in code by inheriting from the *UserControl* class, as shown here:

```vb
' VB
Public Class myControl
   Inherits UserControl
    ' Add implementation here
End Class
```

```csharp
// C#
public class myControl : UserControl
{
    // Add implementation here
}
```

The subordinate controls that make up the composite control are called constituent controls. You can add constituent controls to your composite control in the same way that you would add a control to a form—by dragging it onto the design surface from the Toolbox. You can configure these constituent controls in the same way that you would configure them in a form—you can set properties, alter the visual appearance, and create methods that handle control events. When the composite control is built, the functionality that you have coded will be built into the composite control.

Adding Methods, Properties, and Events to Controls

In addition to adding constituent controls, you can also add additional functionality to your control in the form of methods, properties, and events.

NOTE **Classes, controls, and composite controls**

The information in this section can be applied to classes and controls of all types, not just to composite controls.

Adding Methods to a Control   You can add a method to a control in the same way that you would add a method to a form or to any other class. Within the bounds of the class declaration in the Code window, add the method declaration and the method body. For a method that does not return a value, create a *Sub* (Visual Basic) or a *void* (C#) method, as shown here:

```vb
' VB
Public Sub DisplayString(ByVal aString As String)
   Msgbox(aString)
End Sub
```

```csharp
// C#
public void DisplayString(string aString)
{
   MessageBox.Show(aString);
}
```

For methods that return a value, create a *Function* (Visual Basic) or specify the *return* type (C#), as shown in this example:

```vb
' VB
Public Function DisplayString(ByVal aString As String, ByVal bString As String) As String
   Return aString & bString
End Function
```

```csharp
// C#
public string DisplayString(string aString, string bString)
{
   return aString + bString;
}
```

Adding Properties to a Control   Adding a property is similar to adding a method. You create a property definition and then implement the functionality required to return and set the value represented by the property. Usually, the underlying value for the property is stored in a private member variable. In Visual Basic, you use the *Property* keyword to create a property. In C#, you simply implement the getter and setter for the property. The following example demonstrates how to implement a property, including a member variable to contain the value.

```vb
' VB
Private mUnitsOnHand
Public Property UnitsOnHand() As Integer
   Get
      Return mUnitsOnHand
   End Get
   Set(ByVal value As Integer)
      mUnitsOnHand = value
   End Set
End Property
```

```csharp
// C#
private int mUnitsOnHand;
public int UnitsOnHand
{
```

```
    get { return mUnitsOnHand; }
    set { mUnitsOnHand = value; }
}
```

You can create a read-only property by using the *ReadOnly* keyword in Visual Basic or by simply omitting the setter in C#. An example is shown here:

```
' VB
Private mUnitsOnHand
Public ReadOnly Property UnitsOnHand() As Integer
   Get
        Return mUnitsOnHand
   End Get
End Property
```

```
// C#
private int mUnitsOnHand;
public int UnitsOnHand
{
    get { return mUnitsOnHand; }
}
```

If creating a read-only property, you must set the member variable that represents the property's value in code.

Adding Events to a Control   You can add events to a control that can be raised to notify the rest of the application that something interesting has happened. Once an event has been added to a class or control, it can be raised in code to send a notification to the rest of the application.

In Visual Basic, you can create an event by using the *Event* keyword and specifying the name and signature of the event, as shown here:

```
' VB
Public Event Bang(ByVal decibels As Integer)
```

On the other hand, C# requires an explicit delegate to be present to specify the signature before the event keyword can be used to create a new event. The following example demonstrates how to create an event in C#:

```
// C#
public delegate void Sound(int decibels);
public event Sound Bang;
```

Note that you specify the delegate itself, not an instance of the delegate.

You can raise an event in code by using the *RaiseEvent* keyword in Visual Basic or by simply calling the Event like you would a method in C#. An example is shown here:

```
' VB
RaiseEvent Bang(100)
```

```
// C#
this.Bang(100);
```

Exposing the Properties of Constituent Controls

When constituent controls are added to a composite control, they are given an access level of Friend in by-default Visual Basic and private in C#. In both cases, the constituent controls will be inaccessible to classes in other assemblies. If you want to allow other assemblies to configure parts of the constituent controls, you must expose the properties of the constituent controls by wrapping them in a property declaration and then writing code in the composite control's property to get and set the value of the constituent control's property. For example, suppose you wanted to expose the *Back-Color* property of a constituent Button. You might create a property in the composite control called *ButtonBackColor*, in which you return the *BackColor* property of the constituent Button in the getter and set the constituent *BackColor* property of the Button in the setter. An example of how you might implement this is shown here:

```
' VB
Public Property ButtonBackColor() As System.Drawing.Color
    Get
        Return Button1.BackColor
    End Get
    Set(ByVal value As System.Drawing.Color)
        Button1.BackColor = value
    End Set
End Property
```

```
// C#
public System.Drawing.Color ButtonBackColor
{
    get { return Button1.BackColor; }
    set { Button1.BackColor = value; }
}
```

Configuring a Control to Be Invisible at Run Time

At times, you might want your control to be invisible at run time. You can create an invisible control by setting the *Visible* property to *False*. Controls that are invisible cannot interact with the user through the user interface, but they can still interact with application and other controls. The following example demonstrates how to set the *Visible* property to *False*:

```
' VB
myUserControl.Visible = False
```

```
// C
myUserControl.Visible = false;
```

Note that the *Visible* property can be set only at run time. To ensure that a control is invisible at startup, set the *Visible* property to *False* in the control's *Load* event handler.

Configuring a Control to Have a Transparent Background

When configuring your control to have a transparent background, there are two types of transparencies to consider. A control can be transparent so that the visible appearance of the form underneath the control is seen through the background of the control. A control can also appear as a transparent window through the form, displaying whatever is on the desktop beneath the form.

To create a control with a transparent background color, all you need to do is set the *BackColor* property to *Color.Transparent*. Whatever is displayed on the form beneath the control will show through the background of the control. You can set the *Back-Color* to *Transparent* in the Properties window at design time, or you can set the *Back-Color* in code, as shown here:

```
' VB
Me.BackColor = Color.Transparent
```

```
// C#
this.BackColor = Color.Transparent;
```

Creating a transparent control that acts as a window through the form is a little more complex. Each form has a property called *TransparencyKey*, which represents a color that will appear as transparent when represented on the form. By setting the *Back-Color* property of the control to the same color as the form's *TransparencyKey* property, you can create a window of transparency through the form. You can set the form's *TransparencyKey* property and the control's *BackColor* property in the Designer at design time or in code, as shown here:

```
' VB
Form1.TransparencyKey = Color.Red
myUserControl.BackColor = Color.Red
```

```
// C#
Form1.TransparencyKey = Color.Red;
myUserControl.BackColor = Color.Red;
```

Providing a Toolbox Bitmap for Your Control

After a control has been built, it automatically appears in the Toolbox if you are using it in the same solution that contains the control, or it can be added to the Toolbox if it was created in a different project. When the control is added to the Toolbox, it appears in the Toolbox as the name of the control next to an icon. If no icon is specified, a generic icon is supplied. You can specify the icon that is displayed next to the name of your control by using the *ToolboxBitmapAttribute*. You can attach instances of the *ToolboxBitmapAttribute* class to your control declaration and use it to specify a 16 by 16 pixel bitmap that will be used to represent your control in the Toolbox.

You can specify the Toolbox bitmap in three different ways. The most straightforward is to simply specify the path to the bitmap that you want to use. Here is an example of how to do this:

```
' VB
<ToolBoxBitmap("C:\myToolboxBitmap.bmp")> Class myControl
    Inherits UserControl
    ' Implementation omitted
End Class
```

```
// C#
[ToolBoxBitmap(@"C:\myToolboxBitmap.bmp")]
class myControl : UserControl
{}
```

You can also use the *ToolboxBitmap* from an existing type. For example, you could specify the same *ToolboxBitmap* as is used by the *Button* control with the following code.

```
' VB
<ToolBoxBitmap(GetType(System.Windows.Forms.Button))> Class myControl
    Inherits UserControl
    ' Implementation omitted
End Class
```

```
// C#
[ToolBoxBitmap(GetType(System.Windows.Forms.Button))]
class myControl : UserControl
{}
```

Finally, you can specify an assembly by specifying a type defined in that assembly and then load an icon resource that is specified by a string name, as shown:

```vb
' VB
<ToolBoxBitmap(GetType(myControl), "myControl.bmp")> Class myControl
    Inherits UserControl
    ' Implementation omitted
End Class
```

```csharp
// C#
[ToolBoxBitmap(GetType(myControl), "myControl.bmp")]
class myControl : UserControl
{}
```

> ## Quick Check
> 1. Briefly explain what a composite control is.
> 2. How can you expose properties of constituent controls to developers?
>
> ### Quick Check Answers
> 1. A composite control, also called a user control, is a control that is made up of other preexisting controls (called constituent controls) bound together in a single interface. Composite controls can incorporate custom functionality to enable the constituent controls to work together.
> 2. You expose properties of constituent controls to developers by wrapping them in user control properties.

Lab: Create a Composite Control

In this lab, you will create a simple composite control that acts as a digital clock. You will add a *Label* control to your composite control that displays the correct time and a *Timer* component that updates the *Label* every second. Finally, you will expose the *Enabled* property of the *Timer* control through your composite control to allow users to enable and disable the clock.

▶ **Exercise 1: Create a Digital Clock**

1. Create a new Windows Forms application in Visual Studio.
2. From the Project menu, choose Add User Control and click Add in the Add New Item dialog box. A new user control is added to your project and opens in the Designer.

3. From the Toolbox, drag a *Label* control onto the user control. Resize the user control so that it is approximately the size of the *Label* control.

4. From the Toolbox, drag a *Timer* component onto the user control.

5. In the Properties window, set the *Interval* property for the *Timer* component to *1000* and the *Enabled* property to *True*.

6. Double-click the *Timer* component to open the Code window to the default event handler for the *Timer.Tick* event and add the following line of code:

```
' VB
Label1.Text = Now.ToLongTimeString
```

```
// C#
label1.Text = DateTime.Now.ToLongTimeString();
```

7. In the Code window, add the following *Property* declaration:

```
' VB
Public Property TimeEnabled() As Boolean
   Get
       Return Timer1.Enabled
   End Get
   Set(ByVal value As Boolean)
       Timer1.Enabled = value
   End Set
End Property
```

```
// C#
public bool TimeEnabled
{
    get { return timer1.Enabled; }
    set { timer1.Enabled = value; }
}
```

8. From the File menu, choose Save All to save your solution.

9. From the Build menu, build your solution.

10. In the Designer, choose the tab for Form1. From the Toolbox, drag a UserControl1 onto the form. An instance of your user control is added to the form and begins keeping time every second. Note that you can pause it by setting the *TimeEnabled* property to *False* in the Properties window.

11. Press F5 to build and run your application. Note that the user control functions the same way at run time as it does in the Designer.

Lesson Summary

- Composite controls, also called user controls, consist of preexisting Windows Forms controls and components bound together by common functionality in a common user interface. Controls that are contained in a composite control are called constituent controls. You can add additional methods, properties, and events to a composite control to create custom functionality.

- Properties of constituent controls are not generally accessible to developers. You can expose properties of constituent controls by wrapping them in new properties of the composite control.

- You can configure a control to be invisible at run time by setting the *Visible* property to *False*. You can create a control with a transparent background by setting the *BackColor* property to *Color.Transparent*. You can create a window through the control and its owning form by setting the control's *BackColor* property to the same color as the *Form*'s *TransparencyKey* property.

- You can provide a Toolbox bitmap for a control by configuring the *ToolboxBitmap* attribute.

Lesson Review

The following questions are intended to reinforce key information presented in this lesson. The questions are also available on the companion CD if you prefer to review them in electronic form.

NOTE Answers

Answers to these questions and explanations of why each choice is right or wrong are located in the "Answers" section at the end of the book.

---

1. Which of the following are characteristics of a composite control? (Choose all that apply.)

    A. Composite controls are made up of preexisting Windows Forms controls.

    B. Composite controls can have custom functionality in the form of new methods, properties, or events.

    C. Composite controls must provide their own rendering code.

    D. Composite controls automatically expose the properties of their constituent controls as their own properties.

2. Which of the following are required to provide a Toolbox bitmap for a control? (Choose all that apply.)

   A. You must provide a 16 by 16 pixel bitmap to act as the Toolbox bitmap.

   B. You must provide a bitmap to act as the Toolbox bitmap, but size is unimportant because the .NET Framework will automatically resize it.

   C. You must set the *Image* property of the control to the appropriate bitmap for the Toolbox bitmap.

   D. You must configure the *ToolboxBitmap* attribute to specify a path, a type, or a type and a resource name.

Lesson 2: Creating Custom Controls

Custom controls provide the highest level of configurability and customization of any of the controls but are also the most time-consuming to develop. There is no default user interface for custom controls, and they must provide all of their own code required to render their graphical appearance. In addition, Designer support for custom controls is limited, allowing you to add components from the Toolbox, but not allowing any graphical design. Because of these issues, custom controls can be the most difficult type of controls to develop but are also the best choice when you want to create a control with a particularly complex visual appearance. In this lesson, you will learn to develop a custom control.

After this lesson, you will be able to:

- Develop a custom control.
- Customize a control to paint and render.

Estimated lesson time: 30 minutes

Overview of Custom Controls

When developing controls, custom controls provide the highest level of configurability. You can design a custom control to have the exact visual appearance that you desire, and you can encode whatever functionality is required to interact with the user.

The custom control Designer is significantly less detailed than the user control design. Custom controls have no default appearance, so the Designer is merely an empty gray window. You can drag components such as *Timers* or *BackgroundWorkers* from the Toolbox onto the Designer and incorporate their functionality into your control. Technically, you can also drag controls onto the Designer and incorporate them as well, but they will not be displayed as part of the custom control. If you want to incorporate preexisting controls into your control, create a user control as described in Lesson 1, "Creating Composite Controls."

Custom controls inherit from the *Control* class. The *Control* class provides a good deal of the functionality required for a control. It provides the base functionality required for the control to interact with the rest of the application. For example, it enables the control to detect the presence of the mouse, and it exposes common events such as *Click*. The *Control* class also includes properties that are useful for defining the user interface such as *ForeColor*, *BackColor*, *Visible*, *Location*, and so on. The *Control* class does not provide any specific control functionality, however.

The key development task in creating a custom control is implementation of the visible user interface. You can create the user interface by implementing the *OnPaint* method, which is called whenever the control is rendered to the screen, and it should include the code required to paint the control. Before implementation of the *OnPaint* method can be discussed, it is necessary to provide an introduction to the graphics and drawing classes of the .NET Framework.

Introduction to the *System.Drawing* Namespaces

The *System.Drawing* namespaces expose a great deal of graphics functionality. Although an exhaustive exploration of these namespaces is not possible within the context of this book, you will learn the basics of the functionality required to implement a user interface for a custom control. The general functions of the classes contained in the *System.Drawing* namespaces are summarized in Table 14-1.

Table 14-1   The *System.Drawing* Namespaces

Namespace	Contains
System.Drawing	Most of the classes involved in rendering graphic content to the screen.
System.Drawing.Design	Classes that provide additional functionality for design-time graphics operations.
System.Drawing.Drawing2D	Classes that are designed to render two-dimensional effects and advanced shapes.
System.Drawing.Imaging	Classes that facilitate manipulation and rendering of images.
System.Drawing.Printing	Classes involved in printing content.
System.Drawing.Text	Classes that facilitate manipulation of fonts.

Most of the classes you will use to render graphics for a control are provided in the *System.Drawing* and *System.Drawing.Drawing2D* namespaces.

The *Graphics* Class   The *Graphics* class is the principal class involved in rendering graphics. An instance of the *Graphics* class represents the drawing surface of a visual element such as a form or control. The *Graphics* class encapsulates the interface between the .NET Framework and the graphics rendering system and is used to render all graphics that represent the visual element.

Because a *Graphics* object must be associated with a visual element, you cannot create a *Graphics* object directly. Instead, you must obtain a reference to a *Graphics* object from the visual element that owns it. Classes that inherit from *Control* (including *Form* and any custom controls you might create) expose a *CreateGraphics* method that returns a reference to the *Graphics* object associated with the control. The following code demonstrates how to access the *Graphics* object of a control named *myControl*:

```
' VB
Dim myGraphics As System.Drawing.Graphics
myGraphics = myControl.CreateGraphics()
```

```
// C#
System.Drawing.Graphics myGraphics;
myGraphics = myControl.CreateGraphics();
```

The *Graphics* class exposes several methods that are used for rendering graphics to the drawing surface that it represents. These methods are divided into methods that are used to draw line structures and methods that are used to draw filled shapes. Some of these methods are summarized in Table 14-2 and Table 14-3.

Table 14-2   Methods for Rendering Line Structures

Method	Description
DrawArc	Draws an arc representing a portion of an ellipse
DrawClosedCurve	Draws a closed curve through a series of points
DrawCurve	Draws an open curve through a series of points
DrawEllipse	Draws an ellipse defined by a bounding rectangle
DrawLine	Draws a line connecting two points
DrawLines	Draws a series of lines connecting an array of points
DrawPath	Draws a *GraphicsPath* object, which usually represents a complex shape
DrawPie	Draws a pie shape representing a slice of an ellipse
DrawPolygon	Draws a polygon created from a series of points

Table 14-2   Methods for Rendering Line Structures

Method	Description
DrawRectangle	Draws a rectangle
DrawRectangles	Draws a series of rectangles

Table 14-3   Methods for Rendering Filled Shapes

Method	Description
FillClosedCurve	Renders a filled closed curve specified by an array of points
FillEllipse	Renders a filled ellipse
FillPath	Renders a filled *GraphicsPath* that usually represents a complex shape
FillPie	Renders a filled pie shape that represents a slice of an ellipse
FillPolygon	Renders a filled polygon specified by an array of points
FillRectangle	Renders a filled rectangle
FillRectangles	Renders a series of filled rectangles
FillRegion	Renders a filled *Region* object that usually corresponds to a complex shape

Each of these methods takes a different set of parameters that specify coordinate points and locations of the shapes to be drawn. Each method requires an object to perform the rendering. For line structures, this is a *Pen* object; for filled shapes, this is a *Brush* object.

Creating *Pen* Objects   A *Pen* is an object that is required to draw line shapes. Like a physical pen, a *Pen* object allows you to draw a line of a specified width. You can create a new instance of a pen from a specified color, as shown here:

```
' VB
Dim myPen As New Pen(Color.Tomato)
```

```
// C#
Pen myPen = new Pen(Color.Tomato);
```

By default, pens created in this manner are one pixel wide. You can also specify a width. The following example demonstrates how to create a *Pen* with a width of 3 pixels.

```
' VB
Dim myPen As New Pen(Color.Tomato, 3)
```

```
// C#
Pen myPen = new Pen(Color.Tomato, 3);
```

Creating Brushes   Like real-life paintbrushes, *Brush* objects render filled shapes and text. A *Brush* object is required for any of the *Graphics* methods that render filled shapes. Although there are several different types of *Brush* classes that can be used to render complex visual effects, the one you will use most frequently is the *SolidBrush*, which is used to render filled shapes of a solid color. The following example demonstrates how to create a *SolidBrush* from a specified color.

```
' VB
Dim myBrush As New SolidBrush(Color.Lime)
```

```
// C#
SolidBrush myBrush = new SolidBrush(Color.Lime);
```

System Brushes and Pens   You can create pens and brushes that represent the colors used by the system to render the user interface by accessing the *SystemPen* and *System-Brush* enumerations. These can be useful when you want to match the look and feel of the system settings or when designing for accessibility to ensure that high-contrast mode will be enabled. The following code example demonstrates how to obtain a reference to a *SystemPen* and *SystemBrush*.

```
' VB
Dim myPen As New Pen = SystemPens.Control
Dim myBrush As New Brush = SystemBrushes.Control
```

```
// C#
Pen myPen = SystemPens.Control;
Brush myBrush = SystemBrushes.Control;
```

Rendering Simple Shapes   You can use the methods provided by the *Graphics* object to render a variety of simple shapes, summarized in Table 14-2 and Table 14-3.

All of the methods that render line shapes require a *Pen* object. Likewise, all of the methods that render filled shapes require a *Brush* object. In addition, you must supply whatever other parameters the method requires, such as coordinates or other objects. When coordinates are specified, they are in the coordinate system of the drawing surface represented by the *Graphics* object. For example, if the *Graphics* object you are using represents a control, then the coordinate (0,0) represents the upper left-hand corner of the control. Note that these coordinates are independent of the location of the control as represented by the *Location* property because the *Location* property defines the location of the upper left-hand corner of control in the coordinate system of its container. The following example demonstrates how to render a filled ellipse using the *Graphics* object of the form.

```vb
' VB
Dim myBrush As New SolidBrush(Color.PapayaWhip)
Dim g As Graphics = Me.CreateGraphics()
Dim myRectangle As New Rectangle(0,0,10,30)
g.FillEllipse(myBrush, myRectangle)
g.Dispose()
myBrush.Dispose()
```

```csharp
// C#
SolidBrush myBrush = new SolidBrush(Color.PapayaWhip);
Graphics g  = this.CreateGraphics();
Rectangle myRectangle = new Rectangle(0,0,10,30);
g.FillEllipse(myBrush, myRectangle);
g.Dispose();
myBrush.Dispose();
```

Note that you should always call *Dispose* on your *Pen*, *Brush*, and *Graphics* objects because they consume system resources, and performance will be degraded if they are not disposed of promptly.

Rendering Text   The *Graphics* object exposes a method called *DrawString*, which can be used to render text. You must specify a font for the text as well as a location for the upper left-hand corner of the text and a *Brush* object. The following example demonstrates how to render text on a Form using the *DrawString* method.

```vb
' VB
Dim g As Graphics = Me.CreateGraphics()
Dim myString As String = "Hello World!"
Dim myFont As New Font("Times New Roman", 36, FontStyle.Regular)
' The final two parameters are the X and Y coordinates of the upper left hand
' corner of the rendered string.
g.DrawString(myString, myFont, SystemBrushes.Highlight, 20, 20)
g.Dispose()
```

```csharp
// C#
Graphics g = this.CreateGraphics();
string myString = "Hello World!";
Font myFont = new Font("Times New Roman", 36, FontStyle.Regular);
// The final two parameters are the X and Y coordinates of the upper left hand
```

```
// corner of the rendered string.
g.DrawString(myString, myFont, SystemBrushes.Highlight, 20, 20);
g.Dispose();
```

Rendering Custom Controls by Overriding the *OnPaint* Method

You can render the visual interface for a custom control by overriding the *OnPaint* method. The *OnPaint* method internally handles the *Paint* method and contains all of the code required to render the visual appearance of the control.

The *OnPaint* method has a single parameter, an instance of *PaintEventArgs*. This instance of *PaintEventArgs* contains two important members. The ClipRectangle parameter contains the rectangle in which painting will take place. The Graphics parameter contains an instance of the *Graphics* class that represents the drawing surface of the control being rendered.

When a control is drawn or refreshed, only the part of the control that needs to be refreshed is drawn. If the entire control needs to be refreshed, the *ClipRectangle* will represent the size of the entire control. If only part of the control needs to be refreshed, however, the *ClipRectangle* object will represent only the region that needs to be redrawn. For the most part, you as the developer will never need to use the *Clip-Rectangle* property—it is used automatically by the *Graphics* object.

The *Graphics* object represents the drawing surface of the control. By using the methods described in the previous section, you can render the visual appearance of the control. All of the methods that render graphics require coordinates for the location of the graphics. The upper left-hand corner of the control is (0,0), and the control is bounded by the *Control.Width* and *Control.Height* properties. The following example demonstrates how to override the *OnPaint* method and render a filled-in blue rectangle that fills the entire control.

```vb
' VB
Protected Overrides Sub OnPaint(ByVal pe As System.Windows.Forms.PaintEventArgs)
   MyBase.OnPaint(pe)
   Dim g As Graphics = pe.Graphics
   g.FillRectangle(Brushes.Blue, 0, 0, Me.Width, Me.Height)
End Sub
```

```csharp
// C#
protected override void OnPaint(PaintEventArgs pe)
{
   base.OnPaint(pe);
   Graphics g = pe.Graphics;
   g.FillRectangle(Brushes.Blue, 0, 0, this.Width, this.Height);
}
```

Note the call to *MyBase.OnPaint* (in Visual Basic) or *base.OnPaint* (in C#). When overriding a method in an inherited class, you should generally call the method in the base class to call any base implementation.

▶ **To create a custom control**

1. Add a new class to your project that inherits from the *Control* class.

2. Override the *OnPaint* method to provide custom rendering code.

3. Implement other functionality for the control.

> ## Quick Check
>
> 1. How is a custom control different from a composite control?
>
> 2. Briefly describe how the *Graphics* and *ClipRectangle* properties of *PaintEventArgs* are used in the *OnPaint* method.
>
> ### Quick Check Answers
>
> 1. A composite control provides a designer and a default visual interface and is composed of other Windows Forms controls bound together by common functionality and in a common interface. A custom control has no default visual interface and has a limited designer by default. Custom controls must provide their own rendering code and generally do not incorporate other Windows Forms controls.
>
> 2. You must override the *OnPaint* method to create the rendering code for a custom control. The *Graphics* property of *PaintEventArgs* represents the drawing surface of the custom control and exposes all of the methods required to render graphics to the user interface. The *ClipRectangle* is the rectangle that will be drawn or redrawn when the control is rendered. It is used by the *Graphics* object but generally does not need to be used by the developer.

Lab: Create a Custom Control

In this lab, you will create another digital clock. Like the control you created in the lab from Lesson 1, it will incorporate a *Timer* component to update the user interface on a regular basis. Unlike the previous lab, however, you will create your own rendering for this control instead of using a *Label* control to do so.

▶ **Exercise 1: Create Another Digital Clock**

1. Create a new Windows Forms application in Visual Studio.

2. From the Project menu, choose Add New Item. Select Custom Control in the Add New Item dialog box and click Add. A new custom control is added to your project and opens in the Designer.

3. In the Designer for CustomControl1, drag a *Timer* component from the Toolbox onto the custom control.

4. In the Properties window, set the *Interval* property for the *Timer* component to *1000* and the *Enabled* property to *True*.

5. Double-click the *Timer* component to open the Code window to the default event handler for the *Timer.Tick* event and add the following line of code.

    ```
    ' VB
    Me.Refresh()
    ```

    ```
    // C#
    this.Refresh();
    ```

6. In the Code window, add the following code to the *OnPaint* method, beneath the call to the base class's *OnPaint* method:

    ```
    ' VB
    pe.Graphics.DrawString(Now.ToLongTimeString, Me.Font, New SolidBrush(Me.ForeColor), 0,
    0)
    ```

    ```
    // C#
    pe.Graphics.DrawString(DateTime.Now.ToLongTimeString(), this.Font, new
    SolidBrush(this.ForeColor), 0, 0);
    ```

7. From the File menu, choose Save All to save your solution.

8. From the Build menu, build your solution.

9. In the Designer, choose the tab for Form1. From the Toolbox, drag a Custom-Control1 onto the form. An instance of your custom control is added to the form and begins keeping time every second.

10. Press F5 to build and run your application. Note that the user control functions the same way at run time as it does in the Designer.

Lesson Summary

- In addition to exposing custom methods, events, and properties, custom controls provide their own rendering code. You must override the *OnPaint* method to provide custom rendering code.

- The *Graphics* class represents a drawing surface and exposes a variety of methods that can be used to render graphical images. Methods that render line drawings require a *Pen* object, whereas methods that render filled shapes require a *Brush* object.

- When rendering a custom control, you use coordinates to reference points in the control. The coordinate (0,0) represents the upper left-hand corner of the control, and the coordinate represented by the (*Width*, *Height*) of the control represents the lower right-hand corner of the control.

Lesson Review

The following questions are intended to reinforce key information presented in this lesson. The questions are also available on the companion CD if you prefer to review them in electronic form.

NOTE Answers

Answers to these questions and explanations of why each choice is right or wrong are located in the "Answers" section at the end of the book.

---

1. Which of the following are true of the *Graphics* class? (Choose all that apply.)

    A. The *Graphics* class encapsulates *Pen*s and *Brush*es that can be used to render graphics.

    B. The *Graphics* class represents a drawing surface, such as one exposed by a form or control.

    C. The *Graphics* class provides a variety of methods that can be used to render line shapes and filled shapes.

    D. You can obtain a reference to an instance of the *Graphics* class by calling *Control.CreateGraphics* or from an instance of *PaintEventArgs* in the *OnPaint* method.

2. Which of the following are characteristics of custom controls? (Choose all that apply.)

   A. Custom controls must provide their own rendering code.

   B. Custom controls can incorporate other Windows Forms components.

   C. Custom controls provide a default visual interface around which the rendering code is built.

   D. Custom controls inherit from the *UserControl* class.

Lesson 3: Creating Extended Controls and Dialog Boxes

In addition to creating composite controls from other Windows Forms controls and custom controls that provide their own visual interface, you can create controls that extend other controls. You can add properties and methods to preexisting controls and, in some cases, even provide a different visual representation for a standard control (for example, a round *Button* control). In this lesson, you will learn to create extended controls and dialog boxes.

After this lesson, you will be able to:

- ■ Create and use custom dialog boxes in Windows Forms applications.
- ■ Develop an extended control (inherited from an existing Windows Forms control).

Estimated lesson time: 30 minutes

Custom Dialog Boxes

Dialog boxes are commonly used to gather information from the application user. For example, Visual Studio provides prebuilt dialog boxes that enable the user to select a file, font, or color. You can create custom dialog boxes to collect specialized information from the user. For example, you might create a dialog box that collects user information and relays it to the main form of the application.

A dialog box generally includes an OK button, a Cancel button, and whatever controls are required to gather information from the user. The general behavior of an OK button is to accept the information provided by the user and then to close the form, returning a result of *DialogResult.OK*. The general behavior of the Cancel button is to reject the user input and close the form, returning a result of *DialogResult.Cancel*.

Visual Studio .NET provides a template for dialog boxes. You can add a new dialog box to your application by selecting the Project Menu, then Add New Item, and then the Dialog Box template. Figure 14-2 shows an example of the Dialog Box template that is added to your application.

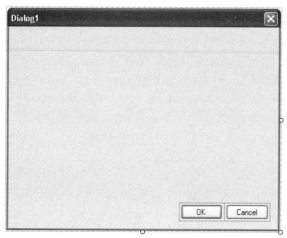

Figure 14-2   The Dialog Box template

You can set the *DialogResult* property for the OK and Cancel buttons in the Properties window. In general, you should set the *DialogResult* for the OK button to *Dialog-Result.OK* and the *DialogResult* for the Cancel button to *DialogResult.Cancel*.

Modal and Modeless Dialog Boxes

A *modal* dialog box is a dialog box that pauses program execution until the dialog box is closed. Conversely, a *modeless* dialog box allows application execution to continue.

Displaying a Dialog Box

You can display a dialog box modelessly by using the *Form.Show* method, as shown here:

```
' VB
Dim aDialog As New DialogForm()
aDialog.Show()
```

```
// C#
DialogForm aDialog = new DialogForm();
aDialog.Show();
```

When shown modelessly, a dialog box does not return a dialog result and does not halt program execution, but you can still retrieve information from the form by examining property values of the form.

You can show a dialog box modally by calling the *Form.ShowDialog* method, as shown here:

```
' VB
Dim aDialog As New DialogForm()
aDialog.ShowDialog()
```

```
// C#
DialogForm aDialog = new DialogForm();
aDialog.ShowDialog();
```

The *ShowDialog* method returns the *DialogResult* value of the button that was clicked to close the form. If the *Button.DialogResult* property is not set, it returns *Dialog-Result.None*. The following example demonstrates how to retrieve the *DialogResult* of a dialog box:

```
' VB
Dim aDialog As New DialogForm()
Dim aResult As DialogResult
aResult = aDialog.ShowDialog()
If aResult = DialogResult.OK Then
    ' Do something with the dialog box information
End If
```

```
// C#
DialogForm aDialog = new DialogForm();
DialogResult aResult;
aResult = aDialog.ShowDialog();
if (aResult == DialogResult.OK)
{
    // Do something with the dialog box information
}
```

Setting the *ParentForm* Property of the Dialog Box

You can also set the *ParentForm* property of the dialog box with the *ShowDialog* method by specifying the parent form as a parameter, as shown in the following example:

```
' VB
Dim aDialog As New DialogForm()
Dim aResult As DialogResult
aResult = aDialog.ShowDialog(Me)
```

```
// C#
DialogForm aDialog = new DialogForm();
DialogResult aResult;
aResult = aDialog.ShowDialog(this);
```

Retrieving Information from the Parent Form

Once the parent form has been set, you can retrieve information from it by casting the *ParentForm* property to the appropriate type and then reading its properties, as shown in the following example. This example assumes an instance of a dialog box called *DialogForm* and that the *ParentForm* property has been set to an instance of a form called Form1.

```vb
' VB
Dim aForm As Form1
aForm = CType(DialogForm.ParentForm, Form1)
' You can now read the information of the parent form
```

```csharp
// C#
Form1 aForm;
aForm = (Form1)DialogForm.ParentForm;
// You can now read the information of the parent form
```

Once a dialog box has been closed it is no longer visible to the user, but its instance remains in memory. You can then retrieve the user input from the dialog box.

Retrieving Dialog Box Information by Using Properties

In general, user input from the dialog box should be exposed through properties of the dialog box. For example, a dialog box that allows the user to input a first name should expose that information through a *FirstName* property. The following example demonstrates how to create a property for a dialog box that takes the user input from a TextBox called txtFirstName and exposes it as a read-only property called First-Name.

```vb
' VB
Public ReadOnly Property FirstName() As String
    Get
        Return txtFirstName.Text
    End Get
End Property
```

```csharp
// C#
public string FirstName
{
    get
    {
        return txtFirstName.Text;
    }
}
```

You can then read the property in the dialog box to retrieve the first name, as shown here:

```
' VB
Dim name As String
name = DialogBox.FirstName
```

```
// C#
string name;
name = DialogBox.FirstName;
```

Creating Extended Controls

Extended controls are user-created controls that extend a preexisting .NET Framework control. By extending existing controls, you can retain all of the functionality of the control but add properties, methods and, in some cases, alter the rendered appearance of the control.

Extending a Control

You can create an extended control by creating a class that inherits the control in question. The following example demonstrates how to create a control that inherits the *Button* class:

```
' VB
Public Class ExtendedButton
    Inherits System.Windows.Forms.Button
End Class
```

```
// C#
public class ExtendedButton : System.Windows.Forms.Button
{}
```

The *ExtendedButton* class created in the previous example has the same appearance, behavior, and properties as the *Button* class, but you can now extend this functionality by adding custom properties or methods. For example, the following demonstrates adding a property called *ButtonValue* that returns an integer.

```
' VB
Public Class ExtendedButton
    Inherits System.Windows.Forms.Button
    Private mValue As Integer
    Public Property ButtonValue() As Integer
    Get
        Return mValue
```

```
      End Get
      Set(ByVal Value As Integer)
         mValue = Value
      End Set
End Class
```

```
// C#
public class ExtendedButton : System.Windows.Forms.Button
{
    int mValue;
    public int ButtonValue
    {
        get
        {
            return mValue;
        }
        set
        {
            mValue = value;
        }
    }
}
```

Overriding Methods

In addition to adding new methods and properties to your control, you can also provide a new implementation for existing methods by overriding. Overriding allows you
to substitute your own implementation for the base implementation of a method or to
add additional functionality to the functionality that is already there. The following
demonstrates how to override the *OnClick* method in a class that inherits from Button.
The new implementation increments a variable called *Clicks* and then calls the base
implementation of *OnClick*.

```
' VB
Protected Overrides Sub OnClick(ByVal e As System.EventArgs)
    Clicks += 1
    MyBase.OnClick(e)
End Sub
```

```
// C#
protected override void OnClick(System.EventArgs e)
{
    Clicks++;
    base.OnClick(e);
}
```

Altering the Appearance of an Inherited Control

For some controls, you can change the visual appearance of the control by overriding the *OnPaint* method. This allows you to either add to or replace the rendering logic of the control. To add to the default rendering of the control, you should call the *MyBase.OnPaint* (Visual Basic) or *base.OnPaint* (C#) method to call the base class's rendering code in addition to your own. To provide a completely custom appearance for the control, you can omit the call to the base class's *OnPaint* method. The following example demonstrates how to create a simple elliptical button. Note, however, that it changes only the shape of the control and does not address subtler rendering tasks such as outlining.

```vb
' VB
Protected Overrides Sub OnPaint(ByVal pevent As System.Windows.Forms.PaintEventArgs)
   Dim x As New System.Drawing.Drawing2D.GraphicsPath
   x.AddEllipse(0, 0, Me.Width, Me.Height)
   Me.Region = New Region(x)
   MyBase.OnPaint(pevent)
End Sub
```

```csharp
// C#
protected overrides void OnPaint(System.Windows.Forms.PaintEventArgs pevent)
{
    System.Drawing.Drawing2D.GraphicsPath x = new System.Drawing.Drawing2D.GraphicsPath();
    x.AddEllipse(0, 0, this.Width, this.Height);
    this.Region = new Region(x);
    base.OnPaint(pevent);
}
```

> ## Quick Check
> 1. How can you retrieve the dialog result of a dialog box?
> 2. Briefly describe how to create an extended control.
>
> ### Quick Check Answers
> 1. You can retrieve the dialog result of a dialog box by creating a variable of type *DialogResult* and assigning to it the value returned by the *ShowDialog* method of the dialog box.
> 2. You can create an extended control by creating a class that inherits a preexisting control. After the extended control has been created, you can add properties and methods as well as override methods in the base class.

Lab: Create an Extended Control

In this lab, you will create a new control by extending the *Button* control. You will create a new button with a property that counts the number of clicks the button receives and displays that number in the lower right-hand corner of the button.

▶ **Exercise 1: Create an Extended *Button* Control**

1. Create a new Windows Forms application in Visual Studio.

2. From the Project menu, choose Add Class. Name the class *ClickButton* and click Add.

3. Modify the class declaration to make ClickButton inherit from the *Button* class, as shown here:

    ```vb
    ' VB
    Public Class ClickButton
        Inherits System.Windows.Forms.Button
    End Class
    ```

    ```csharp
    // C#
    public class ClickButton : System.Windows.Forms.Button
    {}
    ```

4. Add the following member variable and property to the code window to create the *Clicks* property.

    ```vb
    ' VB
    Private mClicks As Integer
    Public ReadOnly Property Clicks() As Integer
        Get
            Return mClicks
        End Get
    End Property
    ```

    ```csharp
    // C#
    int mClicks;
    public int Clicks
    {
        get { return mClicks; }
    }
    ```

5. Override the *OnClick* method to increment the private variable *mClicks* every time the button is clicked, as shown here:

    ```vb
    ' VB
    Protected Overrides Sub OnClick(ByVal e As System.EventArgs)
        mClicks += 1
        MyBase.OnClick(e)
    End Sub
    ```

```csharp
// C#
protected override void OnClick(EventArgs e)
{
    mClicks++;
    base.OnClick(e);
}
```

6. Override the *OnPaint* method to render the number of clicks in the bottom right-hand corner of the control as shown here:

```vb
' VB
Protected Overrides Sub OnPaint(ByVal pevent As System.Windows.Forms.PaintEventArgs)
    MyBase.OnPaint(pevent)
    Dim g As Graphics = pevent.Graphics
    Dim stringsize As SizeF
    stringsize = g.MeasureString(Clicks.ToString, Me.Font, Me.Width)
    g.DrawString(Clicks.ToString, Me.Font, SystemBrushes.ControlText, _
        Me.Width - stringsize.Width - 3, Me.Height - stringsize.Height - 3)
End Sub
```

```csharp
// C#
protected override void OnPaint(System.Windows.Forms.PaintEventArgs pevent)
{
    base.OnPaint(pevent);
    System.Drawing.Graphics g = pevent.Graphics;
    System.Drawing.SizeF stringsize;
    stringsize = g.MeasureString(Clicks.ToString(), this.Font, this.Width);
    g.DrawString(Clicks.ToString(), this.Font,
        System.Drawing.SystemBrushes.ControlText, this.Width -
        stringsize.Width - 3, this.Height - stringsize.Height - 3);
}
```

7. From the File menu, choose Save All to save your solution.

8. From the Build menu, build your solution.

9. In the Designer, select the tab for Form1.

10. From the Toolbox, drag an instance of ClickButton onto the form, and resize it to make it slightly larger.

11. Press F5 to compile and run your application.

12. In the form, click the ClickButton. Note that the number of clicks is displayed in the lower right-hand corner.

Lesson Summary

- Dialog boxes are special forms that are designed to collect information from the user. Dialog boxes can be displayed either modally or modelessly. Modal dialog boxes halt program execution until the dialog box is closed, whereas modeless dialog boxes allow program execution to continue while they are displayed.

- You can use the *ShowDialog* method to set the parent form of a dialog box. You can then retrieve information from the parent form by casting the reference to the parent form to the appropriate type.

- You can create an extended control by creating a class that inherits a preexisting control. Extended controls encapsulate all of the functionality of the inherited control. In addition, you can create new properties, methods, and events for an inherited control or override existing methods to replace preexisting functionality.

- You can alter the appearance of an extended control by overriding the *OnPaint* method. You should call the base class's *OnPaint* method to provide rendering for the base class or omit the call to the base class's *OnPaint* method to provide a completely different rendition for the control.

Lesson Review

The following questions are intended to reinforce key information presented in this lesson. The questions are also available on the companion CD if you prefer to review them in electronic form.

NOTE Answers

Answers to these questions and explanations of why each choice is right or wrong are located in the "Answers" section at the end of the book.

---

1. Which of the following code samples correctly demonstrates how to retrieve the dialog result for a dialog box?

   A. ```
       ' VB
       Dim aResult As DialogResult
       aResult = DialogForm.Show()

       // C#
       DialogResult aResult;
       aResult = DialogForm.Show();
       ```
       ```

B.   ' **VB**
```
Dim aResult As DialogResult
aResult = DialogForm.ShowDialog()
```

```
// C#
DialogResult aResult;
aResult = DialogForm.ShowDialog();
```

C.   ' **VB**
```
Dim aResult As DialogResult
aResult = DialogForm.Show(Me)
```

```
// C#
DialogResult aResult;
aResult = DialogForm.Show(this);
```

D.   ' **VB**
```
Dim aResult As DialogResult
aResult = DialogForm.ShowDialog(DialogResult.OK)
```

```
// C#
DialogResult aResult;
aResult = DialogForm.ShowDialog(DialogResult.OK);
```

2. Which of the following are required to create an extended control?

  A. You must override the *OnPaint* method to provide custom rendering.

  B. You must provide a Toolbox bitmap for the new control.

  C. You must inherit from a preexisting control.

  D. You must expose any necessary properties of the inherited control by wrapping them in new properties.

Chapter Review

To further practice and reinforce the skills you learned in this chapter, you can perform the following tasks:

- Review the chapter summary.
- Review the list of key terms introduced in this chapter.
- Complete the case scenarios. These scenarios set up real-world situations involving the topics of this chapter and ask you to create a solution.
- Complete the suggested practices.
- Take a practice test.

Chapter Summary

- Composite controls, also called user controls, consist of preexisting Windows Forms controls and components bound together by common functionality in a common user interface. Controls that are contained in a composite control are called constituent controls. You can expose properties of constituent controls by wrapping them in new properties of the composite control. You can provide a Toolbox bitmap for a control by configuring the *ToolboxBitmap* attribute.

- The *Graphics* class represents a drawing surface and exposes a variety of methods that can be used to render graphical images. Custom controls must provide their own rendering code. You must override the *OnPaint* method to provide custom rendering code. When rendering a custom control, you use coordinates to reference points in the control.

- Dialog boxes are special forms that are designed to collect information from the user. Dialog boxes can be displayed either modally, which halts program execution, or modelessly, which allows execution to proceed. You can use the *Show-Dialog* method to display a dialog box modally and set the parent form of a dialog box. You can create properties in the dialog box to expose the information collected from the user.

- You can create an extended control by creating a class that inherits a preexisting control. Extended controls encapsulate all of the functionality of the inherited control. In addition, you can create new properties, methods, and events for an inherited control or override existing methods to replace preexisting functionality. You can alter the appearance of an extended control by overriding the *OnPaint* method.

Key Terms

- composite control
- custom control
- extended control
- modal
- modeless
- user control

Case Scenarios

In the following case scenarios, you will apply what you've learned about how to use controls to design user interfaces. You can find answers to these questions in the "Answers" section at the end of this book.

Case Scenario 1: Collecting and Displaying User Data

You've been tasked with the job of designing the user interface of a simple application that accepts input from the user, stores it in a database, and then displays that user input. The key requirements for this project, however, are consistency and code reuse. The look and feel of the user input portion of the application must be the same as the look and feel of the display portion, but the display must be read-only. In addition, several other applications of this sort are planned, and a consistent look and feel is required for all of them with a minimum of developer hours.

Questions

Answer the following questions for your manager:

1. What strategies can you use to build the UI with an eye toward consistency and code reuse?

2. How can you create a read-only display and a read-write input while maintaining the goal of code reuse?

Case Scenario 2: Trey Research Stock Price

The people at Trey Research are very preoccupied with their stock price. So preoccupied, in fact, that they check their stock price online with such frequency that it is starting to have an impact on job performance. As a solution, management would like to create a way to display the stock price graphically and in real time on all the internal Windows Forms applications that they use. You are provided with access to a Web service that provides streaming updates of the stock price.

Technical Requirements

- Stock price must be displayed both as an actual number and as a chart that is updated throughout the day.

- Stock price must be updated in real time every 15 seconds.

- It must be easy to integrate this functionality with a variety of Windows Forms applications.

Questions

- How can this functionality be implemented?

Suggested Practices

- Create a dialog box that collects user information such as first name, last name, address, Zip code, and phone number and exposes that information as properties. Then create a dialog box that collects the same information but exposes the information as a single instance of a class that encapsulates all of that information.

- Extend the composite control created in the lab in Lesson 1 to create an alarm clock that has a property that represents the time an alarm is sounded, allows the user to snooze or reset the alarm, and actually sounds an alarm when that time occurs.

- Create a *Shape* control that draws a simple shape on the screen and allows the user to choose between rectangle, ellipse, triangle, and other simple geometric forms. The control should be fully configurable with regard to color and size.

- Extend the *Button* control to create a round or elliptical button. Implement rendering code to render shading and the appropriate behavior when clicked, using the shading and behavior of the rectangular *Button* control as a guide.

Take a Practice Test

The practice tests on this book's companion CD offer many options. For example, you can test yourself on just the content covered in this chapter, or you can test yourself on all the 70-526 certification exam content. You can set up the test so that it closely simulates the experience of taking a certification exam, or you can set it up in study mode so that you can look at the correct answers and explanations after you answer each question.

MORE INFO   Practice tests

For details about all the practice test options available, see the "How to Use the Practice Tests" section in this book's Introduction.

Chapter 15
Deployment

Once development of your application is complete, it must reach the intended audience. Microsoft Visual Studio provides several methods for deploying your application. ClickOnce technology allows you to quickly and easily deploy your application and provide for automatic updates. For more detailed deployments, Windows Installer technology provides a highly configurable deployment environment. In this chapter, you will learn how to deploy your applications using ClickOnce and Windows Installer technology.

Exam objectives in this chapter:
- Configure the installation of a Windows Forms application by using ClickOnce technology.
  - ❑ Install a Windows Forms application on the client computer by using ClickOnce deployment.
  - ❑ Install a Windows Forms application from a server by using ClickOnce deployment.
  - ❑ Configure the required permissions of an application by using ClickOnce deployment.
- Create a Windows Forms setup application.
  - ❑ Create a Windows Forms application setup project.
  - ❑ Set deployment project properties.
  - ❑ Configure a setup project to add icons during setup.
  - ❑ Configure conditional installation based on operating system versions.
  - ❑ Configure a setup project to deploy the .NET Framework.
- Add functionality to a Windows Forms setup application.
  - ❑ Add a custom action to a setup project.
  - ❑ Add error-handling code to a setup project for custom actions.

664 Chapter 15 Deployment

Lessons in this chapter:

- Lesson 1: Deploying Applications with ClickOnce 665
- Lesson 2: Creating Setup Projects for Deployment. .672

Before You Begin

To complete the lessons in this chapter, you must have:

- A computer that meets or exceeds the minimum hardware requirements listed in the "Introduction" at the beginning of the book.

- Visual Studio 2005 Professional Edition installed on your computer.

- An understanding of Microsoft Visual Basic or C# syntax and familiarity with the Microsoft.NET Framework.

Real World

Matt Stoecker

Deployment can pose some difficult challenges to the developer. I find that it is especially difficult to deploy applications that require frequent updates. ClickOnce addresses this problem and allows me to deploy applications that are updated regularly. And for complex deployments, I still like to use Windows Installer technology, which provides the greatest degree of control and customization.

Lesson 1: Deploying Applications with ClickOnce

ClickOnce is a new deployment technology from Microsoft that has been developed to address several problems with deployment, namely, difficulty in providing regular updates, the inability of nonadministrative users to install applications, and the dependence of multiple programs on shared components. ClickOnce addresses all of these problems and allows you to create a deployment strategy that is easily update-able, isolated from other applications, and installable by nonadministrative users.

After this lesson, you will be able to:

- ■ Install a Windows Forms application on the client computer by using ClickOnce.
- ■ Install a Windows Forms application from a server by using ClickOnce.
- ■ Configure the required permissions of an application by using ClickOnce.

Estimated lesson time: 30 minutes

Overview of ClickOnce

ClickOnce is a new deployment technology that allows you to create self-updating applications that can be installed from a variety of sources and require minimal user interaction. Any Windows Forms application can be published as a ClickOnce application. You can use ClickOnce to create applications that are deployed from a Web site, a file share, or a CD-ROM. You can configure ClickOnce applications to be run only while the user is online or while the user is offline.

You can configure ClickOnce applications to be self-updating. When configured for updates, ClickOnce applications will automatically check for updates at the location from which they were installed and will automatically download updates if they exist.

ClickOnce applications are isolated from the rest of the system. Because they are completely self-contained, they share no components with the rest of the applications installed on the computer and run no risk of breaking other applications' installations. ClickOnce applications, by default, run in the Internet or intranet security zones when run from the remote location, or under full trust if installed on the local computer. Additional permissions, if required, can be requested by the application, giving the installer the opportunity to grant or deny those permissions.

Publishing a ClickOnce Application

You can configure the properties for a ClickOnce application by right-clicking the solution in Solution Explorer, choosing Properties, and then selecting the Publish tab. This displays the Publish properties page, shown in Figure 15-1.

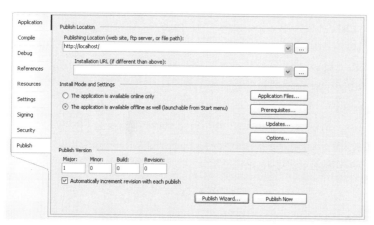

Figure 15-1   The Publish properties page

You can configure the properties for your deployment strategy in this window. Once your properties have been configured, you can publish your application by clicking the Publish Now button.

Specifying the Publishing Location   You can specify the publishing location in the Publishing Location combo box. This should be a file path, a network share, a Hypertext Transfer Protocol (HTTP) address, or a File Transfer Protocol (FTP) address. This is generally the address to which users will go to install the application. You can optionally specify an installation URL for users to install the application from. This is only needed if the ClickOnce application is staged on a different server than the installation location.

Configuring the Install Mode   You can configure a ClickOnce application to be available only when the user is online or when the user is online or offline. By selecting The Application Is Available Online Only in the Install Mode And Settings group of the Publish properties page, you require the application to be run directly from the location specified in the Publishing Location combo box. You can also select The Application Is Available Offline As Well to make the application available offline. In this case, the application will be copied to the local computer and added to the Start menu and the Add/Remove Programs box in the Control Panel.

Configuring Automatic Updates You can configure ClickOnce applications to automatically check for updates. By clicking the Updates button in the Publish properties page, you can open the Application Updates dialog box, shown in Figure 15-2.

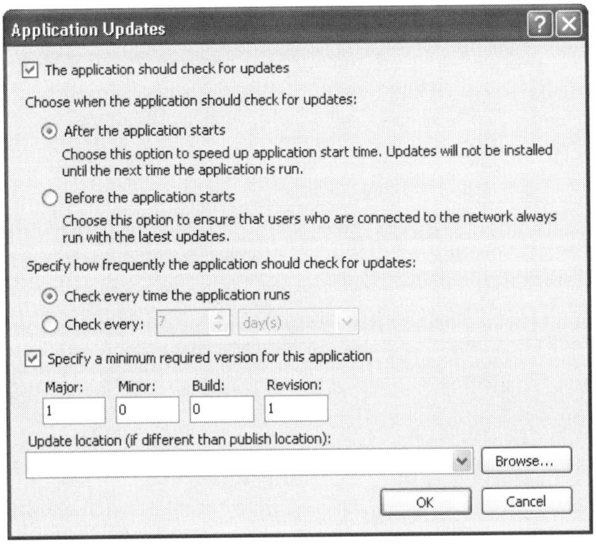

Figure 15-2   The Application Updates dialog box

To enable the application to check for updates, select the check box labeled The Application Should Check For Updates. Doing so enables the other options in the dialog box. You can specify when the application checks for updates by selecting either After The Application Starts or Before The Application Starts. If you select Before The Application Starts, the application will check for new updates every time the application is started. This ensures that the user is always running the most recent version, but it also takes more time at startup. If you select After The Application Starts, you can specify that the application check for updates every time it is run, or at a designated time interval, by choosing the appropriate option under Specify How Frequently The Application Should Check For Updates. You can also specify a minimum required version for the application, and you can specify a different location for updates if your updates will be hosting in a location other than the install location.

Configuring Required Permissions for a ClickOnce Application

By default, ClickOnce applications run from the Internet run in the Internet security zone, and ClickOnce applications run from a file share run in the intranet security zone. For some applications, you might require additional permissions for the application to run. You can configure ClickOnce permissions on the Security tab of the project properties pages. The Security page is shown in Figure 15-3.

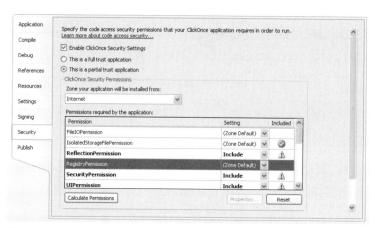

Figure 15-3   The Security properties page

You can either manually select permissions to be granted to the application, or you can calculate the permissions required by the application and configure the application to request those permissions.

▶ **To calculate permissions for a ClickOnce application**

1. On the Security properties page, select the check box labeled Enable ClickOnce Security Settings.

2. Choose the radio button labeled This Is A Partial Trust Application.

3. Click the button labeled Calculate Permissions.

4. The permissions required by your application are added to the permissions that will be requested by your application upon install.

▶ **To manually configure permissions for a ClickOnce application**

1. On the Security properties page, select the check box labeled Enable ClickOnce Security Settings.

2. Choose the radio button labeled This Is A Partial Trust Application.

3. In the Permissions Required By The Application table, find the permission of interest.

4. In the Setting column, choose Include to include the permission as required or Exclude to not require the permission.

Note that any permissions not included in the zone permission set under which the application is installed must be approved by the user before installation is completed.

Installing a ClickOnce Application on a Client Computer

Installing a ClickOnce application is almost as simple as the name implies.

▶ **To install a ClickOnce Application from a Web site**
1. Navigate to the Publish.htm Web page for the ClickOnce application.
2. Click Install and follow the steps (if any) in the Install wizard.

▶ **To install a ClickOnce Application from a file share**
1. Navigate to the file share for the ClickOnce application.
2. Double-click Setup and follow the steps (if any) in the Install wizard.

Quick Check
1. To what locations can you publish a ClickOnce application?
2. How can you determine the required permissions for a ClickOnce application?

Quick Check Answers
1. You can publish a ClickOnce application to a file path, a network share, an HTTP address, or an FTP address.
2. You can determine the required permissions for a ClickOnce application by going to the Security properties page, enabling ClickOnce security settings, setting the application to partial trust, and clicking the Calculate Permissions button. The permissions required by the application will be calculated automatically.

Lab: Publish an Application to a Network Share with ClickOnce

In this lab, you will publish an application to a network share using ClickOnce. You will create a shared folder on your computer, configure that install and those download locations, and then publish the application and download it using ClickOnce.

NOTE Exercise prerequisites

Your computer must be on a network, or you must have run network setup to complete this lesson.

▶ **Exercise 1: Publishing an Application to a Network Share**

1. In the root directory, create a shared directory named C:\ClickOnce.

2. From the Code folder on the companion CD, open the partial solution for Chapter 15, "Deployment." Note that you will use the same partial solution for both Lesson 1 and Lesson 2.

3. In Solution Explorer, right-click the project and then click Properties. Select the Publish tab.

4. In the Publish Location group, set the Publishing Location to C:\ClickOnce.

5. Also in the Publish Location group, set the Installation Location to \\[*computername*]\ClickOnce, where [*computername*] is the name of your computer.

6. Click Publish Now to publish your application to the network share. ClickOnce verifies application requirements and publishes the application. The Publish.htm file opens.

7. Open the C:\ClickOnce folder and then double-click Setup. You might see a security warning; if so, click Install. The application is installed and opens on your computer. Notice that a new group is added to your Start menu.

8. From the Windows Start menu, open the Control Panel and select Add/Remove Programs. Click the icon for your application and select Change/Remove. Follow the on-screen instructions to remove the application from your computer.

Lesson Summary

- ClickOnce is a powerful new deployment technology that enables developers to quickly and reliably publish applications to Web sites, file shares, or FTP sites.

- ClickOnce applications can be configured to automatically find and install updates. You can configure an application to look for updates every time it is run or at a predetermined interval.

- By default, ClickOnce applications are run under the Internet security zone if downloaded from the Web or under the intranet security zone if downloaded from a file share. If additional permissions are required, they can be set by the developer, either manually or by calculating the required permission set, and they can then be approved or denied by the installer.

- Installing a ClickOnce application is as simple as clicking the Setup file or the Install button on a Web page and following the instructions.

Lesson Review

The following questions are intended to reinforce key information presented in this lesson. The questions are also available on the companion CD if you prefer to review them in electronic form.

NOTE Answers

Answers to these questions and explanations of why each choice is right or wrong are located in the "Answers" section at the end of the book.

---

1. Which of the following are required to install an application that has been published to a server for distribution by using ClickOnce technology?

    A. You must manually configure permissions.

    B. You must click the setup project.

    C. You must specify how frequently to check for updates.

    D. You must configure the install mode.

2. What is the default security mode that a ClickOnce application run from an Internet Web page will run under?

    A. Full trust

    B. Intranet zone

    C. Internet zone

    D. Custom zone

Lesson 2: Creating Setup Projects for Deployment

Whereas ClickOnce provides simple and easy deployment for a variety of applications, you might need a more configurable environment for complex programs. *Setup projects* allow you to create highly configurable deployment plans. In this lesson, you will learn how to create a setup project.

After this lesson, you will be able to:

- Create a Windows Forms Application setup project.
- Set Deployment project properties.
- Configure Setup to add icons during setup.
- Configure conditional installation based on operating system versions.
- Configure a setup project to deploy the .NET Framework.
- Add a custom action to a setup project.
- Add error-handling code to a setup project for custom actions.

Estimated lesson time: 45 minutes

Setup Projects

You can add a setup project to a solution to create a Microsoft Installer application for your solution. Setup projects are highly configurable and allow you to create directories on the target computer, copy files, modify the registry, and execute custom actions during installation. When compiled, a setup project produces an .msi file, which incorporates a setup wizard for the application. The .msi file can be distributed by disk, download, or file share. When clicked, the .msi file will launch the application setup wizard and install the application.

▶ **To add a setup project to your solution**

1. From the File menu, choose Add and then New Project to open the Add New Project dialog box.

2. In the Project Types pane, expand Other Project Types and then click Setup And Deployment.

3. In the Templates pane, click Setup Project and then click OK.

Setup Project Editors

Each setup project includes six editors that allow you to configure the contents and the behavior of the setup project. These editors are:

- **File System Editor**   Allows you to configure the installation of your application to the file system of the target computer.
- **Registry Editor**   Allows you to write entries to the registry upon installation.
- **File Types Editor**   Allows you to set associations between applications and file types.
- **User Interface Editor**   Allows you to edit the user interface seen during installation for both regular installation and administrative installation.
- **Custom Actions Editor**   Allows you to define custom actions to be performed during installation.
- **Launch Conditions Editor**   Allows you to set conditions for launching the installation of your setup project.

Adding Files to a Setup Project with the File System Editor

The File System Editor represents the file system on the target computer. You can add output files to various directories, create new directories on the target computer, or create and add shortcuts to the target computer. Figure 15-4 shows the File System Editor.

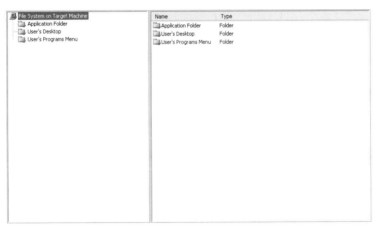

Figure 15-4   The File System Editor

The File System Editor is split into two panes. The left pane represents the directory structure of the target computer. Each folder in the left pane represents a folder on the target computer that exists or will be created by the setup application. The right pane displays the contents of the directory that is selected in the left pane. Initially, the File System Editor consists of three folders: the Application Folder, the User's Desktop, and the User's Program Menu. You can change the folder for a particular file by selecting the file in the right pane and dragging it to the appropriate folder.

You can add additional folders to the File System Editor by right-clicking the left pane and choosing Add Special Folder. The shortcut menu pictured in Figure 15-5 appears. Using this menu, you can add a special folder to the File System Editor or create your own custom folder. If you choose a custom folder, this folder will be created in the target computer's file system upon installation.

Figure 15-5   The Add Special Folder shortcut menu

▶ **To add output from a project to a deployment project**

1. Right-click Application Folder in the left-hand pane of the File System Editor, choose Add, and then choose Project Output. The Add Project Output Group dialog box (pictured in Figure 15-6) opens.

Figure 15-6   The Add Project Output Group dialog box

2. Choose the project outputs that you want to add to your setup project. All .exe and .dll files created by the project are contained in Primary Output. You can also add additional project files to your setup project, such as localized resources, content files, or documentation files, or, less frequently, debug symbols, source files, or XML serialization assemblies. Once you have selected the output to be added to the folder, click OK.

▶ **To create a shortcut and add it to the target computer**

1. In the right-hand pane of the File System Editor, right-click the file for which you want to create a shortcut and choose Create Shortcut. A shortcut to the file is created and added to the pane.

2. Drag the shortcut from the right-hand pane to the appropriate folder in the left-hand pane.

Configuring the Setup Project to Add an Icon During Setup

You can use the File System Editor to associate an icon with your application at install. Shortcuts to your application will be displayed with the icon you specify.

▶ **To associate an icon with an application at setup**

1. In the File System Editor, right-click a folder and choose Add and then select File. The Add Files dialog box opens.

2. Browse to the .ico file you want to associate with a shortcut and click Add to add it to your setup project.

3. Create a shortcut to your application as previously described.

4. In the File System Editor, select the shortcut.

5. In the Properties window, select the *Icon* property and then choose (Browse...). Browse to the icon you want to associate with your application.

6. Select the icon and click OK.

Configuring Conditional Installation Based on the Operating System Version

You can use the system property *VersionNT* to determine the operating system at install time. This allows you to create install conditions that allow the installation to proceed or abort based on the operating system.

The *VersionNT* property is an integer that is calculated by the following formula: MajorVersion * 100 + MinorVersion. Thus, Microsoft Windows 2000 would report a *VersionNT* value of 500 or greater, based on the minor version.

▶ **To configure conditional installation based on the operating system version**

1. In the File System Editor, select the file that contains the primary output for the application.

2. In the Properties window, select the *Condition* property and type a condition that evaluates the operating system based on the formula previously described. For example, if you want to restrict installation to Windows 2000 or later, you would type a condition that read VersionNT>=500.

Setting Setup Project Properties

The setup project properties provide information about your project and set actions relating to versions of your project. The setup project properties are set in the Properties window. Many setup project properties can provide descriptive information about your application. These properties include:

- *AddRemoveProgramsIcon*   Specifies an icon for the Add/Remove Programs dialog box on the client computer.
- *Author*   Contains information about the author of the program.
- *Description*   Contains a description of the application.
- *Keywords*   Contains keywords to be associated with the application.
- *Localization*   Provides the locale information for the application.

- *Manufacturer*   Contains information about the manufacturer of the application. Is commonly used to define the default install folder within the Program Files folder.
- *ManufacturerURL*   Contains the URL of the manufacturer's Web site.
- *ProductName*   Contains the name of the product.
- *Subject*   Contains information about the subject of the application.
- *SupportPhone*   Provides a phone number for support for the application.
- *SupportURL*   Contains a URL for support for the application.
- *TargetPlatform*   Specifies the target platform of the installer: x86, x64, or Itanium.
- *Title*   Contains the title of the application.

Other properties of the setup project are used to determine the behavior of the setup project at install time. These properties include:

- *DetectNewerInstalledVersion*   Looks for a more recent version of the application on the target computer and aborts the installation if one is found.
- *InstallAllUsers*   Specifies whether the package is installed for all users or for only the installing user.
- *PostBuildEvent*   Specifies a command line that is executed after the build ends.
- *PreBuildEvent*   Specifies a command line that is executed before the build begins.
- *RemovePreviousVersion*   Looks for earlier versions of the application and uninstalls them in favor of the new version if one is found.
- *RunPostBuildEvent*   Specifies the condition under which the post-build event runs. The value is either *On Successful Build* or *Always*.
- *SearchPath*   Specifies the path that is used to search for assemblies, files, or merge modules on the development computer.
- *Version*   Holds the information used by the previous two properties to determine versioning.

There are two additional properties: *ProductCode* and *UpgradeCode*. These are used by the setup program and should never be altered manually.

You can change these properties at design time by selecting the project in Solution Explorer and altering the appropriate property in the Properties window.

Configuring a Deployment Project to Deploy the .NET Framework

All applications created with Visual Studio 2005 require .NET Framework 2.0 to run. If you are uncertain of the deployment environment for your applications, you can configure your setup project to install prerequisites such as the .NET Framework as part of the installation. The .NET Framework is configured to be installed by default, but the following procedure allows you to verify that this configuration is still valid.

▶ **To configure a deployment project to deploy the .NET Framework**

1. In Solution Explorer, select the deployment project.

2. From the Project menu, click Properties. The Property Pages dialog box opens.

3. In the Properties dialog box, click Prerequisites to open the Prerequisites dialog box.

4. If it is not already selected, select the check box labeled Create Setup Program To Install Prerequisite Components.

5. In the Choose Which Prerequisites To Install list, select the check box labeled .NET Framework 2.0.

6. In the group labeled Specify The Install Location For Prerequisites, select the radio button labeled Download Prerequisites From The Component Vendor's Web Site.

7. Click OK, and then click OK again in the Property Pages dialog box.

Custom Actions

Custom actions are an advanced installation technology. With the Custom Actions Editor, you can configure code to be executed during installation. Custom action code must be contained in an *Installer* class. You can use custom actions to execute code upon four *Installer* events: *Install, Commit, Rollback,* or *Uninstall.* Install actions occur after the files have been installed but before the installation has been committed. Commit actions occur when an installation is committed on the target machine. Rollback actions are executed when an installation fails and is rolled back, and Uninstall actions are executed when an application is being uninstalled. You can use the Custom Actions Editor, shown in Figure 15-7, to associate code with these Windows Installer events.

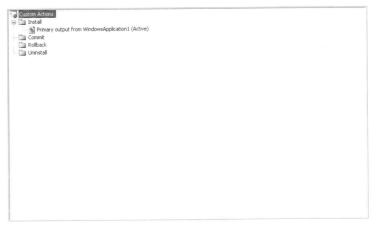

Figure 15-7 The Custom Actions Editor

Any executable code can be executed as a custom action as long as it is contained in an *Installer* class. (Although, technically, it is possible to configure a custom action in code other than an *Installer* class, this text will limit discussion of custom actions to *Installer* classes.) You can add a new custom action in the Custom Action Editor by right-clicking the event in which you want your custom action to run and choosing Add Custom Action from the context menu. This opens the Select Item In Project dialog box, which allows you to select an item in your project to set as a custom action. A new custom action representing the item you selected is added to your setup project.

For the item you select to function as a custom action, it must contain an *Installer* class. *Installer* classes expose methods such as *Install*, *Rollback*, *Uninstall*, and *Commit* that are used by the setup project to execute custom actions. These methods are present in the base *Installer* class and must be overridden in the *Installer* class you create to contain a custom action. For example, the following code example demonstrates how to override the *Install* method of an *Installer* class:

```vb
' VB
Public Overrides Sub Install(ByVal stateSaver As System.Collections.IDictionary)
   MyBase.Install(stateSaver)
      ' Insert code for the custom action here
End Sub
```

```csharp
// C#
public override void Install(System.Collections.IDictionary stateSaver)
{
    base.Install(stateSaver);
    // Insert code for your custom action here
}
```

You can write code for any or all of these methods, but code written in an *Installer* class will not be executed unless the project that contains it has been designated as a Custom Action. Note that the *Installer* class must be added to the project you want to deploy, not to the setup project itself.

▶ **To add an *Installer* class to your project**

  1. In Solution Explorer, select the project that you want to add the *Installer* class to. Note that this should be the project you want to deploy, not the setup project itself.

  2. From the Project menu, select Add New Item and then choose Installer Class in the Add New Item dialog box and click OK.

You can configure the custom action by setting the properties in the Properties window. Custom action properties are shown in Table 15-1.

Table 15-1   Properties of Custom Actions

Property	Description
(Name)	This is the name of the selected custom action.
Arguments	Supplies any required command-line arguments to the application represented by the custom action. This property is applicable only when the custom action is implemented as an executable (.exe).
Condition	Enters a Boolean statement that will be evaluated before the custom action is executed. If the statement is true, the custom action will execute. If the statement is false, the action will not execute. You can use the *Condition* property to evaluate properties chosen in custom dialog boxes.
CustomActionData	Passes any additional required data to the custom action.
EntryPoint	Specifies the name of the method to execute for the custom action. If left blank, the custom action will attempt to execute a method with the same name as the event with which the custom action is associated (for example, *Install*). This property applies only to custom actions implemented in DLLs and is ignored when the *InstallerClass* property is set to *True*.

Table 15-1   **Properties of Custom Actions**

Property	Description
InstallerClass	A Boolean value that represents whether your custom action is implemented in an *Installer* class. This property must be true if the custom action is implemented in an *Installer* and false if it is not.
SourcePath	Contains the actual path on the developer's computer to the file that implements the custom action. This property is read-only.

▶ **To create a custom action**

1. Write, test, and debug the code for the custom action you want to add to your setup project.

2. Add an *Installer* class to the solution you want to deploy.

3. Add the code written in step 1 to the appropriate overridden method (e.g., *Install*, *Rollback*, *Commit*, or *Uninstall*) of the *Installer* class.

4. From the View menu, choose Editors, Custom Actions Editor.

5. Right-click the installation event that you want to associate with your custom action and choose Add Custom Action. The Select Item In Project window opens.

6. Browse to the file that implements your custom action and select it.

7. In the Properties window, configure the properties of the custom action.

Handling Errors in Custom Actions

Although most errors in deployment are handled by Windows Installer, you must write error-handling code to trap errors in custom actions. Because custom actions are executed code, errors that occur and are not handled can cause unexpected results on installation. Use *Try...Catch* blocks to catch and correct any errors that can be corrected. If an error occurs that cannot be corrected, such as a missing file, throw a new *InstallException*. Throwing an *InstallException* will cause the installation to be rolled back without leaving any lasting effect on the system. The following example demonstrates how to test for the existence of a file and throw a new *InstallException* if the file is not found.

```
' VB
Dim myInfo As New System.IO.FileInfo("aFile.txt")
If Not myInfo.Exists Then
```

```
    Throw New System.Configuration.Install.InstallException("File not found")
End If
```

```
// C#
System.IO.FileInfo myInfo = new System.IO.FileInfo("aFile.txt");
if(!(myInfo.Exists))
    throw new System.Configuration.Install.InstallException("File not found");
```

Quick Check

1. How can you associate an icon with an application?

2. How can you roll back installation of a setup project in a custom action?

Quick Check Answers

A. You can associate an icon with your application by creating a shortcut in the File System Editor and then setting the shortcut's *Icon* property to the icon you want to associate with your application. The icon will be automatically added as the shortcut.

B. By throwing an *InstallException*. Custom actions that encounter unrecoverable errors should throw *InstallException* to roll back the installation and prevent harm to the system.

Lab: Create a Setup Project

In this lab, you will create a setup project for the same application that you installed in Lesson 1, "Deploying Applications with ClickOnce." You will use the File System Editor to install files to different directories and create a custom action that displays a message box at install time.

▶ **Exercise 1: Use the File System Editor and Create a Custom Action**

1. From the Code folder on the companion CD, open the partial solution for Chapter 15.

2. From the File menu, choose Add and then choose New Project. The Add New Project dialog box opens.

3. Expand Other Project Types, select Setup and Deployment, and then select Setup Project. Click OK. The Setup Project opens to the File System Editor.

4. In the File System Editor, right-click Application Folder, choose Add, and then choose Project Output.

5. In the File System Editor, right-click the left-hand pane, choose Add Special Folder, and then choose Custom Folder to add a custom folder.

6. In the Add Project Output Group dialog box, select your project and choose Primary Output. Click OK.

7. In the File System Editor, select Custom Folder #1. In the Properties window, set the *DefaultLocation* property to C:\.

8. In the File System Editor, right-click Custom Folder #1, choose Add, and then choose File. Browse to the folder that contains your partial solution and select myFile.txt. Click Open.

9. In Solution Explorer, select your application project (Chapter15BothLabsVB-Partial or Chapter15BothLabsCSPartial).

10. From the Project menu, choose Add New Item. In the Add New Item dialog box, select Installer Class. Then click Add.

11. In the Code Editor, add the following code to override the *Install* method of the *Installer* class.

```
' VB
Public Overrides Sub Install(ByVal stateSaver As System.Collections.IDictionary)
    MyBase.Install(stateSaver)
    MsgBox("Install custom action executed")
End Sub

// C#
public override void Install(System.Collections.IDictionary stateSaver)
{
    base.Install(stateSaver);
    System.Windows.Forms.MessageBox.Show("Install custom action executed");
}
```

12. In Solution Explorer, right-click Installer1 and select View Code to open the Code Editor.

13. In Solution Explorer, right-click Setup1, choose View, and then choose Custom Actions.

14. In the Custom Actions Editor, right-click Install and choose Add Custom Action to open the Select Item In Project dialog box.

15. In the Select Item In Project dialog box, double-click Application Folder and select Primary Output from [*application*], where [*application*] is the project that contains your *Installer* class.

16. From the Build menu, choose Configuration Manager. Make certain that both projects are selected in the Build column and click Close.

17. From the Build menu, choose Build Solution to build your solution.

18. Close Visual Studio. In Windows Explorer, navigate to your solution folder.

19. Open the Setup1\Debug folder and double-click Setup1 to install your application. Follow the instructions in the wizard. Note that a message box appears when the custom action is executed.

20. Navigate to the folder in which you installed your application and double-click your application. It opens and runs.

Lesson Summary

- Setup projects allow you to create Windows Installer applications that you can use to install your solutions. Windows Installer projects are highly configurable and allow a great deal of control over the configuration of the install process.

- Setup projects provide several editors that allow you to edit aspects of the install process, including the File System Editor, the Registry Editor, the File Types Editor, the User Interface Editor, the Custom Actions Editor, and the Launch Conditions editor.

- The File System Editor is used to add output from your projects and other files to your setup project. The File System Editor can create directories on the target system and can install files to those directories. You can also use the File System Editor to install shortcuts and associate icons with your application and install files conditionally, based on the operating system.

- The setup project has several properties that expose descriptive information about the application and affect the behavior of the setup project at install time. You can change these properties by selecting the setup project and changing them in the Properties window.

- Custom actions are code that is executed at install time or uninstall time. You can create a custom action by writing custom code in an *Installer* class, adding the *Installer* class to the project that you want to create a setup application for, and then, finally, designating the project that exposes the custom action in the Custom Actions Editor.

- When errors that are unrecoverable occur in a custom action, you should throw an *InstallException* to roll back installation without damaging the target system.

Lesson Review

The following questions are intended to reinforce key information presented in this lesson. The questions are also available on the companion CD if you prefer to review them in electronic form.

NOTE Answers

Answers to these questions and explanations of why each choice is right or wrong are located in the "Answers" section at the end of the book.

---

1. Which setup project editor is used to add project outputs to a setup project?

    A. File System Editor

    B. File Types Editor

    C. Custom Actions Editor

    D. User Interface Editor

2. Which of the following is an appropriate install condition if you want to restrict installation to Windows 2000 or later?

    A. VersionNT=500

    B. VersionNT>=500

    C. VersionNT<=500

    D. VersionNT<>500

3. Which of the following are required to execute a custom action upon installation of your setup project? (Choose all that apply.)

    A. You must add an *Installer* class to your setup project.

    B. You must add an *Installer* class to the project you want to deploy as a custom action.

    C. You must write your custom action in the *Install* method of an *Installer* class.

    D. You must specify the project that contains the custom action in the Custom Actions Editor.

Chapter Review

To further practice and reinforce the skills you learned in this chapter, you can perform the following tasks:

■ Review the chapter summary.

■ Review the list of key terms introduced in this chapter.

■ Complete the case scenarios. These scenarios set up real-world situations involving the topics of this chapter and ask you to create a solution.

■ Complete the suggested practices.

■ Take a practice test.

Chapter Summary

■ ClickOnce is a powerful new deployment technology that enables developers to quickly and reliably publish applications to Web sites, file shares, or FTP sites. They can be configured to automatically find and install updates and run under default security settings. If additional security permissions are required, they can be set by the developer, either manually or by calculating the required permission set, and they can then be approved or denied by the installer. Installing a ClickOnce application is as simple as clicking the Setup file or the Install button on a Web page and following the instructions.

■ Setup projects allow you to create Windows Installer applications that you can use to install your solutions. Windows Installer projects are highly configurable and allow a great deal of control over the configuration of the install process. The File System Editor is used to add output from your projects and other files to your setup project. The setup project has several properties that expose descriptive information about the application and affect the behavior of the setup project at install time. You can create a custom action by writing custom code in an *Installer* class and adding the *Installer* class to the project that you want to create a Setup application for and then, finally, designating the project that exposes the custom action in the Custom Actions Editor. When errors that are unrecoverable occur in a custom action, you should throw an *InstallException* to roll back installation without damaging the target system.

Key Terms

Do you know what these key terms mean? You can check your answers by looking up the terms in the glossary at the end of the book.

- ClickOnce
- Custom Action
- InstallException
- setup project

Case Scenarios

In the following case scenarios, you will apply what you've learned about deployment. You can find the answers to these questions in the "Answers" section at the end of this book.

Case Scenario 1: Distributing the Document Viewer

Well, here it is! All your work for Fabrikam, Inc., on its document viewer has come to fruition, and the application is ready to distribute to clients! The clients are very excited because this application will allow them to browse and read Fabrikam's massive online library. Unfortunately, the picture is not so rosy. The viewer is full of bugs, and Fabrikam's clients cannot wait any longer. You have to release the buggy version, even though you have a team working around the clock to fix these bugs.

Key Requirements

- You must release the buggy version now.
- You must provide updates that incorporate bug fixes as quickly as possible.
- This application must be installable by the end user who does not have administrative privileges.

Questions

- What is a deployment strategy that will accomplish all of the key requirements?

Case Scenario 2: Installing the Document Core

Fabrikam has decided to make its document server and core database available for sale to some of its higher-end clients, allowing them to host the document library on their own system instead of having to access Fabrikam's. You have been tasked with determining a distribution strategy. You will need to install the server application, create a new directory structure and registry keys, and check for prerequisite files in the install phase.

Questions

- What is a deployment strategy that can accomplish all of these goals?

Suggested Practices

To help you successfully master the exam objectives presented in this chapter, complete the following tasks.

- **Practice 1**   Publish your favorite application to a Web site and a file share using ClickOnce. Experiment with expanded permission requirements and update schedules.

- **Practice 2**   Expand on the lab in Lesson 2, "Creating Setup Projects for Deployment," to include an icon for your application and a custom action that tests for a condition and aborts if the condition is not found.

Take a Practice Test

The practice tests on this book's companion CD offer many options. For example, you can test yourself on just the content covered in this chapter, or you can test yourself on all the 70-526 certification exam content. You can set up the test so that it closely simulates the experience of taking a certification exam, or you can set it up in study mode so that you can look at the correct answers and explanations after you answer each question.

MORE INFO   Practice tests

For details about all the practice test options available, see the "How to Use the Practice Tests" section in this book's Introduction.

Answers

Chapter 1: Lesson Review Answers

Lesson 1

1. **Correct Answer: D**

    A. **Incorrect.** There is no *CreateForm* method on a *Form* class. A new form is created by using the *New* keyword.

    B. **Incorrect.** You must create a new instance of Form1 with the *New* keyword before calling methods on that instance.

    C. **Incorrect.** *myForm* is not declared, and you cannot assign an instance variable to a class, although in Microsoft Visual Basic, "Form1" would return the default instance of Form1.

    D. **Correct.** *myForm* is correctly declared and instantiated.

2. **Correct Answer: C**

    A. **Incorrect.** You must supply the new path as a parameter in the *Region* constructor.

    B. **Incorrect.** You must set the *Region* to the new instance of the path.

    C. **Correct.** This code snippet creates an elliptical GraphicsPath and then creates a new region from that GraphicsPath and assigns it to the *Region* property of the Form.

    D. **Incorrect.** You cannot set the *Region* property to a GraphicsPath. You must first create a new *Region* from the GraphicsPath.

3. **Correct Answer: A**

    A. **Correct.** All properties are set to appropriate values.

    B. **Incorrect.** The *FormBorderStyle* property should be set to a member of the *FormBorderStyle* enumeration, not to a string.

    C. **Incorrect.** The *Opacity* property should be set to a value between *0* and *1*, not to a string value, and the form's *Size* property should be set to a new instance of the *Size* structure.

    D. **Incorrect.** The *Opacity* property should be set to a value between *0* and *1*, not to a string value.

Lesson 2

1. **Correct Answer: C**

   A. **Incorrect.** The *Button* class does not expose a *SetFlowBreak* method.

   B. **Incorrect.** Flow breaks are set by the *FlowLayoutPanel*, not by the hosted control.

   C. **Correct.** Use the *SetFlowBreak* method to set a flow break.

   D. **Incorrect.** You cannot access contained controls as members of a container control.

2. **Correct Answer: D**

   A. **Incorrect.** The *TableLayoutPanel* is best for organizing controls in a tabular style. Although it might be a good choice for a single set of properties, it is not a good choice for separating groups.

   B. **Incorrect.** The *FlowLayoutPanel* is best for organizing controls that re-orient themselves in response to resizing of the control, but it is not a good choice for presenting multiple groups of controls.

   C. **Incorrect.** The *GroupBox* is best used for presenting radio buttons that provide the user with exclusive choices between two or more options.

   D. **Correct.** The *TabControl* is best used for organizing related controls into individual related groups.

3. **Correct Answers: A, B, C, and D**

   A. **Correct.** Each of these methods is valid.

   B. **Correct.** Each of these methods is valid.

   C. **Correct.** Each of these methods is valid.

   D. **Correct.** Each of these methods is valid.

4. **Correct Answer: B**

   A. **Incorrect.** You cannot add a type to the controls collection. You must create an instance of the control first.

   B. **Correct.** You must first instantiate the control and then add it to the form's controls collection.

   C. **Incorrect.** The *Add* method is a member of the *Form.Controls* collection, not a member of Form itself.

D. **Incorrect.** The *Add* method is a member of the *Form.Controls* collection, not a member of Form itself.

5. **Correct Answer: D**

   A. **Incorrect.** You cannot add panels to the *SplitContainer* control.

   B. **Incorrect.** You cannot add panels to the *SplitContainer* control.

   C. **Incorrect.** You cannot add panels to the *SplitContainer* control.

   D. **Correct.** You cannot add additional panels to the *SplitContainer* control, although you can add new panels to the individual *SplitterPanel* controls.

Chapter 1: Case Scenario Answers

Case Scenario 1: Designing a User Interface

The *SplitContainer* control can be used to simulate the look and feel of Web page frames by creating a visible, resizable division in the UI. Each *SplitterPanel* control in the *SplitControl* can then host additional container controls. A *FlowLayoutPanel* control will reproduce the flow-style layout of a Web page, and controls that appear in tables can be reproduced in *TableLayoutPanel* controls.

Case Scenario 2: Designing a Web Browser

The *TabContainer* control can be used to display multiple pages of information and allow the user to switch between pages while keeping the information static. You can create a *TabControl* control with a *TabPage* that contains the *WebBrowser* control. When a new Web page is required, you can add an additional *TabPage* to the *TabControl*, which will allow the user to navigate to a new Web page without losing the current one.

Chapter 2: Lesson Review Answers

Lesson 1

1. **Correct Answers: A and D**

   A. **Correct.** You can resize controls by grabbing and dragging the edges.

   B. **Incorrect.** You cannot alter individual controls from the View menu.

C. **Incorrect.** Smart tags do not appear on all controls and generally do not allow you to resize controls when they are present.

D. **Correct.** You can directly modify the *Size* property in the Properties window.

2. **Correct Answers: A, B, and C**

A. **Correct.** You can set the *Location* property in the Properties window.

B. **Correct.** Grabbing the control and repositioning it with the mouse is the most natural way to relocate a control.

C. **Correct.** The Layout toolbar allows you to adjust the spacing and alignment of controls on your form.

D. **Incorrect.** There is no Location window.

3. **Correct Answer: C**

A. **Incorrect.** The control will maintain a constant distance from the top edge.

B. **Incorrect.** The control will maintain a constant distance from the top and bottom edges.

C. **Correct.** The control is not anchored to any edge and will float when the form is resized.

D. **Incorrect.** The control will maintain a constant distance from the right and left edges.

4. **Correct Answer: B**

A. **Incorrect.** This setting will dock the control to the top edge of the control.

B. **Correct.** A value of *Fill* will cause the control to fill the form or container control.

C. **Incorrect.** The dock property can be set to only a single value. A value of *Top, Left, Bottom, Right* is invalid.

D. **Incorrect.** The *Anchor* property does not allow you to fill a Form or container control.

Lesson 2

1. **Correct Answers: A and C**

A. **Correct.** The *Click* event responds to the left click of the mouse as well as to some keyboard events if the button has the focus.

B. **Incorrect.** The *LinkClicked* event exists in the *LinkLabel* control but not in the *Button* control.

C. **Correct.** The *MouseDown* event can respond to any button that a mouse has.

D. **Incorrect.** The *MouseOver* event does not respond to clicks.

2. **Correct Answer: D**

A. **Incorrect.** The *FlatAppearance.MouseOverBackColor* property controls the *BackColor* of the button when the mouse pointer is on the button.

B. **Incorrect.** The *FlatAppearance.MouseDownBackColor* property controls the *BackColor* of the button when the mouse clicks the button.

C. **Incorrect.** The *FlatAppearance.BorderSize* property controls the width of the border when *FlatStyle* is set to *Flat*.

D. **Correct.** The appearance of the text does not change when the *FlatStyle* property is set to *Flat*.

3. **Correct Answers: A, B, and C**

A. **Correct.** You must set the *TabOrder* property, the *UseMnemonic* property, and the *Text* property with appropriate values.

B. **Correct.** You must set the *TabOrder* property, the *UseMnemonic* property, and the *Text* property with appropriate values.

C. **Correct.** You must set the *TabOrder* property, the *UseMnemonic* property, and the *Text* property with appropriate values.

D. **Incorrect.** The *CausesValidation* property is not required to create an access key.

4. **Correct Answers: A and C**

A. **Correct.** The *ActiveLinkColor* property determines the color of the link when clicked.

B. **Incorrect.** *LinkLabel_LinkClicked* is the event that is raised when the link is clicked, but it does not, in and of itself, affect the color of the link.

C. **Correct.** The *VisitedLinkColor* determines the color of the link after the *LinkVisited* property is set to *True*.

D. **Incorrect.** The *LinkBehavior* property affects how the link is underlined, but it does not affect the color.

Lesson 3

1. **Correct Answer: D**

    A. **Incorrect.** The *MultiLine* property allows you to enter and display multiple lines but has no effect on the actual length of text entry.

    B. **Incorrect.** The *WordWrap* property affects how text is displayed in a multi-line text box but has no impact on the maximum length of the string.

    C. **Incorrect.** The *ScrollBars* property influences whether scroll bars are displayed but does not affect the maximum length of the text.

    D. **Correct.** The *MaxLength* property is the only property that affects the maximum length of the *Text* property.

2. **Correct Answer: C**

    A. **Incorrect.** The 9 character indicates an optional numeric character in the *MaskedTextBox*. All entries for a social security number should be required.

    B. **Incorrect.** The 9 character indicates an optional numeric character in the *MaskedTextBox*. All entries for a social security number should be required. Additionally, the slash (/) character represents a date separator and is inappropriate in this context.

    C. **Correct.** The zero (0) character indicates a required numeric character. Additionally, the hyphen (-) is a literal character that is traditional for formatting social security numbers.

    D. **Incorrect.** The slash (/) character represents a date separator and is inappropriate in this context. The hyphen (-) character literal is more appropriate.

3. **Correct Answer: B**

    A. **Incorrect.** If the *CutCopyMaskFormat* property is set to *ExcludePromptAndLiterals*, the hyphen (-) literal character will be excluded. If the *TextMaskFormat* property is set to *IncludeLiterals*, the hyphen (-) literal character will not be excluded from the *Text* property.

    B. **Correct.** The *CutCopyMaskFormat* property should be set to *IncludeLiterals* to include the literal characters, and the *TextMaskFormat* property should be set to *ExcludePromptAndLiterals* to exclude all but the user input.

    C. **Incorrect.** If the *CutCopyMaskFormat* property is set to *ExcludePromptAndLiterals*, the hyphen (-) literal character will be excluded. If the *TextMaskFormat* property is set to *IncludePrompt*, the hyphen (-) literal character will be excluded from the *Text* property, but any prompt characters that remain in the *MaskedTextBox* will be incorporated into the *Text* property as well.

    D. **Incorrect.** If the *TextMaskFormat* property is set to *IncludeLiterals*, the hyphen (-) literal character will not be excluded from the *Text* property.

Chapter 2: Case Scenario Answers

Case Scenario 1: Designing a Simple User Interface

You can use *TextBox* controls to receive input for the interest rate and time span parameters and a *MaskedTextBox* that uses the currency symbol for the current investment value parameter. Labels should be used to clearly identify each input control.

You can set the *TabOrder* property for each control to provide an ordered means of navigating with the *Tab* key. In addition, you can use the *Label* controls to create access keys for the *TextBox* and *MaskedTextBox* controls in your user interface.

Case Scenario 2: Designing a User Interface

For the name and address fields, *TextBox* controls are most appropriate. For fields that have a defined format, such as Zip Code and credit card number, use *MaskedTextBox* controls. A multiline text box will make general comments easier to enter and read. Labels should be used to clearly name each control.

By setting the *PasswordChar* property of the *MaskedTextBox*, you can keep the credit card information from displaying inappropriately. Although this might make it more difficult to ensure that the correct data was entered, the problem could be overcome by requiring that this data be entered twice and that both entries match.

Chapter 3: Lesson Review Answers

Lesson 1

    1. **Correct Answers: B and C**

        A. **Incorrect.** The *IndexOf* method returns the index of an object to which you have a reference but does not detect selected objects.

        B. **Correct.** The *SelectedIndex* property will return the selected index. Note that if more than one item is selected, this property might return any of them.

C. **Correct.** The *SelectedIndices* property will return all selected indexes.

D. **Incorrect.** The *Select* method will programmatically select an object in the *ListBox* but does not detect which index is selected.

2. **Correct Answer: D**

A. **Incorrect.** The *Items.Add* method adds a specified item to the *Items* collection.

B. **Incorrect.** The *Items.Insert* method adds a specified item to the *Items* collection at a specified index.

C. **Incorrect.** The *Items.AddRange* method can be used to add an array of objects to the *Items* collection.

D. **Correct.** The *Items.Contains* method is used to determine if a collection contains a specified item, not to add items to a collection.

3. **Correct Answer: C**

A. **Incorrect.** Setting the *View* property to *LargeIcon* displays the *ListViewItems* with their associated large icons.

B. **Incorrect.** Setting the *View* property to *Details* will display the *ListViewItems* with its associated *SubItems*.

C. **Correct.** The *ListView* property cannot be used for displaying hierarchical data. For items with a tree structure, use the *TreeView* control.

D. **Incorrect.** Setting the *View* property to *SmallIcon* displays the *ListViewItems* with their associated small icons.

Lesson 2

1. **Correct Answers: B and E**

A. **Incorrect.** The *Checked* property is a Boolean value and can be only *True* or *False*. The *CheckState* property can be set to *Checked*, however.

B. **Correct.** The *Checked* property is a Boolean value and can be only *True* or *False*.

C. **Incorrect.** The *Checked* property is a Boolean value and can be only *True* or *False*. The *CheckState* property can be set to *Indeterminate*, however.

D. **Incorrect.** The *Checked* property is a Boolean value and can be only *True* or *False*. The *CheckState* property can be set to *Unchecked*, however.

E. **Correct.** The *Checked* property is a Boolean value and can be only *True* or *False*.

F. **Incorrect.** The *Checked* property is a Boolean value and can be only *True* or *False*. No property of the *CheckBox* control can be set to *NotChecked*.

2. **Correct Answers: A, C, and D**

A. **Correct.** The *MaxSelectionCount* property determines the number of days that can be chosen in the *SelectionRange* property.

B. **Incorrect.** The *SelectionRange* property will be set to a new value when the user chooses dates, so setting it at design time will not facilitate this scenario.

C. **Correct.** The *MinDate* property determines the earliest date that can be chosen, so setting it to the first day of the month in question will prevent the user from choosing any date before this day.

D. **Correct.** The *MaxDate* property determines the latest date that can be chosen, so setting it to the last day of the month in question will prevent the user from choosing any date after this day.

3. **Correct Answers: C and D**

A. **Incorrect.** The *Image* property directly sets an image for the control and cannot be set to an *ImageList*.

B. **Incorrect.** The *ImageKey* property takes a string and indicates the key for the image in the associated *ImageList* component. You cannot set the *ImageKey* property to a value of *Image*.

C. **Correct.** You can set the *ImageList* property of the control to the *ImageList* in question and set the *ImageIndex* property to the index of the image in the *ImageList.Items* collection.

D. **Correct.** You can set the *ImageList* property of the control to the *ImageList* in question and set the *ImageKey* property to the key of the image in the *ImageList.Items* collection.

Lesson 3

1. **Correct Answers: A, B, and C**

A. **Correct.** The *Print* method prints the current document.

B. **Correct.** The *ShowPrintDialog* method displays the print dialog box and allows the user to set options before printing.

C. **Correct.** The *ShowPrintPreview* method displays the print preview dialog box and allows the user to preview the document before printing.

D. **Incorrect.** The *ShowPropertiesDialog* method displays the properties for the current document but does not facilitate printing.

2. **Correct Answers: A, B, and C**

A. **Correct.** The *BalloonTipIcon* property can be set to *Error*, *Warning*, or *Info*, which can set the level of warning for the *BalloonTip*.

B. **Correct.** The *BalloonTipText* property can provide detailed information about the problem to the user and suggest a possible remedy.

C. **Correct.** The *BalloonTipTitle* property can provide a clear indication of the problem to the user.

D. **Incorrect.** The *Text* property is displayed when the user mouses over the *NotifyIcon* in the system tray and should not be used for displaying critical information.

3. **Correct Answers: B, C, and D**

A. **Incorrect.** Although the access key will not function if the control is not enabled, setting the *Enabled* property to *False* does not prevent the creation of an access key at design time.

B. **Correct.** The *Text* property allows the user to define the key that is to be the access key.

C. **Correct.** The *UseMnemonic* property indicates that the control should use the key preceded by the ampersand (&) symbol in the *Text* property as the access key.

D. **Correct.** If the control cannot inherently receive the focus, you cannot create an access key for it.

Chapter 3: Case Scenario Answers

Case Scenario 1: Incorporating List-Based Controls into the User Interface

The primary control of this user interface would be the *TreeView* control, which can be used to display hierarchical information, such as an organization chart, to the user. Individual nodes in the organization can be expanded or collapsed, and the user can easily browse the interface. You can use other controls to display detailed information about a selected employee.

You can create an *ImageList* that contains icon photos of each employee and set the *ImageList* property of the *TreeView* to read these images. By setting the *ImageKey* or *ImageIndex* property of each *TreeNode*, an individual icon will be displayed in the *TreeView*. In the details view, you can use the *PictureBox* control to display a full-size image.

Case Scenario 2: Working with Files and Background Processes

The *NotifyIcon* component can be used to inform the user without creating an obtrusive user interface. An icon in the system tray will let the user know the application is running. If there is a problem, this can be communicated to the user through the balloon tip. The *BalloonTipIcon* property can be set to the appropriate level (*Error*, *Warning*, or *Info*), and additional information can be provided to the user through the *BalloonTipText*.

If launching the user interface is required, we can enable that by associating a *ContextMenuStrip* with the *NotifyIcon*. The user can right-click the *NotifyIcon* and choose a command from the context menu.

The *WebBrowser* component contains all of the functionality necessary to examine, print, and save files. We can design the interface so that the user can view the file in the *WebBrowser* and then call the *WebBrowser.Print* or *WebBrowser.ShowSaveAsDialog* methods as necessary to print and save the document.

Chapter 4: Lesson Review Answers

Lesson 1

A. **Correct Answer: B**

A. **Incorrect.** The *ToolStrip* class does not have a *Merge* method. You must use the *ToolStripManager* class.

B. **Correct.** Use the static *ToolStripManager* class to merge tool strips.

C. **Incorrect.** The *ToolStripManager* class is static and, thus, cannot be instantiated.

D. **Incorrect.** The *ToolStrip* class does not have a *Merge* method. You must use the *ToolStripManager* class.

B. **Correct Answer: A**

   A. **Correct.** Use the *Add* method of the *Items* collection to add a new item at run time.

   B. **Incorrect.** The *ToolStripManager* class is used to manage the tool strips themselves, not the items they contain.

   C. **Incorrect.** The *ToolStrip* class contains a single collection, *Items*, for all the tool strip items and does not contain a separate collection for each type of tool strip item.

   D. **Incorrect.** Use the *Items.Add* method to add a new item. There is no *Items.NewItem* method.

Lesson 2

1. **Correct Answer: C**

   A. **Incorrect.** *ToolStripMenuItem* controls have no *UseMnemonic* property and create access keys automatically when a letter is preceded by an ampersand.

   B. **Incorrect.** *ToolStripMenuItem* controls have no *AccessKeys* property and create access keys automatically when a letter is preceded by an ampersand.

   C. **Correct.** *ToolStripMenuItem* controls create access keys automatically when a letter is preceded by an ampersand.

   D. **Incorrect.** The *ShortcutKeys* property creates shortcut keys, which provide direct access to the command. Access keys are defined by preceding a letter in the *Text* property with an ampersand.

2. **Correct Answer: D**

   A. **Incorrect.** The *ToolStripManager* does not contain a *Menus* collection.

   B. **Incorrect.** The *ToolStripManager.Merge* method is used for merging two tool strips or menus, not for adding a menu to a form.

   C. **Incorrect.** The *ToolStripManager* does not contain a *Controls* collection.

   D. **Correct.** To add a menu to a form at run time, you add it through the form's *Controls* collection.

3. **Correct Answer: A**

   A. **Correct.** All that is required to enable a context menu for a control is to set that control's *ContextMenuStrip* property.

   B. **Incorrect.** Controls do not have a *ShowPopUp* property.

      C. **Incorrect.** *ContextMenuStrip* controls do not have a *ShowPopUp* method.

      D. **Incorrect.** *ContextMenuStrip* controls do not have a *Control* property.

Lesson 3

  1. **Correct Answers: A, B, C, and D**

      A. **Correct.** The *Control* property returns a Boolean value that indicates if the *Ctrl* key has been pressed.

      B. **Correct.** The *KeyCode* property returns a value representing the code of the key that has been pressed. The *Ctrl* key will send a code to this property.

      C. **Correct.** The *KeyData* property returns data representing all keys and modifiers that have been pressed.

      D. **Correct.** The *Modifiers* property returns all of the modifier keys that have been pressed.

  2. **Correct Answer: C**

      A. **Incorrect.** In Visual Basic, you use the standalone keyword *AddHandler* to add an event handler at run time. However, AddHandler is not a method. In C#, you use the += operator, but you must specify the event name, not the name of the event handler.

      B. **Incorrect.** In Visual Basic, you must use the *AddressOf* operator to create a delegate at run time to assign to an event. In C#, you must use the += operator to add an event handler.

      C. **Correct.** In Visual Basic, you use the standalone keyword *AddHandler* to add an event handler at run time. In C#, you use the += operator.

      D. **Incorrect.** In Visual Basic, you use the standalone keyword *AddHandler* to add an event handler at run time, not *AddressOf*. In C#, you use the += operator, not ++.

Chapter 4: Case Scenario Answers

Case Scenario 1: Designing a Complex User Interface

The answer to both questions lies in the design of the user interface. All commands and options should be exposed in the main menu, with menu options changing as the application conditions require. Frequently used commands should be segregated into groups and programmed into toolbars that can be added or removed from the UI at the user's option. The use of familiar icons for toolbar commands will break up the monotony of the UI and make it easier to use and learn. Context menus that duplicate key commands can reinforce application integrity and make the program easier to use.

Case Scenario 2: More Humongous Requirements

Menu items are no problem, of course. Access keys are automatically created by preceding the desired key in the *Text* property with the ampersand (&) symbol. Likewise, shortcut keys can be created by setting the *ShortcutKeys* property of each menu item. To auto-fill a *TextBox* on a command keystroke, you should handle the *TextBox.KeyDown* event and determine if an appropriate combination of a key plus a modifier key has been pressed. If so, you can set the *Text* property for the *TextBox* in the event handler.

Chapter 5: Lesson Review Answers

Lesson 1

1. **Correct Answer: C**

   A. **Incorrect.** The application configuration can contain the connection string information but not the actual connection object.

   B. **Incorrect.** The Data Sources window displays the objects in a dataset, not the actual connection object.

   C. **Correct.** The dataset code file is where the code that defines the connection object is located.

   D. **Incorrect.** The generated form code does not contain the connection object.

2. **Correct Answers: B and C**

   A. **Incorrect.** Use the *OracleConnection* object to connect to Oracle databases.

   B. **Correct.** Use the *OleDbConnection* object to connect to Office Access databases.

   C. **Correct.** Use the *OleDbConnection* object when connecting to Microsoft SQL Server 6.x databases.

   D. **Incorrect.** Use the *SqlConnection* object when connecting to SQL Server 2000 databases.

3. **Correct Answer: C**

    A. **Incorrect.** Connections can be created while running the Data Source Configuration Wizard, but it is not the wizard that actually creates the connection.

    B. **Incorrect.** Server Explorer displays connections but is not used to actually create connections.

    C. **Correct.** The Add Connection dialog box creates connections whether using Server Explorer or a data wizard.

    D. **Incorrect.** The Properties window can display connection information, and it can be an entry point into the Add Connection dialog box, but it is not used to actually create connections.

Lesson 2

1. **Correct Answers: A and D**

    A. **Correct.** The connection string must have information about the data source to connect to.

    B. **Incorrect.** The provider name is not required to connect to SQL Server 2000 and SQL Server 2005.

    C. **Incorrect.** A valid filepath is not required when connecting to SQL Server 2000 or SQL Server 2005.

    D. **Correct.** Appropriate credentials or Integrated Security settings are required to connect to a SQL Server database.

2. **Correct Answers: B, C, and D**

    A. **Incorrect.** The connection is not destroyed, although it may be released and marked ready for garbage collection.

    B. **Correct.** The connection is returned to the pool.

    C. **Correct.** When closing a connection, the *StateChange* event is fired and the *Connection.CurrentState* property is set to *Closed*.

    D. **Correct.** When closing a connection, all pending transactions that have not been explicitly committed are automatically rolled back.

3. **Correct Answer: C**

    A. **Incorrect.** Information regarding the current state of a connection is accessed through the connection's *CurrentState* property.

B. **Incorrect.** High-severity SQL Server errors (severity 17 and above) are not available through the *InfoMessage* event.

C. **Correct.** Low-severity SQL Server errors (severity 10 and below) will cause the *InfoMessage* event to fire.

D. **Incorrect.** Network errors that are encountered when attempting to open a connection are not exposed through the *InfoMessage* event.

Lesson 3

1. **Correct Answers: A and B**

   A. **Correct.** The connection string is used to determine which connection pool to use.

   B. **Correct.** The identity or credential of a user is used to determine which connection pool to use.

   C. **Incorrect.** The database being connected to does not determine the connection pool to use.

   D. **Incorrect.** The connection object used to connect to the database does not determine the connection pool to use.

2. **Correct Answers: B and C**

   A. **Incorrect.** The *OLE DB Services* connection string keyword is not used for SQL Server 2000 or SQL Server 2005.

   B. **Correct.** Opening a connection and not explicitly disabling pooling. Connection pooling is on by default with all the .NET Data Providers, so you can just open a connection to use connection pooling.

   C. **Correct.** Setting the connection string keyword *Pooling* = *True* in the connection string. This is how to explicitly turn on connection pooling in SQL Server 2000 and SQL Server 2005.

   D. **Incorrect.** The Connection Pooling tab of the ODBC Data Source Administrator dialog box is used only for ODBC data sources. Although SQL Server can be connected through ODBC it is better to use the .NET Framework Data Provider for SQL Server when connecting to SQL Server.

3. **Correct Answer: C**

   A. **Incorrect.** Setting the *OLE DB Services* connection string keyword to *0* turns all services off (including connection pooling).

B. **Incorrect.** Setting the *OLE DB Services* connection string keyword to *-4* turns on all services except pooling and auto-enlistment of transactions.

C. **Correct.** Setting the *OLE DB Services* connection string keyword to *-1* turns on all services, including pooling.

D. **Incorrect.** Setting the *OLE DB Services* connection string keyword to *-7* turns on all services except pooling, auto-enlistment, and Client Cursor.

Lesson 4

1. **Correct Answers: C and D**

   A. **Incorrect.** When errors with a severity level of 1 through 9 are encountered, the connection will typically remain open.

   B. **Incorrect.** When errors with a severity level of 10 through 19 are encountered, the connection will typically remain open.

   C. **Correct.** When errors with a severity level of 20 or greater are encountered, the connection will typically close.

   D. **Correct.** When errors with a severity level of 30 or greater are encountered, the connection will typically close.

2. **Correct Answers: B and D**

   A. **Incorrect.** The *SqlException.Source* property contains the name of the provider that generated the error, not the actual error.

   B. **Correct.** The *SqlException.Message* property contains the error message returned by SQL Server.

   C. **Incorrect.** The *SqlError.Class* property contains the severity of the error, but not the actual error message.

   D. **Correct.** The *SqlError.Message* property contains the error message returned by SQL Server.

Lesson 5

A. **Correct Answer: C**

   A. **Incorrect.** *VisibleSqlServers* is the instance name of the *DataGridView* in this lesson's example and not the object that returns the list of servers.

   B. **Incorrect.** *GetDataSources* is the method on the *SqlDataSourceEnumerator* and not the object that returns the list of servers.

    C. **Correct.** The *SqlDataSourceEnumerator* is the object used to return the list of visible SQL servers.

    D. **Incorrect.** The *ServerName* is a column name in the *DataTable* returned by the *GetDataSources* method call.

B. **Correct Answers: A, B, and C**

    A. **Correct.** The computer's firewall settings can block the visibility of the SQL server to your application.

    B. **Correct.** The amount of network traffic can cause a timeout before your application is able to retrieve information about the SQL server.

    C. **Correct.** The availability of the SQL Browser service can affect the ability of your application to see any SQL servers.

    D. **Incorrect.** There is no *Visibility* property of a SQL server.

C. **Correct Answers: A, C, and D**

    A. **Correct.** The name of the server is available in the *ServerName* column of the *DataTable* returned by the *GetDataSources* method.

    B. **Incorrect.** The number of databases is not provided by the *SqlServer-Enumerator* object.

    C. **Correct.** The name of the version is available in the Version column of the *DataTable* returned by the *GetDataSources* method.

    D. **Correct.** The name of the instance is available in the InstanceName column of the *DataTable* returned by the *GetDataSources* method.

Lesson 6

1. **Correct Answers: B and C**

    A. **Incorrect.** *Integrated security = yes* is used for ODBC connections.

    B. **Correct.** *Integrated Security = SSPI* can be used for both SQL Server and OLE DB.

    C. **Correct.** *Integrated Security = True* is used for SQL Server 2000 and SQL Server 2005 connections.

    D. **Incorrect.** *Trusted_Connection = yes* is used for Oracle connections.

2. **Correct Answer: B**

   A. **Incorrect.** Compiled in the application is not where you should store sensitive information. The application can be decompiled, which can compromise the security of the data.

   B. **Correct.** An encrypted application configuration file is the recommended location for storing sensitive information.

   C. **Incorrect.** A resource file deployed with the application is not secure and can compromise the security of your data.

   D. **Incorrect.** The registry is not a recommended location for storing sensitive information.

3. **Correct Answer: C**

   A. **Incorrect.** Encrypting the data in the application configuration file is a way to secure sensitive information if it must be included in the application, but the recommended method is to use integrated security.

   B. **Incorrect.** Using a code obfuscator is not the recommended method for securing sensitive connection string information.

   C. **Correct.** Using integrated security (Windows Authentication) is the recommended method for securing sensitive connection string information.

   D. **Incorrect.** Querying the user for his or her credentials at run time is not the recommended method for securing sensitive connection string information.

Chapter 5: Case Scenario Answers

Case Scenario 1: Troubleshooting a SQL Connection

The modifications to the application are as follows:

- Locate every line of code that opens connections to the SQL server and surround those lines of code with a try-catch block.

- Add code to catch the errors using the *SqlException* and *SqlError* classes.

- Add code to handle the errors and provide comprehensive error messages so users understand the cause of the errors and know the course of action they can follow.

Case Scenario 2: Securing Sensitive Data

The recommendations to upper management are as follows:

- Remove the sensitive information from the code and modify all connection strings to use integrated security.

- Remove the sensitive information from the code and move it to the application configuration file where it can be encrypted.

Chapter 6: Lesson Review Answers

Lesson 1

1. **Correct Answers: B and D**

    A. **Incorrect.** *CommandType* = Text, *CommandText* = stored procedure name are not valid settings because the *CommandType* needs to be set to *StoredProcedure*.

    B. **Correct.** *CommandType* = Text, *CommandText* = SQL syntax to execute the stored procedure is not the recommended way to execute a stored procedure, but setting *CommandType* = Text allows you to execute any valid SQL statement.

    C. **Incorrect.** *CommandType* = StoredProcedure, *CommandText* = SQL syntax to execute the stored procedure are not valid settings because the *CommandText* needs to be the name of the stored procedure.

    D. **Correct.** *CommandType* = *StoredProcedure*, *CommandText* = stored procedure name is the recommended way to execute a stored procedure with a *Command* object.

2. **Correct Answers: B and D**

    A. **Incorrect.** Calling the *EndExecuteNonQuery* method before the *StatementCompleted* event fires is incorrect because *BeginExecuteNonQuery* does not return any data.

    B. **Correct.** Calling the *EndExecuteReader* method before the *StatementCompleted* event fires causes the process to wait for the query to return and allows you to access the data afterward.

C. **Incorrect.** Waiting for the *StatementCompleted* event to fire and then iterating through the *DataReader* is incorrect because you need to call *EndExecuteReader* to return the *DataReader*.

D. **Correct.** Waiting for the *StatementCompleted* event to fire, calling the *EndExecuteReader* method, and then iterating through the *DataReader* is the correct sequence to follow to execute a command asynchronously and access tabular data.

3. **Correct Answer: C**

A. **Incorrect.** Calling the *ExecuteReader* method of two *Command* objects and assigning the results to the same instance of a *DataReader* is the same as executing two commands. If you do not iterate through the *DataReader* after the first command is executed, the results of the second command will overwrite the contents of the reader.

B. **Incorrect.** Calling the *ExecuteReader* method of a single *Command* object twice will yield only the results of the second call.

C. **Correct.** Set the *Command.CommandText* property to multiple SQL statements delimited by a semicolon and iterate through the *DataReader*. Use *DataReader.NextResult* to check for any more result sets in the *DataReader*.

D. **Incorrect.** Setting the *Command.CommandType* property to multiple result sets is not valid.

       wers: B and C

A.   Incorrect. When the parameter value is created based on user input, it can definitely use an *Input* parameter, but it does not have to.

B. **Correct.** Using the parameter to send data from the application to the database could be the common definition of an *Input* parameter. It is a parameter used to send data to the database to run a query.

C. **Correct.** Setting the command to execute a statement with a *Where* clause is also a typical use of an *Input* parameter.

D. **Incorrect.** Passing the parameter value to an *Insert* statement can also use an *Input* parameter but is not the typical definition.

2. **Correct Answer: D**

   A. **Incorrect.**

   B. **Incorrect.**

   C. **Incorrect.**

   D. **Correct.** *Input, Output,* and *InputOutput* are the primary types of parameters you can use in a .NET Framework Data Provider.

3. **Correct Answer: B**

   A. **Incorrect.** The .NET Framework data type in your application that the parameter represents is not the correct type for the *SqlParameter.SqlDbType* property.

   B. **Correct.** It is the type of column or data in SQL Server that the command expects.

   C. **Incorrect.** The type of column in a *DataTable* that it represents is only a valid data type for the application.

   D. **Incorrect.** All types defined in the *SqlDbDataType* enumeration correspond to the SQL Server types, but you must pick the correct one for your parameter.

Lesson 3

1. **Correct Answers: A and C**

   A. **Correct.** BLOB data is typically transferred with a "stream" object, which presents a more challenging programming task.

   B. **Incorrect.** Whether BLOB data is in a readable format is not why it is complex to work with.

   C. **Correct.** That BLOB data tends to be large, and typically needs to be transferred in smaller pieces, is primarily why working with BLOBs is complex.

   D. **Incorrect.** BLOB data can be read into a *DataReader*.

2. **Correct Answer: D**

   A. **Incorrect.** By setting its *Connection* property to read binary data

   B. **Incorrect.** By calling the *ExecuteNonQuery* method and reading the results into a *BinaryReader*

   C. **Incorrect.** By calling the *ExecuteReader* method and casting the *DataReader* to a *BufferedStream*

    D. **Correct.** By setting the *CommandBehavior* to *SequentialAccess* in the *Execute-Reader* methods constructor

3. **Correct Answer: C**

    A. **Incorrect.** Calling the *DataReader.GetData* method is incorrect.

    B. **Incorrect.** Calling the *DataReader.Read* method and accessing the bytes through a column ordinal is incorrect.

    C. **Correct.** Calling the *DataReader.GetBytes* method and adding the results to the byte array is the correct way to reconstruct the binary data from the *DataReader* results.

    D. **Incorrect.** Calling the *DataReader.GetSqlByte* method and adding the results to the byte array is not the correct way to reconstruct the BLOB.

Lesson 4

1. **Correct Answers: A and C**

    A. **Correct.** One connection for each database the application needs to connect to.

    B. **Incorrect.** Although the *SqlBulkCopy* object does not require two connections for each database to connect to, it might coincidentally end up using two connections to the same database if you are moving data within the same database. In other words, you might use two connections to the same database in the rare occurrence of copying data within a single database, but you do not need two connections for each database when more than one database is involved in the bulk copy operation.

    C. **Correct.** Two connections total—one connection for the source database and one connection for the destination database—is the correct answer, but, as seen in this example, the connections might point to the same data source.

2. **Correct Answer: A**

    A. **Correct.** The BULK INSERT statement uses a data file created with the .bcp utility as the source of its data.

    B. **Incorrect.** The BULK INSERT statement does not get its data from a query executed by a *Command* object.

    C. **Incorrect.** The BULK INSERT statement does not get its data from a *Data-Reader*.

D. **Incorrect**. The BULK INSERT statement does not get its data from a database table in either the same or another database.

3. **Correct Answer: B**

A. **Incorrect**. This condition is correct only if the first record in a batch fails; otherwise, it is incorrect.

B. **Correct**. It depends on the batch size and how many successful batches were copied before the transaction failed. Transactions are performed in batches, and each successful batch is, in turn, successfully copied and is, therefore, not subject to being rolled back.

C. **Incorrect**. Because the batches after a failed transaction are not attempted, this answer is incorrect.

D. **Incorrect**. Because transactions are performed in batches, and each successful batch is, in turn, successfully copied and not subject to rollback, this answer is incorrect.

Lesson 5

1. **Correct Answer: A**

A. **Correct**. Assigning a transaction variable, the return value of the *Connection.BeginTransaction* method is the correct way to create and start a transaction.

B. **Incorrect**. There is no constructor to declare a new instance of the *Transaction* class.

C. **Incorrect**. There is no *Command.CreateTransaction* method.

D. **Incorrect**. The *Command.Transaction* property is where you set the transaction for the command to participate in.

2. **Correct Answer: D**

A. **Incorrect**. The transaction does not validate that multiple commands complete successfully.

B. **Incorrect**. The transaction does not handle exceptions that may occur on the database during command execution.

C. **Incorrect**. The transaction can abort the outcome of an executed command and return data to the state it was in prior to the transaction, but it does so only if the *transaction.Rollback* method is called.

    D. **Correct**. The main purpose of a transaction is to provide an option to abort the outcome of executed commands and return data to the state it was in prior to the transaction.

3. **Correct Answer: C**

    A. **Incorrect**. Local transactions are performed on a single database table, whereas distributed transactions are performed on multiple database tables.

    B. **Incorrect**. Local transactions are performed on a single database, whereas distributed transactions are performed on multiple databases on the same server.

    C. **Correct**. Local transactions are performed on a single database server, whereas distributed transactions can be performed across multiple database servers.

    D. **Incorrect**. Local transactions are performed on a database on the local machine, whereas distributed transactions are performed on a database on a remote machine.

Chapter 6: Case Scenario Answers

Case Scenario 1: Troubleshooting a Non-Performing Application

The possible improvements are as follows:

- Add parameters to the existing queries in an effort to reduce the number of records returned.
- Create a nightly job that bulk copies batches of records so archiving is more efficient.

Case Scenario 2: Preventing the Inventory System from Selling Unavailable Products

The modification to the application is as follows:

- Create a distributed transaction that can query the manufacturers' systems as well as the local warehouse and does not allow the sale to complete if the inventory is unavailable at all locations.

Chapter 7: Lesson Review Answers

Lesson 1

1. Correct Answers: **B and C**

    A. **Incorrect.** A *DataSet* is not a pointer to a remote or local database.

    B. **Correct.** A *DataSet* can be described as a collection of *DataTable* and *DataRelation* objects.

    C. **Correct.** A *DataSet* can be described as an in-memory cache of data.

    D. **Incorrect.** A collection of records from a database can be stored in a *DataTable*, but it is not the definition for a *DataSet*.

2. Correct Answer: **B**

    A. **Incorrect.** A *DataAdapter* is not part of a *DataSet*.

    B. **Correct.** A *DataSet* is made up of *DataTable*, *DataColumn*, and *DataRelation* objects.

    C. **Incorrect.** A constraint is not part of the *DataSet* object.

    D. **Incorrect.** Type is not a main object in a *DataSet*.

3. Correct Answer: **C**

    A. **Incorrect.** The *GetParentRow* and *GetChildRows* methods are not members of the *DataSet*.

    B. **Incorrect.** The *GetParentRow* and *GetChildRows* methods are not members of the *DataTable*.

    C. **Correct.** Calling the *GetParentRow* and *GetChildRows* methods of a *DataRow* is the correct way to programmatically access related records in *DataTable* objects.

    D. **Incorrect.** The *ParentColumns* and *ChildColumns* are collections of the columns that participate in the relation.

Lesson 2

1. Correct Answer: **B**

    A. **Incorrect.** Running the Data Source Configuration Wizard and selecting to create a Database data source will create *DataTable* objects based on the database objects you select in the wizard but is not part of programmatically creating a *DataTable*.

B. **Correct.** Instantiating a new *DataTable* and adding *DataColumn* objects to the *DataTable.Columns* collection is the correct way to create a *DataTable*.

C. **Incorrect.** Adding a new *DataSet* object to your project does not automatically create *DataTable* objects.

D. **Incorrect.** Instantiating a new *DataSet* object still requires you to add *DataTable* objects to its *Tables* collection.

2. **Correct Answer: B**

A. **Incorrect.** The *DataSet* properties do not set the primary key.

B. **Correct.** The *DataTable.PrimaryKey* property is assigned an array of *DataColumn* objects that make up the primary key.

C. **Incorrect.** The *DataColumn* properties do not set the primary key.

D. **Incorrect.** The *DataRelation* properties do not set the primary key.

3. **Correct Answer: C**

A. **Incorrect.** The *DataColumn* does not have a *ForeignKey* property.

B. **Incorrect.** The *DataTable* does not have a *ForeignKey* property.

C. **Correct.** Instantiating a new *ForeignKey* class and adding it to the *DataTable.Constraints* collection is the correct way to configure a foreign key in a *DataTable*.

D. **Incorrect.** The *DataRelation* does not define the foreign key.

Lesson 3

1. **Correct Answer: B**

A. **Incorrect.** *DataAdapter* objects do not contain *DataTable* objects.

B. **Correct.** *DataAdapter* objects are made up of *Connection* and *Command* objects.

C. **Incorrect.** *DataAdapter* objects do not contain *DataTable* or *DataSet* objects.

D. **Incorrect.** *DataAdapter* objects do not contain *DataSet* objects.

2. **Correct Answers: A and C**

A. **Correct.** Instantiate a *CommandBuilder* object and pass it a *DataAdapter* with a configured Select command to generate the Insert, Update, and Delete commands for a *DataAdapter*.

B. **Incorrect.** Calling the *DataAdapter.Update* method attempts to save changes to a database, but the *DataAdapter* must already have valid update commands configured.

C. **Correct.** Assigning valid *Command* objects to the *DataAdapter* object's *InsertCommand*, *UpdateCommand*, and *DeleteCommand* properties is one way to configure a *DataAdapter* to save changes.

D. **Incorrect.** Calling the *DataAdapter.Fill* method attempts to load the *DataAdapter* with data, but the *DataAdapter* must already have valid update commands configured.

3. **Correct Answer: C**

A. **Incorrect.** The *DataSet* does not have a *Fill* method.

B. **Incorrect.** The *DataSet* does not have a *DataSource* property.

C. **Correct.** Calling the *DataAdapter.Fill* method and passing the Recordset as an argument is the correct way to fill a *DataTable* with a Recordset.

D. **Incorrect.** The *DataAdapter* commands do not provide access to a Recordset.

Lesson 4

1. **Correct Answer: B**

A. **Incorrect.** Creating an instance of a *DataRow* and calling the *DataAdapter* object's *Update* method will not add a new row to the table.

B. **Correct.** Creating an instance of a *DataRow* (or typed row) and adding it to the *Rows* collection of the *DataTable* is the correct way to add a row to a table.

C. **Incorrect.** Calling the *DataTable.NewRow* method does not add a row to the table.

D. **Incorrect.** Creating an instance of a *DataRow* (or typed row) does not automatically add the row to the table.

2. **Correct Answer: C**

A. **Incorrect.** OriginalValue = DataRow("CustomerID"). DataRowVersion.Original is not the correct way to access the original value in a column.

B. **Incorrect.** OriginalValue = DataColumn("CustomerID"). Original is not the correct way to access the original value in a column.

C. **Correct.** Passing the desired *DataRowVersion* as an argument to the Column index is the correct way to access specific row versions.

   D. **Incorrect.** OriginalValue = DataRow("CustomerID") is not the correct way to access the original value in a column.

3. **Correct Answers: B and D**

   A. **Incorrect.** The *ColumnChanged* event is raised after the value has already changed, so it is too late to reject the change.

   B. **Correct.** The *ColumnChanging* event is the correct event to add validation to.

   C. **Incorrect.** The *RowChanged* event is raised after the value has already changed, so it is too late to reject the change.

   D. **Correct.** The *RowChanging* event can be used to validate column changes as well.

Lesson 5

1. **Correct Answer: C**

   A. **Incorrect.** Calling the *GetXmlSchema* method is incorrect. The *GetXml-Schema* method returns the schema as an XML string from a *DataSet*.

   B. **Incorrect.** Calling the *ReadXml* method is how you load data from an XML document into a *DataSet*, not how you retrieve schema information.

   C. **Correct.** Calling the *ReadXmlSchema* method and passing in the path to the .xsd file is the correct way to load schema information from an .xsd file to a *DataSet*.

   D. **Incorrect.** Setting the *Name* property of the *DataSet* is not how you retrieve schema information.

2. **Correct Answer: B**

   A. **Incorrect.** Passing the *XmlDataDocument* to the *DataSet.GetXml* method is incorrect.

   B. **Correct.** Declaring a new instance of an *XmlDataDocument* and passing in the name of the *DataSet* to synchronize with is the correct way to synchronize a *DataSet* with an *XmlDataDocument*.

   C. **Incorrect.** Calling the *XmlDataDocument.Load* method is incorrect.

   D. **Incorrect.** Calling the *XmlDataDocument.Synch* method is incorrect.

3. **Correct Answer: C**

   A. **Incorrect.** Passing the XPath query as a string to the *DataTable.Select* method is not correct.

B. **Incorrect.** Synchronizing with an XML document and performing the XPath query on the raw XML is not correct.

C. **Correct.** Passing the XPath query as a string to the *DocumentElement.SelectNodes* method is the correct way to execute an XPath query against a *DataSet*.

D. **Incorrect.** Passing the XPath query as a string to the *DataTable.Find* method is not correct.

Lesson 6

1. **Correct Answers: C and D**

   A. **Incorrect.** The *DataColumn* in the *DataTable* is not the correct way to access individual values in a *DataView*.

   B. **Incorrect.** The associated *DataTable* object's *DataRow* is not the correct way to access individual columns in a *DataView*.

   C. **Correct.** Through the indexer of a *DataRowView* object is the correct way to access an individual column value in a *DataView*.

   D. **Correct.** The *DataView* uses the *DataTable* as its data source, so the columns are the same.

2. **Correct Answer: B**

   A. **Incorrect.** The *Find* method does not return an individual *DataRow*.

   B. **Correct.** The *Find* method returns the index of the "found" row in the *DataView*.

   C. **Incorrect.** The *Find* method does not return an individual *DataRowView*.

   D. **Incorrect.** The *Find* method does not return a collection of *DataRow* objects.

3. **Correct Answer: C**

   A. **Incorrect.** Calling the *GetChildRows* method of the *DataView* is not the correct way to access related records in a *DataView*.

   B. **Incorrect.** Calling the *CreateChildView* method of the *DataView* is not the correct way to access related records in a *DataView*.

   C. **Correct.** The correct way to access related records using a *DataView* is to call the *CreateChildView* method of the *DataRowView*.

   D. **Incorrect.** Calling the *GetParentRow* method of the *DataView* is not the correct way to access related records in a *DataView*.

Chapter 7: Case Scenario Answers

Case Scenario 1: Upgrading an Old Application

The possible improvements are as follows:

- Start substituting the temporary files with either XML documents or, possibly, *DataView* objects, depending on the overall restrictions of the existing application architecture.

- Replace the existing object model with strongly typed *DataSet* objects where appropriate.

Case Scenario 2: Slow System Performance

The possible improvements are as follows:

- Use *DataSet* and *DataTable* objects to divide the inventory list into smaller chunks.

- Use *DataView* filtering to reduce the amount of data the application needs to parse through during a transaction.

Chapter 8: Lesson Review Answers

Lesson 1

1. **Correct Answers: A, C, and D**

   A. **Correct.** Selecting Add New Data Source from the Data Sources window starts the Data Source Configuration Wizard and populates the Data Sources window with the configured data source.

   B. **Incorrect.** Dragging a *DataSet* from the Toolbox onto a form will not add items to the Data Sources window.

   C. **Correct.** Selecting Add New Data Source from the Data menu starts the Data Source Configuration Wizard and populates the Data Sources window with the configured data source.

   D. **Correct.** Running the Data Source Configuration Wizard populates the Data Sources window with the configured data source.

2. **Correct Answer: B**

    A. **Incorrect.** Dragging items from Server Explorer onto the Dataset Designer adds items to the typed dataset; it does not create data-bound controls on a form.

    B. **Correct.** Dragging items from the Data Sources window onto a form creates data-bound controls.

    C. **Incorrect.** Dragging items from the ToolBox onto a form does not create data-bound controls

    D. **Incorrect.** Setting properties in the Properties window does not create data-bound controls.

3. **Correct Answer: B**

    A. **Incorrect.** Selecting the main node of the related table in the Data Sources window and dragging it onto a form binds controls to the entire table, not just to the related records.

    B. **Correct.** Selecting the child node in the Data Sources window and dragging it onto a form is the correct way to bind controls to related data.

    C. **Incorrect.** Dragging a *Relation* object onto the Dataset Designer creates a relationship between tables in your dataset but does not create bound controls.

    D. **Incorrect.** Binding to the child *DataTable* in the *DataSet* binds to the entire table, not just to the related records.

Lesson 2

1. **Correct Answer: D**

    A. **Incorrect.** That the control displays only a single column of data is incorrect because controls such as a *ComboBox* might display only a single column of data but can really be bound to several columns through additional data-binding properties.

    B. **Incorrect.** Although a *TextBox* displaying a string might be a simple-bound control, it is not the definition of simple data binding.

    C. **Incorrect.** That the control can display only native data types is incorrect.

    D. **Correct.** That the control has a single property bound to a single column of data correctly describes simple binding.

2. **Correct Answer: C**

   A. **Incorrect.** The name of the database and the name of the data table are not enough information to set up complex data binding.

   B. **Incorrect.** The name of the database and the name of the dataset are not enough information to set up complex data binding.

   C. **Correct.** The object data source, such as a *BindingSource* or a *DataSet*, and the list to display, such as a *DataTable*, are the correct bits of information needed to set up complex data binding.

   D. **Incorrect.** The name of the *DataSet* and the name of the control is not enough information to set up complex data binding.

3. **Correct Answers: A and B**

   A. **Correct.** The *BindingSource* component provides a level of abstraction between bound controls and a data source, simplifying the process of redirecting your application to use a different data source; it is the main reason to use a *BindingSource* component.

   B. **Correct.** The *BindingSource* component contains the methods necessary for navigating through a *DataTable*, which might be a reason to use a *BindingSource* component.

   C. **Incorrect.** The *BindingSource* component does not contain the methods necessary for sending updates back and forth between the application and the database. The *TableAdapter* or *DataAdapter* component contains the update commands.

   D. **Incorrect.** The *BindingSource* does not provide events through which you can add validation logic to your code. The *DataTable* events are a more likely place to add validation logic to your application.

Lesson 3

1. **Correct Answer: B**

   A. **Incorrect.** Using the column and row indexes of the selected cell is not the best way to determine the currently selected cell.

   B. **Correct.** Using the *DataGridView.CurrentCell* property is the best way to determine the currently selected cell.

C. **Incorrect.** Using the cursor position's *x* and *y* coordinates is not the best way to determine the currently selected cell.

D. **Incorrect.** Using the currently selected column and row in the bound *DataTable* to determine the clicked cell is incorrect.

2. **Correct Answer: C**

A. **Incorrect.** Adding validation code to the *CellPainting* event handler is not the preferred method to validate data in the *DataGridView*.

B. **Incorrect.** Adding validation code to the *DataGridView.CellClick* event handler is not the preferred method to validate data in the *DataGridView*.

C. **Correct.** Adding your validation code to the *DataGridView.CellValidating* event handler is the correct way to validate value changes in cells in a *Data-GridView*.

D. **Incorrect.** Adding code to the *DataGridView* partial class file is not the preferred method to validate data in the *DataGridView*.

3. **Correct Answer: B**

A. **Incorrect.** Configuring a *DataGridViewTextBoxColumn* to display *True* or *False* is one way to display a Boolean value but not the preferred way.

B. **Correct.** Configuring a *DataGridViewCheckBoxColumn* to display a check box that indicates checked or unchecked is the preferred way to display Boolean values in the *DataGridView*.

C. **Incorrect.** Configuring a *DataGridViewButtonColumn* class to display a button that indicates pressed or unpressed is not correct.

D. **Incorrect.** Configuring a custom column to display *Yes* or *No* is also one way to present a Boolean value but not the preferred method.

Chapter 8: Case Scenario Answers

Case Scenario 1: Upgrading an Old Application

The possible improvements are as follows:

- Display all records in a *DataGridView* on a single form.
- Implement data-bound controls to eliminate the extra component.

Case Scenario 2: Preventing Recompilation of a Large Application

The application will implement the following:

- *BindingSource* components
- Moving the connections to be configured to the application configuration file

Chapter 9: Lesson Review Answers

Lesson 1

1. **Correct Answer: C**

   A. **Incorrect.** The *XmlReader* class is an abstract class and has no constructor. Thus, the *New* (new) keyword cannot be used.

   B. **Incorrect.** You must specify a source for the XML when creating an instance of *XmlReader* with the *XmlReader.Create* method.

   C. **Correct.** You use the *XmlReader.Create* method to obtain an instance of a default implementation of *XmlReader*, and you must specify a source for the XML.

   D. **Incorrect.** The *XmlReader* class is an abstract class and has no constructor. Thus, the *New* (new) keyword cannot be used.

2. **Correct Answers: A, B, and C**

   A. **Correct.** The *MoveToAttribute* method allows you to specify either an attribute name or index. The attribute value is then exposed in the *XmlReader.Value* method.

   B. **Correct.** The *MoveToAttribute* method allows you to specify either an attribute name or index. The attribute value is then exposed in the *XmlReader.Value* method.

   C. **Correct.** The *MoveToAttribute* method allows you to specify either an attribute name or index. The attribute value is exposed via the *InnerXml* property.

   D. **Incorrect.** When positioned on an attribute, the *OuterXml* property returns the name of the attribute as well as the value.

3. **Correct Answer: A**

   A. **Correct.**

B. **Incorrect.** You do not need to supply the element name when calling *Write-EndElement.*

C. **Incorrect.** You should use *WriteStartElement* and *WriteEndElement* to create opening and closing tags with content in between.

D. **Incorrect.** For a simple element, you should use *WriteElementString* instead of *WriteStartElement.*

Lesson 2

1. **Correct Answer: A**

    A. **Correct.** This will create a new element named *Test* and add it as a child of *myNode.*

    B. **Incorrect.** You must create a variable to hold the reference to the newly created node and then append that node to *myNode.*

    C. **Incorrect.** This will make the *Test* element a child of *myDoc*, not of *myNode.*

    D. **Incorrect.** The *XmlNode* class does not expose a *CreateElement* method.

2. **Correct Answer: B**

    A. **Incorrect.** The *ReplaceChild* method requires two *XmlNode* objects and cannot accept a string.

    B. **Correct.** This will replace the child of *Node1* with the XML contained in *aString.*

    C. **Incorrect.** The *Value* property refers to the actual value of the node, not to the child nodes.

    D. **Incorrect.** The *OuterXml* property includes the parent nodes as well as the child nodes.

Chapter 9: Case Scenario Answers

Case Scenario 1: Report Archiving

You can parse the incoming reports by using the *XmlReader.Read* method to read each element in turn and process it as appropriate through the compression API.

By using the *XmlValidatingReader* or by creating an *XmlReader* that validates and referencing our schema in each report, we can validate the contents of the report against the schema. An error will be raised if the report does not conform to the schema.

In the *ValidationError* event handler, we can save the XML file as is instead of processing it and add it to a queue of items that must be hand-examined.

Case Scenario 2: The Merger

By designing our application around the *XmlDocument* class, we can accomplish this quickly and easily. Each document can be loaded into an instance of the *XmlDocument* class. We can retrieve the nodes in question by using the *XmlDocument.GetElementsByTagName*. Because these elements wrap text, we can use the *XmlNode.ReplaceChild* method to replace the child text elements with the text we specify.

Chapter 10: Lesson Review Answers

Lesson 1

1. **Correct Answer: C**

    A. **Incorrect.** The *PrintPreviewDialog* represents a print preview form but does not allow the user to add printers.

    B. **Incorrect.** The *PageSetupDialog* represents a page setup form but does not allow the user to add printers.

    C. **Correct.** Users can add printers from the *PrintDialog*.

    D. **Incorrect.** The *PrintPreviewControl* can be used to create customized print preview components but does not allow the user to add printers.

2. **Correct Answers: A and C**

    A. **Correct.** You must set the *Document* property to the *PrintDocument* you want to preview.

    B. **Incorrect.** The *PrintPreviewDialog* automatically generates the output for the *PrintDocument* component and displays it. No additional method or event is necessary to generate the previewed document.

    C. **Correct.** You must display the form to preview the document.

    D. **Incorrect.** The *PrintPreviewDialog* automatically generates the output for the *PrintDocument* component and displays it. No additional method or event is necessary to generate the previewed document.

3. **Correct Answer: C**

    A. **Incorrect.** Users can set the page orientation from the *PageSetupDialog* component.

B. **Incorrect.** Users can set the paper tray from the *PageSetupDialog* component.

C. **Correct**. The user can add a printer within the PrintDialog box only.

D. **Incorrect.** Users can set the page margins from the *PageSetupDialog* component.

Lesson 2

1. **Correct Answer: B**

    A. **Incorrect.** *PrintPages* is the event that is raised to print pages, but it cannot be called like a method.

    B. **Correct.** Set the *HasMorePages* property to *True* to raise the *PrintPages* event again and print multiple pages.

    C. **Incorrect.** *HasMorePages* is a property, not a method.

    D. **Incorrect.** The *Cancel* property can be set to *True* to cancel the current print job, but setting it to *False* does not automatically print additional pages.

2. **Correct Answer: A**

    A. **Correct.** To find the total lines on the printed page, you divide the height of the MarginBounds by the height of the Font.

    B. **Incorrect.** The *GetHeight* method requires a *Graphics* object as a parameter.

    C. **Incorrect.** *GetHeight* is not a member of the *Graphics* object.

    D. **Incorrect.** Using the height of the *PageBounds* will calculate the total number of lines in the page, including the excluded areas of the header and footer.

3. **Correct Answer: B**

    A. **Incorrect.** The *BeginPrint* event occurs at the beginning of a print job.

    B. **Correct.** The *EndPrint* event occurs after all pages have been printed, and it is the appropriate event to handle to notify the user that a print job is complete.

    C. **Incorrect.** The *PrintPages* event is used to send data to the printer.

    D. **Incorrect.** The *QueryPageSettings* event occurs before each page is printed to allow the user to use different page settings for each page.

Lesson 3

1. **Correct Answer: C**

    A. **Incorrect.** In the *Zoom* property, a value of *1* represents 100 percent normal size. Thus, *250* would correspond to a zoom of 25,000 percent.

B. **Incorrect.** In the *Zoom* property, a value of *1* represents 100 percent normal size. Thus, *25* would correspond to a zoom of 2,500 percent.

C. **Correct.** In the *Zoom* property, a value of *1* represents 100 percent normal size. Thus, *2.5* would correspond to a zoom of 250 percent.

D. **Incorrect.** In the *Zoom* property, a value of *1* represents 100 percent normal size. Thus, *.25* would correspond to a zoom of 25 percent.

2. **Correct Answer: B**

A. **Incorrect.** *UseAntiAlias* is a property, not a method.

B. **Correct.** To smooth the appearance, set the *UseAntiAlias* property to *True*.

C. **Incorrect.** *UseAntiAlias* is a property, not a method, and it exists in the *PrintPreviewControl* class, not on the *Document* property.

D. **Incorrect.** *UseAntiAlias* exists in the *PrintPreviewControl* class, not on the *Document* property.

Chapter 10: Case Scenario Answers

Case Scenario 1: A Better *PrintPreview* Control

To create a component like the one described, you would start by creating a new form that contains a *PrintPreviewControl* that would be used to display the document. By adding a *Timer* component, you can change the *PrintPreviewControl.StartPage* property at regular intervals to cycle through the pages. One way of implementing page skipping would be to subclass the *PrintPreviewControl* and add a property that indicated the step to take when skipping pages.

Case Scenario 2: A Simple Report Tool

Because the form is already the size of a piece of paper, the task is quite simplified. In the method handling the *PrintPages* event, you can loop through the controls on the form. For the label controls, you can use the *Graphics.DrawString* method to print the string in the label using the same font and location as the label itself. For image controls, you can likewise print the image using the *Graphics.DrawImage* method to draw the image at the location specified by the image control.

You can print a report for each record in the database by iterating through the records in the *PrintPage* event handler. After a page has been printed, the method should check to see if any more records exist. If so, the *e.HasMorePages* property should be set to *True* and the next record printed.

Chapter 11: Lesson Review Answers

Lesson 1

1. Correct Answer: D

    A. **Incorrect.** Although most drag-and-drop operations begin in the *Mouse-Down* event on the source control, it is not required that they begin here.

    B. **Incorrect.** Although most drag-and-drop operations end with the mouse button being released, this is handled by the *DragDrop* event.

    C. **Incorrect.** The *DragLeave* event is used to execute code when data is dragged out of a control, but it is not necessary for the drag-and-drop operation.

    D. **Correct.** The *DragDrop* event must be handled to complete a drag-and-drop-operation.

2. Correct Answers: A, B, C, and D

    A. **Correct.** The *DoDragDrop* method begins the drag-and-drop operation.

    B. **Correct.** If the target control does not allow one of the specified effects, the operation will not be completed.

    C. **Correct.** If the data format is not correct, the operation cannot be completed.

    D. **Correct.** If *AllowDrop* is set to *False*, no drag-and-drop operation may occur.

3. Correct Answer: B

    A. **Incorrect.** Whereas the *MouseDown* event is used to initiate most drag-and-drop operations, the *ItemDrag* event is used to initiate a drag-and-drop operation in a *TreeView* control.

    B. **Correct.** Use the *ItemDrag* event to call the *DoDragDrop* method.

    C. **Incorrect.** The *TreeView.DragEnter* event should be used to set the effect allowed for the drag-and-drop operation, but it will not be raised if a drag-and-drop operation has not already been started.

    D. **Incorrect.** The *TreeView.DragDrop* event is used to complete the drag-and-drop operation.

Lesson 2

1. Correct Answer: C

    A. **Incorrect.** *CurrentUICulture* determines the localized version of the form that is loaded but does not control data formatting.

B. **Incorrect.** Culture is set by the thread, not by the form.

C. **Correct.** The *CurrentCulture* setting determines the formatting methods used for application data.

D. **Incorrect.** Culture is set by the thread, not by the form.

2. **Correct Answers: C and D**

A. **Incorrect.** Because the default value for the *RightToLeft* property is *Inherit*, you only need to set the *Form.RightToLeft* property to *True* for the control text to be displayed right to left.

B. **Incorrect.** Because the default value for the *RightToLeft* property is *Inherit*, you only need to set the *Form.RightToLeft* property to *True* for the control text to be displayed right to left.

C. **Correct.** Setting the *Form.RightToLeft* property to *True* will cause all controls with a *RightToLeft* property value of *Inherit* to display text right to left.

D. **Correct.** Setting the *Form.RightToLeftLayout* property to *True*, along with setting the *Form.RightToLeft* property to *True*, will cause the entire form to lay out in a right-to-left manner.

Lesson 3

1. **Correct Answers: A and C**

A. **Correct.** You must create a parent form by setting the *IsMdiParent* property to *True*.

B. **Incorrect.** The *ActiveMdiForm* property is to determine which child form is active, but it is not required to create a child form.

C. **Correct.** You create a child form by setting the *MdiParent* property to an appropriate parent form.

D. **Incorrect.** It is not necessary to create a window list menu to create a child form.

2. **Correct Answer: D**

A. **Incorrect.** This method is used to activate a child form, not to get a reference to the active form.

B. **Incorrect.** This method adds an owned form but does not return a reference to it.

C. **Incorrect.** This property reports whether the form is a child form but does not return a reference.

D. **Correct.** The *ActiveMdiChild* property holds a reference to the currently active MDI form.

Chapter 11: Case Scenario Answers

Case Scenario 1: Still More Document Control

By using an MDI application, you can enable users to view multiple child documents while containing and organizing them in a single form. The parent form can include a *TreeView* control to display the documents in the table of contents, and the documents can be loaded as child forms when viewing is required. You can use drag-and-drop functionality to enable reordering of the table of contents in the *TreeView* control at run time.

Case Scenario 2: Fabrikam Goes International

You can create an MDI form that displays two child forms simultaneously: one for the European market and one for the U.S. market. You can ensure that market data is formatted appropriately by setting the *CurrentCulture* property to an appropriate culture before creating the form.

You can create localized versions of the user interface by researching what locales the application will be deployed in and creating localized strings and other resources for the user interface. You can then use these strings to create localized versions of the form. At run time, the application will retrieve the *CurrentUICulture* from the system and automatically display the correctly localized user interface. If desired, you can also allow the user to manually switch locales by setting the *CurrentUICulture* property in code.

Chapter 12: Lesson Review Answers

Lesson 1

1. **Correct Answers: A, B, and D**

   A. **Correct.** A user interface should be flexible to accommodate a variety of accessibility styles.

   B. **Correct.** Consistency allows your application to interact with the system in a predictable manner, thus enhancing accessibility.

C. **Incorrect.** An accessible interface does not have to be a simple interface. Even complicated interfaces can be made accessible.

D. **Correct.** Accessible interfaces should be compatible with accessibility aids.

2. **Correct Answer: A**

A. **Correct.** Although sound can be helpful, no information should be conveyed by sound alone.

B. **Incorrect.** This is an accessibility best practice.

C. **Incorrect.** This is an accessibility best practice.

D. **Incorrect.** This is an accessibility best practice.

Lesson 2

1. **Correct Answers: A and C**

A. **Correct.** The *PerformStep* method will increment the value to whatever the *Step* property is set to.

B. **Incorrect.** After the *Step* property is set, you must call *PerformStep* to advance the value.

C. **Correct.** The *Increment* method advances the *Value* by the value indicated.

D. **Incorrect.** The *Increment* method requires a value for the *Value* property to be advanced. It does not use the value of the *Step* property.

2. **Correct Answers: A, B, and C**

A. **Correct.** If the next control that is navigated to after the text box does not have the *CausesValidation* property set to *True*, the *Validating* event on the text box will not be fired.

B. **Correct.** To display the error icon, you must call the *SetError* method and set the error to an informative string.

C. **Correct.** To cancel the error, you must call the *SetError* method and set the error string to an empty string.

D. **Incorrect.** The *ErrorProvider* component does not have inherent validation capabilities.

3. **Correct Answer: B**

A. **Incorrect.** Although you must call *SetShowHelp*, you must also set the *Help-Navigator* to *Find*.

B.   **Correct.** You must call the *SetShowHelp* method to set *ShowHelp* to *True*, and you must set the *HelpNavigator* to *Find* to open the search page.

C.   **Incorrect.** Whereas you must call the *SetShowHelp* method to set *ShowHelp* to *True*, setting the *HelpNavigator* to *Topic* will open help to a topic, not to the search page.

D.   **Incorrect.** Setting the *HelpString* will not have any effect when the *HelpNavigator* has been set.

Chapter 12: Case Scenario Answers

Case Scenario 1: Putting the Final Touches on the Document Management System

You can use the *HScrollBar* or *VScrollBar* to build an interface that provides rapid navigation through the long list of files. By tying the value of the scroll bar to the location in the file list, you can allow the user to rapidly navigate to the approximate location of the desired file and then use fine adjustments to find the exact location.

You can use the *ProgressBar* control to provide feedback for the download status. When download is complete, you can notify the user by playing a beep from *SystemSounds*.

You can provide help for the application by creating a compiled help file (.chm) and using the *HelpProvider* component to connect it to your application. For more immediate and less in-depth help, you can use the *ToolTip* component to provide informative tooltips for the controls on your application. The *ErrorProvider* component can be used to provide feedback for invalid user input.

Case Scenario 2: Making the Document Management Application Accessible

By using only system colors, you can support high-contrast mode. If nonsystem colors are desired for the regular application interface, the application should detect if the system is in high-contrast mode and replace nonstandard colors with system colors.

No information should be conveyed by sound alone, so when file downloads are complete, for example, you should provide a visual cue as well as an audible cue.

Access keys should be used to enable keyboard access to all important functionality in the application, and this keyboard access should be fully documented.

System settings should be used throughout the application to support interaction with usability aids. In addition, the *AccessibleDescription*, *AccessibleName*, and *AccessibleRole* properties should be set to appropriate values.

Chapter 13: Lesson Review Answers

Lesson 1

1. **Correct Answers: A and B**

   A. **Correct.** The *RunWorkerAsync* process fires the *DoWork* event, which contains the code that is executed on a background process.

   B. **Correct.** The *DoWork* event handler contains the code that is executed on the background process.

   C. **Incorrect.** The *ProgessChanged* event is fired when the *ReportsProgress* method is called, but it is not required for the background process to be run.

   D. **Incorrect.** The *WorkerSupportsCancellation* property indicates whether the *BackgroundWorker* supports cancellation of the background process, but it is not required for the background process to run.

2. **Correct Answers: A, B, and C**

   A. **Correct.** You must set the *WorkerSupportsCancellation* property to *True* to allow the process to be cancelled.

   B. **Correct.** You must implement your own code to poll the *CancellationPending* property and cancel the process.

   C. **Correct.** The *CancelAsync* method sets the *CancellationPending* property to *True*.

   D. **Incorrect.** You cannot set the *CancellationPending* property directly. You must instead call the *CancelAsync* method.

3. **Correct Answers: A, B, and D**

   A. **Correct.** The *ReportProgress* method raises the *ProgressChanged* event and allows you to specify a percentage of progress.

   B. **Correct.** You must handle the *ProgressChanged* event to implement code that is executed when progress is reported.

   C. **Incorrect.** It is unnecessary to poll the *IsBusy* property to report progress.

   D. **Correct.** You cannot call the *ReportProgress* method unless the *WorkerReportsProgress* property is set to *True*.

Lesson 2

1. **Correct Answer: B**

   A. **Incorrect.** The *Invoke* method is used to execute a method call synchronously.

   B. **Correct.** The *BeginInvoke* method calls the method on a separate process thread.

   C. **Incorrect.** Although commonly used to complete an asynchronous method call, *EndInvoke* is required to complete the call only if a method result is required.

   D. **Incorrect.** The *DynamicInvoke* method is used to call methods synchronously using late binding.

2. **Correct Answers: A and B**

   A. **Correct.** *Thread* objects are instances of the *Thread* class, and each thread must be individually created.

   B. **Correct.** The *Thread.Start* method starts the new background process.

   C. **Incorrect.** Although you can provide an *Object* parameter to the new thread, you can also start a thread with a method that takes no parameters.

   D. **Incorrect.** Once execution of a thread completes, the thread will stop. Calling *Thread.Abort* is required only to stop a thread that is still running.

3. **Correct Answers: B and C**

   A. **Incorrect.** Calls to controls from background threads are inherently unsafe and must be called through *Control.Invoke*.

   B. **Correct.** The *InvokeRequired* property can be queried from any thread to determine if it is safe to make a direct call or whether *Control.Invoke* must be used.

   C. **Correct.** The *Control.Invoke* method can be used to make safe calls to controls from background threads.

   D. **Incorrect.** The *Control.IsAccessible* property indicates if the control is accessible to accessibility aids and is not related to calls from background threads.

Chapter 13: Case Scenario Answers

Case Scenario 1: The Publishing Application

The central issue in this application design is the list of documents for download. Both the UI thread and the background downloading thread must access this list. You should protect access to this list by using *SyncLock* or *lock* blocks where appropriate to allow access to the list by only one thread at a time. A background thread should be used to download the documents. When download of a particular document is complete, the UI should be updated through the thread-safe *Control.Invoke* method.

Case Scenario 2: Creating a Simple Game

The *BackgroundWorker* component allows you to implement separate process threads with relative ease. In the preceding example, you could create a single *Background-Worker* component that takes the path to the file to play as a parameter and then plays the sound on a background thread. When finished, the *BackgroundWorker* component can be used again without reinitializing.

Chapter 14: Lesson Review Answers

Lesson 1

1. **Correct Answers: A and B**

   A. **Correct.** Composite controls consist of preexisting Windows Forms controls bound together by common functionality.

   B. **Correct.** You can add new properties, methods, and events to a composite control.

   C. **Incorrect.** Composite controls provide their own rendering code.

   D. **Incorrect.** Properties of constituent controls are not generally available to the developer. You can wrap the properties of constituent controls in new properties to make them available to the developer, but this is not available by default.

2. **Correct Answers: A and D**

   A. **Correct.** A Toolbox bitmap must be a 16-by-16 pixel bitmap.

    B. **Incorrect.** Size is important. A Toolbox bitmap must be a 16-by-16 pixel bit-map.

    C. **Incorrect.** The *Image* property determines what image is displayed in the control at run time, not what is displayed next to the control in the Toolbox.

    D. **Correct.** The *ToolboxBitmap* attribute allows you to specify a path, a type, or a type and a resource name to specify the Toolbox bitmap.

Lesson 2

1. **Correct Answers: B, C, and D**

    A. **Incorrect.** The methods exposed by the *Graphics* class use *Pen* and *Brush* objects, but the *Graphics* class itself does not encapsulate them.

    B. **Correct.** The *Graphics* class is an in-code representation of the drawing sur-face associated with a visual element.

    C. **Correct.** All actual rendering is done via the *Graphics* class, and it exposes all of the methods necessary to do so.

    D. **Correct.** The *Graphics* class has no constructor and, thus, cannot be directly created, but you can obtain a reference via *PaintEventArgs* or by call-ing the *Control.CreateGraphics* method.

2. **Correct Answers: A and B**

    A. **Correct.** Custom controls must provide all of their own rendering code.

    B. **Correct.** Custom controls can encapsulate other .NET Framework compo-nents and, rarely, even other controls.

    C. **Incorrect.** There is no default visual interface for custom controls.

    D. **Incorrect.** Custom controls inherit from the *Control* class. Composite con-trols inherit from the *UserControl* class.

Lesson 3

1. **Correct Answer: B**

    A. **Incorrect.** The *Form.Show* method does not return a *DialogResult*.

    B. **Correct.** The *Form.ShowDialog* method returns a *DialogResult* value.

    C. **Incorrect.** The *Form.Show* method does not return a *DialogResult*, nor does it allow you to specify the parent form as a parameter.

D. **Incorrect.** The *Form.ShowDialog* method does not allow you to specify a dialog result as a parameter.

2. **Correct Answer: C**

A. **Incorrect.** Although you must override the *OnPaint* method to provide a new appearance for an extended control, you are not required to provide a new appearance.

B. **Incorrect.** If a Toolbox bitmap is not provided, the control will use the bitmap used by the inherited control.

C. **Correct.** All that is required to create an extended control is to inherit a base control. All other steps are optional.

D. **Incorrect.** The extended control will expose all of the same properties and methods as the control it inherits.

Chapter 14: Case Scenario Answers

Case Scenario 1: Collecting and Displaying User Data

The best way to approach this problem is to create a composite control consisting of *TextBox* controls to receive the user input. This control can be hosted in a dialog box to receive user input and in the general application to display user input. The *ReadOnly* property of the *TextBox* controls can be wrapped in new properties in the composite control to allow developers to determine when the control is read-only and when it is read-write. Finally, by creating a composite control, you will be able to reuse it in subsequent applications, thereby minimizing developer hours.

Case Scenario 2: Trey Research Stock Price

The best approach here is to create a custom control that accesses the Web service. The custom control can encapsulate a *Timer* component that is set to sample the Web service every 15 seconds. Custom rendering code can be provided to render the stock price and the graph. Because it is a control, it can easily be integrated with any Windows Forms application.

Chapter 15: Lesson Review Answers

Lesson 1

1. **Correct Answer: B**

   A. **Incorrect.** Required permissions will be determined when the application is published. You might be asked to approve a permission set, but you do not need to configure permissions.

   B. **Correct.** To install a Click-Once application, you need only to click the Setup file and follow any instructions.

   C. **Incorrect.** The developer will determine how frequently the application will check for updates before the application is published.

   D. **Incorrect.** The install mode is configured before the application is published.

2. **Correct Answer: C**

   A. **Incorrect.** Applications run from the Internet run under the Internet security zone by default.

   B. **Incorrect.** Applications run from the Internet run under the Internet security zone by default. Applications run from file shares are run under the intranet security settings by default.

   C. **Correct.** Applications run from the Internet run under the Internet security zone by default.

   D. **Incorrect.** Applications run from the Internet run under the Internet security zone by default.

Lesson 2

1. **Correct Answer: A**

   A. **Correct.** The File System Editor is used to determine which files will be distributed by a setup project.

   B. **Incorrect.** The File Types Editor is used to set associations between file types and applications.

   C. **Incorrect.** The Custom Actions Editor is used to add custom actions to your application.

   D. **Incorrect.** The User Interface Editor is used to edit the user interface of the setup wizard.

2. **Correct Answer: B**

   A. **Incorrect.** This specifies a particular value for the operating system version that may not actually exist. You should use >= to specify that the operating system should be greater than a specified version.

   B. **Correct.** You should use >= to specify that the operating system should be greater than a specified version.

   C. **Incorrect.** This requires the operating system to be earlier than Windows 2000. You should use >= to specify that the operating system should be greater than a specified version.

   D. **Incorrect.** This allows installation for any operating system except a particular version of Windows 2000. You should use >= to specify that the operating system should be greater than a specified version.

3. **Correct Answer: B, C, and D**

   A. **Incorrect.** The *Installer* class should be added to the project you want to deploy, not to the setup project itself.

   B. **Correct.** You must add an *Installer* class to the project you want to deploy as a custom action.

   C. **Correct.** You must write your custom action in the *Install* method of an *Installer* class.

   D. **Correct.** You must specify the project that contains the custom action in the Custom Actions Editor.

Chapter 15: Case Scenario Answers

Case Scenario 1: Distributing the Document Viewer

Using Click-Once technology, you can provide the version that is available now through a Web site that is accessible by your clients. By setting the application to check for updates every time the application is run, you can ensure that your clients receive the most up-to-date version every time they run the application. In addition, with a Click-Once application, your clients do not have to be administrative users to install the application.

Case Scenario 2: Installing the Document Core

By creating a setup project to install the document core, you can create a setup environment that accomplishes all of these goals. Directory structures can be defined in the File System Editor, and registry keys can be created through the Registry Editor. You can check for prerequisites in a custom action and, if they are not found, use the custom action to either install the prerequisites, if possible, or throw an *InstallException* to abort installation if it is not possible to install them.

Glossary

access keys   A combination of multiple key presses that defines a keyboard shortcut for a particular control.

accessible design   The principle of designing a user interface to conform to certain principles that allow the application to be accessible by people with differing abilities.

application scope   When referring to application settings, settings with application scope are read-only at run time.

BindingSource   A Windows Form component that facilitates data binding controls to a data source.

BLOB   A BLOB is a binary large object; a byte array that represents large items such as graphics, music files, executable files, or any large item represented in binary form.

ClickOnce   A new deployment technology that allows you to quickly publish any application to a Web site or file share, or to install an application on a computer. ClickOnce applications typically run under default security settings.

composite control   A user-authored control that is made up of other controls and inherits from the *UserControl* base class.

Connection **object**   A representation of a connection to a data source.

connection pool   A collection of connections available for reuse that reduce the overhead of continuously creating and disposing connections.

connection string   The information required to connect to a data source, such as database server name, database name, type of credentials to use, and so on.

container control   A control that can contain other controls, such as a *Panel* control, a *GroupBox* control, or a *TabControl* control.

control   A component that has a visual interface and can be hosted in a form or container control. Controls contain properties, methods, and events that act together to create a common functionality. Examples of controls include *Button*, *TextBox*, and *Label*.

custom action   Code that is executed in the Install, Commit, Rollback, or Uninstall phase of a Windows Installer installation. Custom actions are written in *Installer* classes and added to the projects that are to be installed.

custom control   A user-authored control that supplies its own code for rendering the user interface.

DataAdapter   Represents a set of SQL commands and a database connection that are used to fill the *DataSet* and update the data source.

data binding   The concept of displaying data in a control on a form that implements two-way communication between the control and the data source. Changes in one are reflected in the other.

DataColumn   The object in a *DataTable* that represents the column in a database table.

DataSet   An in-memory cache of data that is structured like a relational database with tables and relationships.

DataTable   The object in a *DataSet* that represents a single set of returned data.

DataView   A customizable view of the data in a *DataTable* that can be sorted, filtered, and set to display records in a specific state, such as all deleted records.

delegate   A type-date function pointer that can be used to call a method synchronously or asynchronously.

drag-and-drop   An operation by which the user grabs data on a form by pressing the left mouse button, drags it across the form, and drops it onto another control by releasing the left mouse button.

encryption   The process of altering data into an unreadable form that must be decrypted to be readable.

event   A message from a control that is sent to the rest of the application and can be handled by methods that have the same signature as the event.

event handler   The method that is executed when an event is fired. An event handler must have the same signature as its event.

extended control   A user-authored control that inherits a preexisting control and incorporates that control's functionality.

globalization   The process of formatting application data in a locale-specific manner.

Graphics **object**   An object that represents a drawing surface. When printing, the *Graphics* object is used to draw content to the printed page.

InstallException   An exception that can be thrown by an *Installer* class. Throwing an *InstallException* in a custom action will result in the installation being rolled back.

integrated security   Also known as Windows Authentication. This method of security uses existing domain credentials to access a data source.

list   A group of related objects that are available to an application, usually exposed through a collection. A control that works with a list will typically have methods to add, remove, and otherwise manage members of the list.

list-based control   A control that is designed to expose or display a list of items. Common examples include the *ListBox*, *ComboBox*, and *CheckedListBox* controls.

localization   The process of displaying a user interface that is customized in a locale-specific manner.

mask   The format for text entry and display in a *MaskedTextBox*.

MDI child   A form that is contained in an MDI parent form.

MDI parent   A form that contains, hosts, and organizes MDI child forms.

MenuStrip   A specialized *ToolStrip* control that is specialized to host *ToolStripMenuItem* controls.

modal   A mode of dialog box display. When a dialog box is displayed modally, the main thread of application execution is halted until the dialog box is closed.

modeless   A mode of dialog box display. When a dialog box is displayed modelessly, the main thread of application execution may continue while the dialog box is open.

parameter   When creating database queries, a variable used to provide alternate values to expressions such as SQL statements and stored procedures.

PrintDocument   The primary component in printing. A *PrintDocument* component represents a printed document.

PrintPreview   An on-screen preview of a printed document. You can preview a *PrintDocument* component in either a *PrintPreviewDialog* or a *PrintPreviewControl*.

setting   A value that properties can be bound to that is persisted between application sessions. Also called application setting.

setup project   A project that produces a Windows Installer application. A setup project provides a highly configurable and controllable environment for creating deployments.

snaplines   Visual aids that appear in the IDE to aid control alignment.

thread   An operation that occurs concurrently with other operations in an application. Can also refer to an instance of the *Thread* class, which is used to create and manage a thread.

Toolbox   A window in the Microsoft Visual Studio IDE from which a control can be dragged onto the designer.

ToolStrip   A control that is used to host *ToolStripItems* and can be easily configured by the user at run time.

ToolStripItem   A control that can be hosted in a *ToolStrip*. It can represent a menu item, or any of a number of controls that can be hosted in the *ToolStrip*.

ToolStripMenuItem   A control that represents a menu item and is usually hosted in a *MenuStrip*.

transaction   A logical set of commands executed as a group.

user control   Another term for composite control.

user scope   When referring to application settings, settings that are read-write at run time.

value-setting control   A control that allows the user to set a value in the user interface. Common examples include *CheckBox*, *RadioButton*, and *TrackBar* controls.

XmlDocument   A class that provides an in-memory representation of XML data.

XmlNode   An in-memory representation of an XML node, including child nodes, if any.

XmlReader   An abstract class that provides non-cached, forward-only access to an XML file or stream.

XmlWrite   An abstract class that provides a forward-based XML writing model.

Index

Symbols

A

B

System Requirements

We recommend that you use a computer that is not your primary workstation to do the practice exercises in this book because you will make changes to the operating system and application configuration.

Hardware Requirements

The following hardware is required to complete the practice exercises:

- Computer with a 600 MHz or faster processor
- 192 MB of RAM or more
- 2 GB of available hard disk space
- DVD-ROM drive
- 1,024 x 768 or higher resolution display with 256 colors
- Keyboard and Microsoft mouse, or compatible pointing device

Software Requirements

The following software is required to complete the practice exercises:

- One of the following operating systems:
    - Windows 2000 with Service Pack 4
    - Windows XP with Service Pack 2
    - Windows XP Professional x64 Edition (WOW)
    - Windows Server 2003 with Service Pack 1
    - Windows Server 2003, x64 Editions (WOW)
    - Windows Server 2003 R2
    - Windows Server 2003 R2, x64 Editions (WOW)
    - Microsoft Windows Vista
- Visual Studio 2005 (A 90-day evaluation edition of Visual Studio 2005 Professional Edition is included on DVD with this book.)